The Interpersonal Communication Book

12th Edition

The Interpersonal Communication Book

Joseph A. DeVito

Hunter College of the City University of New York

PEARSON

Boston   New York   San Francisco
Mexico City   Montreal   Toronto   London
Madrid   Munich   Paris
Hong Kong   Singapore   Tokyo   Cape Town   Sydney

Acquisitions Editor: Jeanne Zalesky
Editorial Assistant: Megan Lentz
Development Editor: Hilary Jackson
Marketing Manager: Suzan Czajkowski
Editorial Production Service: Tom Conville for Nesbitt Graphics, Inc.
Manufacturing Buyer: JoAnne Sweeney
Electronic Composition: Nesbitt Graphics, Inc.
Interior Design: Nesbitt Graphics, Inc.
Photo Researcher: Kate Cebik
Cover Administrator: Joel Gendron

For related titles and support materials, visit our online catalog at www.pearsoned.com.

Between the time website information is gathered and then published, it is not unusual for some sites to have closed. Also, the transcription of URLs can result in typographical errors. The publisher would appreciate notification where these errors occur so that they may be corrected in subsequent editions.

ISBN-13: 978-0-205-62570-3   ISBN-10: 0-205-62570-3

Library of Congress Cataloging-in-Publication Data
DeVito, Joseph A.
    The interpersonal communication book / Joseph A. DeVito.—Twelfth ed.
        p.   cm.
    Includes bibliographical references and index.
    ISBN-13: 978-0-205-62570-3
    ISBN-10: 0-205-62570-3
    1. Interpersonal communication.   I. Title.
BF637.C45D49 2009
302.2—dc22   2008028946

Printed in the United States of America
10 9 8 7 6 5 4 3 2 1   WEB   11 10 09 08

Brief Contents

Contents

Part 1 Preliminaries to Interpersonal Communication   1

1 Foundations of Interpersonal Communication   1

Part 2 Interpersonal Messages 98

Specialized Contents

Welcome to *The Interpersonal Communication Book*

It is truly a great privilege to present this twelfth edition of *The Interpersonal Communication Book*. Each revision has enabled me to improve and fine-tune the presentation of interpersonal communication so that it accurately reflects what we currently know about the subject and is as clear, interesting, involving, and up-to-date as it can possibly be.

This new edition continues to provide in-depth coverage of interpersonal communication, blending theory and research on the one hand and practical skills on the other. The book's philosophical foundation continues to be the *notion of choice*. Choice is central to interpersonal communication; as speaker, listener, and communication analyst, you are constantly confronted with choice points at every stage of the communication process—and these choices will influence the effectiveness of your messages and your relationships. This text provides you with worthwhile options for a vast array of interpersonal situations and discusses the theory and research evidence bearing on your communication choices. After completing this text, you should thus be better equipped to make more reasoned, more reasonable, and more effective communication choices.

THE TEXT

This twelfth edition retains much of the well-received structure of the previous edition with some significant improvements.

Part 1, "Preliminaries to Interpersonal Communication," covers the foundation concepts that are basic to all forms of interpersonal communication and relationships in four chapters.

- Chapter 1, "Foundations of Interpersonal Communication," discusses the nature and importance of interpersonal communication and its fundamental concepts and principles.
- Chapter 2, "Culture and Interpersonal Communication," presents the central role of culture in all aspects of interpersonal communication, explains the importance and aims of a cultural perspective, explains how cultures differ, and considers the nature and principles of intercultural communication.
- Chapter 3, "Perception and the Self in Interpersonal Communication," discusses the basic dimensions of the self (self-concept, self-awareness, and self-esteem), the nature and principles of perception, impression formation, and impression management.
- Chapter 4, "Listening in Interpersonal Communication," considers the importance of listening, the process of listening, listening barriers, the role of culture and gender in listening, and styles of effective listening.

Part 2, "Interpersonal Messages," also contains four chapters. It covers the varied aspects of verbal and nonverbal messages, explores emotional messages, and brings them all together in a discussion of conversation messages.

- Chapter 5, "Verbal Messages," focuses on the verbal message system, identifying the major principles of verbal messages and offering guidelines for making language more accurate, more logical, and more effective.

- Chapter 6, "Nonverbal Messages," covers the major nonverbal channels and the research on nonverbal communication functions and examines the influence of culture on all aspects of nonverbal communication.
- Chapter 7, "Emotional Messages," new to this edition, explains the basic principles of emotions and emotional messages, the major obstacles to communicating emotions, and the skills for both expressing emotions and responding to the emotions of others.
- Chapter 8, "Conversational Messages," brings the material on messages together in an examination of the conversation process, then considers how conversation works, how it can be managed, the nature and role of self-disclosure, organizational conversations, and how conversational problems can be prevented and repaired.

Part 3, "Interpersonal Relationships," covers in five chapters the nature and stages of interpersonal relationships, the major types of relationships, and the central concepts of conflict and power.

- Chapter 9, "Interpersonal Relationships: Stages and Theories," introduces the characteristics of interpersonal relationships, the stages relationships may pass through, and some of the major theories explaining how relationships work.
- Chapter 10, "Interpersonal Relationships: Development and Deterioration," traces the stages of relationships and the research and theory relevant to each of the stages: development, maintenance, deterioration, repair, and dissolution.
- Chapter 11, "Interpersonal Relationships: Friendship, Love, Family, and Workplace," discusses the major types of interpersonal relationships and especially the role of interpersonal communication in forming and in maintaining these relationships.
- Chapter 12, "Interpersonal Conflict and Conflict Management," covers the principles of interpersonal conflict, the stages people go through in resolving or managing conflict, and the strategies that can aid in more effective conflict management.
- Chapter 13, "Interpersonal Power and Influence," covers the principles of power and influence; relationship power, personal power, and message power; and the misuses of power (as in sexual harassment and power plays).

FEATURES

This text is a complete learning package that will provide you with the opportunity to learn about the research and theory in interpersonal communication and to practice and acquire the skills necessary for effective interpersonal interaction.

Each chapter opens with a photo from a film that visually introduces the topic of the chapter. A connecting paragraph then points out the relationship between the film and the contents of the chapter. In addition, the chapter opener contains a list of the major topics covered in the chapter.

Each chapter has a five-part ending: (1) **Summary**, a numbered propositional summary of the major concepts discussed in the chapter; (2) **Key Terms**, a list of key terms used in the chapter (and also included in the Glossary of Interpersonal Communication Concepts at the end of the text) and the page number on which the term is introduced. (3) **Critical Thinking Questions**, a series of questions providing opportunities to apply the material from the chapter and to extend it to other areas of your personal and professional life; (4) **Choice Points**, a series of scenarios asking you to make interpersonal communication choices, which will help personalize the material discussed in the chapter; and (5) **MyCommunicationLab Explorations**, a guide to experiential vehicles that are especially useful in enabling you to work with the chapter contents and that are easily accessible on www.mycommunicationlab.com/devito.

Two **Glossaries** are included at the end of this text: a glossary of interpersonal communication concepts and a glossary of interpersonal communication skills.

The "Dark Side" of Interpersonal Communication

Research and theory on the dark side of communication have been steadily increasing, and this edition points up the dark side and potential dark side of varied interpersonal topics. Some examples include ignoble purposes of interpersonal communication (Chapter 1); the use of impression management to deceive (Chapter 3); fallacies in reasoning and in language that can be used to mislead (Chapter 4); criticism designed to hurt, disconfirmation (sexism, heterosexism, racism, and ageism), verbal messages used to deceive (Chapter 5); maladaptive emotions and violence (Chapter 7); the misuse of self-disclosures of others (Chapter 8); relationship disadvantages (Chapter 9); jealousy (Chapter 10); relationship violence (Chapter 11); unproductive conflict strategies such as verbal aggressiveness (Chapter 12); and sexual harassment and power plays (Chapter 13).

Popular Myths

Many chapters highlight popular myths about various aspects of communication. Included are general myths about communication as well as the myths that culture is equivalent to race, that high self-esteem leads to academic success, that listening and hearing are the same thing, that meanings are in words, that directness is always better than indirectness, that it is always best to express your feelings, that self-disclosure is necessarily a good thing, that relationships should always be preserved, that love will conquer all, that conflict is bad and that in conflict someone's got to lose and someone's got to win, that power is bad, and that everyone is equal.

Workplace Communication and Relationships

This edition continues to integrate coverage of workplace communication into the various chapters. This integrated approach reflects the increasing importance of interpersonal communication in the workplace and responds to students' growing desire for insights into the ways in which interpersonal communication functions in the business world. For example, different chapters cover romantic relationships in the workplace, mentoring, excuses in the workplace, the grapevine, networking, and organizational conversation.

Culture and Interpersonal Communication

As our knowledge of culture and its relevance to interpersonal communication grows, so must culture's presence in an interpersonal communication textbook and course. An entire chapter devoted to culture (Chapter 2, "Culture in Interpersonal Communication") is presented early in the text as one of the foundation concepts for understanding interpersonal communication. This chapter covers the relationship of culture and interpersonal communication, the ways in which cultures differ, and ways to make intercultural communication more effective. In addition to this separate chapter, the entire text stresses the importance of culture to all aspects of interpersonal communication. Here are some of the more important discussions:

- The cultural dimension of context; culture in complementary and symmetrical relationships, in the principle of adjustment, and in ethical questions (Chapter 1)
- The role of culture in the development of self-concept, accurate perception, implicit personality theory, the self-serving bias, and uncertainty (Chapter 3)
- Listening, culture, and gender (Chapter 4)
- Cultural and gender differences in politeness, directness, and assertiveness; cultural identifiers, sexism, heterosexism, racism, and ageism in language and in listening (Chapter 5)
- Culture and gesture, facial expression, eye communication, color, touch, paralanguage, silence, and time (Chapter 6)

- The influence of culture on emotions; cultural customs as an obstacle to the communication of emotions (Chapter 7)
- Conversational maxims, culture, and gender; culture and expressiveness; the influence of culture on self-disclosure (Chapter 8)
- The influence of culture on interpersonal relationships (Chapter 9)
- Culture and the stages of relationships (Chapter 10)
- Cultural differences in friendship, cultural differences in loving, culture and the family (Chapter 11)
- Cultural influences on conflict and conflict management (Chapter 12)
- The cultural dimension of power (Chapter 13)

People with disabilities may also be viewed from a cultural perspective, and in this edition four special tables offer suggestions for communication between people with and people without disabilities. These tables provide tips for communication between people with and without visual problems (Table 1.2 in Chapter 1); between people with disabilities—such as people who have cerebral palsy or who use wheelchairs—and people without disabilities (Table 2.1 in Chapter 2); between persons with and without hearing deficiencies (Table 4.1 in Chapter 4); and between people with and people without speech and language disorders (Table 8.1 in Chapter 8).

Technology

This edition continues to integrate face-to-face communication with communication involving "technology," a useful but not entirely accurate term. Today all means and channels of communication are used in thorough integration, and it's not always easy to tell what qualifies as technology and what doesn't. Suffice it to say that all forms of interpersonal and relationship interaction—face-to-face, phone, social networking, blogging, IM, and e-mail—are important and consequently are considered here. To be sure, there are differences among the media, and these need to be taken into consideration in any contemporary presentation of interpersonal interaction and relationships.

Another way in which technology is integrated is through the use of an extensive package of electronic supplements that is updated regularly. A listing of available ancillaries may be found at the end of this preface. Frequent updates may be found at www.pearsonhighered.com/devito.

Still another way in which technology is integrated is **The Communication Blog**, available at http://tcbdevito.blogspot. com or through the text website (www.pearsonhighered.com/devito). Come visit.

Self-Tests

Twenty-one self-tests appear throughout the text to help personalize the material. Entitled **Test Yourself**, these quizzes cover such topics as your cultural beliefs and values, how ethnocentric you are, your assertiveness, the kind of lover you are, your verbal aggressiveness and argumentativeness, and your interpersonal power. Approximately half of these self-tests are used regularly in interpersonal communication research; the other half were developed to highlight and preview some part of the text material. Each self-test concludes with a two-part discussion: "How Did You Do?" contains the scoring instructions, and "What Will You Do?" asks what steps you might consider taking as a result of the insights provided by the self-assessment. A complete list of self-tests appears in the Specialized Contents on page xiii.

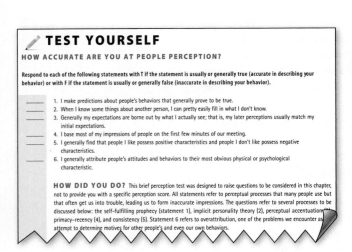

TEST YOURSELF

HOW ACCURATE ARE YOU AT PEOPLE PERCEPTION?

Respond to each of the following statements with T if the statement is usually or generally true (accurate in describing your behavior) or with F if the statement is usually or generally false (inaccurate in describing your behavior).

_____ 1. I make predictions about people's behaviors that generally prove to be true.
_____ 2. When I know some things about another person, I can pretty easily fill in what I don't know.
_____ 3. Generally my expectations are borne out by what I actually see; that is, my later perceptions usually match my initial expectations.
_____ 4. I base most of my impressions of people on the first few minutes of our meeting.
_____ 5. I generally find that people I like possess positive characteristics and people I don't like possess negative characteristics.
_____ 6. I generally attribute people's attitudes and behaviors to their most obvious physical or psychological characteristic.

HOW DID YOU DO? This brief perception test was designed to raise questions to be considered in this chapter, not to provide you with a specific perception score. All statements refer to perceptual processes that many people use but that often get us into trouble, leading us to form inaccurate impressions. The questions refer to several processes to be discussed below: the self-fulfilling prophecy (statement 1), implicit personality theory (2), perceptual accentuation (3), primacy–recency (4), and consistency (5). Statement 6 refers to overattribution, one of the problems we encounter as we attempt to determine motives for other people's and even our own behaviors.

Theory/Research and Skills

Coordinate boxes covering some of the essential theories and research and some of the essential skills in interpersonal communication are presented in each chapter. Each chapter contains an **Understanding Interpersonal Theory and Research** box highlighting a particular area of theory and research in interpersonal communication. Although theories and research are integrated throughout the text, these boxes highlight specific theories and ask you to work with them and apply them to your own experiences. Coordinated with these are boxes that highlight the essential skills of effective interpersonal communication. Each of these **Understanding Interpersonal Skills** boxes contains a discussion of an important aspect of effectiveness and points up ways in which you can better communicate using these qualities of effectiveness. Complete lists of these Understanding Interpersonal Theory and Research and Understanding Interpersonal Skills boxes appear in the Specialized Contents on page xiii.

Ask the Researcher

Each chapter contains an **Ask the Researcher** Q&A to emphasize the close connection between theory and research on the one hand, and practical skills on the other. In these Ask the Researcher features—many of which have been revised for this edition by the authors—nationally and internationally known theorists and researchers respond to questions typical of those students ask about interpersonal communication. You'll find their responses both provocative and practical. A complete list of these Ask the Researcher boxes and their distinguished authors is provided in the Specialized Contents, page xiii.

Ethics in Interpersonal Communication

In each chapter an **Ethics in Interpersonal Communication** box presents a brief discussion of an ethical issue related to the content of the chapter. These ethics discussions cover issues such as culture and ethics, ethical listening, motivational appeals, gossip, lying, interpersonal silence, and your obligation to reveal yourself. A complete list of these Ethics in Interpersonal Communication boxes is provided in the Specialized Contents on page xiii.

ViewPoint

As in the previous edition, the photo captions here contain substantive material rather than the typical brief descriptions of the photos that appear in many texts. These captions, called ViewPoints, present issues to be discussed and should provide useful stimuli for class discussion.

Interactivity

Of course, a printed text cannot be truly interactive; but this edition of *The Interpersonal Communication Book* offers an expanded and improved array of features that invite you to involve yourself, that encourage you to participate actively

UNDERSTANDING INTERPERSONAL THEORY & RESEARCH
The Just World Hypothesis

Many people believe that the world is just: Good things happen to good people and bad things happen to bad people (Aronson, Wilson, & Akert, 2007; Hunt, 2000). Put differently, you get what you deserve! Even when you mindfully dismiss this assumption, you may use it mindlessly when perceiving and evaluating other people. Consider a particularly vivid example: If a woman is raped in certain cultures (for example, in Bangladesh, Iran, or Yemen), she is considered by many in that culture (certainly not all) to have disgraced her family and to be deserving of severe punishment—in many cases, even death. And although you may claim that this is unfair, much research shows that even in this country many people do in fact blame the victim for being raped, especially if the victim is male (Adams-Price, Dalton, & Sumrall, 2004; Anderson, 2004).

The belief that the world is just creates perceptual distortions by leading us to deemphasize the influence of situational factors and to overemphasize the influence of internal factors in our at-

Working with Theories and Research

Using your favorite search engine, search the psychology, sociology, and/or communication databases for "just world." Scan some of the articles. What can you add to the discussion presented here?

UNDERSTANDING INTERPERSONAL SKILLS
Cultural Sensitivity

Cultural sensitivity is an attitude and way of behaving in which you're aware of and acknowledge cultural differences; it's crucial for such global goals as world peace and economic growth as well as for effective interpersonal communication (Franklin & Mizell, 1995). Without cultural sensitivity there can be no effective interpersonal communication between people who are different in gender or race or nationality or affectional orientation. So be mindful of the cultural differences between yourself and the other person. The techniques of interpersonal communication that work well with European Americans may not work well with Asian Americans; what proves effective in Japan may not in Mexico. The close physical distance that is normal in Arab cultures may seem too familiar or too intrusive in much of the United States and northern Europe. The empathy that most Americans welcome may be uncomfortable for most Koreans, Japanese, or Chinese.

Increasing Cultural Sensitivity. This chapter has identified many guidelines for more effective intercultural communication, and among them are recommendations that constitute the best advice for achieving cultural sensitivity:

- Prepare yourself. Read about and listen carefully for culturally influenced behaviors.
- Recognize and face your own fears of acting inappropriately toward members of different cultures.
- Recognize differences between yourself and the culturally different individual.

Working with Interpersonal Skills

How would you rate your own cultural sensitivity? Try to recall situations in which you were and situations in which you weren't culturally sensitive. What happened in each? Can you identify one situation that could have been improved with the additional of cultural sensitivity?

Ask the Researcher
The Importance of Culture in Interpersonal Communication

Culture seems to be a part of all my college courses. But I wonder: Is culture and intercultural communication that important today? Is this knowledge going to help me be more successful in my profession, whatever that will be?

Globalization has made the world more, not less complex, offering us many opportunities to interact with people of other cultures at home and abroad. Intercultural communication engages us at the individual and relational level. Our sense of efficacy in interaction depends to a large degree upon our training, knowledge, and willingness to be open to other cultures. This is the individual level; one may call it self-preparation for

Ethics in Interpersonal Communication
Lying

Lying occurs when you send messages designed to make others believe what you know to be untrue (Ekman, 1985; Burgoon & Hoobler, 2002). You can lie by commission (by making explicitly false statements or even by being evasive or misleading) or by omission (by omitting relevant information and so allowing others to draw incorrect inferences). Similarly, you can lie verbally (in speech or writing) or nonverbally (wearing an innocent facial expression instead of acknowledging the commission of some wrong, or nodding knowingly instead of expressing honest ignorance) (O'Hair, Cody, & McLaughlin, 1981). Lies range from "white lies" and truth stretching to lies that form the basis of relationship infidelity, libel, and perjury. And, not surprisingly, lies have ethical implications.

- Some lies may be considered ethical; for example, lying to a child to protect a fantasy belief in Santa Claus or the tooth fairy, or publicly agreeing with someone to enable the person to save face.
- Some lies may be considered not only ethical but required; for example, lying to protect someone that...

What would you do?

You've been asked to serve as a witness in the trial of someone suspected of robbing a local grocery store. You don't want to get involved—yet you wonder if you can ethically refuse and say you didn't see anything (even though you did). There are other witnesses, and your testimony is not likely to make a significant difference. What would you do?

with the material, and that provide you with lots of material for classroom dialogue. For example:

- *Choice Points* at the end of each chapter present interpersonal dilemmas and invite you to consider how you would respond.
- *Self-tests* in the text provide opportunities for you to examine your own communication behaviors on a wide variety of issues discussed in the text.
- *Ethics in Interpersonal Communication, Understanding Interpersonal Theory and Research,* and *Understanding Interpersonal Skills* boxes all contain questions to help you personalize the concepts.
- *ViewPoint* photo captions also ask for your active involvement in examining selected issues discussed in the text.

GENERAL AND CHAPTER-BY-CHAPTER CHANGES

In addition to new material in many self-tests, Ask the Researcher items, and Ethics in Interpersonal Communication, Understanding Interpersonal Theory and Research, and Understanding Interpersonal Skills boxes, the text of this edition incorporates a variety of new concepts and principles, new research findings, new examples, and new illustrations.

First, here are some general changes:

1. All new chapter openers.
2. Chapters 3 and 4 have been combined into a single chapter (self and perception)
3. Chapters 6, 7, and 8—on verbal and nonverbal messages—have been combined into two chapters (Verbal Messages and Nonverbal Messages)
4. A new chapter on emotional communication (Chapter 7) has been added to Part 2 (Messages)
5. New research has been integrated throughout the text.
6. The Ask Yourself items that were formerly in the margins, augmented by additional items, now make up the new chapter-end section on "choice points"—points at which an interpersonal communication decision needs to be made.
7. The Speaking-Interpersonal-E items have been deleted from the margins; the best of these have been integrated into the text or into the critical thinking questions.
8. Discussions of the myths of various aspects of interpersonal communication have been expanded and highlighted.
9. Key terms are now listed at the end of each chapter with page numbers locating the term's first occurrence and its definition.
10. The dark sides of varied forms of interpersonal communication and relationships are highlighted.

By chapter, the most notable changes are:

- Chapter 1 (Foundations): Clarification of the benefits (divided here into intellectual and practical) of the study of interpersonal communication; explanation of the nature of interpersonal communication in terms of six major characteristics (interdependency, relational nature, continuum, verbal and nonverbal messages, varied forms, and variations in effectiveness); update of the forms of communication (integrating CMC and face-to-face); new figure explaining the interpersonal continuum; and expanded discussion of mindfulness to include specific communication recommendations.
- Chapter 2 (Culture): New 15-item self-test on how cultures differ ("What's Your Cultural Orientation?"); new discussion of high- and low-ambiguity-tolerant cultures; also, ethnocentrism and the accompanying test of ethnocentrism (formerly in the verbal messages chapter) now appear in the culture chapter.

- Chapter 3 (Self and Perception): This chapter is an integration of Chapters 3 (the self) and 4 (perception); expansion of self-esteem discussion with a new self-test (How's Your Self-Esteem?); expansion of self-affirmation in terms of *am*, *can*, and *will* statements; and new section on impression management offering a communication typology of impression management goals and strategies.
- Chapter 4 (Listening): Expanded discussion of the benefits of listening (professional and relationship); reorganization of chapter (e.g., the self-test now appears as a preface to the discussion of the styles of listening); new section on the barriers to listening; and expansion and update of gender differences in listening.
- Chapter 5 (Verbal Messages): Now contains much of the material from the 11th edition's Chapters 6 and 7; a new discussion of politeness now includes discussions of negative and positive face, direct and indirect messages, messages of exclusion and inclusion, and politeness on the Net; discussions of sexism, heterosexism, racism, and ageism have been expanded, and each is now discussed in terms of individual and institutionalized manifestations of these -isms; new summary table of verbal message guidelines, and expanded discussion of metalanguage (in the skills box).
- Chapter 6 (Nonverbal Messages): Myths about nonverbal communication; nonverbal impression formation; new table on nonverbal ways to increase attractiveness; expansion of the immediacy skills box, including both verbal and nonverbal means for increasing immediacy; and expansion of the role of cultural variation in nonverbal communication.
- Chapter 7 (Emotional Messages): A new chapter on emotional messages, including the principles of emotions and emotional messages, obstacles to communicating emotions, skills for expressing emotions, and skills for responding to the emotions of others.
- Chapter 8 (Conversation): The self-disclosure discussion (formerly in Chapter 3) is now included in the conversation chapter under the heading "Conversational Disclosure"; also in this chapter is discussion of organizational messages, both formal (upward, downward, and lateral) and informal (grapevine and, in the ethics box, gossip).
- Chapter 9 (Interpersonal Relationships: Stages and Theories): Added discussion of flirting in relationship development and extended discussion of relationship rules theory in friendship, love, and family.
- Chapter 10 (Interpersonal Relationships; Development and Dissolution): Discussion of the relationship license; streamlined discussion of the causes of relationship deterioration; expansion of "communication in relationships" figure to include all theories discussed in text; new discussion on the reasons for relationship dissolution; expanded discussion of empathy (skills box); expanded discussion of jealousy (theory and research box).
- Chapter 11 (Types of Relationships): Updates and expansions of coverage of technology in friendship, love, family, and workplace relationships; consideration of long-distance relationships; expansion of typology of couple types; and a new discussion of relationship violence (what it is, its effects, and what to do about it—including a self-test).
- Chapter 12 (Conflict): Clarification of the nature of interpersonal conflict; myths about conflict; a new 10-item self-test of verbal aggressiveness.
- Chapter 13 (Power): New principles of power (power can be shared and power generates privilege); restructured discussion of the uses of power, built around power in the relationship, in the person, and in the message; new table on "additional types of harassment"; new interpersonal credibility self-test; and new theory and research box on an alternative typology of compliance-gaining strategies.

The Communication Blog (http://tcbdevito.blogspot.com)

Maintained by the author, this site offers a forum for people teaching basic courses in interpersonal communication as well as hybrid and public speaking courses. Regular posts by the author update the text material and share ideas for teaching.

ANCILLARIES/SUPPLEMENTARY MATERIALS

Instructor Supplements

Print Supplements

- **Instructor's Manual/Test Bank by Janice Stuckey, Jefferson State Community College**
  This Instructor's Manual/Test Bank includes sample syllabi, chapter outlines, classroom activities, discussion questions, and video suggestions. The Test Bank contains more than 1,000 items, including challenging multiple-choice, true/false, and short-answer essay questions along with an answer key that ranks the difficulty level of each item.

Electronic Supplements

- **Computerized Test Bank**
  This user-friendly interface enables instructors to view, edit, and add questions, transfer questions to tests, and print tests in a variety of fonts. Search and sort features allow instructors to locate questions quickly and arrange them in a preferred order. The computerized test bank is available online at www.pearsonhighered.com/irc (access code required).

- **PowerPoint Presentation Package by Nancy Jackson, Community College of Aurora**
  This text-specific package consists of a collection of lecture outlines and graphic images keyed to every chapter in the text. The PowerPoint Presentation is available for download at www.pearsonhighered.com/irc (access code required).

- **MyCommunicationLab**
  This website is an interactive and instructive online solution for inerpersonal communication courses. Designed to be used as a supplement for a traditional lecture course, or completely administer an online course, *MyCommunicationLab* combines multimedia, video case studies and assessments, research support, tests, and quizzes to make teaching and learning fun! Students benefit from a wealth of new video and audio clips specific to interpersonal communication that are accompanied by activities, questions to consider, and helpful tips—all geared to help students learn to communicate more effectively. Go to www.mycommunicationlab.com for more information or contact your local Pearson representative (access code required).

- **VideoWorkshop for Interpersonal Communication—Instructor's Teaching Guide**
  The VideoWorkshop for Interpersonal Communication is a new way to bring video into your course for maximized learning! This total teaching and learning system includes quality video footage on an easy-to-use CD-ROM plus a Student Learning Guide and an Instructor's Teaching Guide. The result? A program that brings textbook concepts to life with ease and that helps your students understand, analyze, and apply the objectives of the course. Go to www.pearsonhighered.com for more details.

- **Allyn & Bacon Interpersonal Communication Video Library**
  This library contains a range of videos from which adopters can choose. Each of the videos features a variety of scenarios that illustrate interpersonal concepts and relationships, including topics such as nonverbal communication, perception, conflict, and listening. Please contact your Pearson representative for details and a complete list of videos and their contents to choose which would be most useful to your class.

- **InterWrite PRS (Personal Response System)**
  This easy-to-use wireless polling system enables you to pose questions, record results, and display those results instantly in your classroom. Designed by teachers, for teachers, PRS is easy to integrate into your lectures.

- **Lecture Questions for Clickers: Interpersonal Communication by Keri Moe, El Paso Community College**

  An assortment of questions and activities covering the principles and axioms of interpersonal communication are presented in PowerPoint slides. These slides will help liven up your lectures and can be used along with the Personal Response System to get students more involved in the material. Available on the Web at www.pearsonhighered.com/irc (access code required).

- **The Communication Blog** (http://tcbdevito.blogspot.com)

  Maintained by the author, this site offers a forum for people teaching basic courses in interpersonal communication as well as the hybrid and public speaking courses. Regular posts by the author update the text material and share ideas for teaching.

Student Supplements

Electronic Supplements

- **MyCommunicationLab**

  MyCommunicationLab is a state-of-the-art, interactive learning solution for your interpersonal communication course. MyCommunicationLab combines a complete E-book, multimedia, video clips, activities, research support, tests, and quizzes to help you succeed in your interpersonal communication course. Go to www.mycommunicationlab.com for more information (access code required).

- **Interpersonal Communication Study Site with online practice tests**

  This site includes multiple choice, true/false, and essay study questions. The website (www.abinterpersonal.com) also includes flashcards and web links.

- **VideoWorkshop for Interpersonal Communication—Student Learning Guide by Christine North, Ohio Northern University**

  The VideoWorkshop for Interpersonal Communication is a new way to bring video into your course for maximized learning! This total learning system includes quality video footage on an easy-to-use CD-ROM plus a Student Learning Guide. The result? A program that brings textbook concepts to life with ease and that helps you understand, analyze, and apply the objectives of the course.

ACKNOWLEDGMENTS

I owe a great debt to the many researchers who responded to my call for responses to a variety of questions and whose answers appear in the Ask the Researcher features throughout the text. Without your cooperation, goodwill, and support, this feature obviously could not have been done. I thank you all (in order of appearance):

Sherwyn P. Morreale (University of Colorado, Colorado Springs)
Molefi Kete Asante (Temple University)
Linda C. Lederman (Arizona State University)
Deborah Borisoff (New York University)
Teresa L. Thompson (University of Dayton)
Kelly A. Rocca (St. John's University)
Elizabeth M. Perse (University of Delaware)
Susan B. Barnes (Rochester Institute of Technology)
Barbara Montgomery (Colorado State University, Pueblo)
Shirlee A. Levin (College of Southern Maryland)
Anita L. Vangelisti (University of Texas)
Carolyn M. Anderson (University of Akron)
John Daly (University of Texas)

I want also to express my appreciation to the many specialists who carefully reviewed the previous edition. Your comments resulted in a large number of changes; I'm extremely grateful. Thank you:

Narrisra Maria Punyanunt-Carter (Texas Tech University)
Robert N. St. Clair (University of Louisville)
Ee Lin Lee (Western Washington University)
Nathan Miczo (Western Illinois University)
Elaine Zelley (La Salle University)

In addition, I wish to express my appreciation to the people at Allyn & Bacon who contributed so heavily to this text, especially Jeanne Zalesky, acquisitions editor; Hilary Jackson, developmental editor; Jay Howland, copy editor; Tom Conville, project editor; and Kate Cebik, photo researcher. I thank them all for making me and this book look good.

Joseph A. DeVito
jadevito@earthlink.net
www.pearsonhighered.com/devito
http://tcbdevito.blogspot.com

The Interpersonal Communication Book

CHAPTER

1

Foundations of Interpersonal Communication

Why Study Interpersonal Communication

The Nature of Interpersonal Communication

Elements of Interpersonal Communication

Principles of Interpersonal Communication

Quantum of Solace

James Bond, here in *Quantum of Solace*, is the quintessential hero—suave, sophisticated, and competent in all interpersonal situations in love and in war. This chapter introduces what it means to be a competent interpersonal communicator and the remaining chapters provide you with the means for acquiring these crucial life skills.

This chapter introduces the study of interpersonal communication and explains why interpersonal communication is so important. The chapter examines the nature of this unique form of communication, its elements, and its principles.

Why Study Interpersonal Communication

Fair questions to ask at the beginning of this text and this course are "What will I get out of this?" and "Why should I study interpersonal communication?" As with any worthwhile study, we can identify two major benefits: intellectual benefits and practical benefits.

Intellectual Benefits

Interpersonal communication is something you do every day:

- talking with coworkers
- giving or responding to a compliment
- making new friends
- asking for a date
- communicating through instant messaging
- maintaining and repairing relationships
- breaking off relationships
- applying for a job
- giving directions
- persuading a supervisor

Understanding these interactions is an essential part of a liberal arts education. Much as an educated person must know geography, history, science, and mathematics, you need to know the how, why, and what of interpersonal communication. It's a significant part of the world in which you live, and it's becoming more significant every day.

If you measured the time you spend in some form of interpersonal communication, it would probably occupy a major (if not the major) part of your day. Understanding the theories and research bearing on this most defining of all human qualities seems essential to a well-rounded education. Without a knowledge of interpersonal communication, it would be impossible to understand a large part of human interaction and human relationships.

Practical Benefits

Interpersonal communication is also an extremely practical art; effectiveness in your personal, social, and professional life is largely dependent on your interpersonal communication knowledge and skills.

For example, in a survey of 1,001 people over 18 years of age, 53 percent felt that a lack of effective communication was the major cause of marriage failure, significantly greater than money (38 percent) and in-law interference (14 percent) (How Americans Communicate, 1999). The relevance of interpersonal communication skills to relationships is, of course, a major theme of this text, and we'll return frequently to this topic.

In a similar way, interpersonal skills are crucial to professional success, a relationship that has been widely documented. Not long ago the *Wall Street Journal* published an article titled "How to get hired: We asked recruiters what M.B.A. graduates are doing wrong. Ignore their advice at your peril" (Alsop, 2004). The article reported that among the 23 attributes ranked as "very important" in hiring decisions, "communication and interpersonal skills" was at the top of the list, noted by 89 percent of the recruiters. This was a far higher percentage of recruiters than noted "content of the core curriculum" (34 percent), or "overall value for the money invested in the recruiting effort" (33 percent).

These findings, although interesting, reveal nothing new. Interpersonal skills have long been recognized as critical to professional success in hundreds of studies (Morreale, Osborn, & Pearson, 2000; Morreale & Pearson, 2008). Interpersonal skills offer a "key career advantage for finance professionals in the next century" (Messmer, 1999), play an important role in preventing workplace violence (Parker, 2004), reduce medical mishaps

Ask the Researcher

The Values of Interpersonal Communication in the Twenty-first Century

I can understand the value of interpersonal communication for lots of people, but I don't know what I'm going to do or be in the future. Why should I study communication?

From an analysis of 93 recent articles, communication skills were found critical to success in life no matter what you do, personally or professionally. *New York Times* columnist and best-selling author Tom Friedman talks about what college graduates need to know and be able to do to succeed in the twenty-first century in his recent book *The World Is Flat*:

> You need to like people. You need to be good at managing or interacting with other people. Although having good people skills has always been an asset in the working world, it will be even more so in a flat world [with advances in technology and communication putting diverse people in touch as never before]. That said, I am not sure how you teach that as part of a classroom curriculum, but someone had better figure it out. (p. 106)

Actually, the answer is simple: We all need to learn to communicate effectively and ethically!

For more information see T. L. Friedman, *The World Is Flat: A Brief History of the Twenty-first Century* (New York: Farrar, Straus & Giroux, 2006); and S. P. Morreale, and J. C. Pearson, "Why Communication Education Is Important: The Centrality of the Discipline in the 21st Century," *Communication Education* 57 (2) (2008).

Sherwyn P. Morreale (Ph.D., University of Denver) is a faculty member and director of graduate studies in communication at the University of Colorado at Colorado Springs. She is the former associate director of the National Communication Association, a textbook author, and a recognized national expert on the nature of communication competence and its importance in U.S. society.

and improve doctor–patient communication (Sutcliffe, Lewton, & Rosenthal, 2004; Smith, 2004), and are one of six areas that define the professional competence of physicians and trainees (Epstein & Hundert, 2002). The importance of interpersonal communication skills extends over the entire spectrum of professions.

Clearly, then, interpersonal skills are vital to your relationship and professional success: They will help you become a more effective relationship partner and a more successful professional, regardless of your specific professional goal.

Understanding the theory and research in interpersonal communication and mastering its skills go hand in hand (Greene & Burleson, 2003). The more you know about interpersonal communication, the more insight and knowledge you'll gain about what works and what doesn't work. The more skills you have within your arsenal of communication strategies, the greater will be your choices for communicating in any situation. In a nutshell, the greater your knowledge and the greater the number of communication choices at your disposal, the greater the likelihood that you'll be successful in achieving your interpersonal goals. This concept of choice figures into many of the principles and skills discussed throughout this book. You might even look at this textbook and your course as enlarging your interpersonal communication choices, giving you a greater number of options than you had before your formal exposure to the study of interpersonal communication.

As a preface to an area of study that will be enlightening, exciting, and extremely practical, examine your assumptions about interpersonal communication by taking the accompanying self-test.

TEST YOURSELF

WHAT DO YOU BELIEVE ABOUT INTERPERSONAL COMMUNICATION?

Respond to each of the following statements with T if you believe the statement is usually true or F if you believe the statement is usually false.

_____ 1. Good communicators are born, not made.

_____ 2. The more you communicate, the better at it you will be.

_____ 3. In your interpersonal communications, a good guide to follow is to be as open, empathic, and supportive as you can be.

_____ 4. The best guide to follow when communicating with people from other cultures is to ignore the differences and treat the other person just as you'd treat members of your own culture.

_____ 5. Fear of meeting new people is detrimental and must be eliminated.

_____ 6. When there is conflict, your relationship is in trouble.

HOW DID YOU DO? As you probably figured out, all six statements are generally false. As you read this text, you'll discover not only why these beliefs are false but also the trouble you can get into when you assume they're true. For now, and in brief, here are some of the reasons each of the statements is generally false: (1) Effective communication is a learned skill; although some people are born brighter or more extroverted, all can improve their abilities and become more effective communicators. (2) It's not the amount of communication people engage in but the quality that matters; if you practice bad habits, you're more likely to grow less effective than more effective, so it's important to learn and follow the principles of effectiveness (J. O. Greene, 2003; Greene & Burleson, 2003). (3) Each interpersonal situation is unique, and therefore the type of communication appropriate in one situation may not be appropriate in another. (4) This assumption will probably get you into considerable trouble, because people from different cultures will often attribute different meanings to a message; members of different cultures also follow different rules for what is and is not appropriate in interpersonal communication. (5) Many people are nervous meeting new people, especially if these are people in authority; managing, not eliminating, the fear will enable you to become effective regardless of your current level of fear. (6) All meaningful relationships experience conflict; relationships are not in trouble when there is conflict, though dealing with conflict ineffectively can often damage the relationship.

WHAT WILL YOU DO? This is perhaps, then, a good place to start practicing the critical thinking skill of questioning commonly held assumptions about interpersonal communication and about yourself as an interpersonal communicator. Consider, for example, what other beliefs you have about communication and about yourself as a communicator. How do these beliefs influence your communication?

The Nature of Interpersonal Communication

Although this entire book is in a sense a definition of interpersonal communication, a working definition is useful at the start. **Interpersonal communication** is *the verbal and nonverbal interaction between two (or sometimes more than two) interdependent people.* This relatively simple definition implies a variety of characteristics.

Interpersonal Communication Involves Interdependent Individuals

Interpersonal communication is the communication that takes place between people who are in some way "connected." Interpersonal communication would thus include what takes place between a son and his father, an employer and an employee, two sisters, a teacher and a student, two lovers, two friends, and so on. Although largely dyadic (two-person) in nature, interpersonal communication is often extended to include small intimate groups such as the family. Even within a family, however, the communication that takes place is often dyadic—mother to child, father to mother, daughter to son, and so on.

Not only are the individuals simply "connected"—they are also interdependent: What one person does has an impact on the other person. The actions of one person have consequences for the other person. In a family, for example, a child's trouble with the police will affect the parents, other siblings, extended family members, and perhaps friends and neighbors.

Interpersonal Communication Is Inherently Relational

Because of this interdependency, interpersonal communication is inevitably and essentially relational in nature; interpersonal communication takes place within a relationship, it impacts the relationship, it defines the relationship. The communication that takes place in a relationship is in part a function of that relationship. That is, the way you communicate is determined in great part by the kind of relationship that exists between you and the other person. You interact differently with your interpersonal communication instructor and your best friend; you interact with a sibling in ways very different from the ways in which you interact with a neighbor, a work colleague, or a casual acquaintance.

But notice also that the way you communicate, the way you interact, will influence the kind of relationship you develop. If you interact with another person in friendly ways, you're likely to develop a friendship. If you regularly exchange hateful and hurtful messages, you're likely to develop an antagonistic relationship. If you regularly express respect and support for each other, a respectful and supportive relationship is likely to develop. This is surely one of the most obvious observations you can make about interpersonal communication. And yet many people seem not to appreciate this very clear relationship between what they say and the relationships that develop (or deteriorate).

Interpersonal Communication Exists on a Continuum

Interpersonal communication exists along a continuum (see Figure 1.1) that ranges from relatively impersonal to highly personal (Miller, 1978, 1990). At the impersonal end of the spectrum, you have simple conversation between people who, we'd say, really don't know each other—the server and the customer, for example. At the highly personal end is the communication that takes place between people who are intimately interconnected—a father and son, two longtime lovers, or best friends, for example. A few characteristics distinguish the impersonal from the personal forms of communication (Miller, 1978).

- *Role versus personal information.* Notice that in the impersonal example, the individuals are likely to respond to each other according to the *roles* they are currently playing; the server treats the customer not as a unique individual but as one of many customers. And the customer, in turn, acts towards the server not as a unique individual but as he or she would react to any server. The father and the son, however, react to each other as unique individuals. They act on the basis of *personal information.*
- *Societal versus personal rules.* Notice too that the server and the customer interact according to the *rules of society* governing the server–customer interaction. The father and the son, on the other hand, interact on the basis of *personally established rules.* The way they address each other, their touching behavior, and their degree of physical closeness, for example, are unique to them and are established by them rather than by society.
- *Predictive versus explanatory data.* The relationships on the left side of the continuum— the more impersonal interactions—offer the individuals some measure of predictability. For example, at the start of a course, you can predict some of the behaviors of the other students in your class. But as you get to observe and interact with your classmates

FIGURE 1.1

An Interpersonal Continuum

Here is one possible interpersonal continuum. Other people would position the relationships differently. You may want to try constructing an interpersonal continuum of your own relationships.

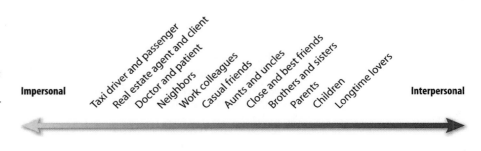

TABLE 1.1 **Face-to-Face and Computer-Mediated Communication**

Throughout this text face-to-face and computer-mediated interpersonal communication are discussed, compared, and contrasted. Here is a brief summary of some communication concepts indicating some of the ways in which face-to-face and computer-mediated communication (CMC) are similar and different. What other similarities and differences would you identify?

Interpersonal Communication Element	Face-to-Face	CMC
Sender (speaking turn, presentation of self, impression management)	Visual appearance communicates who you are; personal characteristics (sex, approximate age, race, etc.) are overt and open to visual inspection; receiver controls the order of what is attended to; disguise is difficult.	You present the self you want others to see; personal characteristics are covert and are revealed when you want to reveal them; speaker controls the order of revelation; disguise or anonymity is easy.
	You compete for the speaker's turn and time with the other person(s); you can be interrupted.	It's always your turn; speaker time is unlimited; you can't be interrupted.
Receiver (number, interests, third party, impression formation)	One or a few who are in your visual field.	One, a few, or as many as you find in a chat room, have on your e-mail list, or can address via bulletin board posts.
	Receivers are limited to those you have the opportunity to meet; finding people who have the same interests you do can be difficult, especially in isolated communities with little mobility.	Receivers are virtually unlimited; you can more easily and quickly find people who match your interests.
	Your messages can be overheard by or repeated to third parties, but not verbatim and not with complete accuracy.	Your messages can be retrieved by others or forwarded verbatim to a third party or to hundreds of third parties (with or without your knowledge).
	Impressions are based on the verbal and nonverbal cues receiver perceives.	Impressions are based (usually) on text messages receiver reads.
Context (physical, temporal, social–psychological, cultural)	Where you both are; together in essentially the same physical space.	Where you and receiver each want to be, separated in space.
	Context happens as it happens; you have little control over the context once you're in a communication situation.	You can more easily choose the timing—when you want to respond.
	Communication is synchronous—messages are exchanged at the same time.	Communication may be synchronous, as in chat rooms and instant messaging, or asynchronous—when messages are exchanged at different times, as in e-mail and bulletin board postings.
Channel	Channels are auditory + visual + tactile + proxemic.	Channel is visual for text (though both auditory and visual for graphics and video are available).
	Two-way channel enables immediate interactivity.	Two-way channels; some enable immediate and some delayed interactivity.
Messages (verbal/nonverbal messages; permanence, purposes)	Spoken words along with gestures, eye contact, accent, paralinguistic cues, space, smell, touch, clothing, hair, and all the other nonverbal cues.	Written words in purely text-based CMC, though that's changing.
	Messages are temporary unless recorded; speech signals fade rapidly.	Messages are permanent unless erased.
	Rarely are abbreviations verbally expressed.	Limited nonverbal cues; some can be created with emoticons or words and some (like smells and touch) cannot.
		CMC uses lots of abbreviations.
Feedforward	Feedforward is conveyed nonverbally and verbally early in the interaction.	In e-mail it's given in the headings and subject line as well as in the opening sentences.
Feedback	Usually immediate, though this can be delayed; immediacy is usually expected.	In e-mail, newsgroup, and discussion list communication, feedback is usually and easily delayed; some delay is expected.
		In chat and instant messaging it is immediate.
Purposes and Effects	All purposes (to learn, to relate, to influence, to play, to help) can be achieved.	All purposes (to learn, to relate, to influence, to play, to help) can be achieved.
	All effects can be achieved.	All effects can be achieved.
	Some purposes may be easier to achieve in face-to-face interaction; for example, affection or support.	Some purposes may be easier to achieve in CMC; for example, information.

| TABLE 1.1 | (Continued) |

Noise	Noise in the context; articulation, pronunciation, and grammatical errors.	Noise in your own surroundings; spelling and grammatical errors.
	Physiological, psychological, and semantic noise are usually present to some extent.	Physiological, psychological, and semantic noise are usually present to some extent.
Ethics and Deception	Presentation of false physical self is difficult but not impossible; false psychological and social selves are easier to present.	Presentation of false physical self as well as false psychological and social selves is relatively easy, though with audio and visual components it gets a bit more difficult.
	Nonverbal leakage cues often give you away when you're lying.	Lying is probably easier.
Competence (oral, written, technological)	Effective speaking techniques.	Effective writing techniques.
	Oral skills aid in interaction management, empathy, other-orientation, etc.	Writing skills aid in interaction management, empathy, other-orientation, etc.
		Technological skills aid in use of media.

over time—that is, as you get to know them better—your accuracy in prediction increases; and, most important, you'll also begin to be able to explain their behaviors (at least to some extent). That is, as you move along the continuum from impersonal to highly personal, your ability to predict and explain behaviors increases.

■ *Social versus personal messages.* Still another difference is found in the messages exchanged. The messages that the server and customer exchange, for example, are themselves *impersonal*; there is little self-disclosure and little emotional content. In the father–son example, the messages may run the entire range and may at times be *highly personal* with lots of disclosure and emotion.

Interpersonal Communication Involves Verbal and Nonverbal Messages

Interpersonal interaction involves the exchange of both verbal and nonverbal messages. The words you use as well as your facial expressions, your eye contact, and your body posture send interpersonal messages. Likewise, you receive interpersonal messages through your sense of hearing as well as through your other senses, especially vision and touch. Even silence sends interpersonal messages. These messages, as you'll see throughout this course, will vary greatly depending on the other factors involved in the interaction. You don't talk to a best friend in the same way you talk to your college professor or your parents.

One of the great myths in communication is that nonverbal communication accounts for more than 90 percent of the meaning of any message. Actually, it depends. In some situations the nonverbal signals will indeed carry more of your meaning than the words you use. In other situations, however, the verbal signals will communicate more information. Most often, of course, they work together. Rather than focusing on which channel communicates the greater percentage of meaning, it's more important to focus on the ways in which verbal and nonverbal messages occur together.

Interpersonal Communication Exists in Varied Forms

Often interpersonal communication takes place face-to-face, as when we talk with other students before class, interact with family or friends over dinner, or trade secrets with intimates. This is the type of interaction that probably comes to mind when you think of interpersonal communication. Today, however, much conversation also takes place online. Online communication, or computer-mediated communication (CMC), is now a major part of people's interpersonal experience throughout the world. Such communications are important personally, socially, and professionally.

The major types of online conversation differ from one another and from face-to-face interaction in important ways. A few of the major similarities and differences may be pointed out here (see Table 1.1).

E-mail is still the most common use of Internet communication. The number of e-mails has been estimated to be approximately 183 billion per day or about two million per second (http://email.about.com accessed April 29, 2008).

E-mail communication is **asynchronous**, meaning that it does not take place in real time. You may send your message today, but the receiver may not read it for a week and may take another week to respond. Consequently, much of the spontaneity created by real-time communication is lost here. You may, for example, be very enthusiastic about a topic when you send your e-mail but practically forget it by the time someone responds. E-mail is also virtually unerasable, a feature that has important consequences we'll discuss later in this chapter.

Through instant messaging or IM you interact in (essentially) real time. The communication messages are **synchronous**—they occur at the same time and are similar to phone communication, except that IM is text-based rather than voice-based. Through IM you can also play games, share files, listen to music, send messages to cell phones, announce company meetings, and do a great deal else with short, abbreviated messages. Among college students, as you probably know, the major purpose of IM seems to be to maintain "social connectedness" (Kindred & Roper, 2004).

In chat groups and social networking groups like Facebook and MySpace, you can also communicate in real time. Some 55 percent of all Americans between the ages of 12 and 17 use social networking sites, and the majority of these users have posted personal profiles. Among their purposes, in order of frequency, are: to stay in touch with friends, to make plans with friends, to make new friends, and to flirt (Lehart & Madden, 2007). Unlike mailing lists, chat communication lets you see a member's message as it is being sent; there's virtually no delay. Whereas e-mail and IM are largely text-based systems, chat and social network communication may include voice, photos, and videos.

Chat groups and social networking sites give you the great advantage of enabling you to communicate with people you would never meet or interact with otherwise. Because many of these groups are international, they provide excellent exposure to other cultures, other ideas, and other ways of communicating; they offer a good introduction to intercultural communication.

Interpersonal Communication Varies in Effectiveness

Like all communication, interpersonal communication may vary greatly in effectiveness and satisfaction. Some interactions (and relationships) are highly successful and some are total failures; some give joy and others give grief. Most are somewhere between these extremes. Part of the purpose of this text and this course is to provide you with options for interacting more effectively and with greater individual satisfaction. Look at it this way: Throughout your interpersonal life and in each interpersonal interaction you're presented with **choice points**—moments when you have to make a choice as to who you communicate with, what you say, what you don't say, how you phrase what you want to say, and so on. This course and this text aim to give you reasons (grounded in communication theory and research discussed throughout the text and highlighted in the Understanding Theory and Research boxes) for the varied choices you'll be called upon to make in your interpersonal interactions. The course also aims to give you the skills you'll need to execute these well-reasoned choices (many of which are written into the text and some of which are highlighted in the Understanding Interpersonal Communication Skills boxes).

Elements of Interpersonal Communication

The model presented in Figure 1.2 is designed to reflect the circular nature of interpersonal communication; both persons send messages simultaneously rather than in a linear sequence where communication goes from person 1 to person 2 to person 1 to person 2 and on and on. Each of the concepts identified in the model and discussed here may be thought of as a **universal of interpersonal communication**, in that it's present in all interpersonal interactions: (1) source–receiver, (2) encoding–decoding, (3) messages, (4) channels, (5) noise, (6) contexts, (7) ethics, and (8) competence.

Source–Receiver

Interpersonal communication involves at least two persons. Each person performs **source** functions (formulates and sends messages) and also performs **receiver** functions (perceives and comprehends messages). The term **source–receiver** emphasizes that both functions are performed by each individual in interpersonal communication.

   Who you are, what you know, what you believe, what you value, what you want, what you have been told, and what your attitudes are all influence what you say, how you say it, what messages you receive, and how you receive them. Likewise, the person you're speaking to and the knowledge that you think that person has will greatly influence your interpersonal messages (Lau, Chiu, & Hong, 2001). Each person is unique; each person's communications are unique.

Encoding–Decoding

Encoding refers to the act of producing messages—for example, speaking or writing. *Decoding* is the reverse and refers to the act of understanding messages—for example, listening or reading. By sending your ideas via sound waves (in the case of speech) or

FIGURE 1.2

A Model of Some Universals of Interpersonal Communication

After you read the section on the elements of interpersonal communication, you may wish to construct your own model of the process. In constructing this model, be careful that you don't fall into the trap of visualizing interpersonal communication as a linear or simple left-to-right, static process. Remember that all elements are interrelated and interdependent. After completing your model, consider, for example: (1) Could your model also serve as a model of intrapersonal communication? A model of small group, public, or mass communication? (2) What elements or concepts other than those noted here might be added to the model?

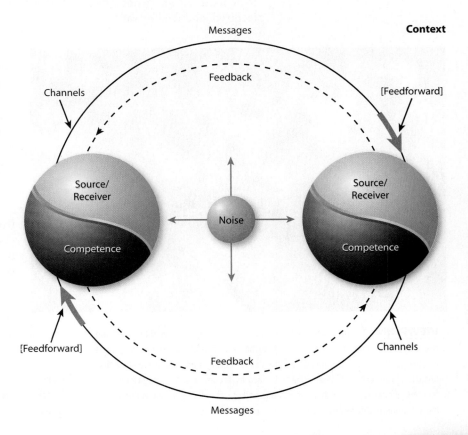

light waves (in the case of writing), you're putting these ideas into a **code**, hence *en*coding. By translating sound or light waves into ideas, you're taking them out of a code, hence *de*coding. Thus, speakers and writers are called **encoders**, and listeners and readers are called **decoders**. The term **encoding–decoding** is used to emphasize that the two activities are performed in combination by each participant. For interpersonal communication to occur, messages must be encoded and decoded. For example, when a parent talks to a child whose eyes are closed and whose ears are covered by stereo headphones, interpersonal communication does not occur because the messages sent are not being received.

Messages

Messages—signals that serve as **stimuli** for a receiver—may be auditory (hearing), visual (seeing), tactile (touching), olfactory (smelling), gustatory (tasting), or any combination. You communicate interpersonally by gesture and touch as well as by words and sentences. The clothes you wear communicate to others and, in fact, to yourself as well. The way you walk communicates, as does the way you shake hands, tilt your head, comb your hair, sit, smile, or frown. These signals are your interpersonal communication messages. Similarly, the colors and types of cell phones, the wallpaper and screen savers on your computer, and even the type and power of your computer communicate messages about you. Interpersonal communication can take place by telephone, through prison cell walls, through webcams, or face-to-face. Increasingly, it's taking place through computers.

Messages may be intentional or unintentional. They may result from the most carefully planned strategy as well as from the unintentional slip of the tongue, lingering body odor, or nervous twitch.

Messages may refer to the world, people, and events as well as to other messages (DeVito, 2003a). Messages that are about other messages are called **metamessages** and represent many of your everyday communications; they include, for example, "Do you understand?" "Did I say that right?" "What did you say?" "Is it fair to say that . . .?" "I want to be honest," "That's not logical." Two particularly important types of metamessages are feedback and feedforward.

VIEWPOINT The "feedback theory of relationships" holds that satisfying friendships or romantic relationships may be characterized by feedback that is positive, person focused, immediate, low in monitoring, and supportive—and that unsatisfying relationships are characterized by feedback that is negative, self-focused, nonimmediate, high in monitoring, and critical. How effective is this theory in explaining relationships with which you're familiar?

Feedback Messages Throughout the interpersonal communication process, you exchange **feedback**—messages sent back to the speaker concerning reactions to what is said (Clement & Frandsen, 1976). Feedback tells the speaker what effect she or he is having on listeners. On the basis of this feedback, the speaker may adjust, modify, strengthen, de-emphasize, or change the content or form of the messages.

Feedback may come from yourself or from others. When you send a message—say, in speaking to another person—you also hear yourself. That is, you get feedback from your own messages: you hear what you say, you feel the way you move, you see what you write. In addition to this self-feedback, you get feedback from others. This feedback can take many forms. A frown or a smile, a yea or a nay, a pat on the back or a punch in the mouth are all types of feedback. Sometimes feedback is easy to identify, but sometimes it isn't (Skinner, 2002). Part of the art of effective communication is to discern feedback and adjust your messages on the basis of that feedback.

Feedforward Messages **Feedforward** is information you provide before sending your primary message (Richards, 1951). Feedforward reveals something about the message to come. Examples of feedforward include the preface or table of contents of a book, the opening paragraph of a chapter, movie previews, magazine covers, and introductions in public speeches. Feedforward may serve a variety of functions. For example, you might use feedforward to express your wish to chat a bit, saying something like "Hey, I haven't seen you the entire week; what's been going on?" Or you might give a brief preview of your main message by saying something like "You'd better sit down for this; you're going to be shocked." Or you might ask others to hear you out before they judge you.

Channel

The communication **channel** is the medium through which messages pass. It's a kind of bridge connecting source and receiver. Communication rarely takes place over only one channel; two, three, or four channels are often used simultaneously. For example, in face-to-face interaction, you speak and listen (vocal–auditory channel), but you also gesture and receive signals visually (gestural–visual channel), and you emit odors and smell those of others (chemical–olfactory channel). Often you communicate through touch (cutaneous–tactile channel). Another way to think about channels is to consider them as the means of communication: for example, face-to-face contact, telephone, e-mail and snail mail, chat groups, instant messaging, news postings, film, television, radio, smoke signals, or fax.

Note that the channel imposes different restrictions on your message construction. For example, in CMC you can pause to think of the right word or phrase, you can go on for as short or as long a time as you want without any threat of interruption or contradiction, and you can edit your speech/message more easily.

It would be a mistake to view the channel as a simple passageway that provides unobstructed connections between two people. In reality, there are "gatekeepers" that allow some messages to get from sender to receiver but prevent others from getting through (Lewin, 1947). The media are among the most well known of gatekeepers; they allow certain messages to air on television and to be dramatized in film while barring others from similar exposure. Editors of newspapers, periodicals, publishing houses, and websites are also gatekeepers (Lewis, 1995; Bodon, Powell, & Hickson, 1999). But a perhaps more important kind of gatekeeping is seen in interpersonal situations. As you were growing up, your parents gave you certain information and withheld other information (Fagan & Barnett, 2003). Depending on the culture in which you were raised, you may have been told about Santa Claus and the Tooth Fairy but not about cancer or mutual funds. When you went to school, your teachers served a similar function. They taught you about certain historical events but not others. Your friends and romantic partners may tell you some things and withhold others. For example, a friend may withhold information about an impending test (that you didn't hear about) because he or she wants you to go to the movies instead of studying. Or a romantic partner may prevent from meeting his or her ex-partners, lest you hear some negative reactions. And you in turn likely function similarly.

Obstruction in the channel is also seen when one or more channels is physiologically damaged. For example, in individuals with visual difficulties, the visual channel is impaired, so adjustments have to be made. Table 1.2 gives you an idea of how such adjustment can make interpersonal communication between persons with and without visual impairment more effective.

Noise

Technically, **noise** is anything that distorts a message, anything that prevents the receiver from receiving the message. At one extreme,

TABLE 1.2 Interpersonal Communication Tips
Between People with and People without Visual Impairments

Louis Braille

Helen Keller

Ray Charles

David Paterson

People vary greatly in their visual abilities; some are totally blind, some are partially sighted, and some have unimpaired vision. Ninety percent of people who are "legally blind" have some vision. All people, however, have the same need for communication and information. Here are some tips for making communication better between those who have visual impairments and those without such difficulties.

If you're the sighted person and are talking with a visually impaired person:

1. Identify yourself. Don't assume the visually impaired person will recognize your voice.

2. Face your listener; you'll be easier to hear. Don't shout. Most people who are visually impaired are not hearing impaired. Speak at your normal volume.

3. Because your gestures, eye movements, and facial expressions cannot be seen by the visually impaired listener, encode into speech all the meanings you wish to communicate.

4. Use audible turn-taking cues. When you pass the role of speaker to a person who is visually impaired, don't rely on nonverbal cues; instead, say something like "Do you agree with that, Joe?"

5. Use normal vocabulary and discuss topics that you would discuss with sighted people. Don't avoid terms like "see" or "look" or even "blind." Don't avoid discussing a television show or the way your new car looks; these are normal topics for all people.

If you are a visually impaired person, interacting with a sighted person:

1. Help the sighted person meet your special communication needs. If you want your surroundings described, ask. If you want the person to read the road signs, ask.

2. Be patient with the sighted person. Many people are nervous talking with people who are visually impaired for fear of offending. Put them at ease in a way that also makes you more comfortable.

Sources: These suggestions were drawn from a variety of sources: www.cincyblind.org, www.abwa.asn.au/, and www.batchelor.edu.au/disability/communication (all accessed April 29, 2008).

noise may prevent a message from getting from source to receiver. A roaring noise or line static can easily prevent entire messages from getting through to your telephone receiver. At the other extreme, with virtually no noise interference, the message of the source and the message received are almost identical. Most often, however, noise distorts some portion of the message a source sends as it travels to a receiver.

Four types of noise are especially relevant. It's important to identify these types of noise and, when possible, to reduce their effects.

- *Physical noise* is interference that is external to both speaker and listener; it impedes the physical transmission of the signal or message. Examples include the screeching of passing cars, the hum of a computer, sunglasses, extraneous messages, illegible handwriting, blurred type or fonts that are too small or difficult to read, misspellings and poor grammar, and pop-up ads.
- *Physiological noise* is created by barriers within the sender or receiver such as visual impairments, hearing loss, articulation problems, and memory loss.
- *Psychological noise* is mental interference in speaker or listener and includes preconceived ideas, wandering thoughts, biases and prejudices, closed-mindedness, and

extreme emotionalism. You're likely to run into psychological noise when you talk with someone who is closed-minded or who refuses to listen to anything he or she doesn't already believe.

■ *Semantic noise* is interference that occurs when the speaker and listener have different meaning systems; examples include language or dialectical differences, the use of jargon or overly complex terms, and ambiguous or overly abstract terms whose meanings can be easily misinterpreted. You see this type of noise regularly in the medical doctor who uses "medicalese" without explanation or in the insurance salesperson who speaks in the jargon of the insurance industry.

As you can see from these examples, noise is anything that hinders your receiving the messages of others or their receiving your messages.

A useful concept in understanding noise and its importance in communication is **signal-to-noise ratio.** In this term the word *signal* refers to information that you'd find useful, and *noise* refers to information that is useless (to you). So, for example, a mailing list or newsgroup that contains lots of useful information would be high on signal and low on noise; messages that contain lots of useless information would be high on noise and low on signal.

All communications contain noise. Noise cannot be totally eliminated, but its effects can be reduced. Making your language more precise, sharpening your skills for sending and receiving nonverbal messages, and improving your listening and feedback skills are some ways to combat the influence of noise.

Context

Communication always takes place in a **context** that influences the form and content of your messages. At times this context isn't obvious or intrusive; it seems so natural that it's ignored—like background music. At other times the context dominates, and the ways in which it restricts or stimulates your messages are obvious. Compare, for example, the differences among communicating in a funeral home, in a football stadium, in a formal restaurant, and at a rock concert. The context of communication has at least four dimensions, all of which interact with and influence each other.

Physical Dimension The *physical dimension* is the tangible or concrete environment in which communication takes place—the room, hallway, or park, the boardroom or the family dinner table. The size of the space, its temperature, and the number of people present in the physical space would also be part of the physical dimension. In print media such as magazines or newspapers, context includes the positioning of stories and news articles; an article on page 37 is identified as less important than an article on page 1 or 2. Even the placement of passages within an article proves relevant. For example, the *New York Times* was once criticized for putting information critical of the way it counted subscriptions (and thus set advertising rates) in the 30th paragraph of an article. Similarly, the political and social preferences of a newspaper can be identified, in part at least, by the physical context in which the editors place stories and news articles (Okrent, 2005).

Temporal Dimension The *temporal dimension* has to do not only with the time of day and moment in history but also with where a particular message fits into the sequence of communication events. For example, a joke about illness told immediately after the disclosure of a friend's sickness will be received differently than the same joke told in response to a series of similar jokes. Also, some channels (for example, face-to-face, chat rooms, and instant messaging) allow for synchronous communication in which messages are sent and received simultaneously. Other channels (for example, letter

VIEWPOINT One study found that 80 percent of young adult women consider a spouse who can communicate his feelings more desirable than a man who earns a good living (www.gallup.com, accessed June 27, 2001). How important, compared to all the other factors you might take into consideration in choosing a partner, is the ability to communicate? What specific communication skills would you consider "extremely important" in a life partner?

writing, e-mail, and bulletin board posts) are asynchronous; messages are sent and received at different times.

Social–Psychological Dimension The *social–psychological dimension* includes, for example, status relationships among the participants, roles and games that people play, norms of the society or group, and the friendliness, formality, or gravity of the situation.

Cultural Dimension The *cultural context* (Chapter 2) includes the cultural beliefs and customs of the people communicating. When you interact with people from different cultures, you may each follow different rules of communication. This can result in confusion, unintentional insult, inaccurate judgments, and a host of other miscommunications. Similarly, communication strategies or techniques that prove satisfying to members of one culture may prove disturbing or offensive to members of another. In fact, research shows that you lose more information in an intercultural situation (approximately 50 percent) than in an intracultural situation (approximately 25 percent) (Li, 1999).

Ethics

Because communication has consequences, interpersonal communication also involves **ethics**; each communication act has a moral dimension, a rightness or wrongness (cf. Jaksa & Pritchard, 1994; Johannesen, 2001). Communication choices need to be guided by ethical considerations as well as by concerns with effectiveness and satisfaction. Some research finds important cross-cultural similarities in this regard; for example, it's been proposed that there are certain universal ethical principles that are held by all cultures, such as that you should tell the truth, have respect for another's dignity, and not harm the innocent (Christians & Traber, 1997). Ethics is therefore included as a universal of interpersonal communication and is presented in this text in the Ethics in Interpersonal Communication boxes. These boxes cover issues such as the differences between subjective and objective approaches to ethics, whether the ends justify the means, the ethical obligations of speakers and listeners, lying, gossip, and unethical speech.

Ethics in Interpersonal Communication

Ethical Questions

Because ethics is relevant to all forms of interpersonal communication, ethical issues are integrated throughout the text in these Ethics in Interpersonal Communication boxes. Here, as a kind of preview, are just a few of the ethical issues raised in these boxes. As you read these questions, think about your own ethical beliefs and how these beliefs influence the way you'd answer the questions.

- What obligations do you have to keep a secret? Can you identify situations in which it would be unethical not to reveal information you promised to keep secret? See Ethics box, Chapter 8.
- What are your ethical obligations as a listener? See Ethics box, Chapter 4.
- Are ethical principles objective or subjective? For example, if lying is unethical, is it unethical in all situations? Or would your answer depend on the circumstances? See Ethics box, Chapter 5.
- What are your ethical obligations to reveal personal information to a relationship partner? See Ethics box, Chapter 9.
- Are there ethical and unethical ways to engage in conflict and conflict resolution? See Ethics box, Chapter 12.

What would you do?

You're ready to enter into a permanent romantic relationship and are being pressured to talk about yourself. What can you ethically keep hidden? What types of information are you ethically obligated to reveal?

Competence

Your ability to communicate effectively is your interpersonal **competence** (Spitzberg & Cupach, 1989; Wilson & Sabee, 2003). Communication competence is a measure of the quality of your intellectual and physical interpersonal performance (Almeida, 2004). Your competence includes, for example, the knowledge that in certain contexts and with certain listeners one topic is appropriate and another isn't. Your knowledge about the rules of nonverbal behavior—for example, the appropriateness of touching, vocal volume, and physical closeness—is also part of your competence. In short, interpersonal competence includes knowing how to adjust your communication according to the context of the interaction, the person with whom you're interacting, and a host of other factors discussed throughout this text.

You learn communication competence much as you learn to eat with a knife and fork—by observing others, by explicit instruction, and by trial and error. Some individuals learn better than others, though, and these are generally the people with whom you find it interesting and comfortable to talk. They seem to know what to say and how and when to say it.

Not surprisingly, there's a positive relationship between interpersonal competence on the one hand and success in college and job satisfaction on the other (Rubin & Graham, 1988; Wertz, Sorenson, & Heeren, 1988). So much of college and professional life depends on interpersonal competence—meeting and interacting with other students, teachers, or colleagues; asking and answering questions; presenting information or argument—that you should not find this connection surprising. Interpersonal competence also enables you to develop and maintain meaningful relationships in friendship, love, family, and work. Such relationships, in turn, contribute to the lower levels of anxiety, depression, and loneliness observed in interpersonally competent people (Spitzberg & Cupach, 1989).

Essential to competence are the skills of interpersonal communication. In this text most of the interpersonal skills are discussed throughout the chapters. Some are highlighted in boxes. As you read these skills, try to personalize them; ask yourself how you might use the skills and in what situations they might prove useful (and in what situations they might prove ineffective). Try them out, consider their effects, and then modify or adjust them as you think necessary.

Table 1.3 on page 16 gives you another view of the field of interpersonal communication by identifying its major divisions or areas, the related academic areas, and some examples of the topics in which interpersonal communication researchers, theorists, and students are interested.

VIEWPOINT In a class discussion of ethics, your instructor presents the following possible ethical guidelines: (1) Behavior is ethical when you feel in your heart that you're doing the right thing, (2) Behavior is ethical when it is consistent with your religious beliefs, (3) Behavior is ethical when it's legal within society, (4) Behavior is ethical when the majority of people would consider it ethical, and (5) Behavior is ethical when the end result is in the interest of the majority. How would you respond to these guidelines? Would you accept any as an accurate statement of what constitutes ethical behavior? Would you reject any? Why?

Principles of Interpersonal Communication

Now that the nature of interpersonal communication and its elements are clear, we can explore some of the more specific axioms or principles that are common to all or most interpersonal encounters. These axioms are largely the work of the transactional researchers Paul Watzlawick, Janet Helmick Beavin, and Don D. Jackson, presented in their landmark *Pragmatics of Human Communication* (1967; Watzlawick 1977, 1978).

Interpersonal Communication Is a Transactional Process

A **transactional perspective** views interpersonal communication as (1) a process with (2) elements that are *inter*dependent. Figure 1.3 on page 17 visually explains this transactional view and distinguishes it from two earlier views of how interpersonal communication works.

TABLE 1.3   The Areas of Interpersonal Communication and Relationships

This table is intended as a guide for identifying some of the important areas in the general topic of "interpersonal communication and relationships" and not as a formal outline of the field. The six areas of interpersonal communication interact and overlap; they're not independent. For example, interpersonal interaction is a part of all the other areas; similarly, intercultural communication can exist in any of the other areas. The related academic areas illustrate the close ties among fields of study and the centrality of communication to all academic areas.

General and Related Areas	Selected Topics
Interpersonal interaction Communication between two people *Related areas:* Psychology, education, linguistics, counseling	Characteristics of effectiveness, conversational processes, self-disclosure, active listening, verbal and nonverbal messages in conversation, e-mail, instant messaging, social networking
Health communication Communication between health professional and patient and between the health profession and the public *Related areas:* Medicine, psychology, counseling, health care	Increasing doctor–patient effectiveness, talking about death, communication and aging, therapeutic communication, counseling, communicating safe-sex guidelines
Family communication Communication within the nuclear or extended family system *Related areas:* Sociology, psychology, family studies, social work	Couple communication, power in the family, dysfunctional families, family conflict, communication in the extended family, heterosexual and homosexual families, parent–child communication
Intercultural communication Communication between members of different nationalities, religions, genders, and generations *Related areas:* Anthropology, sociology, cultural studies, business	Cross-generational communication; male–female communication; black–Hispanic–Asian–Caucasian communication; prejudice and stereotypes; barriers to intercultural communication; the Internet and cultural diversity; sexism, racism, heterosexism, and ageism
Business and organizational communication Communication among workers in an organizational environment *Related areas:* Business, management, public relations, computer science	Interviewing strategies, sexual harassment, upward and downward communication, increasing managerial effectiveness, increasing worker productivity and morale, leadership in business, mentoring and networking, public relations and advertising
Social and personal relationships Communication in close relationships such as friendship and love *Related areas:* Psychology, sociology, anthropology, family studies	Relationship development, maintenance, deterioration, and repair; gender and cultural differences in relationships; increasing intimacy; dealing with relationship breakdowns; verbal abuse and relationship violence

Interpersonal Communication Is a Process   Interpersonal communication is best viewed as an ever-changing process. Everything involved in interpersonal communication is in a state of flux: You're changing, the people you communicate with are changing, and your environment is changing. Sometimes these changes go unnoticed and sometimes they intrude in obvious ways, but they're always occurring.

The process of communication is circular: One person's message serves as the stimulus for another's message, which serves as a stimulus for the first person's message, and so on. Throughout this circular process, each person serves simultaneously as a speaker *and* a listener, an actor *and* a reactor. Interpersonal communication is a mutually interactive process.

Elements Are Interdependent   In interpersonal communication, not only are the individuals interdependent, as noted earlier, but the varied elements of communication also are interdependent. Each element—each part—of interpersonal communication is intimately

FIGURE 1.3

The Transactional View of Interpersonal Communication

The top figure represents a linear view of communication, in which the speaker speaks and the listener listens. The middle figure represents an interactional view, in which speaker and listener take turns speaking and listening; A speaks while B listens and then B speaks while A listens. The bottom figures (left and right) represent a transactional view, in which each person serves simultaneously as speaker and listener; at the same time that you send messages, you also receive messages from your own communications as well as from the reactions of the other person(s).

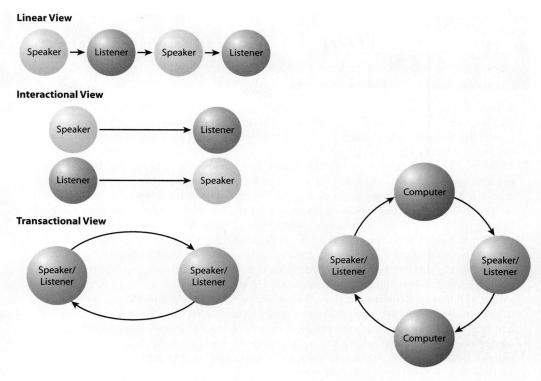

Linear View

Interactional View

Transactional View

Face-to-Face Communication

Computer-Mediated Communication

connected to the other parts and to the whole. For example, there can be no source without a receiver; there can be no message without a source; there can be no feedback without a receiver. Because of interdependency, a change in any one element causes changes in the others. For example, you're talking with a group of fellow students about a recent examination, and your teacher joins the group. This change in participants will lead to other changes—perhaps in the content of what you say, perhaps in the manner in which you express it. But regardless of what change is introduced, other changes result.

Interpersonal Communication Is Purposeful

The interpersonal communication act is purposeful; each interpersonal interaction has a purpose or, more often, a combination of purposes. Five such purposes can be identified: to learn, to relate, to influence, to play, and to help.

To Learn Interpersonal communication enables you to learn, to better understand the external world—the world of objects, events, and other people. Although a great deal of information comes from the media, you probably discuss and ultimately learn or internalize information through interpersonal interactions. In fact, your beliefs, attitudes, and values are probably influenced more by interpersonal encounters than by the media or even by formal education.

Most important, however, interpersonal communication helps you learn about yourself. By talking about yourself with others, you gain valuable feedback on your feelings, thoughts, and behaviors. Through these communications, you also learn how you appear to others—who likes you, who dislikes you, and why.

To Relate Interpersonal communication helps you relate. You communicate your friendship or love through your interpersonal communication; at the same time, you react and respond to the friendship and love messages of others. Such communication is at the heart of one of the greatest needs people have: to establish and maintain close relationships. You

UNDERSTANDING INTERPERSONAL THEORY & RESEARCH

Communication Theories and Research

A **theory** is a generalization that explains how something works—for example, gravity, blood clotting, interpersonal attraction, or communication. Academic writers usually reserve the term *theory* to refer to a well-established system of knowledge about how things work or how things are related that is supported by research findings.

The theories you'll encounter in this book explain how communication works—for example, how you accommodate your speaking style to your listeners, how communication works when relationships deteriorate, or how and why people disclose their normally hidden selves.

Despite their many values, however, theories don't reveal truth in any absolute sense. Rather, theories reveal some degree of accuracy, some degree of truth. In the natural sciences (such as physics and chemistry), theories are extremely high in accuracy. In the social and behavioral sciences (such as communication, sociology, and psychology), the theories are far less accurate in describing or in predicting how things work. Nevertheless, theories provide enormous insights into the world of interpersonal communication and interpersonal relationships.

Not surprisingly, interpersonal communication theories often have practical implications for developing your own skills. For example, theories of interpersonal attraction offer practical insight into how to make yourself more attractive to others; theories of nonverbal communication will help you use and decipher nonverbal behaviors more accurately. The more you know about the theories and research explaining how communication works, the more likely you'll be able to use them to build your own interpersonal communication skills.

Working with Theories and Research

Log on to your favorite electronic database and browse through issues of *Quarterly Journal of Speech, Communication Monographs, Communication Theory, or Journal of Communication* (or scan similar journals in your own field of study). You'll be amazed at the breadth and depth of academic research and theory.

---

want to feel loved and liked, and in turn you want to love and like others. Such relationships help to alleviate loneliness and depression, enable you to share and heighten your pleasures, and generally make you feel more positive about yourself.

To Influence Very likely, you influence the attitudes and behaviors of others in your interpersonal encounters. You may wish others to vote a particular way, try a new diet, buy a new book, listen to a record, see a movie, take a specific course, think in a particular way, believe that something is true or false, or value some idea—the list is endless. A good deal of your time is probably spent in interpersonal persuasion. Some researchers, in fact, would argue that all communication is persuasive and that all our communications seek some persuasive goal. Some examples (Canary, Cody, & Manusov, 2000):

- Self-presentation goals: You communicate to give others the image you want them to have of you.
- Relationship goals: You communicate to form the relationships that will meet your needs.
- Instrumental goals: You communicate to get others to do something for you.

In computer-mediated communication (CMC), a new study called **captology** has arisen. Captology is the study of the ways in which computer technology and computer-mediated communication generally serve persuasive functions. Websites, blogs, and instant messages, for example, persuade you on a variety of topics—for example, urging you to vote for a particular candidate, providing you with guidance on managing finances, or helping you find a relationship partner (http://captology.stanford.edu/index.html, accessed April 29, 2008).

To Play Talking with friends about your weekend activities, discussing sports or dates, telling stories and jokes, and in general just passing the time are play functions. Far from frivolous, this extremely important purpose gives your activities a necessary balance and your mind a needed break from all the seriousness around you. In CMC perhaps the most obvious forms of play are the multiuser domains—MUDs and MOOs, for example—where you interact with other participants in a virtual reality environment in real time and, in the process, interestingly enough, develop useful skills such as the ability take the perspective of another person (Tynes, 2007). And even certain forms of cyberflirting may be viewed as play (Whitty, 2003b).

To Help Therapists of various kinds serve a helping function professionally by offering guidance through interpersonal interaction. But everyone interacts to help in everyday encounters: You console a friend who has broken off a love affair, counsel another student about courses to take, or offer advice to a colleague about work. Even babies as young as six months old can distinguish between helpful and unhelpful behavior (Hamlin, Wynn, & Bloom, 2007). And, not surprisingly, much support and counseling are currently taking place through e-mail and chat groups (Wright & Chung, 2001). Success in accomplishing this helping function, professionally or otherwise, depends on your knowledge and skill in interpersonal communication.

The purposes of interpersonal communication can also be viewed from two other perspectives (see Figure 1.4). First, purposes may be seen as motives for engaging in interpersonal communication. That is, you engage in interpersonal communication to satisfy your need for knowledge or your need to form relationships. Second, these purposes may be viewed in terms of the results you want to achieve. Looked at in this way, you engage in interpersonal communication to increase your knowledge of yourself and others or to exert influence or power over others, for example.

Each of these purposes can serve noble functions—as illustrated below—or ignoble ones. So, for example, interpersonal communication can also be used to teach and learn prejudices and bigotry, to create relationships that are destructive or abusive, or to influence others to do something that is illegal or unethical. Instead of play as we normally think of it—harmless, enjoyable pastime—play can also involve teasing, making fun of others, or sexist or racist joking. And even attempts at helping can go drastically wrong in the hands of an inept social worker, counselor, or therapist.

FIGURE 1.4

Why You Engage in Interpersonal Communication

This figure identifies some of the reasons you communicate. The innermost circle contains the general purposes of interpersonal communication. The middle circle contains the motivations that lead you to communicate. The outer circle contains the results that you might hope to achieve by engaging in interpersonal communication. A similar typology of purposes comes from research on motives for communicating (Graham, Barbato, & Perse, 1993; Rubin & Martin, 1994).

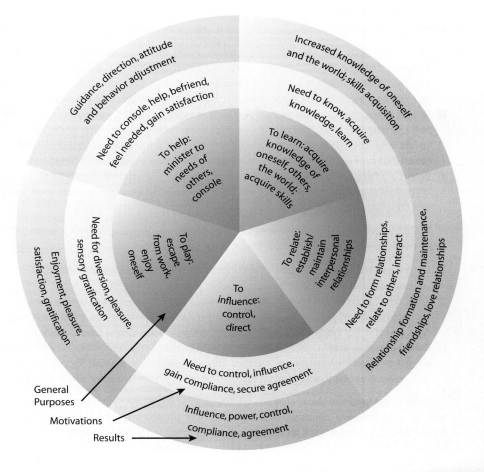

Interpersonal Communication Is Ambiguous

An ambiguous message is a message that can be interpreted as having more than one meaning. Sometimes **ambiguity** occurs because people use words that can be interpreted differently. Informal time terms offer good examples; *soon, right away, in a minute, early, late,* and similar terms can easily be interpreted very differently by different people. The terms are ambiguous. A more interesting type of ambiguity is grammatical ambiguity. You can get a feel for this type of ambiguity by trying to paraphrase—rephrase in your own words—the following sentences:

- What has the cat in its paws?
- Visiting neighbors can be boring.
- They are frying chickens.

UNDERSTANDING INTERPERSONAL SKILLS

Mindfulness

Mindfulness is a state of mental awareness; in a mindful state you're conscious of your reasons for thinking or communicating in a particular way. Its opposite, **mindlessness**, is a lack of conscious awareness of your thinking or communicating (Langer, 1989). To apply interpersonal skills appropriately and effectively, you need to be mindful of the unique communication situation you're in, of your available communication options or choices, and of the reasons why one option is likely to prove better than the others (Langer, 1989; Elmes & Gemmill, 1990; Burgoon, Berger, & Waldron, 2000). You can look at this textbook and this course in interpersonal communication as means of awakening your mindfulness about the way you engage in interpersonal communication. After you complete this course and this text, you should be much more mindful about all your interpersonal interactions, which will prove beneficial in all your interpersonal interactions (Carson, Carson, Gil, & Baucom, 2004; Sagula & Rice, 2004).

Increasing Mindfulness. To increase mindfulness in general, try the following suggestions (Langer, 1989):

- Create and recreate categories. Learn to see objects, events, and people as belonging to a wide variety of categories. Try to see, for example, your prospective romantic partner in a variety of roles—child, parent, employee, neighbor, friend, financial contributor, and so on. Avoid storing in memory an image of a person with only one specific label; if you do, you'll find it difficult to recategorize the person later.
- Be open to new information and points of view, even when these contradict your most firmly held stereotypes. New information forces you to reconsider what might be outmoded ways of thinking. New information can help you challenge long-held but now inappropriate beliefs and attitudes. Be willing to see your own and others' behaviors from a variety of viewpoints, especially from the perspective of people very different from yourself.
- Beware of relying too heavily on first impressions (Chanowitz & Langer, 1981; Langer, 1989). Treat your first impressions as tentative—as hypotheses that need further investigation. Be prepared to revise, reject, or accept these initial impressions.

In addition, consider a few suggestions specific to communication (Burgoon, Berger, & Waldron, 2000). To increase mindfulness in communication, ask yourself these questions:

- Can the message be misinterpreted? What can you do to make sure it's interpreted correctly? (For example, you can paraphrase or restate the message in different ways or you can ask the person to paraphrase.)
- When there's a continuous communication pattern—as there is in an escalating conflict in which each person brings up past relationship injustices—ask yourself if this pattern is productive and, if not, what you can do to change it. (For example, you can refuse to respond in kind and thereby break the cycle.)
- Remind yourself of what you already know about a situation, recall that all communication situations are different, and ask yourself how you can best adapt your messages to this unique situation. (For example, you may want to be especially positive to a friend who is depressed but not so positive to someone who betrayed a confidence.)

Perhaps most important, think before you act. Especially in delicate situations (for example, when expressing anger or when conveying commitment messages), it's wise to pause and think over the situation mindfully (DeVito, 2003b). In this way you'll stand a better chance of acting and reacting appropriately.

Working with Interpersonal Skills

Reflect on your own tendencies to communicate mindlessly and mindfully. In which situations are you more apt to communicate mindlessly? In which situations are you more apt to communicate mindfully? Do you communicate mindfully with certain people and mindlessly with others?

Each of these ambiguous sentences can be interpreted and paraphrased in at least two different ways:

- What monster has the cat in its paws? What is the cat holding in its paws?
- To visit neighbors is boring. Neighbors who visit are boring.
- Those people are frying chickens. Those chickens are for frying.

Although these examples are particularly striking—and are the work of linguists who analyze language—some degree of ambiguity exists in all interpersonal communication: All messages are ambiguous to some degree. When you express an idea you never communicate your meaning exactly and totally; rather, you communicate your meaning with some reasonable accuracy—enough to give the other person a reasonably clear idea of what you mean. Sometimes, of course, you're less accurate than you anticipated. Perhaps your listener "gets the wrong idea" or "gets offended" when you only meant to be humorous, or the listener "misunderstands your emotional meaning." Because of this inevitable uncertainty, you may qualify what you're saying, give an example, or ask, "Do you know what I mean?" These additional explanations help the other person understand your meaning and reduce uncertainty (to some degree).

Similarly, all relationships contain uncertainty. Consider one of your own close interpersonal relationships and answer the following questions, using a six-point scale with "1" meaning that you are completely or almost completely uncertain about the answer and "6" meaning that you are completely or almost completely certain of the answer.

- What can or cannot you say to each other in this relationship?
- Do you and your partner feel the same way about each other?
- How would you and your partner describe this relationship?
- What is the future of the relationship?

It's very likely that you were not able to respond with 6s for all four questions, and equally likely that the same would be true for your relationship partner. Your responses to these questions—adapted from a relationship uncertainty scale (Knoblock & Solomon, 1999)—and similar other questions illustrate that you probably experience some degree of uncertainty about (1) the norms that govern your relationship communication (question 1), (2) the degree to which you and your partner see the relationship in similar ways (question 2), (3) the definition of the relationship (question 3), and (4) the relationship's future (question 4).

The skills of interpersonal communication presented throughout this text may be looked at as means for appropriately reducing ambiguity and making your meaning as unambiguous as possible.

Interpersonal Relationships May Be Symmetrical or Complementary

Interpersonal relationships can be described as either symmetrical or complementary (Bateson, 1972; Watzlawick, Beavin, & Jackson, 1967). In a **symmetrical relationship**, the two individuals mirror each other's behavior (Bateson, 1972). If one member nags, the other member responds in kind. If one member is passionate, the other member is passionate. If one member expresses jealousy, the other member also expresses jealousy. If one member is passive, so is the other. The relationship is one of equality, with the emphasis on minimizing the differences between the two individuals.

Note, however, the problems that can arise in this type of relationship. Consider the situation of a couple in which both members are very aggressive. The aggressiveness of one person fosters aggressiveness in the other, which fosters increased aggressiveness in the first individual. As this cycle escalates, the aggressiveness can no longer be contained, and the relationship is consumed by the aggression.

In a **complementary relationship**, the two individuals engage in different behaviors. The behavior of one serves as the stimulus for the other's complementary behavior. In complementary relationships, the differences between the parties are maximized. The people occupy different positions, one superior and the other inferior, one passive and the other active, one strong and the other weak. At times, cultures establish such relationships—for example, the complementary relationship between teacher and student or between employer and employee.

Early marriages are likely to be complementary relationships in which each person tries to complete him- or herself. When such couples separate and the members form new relationships, these new relationships are more likely to be symmetrical and to involve a kind of reconfirmation of the partners' own identities (Prosky, 1992). Generally, research finds that complementary couples have a poorer marital adjustment level than do symmetrical couples (Main & Oliver, 1988; Holden, 1991).

Interpersonal Communication Refers to Content and Relationship

Messages may refer to the real world; for example, to the events and objects you see before you. At the same time, however, they also may refer to the relationship between the people communicating. For example, a judge may say to a lawyer, "See me in my chambers immediately." This simple message has both a content aspect, which refers to the response expected (namely, that the lawyer will see the judge immediately), and a relationship aspect, which says something about the relationship between the judge and the lawyer and, as a result of this relationship, about how the communication is to be dealt with. Even the use of the simple command shows that there is a status difference between the two parties. This difference can perhaps be seen most clearly if you imagine the command being made by the lawyer to the judge. Such a communication appears awkward and out of place because it violates the normal relationship between judge and lawyer.

In any two communications, the content dimension may be the same, but the relationship aspect may be different, or the relationship aspect may be the same and the content dimension different. For example, the judge could say to the lawyer, "You had better see me immediately" or "May I please see you as soon as possible?" In both cases, the content is essentially the same; that is, the message about the expected response is the same. But the relationship dimension is quite different. The first message signifies a definite superior–inferior relationship; the second signals a more equal relationship, one that shows respect for the lawyer.

Similarly, at times the content is different but the relationship is essentially the same. For example, a daughter might say to her parents, "May I go away this weekend?" or "May I use the car tonight?" The content of the two questions is clearly very different. The relationship dimension, however, is the same. Both questions clearly reflect a superior–inferior relationship in which permission to do certain things must be secured.

Many problems between people result from failure to recognize the distinction between the **content and relationship dimensions** of communication. For example, consider the couple arguing because Pat made plans to study with friends during the weekend without first asking Chris if that would be all right. Probably both would agree that to study over the weekend is the right decision. Thus, the argument isn't primarily concerned with the content level. It centers on the relationship level; Chris expected to be consulted about plans for the weekend. Pat, in not doing so, rejected this definition of their relationship. Similar situations occur when one member of a couple buys something, makes dinner plans, or invites a guest to dinner without first asking the other person. Even though the other person might have agreed with the decision, the couple argues because of the message communicated on the relationship level.

Consider the following interchange:

Dialogue	*Comments*
He: I'm going bowling tomorrow. The guys at the plant are starting a team.	He focuses on the content and ignores any relationship implications of the message.

She: Why can't we ever do anything together?	She responds primarily on a relationship level, ignores the content implications of the message, and expresses her displeasure at being ignored in his decision.
He: We can do something together anytime; tomorrow's the day they're organizing the team.	Again, he focuses almost exclusively on the content.

This example reflects research findings that men generally focus more on the content while women focus more on the relationship dimensions of communication (cf. Pearson, West, & Turner, 1995; Wood, 1994; Ivy & Backlund, 2000). Once you recognize this difference, you may be better able to remove a potential barrier to communication between the sexes by being sensitive to the orientation of the opposite sex. Here is essentially the same situation but with added sensitivity:

Dialogue	*Comments*
He: The guys at the plant are organizing a bowling team. I'd sure like to be on the team. Would it be a problem if I went to the organizational meeting tomorrow?	Although focused on content, he is aware of the relationship dimensions of his message and includes both in his comments—by acknowledging their partnership, asking if there would be a problem, and expressing his desire rather than his decision.
She: That sounds great, but I was hoping we could do something together.	She focuses on the relationship dimension but also acknowledges his content orientation. Note, too, that she does not respond as though she has to defend her emphasis on relationship aspects.
He: How about your meeting me at Joe's Pizza, and we can have dinner after the organizational meeting?	He responds to the relationship aspect—without abandoning his desire to join the bowling team—and incorporates it.
She: That sounds great. I'm dying for pizza.	She responds to both messages, approving of his joining the team and their dinner date.

Arguments over the content dimension are relatively easy to resolve. Generally, you can look up something in a book or ask someone what actually took place. It is relatively easy to verify disputed facts. Arguments on the relationship level, however, are much more difficult to resolve, in part because you may not recognize that the argument is in fact a relational one. Once you realize that, you can approach the dispute appropriately and deal with it directly.

Interpersonal Communication Is a Series of Punctuated Events

Communication events are continuous transactions. There is no clear-cut beginning and no clear-cut end. As participants in or observers of the communication act, you segment this continuous stream of communication into smaller pieces. You label some of these pieces causes or stimuli and others effects or responses.

Consider an example. A married couple is in a restaurant. The husband is flirting with another woman, and the wife is talking to her sister on her cell phone. Both are scowling at each other and are obviously in a deep nonverbal argument. Recalling the situation later, the husband might observe that the wife talked on the phone, so he innocently flirted with the other woman. The only reason for his behavior (he says) was his anger over her talking on the phone when they were supposed to be having dinner together. Notice that he sees his behavior as a response to her behavior. In recalling the same incident, the wife might say that she phoned her sister when he started flirting. The more he flirted, the longer she

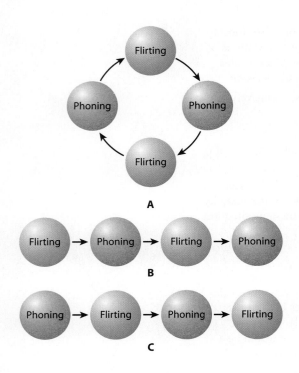

FIGURE 1.5

Punctuation and the Sequence of Events

(A) Shows the actual sequence of events as a continuous series of actions with no specific beginning or end. Each action (phoning and flirting) stimulates another action, but no initial cause is identified.

(B) Shows the same sequence of events as seen by the wife. She sees the sequence as beginning with the husband's flirting and her phoning behavior as a response to that stimulus.

(C) Shows the same sequence of events from the husband's point of view. He sees the sequence as beginning with the wife's phoning and his flirting as a response to that stimulus.

Try using this three-part figure, discussed in the text, to explain what might go on when a supervisor complains that workers are poorly trained for their jobs and when the workers complain that the supervisor doesn't know how to supervise.

talked. She had no intention of calling anyone until he started flirting. To her, his behavior was the stimulus and hers was the response; he caused her behavior. Thus, the husband sees the sequence as going from phoning to flirting, and the wife sees it as going from flirting to phoning. This example is depicted visually in Figure 1.5 above and is supported by research showing that, among marrieds at least, the individuals regularly see their partner's behavior as the cause of conflict (Schutz, 1999).

This tendency to divide communication transactions into sequences of stimuli and responses is referred to as **punctuation** (Watzlawick, Beavin, & Jackson, 1967). Everyone punctuates the continuous sequences of events into stimuli and responses for convenience. Moreover, as the example of the husband and wife illustrates, punctuation usually is done in ways that benefit the self and are consistent with a person's self-image.

Understanding how another person interprets a situation, how he or she punctuates, is a crucial step in interpersonal understanding. It is also essential in achieving empathy (feeling what the other person is feeling). In all communication encounters, but especially in conflicts, try to see how others punctuate the situation.

Interpersonal Communication Is Inevitable, Irreversible, and Unrepeatable

Interpersonal communication cannot be prevented (is inevitable), cannot be reversed (is irreversible), and cannot be repeated (is unrepeatable). Let's look briefly at each of these qualities and their implications.

Inevitability Often communication is thought of as intentional, purposeful, and consciously motivated. In many instances it is. But the **inevitability** principle means that in many instances you're communicating even though you might not think you are or might not even want to be. Consider, for example, the new editorial assistant sitting at the desk with an "expressionless" face, perhaps staring out the window. Although this assistant might say that she or he is not communicating with the manager, the manager may derive any of a variety of messages from this behavior—for example, that the assistant lacks interest, is bored, or is worried about something. In any event, the manager is receiving messages even though the assistant might not intend to communicate. In an interactional situation, all behavior is potentially communication. Any aspect of your behavior may communicate if the other person gives it message value. On the other hand, if the behavior (for example, the assistant's looking out the window) goes unnoticed, then no communication will have taken place (Watzlawick, Beavin, & Jackson, 1967; Motley, 1990a, 1990b; Bavelas, 1990; Beach, 1990).

Further, when you are in an interactional situation, your responses all have potential message value. For example, if you notice someone winking at you, you must respond in some way. Even if you don't respond openly, that lack of response is itself a response and it communicates (assuming it is perceived by the other person).

Irreversibility   The processes of some systems can be reversed. For example, you can turn water into ice and then reverse the process by melting the ice. Moreover, you can repeat this reversal of ice and water as many times as you wish. Other systems, however, are irreversible. In these systems, the process can move in only one direction; it cannot go back again. For example, you can turn grapes into wine, but you cannot reverse the process and turn the wine back into grapes.

Interpersonal communication is irreversible. This quality of **irreversibility** means that what you have communicated remains communicated; you cannot *un*communicate. Although you may try to qualify, negate, or somehow reduce the effects of your message, once it has been sent and received, the message itself cannot be reversed. In interpersonal interactions (especially in conflict), you need to be especially careful that you don't say things you may wish to withdraw later. Similarly, commitment messages, such as "I love you," must be monitored lest you commit yourself to a position you may be uncomfortable with later.

Face-to-face communication is evanescent; it fades after you have spoken. There is no trace of your communications outside of the memories of the parties involved or of those who overheard your conversation. In computer-mediated communication, however, the messages are written and may be saved, stored, and printed. Both face-to-face and computer-mediated messages may be kept confidential or revealed publicly. But computer messages may be made public more easily and spread more quickly than face-to-face messages. Written messages provide clear evidence of what you have said and when you said it.

Because electronic communication often is permanent, you may wish to be cautious when you're e-mailing or posting your profile or posting a message. Specifically:

- Electronic messages are virtually impossible to destroy. Often e-mails that you think you deleted or a post you wrote in anger will remain on servers and workstations and may be retrieved by a clever hacker or may simply be copied and distributed to people you'd rather not have see what you wrote.
- Electronic messages can easily be made public. Your post on your blog or on a social networking site can be sent to anyone. Your rant about a former employer may reach a prospective employer, who may see you as a complainer and reject your job application. In fact, employers regularly search such sites for information about job candidates.
- Electronic messages are not privileged communication; they can easily be accessed by others and be used against you. And you'll not be able to deny saying something; it will be there in black and white.

Unrepeatability   In addition to being inevitable and irreversible, interpersonal communication is unrepeatable. The reason for this quality of **unrepeatability** is simple: Everyone and everything is constantly changing. As a result, you can never recapture the exact same situation, frame of mind, or relationship dynamics that defined a previous interpersonal act. For example, you can never repeat the experience of meeting a particular person for the first time, comforting a grieving friend, or resolving a specific conflict. And, as you surely know, you never get a second chance to make a first impression.

You can, of course, try again, as when you say, "I'm sorry I came off so forward; can we try again?" But notice that even when you say this, you don't erase the initial impression. Instead, you try to counteract the initial (and perhaps negative) impression by going through the motions once more. In doing so, you try to create a more positive impression, which you hope will lessen the original negative effect—and which often does.

Summary

These chapter summaries are designed to refresh your memory of the topics covered in the chapter. Note that the major heads of the chapter are repeated here to better connect them and the summary propositions.

This chapter introduced the importance of interpersonal communication, its essential nature, its elements, and some of its major principles.

Why Study Interpersonal Communication

1. Intellectual benefits include a deeper understanding of yourself and others and of relationships.
2. Practical benefits include personal, social or relationship, and professional benefits.

The Nature of Interpersonal Communication

3. Interpersonal communication is communication between two or more interdependent individuals.
4. Interpersonal communication is inherently relational.
5. Interpersonal communication exists on a continuum from relatively impersonal to intimate.
6. Interpersonal communication involves both verbal and nonverbal messages.
7. Interpersonal communication can take place, and interpersonal relationships can develop, through face-to-face interactions as well as those you have on the Internet.
8. Interpersonal communication can range from extremely ineffective to extremely effective.

Elements of Interpersonal Communication

9. The source–receiver concept emphasizes that you send and receive interpersonal messages simultaneously.
10. Encoding–decoding involves putting meaning into verbal and nonverbal messages and deriving meaning from the messages you receive from others.
11. Messages are the signals that serve as stimuli for a receiver; metamessages are messages about other messages. Feedback messages are messages that are sent back by the receiver to the source in response to the source's messages. Feedforward messages are messages that preface other messages and ask that the listener approach future messages in a certain way.
12. Channels are the media through which messages pass and which act as a bridge between source and receiver; for example, the vocal–auditory channel used in speaking or the cutaneous–tactile channel used in touch.

13. Noise is the inevitable physical, physiological, psychological, and semantic interference that distorts messages.
14. Context is the physical, social–psychological, temporal, and cultural environment in which communication takes place.
15. Ethics is the moral dimension of communication, the study of what makes behavior moral or good as opposed to immoral and bad.
16. Competence is the knowledge of and ability to use effectively your own communication system.

Principles of Interpersonal Communication

17. Interpersonal communication is a transactional process. Interpersonal communication is a process, an ongoing event, in which the elements are interdependent; communication is constantly occurring and changing. Don't expect clear-cut beginnings or endings or sameness from one time to another.
18. Interpersonal communication is purposeful. Five purposes may be identified: to learn, relate, influence, play, and help.
19. Interpersonal communication is ambiguous. All messages are potentially ambiguous; different people will derive different meanings from the "same" message. There is ambiguity in all relationships.
20. Interpersonal relationships may be symmetrical or complementary; interpersonal interactions may stimulate similar or different behavior patterns.
21. Interpersonal communication refers both to content and to the relationship between the participants.
22. Interpersonal communication is punctuated; that is, everyone separates communication sequences into stimuli and responses on the basis of his or her own perspective.
23. Interpersonal communication is inevitable, irreversible, and unrepeatable. When in an interactional situation, you cannot not communicate; you cannot uncommunicate; and you cannot repeat exactly a specific message.

Key Terms

These are the key terms discussed in this chapter. If you're in doubt about the definition of any of these terms, look them up; the pages on which these terms are introduced and defined are shown here, and the terms also appear in the Glossary of Interpersonal Communication Concepts.

ambiguity, **20**	context, **13**	interpersonal communication, **4**	relationship dimension, **22**
asynchronous communication, **8**	decoder, **10**	irreversibility, **25**	source–receiver, **9**
captology, **18**	encoder, **10**	messages, **10**	symmetrical relationship, **21**
channel, **11**	encoding–decoding, **10**	metamessages, **10**	synchronous communication, **8**
choice point, **8**	ethics, **14**	mindfulness, **20**	theory, **18**
competence, **15**	feedback, **10**	mindlessness, **20**	transactional perspective, **15**
complementary relationship, **21**	feedforward, **11**	noise, **11**	unrepeatability, **25**
content dimension, **22**	inevitability, **24**	punctuation, **24**	

Critical Thinking Questions

These questions are designed to stimulate further exploration of the concepts discussed in the chapter and to encourage you to think more personally about these ideas.

1 How would you explain interpersonal communication or interpersonal relationships in terms of metaphors such as a see-saw, a ball game, a flower, ice skates, a microscope, a television sitcom, a work of art, a long book, a rubber band, or a software program?

2 What kinds of feedforward can you find in this book? What additional feedforward messages would you find useful in a textbook? In a lecture?

3 What characters in television sitcoms or dramas do you think demonstrate superior interpersonal competence? What characters demonstrate obvious interpersonal incompetence?

4 How would you describe one of your interpersonal relationships in terms of symmetrical and complementary interactions? For example, is the relationship defined by the differences or by the similarities between you and the other person? Is there equality between you, or is one of you superior? Are you dependent on each other or independent? Is the power shared, or is one person in control?

5 How would you describe the optimum level of relationship ambiguity? For example, would you want to be certain about everything? Be kept in the dark about certain things?

Choice Points

The items presented as Choice Points present brief scenarios asking you to make an interpersonal communication choice or decision. Use these items to help you personalize the material presented in the text and relate it to your own interpersonal communication experiences.

1 *Reducing Relationship Ambiguity.* You've gone out with some-one for several months and want to reduce ambiguity about the future of the relationship and discover your partner's level of commitment. But you don't want to scare your partner. Ask yourself: What are some things you can say or do to find answers to your very legitimate questions?

2 *Strengthening Similarities.* You're dating a person you really like, but you are both so different—in values, politics, religion, and just about everything else. In fact, you're almost direct opposites. But you enjoy each other more than you do anyone else. Ask yourself: What can you do to encourage greater similarity while not losing the excitement created by the differences?

3 *Communicating an Image.* A new position is opening at work, and you want it. Your immediate supervisor will likely be the one to make the final decision. Ask yourself: What can you do to help secure this new position?

4 *Lessening the Negative Impact.* You write a gossipy e-mail about Ellen to your mutual friend Elle (revealing things about Ellen that you promised to keep secret) but inadvertently send the e-mail to Ellen herself. Ask yourself: What options do you have to correct this problem? What seems your best option?

5 *The Irreversibility of Interpersonal Communication.* You accidentally refer to your best friend's current romantic partner with the name of the friend's ex-partner. From both their expressions you can tell your friend never mentioned the ex. Ask yourself: What can you say to get your friend out of the trouble you just created?

MyCommunicationLab
Explorations

A variety of exercises, identified at the end of each chapter and available on the MyCommunicationLab website, will help you gain a deeper understanding of the concepts in this chapter and help you to apply this material to your own interpersonal interactions.

❶ Models of Interpersonal Communication asks you to draw a model of interpersonal communication that will visualize and explain a specific interpersonal situation. ❷ How Would You Give Feedback? and ❸ How Would You Give Feedforward? provide practice in examining the types of feedback and feedforward you have available. ❹ Ethics in Interpersonal Communication asks you to consider what you feel is an ethical response in a variety of interpersonal situations. ❺ How Can You Respond to Contradictory Messages? looks at types of situations that may call for you to respond to contradictory meanings. ❻ I'd Prefer to Be is an icebreaker that will help you get to know others in the class and at the same time explore factors that can influence your interpersonal communication. ❼ Applying the Axioms and ❽ Analyzing an Interaction provide opportunities to examine how the axioms may be applied to actual interpersonal situations.

2 Culture and Interpersonal Communication

Culture

How Cultures Differ

Principles of Intercultural
Communication

Persepolis

In *Persepolis* we see the strong influence of culture and how it can offer both comfort and discomfort, both satisfaction and dissatisfaction, through the eyes of a young Iranian girl, Marjane Satrapi. This chapter focuses on culture and aims to explain the role that culture plays in interpersonal communication.

This chapter discusses one of the foundation concepts of interpersonal communication, culture—an often misunderstood concept. More specifically, this chapter explains the nature of culture and its relationship to interpersonal communication, the major differences among cultures and how these differences affect interpersonal communication, and the ways you can improve your own intercultural communication.

As a preface consider two general views on culture: cultural evolution and cultural relativism. The *cultural evolution* approach (often called social Darwinism) holds that much as the human species evolved from earlier life forms to Homo sapiens, cultures also evolve. Consequently, some cultures may be considered advanced and others primitive. Most contemporary scholars reject this view, however, because the judgments that distinguish one culture from another have no basis in science and are instead based on individual values and preferences.

Cultural relativism theory, on the other hand, holds that all cultures are different but that no culture is either superior or inferior to any other (Berry, Poortinga, Segall, & Dasen, 1992; Mosteller, 2008). Today cultural relativism is generally accepted, and this view guides the infusion of cultural materials into contemporary textbooks on all academic levels (Jandt, 2007). As explained below, this view does not necessitate that you accept or approve of all cultural practices, however.

Culture

Culture (introduced briefly in Chapter 1) consists of (1) the relatively specialized lifestyle of a group of people (2) that is passed on from one generation to the next through communication, not through genes.

(1) Included in a social group's "culture" is everything that members of that group have produced and developed—their values, beliefs, artifacts, and language; their ways of behaving and ways of thinking; their art, laws, religion, and, of course, communication theories, styles, and attitudes.

(2) Culture is passed on from one generation to the next through communication, not through genes. Culture is not synonymous with race or nationality. The term *culture* does not refer to color of skin or shape of eyes, as these are passed on through genes, not communication. Of course, because members of a particular ethnic or national group are often taught similar beliefs, attitudes, and values, it's possible to speak of "Hispanic culture" or "African American culture." It's important to realize, however, that within any large group—especially a group based on race or nationality—there will be enormous differences. The Kansas farmer and the Wall Street executive may both be, say, German American, but may differ widely in their attitudes, beliefs, and lifestyles. In some ways the Kansas farmer may be closer in attitudes and values to a Chinese farmer than to the New York financier.

In ordinary conversation *sex* and *gender* are often used synonymously. In academic discussions of culture, however, they're more often distinguished. *Sex* refers to the biological distinction between male and female; sex is determined by genes, by biology. *Gender*, on the other hand, refers to the "social construction of masculinity and femininity within a culture" (Stewart, Cooper, & Stewart, 2003). Gender (masculinity and femininity) is what boys and girls learn from their culture; it's the attitudes, beliefs, values, and ways of communicating and relating to one another that boys and girls learn as they grow up.

Because of this, although sex is transmitted genetically and not by communication, gender may be considered a cultural variable—largely because cultures teach boys and girls different attitudes, beliefs, values, and ways of communicating and relating to others. Thus, you act like a man or a woman in part because of what your culture has taught you about how men and women should act. This does not, of course, deny that biological differences also play a role in the differences between male and female behavior. In fact, research continues to uncover biological roots of male/female differences we once thought were entirely learned (McCroskey, 1998).

Enculturation, Ethnic Identity, and Acculturation

Culture is transmitted from one generation to another through **enculturation**, the process by which you learn the culture into which you're born (your native culture). Parents, peer groups, schools, religious institutions, and government agencies are the main teachers of culture.

Through enculturation you develop an **ethnic identity**, a commitment to the beliefs and philosophy of your culture that, not surprisingly, can act as a protective shield against discrimination (Chung & Ting-Toomey, 1999; R.M. Lee, 2005). The degree to which you identify with your cultural group can be measured by your responses to questions such as the following (from Ting-Toomey, 1981). Using a five-point scale with 1 meaning "strongly disagree" and 5 meaning "strongly agree," indicate how true of you these statements are:

_____ **1.** I am increasing my involvement in activities with my ethnic group.
_____ **2.** I involve myself in causes that will help members of my ethnic group.
_____ **3.** It feels natural being part of my ethnic group.
_____ **4.** I have spent time trying to find out more about my own ethnic group.
_____ **5.** I am happy to be a member of my ethnic group.
_____ **6.** I have a strong sense of belonging to my ethnic group.
_____ **7.** I often talk to other members of my group to learn more about my ethnic culture.

High scores (say, 4s and 5s) indicate a strong commitment to your culture's values and beliefs; low numbers (1s and 2s) indicate a relatively weak commitment.

As you can imagine, you acquire your ethnic identity from family and friends who observe ethnic holidays, patronize ethnic parades, and eat ethnic foods; from your schooling where you learn about your own culture and ethnic background; and from your own media and Internet exposure. Ethnic identity can turn into ethnocentrism (see pp. 48–51) if you begin looking at your culture's practices as the only right ways to behave or seeing the practices of other cultures as inferior.

A different process of learning culture is **acculturation**, the process by which you learn the rules and norms of a culture different from your native culture. In acculturation your original or native culture is modified through direct contact with or exposure to a new and different culture. For example, when immigrants settle in the United States (the host culture), their own culture becomes influenced by the host culture. Gradually, the values, ways of behaving, and beliefs of the host culture become more and more a part of the immigrants' culture. At the same time, of course, the host culture also changes as it interacts with the immigrants' culture. Generally, however, the culture of the immigrant changes more. The reasons for this are that the host country's members far outnumber the immigrant group and that the media are largely dominated by and reflect the values and customs of the host culture (Kim, 1988).

New citizens' acceptance of the new culture depends on many factors (Kim, 1988). Immigrants who come from cultures similar to the host culture will become acculturated more easily. Similarly, those who are younger and better educated become acculturated more quickly than do older and less well educated people. Personality factors also play a part. Persons who are risk takers and open-minded, for example, have greater acculturation potential. Also, persons who are familiar with the host culture before immigration— through interpersonal contact or through media exposure—will be acculturated more readily.

Cultural Beliefs and Values

Before exploring further the role of culture in communication, consider your own cultural values and beliefs by taking the self-test, p. 32. This test illustrates how your own cultural values and beliefs may influence your interpersonal, small group, and public communications— both the messages you send and the messages to which you listen.

WHAT ARE YOUR CULTURAL BELIEFS AND VALUES?

The extremes of different cultural attitudes on six topics are identified below. For each topic indicate your own values. If your values are very similar to the extremes, select 1 or 7. If your values are quite similar to the extremes, select 2 or 6. If your values are fairly similar to the extremes, select 3 or 5. If you're in the middle, select 4.

Men and women are equal and are entitled to equality in all areas.	**Gender Equality** 1 2 3 4 5 6 7	Men and women should stick to their specific and different cultural roles.
Religion is the final arbiter of what is right and wrong; your obligation is to abide by your religion's rules.	**Religion** 1 2 3 4 5 6 7	Religion is like any other social institution; it's not inherently moral or right just because it's a religion.
Your first obligation is to your family; each person is responsible for the welfare of her or his family.	**Family** 1 2 3 4 5 6 7	Your first obligation is to yourself; each person is responsible for her- or himself.
Work hard now for a better future.	**Time Orientation** 1 2 3 4 5 6 7	Live in the present; the future may never come.
Money should be a major consideration in just about any decision you make.	**Money** 1 2 3 4 5 6 7	Money should not enter into life's really important decisions such as what relationship to enter or what career to pursue.
The world is just; bad things happen to bad people and good things happen to good people.	**Belief in a Just World** 1 2 3 4 5 6 7	The world is random; bad and good things happen to people without reference to whether they're good or bad.

HOW DID YOU DO? As demonstrated throughout this text and as research shows, your cultural values and beliefs influence your interpersonal communications as well as your decision making, your assessments of coworkers, your approach to teamwork, your level of trust in others, the importance you place on diversity in the workplace, and your attitudes toward the role of women in the workplace (Stephens & Greer, 1995; Bochner & Hesketh, 1994). For example, your beliefs and values about gender equality will influence the way in which you communicate with and about the opposite sex. Your beliefs about family will influence how you interact with family members.

WHAT WILL YOU DO? There are no right or wrong answers to this test. What makes this particular test of value for our purposes is that it asks you to examine your own cultural values and beliefs and hopefully stimulates you to go the next step and ask yourself how these values and beliefs influence your interpersonal communication. As you review your feelings about the six topics, try to identify at least one specific way in which your attitudes on each topic named in the self-test influence your interpersonal communication.

The Relevance of Culture

Because of (1) demographic changes, (2) increased sensitivity to cultural differences, (3) economic interdependency, (4) advances in communication technology, and (5) the fact that communication competence is specific to a culture (what works in one culture will not necessarily work in another), it's impossible to communicate effectively without being aware of how culture influences human communication.

Demographic Changes Most obvious, perhaps, are the vast demographic changes taking place throughout the United States. Whereas at one time the United States was a country largely populated by Europeans, it's now a country greatly influenced by the enormous number of new citizens from Latin and South America, Africa, and Asia. The same demographic shift is noticeable on college campuses. These changes have brought different interpersonal customs and the need to understand and adapt to new ways of looking at communication.

Ask the Researcher

The Importance of Culture in Interpersonal Communication

Culture seems to be a part of all my college courses. But I wonder: Is culture and intercultural communication that important today? Is this knowledge going to help me be more successful in my profession, whatever that will be?

Globalization has made the world more, not less complex, offering us many opportunities to interact with people of other cultures at home and abroad. Intercultural communication engages us at the individual and relational level. Our sense of efficacy in interaction depends to a large degree upon our training, knowledge, and willingness to be open to other cultures. This is the individual level; one may call it self-preparation for interaction. At the relational level we may be engaged in intercultural communication in several dimensions: advocacy, conversation, implementation of programs, deliberation, participation, presentation, and organization.

Knowledge of other cultures is fundamental to understanding how the world functions at the macro level. The more you build your capacity to engage different cultures, the greater your opportunity for success in your profession in the twenty-first century. Openness and humility are the keys to an effective interaction with others in your profession and in life.

For more information see Molefi Kete Asante, *Rhetoric, Race and Identity: The Architecton of Soul* (Amherst, MA: Prometheus Books, 2005) and Robert Shuter, "The Cultures of Rhetoric," in A. Gonzales and D. Tanno (eds.), *Rhetoric in Intercultural Contexts* (Thousand Oaks, CA: Sage, 2000), pp. 11–17.

Molefi Kete Asante (Ph.D., University of California, Los Angeles) is professor of African American studies at Temple University and the editor of the *Handbook of International and Intercultural Communication*. Dr. Asante is an international consultant on intercultural and international issues and the author of 60 books on culture and communication, including *Erasing Racism: The Survival of the American Nation* (Amherst, MA: Prometheus Books, 2003).

Sensitivity to Cultural Differences As a people we've become increasingly sensitive to cultural differences. American society has moved from an assimilationist attitude (people should leave their native culture behind and adapt to their new culture) to a perspective that values cultural diversity (people should retain their native cultural ways). We have moved from the metaphor of the melting pot, in which different cultures blended into one, to a metaphor of a spaghetti bowl or tossed salad, in which there is some blending but specific and different tastes and flavors still remain. In this diverse society, and with some notable exceptions—hate speech, racism, sexism, homophobia, and classism come quickly to mind—we are more concerned with saying the right thing and ultimately with developing a society where all cultures can coexist and enrich one another. The ability to interact effectively with members of other cultures often translates into financial gain and increased employment opportunities and advancement prospects as well.

Economic and Political Interdependence Today, most countries are economically dependent on one another. Our economic lives depend on our ability to communicate effectively across different cultures. Similarly, our political well-being depends in great part on that of other cultures. Political unrest in any part of the world—South Africa, Eastern Europe, Asia, and the Middle East, to take a few examples—affects our own security. Intercultural communication and understanding seem more crucial now than ever.

Spread of Technology The rapid spread of technology has made intercultural communication as easy as it is inevitable. News from foreign countries is commonplace. You see nightly—in vivid detail—what is going on in remote countries, just as you see what's happening in your own city and state. Of course, the Internet has made intercultural communication

as easy as writing a note on your computer. You can now communicate just as easily by e-mail with someone in Asia or Europe, for example, as you can with someone in another U.S. city or state.

Culture-Specific Nature of Interpersonal Communication Still another reason why culture is so important is that interpersonal competence is culture specific; what proves effective in one culture may prove ineffective in another. Many Asians, for example, often find that the values they were taught—values that promote cooperation and face-saving but discourage competitiveness and assertiveness—work against them in cultures that value competition and outspokenness (Cho, 2000). In another example, in the United States corporate executives get down to business during the first several minutes of a meeting. In Japan business executives interact socially for an extended period and try to find out something about one another. Thus, the communication principle influenced by U.S. culture would advise participants to get down to the meeting's agenda during the first five minutes. The principle influenced by Japanese culture would advise participants to avoid dealing with business until everyone has socialized sufficiently and feels well enough acquainted to begin negotiations. A third example: Giving a birthday gift to a close friend would be appreciated by many; but Jehovah's Witnesses would frown on this act, because they don't celebrate birthdays (Dresser, 2005). Neither principle is right, and neither is wrong. Each is effective within its own culture and ineffective outside its own culture.

The Aim of a Cultural Perspective

Because culture permeates all forms of communication, it's necessary to understand its influences if you're to understand how communication works and master its skills. As illustrated throughout this text, culture influences communications of all types (Moon, 1996; Jandt, 2007). It influences what you say to yourself and how you talk with friends, lovers, and family in everyday conversation (for example, Shibazaki & Brennan, 1998). It influences how you interact in groups and how much importance you place on the group versus the individual. It influences the topics you talk about and the strategies you use in communicating information or in persuading. It influences how you use the media and the credibility you attribute to them.

Consider attitudes toward age. If you were raised in the United States, you probably grew up with a youth bias (young is good, old is not so good)—an attitude the media reinforce daily—and might well assume that this preference for youth would be universal across all cultures. But it isn't; and if you assume it is, you may be in for intercultural difficulties. A good example is the case of the American journalist in China who remarked that the government official he was talking with was probably too young to remember a particular event, a comment that would be taken as a compliment by most youth-oriented Americans. But to the Chinese official the comment appeared to be an insult, a suggestion that the official was too young to deserve respect (Smith, 2002).

You need cultural understanding to communicate effectively in the wide variety of intercultural situations. Success in interpersonal communication—at your job and in your social and personal life—will depend in great part on your understanding of and your ability to communicate effectively with persons who are culturally different from yourself. Daily the media bombard you with evidence of racial tensions; religious disagreements; sexual bias; and, in general, the problems caused when intercultural communication fails.

This emphasis on culture does not imply that you should accept all cultural practices or that all cultural practices will necessarily be equal in terms of your own values and beliefs (Hatfield & Rapson, 1996). Nor does it imply that you have to accept or follow all of the practices of your own culture. For example, even if the majority in your culture find cockfighting acceptable, you need not agree with or follow the practice. Nor need you consider this practice equal to a cultural practice in which animals are treated kindly. You can reject capitalism or communism or socialism regardless of the culture in which you were raised. Of course, going against your culture's traditions and values is often very difficult. But it's important to realize that culture influ-

Culture and Ethics

One of the most shocking revelations to come to world attention after the events of September 11, 2001, was the way in which women were treated under Taliban rule in Afghanistan: Females could not be educated or even go out in public without a male relative escort, and when in public had to wear garments that covered their entire body.

Throughout history there have been cultural practices that today would be judged unethical. Sacrificing virgins to the gods, burning people who held different religious beliefs, and sending children to fight religious wars are obvious examples. But even today there are practices woven deep into the fabric of different cultures that you might find unethical. A few examples:

- bronco riding and bullfighting, practices involving inflicting pain and even causing the death of horses and bulls
- "female circumcision," in which part or all of a young girl's genitals are surgically altered so that she can never experience sexual intercourse without extreme pain, a practice designed to keep her a virgin until marriage
- the belief and practice that a woman must be subservient to her husband's will
- the practice of wearing fur—which in some cases means killing wild animals and in others raising animals so they can be killed when their pelts are worth the most money

What would you do?

You're talking with new work colleagues, and one of the above-mentioned practices is discussed with approval; your colleagues argue that each culture has a right to its own practices and beliefs. Given your own beliefs about these issues and about cultural diversity, what ethical obligations do you have to speak your mind without—you hope—jeopardizing your new position?

ences, it does not determine, your values or behavior. Often personality factors (your degree of assertiveness, extroversion, or optimism, for example) will prove more influential than culture (Hatfield & Rapson, 1996).

As demonstrated throughout this text, cultural differences exist throughout the interpersonal communication spectrum—from the way you use eye contact to the way you develop or dissolve a relationship (Chang & Holt, 1996). Culture even influences your level of happiness, which in turn influences your attitudes and the positivity and negativity of your messages (Kirn, 2005). But these differences should not blind you to the great number of similarities existing among even the most widely separated cultures. When discussing differences, remember that these are usually questions of degree rather than all-or-none. For example, most cultures value honesty, but some cultures give it greater emphasis than others. In addition, advances in media and technology and the widespread use of the Internet are influencing cultures and cultural change and are perhaps homogenizing different cultures to some extent, lessening differences and increasing similarities.

How Cultures Differ

Cultures, of course, differ in a wide variety of ways; and for purposes of communication, the difference that probably comes to mind first is that of languages. Certainly, cultures do differ in the languages spoken and understood. In fact, one of the most popular theories in intercultural communication, the language relativity hypothesis, argued that the language you speak influences your thoughts and behaviors and that because cultures differ so widely in their languages, they also will differ in their ways of thinking and behaving.

Subsequent research and theory, however, did not support the extreme claims made by linguistic relativity researchers (Pinker, 1994; Niemeier & Dirven, 2000; Durst, 2003). A more modified hypothesis is currently supported: The language you speak helps to *highlight* what you see and how you talk about it. For example, if you speak a language that is rich in color terms (English is a good example), you will find it easier to highlight and talk about nuances of color than will someone from a culture that has fewer color terms (some cultures distinguish only two or three or four parts of the color spectrum). This does not mean, however, that people *see* the world differently; only that their language helps (or

VIEWPOINT The theory of cultural imperialism argues that certain developed countries such as those of North American and Western Europe dominate the cultures of countries importing their products, especially their media. This cultural dominance is also seen in computer communication, in which the United States and the English language dominate. What do you think of the influence that media and the Internet from the United States and Western Europe are having on native cultures throughout the world? How do you evaluate this trend? Do you see advantages? How does this influence what you believe and feel about cultures other than your own?

doesn't help) them to focus on certain variations in nature and makes it easier (or more difficult) to talk about them. Nor does it mean that people speaking widely differing languages are doomed to misunderstanding each other. Translation enables us to understand a great deal of the meaning in a foreign-language message. We also have a ready arsenal of communication skills, which you'll encounter throughout this course, that can help bridge the communication gap between members of different cultures.

Language differences are not the only differences between cultures that will influence intercultural communication. Let's take a look at five such differences: power distances, masculine and feminine orientation, high and low tolerance for ambiguity, collectivism and individualism, and high and low context (Gudykunst, 1991; Hall & Hall, 1987; Hofstede, 1997). As you review these differences, recognize that they are matters of degree. Characteristics aren't necessarily present in one culture and absent in the other; rather they're present in both but to different degrees. And that's what this discussion focuses on: degrees of differences, not absolute differences.

Before reading about these dimensions, take the following self-test; it will help you think about your own cultural orientation and will personalize the text discussion and make it more meaningful.

Power Distances

In some cultures power is concentrated in the hands of a few, and there is a great difference between the power held by these people and that held by the ordinary citizen. These are called high-power-distance cultures; examples are Mexico, Brazil, India, and the Philippines (Hofstede, 1983, 1997). In low-power-distance cultures, power is more evenly distributed throughout the citizenry; examples include Denmark, New Zealand, Sweden, and to a lesser extent the United States. These different **power distances** affect interpersonal communication and relationships in a variety of ways.

Friendship and dating relationships will be influenced by the power distance between groups (Andersen, 1991). For example, in India (high power distance), friendships and romantic relationships are expected to take place within your cultural class; in Sweden (low power distance), a person is expected to select friends and romantic partners not on the basis of class or culture, but on individual factors such as personality, appearance, and the like.

In low-power-distance cultures there is a general feeling of equality that is consistent with acting assertively, and so you're expected to confront a friend, partner, or supervisor assertively (Borden, 1991). In high-power-distance cultures, direct confrontation and assertiveness may be viewed negatively, especially if directed at a superior (Morrison, Chen, & Salgado, 2004).

In high-power-distance cultures you're taught to have great respect for authority; people in these cultures see authority as desirable and beneficial, and challenges to authority are generally not welcomed (Westwood, Tang, & Kirkbride, 1992; Bochner & Hesketh, 1994). For example, in one study Asian adolescents (high-power-distance culture) had greater difficulty discussing problems with their parents than did Caucasians (low-power-distance culture) (Rhee, Chang, & Rhee, 2003). In low-power-distance cultures, there's a certain distrust for authority; it's seen as a kind of necessary evil that should be limited as much as possible. This difference in attitudes toward authority can be seen right in the classroom. In

TEST YOURSELF

WHAT'S YOUR CULTURAL ORIENTATION?

For each of the items below, select either *a* or *b*. In some cases, you may feel that neither *a* nor *b* describes you accurately; in these cases simply select the alternative that is closer to your feeling. As you'll see when you read this section, these are not *either/or* preferences, but *more-or-less* preferences.

_____ 1. I'd enjoy working in most groups
- a. in which there is little distinction between leaders and members.
- b. in which there is a clearly defined leader.

_____ 2. As a student (and if I feel well-informed)
- a. I'd feel comfortable challenging a professor.
- b. I'd feel uncomfortable challenging a professor.

_____ 3. In choosing a life partner or even close friends, I'd feel more comfortable
- a. with just about anyone, not necessarily one from my own culture and class.
- b. with those from my own culture and class.

_____ 4. Of the following characteristics, the ones I value more highly are
- a. aggressiveness, material success, and strength.
- b. modesty, tenderness, and quality of life.

_____ 5. In a conflict situation, I'd be more likely to
- a. confront conflicts directly and seek to win.
- b. confront conflicts with the aim of compromise.

_____ 6. If I were a manager of an organization I would stress
- a. competition and aggressiveness.
- b. worker satisfaction.

_____ 7. Generally, I'm
- a. comfortable with ambiguity and uncertainty.
- b. uncomfortable with ambiguity and uncertainty.

_____ 8. As a student, I'm more comfortable with assignments in which
- a. there is freedom for interpretation.
- b. there are clearly defined instructions.

_____ 9. Generally, when approaching an undertaking with which I've had no experience, I'd feel
- a. comfortable.
- b. uncomfortable.

_____ 10. Success, to my way of thinking, is better measured by
- a. the extent to which I surpass others.
- b. my contribution to the group effort.

_____ 11. My heroes are generally
- a. people who stand out from the crowd.
- b. team players.

_____ 12. The values I consider more important are
- a. achievement, stimulation, enjoyment.
- b. tradition, benevolence, conformity.

_____ 13. Generally, in my business transactions, I feel comfortable
- a. relying on oral agreements.
- b. relying on written agreements.

_____ 14. If I were a manager, I would likely
- a. reprimand a worker in public if the occasion warranted.
- b. always reprimand in private regardless of the situation.

_____ 15. In communicating, it's generally more important to be
- a. polite than accurate or direct.
- b. accurate and direct rather than polite.

high-power-distance cultures there's a great power distance between students and teachers; students are expected to be modest, polite, and totally respectful. In low-power-distance cultures students are expected to demonstrate their knowledge and command of the subject matter, participate in discussions with the teacher, and even challenge the teacher, something many high-power-distance culture members wouldn't even think of doing. The same is true for parents and their children's teachers; parents from high-power-distance cultures would be reluctant to question or even imply that they were questioning a teacher's decisions. A teacher who comes from a low-power-distance culture may see this parental behavior as a reluctance to get involved or as a lack of interest (Gibbs, 2005). The same differences can be seen in patient–doctor communication. Patients from high-power-distance cultures are less likely to challenge their doctors or admit that they don't understand the medical terminology than would patients in low-power-distance cultures.

High-power-distance cultures rely more on symbols of power. For example, titles (Dr., Professor, Chef, Inspector) are more important in high-power-distance cultures. Failure to include these in forms of address is a serious breach of etiquette. Low-power-distance cultures rely less on symbols of power, and less of a problem is created if you fail to use a respectful title (Victor, 1992). But even in low-power-distance cultures you may create problems if, for example, you call a medical doctor, police captain, military officer, or professor Ms. or Mr.

In the United States, two people quickly move from Title plus Last Name (Mr. or Ms. Smith) to First Name (Pat). In low-power-distance cultures less of a problem is created if you're too informal or if you presume to exchange first names before sufficient interaction has taken place. In high-power-distance cultures too great an informality—especially between those differing greatly in power—would be a serious breach of etiquette. Again, in even the lowest power-distance culture, you may still create problems if you call your English professor Pat.

Because the Internet and its information are available to vast numbers of people—not just to those in positions of power—it's been argued that power distances, especially in organizations, will change in the direction of becoming more egalitarian. Others have argued that this will not happen, simply because the hierarchical structure of most organizations serves them well; it's efficient and it encourages workers to climb the organizational ladder (Leavitt, 2005).

Masculine and Feminine Cultures

A popular classification of cultures is in terms of their masculinity and femininity (Hofstede, 1997, 1998, 2000; Imwalle & Schillo, 2004). When denoting cultural orientations, the terms "masculine" and "feminine" should be taken not as perpetuating stereotypes, but as a reflection of some of the commonly held assumptions of a sizable number of people throughout the world. "Masculinity" and "femininity" are the terms under which the research is conducted, and it is these words that you'd use to search the electronic databases.

For these reasons, these terms are used here. Some intercultural theorists, although continuing to use "masculine" and "feminine," note that equivalent terms would be "achievement" and "nurturance" (Lustig & Koester, 2006).

In a highly "masculine" culture men are viewed as assertive, oriented to material success, and strong; women on the other hand are viewed as modest, focused on the quality of life, and tender. In a highly "feminine" culture, both men and women are encouraged to be modest, oriented to maintaining the quality of life, and tender. The 10 countries with the highest masculinity score (beginning with the highest) are Japan, Austria, Venezuela, Italy, Switzerland, Mexico, Ireland, Jamaica, Great Britain, and Germany. The 10 countries with the highest femininity score (beginning with the highest) are Sweden, Norway, Netherlands, Denmark, Costa Rica, Yugoslavia, Finland, Chile, Portugal, and Thailand. Out of 53 countries ranked, the United States ranks 15th most masculine (Hofstede, 1997).

Masculine cultures emphasize success and socialize their people to be assertive, ambitious, and competitive. Members of masculine cultures are thus more likely to confront conflicts directly and to competitively fight out any differences; they're more likely to emphasize win–lose conflict strategies. **Feminine cultures** emphasize the quality of life and socialize their people to be modest and to emphasize close interpersonal relationships. Members of feminine cultures are thus more likely to emphasize compromise and negotiation in resolving conflicts; they're more likely to seek win–win solutions. Not surprisingly, people in feminine nations score significantly lower on depression levels (Arrindell, Steptoe, & Wardle, 2003).

Organizations also can be viewed in terms of masculinity or femininity. Masculine organizations emphasize competitiveness and aggressiveness. They focus on the bottom line and reward their workers on the basis of their contribution to the organization. Feminine organizations are less competitive and less aggressive. They're more likely to emphasize worker satisfaction and to reward their workers on the basis of need; those who have large families, for example, may get better raises than the single people, even if the singles have contributed more to the organization.

High-Ambiguity-Tolerant and Low-Ambiguity-Tolerant Cultures

In some cultures, people do little to avoid uncertainty, and they have little anxiety about not knowing what will happen next. In some other cultures, however, uncertainty is strongly avoided and there is much anxiety about uncertainty.

High-Ambiguity-Tolerant Cultures
Members of cultures with **high ambiguity tolerance** don't feel threatened by unknown situations; uncertainty is a normal part of life, and people accept it as it comes. Examples of such low-anxiety cultures include Singapore, Jamaica, Denmark, Sweden, Hong Kong, Ireland, Great Britain, Malaysia, India, Philippines, and the United States.

Because high-ambiguity-tolerant cultures are comfortable with ambiguity and uncertainty, they minimize the importance of rules governing communication and relationships (Hofstede, 1997; Lustig & Koester, 2006). People in these cultures readily tolerate individuals who don't follow the same rules as the cultural majority, and may even encourage different approaches and perspectives.

Students from high-ambiguity-tolerant cultures appreciate freedom in education and prefer assignments that allow for creativity without specific timetables or length restrictions. These students want to be rewarded for creativity and readily accept an instructor's lack of knowledge.

Low-Ambiguity-Tolerant Cultures
Members of cultures with **low ambiguity tolerance** do much to avoid uncertainty and have a great deal of anxiety about not knowing what will happen next; they see uncertainty as threatening and as something that must be counteracted. Examples of such low-ambiguity-tolerant cultures include Greece, Portugal, Guatemala,

Uruguay, Belgium, El Salvador, Japan, Yugoslavia, Peru, France, Chile, Spain, and Costa Rica (Hofstede, 1997).

Low-ambiguity-tolerant cultures create very clear-cut rules for communication that must not be broken. For example, students from strong-uncertainty-avoidance cultures prefer highly structured experiences with little ambiguity; they prefer specific objectives, detailed instructions, and definite timetables. An assignment to write a term paper on "anything" would be cause for alarm; it would not be clear or specific enough. These students expect to be judged on the basis of the right answers and expect the instructor to have all the answers all the time (Hofstede, 1997).

Individualist and Collectivist Orientations

Cultures also differ in the extent to which they promote individualist values (for example, power, achievement, hedonism, and stimulation) versus collectivist values (for example, benevolence, tradition, and conformity). The countries with the highest **individualist orientation** (beginning with the highest) are the United States, Australia, Great Britain, Canada, Netherlands, New Zealand, Italy, Belgium, Denmark, Sweden, France, and Ireland. Countries with the highest **collectivist orientation** (beginning with the highest) are Guatemala, Ecuador, Panama, Venezuela, Colombia, Indonesia, Pakistan, Costa Rica, Peru, Taiwan, and South Korea (Hofstede, 1983, 1997; Hatfield & Rapson, 1996; Kapoor, Wolfe, & Blue, 1995). For the most part the individualist countries are wealthy and the collectivist countries are poor, but there are a few notable exceptions. For example, Japan and Hong Kong—which score in the middle—are wealthier than many of the most individualist countries.

One of the major differences between these two orientations is in the extent to which an individual's goals or the group's goals are given precedence. Individualist and collectivist tendencies are, of course, not mutually exclusive; this is not an all-or-none orientation but rather one of emphasis. You probably have both tendencies. For example, you may compete with other members of your basketball team for most baskets or most valuable player award (and thus emphasize individual goals). At the same time, however, you will—in a game—act in a way that will benefit the entire team (and thus emphasize group goals). In actual practice both individual and collective tendencies will help you and your team each achieve your goals. Yet most people and most cultures have a dominant orientation; they're more individually oriented (they see themselves as independent) or more collectively oriented (they see themselves as interdependent) in most situations, most of the time (cf. Singelis, 1994).

In some instances, however, these tendencies may come into conflict. For example, do you shoot for the basket and try to raise your own individual score, or do you pass the ball to another player who is better positioned to score and thus benefit the team as a whole? You make this distinction in everyday conversation when you call someone a team player (collectivist orientation) or an individual player (individualist orientation).

In an **individualist culture** members are responsible for themselves and perhaps their immediate family. In a **collectivist culture** members are responsible for the entire group.

In an individualist culture success is measured by the extent to which you surpass other members of your group; you would take pride in standing out from the crowd. Your heroes—in the media, for example—are likely to be those who are unique and who stand apart. In a collectivist culture success is measured by your contribution to the achievements of the group as a whole; you would take pride in your similarity to other members of your group. Your heroes are more likely to be team players who do not stand out from the rest of the group's

VIEWPOINT In 1995 the Emma Lazarus poem inscribed on the Statue of Liberty was changed. The original last five lines of the poem, "The New Colossus," had been as follows, but in 1995 the words in brackets were deleted:

Give me your tired, your poor,
Your huddled masses yearning to breathe free,
[The wretched refuse of your teeming shore,]
Send these, the homeless, tempest-tost, to me:
I lift my lamp beside the golden door.

The late Harvard zoologist Stephen Jay Gould, commenting on this change, noted that the poem no longer represented what Lazarus wrote. "The language police triumph and integrity bleeds," said Gould (1995). Yet it is true that calling immigrants "wretched refuse" is insulting; if Lazarus had been writing in 1995, she probably wouldn't have used that phrase. Would you have supported deleting the line?

members. Not surprisingly, advertisements in individualist cultures emphasize individual preferences and benefits, independence, and personal success; advertisements in collectivist cultures emphasize group benefits, family integrity, and group harmony (Han & Shavitt, 1994).

In an individualist culture you're responsible to your own conscience, and responsibility is largely an individual matter; in a collectivist culture you're responsible to the rules of the social group, and responsibility for an accomplishment or a failure is shared by all members. Competition is fostered in individualist cultures, whereas cooperation is promoted in collectivist cultures. Not surprisingly, people in collectivist cultures are more willing to forgive others than are those in individualist cultures (Fu, Watkins, & Hui, 2004).

In an individualist culture you might compete for leadership in a small group setting, and there would likely be a very clear distinction between leaders and members. In a collectivist culture leadership would be shared and rotated; there is likely to be little distinction between leader and members. These orientations will also influence the kinds of communication members consider appropriate in an organizational context. For example, individualist members will favor clarity and directness, whereas collectivists will favor "face-saving" and the avoidance of hurting others or arousing negative evaluations (Kim & Sharkey, 1995).

Distinctions between in-group members and out-group members are extremely important in collectivist cultures. In individualist cultures, which prize each person's individuality, the distinction is likely to be less important.

High- and Low-Context Cultures

Cultures also differ in the extent to which information is made explicit or is assumed to be in the context or in the persons communicating. In a **high-context culture** much of the information in communication is in the context or in the person—for example, information that was shared through previous communications, through assumptions about one another, and through shared experiences. The information is thus known by all participants but isn't explicitly stated in the verbal messages. In a **low-context culture** most of the information is explicitly stated in the verbal message. In formal transactions it would be stated in written (or contract) form.

High-context cultures are also collectivist cultures (Gudykunst & Ting-Toomey, 1988; Gudykunst & Kim, 1992). These cultures (Japanese, Arabic, Latin American, Thai, Korean, Apache, and Mexican are examples) place great emphasis on personal relationships and oral agreements (Victor, 1992). Low-context cultures are also individualist cultures. These cultures (German, Swedish, Norwegian, and American are examples) place less emphasis on personal information and more emphasis on verbalized, explicit explanation and on written contracts in business transactions.

Members of high-context cultures spend lots of time getting to know one another interpersonally and socially before any important transactions take place. Because of this prior personal knowledge, a great deal of information is shared by the members and therefore does not have to be explicitly stated. Members of low-context cultures spend much less time getting to know one another and hence don't have that shared knowledge. As a result everything has to be stated explicitly.

This difference between high- and low-context orientation is partly responsible for the differences observed in Japanese and American business groups (mentioned earlier in this chapter). The Japanese spend lots of time getting acquainted before conducting actual business, whereas Americans get down to business very quickly. The Japanese (and members of other high-context cultures) want to get to know one another because important information isn't made explicit. They have to know you so they can read your nonverbals, for example (Sanders, Wiseman, & Matz, 1991). Americans can get right down to business because all important information will be stated explicitly.

To high-context cultural members, what is omitted or assumed is a vital part of the communication transaction. Silence, for example, is highly valued (Basso, 1972). To low-context cultural members, what is omitted creates ambiguity, but this ambiguity is simply something that will be eliminated by explicit and direct communication. To high-context cultural members, ambiguity is something to be avoided; it's a sign that the interpersonal and social interactions have not proved sufficient to establish a shared base of information (Gudykunst, 1983).

When this simple difference isn't understood, intercultural misunderstandings can easily result. For example, the directness characteristic of the low-context culture may seem insulting, insensitive, or unnecessary to the high-context cultural member. Conversely, to the low-context member, the high-context cultural member may appear vague, underhanded, or dishonest in his or her reluctance to be explicit or to engage in communication that a low-context member would consider open and direct.

Members of high-context cultures are reluctant to say no, for fear of offending and causing the person to lose face. Thus, it's necessary to be able to read when a Japanese executive's "yes" means yes and when it means no. The difference isn't in the words used but in the way in which they're used.

Members of high-context cultures also are reluctant to question the judgments of their superiors. In a company, for example, if a product were being manufactured with a defect, workers might be reluctant to communicate this back to management (Gross, Turner, & Cederholm, 1987). Similarly, workers might detect problems in procedures proposed by management but never communicate their concerns to their supervisors. In an intercultural organization knowledge of this tendency would alert a low-context management to look more deeply into the absence of communication, especially the absence of messages that might appear critical or negative.

Principles of Intercultural Communication

Understanding the role of culture in communication is an essential foundation for understanding intercultural communication as it occurs in an interpersonal context.

As a preface to this discussion, consider the following situations. How willing and open you would be to

- initiate a conversation with a culturally different person while waiting alone for a bus?
- have a close friendship with a culturally different person?
- have a long-term romantic relationship with a culturally different person?

UNDERSTANDING INTERPERSONAL SKILLS

Cultural Sensitivity

Cultural sensitivity is an attitude and way of behaving in which you're aware of and acknowledge cultural differences; it's crucial for such global goals as world peace and economic growth as well as for effective interpersonal communication (Franklin & Mizell, 1995). Without cultural sensitivity there can be no effective interpersonal communication between people who are different in gender or race or nationality or affectional orientation. So be mindful of the cultural differences between yourself and the other person. The techniques of interpersonal communication that work well with European Americans may not work well with Asian Americans; what proves effective in Japan may not in Mexico. The close physical distance that is normal in Arab cultures may seem too familiar or too intrusive in much of the United States and northern Europe. The empathy that most Americans welcome may be uncomfortable for most Koreans, Japanese, or Chinese.

Increasing Cultural Sensitivity. This chapter has identified many guidelines for more effective intercultural communication, and among them are recommendations that constitute the best advice for achieving cultural sensitivity:

- Prepare yourself. Read about and listen carefully for culturally influenced behaviors.
- Recognize and face your own fears of acting inappropriately toward members of different cultures.
- Recognize differences between yourself and culturally different individuals.
- At the same time, recognize that there are often enormous differences within any given cultural group.
- Recognize differences in meaning; words rarely mean the same thing to members of different cultures.
- Become conscious of the cultural rules and customs of others.

Working with Interpersonal Skills

How would you rate your own cultural sensitivity? Try to recall situations in which you were and situations in which you weren't culturally sensitive. What happened in each? Can you identify one situation that could have been improved with the additional of cultural sensitivity?

FIGURE 2.1

A Model of Intercultural Communication

This model of intercultural communication illustrates that culture is a part of every communication act. More specifically, it illustrates that the messages you send and the messages you receive will be influenced by your cultural beliefs, values, and attitudes. Note also that the circles overlap to some degree, illustrating that no matter how different the cultures of the two individuals are, there will always be some commonalities, some similarities, along with differences.

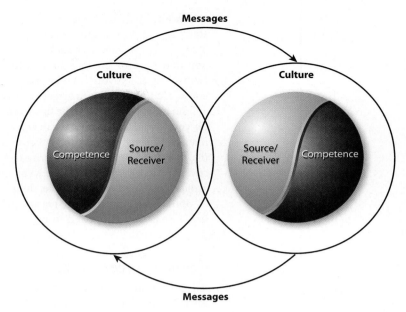

■ listen fairly to a conversation conducted by a culturally different person?
■ ascribe a level of credibility to a culturally different person identical to that you would ascribe to a culturally similar person—all other things being equal?

The term **intercultural communication** refers to communication between persons who have different cultural beliefs, values, or ways of behaving. The model in Figure 2.1 illustrates this concept. The circles represent the cultures of the individual communicators. The inner circles identify the communicators (the sources/receivers). In this model each communicator is a member of a different culture. In some instances the cultural differences are relatively slight—say, between persons from Toronto and New York. In other instances the cultural differences are great—say, between persons from Borneo and Germany, or between persons from rural Nigeria and industrialized England.

Every message originates from a specific and unique cultural context, and that context influences the message's content and form. You communicate as you do largely as a result of your culture. Culture (along with the processes of enculturation and acculturation) influences every aspect of your communication experience.

Murphy's Law ("Anything that can go wrong will go wrong") is especially applicable to intercultural communication. Intercultural communication is, of course, subject to all the same barriers and problems as are the other forms of communication discussed throughout this text. Drawing on the work of numerous intercultural researchers, let's consider several guidelines designed to counteract the barriers that are unique to intercultural communication (Barna, 1997; Ruben, 1985; Spitzberg, 1991).

Educate Yourself

There's no better preparation for intercultural communication than learning about the other culture. Fortunately, there are numerous sources to draw on. View a documentary or movie that presents a realistic view of the culture. Read material about the culture by persons from that culture as well as by "outsiders" (e.g., Foster, 2004). Scan magazines and websites from the culture. Talk with members of the culture. Chat in international chat rooms. Read materials addressed to people who need to communicate with those from other cultures. For example, books on the subject include: *Essential Do's and Taboos: The Complete Guide to International Business and Leisure Travel* (Axtell, 2007); *Behave Yourself!: The Essential Guide to International Etiquette* (Powell, 2005); *Global Business Etiquette: A Guide to International Communication and Customs* (Martin & Chaney, 2008); and *Cultural Dimensions of International Business* (Ferraro, 2005). You can find a great many more such works at Amazon.com (www.amazon.com) or Barnes and Noble (www.bn.com), for example.

Another part of this preparation is to recognize and face your own fears, which can stand in the way of effective intercultural communication (Gudykunst, 1994; Stephan & Stephan, 1985; Shelton & Richeson, 2005). For example, you may fear for your self-esteem. You may become anxious about your ability to control the intercultural situation, or you may worry about your own level of discomfort. You may fear saying something that will be considered politically incorrect or culturally insensitive and thereby losing face.

You may fear that you'll be taken advantage of by a member of another culture. Depending on your own stereotypes, you may fear being lied to, financially duped, or made fun of. You may fear that members of this other group will react to you negatively. You may fear, for example, that they will not like you or may disapprove of your attitudes or beliefs or perhaps even reject you as a person. Conversely, you may fear negative reactions from members of your own group. They might, for example, disapprove of your socializing with the culturally different.

Some fears, of course, are reasonable. In many cases, however, such concerns are groundless. Either way, they need to be assessed logically and their consequences weighed carefully. Then you'll be able to make informed choices about your communications.

Reduce Uncertainty

All communication interactions involve uncertainty and ambiguity. Not surprisingly, uncertainty and ambiguity are greater when there are large cultural differences (Berger & Bradac, 1982; Gudykunst, 1989, 1993). Because of this greater uncertainty in intercultural communication, more time and effort are required to reduce it and thus to communicate meaningfully. Reducing your uncertainty about another person not only will make your communication more effective; it also will increase your liking for the person and make the interaction more satisfying (Neuliep & Grohskopf, 2000; Douglas, 1994). In situations of great uncertainty the techniques of effective communication (for example, active listening, perception checking, being specific, and seeking feedback) take on special importance.

Active listening (Chapter 4) and perception checking techniques (Chapter 3) help you to verify the accuracy of your perceptions and allow you to revise and amend any incorrect perceptions. Being specific reduces ambiguity and the chances of misunderstandings. For example, misunderstanding is a lot more likely in a conversation about "neglect" (a highly abstract concept) than in a discussion about "forgetting your last birthday" (a specific event).

Seeking feedback helps you to correct any possible misconceptions almost immediately. Seek feedback on whether you're making yourself clear ("Does that make sense?" "Do you see where to put the widget?"). Similarly, seek feedback to make sure you understand what the other person is saying ("Do you mean that you'll never speak with them again? Do you mean that literally?").

Although you're always in danger of misperceiving and misevaluating another person, you're in special danger in intercultural situations. Therefore, try to resist your natural tendency to judge others quickly and permanently. A judgment made early is likely to be based on too little information. Because of this, flexibility and a willingness to revise opinions are essential intercultural skills.

VIEWPOINT One of the current controversies in education centers on the teaching of evolution (humans evolved from earlier forms of animals) versus creationism (God created humans as they are now). Although the scientific evidence and most scientists support evolution and argue that therefore this is what should be taught in the schools, many influential religious leaders have argued that creationism is an equally plausible explanation and have pressured some publishers to present evolution as just one theory and creationism as another (Lemonick, 2005b). How do you feel about this issue?

Recognize Differences

To communicate interculturally you need to recognize the differences between yourself and people from other cultures, the differences within the other cultural group, and the numerous differences in meaning.

UNDERSTANDING INTERPERSONAL THEORY & RESEARCH

Culture Shock

Culture shock is the psychological reaction you experience when you're in a culture very different from your own (Ward, Bochner, & Furnham, 2001; Wan, 2004). Culture shock is normal; most people experience it when entering a new and different culture. Nevertheless, it can be unpleasant and frustrating. Part of this results from feelings of alienation, conspicuousness, and difference from everyone else. When you lack knowledge of the rules and customs of the new society, you cannot communicate effectively. You're apt to blunder frequently and seriously. In your culture shock you may not know such basic things as how to ask someone for a favor or pay someone a compliment, how to extend or accept an invitation for dinner, or how early or how late to arrive for an appointment.

Culture shock occurs in four stages (Oberg, 1960). These stages are useful for examining many encounters with the new and the different. Going away to college, moving in together, or joining the military, for example, can also result in culture shock.

- **Stage One: The Honeymoon.** At first you experience fascination, even enchantment, with the new culture and its people.
- **Stage Two: The Crisis.** Here, the differences between your own culture and the new setting create problems. Feelings of frustration and inadequacy come to the fore. This is the stage at which you experience the actual shock of the new culture.
- **Stage Three: The Recovery.** During this period you gain the skills necessary to function effectively. You learn the language and ways of the new culture. Your feelings of inadequacy subside.
- **Stage Four: The Adjustment.** At this final stage, you adjust to and come to enjoy the new culture and the new experiences. You may still experience periodic difficulties and strains, but on the whole, the experience is pleasant.

People may also experience culture shock when they return to their original culture after living in a foreign culture, a kind of reverse culture shock (Jandt, 2004). Consider, for example, Peace Corps volunteers who work in rural and economically deprived areas. On returning to Las Vegas or Beverly Hills, they too may experience culture shock. A sailor who serves long periods aboard ship and then returns to an isolated farming community may experience culture shock. In these cases, however, the recovery period is shorter and the sense of inadequacy and frustration is less.

Working with Theories and Research

Among the ways recommended to manage the inevitable culture shock are: (1) Familiarize yourself with the host nation, (2) form friendship networks to assist you in adjusting, (3) interact with members of the culture and your hosts, and (4) be open to seeking professional help in adjusting to cultural problems (Constantine, Anderson, Berkel, Caldwell, & Utsey, 2005; Britnell, 2004; Chapdelaine & Alexitch, 2004). In what other ways might you effectively manage culture shock?

Differences between Yourself and the Culturally Different A common barrier to intercultural communication occurs when you assume that similarities exist and that differences do not. This is especially true of values, attitudes, and beliefs. You might easily accept different hairstyles, clothing, and foods. In basic values and beliefs, however, you may assume that deep down all people are really alike. They aren't. When you assume similarities and ignore differences, you'll fail to notice important distinctions and when communicating will convey to others that your ways are the right ways and that their ways are not important to you. Consider this example. An American invites a Filipino coworker to dinner. The Filipino politely refuses. The American is hurt and feels that the Filipino does not want to be friendly. The Filipino is hurt and concludes that the invitation was not extended sincerely. Here, it seems, both the American and the Filipino assume that their customs for inviting people to dinner are the same when, in fact, they aren't. A Filipino expects to be invited several times before accepting a dinner invitation. When an invitation is given only once it's viewed as insincere.

Here's another example. An American college student hears the news that her favorite uncle has died. She bites her lip, pulls herself up, and politely excuses herself from the group of foreign students with whom she is having dinner. The Russian thinks: "How unfriendly." The Italian thinks: "How insincere." The Brazilian thinks: "How unconcerned." To many Americans, it's a sign of bravery to endure pain (physical or emotional) in silence and without any outward show of emotion. To members of other groups, such silence is often interpreted negatively to mean that the individual does not consider them friends who can share such sorrow. In other cultures, people are expected to reveal to friends how they feel.

Differences within the Culturally Different Group Within every cultural group there are vast and important differences. As all Americans are not alike, neither are all Indonesians, Greeks, Mexicans, and so on. When you ignore these differences—when you assume that all persons covered by the same label (in this case a national or racial label) are the same—you're guilty of stereotyping. A good example of this is seen in the use of the term "African American." The term stresses the unity of Africa and of those who are of African descent and is analogous to "Asian American" or "European American." At the same time, it ignores the great diversity within the African continent when, for example, it's used as analogous to "German American" or "Japanese American." More analogous terms would be "Nigerian American" or "Ethiopian American." Within each culture there are smaller cultures that differ greatly from each other and from the larger culture.

Differences in Meaning Meaning exists not in words but in people (a principle we'll return to in Chapter 5). Consider, for example, the differences in meaning that exist for words such as *woman* to an American and a Muslim, *religion* to a born-again Christian and an atheist, and *lunch* to a Chinese rice farmer and a Madison Avenue advertising executive. Even though the same word is used, its meanings will vary greatly depending on the listeners' cultural definitions.

Nonverbal differences in meaning also exist. For example, a left-handed American who eats with the left hand may be seen by a Muslim as obscene. To the Muslim, the left hand isn't used for eating or for shaking hands but to clean oneself after excretory functions. So using the left hand to eat or to shake hands is considered insulting and obscene.

Confront Your Stereotypes

Stereotypes, especially when they operate below the level of conscious awareness, can create serious communication problems (Lyons & Kashima, 2003). Originally, the word *stereotype* was a printing term that referred to the plate that printed the same image over and over. A sociological or psychological **stereotype** is a fixed impression of a group of people. Everyone has attitudinal stereotypes—images of national groups, religious groups, or racial groups or perhaps of criminals, prostitutes, teachers, or plumbers. Consider, for example, if you have any stereotypes of, say, bodybuilders, the opposite sex, a racial group different from your own, members of a religion very different from your own, hard drug users, or college professors. It is very likely that you have stereotypes of several or perhaps even of all of these groups. Although we often think of stereotypes as negative ("They're lazy, dirty, and only interested in getting high"), stereotypes also may be positive ("They're smart, hardworking, and extremely loyal").

If you have these fixed impressions, you may, on meeting a member of a particular group, see that person primarily as a member of that group. Initially this may provide you with some helpful orientation. However, it creates problems when you apply to that person all the characteristics you assign to members of that group without examining the unique individual. If you meet a politician, for example, you may have a host of characteristics for politicians that you can readily apply to this person. To complicate matters further, you may see in the person's behavior the manifestation of various characteristics that you would not see if you did not know that the person was a politician. In online communication, because there are few visual and auditory cues, it's not surprising to find that people form impressions of online communication partners with a heavy reliance on stereotypes (Jacobson, 1999).

Consider, however, another kind of stereotype: You're driving along a dark road and are stopped at a stop sign. A car pulls up beside you and three teenagers jump out and rap on your window. There may be a variety of possible explanations.

VIEWPOINT Some people feel that media portrayals of cultural groups often perpetuate stereotypes. Thus, for example, *The Sopranos*, the HBO series pictured here, has been accused of perpetuating the stereotype of Italian Americans as gangsters or of gangsters as Italian. How do you feel about the media's portrayals of your own cultural groups? Do the media create and perpetuate stereotypes of your groups? If so, are they basically positive or negative?

Perhaps they need help or they want to ask directions. Or they may be about to engage in carjacking. Your self-protective stereotype may help you decide on "carjacking" and may lead you to pull away and into the safety of a busy service station. In doing that, of course, you may have escaped being carjacked—or you may have failed to help people who needed assistance.

Stereotyping can lead to two major barriers. The tendency to group a person into a class and to respond to that person primarily as a member of that class can lead you to perceive that a person possesses certain qualities (usually negative) that you believe characterize the group to which he or she belongs. Then you will fail to appreciate the multifaceted nature of all people and all groups. For example, consider your stereotype of someone who is deeply into computers. Very likely your image is quite different from the research findings on such individuals, which show that in fact they are as often female as male and are as sociable, popular, and self-assured as their peers who are not into heavy computer use (Schott & Selwyn 2000).

Stereotyping also can lead you to ignore the unique characteristics of an individual; you therefore may fail to benefit from the special contributions each person can bring to an encounter.

Adjust Your Communication

Intercultural communication (in fact, all interpersonal communication) takes place only to the extent that one person can understand the words and nonverbals of the other—that is, only to the extent that the two individuals share the same system of symbols. Because no two people share the identical meaning system for symbols, adjustments have to be made in all interpersonal interactions, but especially, perhaps, in intercultural interactions. Figure 2.2 illustrates the connection between degrees of cultural difference and the degree of adjustment that will be necessary for successful communication.

Parents and children, for example, not only have different vocabularies but also, even more important, have different meanings for some of the terms they have in common. People in close relationships—either as intimate friends or as romantic partners—realize that learning the other person's signals takes a long time and, often, great patience. If you want to understand what another person means—by smiling, by saying "I love you," by arguing about trivial matters, by self-deprecating comments—you have to learn their system of signals.

This principle is especially important in intercultural communication, largely because people from different cultures use different signals and/or use the same signals to signify quite different things. Focused eye contact means honesty and openness in much of the United States. But in Japan and in many Hispanic cultures that same behavior may signify arrogance or disrespect if it occurs between a youngster and someone significantly older.

Part of the art of intercultural communication is learning the other person's signals, how they're used, and what they mean. Furthermore, you have to share your own system of signals with others so that they can better understand you. Although some people may know what you mean by your silence or by your avoidance of eye contact, others may not. You cannot expect others to decode your behaviors accurately without help.

An interesting theory largely revolving around adjustment is *communication accommodation theory*. This theory holds that speakers will adjust to or accommodate the speaking style of their listeners to gain, for example, social approval and greater communication efficiency (Giles, 2008; Giles & Ogay, 2007). For example, research shows that when two people have a similar speech rate, they're attracted more to each other than to people with dissimilar rates (Buller, LePoire, Aune, & Eloy, 1992). Also, the speaker who uses language intensity or forcefulness similar to that of listeners is judged to have greater credibility than the speaker who uses intensity different from that of listeners (Aune & Kikuchi, 1993).

VIEWPOINT Assume you're a judge and the following case is presented to you (*Time*, December 2, 1993, p. 61): A Chinese immigrant killed his wife in New York because he suspected her of cheating. A "cultural defense" was offered, essentially claiming that infidelity so shames a man that he is uncontrollable in his anger. Would this cultural defense have influenced your judgment? In the actual case, influenced by an anthropologist's testimony that infidelity is so serious in Chinese culture that it pushed the defendant to commit the crime, the judge sentenced the defendant to five years' probation. How do you feel about "cultural defenses" in general? Are there some cultural defenses you'd accept and others you would not?

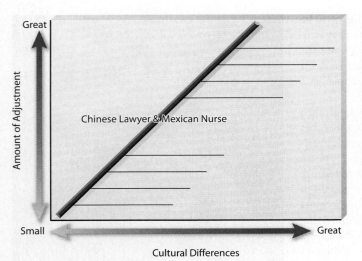

FIGURE 2.2

Cultural Differences and Interpersonal Adjustment

As you can see from this diagram, the greater the cultural differences, the greater the communication adjustment you'll need to make in order to accomplish your interpersonal goal. Note that in the middle of the graph a specific dyad is identified (Chinese lawyer and Mexican nurse). Try to fill in the graph with dyads that you think indicate greater cultural differences and hence require greater communication adjustment as well as with other dyads you think indicate less cultural differences and hence less adjustment.

Another study found that roommates who were similar in communication competence and low in verbal aggressiveness were highest in roommate liking and satisfaction (Martin & Anderson, 1995). People even accommodate in their e-mail. In still another study, for example, responses to messages that contained politeness cues were significantly more polite than responses to e-mails that did not contain such cues (Bunz & Campbell, 2004).

In some instances intermediaries may "broker" accommodation in an effort to make communication easier between two different groups. For example, among Chinese immigrants in New Zealand, many grandparents speak only Chinese and know only the Chinese culture, but their grandchildren speak only English and know only the New Zealand culture. In such situations the parents of the children (who know both languages and cultures) often serve as intermediaries or brokers between grandparents and grandchildren and help each group accommodate their communication toward the other (Ng, He, & Loong, 2004).

As you adjust your communications, recognize that each culture has its own rules and customs for communicating (Barna, 1997; Ruben, 1985; Spitzberg, 1991). These rules identify what is appropriate and what is inappropriate (Serewicz & Petronio, 2007). Thus, for example, in American culture you would call a person you wished to date three or four days in advance; in certain Asian cultures you might call the person's parents weeks or even months in advance. In American culture you say, as a general friendly gesture and not as a specific invitation, "Come over and pay us a visit." To members of other cultures, this comment is sufficient for the listeners to actually visit at their convenience. In some cultures people show respect by avoiding direct eye contact with the person to whom they're speaking; in other cultures this same eye avoidance would signal disinterest. If a young American girl is talking with an older Indonesian man, for example, she's expected to avoid direct eye contact. Among Indonesians direct eye contact in this situation would be considered disrespectful. In some southern European cultures men walk arm in arm. In American culture this is considered inappropriate.

A good example of a series of rules for an extremely large and important culture appears in Table 2.1, "Interpersonal Communication Tips between People with and without Disabilities."

Reduce Your Ethnocentrism

Before reading about this important concept, examine your own ethnocentrism by taking the self-test, p. 50.

As you've probably gathered from taking this test, **ethnocentrism** is the tendency to evaluate the values, beliefs, and behaviors of your own culture as being more positive, logical, and natural than those of other cultures. Although normally thought of negatively, ethnocentrism has its positive aspects. For example, if a group is under attack, ethnocentrism will help create cohesiveness. It has also been argued that it forms the basis of patriotism and a willingness to sacrifice for the benefit of the group (Neuliep & McCroskey, 1997).

TABLE 2.1 Interpersonal Communication Tips
Between People with and without Disabilities

| Franklin Delano Roosevelt | Stephen Hawking | Christopher Reeve | Trevor Snowden |

Other "Tips" tables focus on visual impairment (Chapter 1), hearing loss (Chapter 4), and speech and language disorders (Chapter 8); here we look at communication between those with general disabilities—for example, people in wheelchairs or with, say, cerebral palsy—and those who have no such disability. The suggestions offered here are considered appropriate in the United States, although not necessarily in other cultures. For example, most people in the United States accept the phrase "person with mental retardation," but the term is considered offensive to many in the United Kingdom (Fernald, 1995).

If you're the person without a general disability:

1. Avoid negative terms and terms that define the person as disabled, such as "the disabled man" or "the handicapped child." Instead use "person-first" language and say "person with a disability," always emphasizing the person rather than the disability. Avoid describing the person with a disability as abnormal; when you define people without disabilities as "normal," you in effect say that the person with a disability isn't normal.

2. Treat assistive devices such as wheelchairs, canes, walkers, or crutches as the personal property of the user. Don't move these out of your way; they're for the convenience of the person with the disability. Avoid leaning on a person's wheelchair; it's similar to leaning on a person.

3. Shake hands with the person with the disability if you shake hands with others in a group. Don't avoid shaking hands because the individual's hand is crippled, for example.

4. Avoid talking about the person with a disability in the third person. For example, avoid saying, "Doesn't he get around beautifully with the new crutches." Direct your comments directly to the individual.

5. Don't assume that people who have a disability are intellectually impaired. Slurred speech—such as may occur with people who have cerebral palsy or cleft palate—should not be taken as indicating a low-level intellect. So be careful not to talk down to such individuals as, research shows, many people do (Unger, 2001).

6. When you're not sure of how to act, ask. For example, if you're not sure if you should offer walking assistance, say, "Would you like me to help you into the dining room?" And, more important, accept the person's response. If he or she says no, then that means no; don't insist.

7. Maintain similar eye level. If the person is in a wheelchair, for example, it might be helpful for you to sit down or kneel down to get onto the same eye level.

If you're the person with a general disability:

1. Let the other person know if he or she can do anything to assist you in communicating. For example, if you want someone to speak in a louder voice, ask. If you want to relax and have someone push your wheelchair, say so.

2. Be patient and understanding. Many people mean well but may simply not know how to act or what to say. Put them at ease as best you can.

3. Demonstrate your own comfort. If you detect discomfort in the other person, you might talk a bit about your disability to show that you're not uncomfortable about it—and that you understand that others may not know how you feel. But you're under no obligation to educate the public, so don't feel this is something you should or have to do.

Sources: These suggestions are based on a wide variety of sources, including www.empowermentzone.com/etiquet.txt (the website for the National Center for Access Unlimited), www.disabilityinfo.gov, www.drc.uga.edu, and www.ucpa.org/ (all accessed April 30, 2008).

Here are 18 statements representing your beliefs about your culture. For each statement indicate how much you agree or disagree, using the following scale: 5 = strongly agree, 4 = agree, 3 = neither agree nor disagree, 2 = disagree, 1 = strongly disagree.

_____   1. Most cultures are backward compared to my culture.

_____   2. My culture should be the role model for other cultures.

_____   3. Lifestyles in other cultures are just as valid as those in my culture.

_____   4. Other cultures should try to be like my culture.

_____   5. I'm not interested in the values and customs of other cultures.

_____   6. People in my culture could learn a lot from people in other cultures.

_____   7. Most people from other cultures just don't know what's good for them.

_____   8. I have little respect for the values and customs of other cultures.

_____   9. Most people would be happier if they lived like people in my culture.

_____   10. People in my culture have just about the best lifestyles of anywhere.

_____   11. Lifestyles in other cultures are not as valid as those in my culture.

_____   12. I'm very interested in the values and customs of other cultures.

_____   13. I respect the values and customs of other cultures.

_____   14. I do not cooperate with people who are different.

_____   15. I do not trust people who are different.

_____   16. I dislike interacting with people from different cultures.

_____   17. Other cultures are smart to look up to my culture.

_____   18. People from other cultures act strange and unusual when they come into my culture.

HOW DID YOU DO? This test was presented to give you the opportunity to examine some of your own cultural beliefs, particularly those cultural beliefs that contribute to ethnocentrism. The person low in ethnocentrism would have high scores (4s and 5s) for items 3, 6, 12, and 13 and low scores (1s and 2s) for all the others. The person high in ethnocentrism would have low scores for items 3, 6, 12, and 13 and high scores for all the others.

WHAT WILL YOU DO? Use this test to bring your own cultural beliefs to consciousness so you can examine them logically and objectively. Ask yourself if your beliefs are productive beliefs that will help you achieve your professional and social goals, or if they're counterproductive beliefs that will actually hinder your progress.

Source: This test is taken from James W. Neuliep, Michelle Chaudoir, and James C. McCroskey (2001). A cross-cultural comparison of ethnocentrism among Japanese and United States college students. *Communication Research Reports* 18 (Spring):137–146. Copyright © 2001 by Taylor & Francis Informa UK Ltd.—Journals. Reproduced with permission of Taylor & Francis Informa UK Ltd.—Journals in the format Textbook via Copyright Clearance Center.

But ethnocentrism also can create considerable problems. Although the research is not conclusive, it appears that it may create obstacles to communication with those who are culturally different from you. It can also lead to hostility toward outside groups and may blind you to seeing other perspectives, other values, other ways of doing things (Neuliep & McCroskey, 1997; Cashdan, 2001; Jörn, 2004).

Ethnocentrism exists on a continuum (see Table 2.2). People aren't either ethnocentric or not ethnocentric; rather, most are somewhere between these polar opposites. Of course, your degree of ethnocentrism varies, depending on the group on which you focus. For example, if you're Greek American, you may have a low degree of ethnocentrism when dealing with Italian Americans but a high degree when dealing with Turkish Americans or Japanese Americans. Most important for our purposes is that your degree of ethnocentrism (and we are all ethnocentric to at least some degree) will influence your interpersonal interactions.

There is nothing wrong with classifying. In fact, it's an extremely useful method of dealing with any complex matter; it puts order into thinking. The problem arises not from classification itself but from applying an evaluative label to a class and using that label as an "adequate" map for each and every individual in the group.

| Table 2.2 | The Ethnocentric Continuum |

This table summarizes some of the interconnections between ethnocentrism and communication. In this table, five degrees of ethnocentrism are identified; in reality, there are as many degrees as there are people. The "communication distances" are general terms that highlight the attitude that dominates that level of ethnocentrism. Under "communications" are some of the major ways people might interact given their particular degree of ethnocentrism. Can you identify your own ethnocentrism on this table? For example, are there groups to which you have low ethnocentrism? Middle? High? What accounts for these differences? This table draws on the work of several intercultural researchers (Lukens, 1978; Gudykunst & Kim, 1992; Gudykunst, 1991).

Degree of Ethnocentrism	Communication Distance	Communications
Low	Equality	You treat others as equals; you view different customs and ways of behaving as equal to your own.
	Sensitivity	You want to decrease distance between yourself and others.
	Indifference	You lack concern for others; you prefer to interact in a world of similar others.
	Avoidance	You avoid and limit communications, especially intimate ones with interculturally different others.
High	Disparagement	You engage in hostile behavior and belittle others; you view different cultures and ways of behaving as inferior to your own.

Summary

This chapter explored the nature of culture and identified some key concepts and principles that explain the role of culture in interpersonal communication.

Culture

1. Culture is the relatively specialized lifestyle of a group of people (values, beliefs, artifacts, ways of behaving) that is passed from one generation to the next by means of communication, not through genes.
2. Enculturation is the process through which you learn the culture into which you're born; ethnic identity is a commitment to the ways and beliefs of your culture; and acculturation is the process by which you learn the rules and norms of a culture that is different from your native culture and that modifies your original or native culture.
3. An individual's cultural beliefs and values will influence all forms of interpersonal communication and therefore need to be considered in any full communication analysis.
4. Culture is especially relevant today because of the demographic changes, increased sensitivity to cultural variation, economic interdependency among nations, advances in communication technology which make intercultural communication easy and inexpensive, and the fact that communication effectiveness in one culture may not be effective in another.

How Cultures Differ

5. In high-power-distance cultures, power is concentrated in the hands of a few and there is a great difference between those with

and those without power. In low-power-distance cultures, the power is more equally shared throughout the citizenry.
6. Highly masculine cultures view men as strong, assertive, and focused on success and view women as modest, tender, and focused on the quality of life. Highly feminine cultures view men and women more similarly.
7. Cultures differ greatly in their level of tolerance for ambiguity.
8. A collectivist culture emphasizes the group and subordinates the individual's goals to those of the group. An individualist culture emphasizes the individual and subordinates the group's goals to the individual's.
9. In high-context cultures, much of the information is in the context; in low-context cultures, information is explicitly stated in the verbal message.

Principles of Intercultural Communication

10. Intercultural communication is communication between people who have different cultures, beliefs, values, and ways of behaving.
11. Some intercultural communication guidelines include: Educate yourself; reduce uncertainty; recognize differences (between yourself and others, within the culturally different group, and in meanings); confront your stereotypes; adjust your communication; and reduce your ethnocentrism.

Key Terms

Critical Thinking Questions

1 In this age of multiculturalism, how do you feel about Article II, Section 1 of the United States Constitution? The relevant section reads: "No person except a natural-born citizen, or citizen of the United States at the time of the adoption of this Constitution, shall be eligible to the office of President."

2 It's been argued that in the United States women are more likely to view themselves as interdependents, having a more collectivist orientation, whereas men are more likely to view themselves as independents, having a more individualist orientation (Cross & Madson, 1997). Does your experience support this?

3 Informal time terms (e.g., *soon, right away, early, in a while, as soon as possible*) seem to create communication problems because they're ambiguous; different people will often give the terms different meanings. How might you go about reducing or eliminating the ambiguity created by these terms?

4 You're more likely to help someone who is similar to you in race, attitude, and general appearance. Even the same first name is significant. For example, when an e-mail (asking receivers to fill out surveys of their food habits) identified the sender as having the same name as the receiver, there was a greater willingness to comply with the request (Gueguen, 2003). Do you think people do react this way, and if so, why? Do you do this?

5 Has anyone ever assumed something untrue about you because you were a member of a particular culture? Did you find this disturbing?

6 One study finds that lonely people are more likely to use the Internet to obtain emotional support than are those who are not lonely. Further, lonely people are more satisfied with their online relationships than are those who are not lonely (Morahan-Martin & Schumacher, 2003). How would you explain these findings?

7 Consider how cultural differences underlie some of the most hotly debated topics in the news today. The following, for example, is a brief list of some of these topics. How would you respond to the various questions raised? How do your cultural attitudes, beliefs, and values influence your responses?

- Should Christian Science parents be prosecuted for preventing their children from receiving lifesaving treatments such as blood transfusions or insulin? Some states, such as Connecticut and Arizona, grant Christian Scientists special rights in this regard. Should this special treatment be adopted by all states? Should it be eliminated?

- Should cockfighting be permitted in all states? Or should it be declared illegal as "cruelty to animals"? Some Latino Americans have argued that cockfighting is a part of their culture and should be permitted. Cockfighting is illegal in most of the United States, but in five states and in Puerto Rico, it is legal.

- Should safe sex practices be taught in the elementary schools, or is this a matter for the home?

- Should those who commit crimes because of hate or bias be given harsher sentences?

- Should doctor-assisted suicides be legalized?

- In adoption decisions, should the race of the child and that of the adopting parents be an issue?

Choice Points

1 *Putting Your Foot in Your Mouth.* At work you tell an ageist joke, only to discover later that it has been resented and clearly violated the organizational norms for polite and unbiased talk. Ask yourself: What might you say to make this situation a little less awkward and less potentially damaging to your relationships with coworkers?

2 *Misusing Linguistic Privilege.* You enter a group of racially similar people who are using terms normally considered offensive to refer to themselves. Trying to be one of the group, you too use such terms—but are met with extremely negative nonverbal feedback. Ask yourself: What are some things you might say to lessen this negative reaction and to let the group know that you don't normally use such racial terms?

3 *Clashing Cultural Rules.* Your friend is pressed for time and asks you to do the statistical analyses for a term project. Your first impulse is to say yes, because in your culture it would be extremely impolite to refuse a favor to someone you've known for so long. Yet you're aware that doing work for others is considered unethical at colleges in the United States. Ask yourself: What might you say that would enable you to help your friend but would not involve behavior that would be considered deceitful and might be severely punished?

4 *Violating Cultural Norms.* You're invited to a holiday party by people you recently met at school. Having lots of money yourself and not knowing much about anyone else, you buy a really expensive present. As the gifts are being opened, you notice that everyone gave very inexpensive items—a photograph, a book, a scented candle. Your gift is next. Ask yourself: What can you do to lessen the effect of your choice, which is sure to seem very strange to everyone else?

5 *Giving Directions in High- and Low-Context Situations.* To further appreciate the distinction between high and low context, consider giving directions to some specific place on campus (such as the cafeteria) to someone who knows the campus and who you can assume knows the local landmarks (which would resemble a high-context situation) and to a newcomer who you cannot assume is familiar with campus landmarks (which would resemble a low-context situation). Suppose a newcomer asks you directions to the cafeteria from where you are now. What do you say?

MyCommunicationLab Explorations

PEARSON **mycommunicationlab** www.mycommunicationlab.com

These exercises enable you to explore a wide variety of cultural issues and their relationships to interpersonal communication. ❶ Random Pairs sets up specific intercultural dyads and asks you to consider how these dyads might influence communication. ❷ Cultural Beliefs asks you to examine some of your own cultural beliefs. ❸ From Culture to Gender explores the relationship of culture to gender beliefs. ❹ Cultural Identities lets you explore the strengths in the cultures represented by class members and others. ❺ The Sources of Your Cultural Beliefs explores the origins of your own beliefs about a wide variety of issues. ❻ Confronting Intercultural Obstacles presents situations that can cause intercultural conflict and asks you how you'd head off potential conflicts or resolve them.

3

Perception and the Self in Interpersonal Communication

The Bourne Ultimatum

One of the major themes of *The Bourne Ultimatum*, and of the entire *Bourne* trilogy, is the search for self. Jason Bourne has lost memory of who he is and sets out on a mission to discover who he is and what he has done. In this Bourne is not unlike anyone else. We all want to know ourselves better, perhaps with such knowledge we know we can be more effective. This self-understanding is one of the topics in this chapter.

This chapter discusses two interrelated topics—the self and perception. After exploring the nature of the self (self-concept, self-awareness, and self-esteem) and the nature of perception, we look at the ways in which you form impressions of others and how you manage the impressions that you convey to others.

The Self in Interpersonal Communication

Let's begin this discussion by focusing on several fundamental aspects of the self: self-concept (the way you see yourself), self-awareness (your insight into and knowledge about yourself), and self-esteem (the value you place on yourself). In these discussions you'll see how these dimensions influence and are influenced by the way you communicate.

Self-Concept

You no doubt have an image of who you are; this is your self-concept. It consists of your feelings and thoughts about your strengths and weaknesses, your abilities and limitations, and your aspirations and worldview (Black, 1999). Your self-concept develops from at least four sources: (1) the image of you that others have and that they reveal to you, (2) the comparisons you make between yourself and others, (3) the teachings of your culture, and (4) the way you interpret and evaluate your own thoughts and behaviors (see Figure 3.1).

Others' Images According to Charles Horton Cooley's (1922) concept of the *looking-glass self*, when you want to discover, say, how friendly or how assertive you are, you look at the image of yourself that others reveal to you through the way they treat you and react to you (Hensley, 1996). You look especially to those who are most significant in your life. As a child, for example, you look to your parents and then to your teachers. As an adult, you may look to your friends, romantic partners, and colleagues at work. If these important others think highly of you, you'll see this positive image of yourself reflected in their behaviors; if they think little of you, you'll see a more negative image.

FIGURE 3.1

The Sources of Self-Concept

This diagram depicts the four sources of self-concept, the four contributors to how you see yourself—others' images of you; social comparisons; cultural teachings; and your own observations, interpretations, and evaluations. As you read about self-concept, consider the influence of each factor throughout your life. Which factor influenced you most as a preteen? Which influences you the most now? Which will influence you the most 25 or 30 years from now?

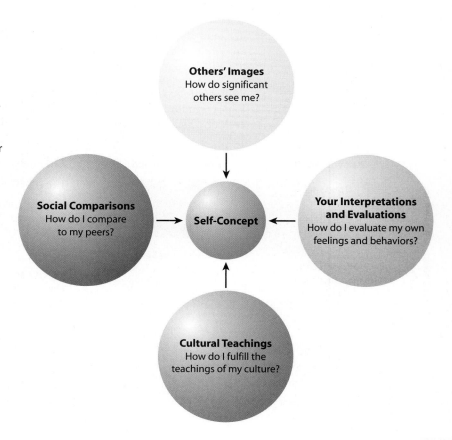

Social Comparisons Another way you develop your self-concept is by comparing yourself with others. When you want to gain insight into who you are and how effective or competent you are, you probably look to your peers. For example, after an examination you probably want to know how you performed relative to the other students in your class. If you play on a baseball team, it's important to compare your batting average with those of others on the team. You gain an additional perspective when you see your score in comparison with the scores of your peers. If you want to feel good about yourself, you may compare yourself to those you know are less effective than you. If you want a more accurate and objective assessment, you'll compare yourself with your peers, with others who are similar to you.

Cultural Teachings Through your parents, teachers, and the media, your culture instills in you a variety of beliefs, values, and attitudes—about success (how you define it and how you should achieve it); about your religion, race, or nationality; about the ethical principles you should follow in business and in your personal life. These teachings provide benchmarks against which you can measure yourself. For example, achieving what your culture defines as success will contribute to a positive self-concept. A perceived failure to achieve what your culture promotes (for example, not being in a permanent relationship by the time you're 30) may contribute to a negative self-concept.

Self-Evaluations Much in the way others form images of you based on what you do, you also react to your own behavior; you interpret and evaluate it. These interpretations and evaluations help to form your self-concept. For example, let us say you believe that lying is wrong. If you lie, you will evaluate this behavior in terms of your internalized beliefs about lying. You'll thus react negatively to your own behavior. You may, for example, experience guilt if your behavior contradicts your beliefs. In contrast, let's say you tutor another student and help him or her pass a course. You will probably evaluate this behavior positively; you will feel good about this behavior and, as a result, about yourself.

Self-Awareness

Your **self-awareness** represents the extent to which you know yourself. Understanding how your self-concept develops is one way to increase your self-awareness: The more you understand about why you view yourself as you do, the more you will understand who you are. Additional insight is gained by looking at self-awareness through the Johari model of the self, or your four selves (Luft, 1984).

Your Four Selves Self-awareness is neatly explained by the model of the four selves, the Johari window. This model, presented in Figure 3.2, has four basic areas, or quadrants, each of which represents a somewhat different self. The Johari model emphasizes that the

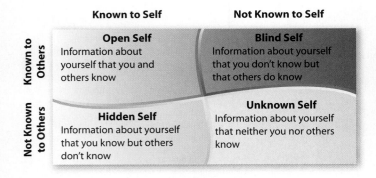

FIGURE 3.2

The Johari Window

Visualize this model as representing your self. The entire model is of constant size, but each section can vary, from very small to very large. As one section becomes smaller, one or more of the others grows larger. Similarly, as one section grows, one or more of the others must get smaller. For example, if you reveal a secret and thereby enlarge your open self, this shrinks your hidden self. Further, this disclosure may in turn lead to a decrease in the size of your blind self (if your disclosure influences other people to reveal what they know about you but that you have not known). How would you draw your Johari window to show yourself when interacting with your parents? With your friends? With your college instructors? The name Johari, by the way, comes from the first names of the two people who developed the model, Joseph Luft and Harry Ingham.

Source: Group Processes: An Introduction to Group Dynamics by Joseph Luft, 1984, p. 60. Reprinted by permission of Mayfield Publishing Company, Mountain View, CA.

several aspects of the self are not separate pieces but are interactive parts of a whole. Each part is dependent on each other part. Like that of interpersonal communication, this model of the self is transactional.

- *The open self* represents all the information about you—behaviors, attitudes, feelings, desires, motivations, and ideas—that you and others know. The type of information included here might range from your name, skin color, and sex to your age, political and religious affiliations, and financial situation. Your open self will vary in size depending on the situation you're in and the person with whom you're interacting. Some people, for example, make you feel comfortable and supported; to them, you open yourself wide, but to others you may prefer to leave most of yourself closed.

- *The blind self* represents all the things about you that others know but of which you're ignorant. These may include relatively insignificant habits like saying "You know," gestures like rubbing your nose when you get angry, or traits such as a distinct body odor; they also may include things as significant as defense mechanisms, fight strategies, or repressed experiences.

- *The hidden self* contains all that you know of yourself and of others that you keep secret. In any interaction, this area includes everything you don't want to reveal, whether it's relevant or irrelevant to the conversation. At the extremes of the hidden self spectrum, we have the overdisclosers and the underdisclosers. The overdisclosers tell all. They tell you their marital difficulties, their children's problems, their financial status, and just about everything else. The underdisclosers tell nothing. They talk about you but not about themselves.

- *The unknown self* represents truths about yourself that neither you nor others know. Sometimes this unknown self is revealed through temporary changes brought about by special experimental conditions such as hypnosis or sensory deprivation. Sometimes

Ask the Researcher

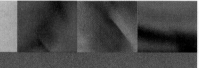

Understanding Self-Talk

I often find myself thinking pretty negative things about myself and telling myself I really can't do something well, even when I can. I think it must be something to do with my self-esteem, but I'm not sure. Can you tell me about it, maybe make some suggestions?

What you're describing is negative self-talk. It's a form of intrapersonal communication; it's communication within the self about the self. Most people self-talk, and it can be negative or positive.

Self-talk is evidence of the relationship a person has with himself or herself and is therefore a pretty important part of building self-esteem. The first thing to do is to take time to really listen to yourself and get a sense of how often and how negative the self-talk is. The next step is to change the negative self-talk to positive talk. You can do this by talking to yourself (or thinking; it doesn't have to be out loud) the way you would to your best friend ("You look hot"). Try it for a week; it takes practice. Give it time and attention, like you give to relationships with others whom you care about. You can start by giving yourself this positive self-talk message: "Yeah, I can do that."

For more information see L. C. Lederman, "Internal Muzak: An Exploration of Intrapersonal Communication," from *Information and Behavior*, reprinted in L. C. Lederman, D. Gibson, and M. Taylor (eds.), *Communication Theory: A Reader*, 2nd ed. (Dubuque, IA: Kendall Hunt, 2005).

Linda C. Lederman (Ph.D., Rutgers) is professor of communication at Arizona State University, where she teaches health communication. Her research examines the role of communication and experience, including intrapersonal communication, in health issues. Her most recent book, coauthored with Lea Stewart, is *Changing the Culture of College Drinking* (Cresskill, NJ: Hampton Press, 2005).

VIEWPOINT ⬆ Your cultural background will significantly influence your responses to this simple "Who Am I?" test. In one study, for example, participants from Malaysia (a collectivist culture) and from Australia and Great Britain (individualist cultures) completed this test. Malaysians produced significantly more group self-descriptions and fewer idiocentric self-descriptions than did the Australian or British respondents (Bochner, 1994; also see Radford, Mann, Ohta, & Nakane, 1993). If you completed the "Who Am I?" test, can you identify responses that were influenced by your cultural orientation, particularly your collectivist-individualist orientation? Did other cultural factors influence your statements?

this area is revealed by certain projective tests or dreams. Mostly, however, it's revealed by the fact that you're constantly learning things about yourself that you didn't know before (things that were previously in the unknown self)—for example, that you become defensive when someone asks you a question or voices disagreement, or that you compliment others in the hope of being complimented back.

Growing in Self-Awareness Here are five ways you can increase your self-awareness:

- *Ask yourself about yourself.* One way to ask yourself about yourself is to take an informal "Who Am I?" test (Bugental & Zelen, 1950; Grace & Cramer, 2003). Title a piece of paper "Who Am I?" and write 10, 15, or 20 times "I am. . . ." Then complete each of the sentences. Try not to give only positive or socially acceptable responses; just respond with what comes to mind first. Take another piece of paper and divide it into two columns; label one column "Strengths" and the other column "Weaknesses." Fill in each column as quickly as possible. Using these first two tests as a base, take a third piece of paper, title it "Self-Improvement Goals," and complete the statement "I want to improve my . . ." as many times as you can in five minutes. Because you're constantly changing, these self-perceptions and goals also change, so update them frequently. Also, see the photo caption on page 000.
- *Listen to others.* You can learn a lot about yourself by seeing yourself as others do. In most interpersonal interactions, people comment on you in some way—on what you do, what you say, how you look. Sometimes these comments are explicit; most often they're found in the way others look at you, in what they talk about, in their interest in what you say. Pay close attention to this verbal and nonverbal information.
- *Actively seek information about yourself.* Actively seek out information to reduce your blind self. You need not be so obvious as to say, "Tell me about myself" or "What do you think of me?" But you can use everyday situations to gain self-information: "Do you think I was assertive enough when asking for the raise?" Or "Would I be thought too forward if I invited myself for dinner?" Do not, of course, seek this information constantly; your friends would quickly find others with whom to interact.
- *See your different selves.* Each person with whom you have an interpersonal relationship views you differently; to each you're a somewhat different person. Yet you are really all of these selves, and your self-concept will be influenced by each of these views as they are reflected back to you in everyday interpersonal interactions. For starters, visualize how you're seen by your mother, your father, your teachers, your best friend, the stranger you sat next to on the bus, your employer, your neighbor's child. The experience will give you new and valuable perspectives on yourself.
- *Increase your open self.* When you reveal yourself to others and increase your open self, you also reveal yourself to yourself. At the very least, you bring into clearer focus what you may have buried within. As you discuss yourself, you may see connections that you had previously missed, and with the aid of feedback from others you may gain still more insight. Also, by increasing the open self you increase the likelihood that a meaningful and intimate dialogue will develop, which will enable you to get to know yourself better. This important process, called self-disclosure, is considered in Chapter 8, along with its advantages and disadvantages.

Self-Esteem

Self-esteem is a measure of how valuable you think you are. If you have high self-esteem, you think highly of yourself; if you have low self-esteem, you tend to view yourself negatively.

Before reading further about this topic, consider your own self-esteem by taking the accompanying self-test, "How's Your Self-Esteem?"

✏ TEST YOURSELF

HOW'S YOUR SELF-ESTEEM?

Respond to each of the following statements with T for true if the statement describes you at least some significant part of the time; with F for false if the statement describes you rarely or never.

_____ 1. Generally, I feel I have to be successful in all things.
_____ 2. Several of my acquaintances are often critical or negative of what I do and how I think.
_____ 3. I often tackle projects that I know are impossible to complete to my satisfaction.
_____ 4. When I focus on the past, I focus more often on my failures than on my successes and on my negative rather than my positive qualities.
_____ 5. I make little effort to improve my personal and social skills.

HOW DID YOU DO? "True" responses to the questions would generally suggest ways of thinking that can get in the way of building positive self-esteem. "False" responses would indicate that you are thinking much like a self-esteem coach would want you to think.

WHAT WILL YOU DO? The following discussion elaborates on these five issues and illustrates why each of them creates problems for the development of healthy self-esteem. So this text is a good starting place. You might also want to log into the National Association for Self-Esteem's website (http://www.self-esteem-nase.org). There you'll find a variety of materials for examining and bolstering self-esteem.

The basic idea behind self-esteem is that when you feel good about yourself—about who you are and what you're capable of doing—you will perform better. When you think like a success, you're more likely to act like a success. Conversely, when you think you're a failure, you're more likely to act like a failure. When you reach for the phone to ask the most popular student in the school for a date and you visualize yourself being successful and effective, you're more likely to give a good impression. If, on the other hand, you think you're going to forget what you want to say or stutter or say something totally stupid, you're less likely to be successful. Here are five suggestions for increasing self-esteem that parallel the questions in the self-test.

Attack Self-Destructive Beliefs Challenge **self-destructive beliefs**—ideas you have about yourself that are unproductive or that make it more difficult for you to achieve your goals (Einhorn, 2006). Here, for example, are some beliefs that are likely to prove self-destructive (Butler, 1981):

- The belief that you have to be perfect; this causes you to try to perform at unrealistically high levels at work, school, and home; anything short of perfection is unacceptable.
- The belief that you have to be strong, which tells you that weakness and any of the more vulnerable emotions—like sadness, compassion, or loneliness—are wrong.
- The belief that you have to please others and that your worthiness depends on what others think of you.
- The belief that you have to hurry up; this compels you to do things quickly, to try to do more than can be reasonably expected in any given amount of time.
- The belief that you have to take on more responsibilities than any one person can be expected to handle.

These beliefs set unrealistically high standards, and therefore almost always end in failure. As a result, you may develop a negative self-image, seeing yourself as someone who constantly fails. So, replace these self-destructive beliefs with more productive ones, such as

"I succeed in many things, but I don't have to succeed in everything" and "It would be nice to be loved by everyone, but it isn't necessary to my happiness."

Seek Out Nourishing People Psychologist Carl Rogers (1970) drew a distinction between noxious and nourshing people. Noxious people criticize and find fault with just about everything. Nourishing people, on the other hand, are positive and optimistic. Most important, they reward us, they stroke us, they make us feel good about ourselves. To enhance your self-esteem, seek out these people. At the same time, avoid noxious people, those who make you feel negatively about yourself. At the same time, seek to become more nourishing yourself so that you can build up others' self-esteem.

Identification with people similar to yourself also seems to increase self-esteem. For example, deaf people who identified with the larger deaf community had greater self-esteem than those who didn't so identify (Jambor & Elliott, 2005). Similarly, identification with your cultural group also seems helpful in fostering positive self-esteem (McDonald, McCabe, Yeh, Lau, Garland, & Hough, 2005).

Work on Projects That Will Result in Success Some people want to fail (or so it seems). Often, they select projects that will result in failure simply because these projects are impossible to complete. Avoid this trap and select projects that will result in success. Each success will help build your self-esteem. Each success, too, will make the next success a little easier. If a project does fail, recognize that this does not mean that you're a failure. Everyone fails somewhere along the line. Failure is something that happens to you; it's not something you've created, and it's not something inside you. Further, failing once does not mean that you will fail the next time. So learn to put failure in perspective.

Remind Yourself of Your Successes Some people have a tendency to focus on and to exaggerate their failures, their missed opportunities, their social mistakes. However, others witnessing these failures give them much less importance (Savitsky, Epley, & Gilovich, 2001). If your objective is to correct what you did wrong or to identify the skills that you need to correct these failures, then focusing on failures can have some positive value. But if you just focus on failure without forming any plans for correction, then you're probably just making life more difficult for yourself and limiting your self-esteem. To counteract the tendency to recall failures, remind yourself of your successes. Recall these successes both intellectually and emotionally. Realize why they were successes, and relive the emotional experience when you sank that winning basketball or aced that test or helped that friend overcome personal problems. And while you're at it, recall your positive qualities.

Secure Affirmation An affirmation is simply a statement asserting that something is true. In discussions of self-concept and self-awareness, the word **affirmation** is used to refer to positive statements about yourself, statements asserting that something good or positive is true of you. It's frequently recommended that you remind yourself of your successes with affirmations—that you focus on your good deeds; on your positive qualities, strengths, and virtues; and on your productive and meaningful relationships with friends, loved ones, and relatives (Aronson, Cohen, & Nail, 1998; Aronson, Wilson, & Akert, 2007).

One useful way to look at self-affirmation is in terms of "I am," "I can," and "I will" statements (www.coping.org accessed May 6, 2008):

- *"I am" statements* focus on your self-image—on how you see yourself—and might include, for example, "I am

VIEWPOINT Despite its intuitive value, self-esteem is not without its critics (for example, Bushman & Baumeister, 1998; Baumeister, Bushman, & Campbell, 2000; Bower, 2001; Coover & Murphy, 2000; Hewitt, 1998; Epstein, 2005). Some researchers argue that high self-esteem is not necessarily desirable: It does nothing to improve academic performance, does not predict success, and may even lead to antisocial (especially aggressive) behavior. Interestingly enough, a surprisingly large number of criminals and delinquents are found to have extremely high self-esteem. And conversely, many people who have extremely low self-esteem have become quite successful in all fields (Owens, Stryker, & Goodman, 2002). How do you feel about the benefits or liabilities of self-esteem?

a worthy person," "I am responsible," "I am capable of loving," and "I am a good team player."

- *"I can" statements* focus on your abilities and might include, for example, "I can accept my past but also let it go," "I can learn to be a more responsive partner," "I can assert myself when appropriate," and "I can control my anger."
- *"I will" statements* focus on useful and appropriate goals you want to achieve and might include, for example, "I will get over my guilty feelings," "I will study more effectively," "I will act more supportively," and "I will not take on more responsibility than I can handle."

The idea behind this advice is that the way you talk to yourself will influence what you think of yourself. If you affirm yourself—if you tell yourself that you're a friendly person, that you can be a leader, that you will succeed on the next test—you will soon come to feel more positively about yourself.

Some researchers, however, argue that such affirmations—although extremely popular in self-help books—may not be very helpful. These critics contend that if you have low self-esteem, you're not going to believe your self-affirmations, because you don't have a high opinion of yourself to begin with (Paul, 2001). According to this view, the alternative to self-affirmation is securing affirmation from others. You'd do this by, for example, becoming more interpersonally competent and interacting with more positive people. In this way, you'd get more positive feedback from others—which, these researchers argue, is more helpful than self-talk in raising self-esteem.

Perception in Interpersonal Communication

Perception is the process by which you become aware of objects, events, and especially people through your senses: sight, smell, taste, touch, and hearing. Perception is an active, not a passive process. Your perceptions result both from what exists in the outside world and from your own experiences, desires, needs and wants, loves and hatreds. Among the reasons perception is so important in interpersonal communication is that it influences your communication choices. The messages you send and listen to will depend on how you see the world, on how you size up specific situations, on what you think of yourself and of the people with whom you interact.

Interpersonal perception is a continuous series of processes that blend into one another. For convenience of discussion we can separate interpersonal perception into five stages: (1) You sense, you pick up some kind of stimulation; (2) you organize the stimuli in some way;

UNDERSTANDING INTERPERSONAL THEORY & RESEARCH

The Just World Hypothesis

Many people believe that the world is just: Good things happen to good people and bad things happen to bad people (Aronson, Wilson, & Akert, 2007; Hunt, 2000). Put differently, you get what you deserve! Even when you mindfully dismiss this assumption, you may use it mindlessly when perceiving and evaluating other people. Consider a particularly vivid example: If a woman is raped in certain cultures (for example, in Bangladesh, Iran, or Yemen), she is considered by many in that culture (certainly not all) to have disgraced her family and to be deserving of severe punishment—in many cases, even death. And although you may claim that this is unfair, much research shows that even in this country many people do in fact blame the victim for being raped, especially if the victim is male (Adams-Price, Dalton, & Sumrall, 2004; Anderson, 2004).

The belief that the world is just creates perceptual distortions by leading us to deemphasize the influence of situational factors and to overemphasize the influence of internal factors in our attempts to explain the behaviors of other people or even our own behaviors.

Working with Theories and Research

Using your favorite search engine, search the psychology, sociology, and/or communication databases for "just world." Scan some of the articles. What can you add to the discussion presented here?

(3) you interpret and evaluate what you perceive; (4) you store it in memory; and (5) you retrieve it when needed.

Stage One: Stimulation

At this first stage, your sense organs are stimulated—you hear a new CD, see a friend, smell someone's perfume, taste an orange, receive an instant message, feel another's sweaty palm. Naturally, you don't perceive everything; rather, you engage in **selective perception**, a general term that includes selective attention and selective exposure:

- In **selective attention**, you attend to those things that you anticipate will fulfill your needs or will prove enjoyable. For example, when daydreaming in class, you don't hear what the instructor is saying until your name is called. Your selective attention mechanism then focuses your senses on your name.
- Through **selective exposure**, you expose yourself to people or messages that will confirm your existing beliefs, contribute to your objectives, or prove satisfying in some way. For example, after you buy a car, you're more apt to read and listen to advertisements for the car you just bought, because these messages tell you that you made the right decision. At the same time, you'll likely avoid advertisements for the cars that you considered but eventually rejected, because these messages would tell you that you made the wrong decision.

Stage Two: Organization

At the second stage, you organize the information your senses pick up. Three interesting ways in which people organize their perceptions are by rules, by schemata, and by scripts. Let's look at each briefly.

Organization by Rules In the organization of perceptions by **rules**, one frequently used rule is that of **proximity** or physical closeness: Things that are physically close to each other are perceived as a unit. Thus, using this rule, you will tend to perceive people who are often together, or messages spoken one immediately after the other, as units, as belonging together.

Another rule is **similarity**: Things that are physically similar (they look alike) are perceived as belonging together and forming a unit. This principle of similarity may lead you to see people who dress alike as belonging together. Similarly, you may assume that people who work at the same jobs, who are of the same religion, who live in the same building, or who talk with the same accent belong together.

The rule of **contrast** is the opposite of similarity: When items (people or messages, for example) are very different from each other, you conclude that they don't belong together; they're too different from each other to be part of the same unit. If you're the only one who shows up at an informal gathering in a tuxedo, you'll be seen as not belonging to the group, because you contrast too much with the other people present.

Organization by Schemata Another way you organize material is by creating **schemata**, mental templates that help you organize the millions of items of information you come into contact with every day (as well as those you already have in memory). A stereotype—discussed in greater detail in Chapter 2—is a type of **schema**. Schemata, the plural of schema, may thus be viewed as general ideas about people (e.g., about Pat and Chris, Japanese people, Baptists, Texans); about yourself (your qualities, abilities, liabilities); or about social roles (the characteristics of a police officer, professor, multibillionaire CEO).

You develop schemata from your own experience—actual as well as via television, reading, and hearsay. You might have a schema for college athletes, for example, and this might include an image of college athletes as strong, ambitious, academically weak, and egocentric. You've probably developed schemata for different religious, racial, and national groups; for men and women; and for people of different affectional orientations. Each of the groups that you have some familiarity with will be represented in your mind by schemata. These schemata help you organize your perceptions by enabling you to classify millions of people into a manageable number of categories or classes.

Organization by Scripts A **script** is really a type of schema, but because it's a different type, it's given a different name. A script is an organized body of information about some action, event, or procedure. It's a general idea of how some event should play out or unfold; it's the rules governing events and their sequence. For example, you probably have a script for eating in a restaurant, with the actions organized into a pattern something like this: Enter, take a seat, review the menu, order from the menu, eat your food, ask for the bill, leave a tip, pay the bill, exit the restaurant. Similarly, you probably have scripts for how you do laundry, how an interview is to be conducted, the stages you go through in introducing someone to someone else, and the way you ask for a date.

As you can see rules, schemata, and scripts are useful shortcuts to simplify your understanding, remembering, and recalling information about people and events. They also enable you to generalize, make connections, and otherwise profit from previously acquired knowledge. If you didn't have these shortcuts, you'd have to treat every person, role, or action differently from each other person, role, or action. This would make every experience a new one, totally unrelated to anything you already know. These shortcuts, however, may mislead you; they may contribute to your remembering things that are consistent with your schemata (even if they didn't occur) and to your distorting or forgetting information that is inconsistent.

Stage Three: Interpretation–Evaluation

The **interpretation–evaluation** step in perception (a combined term because the two processes cannot be separated) is greatly influenced by your experiences, needs, wants, values, beliefs about the way things are or should be, expectations, physical and emotional state, and so on. Your interpretation–evaluation will be influenced by your rules, schemata, and scripts as well as by your gender; for example, women have been found to view others more positively than men (Winquist, Mohr, & Kenny, 1998).

For example, on meeting a new person who is introduced to you as Ben Williams, a college football player, you're likely to apply your schema to this person and view him as strong, ambitious, academically weak, and egocentric. You will, in other words, see this person through the filter of your schema and evaluate him according to your schema for college athletes. Similarly, when viewing someone performing some series of actions (say, eating in a restaurant), you apply your script to this event and view the event through the script. You will interpret the actions of the diner as appropriate or inappropriate depending on your script for this behavior and the ways in which the diner performed the sequence of actions.

Judgments about members of other cultures are often ethnocentric; because your schemata and scripts are created on the basis of your own cultural beliefs and experiences, you can easily (but inappropriately) apply these to members of other cultures. And so it's easy to infer that when members of other cultures do things that conform to your own scripts, they're right, and when they do things that contradict your scripts, they're wrong—a classic example of ethnocentric thinking. This tendency can easily contribute to intercultural misunderstandings.

A similar problem arises when you base your scripts for different cultural groups on stereotypes that you may have derived from television or movies. For example, you may have schemata for religious Muslims that you derived from the stereotypes presented in the media. If you apply these schemata to all Muslims, you risk interpreting what you see through these schemata and distorting what does not conform.

VIEWPOINT In making evaluations of events or people, it would seem logical that we would first think about the event or person and then make the evaluation. Some research claims, however, that we really don't think before assigning any perception a positive or negative value. This research argues that all perceptions have a positive or negative value attached to them and that these evaluations are most often automatic and involve no conscious thought. Immediately upon perceiving a person, idea, or thing, we attach a positive or negative value (*New York Times*, August 8, 1995, pp. C1, C10). What do you think of this? One bit of evidence against this position would be the ability to identify several things, ideas, or people about which you feel *completely* neutral. Can you do it?

Stage Four: Memory

Your perceptions and their interpretations–evaluations are put into **memory**; they're stored so that you may ultimately retrieve them at some later time. So, for example, you have in memory your schema for college athletes and the fact that Ben Williams is a football player. Ben Williams is then stored in memory with "cognitive tags" that tell you that he's strong, ambitious, academically weak, and egocentric. Despite the fact that you've not witnessed Ben's strength or ambitions and have no idea of his academic record or his psychological profile, you still may store your memory of Ben along with the qualities that make up your schema for "college athletes."

Now let's say that at different times you hear that Ben failed Spanish I, normally an A or B course at your school; that Ben got an A in chemistry (normally a tough course); and that Ben is transferring to Harvard as a theoretical physics major. Schemas act as filters or gatekeepers; they allow certain information to get stored in relatively objective form, much as you heard or read it, and may distort other information or prevent it from getting stored. As a result, these three items of information about Ben may get stored very differently in your memory.

For example, you may readily store the information that Ben failed Spanish, because it's consistent with your schema; it fits neatly into the template you have of college athletes. Information that's consistent with your schema—as in this example, strengthens your schema and make it more resistant to change (Aronson, Wilson, & Akert, 2007). Depending on the strength of your schema, you may also store in memory (even though you didn't hear it) that Ben did poorly in other courses as well. The information that Ben got an A in chemistry, because it contradicts your schema (it just doesn't seem right), may easily be distorted or lost. The information that Ben is transferring to Harvard, however, is a bit different. This information is also inconsistent with your schema, but it is so drastically inconsistent that you begin to look at this mindfully and may even begin to question your schema or perhaps view Ben as an exception to the general rule. In either case, you're going to etch Ben's transferring to Harvard very clearly in your mind.

Stage Five: Recall

The **recall** stage involves accessing the information you have stored in memory. Let's say that at some later date you want to retrieve your information about Ben, because he's the topic of discussion among you and a few friends. As we'll see in our discussion of listening in the next chapter, memory isn't reproductive; you don't simply reproduce what you've heard or seen. Rather, you reconstruct what you've heard or seen into a whole that is meaningful to you—depending in great part on your schemata and scripts. It's this reconstruction that you store in memory. When you want to retrieve this information, you may recall it with a variety of inaccuracies:

- You're likely to recall information that is consistent with your schema; in fact, you may not even be recalling the specific information (say, about Ben) but may actually just be recalling your schema (which contains information about college athletes and, because of this, also about Ben).
- But you may fail to recall information that is inconsistent with your schema; you have no place to put that information, so you easily lose it or forget it.
- However, you may recall information that drastically contradicts your schema, because it forces you to think (and perhaps rethink) about your schema and its accuracy; it may even force you to revise your schema for college athletes in general.

Impression Formation

Impression formation (sometimes referred to as *person perception*) consists of a variety of processes that you go through in forming an impression of another person. Each of these perception processes has pitfalls and potential dangers. Before reading about these processes that you use in perceiving other people, examine your own perception strategies by taking the accompanying self-test, "How Accurate Are You at People Perception?"

TEST YOURSELF

HOW ACCURATE ARE YOU AT PEOPLE PERCEPTION?

Respond to each of the following statements with T if the statement is usually or generally true (accurate in describing your behavior) or with F if the statement is usually or generally false (inaccurate in describing your behavior).

_____ 1. I make predictions about people's behaviors that generally prove to be true.

_____ 2. When I know some things about another person, I can pretty easily fill in what I don't know.

_____ 3. Generally my expectations are borne out by what I actually see; that is, my later perceptions usually match my initial expectations.

_____ 4. I base most of my impressions of people on the first few minutes of our meeting.

_____ 5. I generally find that people I like possess positive characteristics and people I don't like possess negative characteristics.

_____ 6. I generally attribute people's attitudes and behaviors to their most obvious physical or psychological characteristic.

HOW DID YOU DO? This brief perception test was designed to raise questions to be considered in this chapter, not to provide you with a specific perception score. All statements refer to perceptual processes that many people use but that often get us into trouble, leading us to form inaccurate impressions. The questions refer to several processes to be discussed below: the self-fulfilling prophecy (statement 1), implicit personality theory (2), perceptual accentuation (3), primacy–recency (4), and consistency (5). Statement 6 refers to overattribution, one of the problems we encounter as we attempt to determine motives for other people's and even our own behaviors.

WHAT WILL YOU DO? As you read this chapter, think about these processes and consider how you might use them more accurately and not allow them to get in the way of accurate and reasonable people perception. At the same time, recognize that situations vary widely and that strategies for clearer perception will prove useful most of the time but not all of the time. In fact, you may want to identify situations in which you shouldn't follow the suggestions that this text will offer.

Impression Formation Processes

The way in which you perceive another person and ultimately come to some kind of evaluation or interpretation of this person is not a simple logical sequence. Instead, your perceptions seem to be influenced by a variety of processes. Here we consider some of the more significant: the self-fulfilling prophecy, implicit personality theory, perceptual accentuation, primacy–recency, consistency, and attribution.

Self-Fulfilling Prophecy   A **self-fulfilling prophecy** is a prediction that comes true because you act on it as if it were true. Put differently, a self-fulfilling prophecy occurs when you act on your schema as if it were true and in doing so make it true. Self-fulfilling prophecies occur in such widely different situations as parent–child relationships, educational settings, and business (Merton, 1957; Rosenthal, 2002; Madon, Guyll, & Spoth, 2004; Tierney & Farmer, 2004). There are four basic steps in the self-fulfilling prophecy:

1. You make a prediction or formulate a belief about a person or a situation. For example, you predict that Pat is friendly in interpersonal encounters.
2. You act toward that person or situation as if that prediction or belief were true. For example, you act as if Pat were a friendly person.

3. Because you act as if the belief were true, it becomes true. For example, because of the way you act toward Pat, Pat becomes comfortable and friendly.
4. You observe your effect on the person or the resulting situation, and what you see strengthens your beliefs. For example, you observe Pat's friendliness, and this reinforces your belief that Pat is in fact friendly.

The self-fulfilling prophecy also can be seen when you make predictions about yourself and fulfill them. For example, suppose you enter a group situation convinced that the other members will dislike you. Almost invariably you'll be proved right; the other members will appear to you to dislike you. What you may be doing is acting in a way that encourages the group to respond to you negatively. In this way, you fulfill your prophecies about yourself.

Self-fulfilling prophecies can short-circuit critical thinking and influence others' behavior (or your own) so that it conforms to your prophecies. As a result, you may see what you predicted rather than what is really there (for example, you may perceive yourself as a failure because you have predicted it rather than because of any actual failures).

Implicit Personality Theory Each person has a subconscious or implicit theory that says which characteristics of an individual go with other characteristics. Consider, for example, the following brief statements. Note the word in parentheses that you think best completes each sentence.

Carlo is energetic, eager, and (intelligent, stupid).
Kim is bold, defiant, and (extroverted, introverted).
Joe is bright, lively, and (thin, heavy).
Eve is attractive, intelligent, and (likable, unlikable).
Susan is cheerful, positive, and (outgoing, shy).
Angel is handsome, tall, and (friendly, unfriendly).

What makes some of these choices seem right and others wrong is your **implicit personality theory**, the system of rules that tells you which characteristics go together. Your theory may, for example, have told you that a person who is energetic and eager is also intelligent, not stupid—although there is no logical reason why a stupid person could not be energetic and eager.

The widely documented **halo effect** is a function of the implicit personality theory (Dion, Berscheid, & Walster, 1972; Riggio, 1987). If you believe a person has some positive qualities, you're likely to infer that she or he also possesses other positive qualities. There is also a reverse halo (or "horns") effect: If you know a person possesses several negative qualities, you're more likely to infer that the person also has other negative qualities. For example, you're more likely to perceive attractive people as more generous, sensitive, trustworthy, and interesting than those less attractive. And the "horns effect" or "reverse halo effect" will lead you to perceive those who are unattractive as mean, dishonest, antisocial, and sneaky (Katz, 2003).

In using implicit personality theories, apply them carefully and critically so as to avoid perceiving qualities in an individual that your theory tells you should be present but aren't or seeing qualities that are not there (Plaks, Grant, & Dweck, 2005).

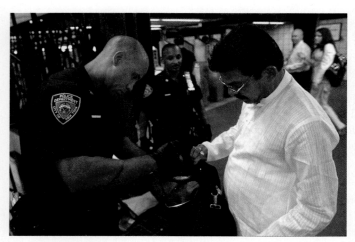

VIEWPOINT Racial profiling (the practice whereby the police focus on members of specific races as possible crime suspects) has been widely reported and widely condemned as racist. In the aftermath of the attack on the World Trade Center and the Pentagon on September 11, 2001, profiling of Muslims and of people who looked "Arab" became viewed by many as necessary for preventing further acts of terrorism. How do you feel about racial, ethnic, or religious profiling?

Perceptual Accentuation When poor and rich children were shown pictures of coins and later asked to estimate their size, the poor children's size estimates were much greater than the rich children's. Similarly, hungry people need fewer visual cues to perceive food objects and food terms than do people who are not hungry. This process, called **perceptual accentuation**, leads you to see what you expect or want to see. You see people you like as better looking and smarter than those you don't like. You magnify or accentuate what will satisfy your needs and desires: The thirsty person sees a mirage of water, the sexually deprived person sees a mirage of sexual satisfaction.

Perceptual accentuation can lead you to perceive what you need or want to perceive rather than what is really there, and to fail to perceive what you don't want to perceive. For example, you may not perceive signs of impending relationship problems, because you're only seeing what you want to see. Another interesting distortion created by perceptual accentuation is that you may perceive certain behaviors as indicative that someone likes you simply because you want to be liked. For example, general politeness and friendly behavior used as a persuasive strategy (say, by a salesperson) are frequently seen as indicating genuine personal liking.

Primacy–Recency Assume for a moment that you're enrolled in a course in which half the classes are extremely dull and half extremely exciting. At the end of the semester, you evaluate the course and the instructor. Will your evaluation be more favorable if the dull classes occurred in the first half of the semester and the exciting classes in the second? Or will it be more favorable if the order is reversed? If what comes first exerts the most influence, you have a **primacy effect**. If what comes last (or most recently) exerts the most influence, you have a **recency effect**.

In the classic study on the effects of **primacy–recency** in interpersonal perception, college students perceived a person who was described as "intelligent, industrious, impulsive, critical, stubborn, and envious" more positively than a person described as "envious, stubborn, critical, impulsive, industrious, and intelligent" (Asch, 1946). Notice that the descriptions are identical; only the order was changed. Clearly, we have a tendency to use early information to get a general idea about a person and to use later information to make this impression more specific. The initial information helps us form a schema for the person. Once that schema is formed, we're likely to resist information that contradicts it.

One interesting practical implication of primacy–recency is that the first impression you make is likely to be the most important—and is likely to be made very quickly (Sunnafrank & Ramirez, 2004; Willis & Todorov, 2006). The reason for this is that the schema that others form of you functions as a filter to admit or block additional information about you. If the initial impression or schema is positive, others are likely (1) to readily remember additional positive information, because it confirms this original positive image or schema; (2) to easily forget or distort negative information, because it contradicts this original positive schema; and (3) to interpret ambiguous information as positive. You win in all three ways—if the initial impression is positive.

Our tendency to give greater weight to early information and to interpret later information in light of early impressions can lead us to formulate a total picture of an individual on the basis of initial impressions that may not be typical or accurate. For example, if you judge a job applicant as generally nervous when he or she may simply be showing normal nervousness at being interviewed for a much-needed job, you will have misperceived this individual. Similarly, this tendency can lead you to discount or distort subsequent perceptions so as not to disrupt your initial impression or upset your original schema. For example, you may fail to see signs of deceit in someone you like because of your early impression that this person is a good and honest individual.

Consistency The tendency to maintain balance among perceptions or attitudes is called **consistency** (McBroom & Reed, 1992). People expect certain things to go together and other things not to go together. On a purely intuitive basis, for example, respond to the following sentences by noting your expected response.

1. I expect a person I like to (like, dislike) me.
2. I expect a person I dislike to (like, dislike) me.
3. I expect my friend to (like, dislike) my friend.
4. I expect my friend to (like, dislike) my enemy.
5. I expect my enemy to (like, dislike) my friend.
6. I expect my enemy to (like, dislike) my enemy.

According to most consistency theories, your expectations would be as follows: You would expect a person you liked to like you (1) and a person you disliked to dislike you (2).

You would expect a friend to like a friend (3) and to dislike an enemy (4). You would expect your enemy to dislike your friend (5) and to like your other enemy (6). All these expectations are intuitively satisfying.

Further, you would expect someone you liked to possess characteristics you liked or admired and would expect your enemies not to possess characteristics you liked or admired. Conversely, you would expect people you liked to lack unpleasant characteristics and those you disliked to possess unpleasant characteristics.

Uncritically assuming that an individual is consistent can lead you to ignore or distort perceptions that are inconsistent with your picture of the whole person. For example, you may misinterpret Karla's unhappiness because your image of Karla is "happy, controlled, and contented."

Attribution of Control   Research on **attribution** shows that another way in which we form impressions is through the attribution of control. For example, suppose you invite your friend Desmond to dinner for 7:00 p.m. and he arrives at 9:00. Consider how you would respond to each of these reasons:

Reason 1: "I just couldn't tear myself away from the beach. I really wanted to get a great tan."
Reason 2: "I was driving here when I saw some young kids mugging an old couple. I broke it up and took the couple home. They were so frightened that I had to stay with them until their children arrived. Their phone was out of order and my cell battery died, so I had no way of calling to tell you I'd be late."
Reason 3: "I got in a car accident and was taken to the hospital."

Depending on the reason, you would probably attribute very different motives to Desmond's behavior. With reasons 1 and 2, you'd conclude that Desmond was in control of his behavior; with reason 3, that he was not. Further, you would probably respond negatively to reason 1 (Desmond was selfish and inconsiderate) and positively to reason 2 (Desmond was a Good Samaritan). Because Desmond was not in control of his behavior in reason 3, you would probably not attribute either positive or negative motivation to his behavior. Instead, you would probably feel sorry that he got into an accident.

You probably make similar judgments based on control in numerous situations. Consider, for example, how you would respond to the following situations:

- Doris fails her history midterm exam.
- Sidney's car is repossessed because he failed to keep up the payments.
- Margie is 150 pounds overweight and is complaining that she feels awful.
- Thomas's wife has just filed for divorce and he is feeling depressed.

You would most likely be sympathetic to each of these people if you felt that he or she was not in control of what happened; for example, if the examination was unfair, if Sidney lost his job because of employee discrimination, if Margie had a glandular problem, and if Thomas's wife wanted to leave him for a wealthy drug dealer. On the other hand, you probably would not be sympathetic if you felt that these people were in control of what happened; for example, if Doris partied instead of studying, if Sidney gambled his payments away, if Margie ate nothing but junk food and refused to exercise, and if Thomas had been repeatedly unfaithful and his wife finally gave up trying to reform him.

In perceiving and especially in evaluating other people's behavior, you frequently ask if they were in control of the behavior. Generally, research shows that if you feel a person was in control of negative behaviors, you'll come to dislike him or her. If you believe the person was not in control of negative behaviors, you'll come to feel sorry for and not blame the person.

In your attribution of control—or in attributing motives on the basis of any other reasons (for example, hearsay or observations of the person's behavior) beware of several potential errors: (1) the self-serving bias, (2) overattribution, and (3) the fundamental attribution error.

- We exhibit the **self-serving bias** when we take credit for the positive and deny responsibility for the negative. For example, you're more likely to attribute your positive outcomes (say, you get an A on an exam) to internal and controllable factors—to your personality, intelligence, or hard work. And you're more likely to attribute your negative outcomes (say, you get a D) to external and uncontrollable factors—to the exam's being exceptionally difficult or to your roomate's party the night before (Bernstein, Stephan, & Davis, 1979; Duval & Silva, 2002).

■ **Overattribution** is the tendency to single out one or two obvious characteristics of a person and attribute everything that person does to this one or these two characteristics. For example, if a person is blind or was born into great wealth, there's often a tendency to attribute everything that person does to such factors. And so you might say, "Alex overeats because he's blind," or "Lillian is irresponsible because she never had to work for her money." To avoid overattribution, recognize that most behaviors and personality characteristics result from lots of factors. You almost always make a mistake when you select one factor and attribute everything to it.

■ The **fundamental attribution error** occurs when we assess someone's behavior but overvalue the contribution of internal factors (for example, a person's personality) and undervalue the influence of external factors (for example, the context or situation the person is in). The fundamental attribution error leads us to conclude that people do what they do because that's the kind of people they are, not because of the situation they're in. When Pat is late for an appointment, for example, you're more likely to conclude that Pat is inconsiderate or irresponsible than to attribute the lateness to a bus breakdown or a traffic accident.

Increasing Accuracy in Impression Formation

Successful interpersonal communication depends largely on the accuracy of the impressions you form of others. We've already seen the potential barriers that can arise with each of the perceptual processes, such as the self-serving bias or overattribution. In addition to avoiding these barriers, here are additional ways to increase your accuracy in impression formation.

UNDERSTANDING INTERPERSONAL SKILLS

Other-Orientation

Other-orientation is a quality of interpersonal effectiveness that includes the ability to adapt your messages to the other person (Spitzberg & Hecht, 1984; Dindia & Timmerman, 2003). It involves communicating attentiveness to and interest in the other person and genuine interest in what the person says.

Communicating Other-Orientation. You'll recognize the following behaviors in those with whom you enjoy talking.

■ Show consideration and respect; ask if it's all right to dump your troubles on someone before doing so, or ask if your phone call comes at a good time.

■ Acknowledge the other person's feelings as legitimate: Expressions such as "You're right" or "I can understand why you're so angry" help focus the interaction on the other person and confirm that you're listening.

■ Acknowledge the presence and importance of the other person. Ask for suggestions, opinions, and clarification. This will ensure that you understand what the other person is saying from that person's point of view.

■ Focus your messages on the other person. Use open-ended questions to involve the other person in the interaction (as opposed to questions that merely ask for a yes or no answer), and make statements that directly address the person. Use focused eye contact and appropriate facial expressions; smile, nod, and lean toward the other person.

■ Grant the other person permission to express (or to not express) her or his feelings. A simple statement such as "I know how difficult it is to talk about feelings" opens up the topic of feelings and gives the other person permission either to pursue such a discussion or to say nothing.

Working with Interpersonal Skills

On a 10-point scale, how would you rate your general other-orientation (give yourself a 10 if you are always and everywhere other-oriented)? Can you identify situations in which you are especially likely to forget other-orientation? In what ways might you become more other-oriented?

Analyze Impressions Subject your perceptions to logical analysis, to critical thinking. Here are two suggestions.

- *Recognize your own role in perception.* Your emotional and physiological state will influence the meaning you give to your perceptions. A movie may seem hysterically funny when you're in a good mood but just plain stupid when you're in a bad mood. Understand your own biases; for example, do you tend to perceive only the positive in people you like and only the negative in people you don't like?
- *Avoid early conclusions.* On the basis of your observations of behaviors, formulate hypotheses to test against additional information and evidence; avoid drawing conclusions that you then look to confirm. Look for a variety of cues pointing in the same direction. The more cues point to the same conclusion, the more likely your conclusion will be correct. Be especially alert to contradictory cues that seem to refute your initial hypotheses. At the same time, seek validation from others. Do others see things in the same way you do? If not, ask yourself if your perceptions may be distorted in some way.

Check Perceptions **Perception checking** is another way to reduce uncertainty and to make your perceptions more accurate. The goal of perception checking is to further explore the thoughts and feelings of the other person, not to prove that your initial perception is correct. With this simple technique, you lessen your chances of misinterpreting another's feelings. At the same time, you give the other person an opportunity to elaborate on his or her thoughts and feelings. In its most basic form, perception checking consists of two steps.

1. Describe what you see or hear, recognizing that descriptions are not really objective but are heavily influenced by who you are, your emotional state, and so on. At the same time, you may wish to describe what you think is happening. Try to do this as descriptively (not evaluatively) as you can. Sometimes you may wish to offer several possibilities.
   - You've called me from work a lot this week. You seem concerned that everything is all right at home.
   - You've not wanted to talk with me all week. You say that my work is fine, but you don't seem to want to give me the same responsibilities that other editorial assistants have.
2. Seek confirmation: Ask the other person if your description is accurate. Avoid mind reading; that is, don't try to read the thoughts and feelings of another person just from observing their behaviors. Regardless of how many behaviors you observe and how carefully you examine them, you can only guess what is going on in someone's mind. A person's motives are not open to outside inspection; you can only make assumptions based on overt behaviors. So be careful that your request for confirmation does not sound as though you already know the answer. Avoid phrasing your questions defensively, as in, for example, "You really don't want to go out, do you? I knew you didn't when you turned on that lousy television." Instead, ask for confirmation in as supportive a way as possible.
   - Would you rather watch TV?
   - Are you worried about me or the kids?
   - Are you displeased with my work? Is there anything I can do to improve my job performance?

Reduce Uncertainty In every interpersonal situation there is some degree of uncertainty. A variety of strategies can help reduce uncertainty (Berger & Bradac, 1982; Gudykunst, 1993; Brashers, 2007).

- Observing another person while he or she is engaged in an active task, preferably interacting with others in an informal social situation, will often reveal a great deal about the person, as people are less apt to monitor their behaviors and more likely to reveal their true selves in informal situations.
- You can sometimes manipulate situations so as to observe the person in more specific and revealing contexts. Employment interviews, theatrical auditions, and student teaching are good examples of situations arranged to provide an accurate view of the person in action.

- When you log on to an Internet chat group and lurk, reading the exchanges between the other group members before saying anything yourself, you're learning about the people in the group and about the group itself, thus reducing uncertainty. When uncertainty is reduced, you're more likely to make contributions that will be appropriate to the group and less likely to violate the group's norms.
- Learn about a person through asking others. You might inquire of a colleague if a third person finds you interesting and might like to have dinner with you.
- Interact with the individual. For example, you can ask questions: "Do you enjoy sports?" "What did you think of that computer science course?" "What would you do if you got fired?" You also gain knowledge of another by disclosing information about yourself. These disclosures help to create an environment that encourages disclosures from the person about whom you wish to learn more.

Increase Cultural Sensitivity Cultural sensitivity—recognizing and being sensitive to cultural differences—will help increase your accuracy in perception. For example, Russian or Chinese artists such as ballet dancers will often applaud their audience by clapping. Americans seeing this may easily interpret this as egotistical. Similarly, a German man will enter a restaurant before the woman in order to see if the place is respectable enough for the woman to enter. This simple custom can easily be interpreted as rude when viewed by people from cultures in which it's considered courteous for the woman to enter first (Axtell, 1994, 2007).

Within every cultural group there are wide and important differences. As all Americans are not alike, neither are all Indonesians, Greeks, or Mexicans. When you make assumptions that all people of a certain culture are alike, you're thinking in stereotypes. Recognizing differences between another culture and your own, and among members of the same culture, will help you perceive situations more accurately.

Cultural sensitivity will help counteract the difficulty most people have in understanding the nonverbal messages of people from other cultures. For example, it's easier to interpret the facial expressions of members of your own culture than those of members of other cultures (Weathers, Frank, & Spell, 2002). This "in-group advantage" will assist your perceptional accuracy for members of your own culture but will often hinder your accuracy for members of other cultures (Elfenbein & Ambady, 2002).

The suggestions for improving intercultural communication offered in Chapter 2 (pp. 42–50) are applicable to increasing your cultural sensitivity in perception. For example, educate yourself; reduce uncertainty; recognize differences (between yourself and people from other cultures, among members of other cultures, and between your meanings and the meanings that people from other cultures may have); confront your stereotypes; and adjust your communication.

Impression Management: Goals and Strategies

Impression management (some writers use the term "self-presentation" or "identity management") has to do with the processes you go through to communicate the impression you want others to have of you.

The impression you make on others is largely the result of the messages you communicate. In the same way that you form impressions of others largely on the basis of how they communicate, verbally and nonverbally, you also convey an impression of yourself through what you say (your verbal messages) and how you act and dress as well as how you decorate your office or apartment (your nonverbal messages). Communication messages, however, are not the only means for impression formation and management. For example, you also communicate your self-image by the people with whom you associate (and judge others the same way); if you associate with A-list people, then surely you must be A-list yourself, the theory goes. Also, as illustrated in the discussion of stereotypes, you may form an impression of someone on the basis of that person's age or gender or ethnic origin. Or you may rely on what others have said about the person and form impressions

Ethics in Interpersonal Communication

Perspectives on Ethics

Are ethical principles objective or subjective? An objective view argues that morality is absolute and exists apart from the values or beliefs of any individual or culture: The same standards apply to all people in all situations at all times. In this view, if lying, false advertising, using illegally obtained evidence, or revealing secrets is unethical, then any such behavior is unethical regardless of the circumstances surrounding it or the context in which it occurs. In a strict objective view, the end doesn't justify the means; you cannot justify an unethical act regardless of how good or beneficial its results (or ends) might be.

A subjective view argues that what is or is not ethical depends on the culture's values and beliefs as well as the particular circumstances. Thus, a subjective position would claim that lying may be wrong to win votes or sell cigarettes, but that white lies may be quite ethical if their purpose is to make someone feel better and if the deceptions do no harm.

What would you do?

After an examination, the instructor accuses a student of cheating and asks you if you witnessed it. Although you believe that both cheating and lying are unethical and you did witness the cheating, you don't want to make trouble for the student (or for yourself). Besides, the examination wasn't announced in advance, and it counted only a few points toward the final grade. What would you do in this situation if you took an objective view of ethics? What would you do if you took a subjective view?

---

that are consistent with these comments. And, of course, the others may well do the same in forming impressions of you.

Part of the art and skill of interpersonal communication is to understand and be able to manage the impressions you give to others; mastering the art of impression management will enable you to present yourself as you want others to see you, at least to some extent.

The strategies you use to achieve this desired impression will depend on your specific goal. Here is an interpersonal typology of seven major communication goals and strategies of impression management. As you read about these goals and strategies, and about how these strategies can backfire, consider your own attempts to communicate the "right" impression to others and what you do (that is, the strategies you use) to achieve this unique kind of communication.

To Be Liked: Immediacy and Affinity-Seeking Strategies

If you want to be liked—say, you're new at school or on the job and you want to be well liked, to be included in the activities of other students or work associates, and to be thought of highly by these other people—you'll likely use two sets of strategies: **immediacy strategies** (these are discussed in the Understanding Interpersonal Skills box in Chapter 6, p. 134) and **affinity-seeking strategies**.

As you can see from examining the list of affinity-seeking strategies that follows, the use of these techniques is likely to increase your chances of being liked (Bell & Daly, 1984). Such strategies are especially important in initial interactions, and their use by teachers has even been found to increase student motivation (Martin & Rubin, 1998; Myers & Zhong, 2004; Wrench, McCroskey, & Richmond, 2008).

- Be of help to Other (the other person).
- Appear to be "in control" as a leader, as one who takes charge.
- Present yourself as socially equal to Other.
- Present yourself as comfortable and relaxed when with Other.
- Allow Other to assume control over relational activities.
- Follow the cultural rules for polite, cooperative conversation with Other.

- Appear active, enthusiastic, and dynamic.
- Stimulate and encourage Other to talk about himself or herself; reinforce disclosures and contributions of Other.
- Ensure that activities with Other are enjoyable and positive.
- Include Other in your social activities and groupings.
- Show that your relationship with Other is closer than it really is.
- Listen to Other attentively and actively.
- Communicate interest in Other.
- Engage in self-disclosure with Other.
- Appear optimistic and positive rather than pessimistic and negative.
- Appear to Other as an independent and freethinking individual.
- Appear to Other as being as physically attractive as possible.
- Appear to Other as an interesting person to get to know.
- Appear as someone who is able to reward Other for associating with you.
- Show respect for Other, and help Other to feel positively about himself or herself.
- Arrange circumstances so that you and Other come into frequent contact.
- Communicate warmth and empathy to Other.
- Demonstrate that you share significant attitudes and values with Other.
- Communicate supportiveness in Other's interpersonal interactions.
- Appear to Other as honest and reliable.

And, not surprisingly, plain old flattery goes a long way toward making you liked. Flattery has also been found to increase your chances for success in a job interview, increase the tip a customer is likely to leave, and even increase your perceived credibility (Varma, Toh, & Pichler, 2006; Seiter, 2007; Vonk, 2002).

There is also, however, a negative effect that can result from the use of affinity-seeking strategies—as there is for all of the strategies discussed in this section. Using affinity-seeking strategies too often or in ways that may appear insincere may lead people to see you as attempting to ingratiate yourself for your own advantage and not really meaning "to be nice."

To Be Believed: Credibility Strategies

Let's say you're a politician and you want people to vote for you or to support a particular proposal you're advancing. In this case you'll probably use **credibility strategies**—a concept that goes back some 2300 years and is supported by contemporary research—and seek to establish your competence, your character, and your charisma. For example, to establish your competence, you may mention your great educational background or the courses you took that qualify you as an expert. To establish that you're of good character, you may mention how fair and honest you are or speak of your concern for enduring values or your concern for others. And to establish your charisma—your take-charge, positive personality—you may demonstrate enthusiasm, be emphatic, or focus on the positive while minimizing the negative. Additional methods for being believed are offered in Chapter 13 (pp. 306–307).

Of course, if you stress your competence, character, and charisma too much, you risk being perceived as too eager—as someone who is afraid of being exposed as lacking the very qualities that you seek to present to others. For example, generally, people who are truly competent need say little directly about their own competence; their knowledgeable, insightful, and logical messages reveal their competence.

To Excuse Failure: Self-Handicapping Strategies

If you were about to tackle a difficult task and were concerned that you might fail, you might use what are called **self-handicapping strategies**. In the more extreme type of self-handicapping strategy, you actually set up barriers or obstacles to make the task impossible so that when you fail, you won't be blamed or thought ineffective—after all, the task was impossible. Let's say you aren't prepared for your interpersonal communication exam and you feel you're going to fail. Well, using this extreme type of self-handicapping strategy, you might go out and party the night before so that when you do poorly in the exam, you can blame it on the all-night party rather than on your intelligence or knowledge. The less extreme type involves manufacturing excuses for failure and having them ready if you do fail. "The exam was unfair" is one such popular excuse. Or you might blame a long period without a date on your being too intelligent or too shy or too poor, or a poorly cooked dinner on your defective stove.

On the negative side, using self-handicapping strategies too often may lead people to see you as incompetent or foolish—after all, partying late into the night before an exam for which you is already unprepared doesn't make a whole lot of sense and can easily reflect on your overall competence.

To Secure Help: Self-Deprecating Strategies

If you want to be taken care of and protected or simply want someone to come to your aid, you might use **self-deprecating strategies**. Confessions of incompetence and inability often bring assistance from others. And so you might say, "I just can't fix that drain and it drives me crazy; I just don't know anything about plumbing" with the hope that the other person will offer help.

But be careful: Using self-deprecating strategies may convince people that you are in fact as incompetent as you say you are. Or people may see you as someone who doesn't want to do something and so confesses incompetence to get others to do it for you. This is not likely to get you help in the long run.

To Hide Faults: Self-Monitoring Strategies

Much impression management is devoted not merely to presenting a positive image but to suppressing the negative via **self-monitoring strategies**. Here you carefully monitor (self-censor) what you say or do. You avoid your normal slang so as to make your colleagues think more highly of you; you avoid chewing gum so you don't look juvenile or unprofessional. While you readily disclose favorable parts of your experience, you actively hide the unfavorable parts.

But if you self-monitor too often or too obviously, you risk being seen as unwilling to reveal yourself, perhaps because you don't trust others enough to feel comfortable disclosing your weaknesses as well as your strengths. In more extreme cases you may be seen as dishonest, as hiding your true self or as trying to fool other people.

To Be Followed: Influencing Strategies

In many instances you'll want to get people to see you as a leader, as someone to be followed in thought and perhaps in behavior. Here you can use a variety of **influencing strategies**. One set of such strategies are those normally grouped under power. So, for example, to gain influence you may stress your knowledge (information power); your expertise (expert power); and/or your right to lead by virtue of your position as, say, a doctor or judge or accountant (legitimate power). These "bases of power" are discussed in greater detail in Chapter 13 (pp. 302–311). Another set of influencing strategies are those of leadership, in which you might stress your prior experience, your broad knowledge, or your previous successes.

Influencing strategies, too, can easily backfire. If your influence attempts fail—for whatever reason—you will lose general influence. That is, if you try but fail to influence someone, you'll be seen to have less power than before you tried the failed influence attempt. And, of course, if you're perceived as trying to influence others for self-gain, your persuasive attempts are likely to be rejected and perhaps even seen as self-serving and resented.

To Confirm Self-Image: Image-Confirming Strategies

At times you communicate to confirm your self-image. As an example of the use of **image-confirming strategies**, if you see yourself as the life of the party, you'll tell jokes and try to amuse people. By doing so you'll confirm your own self-image; you'll also let others know that this is who you are, this is how you want to be seen. At the same time that you reveal aspects of yourself that confirm your desired image, you will probably suppress revealing aspects of yourself that would disconfirm this image.

If you use image-confirming strategies too frequently, however, you risk being seen as "too perfect to be for real." If you try to project an all-positive image, it's likely to turn people off—people want to see their friends and associates as having some faults, some imperfections. Also recognize that image-confirming strategies invariably involve your talking about yourself, and with that comes the risk of appearing self-absorbed.

A knowledge of these impression management strategies and the ways in which they are effective and ineffective will give you a greater number of choices for achieving such widely diverse goals as being liked, being believed, excusing failure, securing help, hiding faults, being followed, and confirming your self-image.

At the same time, recognize that these very same impression management strategies may be used unethically and for less-than-noble purposes. For example, people may use affinity-seeking strategies to get you to like them so that they can extract favors from you. In order to get votes, politicians frequently present themselves as credible (competent, moral, and charismatic) when in fact they are not. And of course the same could be said of the stereotypical used-car salesperson or the insurance agent. Some people will use self-handicapping strategies or self-deprecating strategies to get you see their behavior from a perspective that benefits them rather than you. Self-monitoring strategies are most often deceptive and are designed to present a more polished image than one that might come out without this self-monitoring. And, of course, influence strategies have throughout history been used in deception as well as in truth. Even image-confirming strategies can be used to deceive, as when people exaggerate their positive qualities (or make them up) and hide their negative traits.

Summary

This chapter looked at the self and perception in interpersonal communication.

The Self in Interpersonal Communication

1. Self-concept is the image you have of who you are. Sources of self-concept include others' images of you, social comparisons, cultural teachings, and your own interpretations and evaluations.

2. Self-awareness is your knowledge of yourself; the extent to which you know who you are. A useful way of looking at self-awareness is with the Johari window, which consists of four parts. The open self holds information known to self and others; the blind self holds information known only to others; the hidden self holds information known only to self; and the unknown self holds information known to neither self nor others.

3. To increase self-awareness, ask yourself about yourself, listen to others, actively seek information about yourself, see your different selves, and increase your open self.

4. Self-esteem is the value you place on yourself; your perceived self-worth.

5. To increase self-esteem, try attacking your self-destructive beliefs, seeking affirmation, seeking out nourishing people, and working on projects that will result in success.

Perception in Interpersonal Communication

6. Perception is the process by which you become aware of objects and events in the external world.

7. Perception occurs in five stages: (1) stimulation, (2) organization, (3) interpretation–evaluation, (4) memory, and (5) recall.

Impression Formation

8. Six important processes influence the way you form impressions: Self-fulfilling prophecies may influence the behaviors of others; implicit personality theory allows you to conclude that certain characteristics go with certain other characteristics; perceptual accentuation may lead you to perceive what you expect to perceive instead of what is really there; primacy–recency may influence you to give extra importance to what occurs first (a primacy effect) and may lead you to see what conforms to this judgment and to distort or otherwise misperceive what contradicts it; the tendency to seek and expect consistency may influence you to see what is consistent and not to see what is inconsistent; and attributions, through which you try to understand the behaviors of others, are made in part on the basis of your judgment of control.

9. Among the major errors of attribution are the self-serving bias, overattribution, and the fundamental attribution error.

10. In increasing your accuracy in impression formation: Analyze your impressions and recognize your role in perception; check your impressions; reduce uncertainty; and become culturally sensitive by recognizing the differences between you and others and also the differences among people from other cultures.

Impression Management: Goals and Strategies

11. Among the goals and strategies of impression management are: to be liked (immediacy and affinity-seeking strategies); to be believed (credibility strategies that establish your competence, character, and charisma); to excuse failure (self-handicapping

strategies); to secure help (self-deprecating strategies); to hide faults (self-monitoring strategies); to be followed (influencing strategies); and to confirm your self-image (image-confirming strategies).

12. Each of these impression management strategies can backfire and give others negative impressions. Also, each of these strategies may be used to reveal your true self or to present a false self and deceive others in the process.

Key Terms

affirmation, **60**

attribution, **68**

cultural sensitivity, **71**

fundamental attribution error, **69**

implicit personality theory, **66**

impression formation, **64**

impression management, **71**

interpretation–evaluation, **63**

memory, **64**

other-orientation, **69**

overattribution, **69**

perception, **61**

primacy–recency, **67**

recall, **64**

rules, **62**

schema, **62**

schemata, **62**

script, **63**

self-awareness, **56**

self-destructive beliefs, **59**

self-esteem, **58**

self-fulfilling prophecy, **65**

self-serving bias, **68**

Critical Thinking Questions

1 How satisfied are you with your self-concept? How satisfied are you with your current level of self-esteem? If you're unsatisfied, what are you going to do about it?

2 Do you engage in downward social comparison (comparing yourself to those you know are inferior to you in some way) or in upward social comparison (comparing yourself to those who you think are better than you) (Aspinwall & Taylor, 1993)? What are the purposes of these comparisons?

3 Although most of the research on the self-fulfilling prophecy illustrates its distorting effect on behavior, consider how you might go about using the self-fulfilling prophecy to encourage behaviors you want to increase in strength and frequency. For example, what might you do to encourage persons who are fearful of communicating to speak up with greater confidence? What might you do to encourage people who are reluctant to self-disclose to reveal more of their inner selves?

4 Writers to advice columnists generally attribute their problems to external sources, whereas the columnists' responses often focus on internal sources, and their advice is therefore directed at the writer (you shouldn't have done that; apologize; get out of the relationship) (Schoeneman & Rubanowitz, 1985). Do you observe the same pattern when people discuss their problems with you, whether face-to-face, in letters, or in e-mail? Do you generally respond in the same way as the columnists?

5 What one suggestion for increasing accuracy in impression formation do you wish others would follow more often when they make judgments about you?

6 Ostracizing someone in face-to-face communication proves psychologically painful for the ignored person. One study argues that the same effects are present in online ostracism (Smith & Williams, 2004). How does online ostracism differ from face-to-face ostracism?

7 For the next several days, record all examples of people perception on your part—all instances in which you drew a conclusion about another person. Try to classify these in terms of the processes identified in this chapter; for example, processes such as implicit personality theory and attribution of control. Record also the specific context in which the instances occurred. After you've identified the various processes, share your findings in groups of five or six or with the entire class. As always, disclose only what you wish to disclose. What processes most frequently characterize your perceptions? Do these processes create any barriers to accurate perception?

8 To what extent are you willing to manipulate the image of yourself that you present to other people? For example, would you be willing to deceive people by being friendly when you really disliked them? Or suppose you were anxious to date a particular person. If you knew the kind of person your prospective date liked, and you had the ability to communicate that you were that kind of person, would it be ethical for you to do this? What if the situation were at a job interview? Would it be ethical for you to communicate an image of yourself that the interviewer wanted but that wasn't really you? In general, how authentic must you be to be ethical?

Choice Points

1 *Understanding Rejection.* You've asked several different people at school for a date, but so far all you've received have been rejections. Something's wrong; you're not that bad. Ask yourself: What might you do to gain insight into the possible reasons for these rejections?

2 *Lowering Self-Esteem.* Your brother has entered a relationship with someone who constantly puts him down; this has lowered his self-esteem to the point where he has no self-confidence. If this continues, you fear your brother may again experience bouts of severe depression. Ask yourself: What options do you have for dealing with this problem? What, if anything, would you do?

3 *Face-to-Face.* You've been communicating with Pat over the Internet for the past seven months, and you finally have decided to meet for coffee. You really want Pat to like you. Ask yourself: What impression management strategies might you be likely to use?

4 *Interviewing for a Job.* You're planning to go for a job interview, and you really want the interviewer to see you as credible

and influential. Ask yourself: What specific strategies might prove helpful at the interview?

5 *Reversing a First Impression.* You made a really bad first impression in your interpersonal communication class. You meant to be sarcastically funny but came off as merely sarcastic. Ask yourself: What might you say and do to lessen the impact of this first impression?

MyCommunicationLab
Explorations

PEARSON
mycommunicationlab www.mycommunicationlab.com

These exercises enable you to further explore the concepts of the self and perception, discussed in this chapter.

❶ How Can You Attack Self-Defeating Impulses? asks you to consider your own self-destructive beliefs and how you deal with them. Other exercises focus on sensitizing you to the influences on your perceptions and on helping you make your perceptions more accurate: ❷ Perceiving My Selves invites you to consider how you see yourself and how you think others see you; this exercise is also an excellent icebreaker. ❸ How Might You Perceive Others'

Perceptions? presents a variety of situations in which people are likely to see things very differently and sensitizes you to the variety of perceptions possible from the "same" event. ❹ How Do You Make Attributions? looks at a few specific situations and asks how you might make attributions in explaining the reasons for the behaviors. ❺ Barriers to Accurate Perception presents a dialogue containing a variety of perceptual errors and asks you to identify them. ❻ Perspective Taking asks you to take positive and negative perspectives on the same situations to help you explore the different conclusions people may draw from the same incident.

4 Listening in Interpersonal Communication

The Importance of Listening: Professional and Relationship Benefits

The Process of Listening

Listening Barriers

Culture, Gender, and Listening

Styles of Effective Listening

Ratatouille

In *Ratatouille* one of the great communication lessons that Linguini fortunately learns is to listen, regardless of what you may think at first. It's a useful principle to follow in interpersonal communication as well—as is demonstrated in this chapter on listening, what listening is, and how to do it better.

Listening is surely one of the most important of all interpersonal communication skills. Just think of your own listening behavior during an average day. You wake up to the alarm radio, put on the television to hear the weather and the news, check your computer and listen to the latest entries on YouTube and the advertising pop-ups, go to school while talking on your cell phone, listen to fellow students and instructors, listen to music or watch television, and listen to family members at dinner. Surely listening occupies a good part of your communication day.

The Importance of Listening: Professional and Relationship Benefits

The skills of listening will prove crucial to you in both your professional and relationship lives. First, in today's workplace, listening is regarded as a crucial skill. For example, one study concluded that in this era of technological transformation, employees' interpersonal skills are especially significant; workers' advancement will depend on their ability to speak and write effectively, to display proper etiquette, and *to listen attentively*. And in a survey of 40 CEOs of Asian and Western multinational companies, respondents cited a lack of listening skills as *the major shortcoming* of top executives (Witcher, 1999).

Another important professional benefit of listening is to establish and communicate power. In much the same way that you communicate power with your words or gestures, you also communicate your power through listening (a topic more fully examined in our discussion of power in Chapter 13).

It's also interesting to note that the effective listener is more likely to emerge as a group leader and is often a more effective salesperson, a more attentive and effective healthcare worker, and a more effective manager (Johnson & Bechler, 1998; Kramer, 1997; Castleberry & Shepherd, 1993; Lauer, 2003; Stein & Bowen, 2003; Levine, 2004). Recently medical educators, claiming that doctors are not trained to listen to their patients, have introduced what they call "narrative medicine" to teach doctors not only to listen more effectively but also to recognize how their perceptions of their patients are influenced by their own emotions (D. Smith, 2003).

And there can be little doubt that listening skills play a crucial role as we develop and maintain a variety of interpersonal relationships (Brownell, 2006). When asked what they want in a partner, women overwhelmingly identify "a partner who listens." And most men would agree that they too want a partner who listens. Among friends, listening skills consistently rank high; in fact, it would be hard to think of a person as a friend if that person was not also a good listener. Children need to learn to listen to their parents and also need their parents to listen to them. And parents need to learn to listen to their children.

Another way to appreciate the importance of listening is to consider its purposes and the benefits that accrue for each of these purposes. These purposes, of course, are the same as those of communication generally, as identified in Chapter 1: to learn, to relate, to influence, to play, and to help.

- *To learn:* One purpose of listening is to learn, something you do regularly as you listen to lectures in college. You also listen in order to learn about and understand other people and perhaps to avoid problems and make more reasonable decisions. For example, listening to how your friend dealt with an overly aggressive lover may suggest options to you or to those you know. Listening to your sales staff discuss their difficulties may help you offer more pertinent sales training.
- *To relate:* One of the communication skills most important to healthy relationships is the ability to listen to friends, romantic partners, family members, colleagues, and just about anyone you with whom you come into contact. In fact, as we'll see in the discussion of relationships in Chapter 11, women rate listening as one of the most important qualities in a partner. We all use listening to gain social acceptance and popularity and to make people like us. As you know from your own experience, the people you want to talk most with are the people who know how to listen. When you listen attentively and supportively, you communicate a genuine concern for others; it's a way of telling others that you care about them.

- *To influence:* You also listen to influence other people's attitudes, values, beliefs, opinions, and behaviors. While at first this relationship may seem strange, think about the people who are influential in your life: Very likely these are the people who listen to you, who know you and understand you. You're more likely to follow someone's advice once you feel that you've really been listened to, that your insights and concerns have been heard and understood.

- *To play:* Listening to music or the rustle of leaves often serves a play purpose. Here listening doesn't have to have a profitable outcome; it merely has to be enjoyable for the moment. Listening to the amusing stories of family members and the anecdotes of coworkers will allow you to gain a more comfortable balance between the world of work and the world of play.

- *To help:* Listening to help is something we experience growing up when our parents listen (or, sometimes, don't listen) to our concerns and help us solve our problems. Sometimes just listening—with no advice and no suggestions—proves extremely helpful. Supportive and noninfluential listening helps the other person clarify his or her thoughts and enables them to be seen more objectively. And of course listening is almost always a prerequisite to offering advice or help of any specific kind; after all, you really can't offer useful aid without first knowing and listening to the individual.

The Process of Listening

Listening can be defined as the process of: (1) receiving (hearing and attending to the message), (2) understanding (deciphering meaning from the message you hear), (3) remembering (retaining what you hear in memory), (4) evaluating (thinking critically about and judging the message), and (5) responding (answering or giving feedback to the speaker). This five-step process is visualized in Figure 4.1.

All five listening stages overlap; when you listen, you're performing all five processes at essentially the same time. For example, when listening in conversation, you're not only remaining attentive to what the other person is saying but also critically evaluating what he or she just said and perhaps giving feedback.

Listening is never perfect. There are lapses in attention, misunderstandings, lapses in memory, inadequate critical thinking, and inappropriate responding. The goal is to reduce these obstacles as best you can.

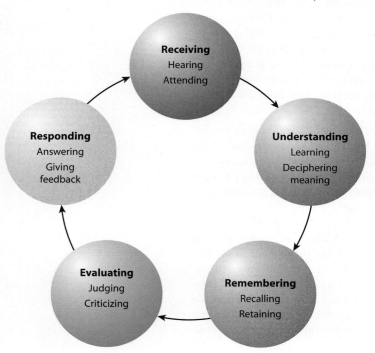

FIGURE 4.1

A Five-Stage Model of Listening

Recognize that at each stage of listening there will be lapses. Thus, for example, at the receiving stage a listener receives part of the message but, because of noise and perhaps for other reasons, fails to receive other parts. Similarly, at the stage of understanding, a listener understands part of the message but, because of each person's inability to share another's meanings exactly, fails to understand other parts. The same is true for remembering, evaluating, and responding. This model draws on a variety of previous models that listening researchers have developed (for example, Alessandra, 1986; Barker, 1990; Brownell, 2006).

Note that the listening process is circular. The responses of Person A serve as the stimuli for Person B, whose responses in turn serve as the stimuli for Person A, and so on. As will become clear in the following discussion of the five steps, listening is not a process of transferring an idea from the mind of a speaker to the mind of a listener. Rather, it is a process in which speaker and listener work together to achieve a common understanding.

Figure 4.1 emphasizes that listening involves a collection of skills: attention and concentration (receiving), learning (understanding), memory (remembering), critical thinking (evaluation), and competence in giving feedback (responding). Listening can go wrong at any stage—but you can improve your listening ability by strengthening the skills needed at each step of the listening process. Consequently, suggestions for listening improvement are offered with each of the five stages.

Stage One: Receiving

Listening begins with hearing, the process of receiving the messages the speaker sends. One of the great myths about listening is that it's the same as hearing. It isn't. Hearing is just the first stage of listening; it's equivalent to receiving. Hearing (and receiving) is a physiological process that occurs when you're in the vicinity of vibrations in the air and these vibrations impinge on your eardrum. Hearing is basically a passive process that occurs without any attention or effort on your part; hearing is mindless. Listening, as you'll see, is very different; listening is mindful.

At the **receiving** stage, you note not only what is said (verbally and nonverbally) but also what is omitted. You receive, for example, your boss's summary of your accomplishments as well as the omission of your shortcomings. To improve your receiving skills:

1. Focus your attention on the speaker's verbal and nonverbal messages, on what is said and on what isn't said. Avoid focusing your attention on what you'll say next; if you begin to rehearse your responses, you're going to miss what the speaker says next.
2. Avoiding distractions in the environment; if necessary, shut off the stereo or tell your assistant to hold your calls.
3. Maintain your role as listener and avoid interrupting. Avoid interrupting as much as possible. It will only prevent you from hearing what the speaker is saying.

In this brief discussion of receiving—and, in fact, throughout this entire chapter on listening—the unstated assumption is that both individuals can receive auditory signals without difficulty. But for the many people who have hearing impairments, listening presents a variety of problems. Table 4.1 provides tips for communication between people who have and people who do not have hearing difficulties.

Stage Two: Understanding

Understanding is the stage at which you learn what the speaker means, the stage at which you grasp both the thoughts and the emotions expressed. Understanding one without the other is likely to result in an unbalanced picture.

You can improve your listening understanding in a variety of ways.

1. Avoid assuming you understand what the speaker is going to say before he or she actually says it. If you do make assumptions, these will likely prevent you from accurately listening to what the speaker wants to say.
2. See the speaker's messages from the speaker's point of view. Avoid judging the message until you fully understand it as the speaker intended it.
3. Ask questions for clarification, if necessary; ask for additional details or examples if they're needed. This shows not only that you're listening—which is always nice for the speaker—but also that you want to learn more. Material that is not clearly understood is likely to be easily lost.
4. Rephrase (paraphrase) the speaker's ideas in your own words. This can be done silently or aloud. If done silently, it will help you rehearse and learn the material; if done aloud, it also helps you confirm your understanding of what the speaker is saying.

TABLE 4.1 Interpersonal Communication Tips
Between People with and without Hearing Difficulties

| Ludwig van Beethoven | Thomas Edison | Pete Townshend | Marlee Matlin |

People with hearing loss differ greatly in their hearing ability: Some are totally deaf and can hear nothing, others have some hearing loss and can hear some sounds, and still others have impaired hearing but can hear most speech. Although people with profound hearing loss can speak, their speech may appear labored and may be less clear than the speech of those with unimpaired hearing. Here are some suggestions for more effective communication between people who hear well and those who have hearing problems.

If you have unimpaired hearing:

1. Set up a comfortable context. Reduce the distance between yourself and the person with a hearing impairment. Reduce background noise: Turn off the television and even the air conditioner.

2. Avoid interference. Make sure the visual cues from your speech are clearly observable; for example, face the person squarely and avoid smoking, chewing gum, or holding your hand over your mouth. Make sure the lighting is adequate.

3. Speak at an adequate volume. But avoid shouting, which can distort your speech and may insult the person. Be careful to avoid reducing volume at the ends of your sentences.

4. Phrase ideas in different ways. Because some words are easier to lip-read than others, it often helps if you can rephrase your ideas in different words.

5. Avoid overlapping speech. In group situations only one person should speak at a time. Similarly, direct your comments to the person with hearing loss himself or herself; don't talk to the person through a third party. Elementary school teachers, for example, have been found to direct fewer comments to deaf children than to hearing students (Cawthon, 2001).

6. Ask for additional information. Ask the person if there is anything you can do to make it easier for him or her to understand you.

7. Don't avoid common terms. Use terms like *hear, listen, music,* or *deaf* when they're relevant to the conversation. Trying to avoid these common terms will make your speech sound artificial.

8. Use nonverbal cues. Nonverbals can help communicate your meaning; gestures indicating size or location and facial expressions indicating emotions and feelings are often helpful.

If you have impaired hearing:

1. Do your best to eliminate background noise.

2. Move closer to the speaker if this helps you hear better. Alert the speaker that this closer distance will help you hear better.

3. Ask for adjustments. If you feel the speaker can make adjustments to ease your comprehension, ask. For example, ask the speaker to repeat a message, to speak more slowly or more distinctly, or to increase his or her volume.

4. Position yourself for best reception. If you hear better in one ear than another, position yourself accordingly and, if necessary, clue the speaker in to this fact.

5. Ask for additional cues. If necessary, ask the speaker to write down certain information, such as phone numbers or website addresses. Carrying a pad and pencil will prove helpful for this and in the event that you wish to write something down for others.

Sources: These suggestions were drawn from a variety of sources: Tips for Communicating with Deaf People (Rochester Institute of Technology, National Technical Institute for the Deaf, Division of Public Affairs), http://www.his.com/~lola/deaf.html, http://www.zak.co.il/deaf-info/old/comm_strategies.html, http://www.agbell.org/, http://www.dol.gov/odep/pubs/fact/comucate.htm, and http://spot.pcc.edu/~rjacobs/career/communication_tips.htm (all websites accessed May 7, 2008).

Stage Three: Remembering

Effective listening depends on **remembering**. For example, when Susan says she is planning to buy a new car, the effective listener remembers this and at a later meeting asks about the car. When Joe says his mother is ill, the effective listener remembers this and inquires about her health later in the week.

In some small group and public speaking situations, you can augment your memory by taking notes or by taping the messages. And in many work situations, taking notes is common and may even be expected. In most interpersonal communication situations, however, note taking is inappropriate—although you often do write down a telephone number, an appointment, or directions.

Perhaps the most important point to understand about memory is that what you remember is not what was said but what you remember was said. Memory for speech is not reproductive; you don't simply reproduce in your memory what the speaker said. Rather, memory is reconstructive; you actually reconstruct the messages you hear into a system that makes sense to you.

If you want to remember what someone says or the names of various people, this information needs to pass from your **short-term memory** (the memory you use, say, to remember a phone number just long enough to write it down) into long-term memory. Short-term memory is very limited in capacity—you can hold only a small amount of information there. **Long-term memory** is unlimited. To facilitate the passage of information from short- to long-term memory, try the following suggestions:

VIEWPOINT The term *false memory syndrome* refers to a phenomenon in which a person "remembers" past experiences that never actually occurred. Most of the studies on false memory syndrome have centered on erroneous recollections of abuse and other traumatic experiences. Often these false memories are implanted by therapists and interviewers, whose persistent questioning over a period of time can create such a realistic scenario that an individual comes to believe these things actually occurred (Porter, Brit, Yuille, & Lehman, 2000). In what other, less dramatic ways can false memory syndrome occur?

1. Identify the central ideas. Even in the most casual of conversations, there are central ideas. Fix these in your mind. Repeat these ideas to yourself as you continue to listen.
2. Summarize the message in a more easily retained form, but take care not to ignore crucial details or qualifications. If you chunk the material into categories, you'll be able to remember more information. For example, if you want to remember 15 or 20 items to buy in the supermarket, you'll remember more if you group them into chunks—say, produce, canned goods, and meats.
3. Repeat names and key concepts to yourself or, if appropriate, aloud. By repeating the names or key concepts, you in effect rehearse these names and concepts, and as a result they'll be easier to learn and remember. If you're introduced to Alice, you'll stand a better chance of remembering her name if you say, "Hi, Alice" than if you say just "Hi."

Stage Four: Evaluating

Evaluating consists of judging the messages in some way. At times you may try to evaluate the speaker's underlying intentions or motives. Often this evaluation process goes on without much conscious awareness. For example, Elaine tells you that she is up for a promotion and is really excited about it. You may then try to judge her intention: Perhaps she wants you to use your influence with the company president, or maybe she's preoccupied with the promotion and so tells everyone, or possibly she's looking for a compliment.

In other situations your evaluation is more in the nature of critical analysis. For example, in listening to proposals advanced in a business meeting, you may ask: Are the proposals practical? Will they increase productivity? What's the evidence? Is there contradictory evidence?

In evaluating consider these suggestions.

1. Resist evaluation until you fully understand the speaker's point of view? This is not always easy, but it's almost always essential. If you put a label on what the speaker is saying (ultraconservative, bleeding-heart liberal), you'll hear the remainder of the messages through these labels.
2. Distinguish facts from opinions and personal interpretations by the speaker. And, most important, fix these labels in mind with the information; for example, try to remember that *Jesse thinks Pat did XYZ*, not just that *Pat did XYZ*.

Ethics in Interpersonal Communication

Ethical Listening

As a listener you have at least these two ethical obligations:

1. You owe it to the speaker to give an honest hearing, without prejudgment, putting aside prejudices and preconceptions as best you can. At the same time, you owe the speaker your best effort at understanding emotionally as well as intellectually what he or she means.

2. Second, you owe the speaker honest responses. Just as you should be honest with the listener when speaking, you should be honest with the speaker when listening. This means giving open and honest feedback and also reflecting honestly on the questions that the speaker raises.

What would you do?

Your friend begins revealing deeply personal secrets—problems at home, a lack of money, no friends, and on and on. You don't want to hear all this; it depresses you. You want to avoid having to listen to these disclosures. At the same time, however, you wonder if you have an ethical obligation to listen openly and respond honestly to your friend. What would you do in this situation?

---

3. Identify any biases, self-interests, or prejudices that may lead the speaker to slant unfairly what is said. It's often wise to ask if the material is being presented fairly or if this person is slanting it in some way.

4. Recognize some of the popular but fallacious forms of "reasoning" speakers may employ, such as:

   - *Name-calling:* applying a favorable or unfavorable label to color your perception— "democracy" and "soft on terrorism" are two currently popular examples
   - *Testimonial:* using positively or negatively viewed spokespersons to encourage your acceptance or rejection of something—such as a white-coated actor to sell toothpaste or a disgraced political figure associated with an idea the speaker wants rejected
   - *Bandwagon:* arguing that you should believe or do something because "everyone else does"

Stage Five: Responding

Responding occurs in two phases: responses you make while the speaker is talking and responses you make after the speaker has stopped talking. These responses are feedback—information that you send back to the speaker and that tells the speaker how you feel and what you think about his or her messages.

Supportive responses made while the speaker is talking are usually most effective; they acknowledge that you're listening and that you're with the speaker. These responses include what nonverbal researchers call *back-channeling cues*—comments such as "I see," "yes," "uh-huh," and similar signals. Back-channeling cues are especially important in face-to-face conversation and are considered in detail in Chapter 8.

Responses made after the speaker has stopped talking are generally more elaborate and might include expressing empathy ("I know how you must feel"), asking for clarification ("Do you mean that this new health plan is to replace the old one?"), challenging ("I think your evidence is weak here"), or agreeing ("You're absolutely right on this; I'll support your proposal").

Here are a few suggestions for making your listening responses more effective.

1. Support the speaker throughout the speaker's conversation by using and varying your listening cues, such as head nods and minimal responses such as "I see" or "mm-hmm."

2. Own your responses. Take responsibility for what you say. Instead of saying, "Nobody will want to do that" say something like "I don't think I'll do that."

3. Resist "responding to another's feelings" with "solving the person's problems" (as men are often accused of doing) unless, of course, you're asked for advice (Tannen, 1990).

TABLE 4.2 Problem-Causing Listening Responses and How to Correct Them

Here are just a few examples of listening responses that can present effective and satisfying interpersonal communication.

Problem-Causing Responses	Correctives
The *static listener* gives no feedback, remains relatively motionless, reveals no expression.	Give feedback as appropriate: Smile, nod, and otherwise appropriately respond to the content and feeling of the message.
The *monotonous feedback giver* seems responsive, but the responses never vary; regardless of what you say, the response is the same.	Give varied feedback that is relevant to the conversation.
The *overly expressive listener* reacts to just about everything with extreme responses.	React in a tone consistent with the other's message.
The *eye avoider* looks all around the room and at others but never at you.	Look at the speaker; don't stare, but make the speaker your eyes' main focus.
The *preoccupied listener* listens to other things at the same time, often with headphones with the sound so loud that it interferes with your own thinking.	Show the speaker that he or she is your primary focus. Take off headphones; shut down the iPhone and the television; turn away from the computer screen.
The *waiting listener* listens for a cue to take over the speaking turn.	Hear the speaker out and then speak; refrain from giving cues that you want to speak while the speaker is in the middle of saying something.
The *thought-completing listener* listens a little and then finishes your thought.	Express respect by allowing the speaker to complete his or her thoughts. Completing someone's thoughts often communicates the message that nothing important is going to be said ("I already know it").
The *critical listener* evaluates everything you say, often negatively.	Avoid criticism (unless the situation calls for it); as far as possible, always stress the positive.
The *advising listener* gives you advice at the first mention of a problem or decision.	Avoid giving advice unless specifically asked, and resist what is supposedly the male tendency to solve problems.
The *never-ending listener* just wants you to keep talking, often long after you've said what you want to say.	Learn to exchange speaking and listening roles; they are each best when relatively short. And allow conversations to end naturally instead of unnecessarily prolonging them.

For another way of looking at responding, see Table 4.2, which identifies a variety of problem-causing listening responses.

Listening Barriers

In addition to practicing the various skills for each stage of listening, consider some of the common general barriers to listening. Here are just four such barriers and some suggestions for dealing with them as both listener and speaker—because both speaker and listener are responsible for effective listening.

Distractions: Physical and Mental

Physical barriers to listening may include, for example, hearing impairment, a noisy environment, or loud music. Multitasking (watching TV while listening to someone with the aim of being supportive, say) simply doesn't work. As both listener and speaker, try to remove whatever physical barriers can be removed; for those that you can't remove, adjust your listening and speaking to lessen the effects as much as possible. As a listener, focus on the speaker; you can attend to the room and the other people later.

Mental distractions are in many ways similar to physical distractions; they get in the way of focused listening. Typical mental distractions, for example, are thinking about your upcoming Saturday night date or becoming too emotional to think (and listen) clearly. In listening, recognize that you can think about your date later. In speaking, make what you say compelling and relevant to the listener.

Biases and Prejudices

Biases and prejudices against groups, or against individuals who are members of such groups, will invariably distort listening. For example, a gender bias that assumes that only one sex has anything useful to say about certain topics will likely distort incoming messages that contradict this bias. As a listener, be willing to subject your biases and prejudices to contradictory information; after all, if they're worth having, they should stand up to differences of opinion. When you as a speaker feel that you may be facing bias, ask your listeners to suspend their attitude for the moment—*I know you don't like the Martins, and I can understand why. But, just listen to . . . .*

Another type of bias is closed-mindedness, which is seen, for example, in the person who refuses to hear any feminist argument or anything about gay marriage. As a listener, assume that what the speaker is saying will be useful in some way. As a speaker, anticipate that many people will be closed-minded on a variety of issues and remember that it often helps to simply ask for openness—*I know this is contrary to what many people think, but let's look at this logically.*

VIEWPOINT Research indicates that overheard cell phone conversations are rated as more intrusive than overheard conversations between two people talking face-to-face (Monk, Fellas, & Ley, 2004); one researcher argues that cell conversations are particularly annoying because you can hear only one side of the dialogue. Do you find the cell phone conversations of people near you on a bus or in a store annoying? If you do, why?

Lack of Appropriate Focus

Focusing on what a person is saying is obviously necessary for effective listening. And yet there are many influences that can lead you astray. For example, listeners often get lost because they focus on irrelevancies; say, on an especially vivid example that conjures up old memories. As a listener, try not to get detoured from the main idea; don't get hung up on unimportant details. Try to repeat the idea to yourself and see the details in relation to this main concept. As a speaker, try to avoid language or examples that may divert attention from your main idea.

At times people will listen only for information with an obvious relevance to them. But this type of listening only prevents you from expanding your horizons. After all, it's quite possible that information that you originally thought irrelevant will eventually prove helpful. Avoid interpreting everything in terms of what it means to you; see other perspectives. As a speaker, be sure to make what you say relevant to your specific listener.

Another mistake is for the listener to focus on the responses he or she is going to make while the speaker is still speaking. Anticipating how you're going to respond or what you're going to say (and perhaps even interrupting the speaker) just prevents you from hearing the message in full. Instead, make a mental note of something and then get back to listening. As a speaker, when you feel someone is preparing to argue with you, ask them to hear you out—*I know you disagree with this, but let me finish and we'll get back to that.*

Premature Judgment

Perhaps the most obvious form of premature judgment is assuming you know what the speaker is going to say—so there's no need to really listen. Let the speaker say what he or she is going to say before you decide that you already know it. As a speaker, of course, it's often wise to assume that listeners will do exactly this, so it may be helpful to make clear that what you're saying will be unexpected.

A common listener reaction is to draw conclusions or judgments on incomplete evidence. Sometimes listeners will stop listening after hearing a speaker, for example, express an attitude they disagree with or make some sexist or culturally insensitive remark. Instead, this is a situation that calls for especially concentrated listening so that you don't rush to judgment. Instead, wait for the evidence or argument; avoid making judgments before you gather all the information. Listen first, judge second. As a speaker, be aware of this tendency and when you feel this is happening, ask for a suspension of judgment. A simple *Hear me out* is often sufficient to prevent a too-early judgment on the part of listeners.

UNDERSTANDING INTERPERSONAL SKILLS

Openness

Openness in interpersonal communication is a person's willingness to self-disclose—to reveal information about himself or herself as appropriate (see Chapter 8, pp. 193–199). Openness also includes a willingness to listen openly and to react honestly to the messages of others. This does not mean that openness is always appropriate. In fact, too much openness is likely to lead to a decrease in your relationship satisfaction (Dindia & Timmerman, 2003).

Communicating Openness. Consider these few ideas.

■ Self-disclose when appropriate. Be mindful about whatever you say about yourself. There are benefits and dangers to this form of communication (see Chapter 8, pp. 195–196).

■ Respond to those with whom you're interacting with spontaneity and with appropriate honesty—though also with an awareness of what you're saying and of what the possible outcomes of your messages might be.

■ Own your own feelings and thoughts. Take responsibility for what you say. Use I-messages instead of you-messages. Instead of saying, "You make me feel stupid when you don't ask my opinion," own your feelings and say, for example, "I feel stupid when you ask everyone else what they think but don't ask me." When you own your feelings and thoughts—when you use I-messages—you say, in effect, "This is how I feel," "This is how I see the situation." I-messages make explicit the fact that your feelings result from the interaction between what is going on outside your skin (what others say, for example) and what is going on inside your skin (your preconceptions, attitudes, and prejudices, for example).

Working with Interpersonal Skills

On a scale from 1 to 10, how would you describe your communication with friends at school in terms of closedness (1) versus openness (10)? Your communication with your family? With your best friends or romantic partner? What do you notice are the advantages of openness? What are some of the dangers?

Culture, Gender, and Listening

Listening is difficult, in part, because of the inevitable differences in communication systems between speaker and listener. Because each person has had a unique set of experiences, each person's meaning system is going to be different from every other person's. When speaker and listener come from different cultures or are of different genders, these differences and their effects are naturally much greater. Consider culture first.

Culture and Listening

In a global environment in which people from very different cultures work together, it's especially important to understand the ways in which cultural differences can influence listening. Three such factors may be singled out: (1) language and speech, (2) nonverbal behaviors, and (3) feedback.

Language and Speech   Even when speaker and listener speak the same language, they speak it with different meanings and different accents. No two speakers speak exactly the same language. Speakers of the same language will, at the very least, have different meanings for the same terms because they have had different experiences.

Speakers and listeners who have different native languages and who may have learned English as a second language will have even greater differences in meaning. Translations never fully capture the meaning in the other language. If your meaning for the word *house* was learned in a culture in which everyone lived in their own house with lots of land around it, then communicating with someone for whom the meaning of *house* was learned in a neighborhood of high-rise tenements is going to be difficult. Although you'll each hear the same word, the meanings you'll each develop will be drastically different. In adjusting your listening—especially in an intercultural setting—understand that the speaker's meanings may be very different from yours even though you're speaking in the same language.

In many classrooms throughout the United States, there will be a wide range of accents. Students whose native language is a tonal one, such as Chinese (in which differences in pitch signal important meaning differences), may speak English with variations in pitch that may seem puzzling to others. Those whose native language is Japanese may have trouble distinguishing *l* from *r*, as Japanese does not include this distinction. The native language acts as a filter and influences the accent given to the second language.

Nonverbal Behaviors Speakers from different *cultures* have different **display rules**—cultural rules that govern what nonverbal behaviors are appropriate or inappropriate in a public setting. As you listen to other people, you also "listen" to their nonverbal cues. If nonverbals are drastically different from what you expect on the basis of the verbal message, you may experience them as a kind of noise or interference or even as contradictory messages. Also, of course, different cultures may give very different meanings to the same nonverbal gesture. For example, the thumb and forefinger forming a circle means "OK" in most of the United States; but it means "money" in Japan, "zero" in some Mediterranean countries, and "I'll kill you" in Tunisia.

Feedback Members of some cultures give very direct and very frank feedback. Speakers from these cultures—the United States is a good example—expect feedback to be an honest reflection of what their listeners are feeling. In other cultures—Japan and Korea are good examples—it's more important to be positive than to be truthful, so people may respond with positive feedback (say, in commenting on a business colleague's proposal) even though they don't agree with what is being said. Listen to feedback, as you would all messages, with a full recognition that various cultures view feedback very differently.

Gender and Listening

Men and women learn different styles of listening, just as they learn different styles for using verbal and nonverbal messages. Not surprisingly, these different styles can create major difficulties in opposite-sex interpersonal communication.

Rapport and Report Talk According to Deborah Tannen (1990) in her best-selling *You Just Don't Understand: Women and Men in Conversation*, women seek to build rapport and establish closer relationships and use listening to achieve these ends. Men, on the other hand, will play up their expertise, emphasize it, and use it in dominating the interaction. They will talk about things; they report. Women play down their expertise and are more interested in talking about feelings and relationships and in communicating supportiveness. Tannen argues that the goal of a man in conversation is to be given respect, so he seeks to show his knowledge and expertise. A woman, on the other hand, seeks to be liked, so she expresses agreement.

Listening Cues Men and women feed back to the speaker different types of listening cues and consequently show that they're listening in different ways. In conversation, a woman is more apt to give lots of listening cues—interjecting "Yeah" or "Uh-huh," nodding in agreement, and smiling. A man is more likely to listen quietly, without giving lots of listening cues as feedback. Women also make more eye contact when listening than do men, who are more apt to look around and often away from the speaker (Brownell, 2006). As a result of these differences, women seem to be more engaged in listening than do men.

Amount and Purposes of Listening Tannen argues that men listen less to women than women listen to men. The reason, says

VIEWPOINT The popular belief is that men listen in the way they do to prove themselves superior and that women listen as they do to ingratiate themselves. Although there is no evidence to show that these images are valid, they persist in the assumptions that people make about the opposite sex. What do you believe accounts for the differences in the way men and women listen?

If women and men do appear to listen differently, what can I do to make sure the other person is really listening in ways that I need?

That women appear to be better listeners is probably due to the fact that women, not men, are typically socialized to provide prosocial listening cues and to solve problems. As this chapter suggests, the responsibility to ensure that the other party is listening appropriately is a shared one. To ensure meaningful listening:

1. Determine your listening needs. Do you want advice on how to solve a personal or professional problem? Do you need an empathic ear to vent your frustration about a disappointment? Is it action such as help that you are seeking?
2. Evaluate the timing and place. Important conversations should take place when both parties can devote sufficient time in a setting free of extraneous distractions.
3. Make your needs clear. "I'd like your advice about . . ." or "I need your feedback on . . ." provide critical cues that orient the listener. During interaction, both the speaker and the listener need to check that they are being heard and understood accurately.

For more information see Deborah Borisoff and Dan Hahn, "Gender and Listening: Values Revalued," in M. Purdy and D. Borisoff (eds.), *Listening in Everyday Life: A Personal & Professional Approach*, 2nd ed. (Lanham, MD: University Press of America, 1997); and Judi Brownell, *Listening: Attitudes, Principles and Skills*, 3rd ed. (Boston; Allyn & Bacon, 2006).

Deborah Borisoff (Ph.D., New York University) is professor of culture and communication at New York University and teaches courses and conducts research in the areas of gender and communication, conflict, listening, and organizational communication. Dr. Borisoff also serves as a consultant to various business organizations and educational institutions.

Tannen, is that listening places the person in an inferior position, whereas speaking places the person in a superior position. Men may seem to assume a more argumentative posture while listening, as if getting ready to argue. They also may appear to ask questions that are more argumentative or that seek to puncture holes in your position as a way to play up their own expertise. Women are more likely to ask supportive questions and perhaps offer criticism that is more positive than men. Men and women act this way to both men and women; their customary ways of talking don't seem to change depending on whether the listener is male or female.

It's important to note that not all researchers agree that there is sufficient evidence to make the claims that Tannen and others make about gender differences (Goldsmith & Fulfs, 1999).

Gender differences are changing drastically and quickly; it's best to take generalizations about gender as starting points for investigation and not as airtight conclusions (Gamble & Gamble, 2003). Further, as you no doubt have observed, gender differences—although significant—are far outnumbered by similarities between males and females. It's important to be mindful of both differences and similarities.

Styles of Effective Listening

Before reading about styles of effective listening in interpersonal communication, examine your own listening habits and tendencies by taking the accompanying self-test, "How Do You Listen?"

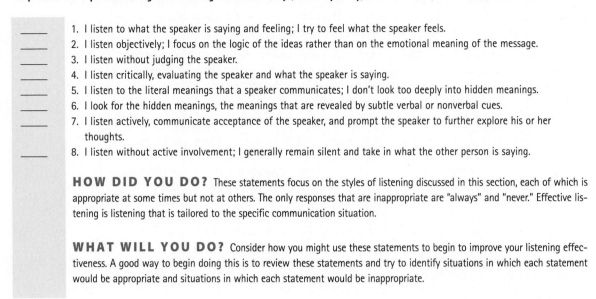

TEST YOURSELF

Respond to each question using the following scale: 1 = always, 2 = frequently, 3 = sometimes, 4 = seldom, and 5 = never.

_____ 1. I listen to what the speaker is saying and feeling; I try to feel what the speaker feels.

_____ 2. I listen objectively; I focus on the logic of the ideas rather than on the emotional meaning of the message.

_____ 3. I listen without judging the speaker.

_____ 4. I listen critically, evaluating the speaker and what the speaker is saying.

_____ 5. I listen to the literal meanings that a speaker communicates; I don't look too deeply into hidden meanings.

_____ 6. I look for the hidden meanings, the meanings that are revealed by subtle verbal or nonverbal cues.

_____ 7. I listen actively, communicate acceptance of the speaker, and prompt the speaker to further explore his or her thoughts.

_____ 8. I listen without active involvement; I generally remain silent and take in what the other person is saying.

HOW DID YOU DO? These statements focus on the styles of listening discussed in this section, each of which is appropriate at some times but not at others. The only responses that are inappropriate are "always" and "never." Effective listening is listening that is tailored to the specific communication situation.

WHAT WILL YOU DO? Consider how you might use these statements to begin to improve your listening effectiveness. A good way to begin doing this is to review these statements and try to identify situations in which each statement would be appropriate and situations in which each statement would be inappropriate.

As the self-test emphasizes, listening is situational; your style of listening should vary with the situation, and each situation will call for a somewhat different combination of listening styles. You do (and should) listen differently depending on your purpose, your conversational partners, and the type of message; in some situations you'll need to be especially critical and in others especially supportive.

Visualize each listening situation as one in which you have to make choices among the four dimensions of listening discussed in this section. Each listening situation should call for a somewhat different configuration of listening responses. The art of effective listening is largely one of making appropriate choices along the following four dimensions: (1) empathic versus objective listening, (2) nonjudgmental versus critical listening, (3) surface versus depth listening, and (4) active versus inactive listening. Let's take a look at each of these dimensions.

Empathic and Objective Listening

If you're to understand what a person means and what a person is feeling, you need to listen with some degree of _empathy_ (Rogers, 1970; Rogers & Farson, 1981). To empathize with others is to feel with them, to see the world as they see it, to feel what they feel. Only when you achieve this can you fully understand another person's meaning. **Empathic listening** will also help you enhance your relationships (Barrett & Godfrey, 1988; Snyder, 1992).

Although for most communication situations empathic listening is the preferred mode of responding, there are times when you need to engage in **objective listening**—to go beyond empathy and measure meanings and feelings against some objective reality. It's important to listen as Peter tells you how the entire world hates him and to understand how Peter feels and why he feels this way. But then you need to look a bit more objectively at Peter and perhaps see the paranoia or the self-hatred. Sometimes you have to put your empathic responses aside and listen with objectivity and detachment.

In adjusting your empathic and objective listening:

Punctuate the message from the speaker's point of view (Chapter 1); see the sequence of events (which events are causes and which are effects) as the speaker does. And try to figure out how this punctuation can influence what the speaker says and does.

Engage in equal, two-way conversation. To encourage openness and empathy, try to eliminate any physical or psychological barriers to equality (for example, step from behind the large desk separating you from your employees). Avoid interrupting the speaker—which sends the signal that what you have to say is more important.

Seek to understand both thoughts and feelings. Don't consider your listening task finished until you've understood what the speaker is feeling as well as thinking.

Avoid "offensive listening," the tendency to listen to bits and pieces of information that will enable you to attack the speaker or find fault with something the speaker has said (Floyd, 1985).

Strive to be objective when listening to friends and foes alike. Your attitudes may lead you to distort messages—to block out positive messages about a foe and negative messages about a friend. Guard against "expectancy hearing," when you fail to hear what the speaker is really saying and hear what you expect to hear instead.

Nonjudgmental and Critical Listening

Effective listening includes both nonjudgmental and critical responses. You need to listen nonjudgmentally—with an open mind with a view toward understanding. But you also need to listen critically—with a view toward making some kind of evaluation or judgment. Clearly, engage in **nonjudgmental listening** first; listen for understanding while suspending judgment. Only after you've fully understood the relevant messages should you evaluate or judge.

Supplement open-minded listening with **critical listening**. Listening with an open mind will help you understand messages better; listening with a critical mind will help you analyze and evaluate the messages. In adjusting your nonjudgmental and critical listening:

Keep an open mind and avoid prejudging. Delay your judgments until you fully understand the intention and the content the speaker is communicating. Avoid both positive and negative evaluation until you have a reasonably complete understanding.

Avoid filtering out or oversimplifying complex messages. Similarly, avoid filtering out undesirable messages. You don't want to hear that something you believe in is untrue, that people you care for are unkind, or that ideals you hold are self-destructive. Yet it's important that you reexamine your beliefs by listening to these messages.

Recognize your own biases. These may interfere with accurate listening and cause you to distort message reception through the process of *assimilation*—the tendency to integrate and interpret what you hear (or think you hear) to fit your own biases, prejudices, and expectations. For example, are your ethnic, national, or religious biases preventing you from appreciating a speaker's point of view?

Avoid sharpening. Recognize and combat the natural human tendency toward sharpening—a process in which one or two aspects of the message become highlighted, emphasized, and perhaps embellished. Often the concepts that are sharpened are incidental remarks that somehow stand out from the rest of the message. Be sure to listen critically to the entire message when you need to make evaluations and judgments.

Recognize the fallacies of language. Take a look at Table 4.3; it identifies four common barriers that challenge critical listening.

Surface and Depth Listening

In Shakespeare's *Julius Caesar*, Marc Antony, in giving the funeral oration for Caesar, says: "I come to bury Caesar, not to praise him. / The evil that men do lives after them; / The good is oft interred with their bones." And later: "For Brutus is an honourable man; / So are they all, all honourable men." If we listen beyond the surface of Marc Antony's words, we can see that he does comes to praise

VIEWPOINT Although empathy is almost universally considered positive, there is some evidence to show that it also can have a negative side. For example, people are most empathic with those who are similar—racially and ethnically as well as in appearance and social status. The more empathy you feel toward your own group, the less empathy—possibly even the more hostility—you feel toward other groups. The same empathy that increases your understanding of your own group decreases your understanding of other groups. So although empathy may encourage group cohesiveness and identification, it also can create dividing lines between your group and "them" (Angier, 1995b). Have you ever experienced or witnessed these negative effects of empathy?

UNDERSTANDING INTERPERSONAL THEORY & RESEARCH

Listening to Lying

In normal listening you assume the speaker is telling the truth. When you do question the speaker's truthfulness, it may be because the speaker exhibits cues that often accompany lying. Research has identified numerous such cues. Typically liars smile less; respond with shorter answers, often a simple yes or no; use fewer specifics and more generalities, such as "we hung out"; shift their posture more; use more self-touching movements; use more and longer pauses; avoid direct eye contact with the listener and blink more often than normal; appear less friendly and attentive; and make more speech errors (Knapp & Hall, 2006; Knapp, 2008; O'Hair, Cody, Goss, & Krayer, 1988; Bond & Atoum, 2000; Al-Simadi, 2000; Burgoon & Bacue, 2003).

But be careful, however, that you don't fall into the trap of thinking that just because someone emits some or all of these cues, he or she is therefore lying. These cues are often used by truth tellers as well as liars. In one study, in fact, people who held stereotypical views of how liars behave (for example, "liars don't look at you" or "liars fidget") were *less* effective in detecting lying than were those who didn't hold such beliefs (Vrij & Mann, 2001).

Furthermore, lie detection is generally unreliable. Whether among nonprofessionals or professional lie detectors (for example, judges, psychiatrists, and police officers), accuracy in judging lying is quite low; accuracy is generally found to be somewhere around 45 to 60 percent (Knapp, 2008).

Most people seem to operate with a truth bias and generally assume that others are telling the truth (Levine, Kim, Park, & Hughes, 2006). But under certain circumstances (with prisoners in prison or when law enforcement personnel interrogate a suspect, for example), there is a "lie bias"; people operate on the assumption that the person is lying. This assumption, not surprisingly, does not increase accuracy in overall lie-detection ability (Knapp, 2008).

Working with Theories and Research

Recall a situation in which you assumed, on the basis of the cues described here (or others), that someone was lying. What happened? Should you want to learn more about lying, log on to an online database and search for lying, deception, and similar terms. It's a fascinating subject of study.

Caesar, and to convince the crowd that Brutus was dishonorable—despite the fact that at first glance his words seem to say quite the opposite.

In most messages there's an obvious meaning that you can derive **surface listening**— from a literal reading of the words and sentences. But there's often another level of meaning. Sometimes, as in *Julius Caesar*, it's the opposite of the literal meaning; at other times it seems totally unrelated. Consider some frequently heard types of messages. For example, Claire asks you how you like her new haircut. On one level the meaning is clear: Do you like the haircut? But **depth listening** can reveal another, perhaps more important, level: Claire is asking you to say something positive about her appearance. In the same way, the parent who complains about working hard at the office or in the home may, on a deeper level, be asking for an expression of appreciation. The child who talks about the unfairness of the other children in the playground may be asking for comfort and love.

To appreciate these other meanings, listen in depth. If you listen only to the surface-level communication (the literal meaning), you'll miss the underlying message and will surely miss the opportunity to make meaningful contact with the other person's feelings and needs. If you say to your parent, "You're always complaining. I bet you really love working so hard," you fail to respond to the call for understanding and appreciation.

In regulating your surface and depth listening:

Focus on both verbal and nonverbal messages. Recognize both consistent and inconsistent "packages" of messages, and use these as guides for drawing inferences about the speaker's meaning. Ask questions when in doubt. Listen also to what is omitted. Remember that speakers communicate by what they leave out as well as by what they include.

Listen for both content and relational messages. The student who constantly challenges the teacher is, on one level, communicating disagreement over content. However, on another level—the relationship level—the student may be voicing objections to the instructor's authority or authoritarianism. The instructor needs to listen and respond to both types of messages.

TABLE 4.3 Listening to Fallacies of Language

Here are four language fallacies that often get in the way of meaningful communication and need to be identified in critical listening. Often these fallacies are used to fool you; they are ways in which language can be used to serve less than noble purposes, to convince or persuade you without giving you any reasons. After reviewing this table, take a look at some of the commercial websites for clothing, books, music, or any such product you're interested in. Can you find examples of these fallacies?

Fallacy	Example	Notes
Weasel words are those terms whose meanings are slippery and difficult to pin down (Hayakawa & Hayakawa, 1989).	A commercial claims that Medicine M works "better than Brand X" but doesn't specify how much better or in what respect Medicine M performs better. It's quite possible that it performs better in one respect but less effectively according to nine other measures.	Other weasel words are "help," "virtually," "as much as," "like" (as in "it will make you feel like new"), and "more economical." Ask yourself, "Exactly what is being claimed?" For example, "What does 'may reduce cholesterol' mean? What exactly is being asserted?"
Euphemisms make the negative and unpleasant appear positive and appealing.	An executive calls the firing of 200 workers "downsizing" or "reallocation of resources." Justin Timberlake refers to the highly publicized act with Janet Jackson during the 2004 Super Bowl as a "wardrobe malfunction."	Often euphemisms take the form of inflated language designed to make the mundane seem extraordinary, the common seem exotic ("the vacation of a lifetime," "unsurpassed vistas"). Don't let words get in the way of accurate firsthand perception.
Jargon is the specialized language of a professional class.	Examples of jargon include the language of the computer hacker, the psychologist, and the advertiser.	When used to intimidate or impress, as when used with people who aren't members of the profession, jargon prevents meaningful communication. Don't be intimidated by jargon; ask questions when you don't understand.
Gobbledygook is overly complex language that overwhelms the listener instead of communicating meaning.	Extra long sentences, complex grammatical constructions, and rare or unfamiliar words can constitute gobbledygook.	Some people just normally speak in complex language. But, others use complexity to confuse and mislead. Ask for simplification when appropriate.

Make special note of self-reflexive statements, statements that refer back to the speaker. People inevitably talk about themselves. Whatever a person says is, in part, a function of who that person is. Attending carefully to those personal, self-referential messages will give you great insight into the person and the person's messages.

At the same time, *don't disregard the literal meaning* in trying to uncover the message's hidden meaning. Balance your listening between the surface and the underlying meaning. Respond to the different levels of meaning in the messages of others as you would like others to respond to yours—be sensitive but not obsessive, attentive but not overly eager to uncover hidden messages.

Active and Inactive Listening

One of the most important communication skills you can learn is that of active listening (Gordon, 1975). Consider the following interaction. You're disappointed that you have to redo your entire report, and you say: "I can't believe I have to rewrite this entire budget report. I really worked hard on this project and now I have to do it all over again." To this, you get three different responses:

HIRO: That's not so bad; most people find they have to redo their first reports. That's the norm here.

MONICA: You should be pleased that all you have to do is a simple rewrite. Sylar and Nathan both had to completely redo their entire projects.

NIKI: You have to rewrite that report you've worked on for the last three weeks? You sound really angry and frustrated.

All three listeners are probably trying to make you feel better. But they go about it in very different ways and, you can be sure, with very different results. Hiro tries to lessen the significance of the rewrite. This well-intended response is extremely common but does little to promote meaningful communication and understanding. Monica tries to give the situation a positive spin. With these responses, however, both these listeners are also suggesting that you should not be feeling the way you do. They're implying that your feelings are not legitimate and should be replaced with more logical feelings.

Niki's response, however, is different from the others. Niki uses active listening. **Active listening** owes its development to Thomas Gordon (1975), who made it a cornerstone of his P-E-T (Parent Effectiveness Training) technique; it is a process of sending back to the speaker what you as a listener think the speaker meant—both in content and in feelings. Active listening, then, is not merely repeating the speaker's exact words, but rather putting together your understanding of the speaker's total message into a meaningful whole.

The Functions of Active Listening

Active listening serves several important functions. First, it helps you as a listener to check your understanding of what the speaker said and, more important, of what he or she meant. Reflecting back perceived meanings to the speaker gives the speaker an opportunity to offer clarification and correct any misunderstandings.

Second, through active listening you let the speaker know that you acknowledge and accept his or her feelings. In the sample responses given, the first two listeners challenged the speaker's feelings. Niki, the active listener, accepted what you were feeling. In addition, she also explicitly identified your feelings: "You sound angry and frustrated," allowing you an opportunity to correct her interpretation if necessary.

Third, active listening stimulates the speaker to explore feelings and thoughts. Niki's response encourages you to elaborate on your feelings, and helps you deal with them by talking them through.

A word of caution: In communicating your understanding back to the person, be especially careful to avoid sending what Gordon (1975) calls "solution messages"—messages that tell the person how he or she should feel or what he or she should do. Four types of messages send solutions, and you'll want to avoid them in your active listening:

- *Ordering messages:* "Do this . . . ." "Don't touch that . . . ."
- *Warning and threatening messages:* "If you don't do this, you'll . . . ." "If you do that, you'll . . . ."
- *Preaching and moralizing messages:* "People should all . . . ." "We all have responsibilities . . . ."
- *Advising messages:* "Why don't you . . . ." "I think you should . . . ."

The Techniques of Active Listening

Three simple techniques will prove useful as you learn to practice active listening: Paraphrase the speaker's meaning, express understanding, and ask questions.

Paraphrase the speaker's meaning. Stating in your own words what you think the speaker means and feels helps ensure understanding and also shows interest in the speaker. Paraphrasing gives the speaker a chance to extend what was originally said. Thus, when Niki echoes your thoughts, you're given the opportunity to elaborate on why rewriting the budget report means so much to you. In paraphrasing, be objective; be especially careful not to lead the speaker in the direction you think he or she should go. Also, be careful that you don't overdo paraphrase; only a very small percentage of statements need paraphrasing. Paraphrase when you feel there's a chance for misunderstanding or when you want to express support for the other person and keep the conversation going.

Express understanding of the speaker's feelings. Echo the feelings the speaker expressed or implied ("You must have felt horrible"). This expression of empathy will help you further check your perception of the speaker's feelings. This will also allow the speaker to see his or her feelings more objectively (especially helpful when they're feelings of anger, hurt, or depression) and to elaborate on them.

Ask questions. Asking questions ensures your own understanding of the speaker's thoughts and feelings and secures additional information ("How did you feel when you read your job appraisal report?"). Ask questions to provide just enough stimulation and support for the speaker to feel he or she can elaborate on these thoughts and feelings. These questions should further confirm your interest and concern for the speaker but not pry into unrelated areas or challenge the speaker in any way.

Active listening, then, is not merely repeating the speaker's exact words, but rather putting together into some meaningful whole your understanding of the speaker's total message. And incidentally, when combined with empathic listening, it proves the most effective mode for success as a salesperson (Comer & Drollinger, 1999).

As noted earlier, listening styles need to be adjusted to the specific situation. Understanding the nature and skills of these styles should help you make more reasoned and more effective listening choices.

Summary

This chapter focused on the nature of listening, the dimensions of listening that you need to consider for effective listening, the influence of culture and gender on listening, and four dimensions of effective listening.

The Importance of Listening: Professional and Relationship Benefits

1. Listening is crucial in a wide range of professions.
2. Listening is crucial to relationship success.

The Process of Listening

3. Listening is an active process of receiving, understanding, remembering, evaluating, and responding to communications.
4. Listening enables you (1) to learn, to acquire information; (2) to relate, to help form and maintain relationships; (3) to influence, to have an effect on the attitudes and behaviors of others; (4) to play, to enjoy yourself; and (5) to help, to assist others.

Listening Barriers

5. Both listener and speaker share in the responsibility for effective listening.
6. Among the obstacles to effective listening are physical and mental distractions, biases and prejudices, lack of appropriate focus, and premature judgment.

Culture, Gender, and Listening

7. Members of different cultures vary on several communication dimensions that influence listening, among them speech and language, nonverbal behavioral differences, and approaches to feedback.
8. Men and women appear to listen differently; generally, women give more specific listening cues to show they're listening than do men.

Styles of Effective Listening

9. The empathic–objective listening dimension has to do with the extent to which you focus on feeling what the speaker is feeling rather than on external reality.
10. The nonjudgmental–critical listening dimension involves the extent to which you accept and support the speaker as opposed to evaluating and analyzing.
11. The surface–depth listening dimension involves the extent to which you focus on obvious surface meanings rather than underlying hidden messages.
12. The active–inactive listening dimension relates to the extent to which you reflect back what you think the speaker means in content and feeling.

Key Terms

active and inactive listening, **94**
display rules, **88**
empathic and objective listening, **90**
evaluating, **83**

listening, **80**
long-term memory, **83**
nonjudgmental and critical listening, **91**
receiving, **81**

remembering, **83**
responding, **84**
short-term memory, **83**

surface and depth listening, **92**
understanding, **81**

Critical Thinking Questions

1 What makes a person deserving of your empathic listening? For example, would you find it more difficult to empathize with someone who was overjoyed because of winning the lottery for $7 million or with someone who was overcome with sadness because of the death of a loved one? How easy would it be for you to empathize with someone who was depressed because an expected bonus of $60,000 turned out to be only $45,000?

2 Using the four styles of listening effectiveness discussed in this chapter (empathic–objective, nonjudgmental–critical, surface–depth, and active–inactive), how would you respond in the following listening situations: (a) Your steady dating partner for the last five years tells you that spells of depression are becoming more frequent and more long lasting; (b) an instructor lectures on the contributions of ancient China to modern civilization; (c) a physician discusses your recent physical tests and makes recommendations; (d) a salesperson tells you the benefits of the new computer; (e) a gossip columnist details the secret life of your favorite movie star.

3 Here are a few situations in which you might want to use paraphrasing to ensure that you understand the speaker's thoughts and feelings. For each situation, (1) identify the thoughts you feel the speaker is expressing, (2) identify the feelings you think the speaker is experiencing, and (3) put these thoughts and feelings into a paraphrase.

■ Did you hear I got engaged to Jerry? Our racial and religious differences are really going to cause difficulties for both of us. But we'll manage.

■ I got a C on that paper. That's the worst grade I've ever received. I just can't believe that I got a C. This is my major. What am I going to do?

■ That rotten, inconsiderate pig just up and left. He never even said goodbye. We were together for six months and after one small argument he leaves without a word. And he even took my bathrobe—that expensive one he bought for my last birthday.

4 Consider this dialogue and note the active listening techniques used throughout:

PAT: That jerk demoted me. He told me I wasn't an effective manager. I can't believe he did that, after all I've done for this place.

CHRIS: I'm with you. You've been manager for three or four months now, haven't you?

PAT: A little over three months. I know it was probationary, but I thought I was doing a good job.

CHRIS: Can you get another chance?

PAT: Yes, he said I could try again in a few months. But I feel like a failure.

CHRIS: I know what you mean. It sucks. What else did he say?

PAT: He said I had trouble getting the paperwork done on time.

CHRIS: You've been late filing the reports?

PAT: A few times.

CHRIS: Is there a way to delegate the paperwork?

PAT: No, but I think I know now what needs to be done.

CHRIS: You sound as though you're ready to give that manager's position another try.

PAT: Yes, I think I am, and I'm going to let him know that I intend to apply in the next few months.

5 What would be an appropriate active listening response for each of these situations?

■ Your friend Phil has just broken up a love affair and is telling you about it. "I can't seem to get Chris out of my mind," he says. "All I do is daydream about what we used to do and all the fun we used to have."

■ A young nephew tells you that he can't talk with his parents. No matter how hard he tries, they don't listen. "I tried to tell them that I can't play baseball and I don't want to play baseball," he confides. "But they ignore me and tell me that all I need is practice."

■ Your mother has been having a difficult time at work. She was recently passed up for a promotion and received one of the lowest merit raises given in the company. "I'm not sure what I did wrong," she tells you. "I do my work, mind my own business, don't take my sick days like everyone else. How could they give that promotion to Helen, who's only been with the company for two years? Maybe I should just quit."

Choice Points

1 *Giving Antilistening Cues.* One of your friends is a storyteller; instead of talking about the world and about people, he tells endless stories—about things that happened a long time ago that he finds funny (though no one else does). You just can't deal with this any longer. Ask yourself: What can you do to get yourself out of these situations?

2 *Listening Actively.* Your six-year-old son comes home from school crying; he says that his new teacher hates him and he hates her and that he doesn't want to ever go back to school. Ask yourself: Instead of reacting with "What did you do wrong?" or some similar expression, you decide to use active listening. What do you say?

3 *Homophobic Language.* At the organization where you work, homophobic language is rampant in small groups but totally absent in formal meetings. You want to point out this hypocrisy but don't want to make enemies or have people think you're going to cause legal problems for them. Ask yourself: What options do you have for accomplishing what you want to without incurring negative reactions?

4 *Giving Listening Cues.* Often you're asked by a speaker if he or she is getting through or making sense. It seems as if speakers doubt that you're listening. But, usually at least, you are. Ask yourself: What might you do to show people you're listening to them and interested in what they're saying?

5 *Support Not Solutions.* You need to make some major decisions in your life, and you need to bounce these off someone, just to clarify things in your own mind. Your romantic partner almost always tries to solve your problems rather than simply listening supportively. Ask yourself: What can you say by way of preface to get your partner to be a supportive listener?

MyCommunicationLab Explorations

PEARSON mycommunicationlab www.mycommunicationlab.com

This group of listening experiences will help you gain new insights into listening and will help to sharpen your listening skills. ❶ Listening to Other Perspectives and ❷ How Might You Listen to New Ideas? present two creative thinking tools to sharpen a variety of skills, especially listening. ❸ Regulating Your Listening Perspective presents different scenarios that call for different types of listening to heighten your awareness of potential listening choices. ❹ Experiencing Active Listening asks you how you'd listen in a variety of situations calling for active listening. ❺ Sequential Communication, which you may recognize as the game of "telephone," will help you identify some of the major errors made in listening. ❻ Reducing Barriers to Listening asks how you'd listen effectively in difficult situations. ❼ Typical Man, Typical Woman explores some of the differences in the way we think of men and women as listeners. ❽ Paraphrasing to Ensure Understanding and ❾ How Can You Express Empathy? provide practice in essential listening skills.

CHAPTER

5 Verbal Messages

| Principles of Verbal Messages | Guidelines for Using Verbal Messages Effectively |

The Great Debaters

The Great Debaters is based on the true story of a debate team from small, largely African American, Wiley College that won debates against teams from some of the most prestigious universities in the country. Throughout the movie you see an emphasis on using language effectively and on the rewards this brings—the topics of this chapter.

As you communicate, you use two major signal systems—the verbal and the nonverbal. **Verbal messages** are those sent with words. The word *verbal* refers to words, not to orality; verbal messages consist of both oral and written words. Verbal messages do not include laughter; vocalized pauses you make when you speak, such as "er," "um," and "ah"; or responses you make to others that are oral but don't involve words, such as "ha-ha," "aha," and "ugh!" These sounds are considered nonverbal—as are, of course, facial expressions, eye movements, gestures, and so on. This chapter focuses on verbal messages; the next focuses on nonverbal messages.

Principles of Verbal Messages

To clarify the nature of verbal messages and the meanings they create in the minds of listeners, let's examine some specific principles: (1) Messages are packaged, (2) meanings are in people, (3) meanings are denotative and connotative, (4) messages vary in abstraction, (5) messages vary in politeness, (6) messages can criticize and praise, (7) messages vary in assertiveness, (8) messages can confirm and disconfirm, and (9) messages vary in cultural sensitivity. Throughout this discussion you'll find lots of useful suggestions for more effective interpersonal communication.

Messages Are Packaged

Both verbal and nonverbal signals occur simultaneously. Usually, verbal and nonverbal behaviors reinforce or support each other. For example, you don't usually express fear with words while the rest of your body relaxes. You don't normally express anger with your body posture while your face smiles. Your entire being works as a whole—verbally and nonverbally—to express your thoughts and feelings. Interestingly enough, this blending of verbal and nonverbal signals seems also to help you think and remember (Iverson & Goldin-Meadow, 1999).

You often fail to notice this "packaging" in others' messages because it seems so natural. But when the nonverbal messages of someone's posture or face contradict what is said verbally, you take special notice. For example, the person who says, "I'm so glad to see you," but avoids direct eye contact and looks around to see who else is present is sending contradictory messages. You also see contradictory or mixed messages when couples say they love each other but seem to go out of their way to hurt each other nonverbally—for example, being late for important dates, flirting with others, or avoiding touching each other.

An awareness of the packaged nature of communication, then, suggests a warning against the too-easy interpretation of another's meaning, especially as revealed in nonverbal behaviors. Before you identify or guess the meaning of any bit of behavior, look at the entire package or cluster of which it's a part, the way in which the cluster is a response to its context, and the role of the specific nonverbal behavior within that cluster. That attractive person winking in your direction may be giving you the come-on—but don't rule out the possibility of ill-fitting contact lenses.

Verbal and nonverbal messages interact with each other in six major ways: to accent, to complement, to contradict, to control, to repeat, and to substitute for each other. A brief overview of these six ways will also serve as a useful introduction to this two-chapter discussion of verbal and nonverbal messages.

- Nonverbal communication is often used to *accent*, to emphasize some part of the verbal message. You might, for example, raise your voice to underscore a particular word or phrase, bang your fist on the desk to stress your commitment, or look longingly into someone's eyes when saying "I love you."

- Nonverbal communication may be used to *complement*, to add nuances of meaning not communicated by your verbal message. Thus, you might smile when telling a story (to suggest that you find it humorous) or frown and shake your head when recounting someone's deceit (to suggest your disapproval).
- You may deliberately *contradict* your verbal messages with nonverbal movements; for example, by crossing your fingers or winking to indicate that you're lying.
- Nonverbal movements may be used to *control*, or to indicate your desire to control, the flow of verbal messages, as when you purse your lips, lean forward, or make hand movements to indicate that you want to speak. You might also put up your hand or vocalize your pauses (for example, with "um") to indicate that you have not finished and aren't ready to relinquish the floor to the next speaker.
- You can *repeat* or restate the verbal message nonverbally. You can, for example, follow your verbal "Is that all right?" with raised eyebrows and a questioning look, or you can motion with your head or hand to repeat your verbal "Let's go."
- You may also use nonverbal communication to *substitute* for verbal messages. You can, for example, signal "OK" with a hand gesture. You can nod your head to indicate yes or shake your head to indicate no.

When you communicate electronically, of course, your message is communicated by means of typed letters without facial expressions or gestures that normally accompany face-to-face communication and without the changes in rate and volume that are a part of normal telephone communication. To compensate for this lack of nonverbal behavior, the emoticon was created. Sometimes called a "smiley" after the ever-present :), the emoticon is a typed symbol that communicates through a keyboard the nuances of the message normally conveyed by nonverbal expression. The absence of the nonverbal channel through which you can clarify your message—for example, smiling or winking to communicate sarcasm or humor—make such typed symbols extremely helpful. Here are some of the more popular emoticons used in computer talk (two excellent websites contain extensive examples of smileys, emoticons, acronyms, and shorthand abbreviations: www.netlingo.com/smiley.cfm and www.netlingo.com/emailsh.cfm):

: -)	= smile; I'm only kidding
: - (	= frown; I'm feeling sad; this saddens me
*	= kiss
:-	= male
>-	= female
{ }	= hug
{ { { ***} } }	= hugs and kisses
; -)	= sly smile
this is important	= underlining, adds emphasis
this is important	= asterisks, adds emphasis
ALL CAPS	= shouting, emphasizing
<G>or<grin>	= grin

Not surprisingly, these symbols aren't used universally (Pollack, 1996). For example, because it's considered impolite for a Japanese woman to show her teeth when she smiles, the Japanese emoticon for a woman's smile is (^ . ^) where the dot signifies a closed mouth. A man's smile is written (^ _ ^). Other emoticons popular in Japan but not used in Europe or the United States are (^ ^ ;) for "cold sweat," (^ o ^ ; Ò) for "excuse me," and (^ o ^) for "happy."

Message Meanings Are in People

Meaning depends not only on the packaging of messages (the combined verbal and nonverbal elements) but also on the interaction of these messages and the receiver's own thoughts and feelings. You don't "receive" meaning; you create meaning. You construct meaning out of the messages you receive combined with your own social and cultural perspectives (beliefs, attitudes, and values, for example) (Berger & Luckmann, 1980; Delia, 1977; Delia, O'Keefe, & O'Keefe, 1982). Words don't mean; people mean.

For example, if you wanted to know the meaning of the word *love*, you'd probably turn to a dictionary. There you'd find, according to Webster's: "the attraction, desire, or affection felt for a person who arouses delight or admiration." But where would you turn if you wanted to know what Pedro means when he says, "I'm in love"? Of course, you'd turn to Pedro to discover his meaning. It's in this sense that meanings are not in words but in people. Consequently, to uncover meaning, you need to look into people and not merely into words.

Also recognize that as you change, you also change the meanings you create. That is, although the message sent may not have changed, the meanings you created from it yesterday and the meanings you create today may be quite different. Yesterday, when a special someone said, "I love you," you created certain meanings. But today, when you learn that the same "I love you" was said to three other people or when you fall in love with someone else, you drastically change the meanings you draw from those three words.

Because meanings are in people—and each person is unique and different from every other person—no word or message will mean the same thing to two different people. And this is why, for example, the same message may be perceived as controlling by one person and as a simple request by another. As you can appreciate, this type of misunderstanding can easily lead to interpersonal conflict if we fail to recognize that the meaning is not in the words; it's in the person. As a result, check your perceptions of another's meanings by asking questions, echoing what you perceive to be the other person's feelings or thoughts, seeking elaboration and clarification, and in general practicing the skills identified in the discussions of effective interpersonal perception and listening (Chapters 3 and 4).

A failure to recognize this important principle is at the heart of a common pattern of miscommunication called *bypassing*. **Bypassing** is "the miscommunication pattern which occurs when the sender (speaker, writer, and so on) and the receiver (listener, reader, and so forth) miss each other with their meanings" (Haney, 1973). Bypassing can take either of two forms.

Bypassing: Different Words, Same Meaning One type of bypassing occurs when two people use different words but give them the same meaning; on the surface there's disagreement, but at the level of meaning there's agreement. The two people actually agree but assume, because they use different words (some of which may actually never be verbalized), that they disagree. Here's an example:

> **PAT:** I'm not interested in one-night stands. I want a permanent relationship. [Meaning: I want an exclusive dating relationship.]
> **CHRIS:** I'm not ready for that. [Meaning: I'm not ready for marriage.]

Bypassing: Same Words, Different Meaning The second type is more common and occurs when two people use the same words but give the words different meanings. On the surface it looks like the two people agree (simply because they're using the same words). But if you look more closely, you see that the apparent agreement masks real disagreement, as in this example:

> **PAT:** I don't really believe in religion. [Meaning: I don't really believe in God.]
> **CHRIS:** Neither do I. [Meaning: I don't really believe in organized religions.]

Here Pat and Chris assume that they agree, but actually they disagree. At some later date the implications of these differences may well become crucial. Numerous other examples could be cited. Couples who say they're "in love" may mean very different things; one person may be thinking about "a permanent and exclusive commitment," whereas the other may be referring to "a sexual involvement." "Come home early" may mean one thing to an anxious parent and quite another to a teenager.

Because of bypassing it is a mistake to assume that when two people use the same word, they mean the same thing, or that when they use different words, they mean different things. Once again, words in themselves don't have meaning; meaning is in the people who use those words. Therefore, people can use different words but mean the same thing or use the same words but mean different things.

Meanings Are Denotative and Connotative

Consider a word such as *death*. To a doctor this word may mean the moment at which the heart stops beating. This is denotative meaning, a rather objective description of an event. To a mother whose son has just died, however, the word means much more. It recalls the son's youth, his ambitions, his family, his illness, and so on. To her, the word is emotional, subjective, and highly personal. These emotional, subjective, and personal associations are the word's connotative meaning. The **denotation** of a word is its objective definition; the **connotation** is its subjective or emotional meaning. Take another example: Compare the term *migrant* (to designate Mexicans coming into the United States to better their economic condition) with the term *settlers* (to designate Europeans who came to the United States for the same reason) (Koppelman, 2005). Though both terms describe essentially the same activity (and are essentially the same denotatively), one is often negatively evaluated and the other is more often positively valued (and so differ widely in their connotations).

Now consider a simple nod of the head in answer to the question, "Do you agree?" This gesture is largely denotative and simply says yes. But what about a wink, a smile, or an overly rapid speech rate? These nonverbal expressions are more connotative; they express your feelings rather than objective information. The denotative meaning of a message is universal; most people would agree with the denotative meanings and would give similar definitions. Connotative meanings, however, are extremely personal, and few people would agree on the precise connotative meaning of a word or nonverbal behavior.

"Snarl words" and "purr words" may further clarify the distinction between denotative and connotative meaning (Hayakawa & Hayakawa, 1989; Hoffmann, 2005). Snarl words are highly negative ("She's an idiot," "He's a pig," "They're a bunch of losers"). Sexist, racist, and heterosexist language and hate speech provide lots of other examples. Purr words are highly positive ("She's a real sweetheart," "He's a dream," "They're the greatest"). Although they may sometimes seem to have denotative meaning and refer to the "real world," snarl and purr words are actually connotative in meaning. They don't describe people or events; rather, they reveal the speaker's feelings about these people or events.

In connection with this principle, also keep in mind that verbal and nonverbal messages occur in a context that, to a large extent, determines their meaning (both denotative and connotative). The same words or behaviors may have totally different meanings when they occur in different contexts. For example, the greeting, "How are you?" means "Hello" to someone you pass regularly on the street but means "Is your health improving?" when said to a friend in the hospital. A wink to an attractive person on a bus means something completely different from a wink that signifies a put-on or a lie. The same message may be considered gracious in one culture and offensive in another culture.

Similarly, the meaning of a given signal depends on the other behavior it accompanies or is close to in time. Pounding a fist on the table during a speech in support of a politician means something quite different from that same gesture in response to news of a friend's death. Divorced from the context, both the denotative and the connotative meanings of messages can be hard to determine. Of course, even if you know the context in detail, you still may not be able to decipher the meaning of the message as the speaker intended. But understanding the context helps and raises the chances of our accurately understanding the speaker's message.

Understanding the distinction between denotation and connotation should encourage you to clarify connotative meanings (or ask for clarification) when you anticipate potential misunderstandings; misunderstandings are almost always centered on connotative differences.

Messages Vary in Abstraction

Consider the following list of terms:

- entertainment
- film
- American film
- classic American film
- *All about Eve*

UNDERSTANDING *INTERPERSONAL SKILLS*

Metacommunication

The prefix *meta-* can mean a variety of things, but as used in communication, philosophy, and psychology, its meaning is best translated as *about*. Thus, **metacommunication** is communication *about* communication, *metalanguage* is language *about* language, and a *metamessage* is a message *about* a message.

Look at it this way. You can communicate about the world—about the desk you're sitting at, the computer you're using, or the passage you're reading right now. This is called *object communication*; you're talking about objects. And the language you're using is called *object language*. But you're not limited to talking about objects. You can also talk about your talk; you can communicate about your communication. And this is referred to as metacommunication. In the same way, you can use language (that is, metalanguage) to talk about language (that is, object language). And you can talk about your messages with metamessages.

Actually, you use this distinction every day, perhaps without realizing it. For example, when you send someone an e-mail with a seemingly sarcastic comment and then put a smiley at the end, the smiley communicates about your communication; it says something like "this message is not to be taken literally; I'm trying to be humorous." The smiley is a metamessage; it's a message about a message. When you say, in preface to some comment, "I'm not sure about this, but . . .," you're communicating a message about a message; you're commenting on the message and asking that it be understood with the qualification that you may be wrong. When you conclude a comment with "I'm only kidding" you're metacommunicating; you're communicating about your communication. In relationship communication you often talk in metalanguage and say things like, "We really need to talk about the way we communicate when we're out with company" or "You're too critical" or "I love when you tell me how much you love me."

And, of course, you can also use nonverbal messages to metacommunicate. You can wink at someone to indicate that you're only kidding or sneer after saying "Yeah, that was great," with the sneer contradicting the literal meaning of the verbal message.

Increasing Metacommunication Effectiveness. Here are a few suggestions for increasing your metacommunication effectiveness:

- Explain the feelings that go with your thoughts.
- Give clear feedforward to help the other person get a general picture of the messages that will follow.
- Paraphrase your own complex messages so as to make your meaning extra clear. Similarly, check on your understanding of another's message by paraphrasing what you think the other person means.
- Ask for clarification if you have doubts about another's meaning.
- Use metacommunication when you want to clarify the communication patterns between yourself and another person: "I'd like to talk about the way you talk about me to our friends" or "I think we should talk about the way we talk about sex."

Working with Interpersonal Skills

In what ways do you normally metacommunicate? Are these generally productive? What kinds of metacommunication messages do you wish other people would use more often?

At the top is the general or abstract term *entertainment*. Note that entertainment includes all the items on the list plus various others—television, novels, drama, comics, and so on. *Film* is more specific and concrete. It includes all of the items below it as well as various other items such as Indian film or Russian film. It excludes, however, all entertainment that is not film. *American film* is again more specific and excludes all films that aren't American. *Classic American film* further limits American film to a relatively small group of highly acclaimed films. And *All about Eve* specifies concretely the one item to which reference is made.

The more general term—in this case, *entertainment*—conjures up many different images. One person may focus on television, another on music, another on comic books, and still another on radio. To some, the word *film* may bring to mind the early silent films. To others, it brings to mind high-tech special effects. To still others, it recalls Disney's animated cartoons. *All about Eve* guides the listener still further—in this case to one film. But note that even though *All about Eve* identifies one film, different listeners are likely to focus on different aspects of the film, perhaps its character development, perhaps its love story, perhaps its financial success.

Effective verbal messages include words at many levels of **abstraction**. At times an abstract, general term may suit your needs best; at other times a more concrete, specific term may serve better. Generally, however, the specific term will prove the better choice. As you get more specific—less abstract—you more effectively guide the images that will come into your listeners' minds. In much the same way that you use specific terms to direct your face-to-face listeners' attention to exactly what you want them to focus on, you also use specific terms to direct an Internet search engine to narrow its focus to (ideally) just those items you want to access.

Messages Vary in Politeness

One of the best ways to look at **politeness** (consideration, respect, etc.) in interpersonal communication is in terms of both positive and negative politeness (Goffman, 1967; Brown & Levinson, 1987; Holmes, 1995; Goldsmith, 2007, 2008; Metts & Cupach, 2008). Both of these forms of politeness are responsive to two needs that each person has. (1) Each of us wishes to be viewed positively by others, to be thought of favorably; this is referred to as maintaining **positive face**. And (2) each of us desires to be autonomous, to have the right to do as we wish; this is referred to as maintaining **negative face**. Politeness in interpersonal communication, then, involves behavior that allows others to maintain both positive and negative face.

To be more specific, to help another person maintain *positive face*, you speak respectfully to and about the person; you give the person your full attention; you say "excuse me" when appropriate. In short, you treat the person as you would want to be treated. This is called *positive politeness*. In contrast, you attack the person's positive face when you speak disrespectfully about the person, ignore the person or the person's comments, and fail to use expressions such as *thank you* and *please*. You attack a person's positive

Ask the Researcher

Talking about Difficult Topics

Do you have any suggestions for talking about really difficult relationship topics, like the use of condoms, infidelity, different religious beliefs, and the like?

The key when talking about difficult issues is not being evaluative of the other person or their attitudes—face-saving should always be allowed. Try to be as descriptive and empathic as possible—try to talk about and understand different positions without implying that your attitude is better or that there's something wrong with the other person or their attitudes. Bringing up condom use in any way other than implying that the other person has likely done something wrong usually works. Religious beliefs can be talked about by indicating you're interested in the person's beliefs without implying that yours are better. Infidelity is tough, in that it's a moral issue that implies that someone has done something wrong—betrayed someone else. Even this topic, however, can be discussed with a focus on trying to understand the other person's perspective rather than telling them what they've done wrong. Saving face is harder here. . . .

For more information see B. Reel and T. L. Thompson, "Is It a Matter of Politeness?: Face-Saving Techniques in Discussions of Safer Sex," *Southern Speech Communication Journal* 69 (2004), 99–120.

Teresa L. Thompson (Ph.D., 1980, Temple University) is professor of communication at the University of Dayton. She teaches courses in health communication, interpersonal communication, communication theory, and research methods (Thompson@udayton.edu). She edits the journal *Health Communication*.

face whenever your messages challenge the image that the person holds of himself or herself or wants to portray to others.

To help another person maintain *negative face*, you respect the person's right to be autonomous. So, for example, you request rather than demand that they do something; you say, "Would you mind opening a window?" rather than "Open that window, damn it!" You may also give the person an "out" when making a request, allowing the person to reject your request: "I know this may be a bad time, and if it is please tell me, but I'm really strapped and could use a loan of $100" rather than "Loan me a $100" or "You have to lend me $100." Or you might say, "Would it be possible for you to write me a recommendation for graduate school" rather than "I need you to write me a recommendation for graduate school." In this way you enable the person to maintain negative face through what is called *negative politeness*. Of course, we do this almost automatically, and asking for a favor without any consideration for the person's negative face needs seems totally insensitive. But attacks on negative face do occur, though sometimes in subtle forms. For example, your mother's saying, "Are you going to wear that?"—to use Deborah Tannen's example in *You're Wearing That? Understanding Mothers and Daughters in Conversation* (Random House, 2006) —attacks negative face by criticizing or challenging your autonomy. This comment also attacks positive face by questioning your ability to dress properly.

Politeness and Directness Messages that support or attack face needs (the latter are called "face-threatening acts" or FTAs) are often discussed in terms of direct and indirect language. Directness is usually less polite and may infringe on a person's need to maintain negative face—"Write me the recommendation", "Lend me $100." Indirectness, as discussed, allows the person to maintain autonomy (negative face) and provides an acceptable way for the person to refuse your request.

Indirect messages also allow you to express a desire or preference without insulting or offending anyone; they allow you to observe the rules of polite interaction. So instead of saying, "I'm bored with this group," you say, "It's getting late and I have to get up early tomorrow," or you look at your watch and pretend to be surprised by the time. Instead of saying, "This food tastes like cardboard," you say, "I just started my diet" or "I just ate."

Sometimes indirect messages allow you to ask for compliments in a socially acceptable manner. In saying, "I was thinking of getting my eyes done," you hope to get the response "Your eyes? They're perfect as they are."

As noted in the Understanding Interpersonal Theory and Research box (p. 109), women are more polite in their speech and, not surprisingly, use more indirect statements when making requests than do men. This difference seems to have both positive and negative implications. Indirect statements, in being more polite, are generally perceived positively; yet they may also be perceived negatively if they are seen as being weaker and less authoritative than more direct statements. Partly for cultural reasons, indirect statements also may be seen as manipulative or underhanded, whereas direct statements may be seen as straightforward and honest.

Influences on Politeness Politeness is considered a desirable trait across most cultures (Brown & Levinson, 1988). Cultures differ, however, in how they define politeness. For example, among English speakers politeness involves showing consideration for others and presenting yourself with confidence and polish. In Japanese it involves showing respect, especially for those in higher-status positions, and presenting yourself with modesty (Haugh, 2004). Cultures also vary in how important they consider politeness as compared with, say, openness or honesty. And, of course, cultures differ in the rules for expressing politeness or impoliteness and in the punishments for violating the accepted rules (Mao, 1994; Strecker, 1993). For example, members of Asian cultures, especially those of China and Japan, are often singled out because they emphasize politeness and mete out harsher social punishments for violations than would people in the United States or Western Europe (Fraser, 1990).

In the business world politeness is recognized as an important part of interpersonal interactions. In one study some 80 percent of employees surveyed believed that they did not get respect at work, and 20 percent felt they were victims of weekly incivility. Rudeness in the workplace, it's been argued, reduces performance effectiveness, hurts creativity, and leads to increased worker turnover—all of which is costly for the organization (Tsiantar, 2005).

Culture is, of course, not the only factor influencing politeness. Your personality and your professional training will influence your degree of politeness and how you express politeness (Edstrom, 2004). Politeness also seems to vary with the type of relationship. One researcher, for example, has proposed that politeness varies among strangers, friends, and intimates as depicted in Figure 5.1. And the context of communication will influence politeness; formal situations in which there is considerable power difference call for greater politeness than informal circumstances in which the power differences are minimal (Mullany, 2004). And, as mentioned earlier, gender also influences politeness (see the Understanding Interpersonal Theories and Research box, p. 109).

Politeness in Inclusion and Exclusion Another perspective on politeness can be seen in messages of inclusion and exclusion. Inclusive messages include all people present and acknowledge the relevance of others and are normally considered polite. Exclusive messages shut out specific people or entire cultural groups and are normally considered impolite.

You see messages of exclusion in the use of in-group language in the presence of an out-group member. When doctors get together and discuss medicine, there's no problem. But when they get together with someone who isn't a doctor, they often fail to adjust to this new person. Instead, they may continue with discussions of procedures, symptoms, medications, and so on, excluding others present. Excluding talk also occurs when people of the same nationality get together within a larger, more heterogeneous group and use the language of their nationality. Similarly, references to experiences not shared by all (experiences such as having children, exotic vacations, and people we know) can serve to include some and exclude others. The use of these terms and experiences can exclude outsiders from full participation in the communication act (Sizemore, 2004).

Another form of excluding talk is the use of the terms of your own cultural group as universal, as applying to everyone. In using such terms, you exclude others. For example, *church* refers to the place of worship for specific religions, not all religions. Similarly, *Bible* refers to the Christian religious scriptures and is not a general term for religious scriptures. Nor does the Judeo-Christian tradition include the religious traditions of everyone. Similarly, the terms *marriage, husband,* and *wife* refer to some heterosexual relationships and exclude others; in most of the world they also exclude gay and lesbian relationships.

Consider the vast array of alternative terms that are inclusive rather than exclusive. For example, the Association of American University Presses (Schwartz et al., 1995) recommends using *place of worship* instead of *church* when you wish to include the religious houses of worship of all people. Similarly, *committed relationship* is more inclusive than *marriage, couples therapy* is more inclusive than *marriage counseling,* and *life partner* is more inclusive than *husband* or *wife. Religious scriptures* is more inclusive than *Bible.* Of course, if you're referring to, say, a specific Baptist church or married heterosexual couples, then the terms *church* and *marriage* are perfectly appropriate.

Politeness on the Net The Internet has very specific rules for politeness, called netiquette (Kallos, 2005). Much as the rules of etiquette provide guidance in communicating in face-to-face social situations, the rules of netiquette provide important guidance in communicating over the Net (Berry, 2004; Fuller, 2004; Ford, 2003; Conlin, 2002; Dereshiwsky, Moan, & Gahungu, 2002). These rules not only make Internet communication more pleasant and easier but also improve your personal efficiency. Here are some key netiquette guidelines:

- *Familiarize yourself with the site before contributing.* Before asking questions about the system, read the Frequently Asked Questions (FAQs). Your question has probably been asked before, and you'll put less strain on the system. Lurk before speaking; read posted notices and conversations before you contribute anything yourself. Lurking (which, in CMC, is good) will help you learn the rules of the particular group and will help you avoid saying things you'd like to take back.
- *Be brief.* Communicate only the information that is needed; communicate clearly, briefly, and in an organized way.
- *Don't shout.* WRITING IN CAPS IS PERCEIVED AS SHOUTING. It's okay to use caps occasionally to achieve emphasis. If you wish to give emphasis, highlight _like this_ or *like this*.
- *Don't spam or flame.* Don't send unsolicited mail, repeatedly send the same mail, or post the same message (or irrelevant messages) to lots of newsgroups. Don't make personal attacks on other users. As in face-to-face conflict, personal attacks are best avoided on the Internet.
- *Avoid offensive language.* Refrain from expressions that would be considered offensive to others, such as sexist or racist terms. As you may know, software is available that will scan your e-mail, alert you if you may have broken an organizational rule, and give you a chance to revise your potentially offensive e-mail (Schwartz, 2005).

VIEWPOINT In the classic film *The Graduate*, there's a particularly good example of direct and indirect messages. Benjamin, the graduate (played by Dustin Hoffman) and Mrs. Robinson (Anne Bancroft) are having an affair. Because of the age difference and the fact that Benjamin is actually in love with Mrs. Robinson's daughter, their affair is uncomfortable and awkward. Mrs. Robinson, contrary to the research evidence showing that women are indirect, is very direct in expressing what she wants and what she doesn't want. Benjamin, also contrary to the research, is very indirect, often failing even to voice his feelings. More recently, on *Desperate Housewives*, you see teenager John calling the woman who employs him as a gardener—but with whom he's also having sex—not Gabrielle but "Mrs. Solis." Under what other types of circumstances would you think this direct/indirect pattern would be reversed, with men being the more indirect and women being more direct?

Messages Can Criticize and Praise

Throughout your communication experiences, you're expected to criticize, to evaluate, and otherwise to render judgment on some person or on something someone did or created. Especially in helping professions such as teaching, nursing, or counseling, criticism is an important and frequently used skill. The problem arises when criticism is used outside of its helping function; when it's inappropriate or excessive. An important interpersonal skill is to develop a facility for detecting when a person is asking for criticism and when that person is simply asking for a compliment. For example, when a friend asks how you like his or her new apartment, the friend may be searching for a compliment rather than wanting you to itemize all the things wrong with the place. Similarly, the person who says, "Do I look okay?" may be asking for a compliment.

Sometimes the desire to be liked (or perhaps the need to be appreciated) is so strong that we go to the other extreme and lavish praise on everything. The most ordinary jacket, the most hackneyed thought, the most average meal are given extraordinary praise, way beyond their merits. Both overly critical and overly complimentary individuals soon find that their comments are no longer met with concern or interest.

In expressing praise, keep the following in mind:

- Use I-messages. Instead of saying, "That report was good," say, "I thought that report was good" or "I liked your report."
- Make sure your affect (facial expression of feelings) is positive. Often, when people praise others simply because it's the socially correct response, they may betray their lack of conviction with too little or inappropriate affect.

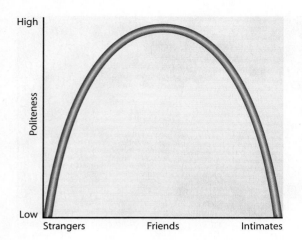

FIGURE 5.1

Wolfson's Bulge Model of Politeness

This figure depicts a proposed relationship between the levels of politeness and intimacy. Politeness, according to this model, is greatest with friends and significantly less with strangers and intimates. On another dimension, how polite is your communication with people in positions of authority—say, professors, supervisors, or police officers—compared with your communication with people in positions similar to your own—say, other students, colleagues, or neighbors? Can you phrase this comparison in the form of a communication rule?

- Name the behavior you're praising. Instead of saying, "That was good," say, "I liked your assertiveness" or "You really made them feel comfortable."
- Take culture into consideration. Many Asians, for example, feel uncomfortable when praised, because they may interpret praise as a sign of veiled criticism (Dresser, 2005).

As an alternative to excessive criticism or praise, consider the principle of honest appraisal. Tell the truth—but note that there is an art to truth telling, just as there is an art to all other forms of effective communication. First, distinguish between instances in which an honest appraisal is sought and those in which the individual needs a compliment. Respond on the appropriate level. Second, if an honest appraisal is desired and if yours is negative, give some consideration to how you should phrase your criticism.

In giving criticism, focus on the event or the behavior rather than on personality; for example, say, "This paper has four typos and has to be redone" rather than "You're a lousy typist; do this over." In offering criticism, be specific. Instead of saying, "This paper is weak," say, "I think the introduction wasn't clear enough. Perhaps a more specific statement of purpose would have worked better."

Try to state criticism positively, if at all possible. Rather than saying, "You look terrible in black," it might be more helpful to say, "You look best in bright colors." In this way, you're also being constructive; you're explaining what can be done to make the situation better. If you do express criticism that seems to prove destructive, it may be helpful to offer a direct apology or to disclaim any harmful intentions (Baron, 1990). In your positive statement of criticism, try to demonstrate that your criticism stems from your caring and concern for the other person (Hornsey, Bath, & Gunthorpe, 2004). Instead of saying, "The introduction to your report is boring," say, "I really want your report to be great; I'd open with some humor to get the group's attention." Or say, "I want you to make a good impression. I think the dark suit would work better."

Avoid implying that because of the criticism approval or affection will be withdrawn (Marano, 2008). When you criticize specific behavior rather than the person as a whole, this is less likely to happen.

Own your thoughts and feelings. Instead of saying, "Your report was unintelligible," say, "I had difficulty following your ideas." At the same time, avoid mind reading. Instead of saying, "Don't you care about the impression you make? This report is terrible," say, "I think I would use a stronger introduction and a friendlier writing style."

Be clear. Many people tend to phrase their criticism ambiguously, thinking that this will hurt less. Research suggests, however, that although ambiguous criticism may appear more polite, it also will appear less honest, less competent, and not necessarily more positive (Edwards & Bello, 2001).

Throughout this text, gender differences are discussed in a wide variety of contexts. In regard to directness, research finds that women are more indirect in giving orders, for example, than are men; they are more likely to say something like "It would be great if these letters could go out today" than "Have these letters out by three." Men are more likely to be indirect when they express weakness, reveal a problem, or admit an error. Generally, men will speak indirectly when expressing meanings that violate the masculine stereotype. Women are generally more polite and will express empathy, sympathy, and supportiveness more than men.

One researcher distinguishes three broad sets of reasons or theories to explain gender differences in communication (Holmes, 1995):

- Some theories argue that gender differences are due to innate *biological differences*. Thus, gender differences in communication, such as in politeness or in listening behavior, are the result of inherited biological factors that have evolved over millions of years.
- Other theories suggest that gender differences are due to different *patterns of socialization*. Thus, the gender differences that you observe in communication are due to the ways in which boys and girls are raised and taught.
- A third group of theories contend that gender differences are due to *inequalities in social power*. For example, because of women's lesser social power, they're more apt to communicate with greater deference and politeness than are men.

Working with Theories and Research

Based on your own observations of and interactions with men and women, what can you add to the discussion here?

Avoid ordering or directing the other person to change (remember that this attacks a person's negative face); try identifying possible alternatives. Instead of saying, "Don't be so forward when you're first introduced to someone," consider saying, "I think they might respond better to a less forward approach." Also, whether with workplace colleagues or in relationships, generally avoid what one writer has called "microinequities"—subtle putdowns, sarcastic remarks, and gestures that imply a lack of concern or interest (Lubin, 2004).

Consider the context of the criticism. Generally, it's best to express criticism in situations where you can interact with the person and express your attitudes in dialogue rather than monologue. By this principle, then, your first choice would be to express criticism face-to-face and your second choice would be by telephone; a distant third choice would be by letter, memo, or e-mail. Also, try to express your criticism in private. This is especially important when you are dealing with members of cultures in which public criticism can result in a serious loss of face.

As a receiver of criticism, consider the motivation behind the criticism. Some criticism, the kind discussed so far, is well intentioned and is designed to help you improve your performance or benefit you in some way. But some criticism is motivated by less noble purposes and may be designed to hurt or to humiliate you. Criticism that is not constructive needs to be examined mindfully. Criticism uttered in conflict or in times of rising emotions may be harsher and more hurtful than criticism given in calmer moments.

Messages Vary in Assertiveness

If you disagree with other people in a group, do you speak your mind? Do you allow others to take advantage of you because you're reluctant to say what you want? Do you feel uncomfortable when you have to state your opinion in a group? Questions such as these speak to your degree of **assertiveness**. Before reading further about this aspect of communication, take the self-test "How Assertive Are Your Messages?"

✎ TEST YOURSELF

HOW ASSERTIVE ARE YOUR MESSAGES?

Indicate how true each of the following statements is about your own communication. Respond instinctively rather than in the way you feel you should respond. Use the following scale: 5 = always or almost always true; 4 = usually true; 3 = sometimes true, sometimes false; 2 = usually false; and 1 = always or almost always false.

_____ 1. I would express my opinion in a group even if my view contradicted the opinions of others.

_____ 2. When asked to do something that I really don't want to do, I can say no without feeling guilty.

_____ 3. I can express my opinion to my superiors on the job.

_____ 4. I can start up a conversation with a stranger on a bus or at a business gathering without fear.

_____ 5. I voice objection to people's behavior if I feel it infringes on my rights.

HOW DID YOU DO? All five items in this test identified characteristics of assertive communication. So high scores (say about 20 and above) would indicate a high level of assertiveness. Low scores (say about 10 and below) would indicate a low level of assertiveness.

WHAT WILL YOU DO? The discussion in this section clarifies the nature of assertive communication and offers guidelines for increasing your own assertiveness. Consider these suggestions as ways to increase your own assertiveness and at the same time to reduce your aggressive tendencies when appropriate.

Assertive people operate with an "I win, you win" philosophy; they assume that both parties can gain something from an interpersonal interaction, even from a confrontation. Assertive people are more positive and score lower on measures of hopelessness than do nonassertive people (Velting, 1999). Assertive people are willing to assert their own rights. Unlike their aggressive counterparts, however, they don't hurt others in the process. Assertive people speak their minds and welcome others doing likewise.

Do realize that as with many other aspects of communication, there will be wide cultural differences when it comes to assertiveness. For example, the values of assertiveness are more likely to be extolled in individualist cultures than in collectivist cultures. Assertiveness will be valued more by those cultures that stress competition, individual success, and independence. It will be valued much less by those cultures that stress cooperation, group success, and the interdependence of all members on one another. American students, for example, are found to be significantly more assertive than Japanese or Korean students (Thompson, Klopf, & Ishii, 1991; Thompson & Klopf, 1991). Thus, for some situations, assertiveness may be an effective strategy in one culture but may create problems in another. Assertiveness with an elder in many Asian and Hispanic cultures may be seen as insulting and disrespectful.

Most people are nonassertive in certain situations. If you're one of these people and if you wish to increase your assertiveness, consider the following steps (Windy & Constantinou, 2005; Bower & Bower, 2005). (If you are always nonassertive and are unhappy about this, then you may need to work with a therapist to change your behavior.)

Analyze Assertive Communications The first step in increasing your assertiveness skills is to understand the nature of assertive communications. Observe and analyze the messages of others. Learn to distinguish the differences among assertive, aggressive, and nonassertive messages. Focus on what makes one behavior assertive and another behavior nonassertive or aggressive. After you've gained some skills in observing the behaviors of others, turn your analysis to yourself. Analyze situations in which you're normally assertive and situations in which you're more likely to act nonassertively or aggressively. What characterizes these situations? What do the situations in which you're normally assertive have in common? How do you speak? How do you communicate nonverbally?

Rehearse Assertive Communications One way to rehearse assertiveness is to use desensitization techniques (Wolpe, 1958; Dwyer, 2005). Select a situation in which you're normally nonassertive. Build a hierarchy that begins with a relatively non-threatening message and ends with the desired communication. For example, let's say that you have difficulty voicing your opinion to your supervisor at work. The desired behavior, then, is to tell your supervisor your opinions. To desensitize yourself, construct a hierarchy of visualized situations leading up to this desired behavior. Such a hierarchy might begin with visualizing yourself talking with your boss. Visualize this scenario until you can do it without any anxiety or discomfort. Once you have mastered this visualization, visualize a step closer to your goal, such as walking into your boss's office. Again, do this until your visualization creates no discomfort. Continue with these successive visualizations until you can visualize yourself telling your boss your opinion. As with the other visualizations, do this until you can do it while totally relaxed. This is the mental rehearsal. You might add a vocal dimension to this by actually acting out (with voice and gesture) your telling your boss your opinion. Again, do this until you experience no difficulty or discomfort. Next, try doing this in front of a trusted and supportive friend or group of friends. Ideally this interaction will provide you with useful feedback. After this rehearsal, you're probably ready for the next step.

Communicate Assertively This step is naturally the most difficult but obviously the most important. Here's a generally effective pattern to follow in communicating assertively:

1. Describe the problem; don't evaluate or judge it. "We're all working on this advertising project together. You're missing half our meetings, and you still haven't produced your first report." Be sure to use I-messages and to avoid messages that accuse or blame the other person.
2. State how this problem affects you; tell the person how you feel. "My job depends on the success of this project, and I don't think it's fair that I have to do extra work to make up for what you're not doing."
3. Propose solutions that are workable and that allow the person to save face. Describe or visualize the situation if your solution were put into effect. "If you can get your report to the group by Tuesday, we'll still be able to meet our deadline. I could give you a call on Monday to remind you."
4. Confirm understanding. "It's clear that we can't produce this project if you're not going to pull your own weight. Will you have the report to us by Tuesday?"

Keep in mind that assertiveness is not always the most desirable response. Assertive people are assertive when they want to be, but they can be nonassertive if the situation calls for it. For example, you might wish to be nonassertive in a situation in which assertiveness might emotionally hurt the other person. Let's say that an older relative wishes you to do something for her or him. You could assert your rights and say no, but in doing so you would probably hurt this person; it might be better simply to do as asked. Of course, there are limits that should be observed. You should be careful, in such a situation, that you're not hurt instead.

A note of caution should be added to this discussion. It's easy to visualize a situation in which, for example, people are talking behind you in a movie, and with your newfound enthusiasm for assertiveness, you tell them to be quiet. It's also easy to see yourself getting smashed in the teeth as a result. In applying the principles of assertive communication, be careful that you don't go beyond what you can handle effectively.

VIEWPOINT Hate speech is speech that is hostile, offensive, degrading, or intimidating to a particular group of people. Women, African Americans, Muslims, Hispanics, and gay men and lesbians are among the major targets of hate speech in the United States. Hate speech often occurs in interpersonal interactions, for example, insulting people because they are from a particular group, posting degrading comments about various groups on social network sites or blogs, or avoiding interacting with people from certain groups or not inviting them to activities to which they would be invited if they were not a member of the hated group. Of course, you also see hate speech in computer games that are configured to target members of minority groups or websites that insult and demean certain groups and at the same time encourage hostility toward members of these groups (Rivlin, 2005). On your college campus, which would be most likely to be considered hate speech: sexist, heterosexist, racist, or ageist language? Which would be least likely? How do you respond when you hear other students using sexist language? Heterosexist language? Racist language? Ageist language?

Messages Can Confirm and Disconfirm

The language behaviors known as confirmation and disconfirmation have to do with the extent to which you acknowledge another person. Consider this situation. You've been living with someone for the last six months and you arrive home late one night. Your partner, let's say Pat, is angry and complains about your being so late. Of the following responses, which are you most likely to give?

1. Stop screaming. I'm not interested in what you're babbling about. I'll do what I want, when I want. I'm going to bed.
2. What are you so angry about? Didn't you get in three hours late last Thursday when you went to that office party? So knock it off.
3. You have a right to be angry. I should have called to tell you I was going to be late, but I got involved in a serious debate at work, and I couldn't leave until it was resolved.

In response 1, you dismiss Pat's anger and even indicate dismissal of Pat as a person. In response 2, you reject the validity of Pat's reasons for being angry, although you do not dismiss either Pat's feelings of anger or of Pat as a person. In response 3, you acknowledge Pat's anger and the reasons for being angry. In addition, you provide some kind of explanation and, in doing so, show that both Pat's feelings and Pat as a person are important and that Pat has the right to know what happened. The first response is an example of disconfirmation, the second of rejection, and the third of confirmation.

Psychologist William James once observed that "no more fiendish punishment could be devised, even were such a thing physically possible, than that one should be turned loose in society and remain absolutely unnoticed by all the members thereof." In this often-quoted observation, James identifies the essence of disconfirmation (Watzlawick, Beavin, & Jackson, 1967; Veenendall & Feinstein, 1995).

Disconfirmation is a communication pattern in which you ignore a person's presence as well as that person's communications. You say, in effect, that the person and what she or he has to say aren't worth serious attention. Disconfirming responses often lead to loss of self-esteem (Sommer, Williams, Ciarocco, & Baumeister, 2001).

Note that disconfirmation is not the same as rejection. In **rejection**, you disagree with the person; you indicate your unwillingness to accept something the other person says or does. In disconfirming someone, however, you deny that person's significance; you claim that what this person says or does simply does not count.

Confirmation is the opposite communication pattern. In **confirmation**, you not only acknowledge the presence of the other person but also indicate your acceptance of this person, of this person's definition of self, and of your relationship as defined or viewed by this other person. Confirming responses often lead to gains in self-esteem and have been shown to reduce student apprehension in the classroom and indirectly to increase motivation and learning (Ellis, 2004). You can communicate both confirmation and disconfirmation in a wide variety of ways; Table 5.1 shows just a few.

You can gain insight into a wide variety of offensive language practices by viewing them as types of disconfirmation—as language that alienates and separates. We'll explore this important principle by looking at racism, heterosexism, ageism, and sexism. Another significant -ism is **ableism**—discrimination against people with disabilities. This particular practice is handled throughout the text in a series of tables offering tips for communicating between people with and without a variety of disabilities:

- between people who are visually impaired and those who aren't (Chapter 1)
- between people with and without disabilities (Chapter 2)
- between people with and without hearing problems (Chapter 4)
- between people with and without speech and language disorders (Chapter 8)

Racism According to Andrea Rich (1974), "any language that, through a conscious or unconscious attempt by the user, places a particular racial or ethnic group in an inferior position is racist." **Racist language** expresses racist attitudes. It also, however, contributes to the development of racist attitudes in those who use or hear the language. Even when

Table 5.1 Confirmation and Disconfirmation

This table identifies some specific confirming and disconfirming messages. As you review this table, try to imagine a specific illustration for each of the ways of communicating disconfirmation and confirmation (Pearson, 1993; Galvin, Bylund, & Brommel, 2004).

Confirmation	Disconfirmation
Acknowledge the presence and the contributions of the other person by either supporting or taking issue with what he or she says.	Ignore the presence or contributions of the other person; express indifference to what the other person says.
Make nonverbal contact by maintaining direct eye contact and, when appropriate, touching, hugging, kissing, and otherwise demonstrating acknowledgment of the other.	Make no nonverbal contact; avoid direct eye contact; avoid touching and general nonverbal closeness.
Engage in dialogue (communication in which both persons are speakers and listeners; both are involved; both are concerned with and have respect for each other).	Engage in monologue (communication in which one person speaks and one person listens; there is no real interaction; there is no real concern or respect for each other).
Demonstrate understanding of what the other person says and means and reflect your understanding in what you say, or when in doubt ask questions.	Jump to interpretation or evaluation rather than working at understanding what the other person means.
Acknowledge the other person's requests; answer the other person's questions; return phone calls and e-mails.	Ignore the other person's requests; fail to answer questions; don't return phone calls or reply to e-mails.
Encourage the other person to express his or her thoughts and feelings by showing interest and asking questions.	Interrupt or otherwise make it difficult for the other person to express himself or herself.
Respond directly and exclusively to what the other person says.	Avoid responding, or respond tangentially by acknowledging the other person's comment but shifting the focus of the message in another direction.

racism is subtle, unintentional, or even unconscious, its effects are systematically damaging (Dovidio, Gaertner, Kawakami, & Hodson, 2002).

Racism exists on both individual and institutional levels, distinctions made by educational researchers and used throughout this discussion (Koppelman, 2005). **Individual racism** involves the negative attitudes and beliefs that people hold about specific races. The assumption that certain races are intellectually inferior to others or that certain races are incapable of certain achievements are clear examples of individual racism. Prejudice against groups such as American Indians, African Americans, Hispanics, and Arabs have been with us throughout history and is still a part of many people's lives today. Such racism is seen in the negative terms people use to refer to members of other races and to disparage their customs and accomplishments.

Institutionalized racism is seen in patterns such as de facto school segregation, companies' reluctance to hire members of minority groups, and banks' unwillingness to extend mortgages and business loans to members of some races or tendency to charge higher interest rates.

Examine your own language racism. Do you:

- use derogatory terms for members of a particular race?
- perceive and interact with members of other races through stereotypes perpetuated by the media?
- include reference to race when it's irrelevant, as in "the African American surgeon" or "the Asian athlete"?
- attribute individuals' economic or social problems to the individuals' race rather than to institutionalized racism or general economic problems that affect everyone?

Heterosexism Heterosexism also exists on both an individual and an institutional level. **Individual heterosexism** consists of attitudes, behaviors, and language that disparage gay men and lesbians and includes the belief that all sexual behavior that is not heterosexual is unnatural and deserving of criticism and condemnation. These beliefs are at the heart of

What do you feel is the current status of sexism and sexist language in your area of the world? Can you identify specific types of sexism that you've observed? In what types of situations is sexism seen most clearly (for example, on the job, in schools, in the military, in the ministry)?

antigay violence and "gay bashing." Individual heterosexism also includes such beliefs as the notions that homosexuals are more likely to commit crimes than are heterosexuals (there's actually no difference) and to molest children than are heterosexuals (actually, child molesters are overwhelmingly heterosexual, married men) (Abel & Harlow, 2001; Koppelman, 2005). It also includes the belief that homosexuals cannot maintain stable relationships or effectively raise children, beliefs that contradict research evidence (Fitzpatrick, Jandt, Myrick, & Edgar, 1994; Johnson & O'Connor, 2002).

Institutional heterosexism is easy to identify. For example, the ban on gay marriage in many states and the fact that at this time only one state (Massachusetts) allows gay marriage is a good example of institutional heterosexism. Other examples include the Catholic Church's ban on homosexual priests, the United States military's prohibition barring openly gay people from serving in the armed forces, and the many laws prohibiting adoption of children by gay people. In some cultures homosexual relations are illegal (for example, in India, Malaysia, Pakistan, and Singapore); penalties range from a "misdemeanor" charge in Liberia to life in jail in Singapore and death in Pakistan.

Heterosexist language includes derogatory terms used for lesbians and gay men. For example, surveys in the military showed that 80 percent of those surveyed heard "offensive speech, derogatory names, jokes or remarks about gays" and that 85 percent believed that such derogatory speech was "tolerated" (*New York Times*, March 25, 2000, p. A12). You also see heterosexism in more subtle forms of language usage; for example, when you qualify a professional—as in "gay athlete" or "lesbian doctor"—and, in effect, say that athletes and doctors are not normally gay or lesbian.

Still another form of heterosexism is the presumption of heterosexuality. Usually, people assume the person they're talking to or about is heterosexual. And usually they're correct, because most people are heterosexual. At the same time, however, this presumption denies the lesbian or gay identity a certain legitimacy. The practice is very similar to the presumptions of whiteness and maleness that we have made significant inroads in eliminating.

Here are a few additional suggestions for avoiding heterosexist (or what some call homophobic) language. Do you:

- use offensive nonverbal mannerisms that parody stereotypes when talking about gay men and lesbians? Do you avoid the "startled eye blink" with which some people react to gay couples (Mahaffey, Bryan, & Hutchison, 2005)?
- "compliment" gay men and lesbians by saying that they "don't look it"? To gay men and lesbians, this is not a compliment. Similarly, expressing disappointment that a person is gay—often thought to be a compliment, as in comments such as "What a waste!"—is not really a compliment.
- make the assumption that every gay or lesbian knows what every other gay or lesbian is thinking? It's very similar to asking a Japanese person why Sony is investing heavily in the United States or, as one comic put it, asking an African American, "What do you think Jesse Jackson meant by that last speech?"
- stereotype? Saying things like "Lesbians are so loyal" or "Gay men are so open with their feelings," which ignore the reality of wide differences within any group, are potentially insulting to all groups.
- overattribute, the tendency to attribute just about everything a person does, says, and believes to the fact that the person is gay or lesbian? This tendency helps to activate and perpetuate stereotypes.
- forget that relationship milestones are important to all people? Ignoring anniversaries or birthdays of, say, a relative's partner is resented by everyone.

As you think about heterosexism, recognize not only that heterosexist language will create barriers to communication but also that its absence will foster more meaningful communication: greater comfort, an increased willingness to disclose personal information, and a greater willingness to engage in future interactions (Dorland & Fisher, 2001).

Ageism Although used mainly to refer to prejudice against older people, the word **ageism** can also refer to prejudice against other age groups. For example, if you describe all teenagers as selfish and undependable, you're discriminating against a group purely because of their age, and thus are ageist in your statements. In some cultures—some Asian and some African cultures, for example—the old are revered and respected. Younger people seek them out for advice on economic, ethical, and relationship issues.

Individual ageism is seen in the general disrespect many show toward older people and in negative stereotypes about older people. **Institutional ageism** is seen in mandatory retirement laws and age restrictions in certain occupations (as opposed to requirements based on demonstrated competence). In less obvious forms, ageism is seen in the media's portrayal of old people as incompetent, complaining, and, perhaps most clearly evidenced in both television and films, without romantic feelings. Rarely, for example, does a TV show or film show older people working productively, being cooperative and pleasant, and engaging in romantic and sexual relationships.

Popular language is replete with examples of linguistic ageism; "little old lady," "old hag," "old-timer," "over the hill," "old coot," and "old fogy" are a few examples. As with sexism, qualifying a description of someone in terms of his or her age demonstrates ageism. For example, if you refer to "a quick-witted 75-year-old" or "an agile 65-year-old" or "a responsible teenager," you're implying that these qualities are unusual in people of these ages and thus need special mention. You're saying that "quick-wittedness" and "being 75" do not normally go together. The problem with this kind of stereotyping is that it's simply wrong. There are many 75-year-olds who are extremely quick-witted (and many 30-year-olds who aren't).

You also communicate ageism when you speak to older people in overly simple words, or explain things that don't need explaining. Nonverbally, you demonstrate ageist communication when, for example, you avoid touching an older person but touch others, or when you avoid making direct eye contact with the older person but readily do so with others, or when you speak at an overly high volume (suggesting that all older people have hearing difficulties).

One useful way to avoid ageism is to recognize and avoid the illogical stereotypes that ageist language is based on. Do you:

- talk down to a person because he or she is older? Older people are not mentally slow; most people remain mentally alert well into old age.
- refresh an older person's memory each time you see the person? Older people can and do remember things.
- imply that romantic relationships are no longer important? Older people continue to be interested in relationships.
- speak at an abnormally high volume? Being older does not mean being hard of hearing or being unable to see; most older people hear and see quite well, sometimes with hearing aids or glasses.
- avoid engaging older people in conversation as you would wish to be engaged? Older people are interested in the world around them.

Even though you want to avoid ageist communication, there are times when you may wish to make adjustments when talking with someone who does have language or communication difficulties. The American Speech and Hearing Association offers several useful suggestions (www.asha.org/public/speech/development/communicating-better-with-older-people.htm, accessed June 3, 2006):

- Reduce as much background noise as you can.
- Ease into the conversation by beginning with casual topics and then moving into more familiar topics. Stay with each topic for a while; avoid jumping too quickly from one topic to another.

- Speak in relatively short sentences and questions.
- Give the person added time to respond. Some older people react more slowly and need extra time.
- Listen actively. Practice the skills of active listening discussed in Chapter 4.

Sexism **Individual sexism** consists of prejudicial attitudes and beliefs about men or women based on rigid beliefs about gender roles. These might include such beliefs as the ideas that women should be caretakers, should be sensitive at all times, and should acquiesce to a man's decisions concerning political or financial matters. Sexist attitudes would also include the nations that men are insensitive, interested only in sex, and incapable of communicating feelings.

Institutional sexism, on the other hand, results from customs and practices that discriminate against people because of their gender. Clear examples in business and industry are the widespread practice of paying women less than men for the same job and the discrimination against women in the upper levels of management. Another clear example of institutionalized sexism is the courts' practice of automatically or near-automatically granting child custody to the mother rather than the father.

Of particular interest here is **sexist language**: language that puts down someone because of his or her gender (a term usually used to refer to language derogatory toward women). The National Council of Teachers of English (NCTE) has proposed guidelines for nonsexist (gender-free, gender-neutral, or sex-fair) language. These guidelines concern the use of the generic word *man*, the use of generic *he* and *his*, and sex-role stereotyping (Penfield, 1987). Consider your own communication behavior. Do you

- use *man* generically? Using the term to refer to humanity in general emphasizes maleness at the expense of femaleness. Gender-neutral terms can easily be substituted. Instead of "mankind," say "humanity," "people," or "human beings." Similarly, the use of terms such as *policeman* or *fireman* that presume maleness as the norm—and femaleness as a deviation from this norm—are clear and common examples of sexist language.
- use *he* and *his* as generic? Instead, you can alternate pronouns or restructure your sentences to eliminate any reference to gender. For example, the NCTE Guidelines (Penfield, 1987) suggest that instead of saying, "The average student is worried about his grades," you say, "The average student is worried about grades."
- use sex-role stereotyping? When you make the hypothetical elementary school teacher female and the college professor male or refer to doctors as male and nurses as female, you're sex-role stereotyping, as you are when you include the sex of a professional with terms such as "woman doctor" or "male nurse."

Racist, Heterosexist, Ageist, and Sexist Listening
Just as racist, heterosexist, ageist, and sexist attitudes will influence your language, they can also influence your listening if you hear what speakers are saying through the stereotypes you hold. Prejudiced listening occurs when you listen differently to a person because of his or her gender, race, affectional orientation, or age even though these characteristics are irrelevant to the message.

Racist, heterosexist, ageist, and sexist listening occurs in lots of situations. For example, when you dismiss a valid argument—or attribute validity to an invalid argument—because the speaker is of a particular race, affectional orientation, age group, or gender, you're listening with prejudice.

Of course, there are many instances when these characteristics are relevant and pertinent to your evaluation of a message. For example, the sex of a person who is talking about pregnancy, fathering a child, birth control, or surrogate motherhood is, most would agree, probably relevant to the message. So in these cases it is not sexist listening to take the sex of the speaker into consideration. It is, however, sexist listening to assume that only one sex can be an authority on a particular topic or that one sex's opinions are without value. The same is true in relation to listening through a person's race or affectional orientation.

Messages Vary in Cultural Sensitivity

Recognizing that messages vary in cultural sensitivity is a great step toward developing confirming and avoiding disconfirming messages. Perhaps the best way to develop non-racist, nonheterosexist, nonageist, and nonsexist language is to examine the preferred **cultural identifiers** to use in talking to and about members of different groups. Keep in mind, however, that preferred terms frequently change over time, so keep in touch with the most current preferences. The preferences and many of the specific examples identified here are drawn largely from the findings of the Task Force on Bias-Free Language of the Association of American University Presses (Schwartz, 1995; Faigley, 2009).

Race and Nationality Generally, most African Americans prefer *African American* to *black* (Hecht, Jackson, & Ribeau, 2003), although *black* is often used with *white*, as well as in a variety of other contexts (for example, Department of Black and Puerto Rican Studies, the *Journal of Black History*, and Black History Month). The American Psychological Association recommends that both terms be capitalized, but the *Chicago Manual of Style* (the manual used by most newspapers and publishing houses) recommends using lowercase. The terms *Negro* and *colored*, although used in the names of some organizations (for example, the United Negro College Fund and the National Association for the Advancement of Colored People), are no longer used outside these contexts. *People of color*—a literary-sounding term appropriate perhaps to public speaking but awkward in most conversations—is preferred to *nonwhite*, which implies that whiteness is the norm and nonwhiteness is a deviation from that norm.

White is generally used to refer to those whose roots are in European cultures and usually does not include Hispanics. Analogous to African American (which itself is based on a long tradition of terms such as Irish American and Italian American) is the phrase *European American*. Few European Americans, however, call themselves that; most prefer their national origins emphasized, as in, for example, German American or Greek American. This preference may well change as Europe moves toward becoming a more cohesive and united entity.

Generally, the term *Hispanic* refers to anyone who identifies himself or herself as belonging to a Spanish-speaking culture. *Latina* (female) and *Latino* (male) refer to persons whose roots are in one of the Latin American countries, such as Haiti, the Dominican Republic, Nicaragua, or Guatemala. *Hispanic American* refers to U.S. residents whose ancestry is in a Spanish culture; the term includes people from Mexico, the Caribbean, and Central and South America. In emphasizing a Spanish heritage, however, the term is really inaccurate, because it leaves out the large numbers of people in the Caribbean and in South America whose origins are African, Native American, French, or Portuguese. *Chicana* (female) and *Chicano* (male) refer to persons with roots in Mexico, although it often connotes a nationalist attitude (Jandt, 2004) and is considered offensive by many Mexican Americans. *Mexican American* is generally preferred.

Inuk (plural *Inuit*), also spelled with two n's (*Innuk* and *Innuit*), is preferred to *Eskimo* (the term the U.S. Census Bureau uses), which was applied to the indigenous peoples of Alaska and Canada by Europeans and literally means "raw meat eaters."

The word *Indian* technically refers only to someone from India, not to members of other Asian countries or to the indigenous peoples of North America. *American Indian* or *Native American* is preferred, even though many Native Americans do refer to themselves as *Indians* and *Indian people*. The word *squaw*, used to refer to a Native American woman and still used in the names of some places in the United States and in some textbooks, is clearly a term to be avoided; its usage is almost always negative and insulting (Koppelman, 2005).

In Canada indigenous people are called *first people* or *first nations*. The term *native American* (with a lowercase *n*) is most often used to refer to persons born in the United States. Although technically the term could refer to anyone born in North or South America, people outside the United States generally prefer more specific designations such as *Argentinean*, *Cuban*, or *Canadian*. The term *native* describes an indigenous inhabitant; it is not used to indicate "someone having a less developed culture."

Muslim (rather than the older *Moslem*) is the preferred form to refer to a person who adheres to the religious teachings of Islam. *Quran* (rather than *Koran*) is the preferred term for the scriptures of Islam. *Jewish people* is often preferred to *Jews*, and *Jewess* (a Jewish female) is considered derogatory. Finally, the term *non-Christian* is to be avoided: It implies that people who have other beliefs deviate from the norm.

When history was being written from a European perspective, Europe was taken as the focal point and the rest of the world was defined in terms of its location relative to that continent. Thus, Asia became the East or the Orient, and *Asians* became *Orientals*—a term that is today considered inappropriate or "Eurocentric." Thus, people from Asia are *Asians*, just as people from Africa are *Africans* and people from Europe are *Europeans*.

Affectional Orientation Generally, *gay* is the preferred term to refer to a man who has an affectional orientation toward other men, and *lesbian* is the preferred term for a woman who has an affectional orientation toward other women (Lever, 1995). ("Lesbian" means "homosexual woman," so the term *lesbian woman* is redundant.) Homosexual can refer to both gays and lesbians, but more often describes a same-sex sexual orientation. The terms *gay* and *lesbian* refer to a lifestyle and not just to sexual orientation. *Gay* as a noun, although widely used, may prove offensive in some contexts, as in "We have two gays on the team." Because most scientific thinking holds that sexuality is not a matter of choice, the terms *sexual orientation* and *affectional orientation* are preferred to *sexual preference* or *sexual status* (which is also vague).

Age *Older person* is preferred to *elder*, *elderly*, *senior*, or *senior citizen* (which technically refers to someone older than 65). Usually, however, terms designating age are unnecessary. There are times, of course, when you'll need to refer to a person's age group, but most of the time age is irrelevant—in much the same way that racial or affectional orientation terms are usually irrelevant.

Sex Generally, the term *girl* should be used only to refer to very young females and is equivalent to *boy*. *Girl* is never used to refer to a grown woman, nor is *boy* used to refer to people in blue-collar positions, as it once was. *Lady* is negatively evaluated by many because it connotes the stereotype of the prim and proper woman. *Woman* or *young woman* is preferred.

Guidelines for Using Verbal Messages Effectively

Our examination of the principles governing the verbal messages system has suggested a wide variety of ways to use language more effectively. Here are some additional guidelines for making your own verbal messages more effective and a more accurate reflection of the world in which we live. We'll consider six such guidelines: (1) Extensionalize: avoid intensional orientation; (2) see the individual: avoid allness, (3) distinguish between facts and inferences: avoid fact–inference confusion, (4) discriminate among: avoid indiscrimination, (5) talk about the middle: avoid polarization, and (6) update messages: avoid static evaluation.

Extensionalize: Avoid Intensional Orientation

The term **intensional orientation** refers to a tendency to view people, objects, and events in terms of how they're talked about or labeled rather than in terms of how they actually exist. **Extensional orientation** is the opposite: It's a tendency to look first at the actual people, objects, and events and then at the labels—a tendency to be guided by what you see happening rather than by the way something or someone is talked about or labeled.

Intensional orientation occurs when you act as if the words and labels were more important than the things they represent—as if the map were more important than the territory. In its extreme form, intensional orientation is seen in the person who is afraid of dogs and who begins to sweat when shown a picture of a dog or when hearing people talk about dogs. Here the person is responding to a label as if it were the actual thing. In its more common form, intensional orientation occurs when you see people through your schemata

Ethics in Interpersonal Communication

Lying

Lying occurs when you send messages designed to make others believe what you know to be untrue (Ekman, 1985; Burgoon & Hoobler, 2002). You can lie by commission (by making explicitly false statements or even by being evasive or misleading) or by omission (by omitting relevant information and so allowing others to draw incorrect inferences). Similarly, you can lie verbally (in speech or writing) or nonverbally (wearing an innocent facial expression instead of acknowledging the commission of some wrong, or nodding knowingly instead of expressing honest ignorance) (O'Hair, Cody, & McLaughlin, 1981). Lies range from "white lies" and truth stretching to lies that form the basis of relationship infidelity, libel, and perjury. And, not surprisingly, lies have ethical implications.

- Some lies may be considered ethical; for example, lying to a child to protect a fantasy belief in Santa Claus or the tooth fairy, or publicly agreeing with someone to enable the person to save face.

- Some lies may be considered not only ethical but required; for example, lying to protect someone from harm.

- Other lies are always considered unacceptable and unethical; for example, lying to defraud investors or to falsely accuse someone.

What would you do?

You've been asked to serve as a witness in the trial of someone suspected of robbing a local grocery store. You don't want to get involved—yet you wonder if you can ethically refuse and say you didn't see anything (even though you did). There are other witnesses, and your testimony is not likely to make a significant difference. What would you do?

---

instead of on the basis of their specific behaviors. For example, it occurs when you think of a professor as an unworldly egghead before getting to know the specific professor.

The corrective to intensional orientation is to focus first on the object, person, or event and then on the way in which the object, person, or event is talked about. Labels are certainly helpful guides, but don't allow them to obscure what they're meant to symbolize.

See the Individual: Avoid Allness

The world is infinitely complex, and because of this you can never say all there is to say about anything—at least not logically. This is particularly true when you are dealing with people. You may think you know all there is to know about certain individuals or about why they did what they did, yet clearly you don't know all. You can never know all the reasons you yourself do something, so there is no way you can know all the reasons your parents, friends, or enemies did something.

Suppose, for example, you go on a first date with someone who, at least during the first hour or so, turns out to be less interesting than you would have liked. Because of this initial impression, you may infer that this person is dull, always and everywhere. Yet it could be that this person is simply ill at ease or shy during first meetings. The problem here is that you run the risk of judging a person on the basis of a very short acquaintanceship. Further, if you then define this person as dull, you're likely to treat the person as dull and fulfill your own prophecy.

The parable of the six blind men and the elephant is an excellent example of an **allness** orientation—the tendency to judge the whole on the basis of experience with part of the whole—and its attendant problems. You may recall from elementary school the poem by John Saxe that concerns six learned blind men of Indostan who came to examine an elephant, an animal they had only heard about. The first blind man touched the elephant's side and concluded that an elephant was like a wall. The second felt the tusk and said an elephant must be like a spear. The third held the trunk and concluded that an elephant was much like a snake. The fourth touched the knee and decided that an elephant was like a tree. The fifth felt the ear and said an elephant was like a fan. The sixth grabbed the tail and concluded that an elephant was like a rope. Each of these learned men reached his own conclusion regarding what an elephant was really like. Each argued that he was correct and that the others were wrong.

Many people feel that it's permissible for members of a particular subculture to refer to themselves in terms that if said by outsiders would be considered racist, sexist, or heterosexist. Some researchers suggest a possible problem with this—the idea that these terms may actually reinforce negative stereotypes that the larger society has already assigned to the group (cf. Guerin, 2003). By using these terms members of the group may come to accept the labels with their negative connotations and thus contribute to their own stereotyping and their own deprecation. Others would argue that by using such labels groups weaken the terms' negative impact. Do you refer to yourself using terms that would be considered offensive or politically incorrect if said by "outsiders"? What effects, if any, do you think such self-talk has?

Each, of course, was correct; at the same time, however, all were wrong. The point this parable illustrates is that you can never see all of anything; you can never experience anything fully. You see part of an object, event, or person—and on that limited basis, you conclude what the whole is like. This procedure is universal, and you follow it because you cannot possibly observe everything. Yet recognize that when making judgments of the whole based on only a part, you're actually making inferences that can later be proved wrong. If you assume that you know everything there is to know about something or someone, you fall into the pattern of misevaluation called allness.

Famed British Prime Minister Benjamin Disraeli once said that "to be conscious that you are ignorant is a great step toward knowledge." This observation is an excellent example of a nonallness attitude. If you recognize that there is more to learn, more to see, more to hear, you leave yourself open to this additional information, and you're better prepared to assimilate it.

A useful extensional device that can help you avoid allness is to end each statement, sometimes verbally but always mentally, with an "etc." (et cetera)—a reminder that there is more to learn, know, and say; that every statement is inevitably incomplete. To be sure, some people overuse the "et cetera." They use it as a substitute for being specific, which defeats its purpose. Instead, it should be used to mentally remind yourself that there is more to know and more to say.

Distinguish between Facts and Inferences: Avoid Fact–Inference Confusion

Language enables us to form statements of facts and inferences without making any linguistic distinction between the two. Similarly, when we listen to such statements, we often don't make a clear distinction between statements of facts and statements of inference. Yet there are great differences between the two. Barriers to clear thinking can be created when inferences are treated as facts, a hazard called **fact–inference confusion**.

For example, you can make statements about things that you observe, and you can make statements about things that you have not observed. In form or structure these statements are similar; they cannot be distinguished from each other by any grammatical analysis. For example, you can say, "She is wearing a blue jacket" as well as "She is harboring an illogical hatred." If you diagrammed these sentences, they would yield identical structures, and yet you know that they're different types of statements. In the first sentence, you can observe the jacket and the blue color; the sentence constitutes a *factual statement*. But how do you observe "illogical hatred"? Obviously, this is not a descriptive statement but an *inferential statement*, a statement that you make not solely on the basis of what you observe but on the basis of what you observe plus your own conclusions.

There's no problem with making inferential statements; you must make them if you're to talk about much that is meaningful. The problem arises when you act as though those inferential statements are factual statements. Consider, for example, the following anecdote (Maynard, 1963):

A woman went for a walk one day and met her friend, whom she had not seen, heard from, or heard of in ten years. After an exchange of greetings, the woman said, "Is this your little boy?" and her friend replied, "Yes. I got married about six years ago." The woman then asked the child, "What is your name?" and the little boy replied, "Same as my father's." "Oh," said the woman, "then it must be Peter."

The question, of course, is how did the woman know the boy's father's name? The answer is obvious, but only after you recognize that in reading this short passage you have, quite unconsciously, made an inference that is preventing you from arriving at the answer. You have inferred that the woman's friend is a woman. Actually, the friend is a man named Peter.

You may wish to test your ability to distinguish facts from inferences by taking the accompanying self-test, "Can You Distinguish Facts from Inferences?"

TEST YOURSELF

CAN YOU DISTINGUISH FACTS FROM INFERENCES?

Carefully read the following account, modeled on a report developed by William Haney (1973), and the observations based on it. Indicate whether you think the observations are true, false, or doubtful on the basis of the information presented in the report. Circle T if the observation is definitely true, F if the observation is definitely false, and ? if the observation may be either true or false. Judge each observation in order. Don't reread the observations after you have indicated your judgment, and don't change any of your answers.

A well-liked college teacher had just completed making up the final examinations and had turned off the lights in the office. Just then a tall, broad figure appeared and demanded the examination. The professor opened the drawer. Everything in the drawer was picked up and the individual ran down the corridor. The dean was notified immediately.

T F ?   1. The thief was tall and broad.
T F ?   2. The professor turned off the lights.
T F ?   3. A tall figure demanded the examination.
T F ?   4. The examination was picked up by someone.
T F ?   5. The examination was picked up by the professor.
T F ?   6. A tall figure appeared after the professor turned off the lights in the office.
T F ?   7. The man who opened the drawer was the professor.
T F ?   8. The professor ran down the corridor.
T F ?   9. The drawer was never actually opened.
T F ?   10. Three persons are referred to in this report.

HOW DID YOU DO? After you answer all 10 questions, form small groups of five or six and discuss the answers. Look at each statement from each member's point of view. For each statement, ask yourself "How can you be absolutely certain that the statement is true or false?" You should find that only one statement can be clearly identified as true and only one as false; eight should be marked "?".

WHAT WILL YOU DO? This test is designed to trap you into making inferences and treating them as facts. Statement 3 is true (it's in the report); statement 9 is false (the drawer was opened); but all other statements are inferences and should have been marked "?". Review the remaining eight statements to see why you cannot be certain that any of them are either true or false.

As you read this chapter try to formulate specific guidelines that will help you distinguish facts from inferences as a speaker and as a listener.

Some of the essential differences between factual and inferential statements are summarized in Table 5.2. Distinguishing between these two types of statements does not imply that one type is better than the other. Both types of statements are useful; both are important. The problem arises when you treat an inferential statement as if it were fact. Phrase your inferential statements as tentative. Recognize that such statements may be wrong. Leave open the possibility of other alternatives.

TABLE 5.2 Differences between Factual and Inferential Statements

These differences highlight the important distinctions between factual and inferential statements and are based on the discussions of William Haney (1973) and Harry Weinberg (1959). As you go through this table, consider how you would classify such statements as: "God exists," "Democracy is the best form of government," "This paper is white," "The Internet will grow in size and importance over the next 10 years," and "This table is based on Haney and Weinberg."

Factual Statements	Inferential Statements
May be made only after observation	May be made at any time
Are limited to what has been observed	Go beyond what has been observed
May be made only by the observer	May be made by anyone
May be about only the past or the present	May be about any time—past, present, or future
Approach certainty	Involve varying degrees of probability
Are subject to verifiable standards	Are not subject to verifiable standards

Discriminate Among: Avoid Indiscrimination

Nature seems to abhor sameness at least as much as vacuums, for nowhere in the universe can you find identical entities. Everything is unique. Language, however, provides common nouns, such as *teacher, student, friend, enemy, war, politician, liberal,* and the like, that may lead you to focus on similarities. Such nouns can lead you to group together all teachers, all students, and all friends and perhaps divert attention from the uniqueness of each individual, object, and event.

The misevaluation known as **indiscrimination**—a form of stereotyping (see Chapter 2)—occurs when you focus on classes of individuals, objects, or events and fail to see that each is unique and needs to be looked at individually. Indiscrimination can be seen in such statements as these:

- He's just like the rest of them: lazy, stupid, a real slob.
- I really don't want another ethnic on the board of directors. One is enough for me.
- Read a romance novel? I read one when I was 16. That was enough to convince me.

A useful antidote to indiscrimination is the extensional device called the *index,* a mental subscript that identifies each individual in a group as an individual even though all members of the group may be covered by the same label. For example, when you think and talk of an individual politician as just a "politician," you may fail to see the uniqueness in this politician and the differences between this particular politician and other politicians. However, when you think with the index—when you think not of politician but of $politician_1$ or $politician_2$ or $politician_3$—you're less likely to fall into the trap of indiscrimination and more likely to focus on the differences among politicians. The same is true with members of cultural, national, or religious groups; when you think of $Iraqi_1$ and $Iraqi_2$, you'll be reminded that not all Iraqis are the same. The more you discriminate among individuals covered by the same label, the less likely you are to discriminate against any group.

Talk about the Middle: Avoid Polarization

Polarization, often referred to as the fallacy of "either/or," is the tendency to look at the world and to describe it in terms of extremes—good or bad, positive or negative, healthy or sick, brilliant or stupid, rich or poor, and so on. Polarized statements come in many forms; for example:

- After listening to the evidence, I'm still not clear who the good guys are and who the bad guys are.
- Well, are you for us or against us?
- College had better get me a good job. Otherwise, this has been a big waste of time.

Most people exist somewhere between the extremes of good and bad, healthy and sick, brilliant and stupid, rich and poor. Yet there seems to be a strong tendency to view only the extremes and to categorize people, objects, and events in terms of these polar opposites.

You can easily demonstrate this tendency by filling in the opposites for each of the following words:

		Opposite
tall	___:___:___:___:___:___	_____
heavy	___:___:___:___:___:___	_____
strong	___:___:___:___:___:___	_____
happy	___:___:___:___:___:___	_____
legal	___:___:___:___:___:___	_____

Filling in the opposites should have been relatively easy and quick. The words should also have been fairly short. Further, if various different people supplied the opposites, there would be a high degree of agreement among them. Now try to fill in the middle positions with words meaning, for example, "midway between tall and short," "midway between heavy and light," and so on. Do this before reading any farther.

These midway responses (compared to the opposites) were probably more difficult to think of and took you more time. The responses should also have been long words or phrases of several words. Further, different people would probably agree less on these midway responses than on the opposites.

This exercise clearly illustrates the ease with which we can think and talk in opposites and the difficulty we have in thinking and talking about the middle. But recognize that the vast majority of cases exist between extremes. Don't allow the ready availability of extreme terms to obscure the reality of what lies in between (Read, 2004).

In some cases, of course, it's legitimate to talk in terms of two values. For example, either this thing you're holding is a book or it isn't. Clearly, the classes "book" and "not-book" include all possibilities. There is no problem with this kind of statement. Similarly, you may say that a student either will pass this course or will not, as these two categories include all the possibilities.

You create problems, however, when you use this either/or form in situations in which it's inappropriate; for example, "The supervisor is either for us or against us." The two choices simply don't include all possibilities: The supervisor may be for us in some things and against us in others, or he or she may be neutral. Right now there is a tendency to group people into pro- and antiwar, for example—and into similar pro- and anti- categories on abortion, taxes, and just about every important political or social issue. Similarly, you see examples of polarization in opinions about the Middle East, with some people entirely and totally supportive of one side and others entirely and totally supportive of the other side. But clearly these extremes do not include all possibilities and polarized thinking actually prevents us from entertaining the vast middle ground that exists on all such issues.

Update Messages: Avoid Static Evaluation

Language changes very slowly, especially when compared to the rapid pace at which people and things change. When you retain an evaluation of a person, despite the inevitable changes in the person, you're engaging in **static evaluation**.

Alfred Korzybski (1933) used an interesting illustration in this connection: In a tank there is a large fish and many small fish that are its natural food source. Given freedom in the tank, the large fish will eat the small fish. After some time, the tank is partitioned, with the large fish on one side and the small fish on the other, divided only by glass. For a time, the large fish will try to eat the small fish but will fail; each time it tries, it will knock into the glass partition. After some time it will learn that trying to eat the small fish means difficulty, and it will no longer go after them. Now, however, the partition is removed, and the small fish swim all around the big fish. But the big fish does not eat them and in fact will die of starvation while its natural food swims all around. The large fish has learned a pattern of behavior, and even though the actual territory has changed, the map remains static.

TABLE 5.3 Essential Verbal Message Guidelines

Here is a brief summary of the guidelines for using verbal messages. As you review these principles, try recalling examples and the consequences of the failure to follow these principles from your own recent interactions.

Principles to Follow	Pitfalls to Avoid
Extensionalize	Beware of intensional orientation. Distinguish between the way people and things are talked about and what exists in reality.
See the Individual	Beware of allness. No one can know or say all about anything; always assume there is more to be said, more to learn.
Distinguish Facts from Inferences	Beware of fact–inference confusion. Distinguish between facts and inferences, and treat them differently.
Discriminate Among	Beware of indiscrimination. No two things, people, or cultures are the same. Interpersonal messages frequently oversimplify and often present people and cultures in stereotypes.
Talk about the Middle	Beware of polarization. People and events are often presented in their most extreme manifestations (Gamson, 1998). But extremes don't represent the majority of people. The majority live between the extremes.
Update Messages	Beware of static evaluation. The world and people are constantly changing; what was true six months ago may no longer be true today, so update your conclusions frequently.

While you would probably agree that everything is in a constant state of flux, the relevant question is whether you act as if you know this. Do you act in accordance with the notion of change, instead of just accepting it intellectually? Do you treat your little sister as if she were 10 years old, or do you treat her like the 20-year-old woman she has become? Your evaluations of yourself and others need to keep pace with the rapidly changing real world. Otherwise you'll be left with attitudes and beliefs—static evaluations—about a world that no longer exists.

To guard against static evaluation, use an extensional device called the date: Mentally date your statements and especially your evaluations. Remember that Gerry Smith$_{2002}$ is not Gerry Smith$_{2010}$; academic abilities$_{2006}$ are not academic abilities$_{2010}$. T. S. Eliot, in *The Cocktail Party*, said that "what we know of other people is only our memory of the moments during which we knew them. And they have changed since then . . . at every meeting we are meeting a stranger."

These six guidelines, which are summarized in Table 5.3, will not solve all problems in verbal communication—but they will help you to more accurately align your language with the real world, the world of words and not words; infinite complexity; facts and inferences; sameness and difference; extremes and middle ground; and, perhaps most important, constant change.

Also, recognize that each of these six guidelines contains a warning against verbal messages that can be used to deceive you. For example, when people try to influence you to respond to people in terms of their labels (often racist, sexist, or homophobic), they are using intensional orientation unethically. Similarly, when people present themselves as knowing everything about something (gossip is often a good example), they are using your natural tendency to think in allness terms to achieve their own ends, not to present the truth. When people present inferences as if they are facts (again, gossip provides a good example) to secure your belief, or when they stereotype, they are relying on your tendency to confuse facts and inferences and to fail to discriminate. And when people talk in terms of opposites (polarize) or as if things and people don't change (static evaluation) in order to influence you to believe certain things or to do certain things, they are again assuming you won't talk about the middle or ask for updated messages.

Summary

This chapter introduced the verbal message system and identified some basic principles concerning how the verbal message system works and how it can be used more effectively.

Principles of Verbal Messages

1. Messages are packaged; verbal and nonverbal signals interact to produce one (ideally) unified message. Six major ways nonverbal messages can interact with verbal messages are to: (1) accent, or emphasize a verbal message; (2) complement, or add nuances of meaning; (3) contradict, or deny the verbal message; (4) control, or manage the flow of communication; (5) repeat, or restate the message; and (6) substitute, or take the place of a verbal message.
2. Message meanings are in people; in people's thoughts and feelings, not just in their words.
3. Messages are both denotative and connotative. Denotation is the dictionary-like meaning of a word or sentence. Connotation is the personal meaning of a word or sentence. Denotative meaning is relatively objective; connotative meaning is highly subjective.
4. Messages vary in abstraction; they vary from very specific and concrete to highly abstract and general.
5. Messages vary in politeness from rude to extremely polite and may be viewed in terms of maintaining positive and negative face. Variations in what is considered polite among cultures are often great.
6. Messages can criticize and praise. Criticism that is overly negative or not constructive will normally be resented while praise that is unrealistic or unspecific may be dismissed.
7. Messages vary in assertiveness. Standing up for one's own rights without infringing on the rights of others is the goal of most assertive communication.
8. Messages can confirm and disconfirm. Disconfirmation is communication that ignores another, that denies the other person's definition of self. Confirmation expresses acknowledgment and acceptance of others and avoids racist, heterosexist, ageist, and sexist expressions that are disconfirming.
9. Messages vary in cultural sensitivity.

Guidelines for Using Verbal Messages Effectively

10. Extensionalize; the word is not the thing. Avoid intensional orientation, the tendency to view the world in the way it's talked about or labeled. Instead, respond to things first; look for the labels second.
11. See the individual; avoid allness, our tendency to describe the world in extreme terms that imply we know all or are saying all there is to say. To combat allness, remind yourself that you can never know all or say all about anything; use a mental and sometimes verbal "etc."
12. Distinguish between facts and inferences, and act differently depending on whether the message is factual or inferential.
13. Discriminate among. Avoid indiscrimination, the tendency to group unique individuals or items because they're covered by the same term or label. To combat indiscrimination, recognize uniqueness, and mentally index each individual in a group (teacher$_1$, teacher$_2$).
14. Talk with middle terms; avoid polarization, the tendency to describe the world in terms of extremes or polar opposites. To combat polarization use middle terms and qualifiers.
15. Update messages regularly; nothing is static. Avoid static evaluation, the tendency to describe the world in static terms, denying constant change. To combat static evaluation, recognize the inevitability of change; date statements and evaluations, realizing, for example, that Gerry Smith$_{2006}$ is not Gerry Smith$_{2010}$.

Key Terms

abstraction, **104**
ageist language, **115**
allness, **119**
assertiveness, **109**
bypassing, **101**
confirmation, **112**

connotation, **102**
denotation, **102**
disconfirmation, **112**
extensional orientation, **118**
fact–inference confusion, **120**
heterosexist language, **114**

indiscrimination, **122**
intensional orientation, **118**
metacommunication, **103**
negative face, **104**
polarization, **122**
politeness, **104**

positive face, **104**
racist language, **112**
rejection, **112**
sexist language, **116**
static evaluation, **123**
verbal messages, **99**

Critical Thinking Questions

1 A weasel is a slippery creature; just when you're going to catch it, it slips away. Weasel words, as noted in Table 4.3, are words whose meanings are difficult to pin down. How many weasel words can you identify in a half-hour television show's commercials?

2 Most often people lie to gain some benefit or reward (for example, to increase desirable relationships, to protect their self-esteem, or to obtain money) or to avoid punishment. In an analysis of 322 lies, researchers found that 75.8 percent benefited the liar, 21.7 percent benefited the person who was told the lie, and 2.5 percent benefited a third party (Camden, Motley, & Wilson, 1984). Are lies told to benefit others less unethical than lies told to benefit yourself?

3 Consider the differences in meaning for such words as *woman* to an American and an Iranian, *religion* to a born-again Christian and an atheist, and *lunch* to a Chinese rice farmer and a Wall Street executive. What principles might help such diverse groups understand the different meanings?

4 Many people who practice direct communication see those who communicate indirectly as being manipulative. According to Deborah Tannen (1994b, p. 92), however, calling people "manipulative" "is often just a way of blaming others for our discomfort with their styles." Do you agree with Tannen? Or do you think that indirectness is often intentionally manipulative?

5 How would you describe the level of directness you use when talking face-to-face versus the level you use in e-mail and chat rooms? If you notice differences, to what do you attribute them?

6 A widely held assumption in anthropology, linguistics, and communication is that the importance of a concept to a culture can be measured by the number of words the language has for talking about the concept. So, for example, in English there are lots of words for money or for transportation or communication. With this principle in mind, consider the findings of Julia Stanley, for example. Stanley researched English-language terms indicating sexual promiscuity and found 220 terms referring to a sexually promiscuous woman but only 22 terms for a sexually promiscuous man (Thorne, Kramarae, & Henley, 1983). What does this finding suggest about our culture's attitudes and beliefs about promiscuity in men and women?

Choice Points

1 *Rejecting Directly.* A colleague at work continues to ask you for a date, but you're just not interested. You've used every polite excuse in the book and now feel you have to be more direct and more honest. Ask yourself: In what ways can you express your feelings to achieve your goal and yet not alienate or insult your colleague?

2 *Confronting a Lie.* You ask about the previous night's whereabouts of your romantic partner of two years and are told something you know beyond any doubt to be false. You don't want to break up the relationship over this, but you do want the truth and an opportunity to resolve the problems that contributed to this situation. Ask yourself: What are some of the things you might say to achieve your purposes? What are some types of things you'd definitely want to avoid saying?

3 *Cultural Insensitivity.* You inadvertently say something that you thought would be funny but that turns out to be culturally insensitive, causing offense to a friend. Ask yourself: What might you say to make it clear that you would never intentionally talk this way?

4 *Using Inappropriate Cultural Identifiers.* Your parents use cultural identifiers that would be considered inappropriate among most social groups—not because of prejudice but mainly through ignorance and habit. You want to avoid falling into these patterns yourself. Ask yourself: What steps might you take to achieve your goal?

5 *Criticizing.* You're supervising a group of five interns who have been doing just about nothing. You don't want to discourage them or criticize them too harshly, but at the same time you have to get them to do some work. Ask yourself: What are some of the things you can say to help turn this group around? What are some of the things you should probably avoid saying?

6 *Discouraging Ethnocentricity.* You've been dating a wonderful person for the last few months, but increasingly you are discovering that your "ideal" partner is extremely ethnocentric and sees little value in other religions, other races, other nationalities. Ask yourself: What are some things you can do to educate your possible life partner?

7 *Discouraging Disconfirmation.* For the last several months you've noticed how disconfirming your neighbors are toward their preteen children; it seems the children can never do anything to the parents' satisfaction. Ask yourself: What are some of the things you might say (if you do decide to get involved) to make your neighbors more aware of their communication patterns and the possible negative effects these might have?

MyCommunicationLab
Explorations

This group of experiences will help clarify the interaction and basic principles of verbal messages. ❶ Integrating Verbal and Nonverbal Messages explores some of the connections between verbal and nonverbal messages. ❷ Climbing the Abstraction Ladder and ❸ Using the Abstraction Ladder as a Creative Thinking Tool will clarify the abstraction process and explain a useful creative thinking technique. ❹ How Can You Vary Directness for Greatest Effectiveness? provides practice in varying directness. ❺ How Can You Rephrase Clichés? provides an opportunity to replace trite expressions with more creative and meaningful phrases. ❻ Who? is a class game–experience that asks you to identify characteristics of other people on the basis of their various verbal and nonverbal messages. This exercise can be used as an introduction to the messages section or as a conclusion. ❼ Analyzing Assertiveness provides practice scenarios calling for assertiveness. ❽ Identifying the Barriers to Communication provides a dialogue demonstrating the various barriers discussed in this chapter. ❾ How Do You Talk? As a Woman? As a Man? and ❿ Recognizing Gender Differences look at gender differences in language and at our perceptions of the speech of others. ⓫ Thinking with E-Prime focuses on the difficulties that can be created when you use and think with the verb "to be." ⓬ How Do You Talk about the Middle? illustrates the ways in which our language makes it easy to polarize. ⓭ Confirming, Rejecting, and Disconfirming looks at specific examples of these types of messages. ⓮ "Must Lie" Situations examines scenarios in which many people would consider it ethical, even necessary, to lie.

6 Nonverbal Messages

Channels of Nonverbal Communication

Functions of Nonverbal Communication

Nonverbal Communication
and Culture

The Simpsons Movie

One of the great things about cartoon movies is that the characters always look like their personalities; a cartoon character's physical characteristics reflect his, her or its personality. In *The Simpsons Movie*, as in the television series, you can tell a great deal about each of the Simpsons simply by looking at how they're drawn. With humans, the situation is quite different, and yet we do make inferences about others on the basis of their physical appearance—a tendancy that is just one of the many topics explored in this chapter on nonverbal communication.

Nonverbal communication is communication without words. You communicate nonverbally when you gesture, smile or frown, widen your eyes, move your chair closer to someone, wear jewelry, touch someone, or raise your vocal volume, or even when you say nothing. The crucial aspect of nonverbal communication is that the message you send is in some way received by one or more other people. If you gesture while alone in your room and no one is there to see you, then, most theorists would argue, communication has not taken place. The same, of course, is true of verbal messages: If you recite a speech and no one hears it, then communication has not taken place.

Your ability to use nonverbal communication effectively can yield two major benefits (Burgoon & Hoobler, 2002). First, the greater your ability to send and receive nonverbal signals, the higher your attraction, popularity, and psychosocial well-being are likely to be. Second, the greater your nonverbal skills, the more successful you're likely to be in a wide variety of interpersonal communication situations, including close relationships, organizational communication, teacher-student communication, in intercultural communication, courtroom communication, in politics, and in health care (Richmond, McCroskey, & Hickson, 2008; Riggio & Feldman, 2005).

Perhaps the best way to begin the study of nonverbal communication is to look at your own beliefs. Which of the following statements do you believe are true?

1. Nonverbal communication conveys more meaning than verbal communication.
2. Liars avoid eye contact.
3. Studying nonverbal communication will enable you to detect lying.
4. Unlike verbal communication, nonverbal communication is universal throughout the world.
5. When verbal and nonverbal messages contradict each other, it's wise to believe the nonverbal.

Actually, all of these statements are popular myths about nonverbal communication. Briefly, (1) in some instances nonverbal messages may communicate more meaning than verbal messages but in most cases, it depends on the situation. You won't get very far discussing science and mathematics nonverbally, for example. (2) Some liars do avoid eye contact, but others don't. (3) Lie detection is a far more difficult process than any chapter or even series of courses could accomplish. (4) Actually, the same nonverbal signals may communicate very different meanings in different cultures. (5) People can be deceptive nonverbally as well as verbally; it's best to look at the entire group of signals before making a judgment, but even then detecting deception won't be an easy or sure thing.

Channels of Nonverbal Communication

Focusing on the channels of nonverbal communication, we can distinguish a wide variety of nonverbal messages. Let's look in detail at each nonverbal channel: (1) body communication, (2) facial communication, (3) eye communication, (4) touch communication, (5) paralanguage and silence, (6) spatial messages, (7) artifactual communication, and (8) temporal communication.

Body Communication

Generally, we can consider body communication in two parts—the gestures you make with your body and your body's appearance.

Body Gestures An especially useful classification in **kinesics**, or the study of communication through body movement, identifies five types: emblems, illustrators, affect displays, regulators, and adaptors (Ekman & Friesen, 1969). Table 6.1 summarizes and provides examples of these five types of movements.

Emblems Emblems are substitutes for words; they're body movements that have rather specific verbal translations, such as the nonverbal signs for "OK," "Peace," "Come here," "Go away," "Who, me?" "Be quiet," "I'm warning you," "I'm tired," and "It's cold." Emblems are as arbitrary as any words in any language. Consequently, your present culture's emblems are not

TABLE 6.1 Five Types of Body Movements

Can you identify similar gestures that mean different things in different cultures and that might create interpersonal misunderstandings?

	Name and Function	Examples
	Emblems directly translate words or phrases.	"OK" sign, "Come here" wave, hitchhiker's sign
	Illustrators accompany and literally "illustrate" verbal messages.	Circular hand movements when talking of a circle, hands far apart when talking of something large
	Affect displays communicate emotional meaning.	Expressions of happiness, surprise, fear, anger, sadness, disgust
	Regulators monitor, maintain, or control the speaking of another.	Facial expressions and hand gestures indicating "Keep going," "Slow down," or "What else happened?"
	Adaptors satisfy some need.	Scratching head

necessarily the same as your culture's emblems of 300 years ago or the same as the emblems of other cultures. For example, the sign made by forming a circle with the thumb and index finger may mean "nothing" or "zero" in France, "money" in Japan, and something sexual in certain southern European cultures. But just as the English language is spreading throughout the world, so, too, is the English nonverbal language. The American use of this emblem to mean "OK" is spreading as fast, for example, as English technical and scientific terms.

Illustrators Illustrators accompany and literally illustrate verbal messages. Illustrators make your communications more vivid and help to maintain your listener's attention. They also help to clarify and intensify your verbal messages. In saying, "Let's go up," for example, you probably move your head and perhaps your finger in an upward direction. In describing a circle or a square, you more than likely make circular or square movements with your hands. Research points to another advantage of illustrators: that they increase your ability to remember. People who illustrated their verbal messages with gestures remembered some 20 percent more than those who didn't gesture (Goldin-Meadow, Nusbaum, Kelly, & Wagner, 2001).

We are aware of illustrators only part of the time; at times, they may have to be brought to our attention. Illustrators are more universal than emblems; illustrators will be recognized and understood by members of more different cultures than will emblems.

Affect Displays Affect displays are the movements of the face that convey emotional meaning—the expressions that show anger and fear, happiness and surprise, eagerness and fatigue. They're the facial expressions that give you away when you try to present a false image and that lead people to say, "You look angry. What's wrong?" We can, however, consciously control affect displays, as actors do when they play a role. Affect displays may be unintentional (as when they give you away) or intentional (as when you want to show anger, love, or surprise). A particular kind of affect display is the poker player's "tell," a bit of nonverbal behavior that communicates bluffing; it's a nonverbal cue that tells others that a player is lying. In much the same way that you may want to conceal certain feelings from friends or relatives, the poker player tries to conceal any such tells.

Regulators Regulators monitor, maintain, or control the speaking of another individual. When you listen to another, you're not passive; you nod your head, purse your lips, adjust your eye focus, and make various paralinguistic sounds such as "mm-mm" or "tsk." Regulators are culture-bound: Each culture develops its own rules for the regulation of conversation.

Regulators also include such broad movements as shaking your head to show disbelief or leaning forward in your chair to show that you want to hear more.

Regulators communicate what you expect or want speakers to do as they're talking; for example, "Keep going," "Tell me what else happened," "I don't believe that. Are you sure?" "Speed up," and "Slow down." Speakers often receive these nonverbal signals without being consciously aware of them. Depending on their degree of sensitivity, speakers modify their speaking behavior in accordance with these regulators.

Adaptors Adaptors satisfy some need and usually occur without conscious awareness; they're unintentional movements that usually go unnoticed. Nonverbal researchers identify three types of adaptors based on their focus, direction, or target: self-adaptors, alter-adaptors, and object-adaptors (Burgoon, Buller, & Woodall, 1996).

Self-adaptors usually satisfy a physical need, generally serving to make you more comfortable; examples include scratching your head to relieve an itch, moistening your lips because they feel dry, or pushing your hair out of your eyes. When these adaptors occur in private, they occur in their entirety: You scratch until the itch is gone. But in public these adaptors usually occur in abbreviated form. When people are watching you, for example, you might put your fingers to your head and move them around a bit but probably not scratch with the same vigor as when in private.

Alter-adaptors are the body movements you make in response to your current interactions. Examples include crossing your arms over your chest when someone unpleasant approaches or moving closer to someone you like.

Object-adaptors are movements that involve your manipulation of some object. Frequently observed examples include punching holes in or drawing on a styrofoam coffee cup, clicking a ballpoint pen, or chewing on a pencil. Object-adaptors are usually signs of negative feelings; for example, you emit more adaptors when feeling hostile than when feeling friendly. Further, as anxiety and uneasiness increase, so does the frequency of object-adaptors (Burgoon, Buller, & Woodall, 1996).

Body Appearance Of course, the body communicates even without movement. For example, others may form impressions of you from your general body build; from your height and weight; and from your skin, eye, and hair color. Assessments of your power, your attractiveness, and your suitability as a friend or romantic partner are often made on the basis of your body appearance (Sheppard & Strathman, 1989).

Height, for example, is significant in a wide variety of situations. Tall presidential candidates have a much better record of winning elections than do their shorter opponents. Tall people seem to be paid more and are favored by interviewers over shorter applicants (Keyes, 1980; Guerrero, DeVito, & Hecht, 1999; Knapp & Hall, 2006; Jackson & Ervin, 1992). Taller people also have higher self-esteem and greater career success than do shorter people (Judge & Cable, 2004).

Your body reveals your race, through skin color and tone, and also may give clues as to your more specific nationality. Your weight in proportion to your height will communicate messages to others, as will the length, color, and style of your hair.

Your general attractiveness also is a part of body communication. Attractive people have the advantage in just about every activity you can name. They get better grades in school, are more valued as friends and lovers, and are preferred as coworkers (Burgoon, Buller, & Woodall, 1996). Although we normally think that attractiveness is culturally determined—and to some degree it is—research seems to indicate that definitions of attractiveness are becoming universal (Brody, 1994). That is, a person rated as attractive in one culture is likely to be rated as attractive in other cultures—even in cultures whose people are widely different in appearance.

VIEWPOINT On a 10-point scale, with 1 indicating "not at all important" and 10 indicating "extremely important," how important is body appearance to your own romantic interest in another person? Do the men and women you know conform to the stereotypes that say males are more concerned with the physical and females more concerned with personality?

Facial Communication

Throughout your interpersonal interactions, your face communicates, especially signaling your emotions. In fact, facial movements alone seem to communicate the degree of pleasantness, agreement, and sympathy a person feels; the rest of the body doesn't provide any additional information. For other aspects, however—for example, the intensity with which an emotion is felt—both facial and bodily cues are used (Graham, Bitti, & Argyle, 1975; Graham & Argyle, 1975).

Some nonverbal communication researchers claim that facial movements may communicate at least the following eight emotions: happiness, surprise, fear, anger, sadness, disgust, contempt, and interest (Ekman, Friesen, & Ellsworth, 1972). Others propose that, in addition, facial movements may communicate bewilderment and determination (Leathers & Eaves, 2008).

Of course, some emotions are easier to communicate and to decode than others. For example, in one study, happiness was judged with an accuracy ranging from 55 percent to 100 percent, surprise from 38 percent to 86 percent, and sadness from 19 percent to 88 percent (Ekman, Friesen, & Ellsworth, 1972). Research finds that women and girls are more accurate judges of facial emotional expression than men and boys (Hall, 1984; Argyle, 1988).

As you've probably experienced, you may interpret the same facial expression differently depending on the context in which it occurs. For example, in a classic study, when a smiling face was presented looking at a glum face, the smiling face was judged to be vicious and taunting. But when the same smiling face was presented looking at a frowning face, it was judged peaceful and friendly (Cline, 1956). In general, not surprisingly, people who smile are judged to be more likable and more approachable than people who don't smile or people who pretend to smile (Gladstone & Parker, 2002; Woodzicka & LaFrance, 2005; Kluger, 2005). And women perceive men who are smiled at by other women as being more attractive than men who are not smiled at. But men—perhaps being more competitive—perceive men whom women smile at as being less attractive than men who are not smiled at (Jones, DeBruine, Little, Burriss, & Feinberg, 2007).

Facial Management As you learned the nonverbal system of communication, you also learned certain **facial management techniques** that enable you to communicate your feelings to achieve the effect you want—for example, to hide certain emotions and to emphasize others. Consider your own use of such facial management techniques. As you do so, think about the types of interpersonal situations in which you would use each of these facial management techniques (Malandro, Barker, & Barker, 1989; Metts & Planalp, 2002). Would you

- *intensify*, as when you exaggerate surprise when friends throw you a party to make your friends feel better?
- *deintensify*, as when you cover up your own joy in the presence of a friend who didn't receive such good news?
- *neutralize*, as when you cover up your sadness to keep from depressing others?
- *mask*, as when you express happiness in order to cover up your disappointment at not receiving the gift you expected?
- *simulate*, as when you express an emotion you don't feel?

These facial management techniques help you display emotions in socially acceptable ways. For example, when someone gets bad news in which you may secretly take pleasure, the display rule dictates that you frown and otherwise nonverbally signal your sorrow. If you place first in a race and your best friend barely finishes, the display rule requires that you minimize your expression of pleasure in winning and avoid any signs of gloating. If you violate these display rules, you'll be judged as insensitive. So although facial management techniques may be deceptive, they're also expected—and, in fact, required by the rules of polite interaction.

Facial Feedback When you express emotions facially, a feedback effect is observed. This finding has given rise to what is called the **facial feedback hypothesis**, which holds that your facial expressions influence your physiological arousal (Lanzetta, Cartwright-Smith, & Kleck, 1976;

Zuckerman, Klorman, Larrance, & Spiegel, 1981). For example, in one study, participants held a pen in their teeth to simulate a sad expression and then rated a series of photographs. Results showed that mimicking sad expressions actually increased the degree of sadness the subjects reported feeling when viewing the photographs (Larsen, Kasimatis, & Frey, 1992).

Generally, research finds that facial expressions can produce or heighten feelings of sadness, fear, disgust, and anger. But this effect does not occur with all emotions; smiling, for example, won't make you feel happier. And if you're feeling sad, smiling is not likely to replace your sadness with happiness. A reasonable conclusion seems to be that your facial expressions can influence some feelings, but not all (Burgoon & Bacue, 2003).

Eye Communication

Occulesis is the study of the messages communicated by the eyes, which vary depending on the duration, direction, and quality of the eye behavior. For example, in every culture there are rather strict, though unstated, rules for the proper duration for eye contact. In much of England and the United States, for example, the average length of gaze is 2.95 seconds. The average length of mutual gaze (two persons gazing at each other) is 1.18 seconds (Argyle, 1988; Argyle & Ingham, 1972). When the duration of eye contact is shorter than 1.18 seconds, you may think the person is uninterested, shy, or preoccupied. When the appropriate amount of time is exceeded, you may perceive this as showing high interest.

In much of the United States direct eye contact is considered an expression of honesty and forthrightness. But the Japanese often view eye contact as a lack of respect. The Japanese will glance at the other person's face rarely and then only for very short periods (Axtell, 1994). In many Hispanic cultures, direct eye contact signifies a certain equality and so should be avoided by, say, children when speaking to a person in authority. Try visualizing the potential misunderstandings that eye communication alone could create when people from Tokyo, San Francisco, and San Juan try to communicate.

The direction of the eye also communicates. Generally, in communicating with another person, you will glance alternatively at the other person's face, then away, then again at the face, and so on. When these directional rules are broken, different meanings are communicated—abnormally high or low interest, self-consciousness, nervousness over the interaction, and so on. The quality of the gaze—how wide or how narrow your eyes get during interaction—also communicates meaning, especially interest level and such emotions as surprise, fear, and disgust.

Eye Contact You use eye contact to serve several important functions (Knapp & Hall, 2006; Malandro, Barker, & Barker, 1989; Richmond, McCroskey, & Hickson, 2008).

- **To monitor feedback**. For example, when you talk with others, you look at them intently and try to understand their reactions to what you're saying. You try to read their feedback, and on this basis you adjust what you say. As you can imagine, successful readings of feedback will help considerably in your overall effectiveness.
- **To secure attention**. When you speak with two or three other people, you maintain eye contact to secure the attention and interest of your listeners. When someone fails to pay you the attention you want, you probably increase your eye contact, hoping that this will increase attention.
- **To regulate the conversation**. Eye contact helps you regulate, manage, and control the conversation. With eye movements you can inform the other person that she or he should speak. A clear example of this occurs in the college classroom, where the instructor asks a question and then locks eyes with a student. This type of eye contact tells the student to answer the question.
- **To signal the nature of the relationship**. Eye communication also can serve as a "tie sign" or signal of the nature of the relationship between two people—for example, to indicate positive or negative regard. Depending on the culture, eye contact may communicate your romantic interest in another person, or eye avoidance may indicate respect. Some researchers note that eye contact serves to enable gay men and lesbians to signal their homosexuality and perhaps their interest in someone—an ability referred to as "gaydar" (Nicholas, 2004).

Immediacy

Immediacy is the creation of closeness, a sense of togetherness, of oneness, between speaker and listener. When you communicate immediacy you convey a sense of interest and attention, a liking for and an attraction to the other person.

And, not surprisingly, people respond to communication that is immediate more favorably than to communication that is not. People like people who communicate immediacy. You can increase your interpersonal attractiveness, the degree to which others like you and respond positively toward you, by using immediacy behaviors. In addition there is considerable evidence to show that immediacy behaviors are also effective in, for example, teaching and health care (Richmond, Smith, Heisel, & McCroskey, 2001; Richmond, McCroskey, & Hickson, 2008).

Communicating Immediacy. Immediacy may be communicated both verbally and nonverbally. Here are a few suggestions for communicating immediacy verbally (Mottet & Richmond, 1998) and nonverbally (Richmond, McCroskey, & Hickson, 2008):

- Self-disclose; reveal something significant about yourself.
- Refer to the other person's good qualities of, say, dependability, intelligence, or character—"you're always so reliable."
- Express your positive view of the other person and of your relationship—"I'm sure glad you're my roommate; you know everyone."
- Talk about commonalities, things you and the other person have done together or share.
- Demonstrate your responsiveness by giving feedback cues that indicate you want to listen more and that you're interested—"And what else happened?"
- Express psychological closeness and openness by, for example, maintaining physical closeness and arranging your body to exclude third parties.
- Maintain appropriate eye contact and limit looking around at others.
- Smile and express your interest in the other person.
- Focus on the other person's remarks. Make the speaker know that you heard and understood what was said, and give the speaker appropriate verbal and nonverbal feedback.

At the same time that you'll want to demonstrate these immediacy messages, try also to avoid nonimmediacy messages such as interrupting the other person, avoiding small talk, making potentially offensive or condescending comments, closing off the channels of communication ("I don't have the time to chat"), or talking about things for which the other person has no reference or no experience. Nonverbally, avoid speaking in a monotone, looking away from the person you're talking to, frowning while talking, having a tense body posture, or avoiding gestures (Richmond, McCroskey, & Hickson, 2008).

Not all cultures or all people respond in the same way to immediacy messages. For example, in the United States immediacy behaviors are generally seen as friendly and appropriate. In other cultures, however, the same immediacy behaviors may be viewed as overly familiar—as presuming that a relationship is close when only acquaintanceship exists (Axtell, 1994). Similarly, recognize that some people may take your immediacy behaviors as indicating a desire for increased intimacy in the relationship. So although you may be trying merely to signal a friendly closeness, the other person may perceive a romantic invitation. Also, recognize that because immediacy behaviors prolong and encourage in-depth communication, they may not be responded to favorably by persons who are fearful about communication and/or who want to get the interaction over with as soon as possible (Richmond, McCroskey, & Hickson, 2008).

Working with Interpersonal Skills

How would other people rate you on immediacy? If you have no idea, ask a few friends. How would you rate yourself? In what situations might you express greater immediacy? In what situations might you express less immediacy?

- **To signal status.** Eye contact is often used to signal status and aggression. Among many younger people, prolonged eye contact from a stranger is taken to signify aggressiveness and frequently prompts physical violence—merely because one person looked perhaps a little longer than was considered normal in that specific culture (Matsumoto, 1996).

I'm planning on becoming a teacher. Isn't my ability to communicate information clearly and simply the only real skill I need? Why do I have to be concerned with qualities like immediacy?

Becoming a teacher requires a number of skills. While skill in communicating clearly is extremely important, it should be supplemented by other positive communication behaviors, such as immediacy, to enhance the overall classroom experience.

When students perceive their teachers as immediate, they're more likely to increase their affective learning (they'll like the subject matter and the teacher, important prerequisites for motivation) and their cognitive learning (they'll more effectively learn the ideas and skills you're teaching). When students see their teachers as immediate, they're more likely to go to class, engage in classroom discussions, and ask course-relevant questions. Attendance and participation also increase learning in the classroom, and immediacy can help link the two together. Further, students who perceive their teachers as immediate are more likely to comply with their teachers' wishes, thus reducing discipline problems. So, while clarity is essential to the instructional communication process, other qualities like immediacy also play an important role in enhancing the overall classroom experience.

For more information see S. A. Myers and K. A. Rocca, "The Relationship between College Student Class Participation and Perceived Instructor Communicator Style," *Journal of the Speech and Theatre Association of Missouri* 37(2007): 114–127; K. A. Rocca, "College Student Attendance: Impact of Instructor Immediacy and Verbal Aggression," *Communication Education* 53 (2004): 185–195; and http://www.jamescmccroskey.com for a plethora of research articles on immediacy.

Kelly A. Rocca (Ed.D., West Virginia University) is an associate dean and associate professor at St. John's University, where she teaches courses in interpersonal communication, public speaking, and persuasion (roccak@stjohns.edu). Her research interests include interpersonal, instructional, health, and sports communication.

- **To compensate for physical distance**. Eye contact is often used to compensate for increased physical distance. By making eye contact you overcome psychologically the physical distance between yourself and another person. When you catch someone's eye at a party, for example, you become psychologically closer even though you may be separated by considerable physical distance.

Eye Avoidance   The eyes, sociologist Erving Goffman observed in *Interaction Ritual* (1967), are "great intruders." When you avoid eye contact or avert your glance, you allow others to maintain their privacy. You probably do this when you see a couple arguing in the street or on a bus. You turn your eyes away, as if to say, "I don't mean to intrude; I respect your privacy." Goffman refers to this behavior as **civil inattention**.

Eye avoidance also can signal lack of interest—in a person, a conversation, or some visual stimulus. At times, like the ostrich, we hide our eyes to try to cut off unpleasant stimuli. Notice, for example, how quickly people close their eyes in the face of some extreme unpleasantness. Interestingly enough, even if the unpleasantness is auditory, we tend to shut it out by closing our eyes. At other times, we close our eyes to block out visual stimuli and thus to heighten our other senses; for example, we often listen to music with our eyes closed. Lovers often close their eyes while kissing, and many prefer to make love in a dark or dimly lit room.

Pupil Dilation   In the fifteenth and sixteenth centuries, Italian women used to put drops of belladonna (which literally means "beautiful woman") into their eyes to enlarge the pupils so that they would look more attractive. Research in the field of **pupillometrics** supports the intuitive logic of these women: Dilated pupils are in fact judged more attractive than constricted ones (Hess, 1975; Marshall, 1983).

In one study, for example, photographs of women were retouched (Hess, 1975). In one set of photographs the pupils were enlarged, and in the other they were made smaller. Men were then asked to judge the women's personalities from the photographs. The photos of women with small pupils drew responses such as cold, hard, and selfish; those with dilated pupils drew responses such as feminine and soft. However, the male observers could not verbalize the reasons for the different perceptions. Both **pupil dilation** itself and people's reactions to changes in the pupil size of others seem to function below the level of conscious awareness.

Pupil size also reveals your interest and level of emotional arousal. Your pupils enlarge when you're interested in something or when you're emotionally aroused. When homosexuals and heterosexuals were shown pictures of nude bodies, the homosexuals' pupils dilated more when viewing same-sex bodies, whereas the heterosexuals' pupils dilated more when viewing opposite-sex bodies (Hess, Seltzer, & Schlien, 1965). These pupillary responses are unconscious and are even observed in persons with profound mental retardation (Chaney, Givens, Aoki, & Gombiner, 1989). Perhaps we find dilated pupils more attractive because we judge them as indicative of a person's interest in us. That may be why models, Beanie Babies, and Teletubbies have exceptionally large pupils.

Although belladonna is no longer used, the cosmetics industry has made millions selling eye enhancers—eye shadow, eyeliner, false eyelashes, and tinted contact lenses that change eye color. These items function (ideally, at least) to draw attention to these most powerful communicators.

Touch Communication

Tactile communication, or communication by touch, also referred to as **haptics**, is perhaps the most primitive form of communication. Developmentally, touch is probably the first sense to be used; even in the womb, the child is stimulated by touch. Soon after birth the child is fondled, caressed, patted, and stroked. In turn, the child explores its world through touch. In a very short time, the child learns to communicate a wide variety of meanings through touch. Not surprisingly, touch also varies with your relationship stage. In the early stages of a relationship, you touch little; in intermediate stages (involvement and intimacy), you touch a great deal; and at stable or deteriorating stages, you again touch little (Guerrero & Andersen, 1991).

The Meanings of Touch Touch may communicate five major meanings (Jones & Yarbrough, 1985; Jones, 2005). *Positive emotions* may be communicated by touch, mainly between intimates or others who have a relatively close relationship. Among the most important of these positive emotions are support, appreciation, inclusion, sexual interest or intent, and affection. Additional research found that touch communicated such positive feelings as composure, immediacy, trust, similarity and equality, and informality (Burgoon, 1991). Touch also has been found to facilitate self-disclosure (Rabinowitz, 1991).

Touch often communicates *playfulness*, either affectionately or aggressively. When touch is used in this manner, the playfulness deemphasizes the emotion and tells the other person that it's not to be taken seriously. Playful touches lighten an interaction.

VIEWPOINT Consider, as Nancy Henley asks in her book *Body Politics* (1977), who would touch whom—say, by putting an arm on the other person's shoulder or by putting a hand on the other person's back—in the following dyads: teacher and student, doctor and patient, manager and worker, minister and parishioner, business executive and secretary. Do your answers reveal that the higher-status person initiates touch with the lower-status person? Henley argues that in addition to indicating relative status, touching demonstrates the assertion of male power, dominance, and superior status over women. When women touch men, Henley says, any suggestion of a female-dominant relationship is not acceptable (to men), so the touching is interpreted as a sexual invitation. What do you think of this position?

Touch also may *control* the behaviors, attitudes, or feelings of the other person. Such control may communicate various different kinds of messages. To ask for compliance, for example, we touch the other person to communicate "Move over," "Hurry," "Stay here," or "Do it." Touching to control may also communicate status and dominance (Henley, 1977; DiBaise & Gunnoe, 2004). The higher-status and dominant person, for example, initiates touch. In fact, it would be a breach of etiquette for the lower-status person to touch the person of higher status.

Ritualistic touching centers on greetings and departures. Shaking hands to say hello or goodbye is perhaps the clearest example of ritualistic touching, but we might also hug, kiss, or put an arm around another's shoulder.

Task-related touching is associated with the performance of a function, such as removing a speck of dust from another person's face, helping someone out of a car, or checking someone's forehead for fever. Task-related touching seems generally to be regarded positively. In studies on the subject, for example, book borrowers had a more positive attitude toward the library and the librarian when touched lightly, and customers gave larger tips when lightly touched by the waitress (Marsh, 1988). Similarly, diners who were touched on the shoulder or hand when being given their change in a restaurant tipped more than diners who were not touched (Crusco & Wetzel, 1984; Stephen & Zweigenhaft, 1986; Guéguen & Jacob, 2004).

As you can imagine, touching also can get you into trouble. For example, touching that is too positive (or too intimate) too early in a relationship may send the wrong signals. Similarly, playing too roughly or holding someone's arm to control their movements may be resented. Using ritualistic touching incorrectly or in ways that may be culturally insensitive may likewise get you into difficulty.

Touch Avoidance Much as we have a need and desire to touch and be touched by others, we also have a tendency to avoid touch from certain people or in certain circumstances (Andersen & Leibowitz, 1978; Andersen, 2004). Before reading about the research findings on **touch avoidance**, you may wish to take the accompanying touch avoidance self-test.

✎ TEST YOURSELF

DO YOU AVOID TOUCH?

This instrument is composed of 18 statements concerning how you feel about touching other people and being touched. Please indicate the degree to which each statement applies to you by indicating whether you: 1 = strongly agree, 2 = agree, 3 = are undecided, 4 = disagree, or 5 = strongly disagree.

```
_____   1. A hug from a same-sex friend is a true sign of friendship.
_____   2. Opposite-sex friends enjoy it when I touch them.
_____   3. I often put my arm around friends of the same sex.
_____   4. When I see two friends of the same sex hugging, it revolts me.
_____   5. I like it when members of the opposite sex touch me.
_____   6. People shouldn't be so uptight about touching persons of the same sex.
_____   7. I think it is vulgar when members of the opposite sex touch me.
_____   8. When a member of the opposite sex touches me, I find it unpleasant.
_____   9. I wish I were free to show emotions by touching members of the same sex.
_____  10. I'd enjoy giving a massage to an opposite-sex friend.
_____  11. I enjoy kissing a person of the same sex.
_____  12. I like to touch friends that are the same sex as I am.
_____  13. Touching a friend of the same sex does not make me uncomfortable.
_____  14. I find it enjoyable when my date and I embrace.
_____  15. I enjoy getting a back rub from a member of the opposite sex.
_____  16. I dislike kissing relatives of the same sex.
_____  17. Intimate touching with members of the opposite sex is pleasurable.
_____  18. I find it difficult to be touched by a member of my own sex.
```

Among the important findings is that touch avoidance is positively related to communication apprehension, or fear or anxiety about communicating: People who fear oral communication also score high on touch avoidance. Touch avoidance also is high among those who self-disclose little; touch and self-disclosure are intimate forms of communication, and people who are reluctant to get close to another person by self-disclosure also seem reluctant to get close through touch.

Older people have higher touch avoidance scores for opposite-sex persons than do younger people. Apparently, as we get older we are touched less by members of the opposite sex, and this decreased frequency of touching may lead us to avoid touching. Males score higher than females on same-sex touch avoidance. This accords well with our stereotypes: Men avoid touching other men, but women may and do touch other women. Women, it is found, have higher touch avoidance scores for opposite-sex touching than do men.

Paralanguage

Paralanguage is the vocal but nonverbal dimension of speech. It has to do with the manner in which you say something rather than with what you say. An old exercise used to increase a student's ability to express different emotions, feelings, and attitudes was to have the student say the following sentence while accenting or stressing different words: "Is this the face that launched a thousand ships?" Significant differences in meaning are easily communicated, depending on where the stress is placed. Consider, for example, the following variations:

1. *Is* this the face that launched a thousand ships?
2. Is *this* the face that launched a thousand ships?
3. Is this the *face* that launched a thousand ships?
4. Is this the face that *launched* a thousand ships?
5. Is this the face that launched a *thousand ships*?

Each of these five sentences communicates something different. Each, in fact, asks a totally different question, even though the words used are identical. All that distinguishes the sentences is variation in stress, one of the aspects of paralanguage.

In addition to stress, paralanguage includes such vocal characteristics as **rate** and **volume**. Paralanguage also includes the vocalizations we make when laughing, yelling, moaning, whining, and belching; vocal segregates—sound combinations that aren't words—such as "uh-uh" and "shh"; and **pitch**, the highness or lowness of vocal tone (Argyle, 1988; Trager 1958, 1961).

A good way to appreciate the workings of paralanguage is to examine your own vocal behavior when communicating different meanings. Try reading each of the sentences below first to communicate praise and then to communicate criticism. What changes in your vocal expression communicate the differences in meaning?

1. Now that looks good on you.
2. That was some meal.
3. You're an expert.
4. You're so sensitive.
5. Are you ready?

People Perception When listening to people—regardless of what they're saying—we form impressions based on their paralanguage as to what kind of people they are. It does seem that certain voices are symptomatic of certain personality types or problems and, specifically, that the personality orientation gives rise to the vocal qualities. Our impressions of others from paralanguage cues span a broad range and consist of physical impressions (perhaps about body type and certainly about gender and age), personality impressions (they sound shy, they appear aggressive), and evaluative impressions (they sound like good people, they sound evil and menacing, they have vicious laughs).

One of the most interesting findings on voice and personal characteristics is that listeners can accurately judge the socioeconomic status (high, middle, or low) of speakers after hearing a 60-second voice sample. In fact, many listeners reported that they made their judgments in less than 15 seconds. It has also been found that the speakers judged to be of high status were rated as being of higher credibility than those rated of middle or low status.

It's interesting to note that listeners agree with one another about the personality of the speaker even when their judgments are in error. Listeners seem to have stereotyped ideas about the way vocal characteristics and personality characteristics are related, and they use these stereotypes in their judgments.

Persuasion The rate of speech is the aspect of paralanguage that has received the most research attention—because speech rate is related to persuasiveness. Therefore, it's of interest to the advertiser, the politician, and anyone else who wants to convey information or to influence others orally, especially when time is limited or expensive. The research on rate of speech shows that in one-way communication situations, persons who talk fast are more persuasive and are evaluated more highly than those who talk at or below normal speeds (MacLachlan, 1979). This greater persuasiveness and higher regard holds true whether the person talks fast naturally or the speech is sped up electronically (as in time-compressed speech).

In one experiment, subjects were asked to listen to taped messages and then to indicate both the degree to which they agreed with the message and their opinions as to how intelligent and objective they thought the speaker was (MacLachlan, 1979). Rates of 111, 140, and 191 words per minute were used. Subjects agreed most with the fastest speech and least with the slowest speech. Further, they rated the fastest speaker as the most intelligent and objective and the slowest speaker as the least intelligent and objective. Even in experiments in which the speaker was known to have something to gain personally from persuasion (as would, say, a salesperson), the speaker who spoke at the fastest rate was the most persuasive. Research also finds that faster speech rates increase listeners' perceptions of speaker competence and dominance (Buller, LePoire, Aune, & Eloy, 1992).

Note that whether or not rapid speech rate is more persuasive depends on whether the speaker is speaking for or against your existing position (Smith & Shaffer, 1991, 1995). The rapid speaker who speaks *against* your existing attitudes is generally more effective than the speaker who speaks at a normal rate. But the rapid speaker who speaks *in favor of* your existing attitudes (say, in an attempt to strengthen them) is actually less effective than the speaker who speaks at a normal rate. The reason for this is quite logical. In the case of the speaker speaking against your attitudes, the rapidity of speech doesn't give you the time you need to think of counterarguments to rebut the speaker's position. So you're more likely to be persuaded by the speaker's position, because you don't have the time to consider why the speaker may be incorrect. In the case of the speaker speaking in favor of your attitudes, the rapidity of speech doesn't give you the time you need to mentally elaborate on the speaker's arguments. Therefore, they don't carry as much persuasive force as they would if spoken more slowly, giving you the time to think of reasons to agree with the speaker.

Although generally research finds that a faster than normal speech rate lowers comprehension, a rapid rate may still have the advantage in communicating information (MacLachlan, 1979; Jones, Berry, & Stevens, 2007). For example, people who listened to speeches at 201 words per minute (about 140 is average) comprehended 95 percent of the message, and those who listened to speeches at 282 words per minute (that is, double the normal rate) comprehended 90 percent. Even though the rates increased dramatically, the comprehension rates fell only slightly. These 5 percent and 10 percent losses are more than offset by the increased speed and thus make the faster rates much more efficient in communicating information. If the speech speeds are increased more than 100 percent, however, comprehension falls dramatically.

Exercise caution in applying this research to your own interpersonal interactions (MacLachlan, 1979). Realize that while the speaker is speaking, the listener is generating and framing a reply. If the speaker talks too rapidly, there may not be enough time to compose this reply, and resentment may be generated. Furthermore, the increased rate may seem so unnatural that the listener may come to focus on the speed of speech rather than the thought expressed.

Silence

"Speech," wrote Thomas Mann, "is civilization itself. The word, even the most contradictory word, preserves contact; it's silence which isolates." Philosopher Karl Jaspers, on the other hand, observed that "the ultimate in thinking as in communication is silence," and philosopher Max Picard noted that "silence is nothing merely negative; it's not the mere absence of speech. It's a positive, a complete world in itself."

Ethics in Interpersonal Communication

Interpersonal Silence

Remaining silent is at times your right. At other times, however, it may be unlawful. You have the right to remain silent so as not to incriminate yourself. You have a right to protect your privacy—to withhold information that has no bearing on the matter at hand. For example, your previous relationship history, affectional orientation, or religion is usually irrelevant to your ability to function in a job, and thus may be kept private in most job-related situations. On the other hand, these issues may be relevant when, for example, you're about to enter a more intimate phase of a relationship; then there may be an obligation to reveal information about yourself that could have been kept hidden at earlier relationship stages.

You do not have the right to remain silent and to refuse to reveal information about crimes you've seen others commit. However, psychiatrists, clergy, and lawyers—fortunately or unfortunately—are often exempt from the requirement to reveal information about criminal activities when the information had been gained through privileged communication with clients.

What would you do?

On your way to work, you witness a father verbally abusing his three-year-old child. You worry that he might psychologically harm the child, and your first impulse is to speak up and tell this man that verbal abuse can have lasting effects on the child and often leads to physical abuse. At the same time, you don't want to interfere with his right to speak to his child, and you certainly don't want to make him angrier. What is your ethical obligation in this case? What would you do in this situation?

The one thing on which these contradictory observations agree is that **silence** communicates. Your silence communicates just as intensely as anything you verbalize (Jaworski, 1993; Richmond, McCroskey, & Hickson, 2008).

The Functions of Silence Like words and gestures, silence serves important communication functions. Silence allows the speaker *time to think*, time to formulate and organize his or her verbal communications. Before messages of intense conflict, as well as those confessing undying love, there is often silence. Again, silence seems to prepare the receiver for the importance of these future messages.

Some people use silence as a weapon *to hurt* others. We often speak of giving someone "the silent treatment." After a conflict, for example, one or both individuals may remain silent as a kind of punishment. Silence used to hurt others also may take the form of refusing to acknowledge the presence of another person, as in disconfirmation (see Chapter 5); here silence is a dramatic demonstration of the total indifference one person feels toward the other.

Sometimes silence is used as a *response to personal anxiety*, shyness, or threats. You may feel anxious or shy among new people and prefer to remain silent. By remaining silent you preclude the chance of rejection. Only when you break your silence and attempt to communicate with another person do you risk rejection.

Silence may be used to *prevent communication* of certain messages. In conflict situations, silence is sometimes used to prevent certain topics from surfacing or to prevent one or both parties from saying things they may later regret. In such situations, silence often allows us time to cool off before expressing hatred, severe criticism, or personal attacks that we know are irreversible.

Like the eyes, face, or hands, silence can also be used to *communicate emotional responses* (Ehrenhaus, 1988; Lane, Koetting, & Bishop, 2002). Sometimes silence communicates a determination to be uncooperative or defiant; by refusing to engage in verbal communication, you defy the authority or the legitimacy of the other person's position. Silence is often used to communicate annoyance, usually accompanied by a pouting expression, arms crossed in front of the chest, and nostrils flared. Silence may express affection or love, especially when coupled with long and longing gazes into each other's eyes.

Silence may also be used strategically, to *achieve specific effects*. The pause before making what you feel is an important comment or after hearing about some mishap may be strategically positioned to communicate a desired impression—to make your idea stand out among others or perhaps to give others the impression that you care a lot more than you really do. In some cases a prolonged silence after someone voices disagreement may give the appearance of control and superiority. It's a way of saying, "I can respond in my own time." Generally, research finds that people use silence strategically more with strangers than they do with close friends (Hasegawa & Gudykunst, 1998).

Of course, you also may use silence when you simply have *nothing to say*, when nothing occurs to you, or when you don't want to say anything. James Russell Lowell expressed this well: "Blessed are they who have nothing to say, and who cannot be persuaded to say it."

The Spiral of Silence The **spiral of silence** theory offers a somewhat different perspective on silence. Applying this theory (originally developed to explain the media's influence on opinion) to the interpersonal context, this theory argues that you're more likely to voice agreement than disagreement (Noelle-Neumann, 1973, 1980, 1991; Severin & Tankard, 2001; Scheufele & Moy, 2000). The theory claims that when a controversial issue arises, you estimate the opinions of others and figure out which views are popular and which are not. You also estimate the rewards and the punishments you'd likely get from expressing popular or unpopular positions. You then use these estimates to determine which opinions you'll express and which you won't.

Generally, you're more likely to voice your opinions when you agree with the majority than when you disagree. And there's evidence to show that this effect is stronger for minority group members (Bowen & Blackmon, 2003). You may do this to avoid being isolated from the majority, or for fear of being proved wrong or being disliked, for example. Or you may simply assume that the majority, because they're a majority, must be right.

As people with minority views remain silent, the majority position gets stronger (because those who agree with it are the only ones speaking); so, as the majority position becomes stronger and the minority position becomes weaker, the situation becomes an ever-widening spiral. The Internet (blogs and social network sites, especially) may in some ways act as a counteragent to the spiral of silence, because Internet discussions provide so many free ways for you to express minority viewpoints (anonymously if you wish) and to quickly find like-minded others (McDevitt, Kiousis, & Wahl-Jorgensen, 2003).

Spatial Messages and Territoriality

Space is an especially important factor in interpersonal communication, although we seldom think about it. Edward T. Hall (1959, 1963, 1966), who pioneered the study of spatial communication, called this area **proxemics**. We can examine this broad area by looking at proxemic distances, the theories about space, and territoriality.

Proxemic Distances Four proxemic distances correspond closely to the major types of relationships. They are intimate, personal, social, and public distances (see Table 6.2).

Intimate Distance Within **intimate distance,** ranging from the close phase of actual touching to the far phase of 6 to 18 inches, the presence of the other person is unmistakable. You experience the sound, smell, and feel of the other's breath. The close phase is used for lovemaking and wrestling, for comforting and protecting. In the close phase, the muscles and the skin communicate, while actual words play a minor role. The far phase allows people to touch each other by extending their hands. The individuals are so close that this distance is not considered proper for strangers in public. Because of the feeling of inappropriateness and discomfort (at least for some Americans), if strangers are this close (say, on a crowded bus), their eyes seldom meet but remain fixed on some remote object.

Personal Distance You carry a protective bubble defining your **personal distance,** which allows you to stay protected and untouched by others. Personal distance ranges from

---

TABLE 6.2 Relationships and Proxemic Distances

Note that these four distances can be further divided into close and far phases and that the far phase of one level (say, personal) blends into the close phase of the next level (social). Do your relationships also blend into one another? Or are, say, your personal relationships totally separate from your social relationships?

Relationship		Distance
Intimate relationship		Intimate distance 0 —————————————— 18 inches close phase · · · · far phase
Personal relationship		Personal distance $1\frac{1}{2}$ —————————————— 4 feet close phase · · · · far phase
Social relationship		Social distance 4 —————————————— 12 feet close phase · · · · far phase
Public relationship		Public distance 12 —————————————— 25+ feet close phase · · · · far phase

18 inches to about 4 feet. In the close phase, people can still hold or grasp each other, but only by extending their arms. You can then take into your protective bubble certain individuals—for example, loved ones. In the far phase, you can touch another person only if you both extend your arms. This far phase is the extent to which you can physically get your hands on things; hence, it defines, in one sense, the limits of your physical control over others. At times, you may detect breath odor, but generally at this distance etiquette demands that you direct your breath to some neutral area.

Social Distance At the **social distance,** ranging from 4 to 12 feet, you lose the visual detail you had at the personal distance. The close phase is the distance at which you conduct impersonal business or interact at a social gathering. The far phase is the distance at which you stand when someone says, "Stand away so I can look at you." At this distance, business transactions have a more formal tone than they do when conducted in the close phase. In the offices of high officials, the desks are often positioned so that clients are kept at least this distance away. Unlike the intimate distance, where eye contact is awkward, the far phase of the social distance makes eye contact essential—otherwise, communication is lost. The voice is generally louder than normal at this level. This distance enables you to avoid constant interaction with those with whom you work without seeming rude.

Public Distance **Public distance** ranges from 12 to more than 25 feet. In the close phase, a person seems protected by space. At this distance, you're able to take defensive action should you feel threatened. On a public bus or train, for example, you might keep at least this distance from a drunk. Although you lose the fine details of the face and eyes, you're still close enough to see what is happening.

At the far phase, you see others not as separate individuals but as part of the whole setting. People automatically establish a space of approximately 30 feet around important public figures, and they seem to do this whether or not there are guards preventing their coming closer. The far phase is the distance by which actors on stage are separated from their audience; consequently, their actions and voices have to be somewhat exaggerated.

The specific distance that you'll maintain between yourself and any given person depends on a wide variety of factors (Burgoon, Buller, & Woodall, 1996; Burgoon & Bacue, 2003). Among the most significant are *gender* (women sit and stand closer to each other than do men in same-sex dyads, and people approach women more closely than they approach men); *age* (people maintain closer distances with similarly aged others than they do with those much older or much younger); and *personality* (introverts and highly anxious people maintain greater distances than do extroverts). Not surprisingly, you'll maintain shorter distances with people you're familiar with than with strangers, and with people you like than with those you don't like.

Theories about Space Researchers studying nonverbal communication have offered numerous explanations as to why people maintain the distances they do. Prominent among these explanations are protection theory, equilibrium theory, and expectancy violation theory—rather complex names for simple and interesting concepts.

Protection Theory **Protection theory** holds that you establish a body buffer zone around yourself as protection against unwanted touching or attack (Dosey & Meisels, 1976). When you feel that you may be attacked, your body buffer zone increases; you want more space around you. For example, if you found yourself in a dangerous neighborhood at night, your body buffer zone would probably expand well beyond what it would be if you were in familiar and safe surroundings. If someone entered this buffer zone, you would probably feel threatened and seek to expand the distance by walking faster or crossing the street.

In contrast, when you're feeling secure and protected, your buffer zone becomes much smaller. For example, if you're with a group of close friends and feel secure, your buffer zone shrinks, and you may welcome close proximity and mutual touching.

Equilibrium Theory **Equilibrium theory** holds that intimacy and interpersonal distance vary together: The greater the intimacy, the closer the distance; the lower the intimacy, the greater the distance. This theory says that you maintain close distances with those with whom you have close interpersonal relationships and that you maintain greater distances with those with whom you do not have close relationships (Argyle & Dean, 1965; Bailenson, Blascovich, Beall, & Loomis, 2001).

At times, of course, your interpersonal distance does not accurately reflect your level of intimacy. When this happens, you make adjustments. For example, let's say that you have an intimate relationship with someone, but for some reason you're separated—perhaps because you could not get concert seats next to each other or you're at a party and have each been led to different parts of a large banquet hall. When this happens, you probably try to preserve your psychological closeness by maintaining frequent eye contact or perhaps by facing each other.

At other times, however, you're forced into close distances with someone with whom you're not intimate (or whom you may even dislike)—for example, on a crowded bus or in the dentist's chair. In these situations, you also compensate, but in such cases you seek to make the psychological distance greater. Consequently, you might avoid eye contact and turn in an opposite direction. In the dentist's chair, you probably close your eyes to decrease this normally intimate distance. If seated to the right of a stranger, you might cross your legs and turn your torso to the left.

Expectancy Violations Theory **Expectancy violations theory** explains what happens when you increase or decrease the distance between yourself and another in an interpersonal interaction (Burgoon & Hoobler, 2002; Burgoon & Bacue, 2003). Each culture has certain expectancies for the distance people are to maintain in their conversations. Of course, each person has certain idiosyncrasies. Together, these determine "expected distance." What happens when these expectations are violated?

If you violate the expected distance to a great extent—small violations most often go unnoticed—then the relationship itself comes into focus. The other person begins to turn attention away from the topic of conversation and toward you and your relationship with him or her. It's also interesting to note that those who violate normal expected spatial relationships are judged to be less truthful than those who didn't commit such violations (Feeley & deTurck, 1995), perhaps because their behavior is seen as a sign of discomfort.

If the other person perceives you positively—for example, if you're a high-status person or you're particularly attractive—then you'll be perceived even more positively if you violate the norm. If, however, you're perceived negatively and you violate the norm, you'll be perceived even more negatively. Thus, the positively evaluated person will be perceived more positively if he or she violates the norm, whereas the negatively evaluated person will be more positively perceived if the distance norm is not violated.

Territoriality Another type of communication having to do with space is **territoriality**, the possessive reaction to an area or to particular objects. You interact basically in three types of territories (Altman, 1975):

- **Primary territories**, or **home territories**, are areas that you might call your own; these areas are your exclusive preserve and might include your room, your desk, or your office.
- **Secondary territories** are areas that don't belong to you but that you have occupied; thus, you're associated with them. Secondary territories might include the table in the cafeteria that you regularly eat at, your classroom seat, or your neighborhood turf.
- **Public territories** are areas that are open to all people; they may be owned by some person or organization, but they are used by everyone. Examples include a movie house, a restaurant, or a shopping mall.

When you operate in your own primary territory, you have an interpersonal advantage, often called the **home field advantage.** In their own home or office, people take on a kind of leadership role: They initiate conversations, fill in silences, assume relaxed and comfortable postures, and in conversations maintain their positions with greater conviction. Because the territorial owner is dominant, you stand a better chance of getting your raise, having your point accepted, or getting a contract resolved in your favor if you're in your own territory (your office, your home) rather than in someone else's (your supervisor's office, for example) (Marsh, 1988).

Like animals, humans mark both their primary and secondary territories to signal ownership. Some people—perhaps because they can't own territories—use markers to indicate pseudo-ownership or appropriation of someone else's space, or of a public territory, for their own use (Childress, 2004). Graffiti and the markings of gang boundaries come quickly to mind as examples. In general, three types of **markers** may be identified: central, boundary, and ear markers (Goffman, 1971). **Central markers** are items you place in a territory to reserve it for you—for example, a drink at the bar, books on your desk, or a sweater over a library chair.

Boundary markers set boundaries that divide your territory from that of others. In the supermarket checkout line, the bar that is placed between your groceries and those of the person behind you is a boundary marker, as are fences, the armrests separating chairs, and the contours of the molded plastic seats on a bus.

Ear markers—a term taken from the practice of branding animals on their ears—are identifying marks that indicate your possession of a territory or object. Trademarks, nameplates, and monograms are all examples of ear markers.

Markers are important in giving you a feeling of belonging. For example, students in college dormitories who marked their rooms by displaying personal items stayed in school longer than did those who didn't personalize their spaces (Marsh, 1988).

Again, like animals, humans use territory to signal their status. For example, the size and location of your territory (your home or office, say) indicates something about your status. Status is also signaled by the unwritten law granting the right of invasion, or **territorial encroachment**. Higher-status individuals have a "right" to invade the territory of lower-status persons, but the reverse is not true. The boss of a large company, for example, can barge into the office of a junior executive, but the reverse would be unthinkable. Similarly, a teacher may invade a student's personal space by looking over her or his shoulder as the student writes, but the student cannot do the same to the teacher.

At times, you may want to resist the encroachment on your territory. If so, you can react in several ways (Lyman & Scott, 1967; Richmond, McCroskey, & Hickson, 2008):

- In **withdrawal** you simply leave the scene, whether the country, home, office, or classroom.
- In **turf defense** you defend the territory against the encroachment. This may mean doing something as simple as saying, "This is my seat," or you may start a fight as nations do.
- **Insulation** involves erecting barriers between yourself and those who would encroach on your territory. Putting up a fence around your property or surrounding your desk with furniture so that others can't get close are common examples of insulation.
- **Linguistic collusion** means speaking in a language or jargon that the "invaders" don't understand and thus excluding them from your interactions.

Artifactual Communication

Artifactual communication consists of messages conveyed by objects that are made by human hands. Thus, aesthetics, color, clothing, jewelry, and hairstyle, as well as scents such as perfume, cologne, or incense, all are considered artifactual. We look briefly at each of these.

Space Decoration
That the decoration or surroundings of a place exert influence on perceptions should be obvious to anyone who has ever entered a hospital, with its sterile walls and furniture, or a museum, with its imposing columns, glass-encased exhibits, and brass plaques. Even the way a room is furnished exerts influence on us. In a classic study, researchers attempted to determine if the aesthetic conditions of a room would influence the

judgments people made in it (Maslow & Mintz, 1956; Mintz, 1956). Three rooms were used: one was beautiful, one average, and one ugly. The beautiful room had large windows, beige walls, indirect lighting, and attractive, comfortable furnishings. The average room was a professor's office with mahogany desks and chairs, metal bookcases and filing cabinets, and window shades. The ugly room was painted battleship gray; lighting was provided by an overhead bulb with a dirty, torn shade. The room was furnished to give the impression of a janitor's storeroom in horrible condition. The ashtrays were filled and the window shades torn.

In the three different rooms, students rated art prints in terms of the fatigue/energy and displeasure/well-being depicted in them. As predicted, the students in the beautiful room rated the prints as more energetic and as displaying well-being; the prints judged in the ugly room were rated as displaying fatigue and displeasure, while those judged in the average room were perceived as somewhere between these two extremes.

The way you decorate your private spaces communicates something about who you are. The office with a mahogany desk, bookcases, and oriental rugs communicates importance and status within the organization, just as a metal desk and bare floor communicate a status much farther down in the hierarchy. At home, the cost of your furnishings may communicate your status and wealth, and their coordination may communicate your sense of style. The magazines may communicate your interests. The arrangement of chairs around a television set may reveal how important watching television is. Bookcases lining the walls reveal the importance of reading. In fact, there is probably little in your home that does not send messages to others and that others do not use for making inferences about you. Computers, wide-screen televisions, well-equipped kitchens, and oil paintings of great grandparents, for example, all say something about the people who own them. Likewise, the absence of certain items will communicate something about you. Consider, for example, what messages you would get from a home in which there was no television, telephone, or books.

People also will form opinions about your personality on the basis of room decorations. Research, for example, finds that people will make judgments as to your openness to new experiences (distinctive decorating usually communicates this, as do different types of books and magazines and travel souvenirs) and as to your conscientiousness, emotional stability, degree of extroversion, and agreeableness. Not surprisingly, bedrooms prove more revealing than offices (Gosling, Ko, Mannarelli, & Morris, 2002).

Color Communication When you're in debt, you speak of being "in the red"; when you make a profit, you're "in the black." When you're sad, you're "blue"; when you're healthy, you're "in the pink"; when you're covetous, you're "green with envy." To be a coward is to be "yellow," and to be inexperienced is to be "green." When you talk a great deal, you talk "a blue streak"; when you're angry, you "see red." As revealed through these timeworn clichés, language abounds in color symbolism.

Color communication takes place on many levels. For example, there is some evidence that colors affect us physiologically. Respiratory movements increase in the presence of red light and decrease in the presence of blue light. Similarly, eye blinks increase in frequency when eyes are exposed to red light and decrease when exposed to blue. This seems consistent with our intuitive feelings that blue is more soothing and red more provocative. After a school changed the paint on its walls from orange and white to blue, the students' blood pressure decreased and their academic performance improved.

Colors surely influence our perceptions and behaviors (Kanner, 1989). People's acceptance of a product, for example, is largely determined by its package. In one study, for example, the very same coffee taken from a yellow can was described as weak, from a dark brown can as too strong, from a red can as rich, and from a blue can as mild. Even our acceptance of a person may depend on the colors worn. Consider, for example, the comments of one color expert (Kanner, 1989): "If you have to pick the wardrobe for your defense lawyer heading into court and choose anything but blue, you deserve to lose the case." Black is so powerful that it can work against the lawyer with the jury. Brown lacks sufficient authority. Green will probably elicit a negative response.

Clothing and Body Adornment Clothing serves a variety of functions. It protects you from the weather and, in sports like football, from injury. It helps you conceal parts of your body and so serves a modesty function. In the business world it may communicate your position within the hierarchy and your willingness and desire to conform to the clothing norms of the organization. It also may communicate your professionalism, which seems to be the reason why some organizations favor dress codes (M. H. Smith, 2003). Clothing also serves as a form of **cultural display** (Morris, 2002). It communicates your cultural and subcultural affiliations. In the United States, where there are so many different ethnic groups, you regularly see examples of dress that indicate what country the wearers are from.

The very poor and the very rich don't dress in the same way, nor do white- and blue-collar workers or the young and the old (Lurie, 1983). People dress, in part at least, to identify with the groups of which they are or want to be members. At the same time, they dress to manage the impressions they give to others (Frith & Gleeson, 2004; Keating, 2006). For example, you're likely to dress conservatively if you're interviewing for a job at a conservative firm, to indicate that you share the values of the firm of which you want to be a part. On the other hand, you'd dress very differently if you were going clubbing at one of the trendy hot spots.

Similarly, college students will perceive an instructor dressed informally as friendly, fair, enthusiastic, and flexible, and the same instructor dressed formally as prepared, knowledgeable, and organized (Malandro, Barker, & Barker, 1989).

Clothing also seems to influence your own behavior and the behavior of groups. For example, it has been argued that people who dress casually act more informally (Morand, cited in *Psychology Today,* March/April 1995, p. 16). Therefore, meetings with such casually dressed people are more likely to involve a freer exchange of thoughts and ideas, which in turn may stimulate creativity. This casual attire seems to work well in companies that must rely heavily on creative development, such as computer software companies. Some years ago IBM, for example, relaxed its conservative dress code and allowed some measure of informal dress among its workers (*New York Times,* February 7, 1995, p. B1). And many technology companies like Google, Yahoo, and Apple encourage a more informal, casual style of dress. But banks and insurance companies, which traditionally have resisted change, may prefer a more formal attire that creates distance between workers as well as between employees and customers.

Your jewelry, too, communicates messages about you. Wedding and engagement rings are obvious examples of jewelry designed to communicate very specific messages. College rings and political buttons also communicate specific information. If you wear a Rolex watch or large precious stones, others are likely to infer that you're rich. Men with earrings will be judged differently from men without earrings.

Today body piercings are popular, especially among the young. Nose and nipple rings and tongue and belly-button jewelry send a variety of messages. Although people wearing such jewelry may wish to communicate meanings of their own, those interpreting these messages seem to infer that the wearer is communicating an unwillingness to conform to social norms and a willingness to take greater risks than those without such piercings (Forbes, 2001). It's worth noting that in a study of employers' perceptions, applicants with eyebrow piercings were rated and ranked significantly lower than those without such piercings (Acor, 2001). In another study, nose-pierced job candidates were given lower scores on measures of credibility such as character and trust as well as sociability and hirability (Seiter & Sandry, 2003). And in relation to health, tattoos and piercings may communicate such undesirable traits as impulsiveness, unpredictability, and a tendency toward recklessness or violence (Rapsa & Cusack, 1990; M. H. Smith, 2003).

Tattoos—temporary or permanent—likewise communicate a variety of messages, often the name of a loved one or some symbol of allegiance or affiliation. Tattoos also communicate to the wearers themselves. For example, tattooed students see themselves (and perhaps others do as well) as more adventurous, creative, individualistic, and risk-prone than those without tattoos (Drews, Allison, & Probst, 2000).

The way you wear your hair communicates who you are. Your hair may communicate a concern for being up-to-date, a desire to shock, or perhaps a lack of concern for appearances. Men with long hair will generally be judged as less conservative than men with shorter hair.

In a study on interpersonal attraction, slides of male and female models were shown with and without glasses and were evaluated by men and women. Results indicated that persons with glasses were rated more negatively than the very same persons without glasses (Hasart & Hutchinson, 1993).

Scent Smell is a peculiar aspect of nonverbal communication and is discussed in widely different ways by different writers. Here, because the emphasis is on using scents (for example, perfume or cologne), it's grouped with artifactual communication. But recognize that body odor also communicates, and perhaps that part of smell is best thought of as a form of body communication. You also use smells to make yourself feel better. When the smells are pleasant, you feel better about yourself; when the smells are unpleasant, you feel less good about yourself. In fact, research finds that smells can influence your body's chemistry, which, in turn, influences your emotional state. For example, the smell of chocolate results in the reduction of theta brain waves, which produces a sense of relaxation and a reduced level of attention (Martin, 1998).

Olfactory communication, or olfactics, is extremely important in a wide variety of situations. Scientists estimate that you can smell some 10,000 different odors (Angier, 1995a). There is some, though not conclusive, evidence showing that the smell of lemon contributes to a perception of health; the smells of lavender and eucalyptus seem to increase alertness, and the smell of rose oil seems to reduce blood pressure. Findings such as these have contributed to the growth of aromatherapy and to the profession of aromatherapist (Furlow, 1996). Because humans possess "denser skin concentrations of scent glands than almost any other mammal," it has been argued that it only remains for us to discover how we use scent to communicate a wide variety of messages (Furlow, 1996, p. 41). Some of the most important messages scent seems to communicate involve attraction, taste, memory, and identification.

In many animal species the female gives off a scent that draws males, often from far distances, and thus ensures the continuation of the species. Humans, too, emit sexual *attractants* called sex pheromones, body secretions that arouse sexual desire (Kluger, 2008). Humans, of course, supplement pheromones with perfumes, colognes, after-shave lotions, powders, and the like to further enhance attractiveness and sexuality. Although we often think of women as the primary users of perfumes and scents, increasingly men are using them as well—not only cologne and after-shave lotions but body sprays, which have become big business with a market estimated at $180 million (Dell, 2005). Women, research finds, prefer the scent of men who bear a close genetic similarity to themselves—a finding that may account in part for our attraction to people much like ourselves (Ober, Weitkamp, Cox, Dytch, Kostyu, & Elias, 1997; Wade, 2002).

Without smell, *taste* would be severely impaired. For example, it would be extremely difficult to taste the difference between a raw potato and an apple without the sense of smell. Street vendors selling hot dogs, sausages, and similar foods are aided greatly by the smells that stimulate the appetites of passersby.

Smell is a powerful *memory* aid; you can often recall situations from months and even years ago when you happen upon a similar smell. One reason smell can so effectively recall a previous situation is that it's often associated with significant emotional experiences (Rubin, Groth, & Goldsmith, 1984; Malandro, Barker, & Barker, 1989).

Smell is often used to create an image or an *identity* for a product. Advertisers and manufacturers spend millions of dollars each year creating scents for cleaning products and toothpastes, for example. These scents have nothing to do with the products' cleaning power. Instead, they function solely to help create product images or identities. There also is evidence that we can identify specific significant others by smell. For example, infants find their mothers' breasts through smell, and mothers can identify their newborns solely through smell. In one study young children were able to identify the T-shirts of their brothers and sisters solely on the basis of smell (Porter & Moore, 1981; Angier, 1995a). One researcher goes so far as to advise: "If your man's odor reminds you of Dad or your brother, you may want genetic tests before trying to conceive a child" (Furlow, 1996, p. 41).

Temporal Communication

Temporal communication consists of the messages communicated by your time orientation and treatment of time. Shortly we'll consider the cultural dimension of time differences. Here, let's look at another dimension of time, psychological time. The study of the communicative function of time is often referred to as **chronemics**.

The term **psychological time** refers to a person's emphasis on, or orientation toward, the past, present, or future. In a *past orientation,* you give particular reverence to the past; you might relive old times and regard old methods as the best. Events are seen as circular and recurring, so that the wisdom of yesterday is applicable also to today and tomorrow. In a *present orientation,* you live in the present and for the present. Present activities command your attention; you engage in them not for their future rewards or their past significance but because they're happening now. In its extreme form, this orientation is hedonistic. In a *future orientation,* you give primary attention to the future. You save today, work hard in college, and deny yourself certain enjoyments and luxuries, all because you're preparing for the future.

Researchers have provided some interesting correlations to these different time orientations (Gonzalez & Zimbardo, 1985; Rappaport, Enrich, & Wilson, 1985). Before reading their conclusions, you may wish to take the self-test "What Time Do You Have?"

✎ TEST YOURSELF

WHAT TIME DO YOU HAVE?

For each statement, indicate whether the statement is true (T) of your general attitude and behavior, or untrue (F) of your general attitude and behavior. (A few statements are purposely repeated to facilitate scoring and analyzing your responses.)

1. Meeting tomorrow's deadlines and doing other necessary work comes before tonight's partying.
2. I meet my obligations to friends and authorities on time.
3. I complete projects on time by making steady progress.
4. I am able to resist temptations when I know there is work to be done.
5. I keep working at a difficult, uninteresting task if it will help me get ahead.
6. If things don't get done on time, I don't worry about it.
7. I think that it's useless to plan too far ahead because things hardly ever come out the way you planned anyway.
8. I try to live one day at a time.
9. I live to make better what is rather than to be concerned about what will be.
10. It seems to me that it doesn't make sense to worry about the future, since fate determines that whatever will be, will be.
11. I believe that getting together with friends to party is one of life's important pleasures.
12. I do things impulsively, making decisions on the spur of the moment.
13. I take risks to put excitement in my life.
14. I get drunk at parties.
15. It's fun to gamble.
16. Thinking about the future is pleasant to me.
17. When I want to achieve something, I set subgoals and consider specific means for reaching these goals.
18. It seems to me that my career path is pretty well laid out.
19. It upsets me to be late for appointments.
20. I meet my obligations to friends and authorities on time.
21. I get irritated at people who keep me waiting when we've agreed to meet at a given time.
22. It makes sense to invest a substantial part of my income in insurance premiums.
23. I believe that "a stitch in time saves nine."
24. I believe that "a bird in the hand is worth two in the bush."
25. I believe it is important to save for a rainy day.
26. I believe a person's day should be planned each morning.
27. I make lists of things I must do.
28. When I want to achieve something, I set subgoals and consider specific means for reaching those goals.
29. I believe that "a stitch in time saves nine."

HOW DID YOU DO? This time test measures seven different factors. If you selected true (T) for all or most of the questions within any given factor, you're high on that factor. If you selected untrue (F) for all or most of the questions within any given factor, you're low on that factor.

The first factor, measured by questions 1–5, is a future, work-motivation, perseverance orientation. These people have a strong work ethic and are committed to completing a task despite difficulties. The second factor (questions 6–10) is a present, fatalistic, worry-free orientation. High scorers on this factor live one day at a time, not necessarily to enjoy the day but to avoid planning for the next day.

The third factor (questions 11–15) is a present, pleasure-seeking, partying orientation. These people enjoy the present, take risks, and engage in a variety of impulsive actions. The fourth factor (questions 16–18) is a future, goal-seeking, and planning orientation. These people derive pleasure from planning and achieving a variety of goals.

The fifth factor (questions 19–21) is a time-sensitivity orientation. People who score high are especially sensitive to time and its role in social obligations. The sixth factor (questions 22–25) is a future, practical action orientation. These people do what they have to do—take practical actions—to achieve the future they want.

The seventh factor (questions 26–29) is a future, somewhat obsessive daily planning orientation. High scorers make daily "to do" lists and devote great attention to detail.

WHAT WILL YOU DO? Now that you have some idea of how you treat time, consider how these attitudes and behaviors work for you. For example, will your time orientations help you achieve your social and professional goals? If not, what might you do about changing these attitudes and behaviors?

Source: From A. Gonzalez and P. Zimbardo, "Time in Perspective," *Psychology Today,* March 1985. Reprinted with permission from *Psychology Today Magazine.* Copyright © 1985 by Sussex Publishers, LLC.

One of the findings of the time research is that future income is positively related to future orientation. The more future oriented a person is, the greater that person's income is likely to be. Present orientation is strongest among lowest-income males.

The time orientation you develop depends largely on your socioeconomic class and your personal experiences (Gonzalez & Zimbardo, 1985). For example, parents with unskilled and semiskilled occupations are likely to teach their children a present-oriented fatalism and a belief that enjoying yourself is more important than planning for the future. Parents who are professionals (for example, teachers or managers) teach their children the importance of planning and preparing for the future, along with strategies for future success.

Not surprisingly, time orientation is heavily influenced by culture. Some cultures—individualistic cultures in particular—seem to emphasize a future orientation; members work hard today for a better future and without much regard for the past, for example. Collectivist cultures, on the other hand, have greater respect for the past; the past is often looked to for guidance for the present. According to some intercultural researchers, many Asian cultures (Japanese and Chinese) place great value on the past; Latinos and Native Americans place more emphasis on the present, and European Americans emphasize the future (Lustig & Koester, 2006). Later in this chapter we'll look at additional cultural distinctions concerning time.

Different time perspectives also account for much intercultural misunderstanding, because different cultures often teach their members drastically different time orientations. The future-oriented person who works for tomorrow's goals will frequently regard the present-oriented person who focuses on enjoying today as lazy and poorly motivated. In turn, the present-oriented person may see those with strong future orientations as obsessed with accumulating wealth or rising in status.

Functions of Nonverbal Communication

Now that you have a good idea of the various channels through which meaningful nonverbal signals may be sent, we need to see these varied channels operating together in actual interpersonal communication situations. The best way to do this is to look at some of the functions that nonverbal communication serves.

Although nonverbal communication serves the same functions as verbal communication, researchers have singled out several specific functions in which nonverbal messages are especially significant: (1) forming and managing impressions, (2) forming and defining relationships, (3) structuring conversation and social interaction, (4) influencing and deceiving, and (5) expressing emotions (Burgoon & Hoobler, 2002; Burgoon & Bacue, 2003; Afifi, 2007).

Forming and Managing Impressions

It is largely through the nonverbal communications of others that you form impressions of them. Based on a person's body size, skin color, and dress, as well as on the way the person smiles, maintains eye contact, and expresses himself or herself facially, you form impressions—you judge who the person is and what the person is like.

And, at the same time that you form impressions of others, you are also managing the impressions they form of you. As explained in the discussion of impression management in Chapter 3 (pp. 71–75), you use different strategies to achieve different impressions. And of course many of these strategies involve nonverbal messages. Also, as noted earlier, each of these strategies may be used to present a false self and to deceive others. For example:

- *To be liked* you might smile, pat another on the back, and shake hands warmly. See Table 6.3 for some additional ways in which nonverbal communication may make you seem more attractive and more likeable.
- *To be believed* you might use focused eye contact, a firm stance, and open gestures.
- *To excuse failure* you might look sad, cover your face with your hands, and shake your head.
- *To secure help* by indicating helplessness, you might use open hand gestures, a puzzled look, and inept movements.

TABLE 6.3 **Ten Nonverbal Messages and Attractiveness**

Here are 10 nonverbal messages that help communicate your attractiveness and 10 that will likely create the opposite effect (Andersen, 2004; Riggio & Feldman, 2005).

Do	But Don't
Gesture to show liveliness and animation in ways that are appropriate to the situation and to the message.	Gesture for the sake of gesturing or gesture in ways that may prove offensive to members of other cultures.
Nod and lead forward to signal that you're listening and are interested.	Go on automatic pilot, nodding without any coordination with what is being said, or lean so far forward that you intrude on the other's space.
Smile and otherwise show your interest, attention, and positiveness facially.	Overdo it; inappropriate smiling is likely to be perceived negatively.
Make eye contact in moderation.	Stare, ogle, glare, or otherwise make the person feel that he or she is under scrutiny.
Touch in moderation when appropriate.	Touch excessively or too intimately. When in doubt, avoid touching another.
Use vocal variation in rate, rhythm, pitch, and volume to communicate your animation and involvement in what you're saying.	Fall into a pattern in which, for example, your voice goes up and down, up and down, up and down without any relationship to what you're saying.
Use silence to listen at least the same amount of time as you speak. Show that you're listening with appropriate facial reactions, posture, and back-channeling cues, for example.	Listen motionlessly or in ways that suggest you're listening only halfheartedly.
Stand reasonably close to show connectedness.	Invade the other person's comfort zone.
Present a pleasant smell—and be careful to camouflage the onions, garlic, or smoke that you're so used to you can't smell it.	Overdo the cologne or perfume.
Dress appropriately to the situation.	Wear clothing that proves uncomfortable or that calls attention to itself and hence distracts others from your message.

- *To hide faults* you might avoid self-adaptors.
- *To be followed* you might dress the part of a leader or display your diploma or awards where others can see them.
- *To confirm self-image and to communicate it to others*, you might dress in certain ways or decorate your apartment with things that reflect your personality.

Forming and Defining Relationships

Much of your relationship life is lived nonverbally. You communicate affection, support, and love, in part at least, nonverbally (Floyd & Mikkelson, 2005). At the same time, you also communicate displeasure, anger, and animosity through nonverbal signals.

You also use nonverbal signals to communicate the nature of your relationship to another person; and you and that person communicate nonverbally with each other. These signals that communicate your relationship status are known as "tie signs": They indicate the ways in which your relationship is tied together (Goffman, 1967; Afifi & Johnson, 2005; Knapp & Hall, 2006). Tie signs are also used to confirm the level of the relationship; for example, you might hold hands to see if this is responded to positively. And of course tie signs are often used to let others know that the two of you are tied together.

Tie signs vary in intimacy and may extend from the relatively informal handshake through more intimate forms such as hand holding and arm linking to very intimate contact such as full mouth kissing (Andersen, 2004).

You also use nonverbal signals to communicate your relationship dominance and status (Knapp & Hall, 2006; Dunbar & Burgoon, 2005). The large corner office with the huge desk communicates high status, just as the basement cubicle communicates low status.

Structuring Conversation and Social Interaction

When you're in conversation, you give and receive cues—signals that you're ready to speak, to listen, to comment on what the speaker just said. These cues regulate and structure the interaction. These **turn-taking cues** may be verbal (as when you say, "What do you think?" and thereby give the speaking turn over to the listener). Most often, however, they're nonverbal; a nod of the head in the direction of someone else, for example, signals that you're ready to give up your speaking turn and want this other person to say something. You also show that you're listening and that you want the conversation to continue (or that you're not listening and want the conversation to end) largely through nonverbal signals of posture and eye contact (or the lack thereof).

Influencing and Deceiving

You can influence others not only through what you say but also through your nonverbal signals. A focused glance that says you're committed; gestures that further explain what you're saying; appropriate dress that says, "I'll easily fit in with this organization"—these are just a few examples of ways in which you can exert nonverbal influence.

And with the ability to influence, of course, comes the ability to deceive—to mislead another person into thinking something is true when it's false or that something is false when it's true. One common example of nonverbal deception is using your eyes and facial expressions to communicate a liking for other people when you're really interested only in gaining their support in some endeavor. Not surprisingly, you also use nonverbal signals to detect deception in others. For example, you may well suspect a person of lying if he or she avoids eye contact, fidgets, and conveys inconsistent verbal and nonverbal messages.

VIEWPOINT The "Pygmalion gift" is a gift that is designed to change the recipient into what the donor wants that person to become. For example, the parent who gives a child books or science equipment may be asking the child to be a scholar or a scientist. What messages have you recently communicated in your gift-giving behavior? What messages do you think others have communicated to you by the gifts they gave you?

But be careful. As explained in the Understanding Interpersonal Theory and Research box in Chapter 4, research shows that it is much more difficult to tell when someone is lying than you probably think it is. So use caution in judging deception (Knapp, 2008).

Expressing Emotions

Although people often explain and reveal emotions verbally, nonverbal signals communicate a great part of your emotional experience. For example, you reveal your level of happiness or sadness or confusion largely through facial expressions. Of course, you also reveal your feelings by posture (for example, whether tense or relaxed), gestures, eye movements, and even the dilation of your pupils. Nonverbal messages often help people communicate unpleasant messages that they might feel uncomfortable putting into words (Infante, Rancer, & Womack, 2003). For example, you might avoid eye contact and maintain large distances between yourself and someone with whom you didn't want to interact or with whom you wanted to decrease the intensity of your relationship.

At the same time, you also use nonverbal messages to hide your emotions. You might, for example, smile even though you feel sad so as not to dampen the party spirit. Or you might laugh at someone's joke even though you think it silly.

Nonverbal Communication and Culture

Throughout this chapter we've seen a few cultural and gender differences in nonverbal communication. Cultural variations in certain channels of nonverbal communication, however, have become the focus of sustained research. Here we consider just a sampling of research on the relationship between culture and nonverbal communication expressed through gestures, facial expressions, eye communication, touch, silence, color, and time (Matsumoto, 2006; Matsumoto Yoo, 2005; Matsumoto, Yoo, Hirayama, & Petrova, 2005).

Culture and Gesture

There is much variation in gestures and their meanings among different cultures (Axtell, 2007). Consider a few common gestures that you may often use without thinking, but that could easily get you into trouble if you used them in another culture (also, take a look at Figure 6.1):

- Folding your arms over your chest would be considered defiant and disrespectful in Fiji.
- Waving your hand would be insulting in Nigeria and Greece.
- Gesturing with the thumb up would be rude in Australia.
- Tapping your two index fingers together would be considered an invitation to sleep together in Egypt.
- Pointing with your index finger would be impolite in many Middle Eastern countries.
- Bowing to a lesser degree than your host would be considered a statement of your superiority in Japan.
- Inserting your thumb between your index and middle finger in a clenched fist would be viewed as a wish that evil fall on the person in some African countries.
- Resting your feet on a table or chair would be insulting and disrespectful in some Middle Eastern cultures.

Culture and Facial Expression

The wide variations in facial communication that we observe in different cultures seem to reflect which reactions are publicly permissible rather than a fundamental difference in the way emotions are facially expressed. In one study, for example, Japanese and American students watched a film of a surgical operation (Ekman, 1985). The students were videotaped both during an interview about the film and alone while watching the film. When alone, the students showed very similar reactions; but in the interview the American students displayed facial expressions indicating displeasure, whereas the Japanese students did not show any great emotion. Similarly, it's considered "forward" or inappropriate for Japanese women

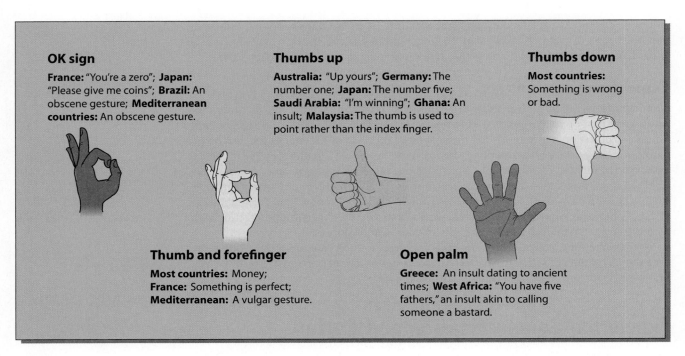

FIGURE 6.1

Some Cultural Meanings of Gestures

Cultural differences in the meanings of nonverbal gestures are often significant. The over-the-head clasped hands that signify victory to an American may signify friendship to a Russian. To an American, holding up two fingers to make a V signifies victory or peace. To certain South Americans, however, it is an obscene gesture that corresponds to the American's extended middle finger. This figure highlights some additional nonverbal differences. Can you identify others?

to reveal broad smiles, so many Japanese women will hide their smile, sometimes with their hands (cf. Ma, 1996). Women in the United States, on the other hand, have no such restrictions and so are more likely to smile openly. Thus, the difference may not be in the way different cultures express emotions but rather in the society's **cultural display rules**, or rules about the appropriate display of emotions in public (cf. Matsumoto, 1991; Aune, 2005). For example, the well-documented finding that women smile more than men is likely due, at least in part, to display rules that allow women to smile more than men (Hall, 2006).

Culture and Eye Communication

Not surprisingly, eye messages vary with both culture and gender. Americans, for example, consider direct eye contact an expression of honesty and forthrightness, but the Japanese often view this as showing a lack of respect. A Japanese person will glance at the other person's face rarely, and then only for very short periods (Axtell, 1990). Interpreting another's eye contact messages according to your own cultural rules is a risky undertaking; eye movements that you may interpret as insulting may have been intended to show respect.

Women make eye contact more and maintain it longer (both in speaking and in listening) than men. This holds true whether women are interacting with other women or with men. This difference in eye behavior may result from women's greater tendency to display their emotions (Wood, 1994). When women interact with other women, they display affiliative and supportive eye contact, whereas when men interact with other men, they avert their gaze (Gamble & Gamble, 2003).

Cultural differences also exist in the ways people decode the meanings of facial expressions. For example, American and Japanese students judged the meaning of a smiling and a neutral facial expression. The Americans rated the smiling face as more attractive, more intelligent, and more sociable than the neutral face. In contrast, the Japanese rated the smiling face as more sociable but not as more attractive—and they rated the neutral face as more intelligent (Matsumoto & Kudoh, 1993).

Culture and Touch

The several functions and examples of touching discussed earlier in this chapter were based on studies in North America; in other cultures these functions are not served in the same way. In some cultures, for example, some task-related touching is viewed negatively and is to be avoided. Among Koreans it is considered disrespectful for a store owner to touch a customer in, say, handing back change; it is considered too intimate a gesture. A member of another culture who is used to such touching may consider the Korean's behavior cold and aloof. Muslim children are socialized not to touch members of the opposite sex; their behavior can easily be interpreted as unfriendly by American children who are used to touching one another (Dresser, 2005).

Some cultures—including many in southern Europe and the Middle East—are contact cultures; others are noncontact cultures, such as those of northern Europe and Japan. Members of contact cultures maintain close distances, touch one another in conversation, face each other more directly, and maintain longer and more focused eye contact. Members of noncontact cultures maintain greater distance in their interactions, touch each other rarely (if at all), avoid facing each other directly, and maintain much less direct eye contact. As a result, of these differences, problems may occur. For example, northern Europeans and Japanese may be perceived as cold, distant, and uninvolved by southern Europeans—who may in turn be perceived as pushy, aggressive, and inappropriately intimate.

VIEWPOINT Consider the operation of the spiral of silence theory on your own interpersonal interactions. For example, if you were talking with a group of new students, would you be more likely to voice opinions that agreed with the majority? Would you hesitate to voice opinions that differed greatly from what the others were expressing?

Culture, Paralanguage, and Silence

Cultural differences also need to be taken into consideration when we evaluate the results of the studies on speech rate, because different cultures view speech rate differently. For example, investigators found that Korean male speakers who spoke rapidly were given unfavorable credibility ratings, unlike Americans who spoke rapidly (Lee & Boster, 1992). Researchers have suggested that in individualist societies a rapid-rate speaker is seen as more competent than a slow-rate speaker, whereas in collectivist cultures a speaker who uses a slower rate is judged more competent.

Similarly, not all cultures view silence as functioning in the same way (Vainiomaki, 2004). In the United States, for example, people often interpret silence negatively. At a business meeting or even in an informal social group, others may wonder if the silent member is not listening, has nothing interesting to add, doesn't understand the issues, is insensitive, or is too self-absorbed to focus on the messages of others.

Other cultures, however, view silence more positively. In many situations in Japan, for example, silence is a response that is considered more appropriate than speech (Haga, 1988). And in this country the traditional Apache regard silence very differently than do European Americans (Basso, 1972). Among the Apache mutual friends do not feel the need to introduce strangers who may be working in the same area or on the same project. The strangers may remain silent for several days. This period enables people to observe one another and to come to a judgment about the other individuals. Once this assessment is made, the individuals talk. When courting, especially during the initial stages, Apache couples remain silent for hours; if they do talk, they generally talk very little. Only after a couple has been dating for several months will they have lengthy conversations. These periods of silence are generally attributed to shyness or self-consciousness. The use of silence is explicitly taught to Apache women, who are especially discouraged from engaging in long discussions with their dates. Silence during courtship is a sign of modesty to many Apache.

Culture and Colors

Colors vary greatly in their meanings from one culture to another. To illustrate this cultural variation, here are some of the many meanings that popular colors communicate in a variety of different cultures (Dreyfuss, 1971; Hoft, 1995; Dresser, 2005; Singh & Pereira, 2005).

As you read this section, you may want to consider your own meanings for these colors and where your meanings came from.

- *Red:* In China red signifies prosperity and rebirth and is used for festive and joyous occasions. In France and the United Kingdom, red indicates masculinity, in many African countries blasphemy or death, and in Japan anger and danger. Red ink, especially among Korean Buddhists, is used only to write a person's name at the time of death or on the anniversary of the person's death; this can create problems when American teachers use red ink to mark homework.
- *Green:* In the United States green signifies capitalism, a signal to go ahead, and envy; in Ireland patriotism; among some Native Americans femininity; to the Egyptians fertility and strength; and to the Japanese youth and energy.
- *Black:* In Thailand black signifies old age, in parts of Malaysia courage, and in much of Europe death.
- *White:* In Thailand white signifies purity, in many Muslim and Hindu cultures purity and peace, and in Japan and other Asian countries death and mourning.
- *Blue:* In Iran blue signifies something negative, in Ghana joy; for the Cherokee it signifies defeat, for the Egyptian virtue and truth, and for the Greek national pride.
- *Yellow:* In China yellow signifies wealth and authority, in the United States caution and cowardice, in Egypt happiness and prosperity, and in many countries throughout the world femininity.
- *Purple:* In Latin America purple signifies death, in Europe royalty, in Egypt virtue and faith, in Japan grace and nobility, in China barbarism, and in the United States nobility and bravery.

Culture and Time

Culture influences our attitudes toward time in a variety of ways. Here we look at two dimensions of **cultural time**: formal versus informal time and monochronism versus polychronism. Another cultural dimension of time, the social clock, is discussed in the Understanding Interpersonal Theory and Research box.

UNDERSTANDING INTERPERSONAL THEORY & RESEARCH

Social and Biological Clocks

Your culture maintains a *social clock*—a time schedule for the right time to do various important things, such as starting dating, finishing college, buying your own home, or having a child. The social clock tells you if you're keeping pace with your peers, are ahead of them, or are falling behind (Neugarten, 1979; Greene, 2003). On the basis of this social clock, which you learned as you grew up, you evaluate your own social and professional development. If you're keeping pace with the rest of your peers (for example, you started dating at the "appropriate" age or you're finishing college at the "appropriate" age), you'll feel well adjusted, competent, and a part of the group. If you're late, you'll probably experience feelings of dissatisfaction. Although today the social clock is becoming more flexible and more tolerant of deviations from the acceptable timetable than it was in past decades, it still exerts pressure on each of us to keep pace with our peers (Peterson, 1996).

Another type of "clock" has to do with biological time or *biorhythms*; the term refers to your body clock, the ways your body functions differently at different times. According to biorhythm research, you function in three different cycles—physical, emotional, and intellectual. Each cycle begins at birth and continues throughout life, constantly repeating itself. Each cycle has an upside, during which you are particularly sharp; a downside, during which you are particularly dull; and a crucial period during which you are at your absolute worst. Detailed explanations and instructions for calculating your own intellectual, physical, and emotional cycles can be found in DeVito (1989); or, even better, you can visit a website that will compute your biorhythms, (such as www.bio-chart.com or www.facade.com/biorhythm (both accessed May 6, 2008).

Working with Theories and Research

How important is the social clock to you? Have you ever felt out of step with your peers in some area? Did your feeling influence your behavior in any way? If you computed your biorhythm chart, how accurate do you find it?

Formal and Informal Time Days are astronomically determined by the earth's rotation on its axis, months by the moon's movement around the earth, and years by the earth's rotation around the sun. But the rest of our time divisions are cultural (largely religious) in origin.

In the United States and in most of the world, formal time divisions include seconds, minutes, hours, days, weeks, months, and years. Some cultures, however, may use seasons or phases of the moon to demarcate their most important time periods. In the United States, if your college is on the semester system, your courses are divided into 50- or 75-minute periods that meet two or three times a week for 14-week periods. Eight semesters of 15 or 16 periods per week equal a college education. As these examples illustrate, formal time units are arbitrary. The culture establishes them for convenience.

Informal time communication involves the use of **informal time terms**—for example, expressions such as "forever," "immediately," "soon," "right away," "as soon as possible." This type of time communication creates the most problems, because informal terms have different meanings for different people. This is especially true when these terms are used interculturally. For example, what does "late" mean when applied to a commuter train that is not on time? Apparently, it depends on your culture. In the New York area, "late" means arriving six minutes or more after the scheduled time; in Britain it means five minutes or more. But in Japan it means one minute. The deadly train crash that killed 90 people in Japan in 2005—the most deadly crash in Japan in 40 years—was attributed to the Japanese concern with time (Onishi, 2005a).

Not only in concepts of lateness but in other respects as well, attitudes toward time vary from one culture to another. In one study, for example, researchers measured the accuracy of clocks in six cultures—in Japan, Indonesia, Italy, England, Taiwan, and the United States. Japan had the most accurate and Indonesia had the least accurate clocks. The investigators also measured the speed at which people in these six cultures walked; results showed that the Japanese walked the fastest, the Indonesians the slowest (LeVine & Bartlett, 1984).

Monochronism and Polychronism Another important distinction is that between **monochronic** and **polychronic time orientations** (Hall, 1959, 1976; Hall & Hall, 1987). Monochronic people or cultures—such as those of the United States, Germany, Scandinavia, and Switzerland—schedule one thing at a time. In these cultures time is compartmentalized and there is a time for everything. On the other hand, polychronic people or cultures—such as those of Latin Americans, Mediterranean peoples, and Arabs—schedule multiple things at the same time. Eating, conducting business with several different people, and taking care of family matters all may occur at the same time.

No culture is entirely monochronic or polychronic; rather, these are general tendencies that are found across a large part of the culture. Some cultures combine both time orientations; for example, both orientations are found in Japan and in parts of American culture. Table 6.4 identifies some of the distinctions between these two time orientations.

TABLE 6.4 Monochronic and Polychronic Time

As you read this table, based on Hall and Hall (1987), note the potential for miscommunication that these differences may create when M-time and P-time people interact. Have any of these differences ever created interpersonal misunderstandings for you?

The Monochronic-Time Person	The Polychronic-Time Person
does one thing at a time	does several things at once
treats time schedules and plans very seriously; feels they may be broken only for the most serious of reasons	treats time schedules and plans as useful (not sacred); feels they may be broken for a variety of causes
considers the job the most important part of life, ahead of even family	considers the family and interpersonal relationships more important than the job
considers privacy extremely important; seldom borrows or lends to others; works independently	is actively involved with others; works in the presence of and with lots of people at the same time

Understanding these culturally different perspectives on time should make intercultural communication a bit easier, especially if these time differences are discussed in a culturally sensitive atmosphere. After all, one view of time is not any more correct than any other. However, like all cultural differences, these different time orientations have consequences. For example, the train crash in Japan might not have happened had it not been for the national obsession with time. And members of future-oriented cultures are more likely to succeed in competitive markets like the United States but may be viewed negatively by members of cultures that stress living in and enjoying the present.

Summary

This chapter explored nonverbal communication and identified the varied channels of nonverbal communication, several functions of nonverbal communication that research has focused on, and the influence of culture on nonverbal messages.

Channels of Nonverbal Communication

1. Among body gestures are emblems, illustrators, affect displays, regulators, and adaptors. General body appearance (e.g., height, weight, and eye and skin colors) can communicate a person's power, level of attractiveness, and suitability as a friend or romantic partner.
2. Facial movements express emotions, such as happiness, surprise, fear, anger, sadness, disgust/contempt, interest, bewilderment, and determination. Some facial movements manage the meanings being communicated by means of intensifying, deintensifying, neutralizing, masking, and simulating.
3. Through eye contact we monitor feedback, maintain interest/attention, signal conversational turns, signal the nature of relationships, signal status, and compensate for physical distance. Through eye avoidance we may give others privacy, signal disinterest, cut off unpleasant stimuli, or heighten other senses. Pupil dilation indicates interest/arousal and increases attractiveness.
4. Among the meanings touch can communicate are positive affect, playfulness, control, ritual functions, and task-relatedness.
5. Paralanguage cues help people form impressions; identify emotional states; and make judgments of speakers' credibility, intelligence, and objectivity.
6. Silence can communicate varied meanings (for example, to hurt, to prevent communication, to achieve special effects). The spiral of silence theory offers an interesting perspective on the influence of silence.
7. The major types of distance that correspond to types of relationships are intimate distance (touching to 18 inches), personal distance (18 inches to 4 feet), social distance (4 to 12 feet), and public distance (12 or more feet).
8. Theories about space include protection theory (you maintain spatial distance to protect yourself); equilibrium theory (you regulate distance according to the intimacy level of your relationship); and expectancy violations theory (increasing or decreasing the expected distance between yourself and another can send important messages).
9. Your territories may be identified as primary (areas you own), secondary (areas that you occupy regularly), and public (areas open to everyone). Like animals, humans often mark their territories with central, boundary, and ear markers as proof of ownership. Your territory (its appearance and the way it's used) also communicates status.
10. Among the artifactual nonverbal cues are space decoration, color, clothing and body adornment, and the use of scent.
11. Three main time orientations can be distinguished: past, present, and future. These orientations influence a wide variety of behaviors, such as your willingness to plan for the future, your tendency to party, and even your potential income.

Functions of Nonverbal Communication

12. Among the major functions of nonverbal communication that researchers have studied are the roles of nonverbal signals in forming and managing impressions, forming and defining relationships, structuring conversation and social interaction, influencing and deceiving, and expressing emotions.

Nonverbal Communication and Culture

13. Researchers have demonstrated some wide cultural differences in nonverbal communication, including the way people gesture and the meanings of such gestures, the rules for expressing emotions facially and the meanings given to such facial expressions, eye messages, preferences for touch behavior (some encouraging lots of touching and some discouraging it), paralinguistic variations and silence, colors, and the ways of dealing with time (for example, differences in the treatment of formal and informal time and in monochronism versus polychronism).

Key Terms

artifactual communication, **145**	facial feedback hypothesis, **132**
body communication, **131**	facial management techniques, **132**
body gestures, **129**	
chronemics, **148**	haptics, **136**
color communication, **146**	immediacy, **134**
eye avoidance, **135**	informal time terms, **157**
eye communication, **133**	kinesics, **129**
facial communication, **132**	monochronic time orientation, **157**

Critical Thinking Questions

1 Research shows that women are perceived to be and in reality are more skilled at both encoding and decoding nonverbal messages (Briton & Hall, 1995a). Do you notice this in your own interactions? Do these differences give women an advantage in conversation? In negotiation? In conflict resolution?

2 A popular defense tactic in sex crimes against women, gay men, and lesbians is to blame the victim by referring to the way the victim was dressed and implying that the victim, by wearing certain clothing, provoked the attack. Currently New York and Florida are the only states that prohibit defense attorneys from referring to the way a sex-crime victim was dressed at the time of the attack (*New York Times*, July 30, 1994, p. 22). What do you think of this? If you don't live in New York or Florida, have there been proposals in your state to similarly limit this defense tactic?

3 Here are a few findings from research on nonverbal gender differences (Burgoon, Buller, & Woodall, 1996; Guerrero, DeVito, & Hecht, 1999; Gamble & Gamble, 2003; Stewart, Cooper, & Stewart, 2003; KroLøkke & Sørensen, 2006): (1) Women smile more than men. (2) Women stand closer to each other than do men and are generally approached more closely than men. (3) Both men and women, when speaking, look at men more than at women. (4) Women both touch and are touched more than men. (5) Men extend their bodies more, taking up greater areas of space, than women. What problems might these differences create when men and women communicate with each other?

4 Interestingly enough, the social or cheek kiss is fast replacing the handshake in the workplace, perhaps because of the Latin influence or perhaps because of growing informality in the business world (Olson, 2006). But because the practice is in transition, it's often difficult to know how to greet people. What nonverbal signals would you look for in deciding whether someone expects you to extend a hand or pucker your lips?

5 As noted in the text, you're likely to dress differently depending on the situation. But exactly how would you dress:

■ to interview for a job at a prestigious and conservative law firm?

■ to appear friendly but serious as you teach your first college class?

■ to appear as the trendiest partygoer at the trendiest spot in town?

■ to make your romantic partner's parents (you've been dating about six months), about whom you know very little, think you're absolutely wonderful?

■ to attend a parent–teacher conference (you're the parent) at your child's preschool and appear very concerned and involved, though in truth you've not participated in any of the school's activities?

6 Test your ability to identify these emotions on the basis of verbal descriptions. Try to "hear" the following voices and to identify the emotions being communicated. Do you hear affection, anger, boredom, or joy (Davitz, 1964)?

■ This voice is soft, with a low pitch, a resonant quality, a slow rate, and a steady and slightly upward inflection. The rhythm is regular, and the enunciation is slurred.

■ This voice is loud, with a high pitch, a moderately blaring quality, a fast rate, an upward inflection, and a regular rhythm.

■ This voice is loud, with a high pitch, a blaring quality, a fast rate, and an irregular up-and-down inflection. The rhythm is irregular, and the enunciation is clipped.

■ This voice is moderate to low in volume, with a moderate-to-low pitch, a moderately resonant quality, a moderately slow rate, and a monotonous or gradually falling inflection. The enunciation is somewhat slurred.

7 Studies show that listeners gaze at speakers more than speakers gaze at listeners (Knapp & Hall, 2006). The percentage of interaction time spent gazing while listening, for example, ranges from 62 percent to 75 percent; the percentage of time spent gazing while talking, however, ranges from 38 percent to 41 percent. When these percentages are reversed—when a speaker gazes at the listener for longer than "normal" periods or when a listener gazes at the speaker for shorter than "normal" periods—the conversational interaction becomes awkward. Try this out with a friend and see what happens. Even with mutual awareness, you'll notice the discomfort caused by this seemingly minor communication change.

Choice Points

1 *Smelling.* Your colleague in the next cubicle wears extremely strong cologne that you find horrendous. You can't continue smelling this horrible scent any longer. Ask yourself: What choices or options do you have to correct this situation?

2 *Criticizing with Kindness.* A close friend is going to an important job interview dressed totally inappropriately and asks, "How do I look?" Ask yourself: What are some of the ways of expressing your response that will help your friend with the interview presentation but also bolster your friend's self-esteem?

3 *Inappropriate Spacing.* As in an episode of *Seinfeld*, your friend is a "close talker" who stands much too close to others when talking and makes others feel uncomfortable. Ask yourself: What (if anything) can you say to help your friend use space to communicate more effectively?

4 *Remaining Silent.* Your college roommate has developed a small business selling term papers and uses your jointly owned computer to store them. You've remained silent about this for some time, but you've become increasingly uncomfortable about the situation and want to distance yourself from what you feel is unethical. Ask yourself: How might you break your silence to distance yourself or, better, sever yourself entirely from this operation without creating too much trouble in the small dorm room you'll have to continue sharing for the rest of the year?

5 *Inviting and Discouraging Conversation.* Sometimes you want to encourage people to come into your office and chat, and at other times you want to be left alone. Ask yourself: What might you do nonverbally to achieve each goal?

6 *Touching.* Your supervisor touches just about everyone. You don't like it and want it to stop—at least as far as you're concerned. Ask yourself: What are some ways you can nonverbally show your aversion to this unwanted touching?

7 *Demonstrating Credibility.* At work people don't attribute any credibility to you, although you're probably as competent as anyone else. You need to increase the nonverbal credibility cues you give off. Ask yourself: What nonverbal cues communicate competence and ability? How might you begin to integrate these into your own communication?

MyCommunicationLab
Explorations

PEARSON
mycommunicationlab www.mycommunicationlab.com

This group of experiences deals with nonverbal messages and provides opportunities to work with these various channels of communication. ❶ Facial Expressions and ❷ Eye Contact focus on the various meanings the face and the eyes communicate. ❸ Interpersonal Interactions and Space and ❹ Sitting at the Company Meeting look at the meanings communicated by the way you use space.

❺ The Meanings of Color helps sensitize you to the various meanings that different colors communicate. ❻ Praising and Criticizing looks at how a variety of meanings can be communicated without words. ❼ Artifacts and Culture: The Case of Gifts illustrates the vast cultural differences in what is considered appropriate gift giving.

CHAPTER

7 Emotional Messages

Principles of Emotions and Emotional Messages

Obstacles to Communicating Emotions

Skills for Expressing Emotions

Skills for Responding to the Emotions of Others

There Will Be Blood

One insightful way to look at the role of emotions in interpersonal communication is to examine a well-written, well-acted movie such as *There Will Be Blood*. Devoid of emotions the film would have no story and no interest. In this respect films and other media are not unlike interpersonal relationships; without emotions, interpersonal interactions and interpersonal relationships would be almost without meaning and certainly uninteresting.

Some of the more difficult interpersonal communication situations are those that involve strong emotions. This chapter addresses this crucial topic; it offers insight into the nature of emotions and emotional expression, discusses some of the obstacles to communicating emotions, and presents suggestions for communicating emotions and for responding to the emotions of others.

Principles of Emotions and Emotional Messages

Communicating **emotions**, or feelings, is both difficult and important. It's difficult because your thinking often gets confused when you're intensely emotional. It's also difficult because you probably weren't taught how to communicate emotions—and you probably have few effective models to imitate.

Communicating emotions is also important, however. Feelings constitute a great part of your meanings. If you leave your feelings out, or if you express them inadequately, you will fail to communicate a great part of your meaning. For example, consider what your communications would be like if you left out your feelings when talking about failing a recent

UNDERSTANDING INTERPERSONAL THEORY & RESEARCH

Theories of Emotions

If you were to describe the events leading up to emotional arousal, you would probably describe three stages: (1) An event occurs. (2) You experience an emotion such as surprise, joy, or anger. (3) You respond physiologically; your heart beats faster, your face flushes, and so on. Figure A depicts this commonsense view of emotions.

Psychologist William James and physiologist Carl Lange offered a different explanation. Their theory places the physiological arousal before the experience of the emotion. The sequence of events according to the **James–Lange theory** is: (1) An event occurs. (2) You respond physiologically. And (3) you experience an emotion; for example, you feel joy or sadness. Figure B depicts the James–Lange view of emotions.

According to a third explanation, the **cognitive labeling theory**, you interpret the physiological arousal and, on the basis of this, experience the emotions of joy, sadness, or whatever (Schachter, 1971; Reisenzein, 1983). The sequence goes like this: (1) An event occurs. (2) You respond physiologically. (3) You interpret this arousal—that is, you decide what emotion you're experiencing. And (4) you experience the emotion. Your interpretation of your arousal will depend on the situation you're in. For example, if you experience an increased pulse rate after someone you've been admiring smiles at you, you may interpret this as joy. If three suspicious-looking strangers approach you on a dark street, however, you may interpret that same increased heartbeat as fear. It's only after you make the interpretation that you experience the emotion; for example, the joy or the fear. Figure C diagrams this sequence of events.

Working with Theories and Research

These theories offer considerable insight into the way in which we experience emotions, though none of them is the total explanation. From an analysis of your own emotional experience, what explanation seems the most logical? Why?

Three Views of Emotion

How would you describe emotional arousal?

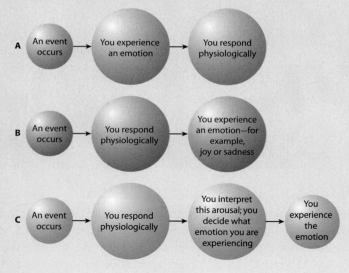

A. An event occurs → You experience an emotion → You respond physiologically

B. An event occurs → You respond physiologically → You experience an emotion—for example, joy or sadness

C. An event occurs → You respond physiologically → You interpret this arousal; you decide what emotion you are experiencing → You experience the emotion

test, winning the lottery, becoming a parent, getting engaged, driving a car for the first time, becoming a citizen, or being promoted to supervisor. Emotional expression is so much a part of communication that even in the cryptic e-mail message style, emoticons are becoming more popular.

So important is **emotional communication** that it is at the heart of what is now called "emotional intelligence" or "social intelligence" (Goleman, 1995a); and the inability to engage in emotional communication—as sender and as receiver—is part of the learning disability known as *dyssemia*, a condition in which individual are unable to appropriately read the nonverbal messages of others or to communicate their own meanings nonverbally (Duke & Nowicki, 2005). Persons suffering from dyssemia, for example, look uninterested, fail to return smiles, and use facial expressions that are inappropriate to the situation and the interaction. As you can imagine, people who are poor senders and receivers of emotional messages will likely have problems in developing and maintaining relationships. When interacting with such people, you're likely to feel uncomfortable because of their inappropriate emotional communication (Goleman, 1995a).

Let's look first at several general principles of emotions and emotional expression; these will establish a foundation for our consideration of the skills of emotional communication.

Emotions May Be Primary or Blended

How would you feel in each of the following situations?

- You won the lottery!
- You got the job you applied for.
- Your best friend just died.
- Your parents tell you they're getting divorced.

You would obviously feel very differently in each of these situations. In fact, each feeling is unique and unrepeatable. Yet amid all these differences, there are some similarities. For example, most people would agree that the first two sets of feelings are more similar to each other than they are to the last two. Similarly, the last two are more similar to each other than they are to the first two.

To capture the similarities among emotions, many researchers have tried to identify basic or **primary emotions.** Robert Plutchik (1980; Havlena, Holbrook, & Lehmann, 1989) developed a most helpful model. In this model there are eight basic emotions (Figure 7.1): joy, acceptance, fear, surprise, sadness, disgust, anger, and anticipation. Emotions that are close to each other on this wheel are also close to each other in meaning. For example, joy and anticipation are more closely related than are joy and sadness or acceptance and disgust. Emotions that are opposite each other on the wheel are also opposite each other in their meaning. For example, joy is the opposite of sadness; anger is the opposite of fear.

In this model there are also blends. These **blended emotions** are combinations of the primary emotions. These are noted outside the emotion wheel. For example, according to this model, love is a blend of joy and acceptance. Remorse is a blend of disgust and sadness.

Emotions Are Influenced by Body, Mind, and Culture

Emotion involves at least three parts: bodily reactions (such as blushing when you're embarrassed); mental evaluations and interpretations (as in calculating the odds of drawing an inside straight at poker); and cultural rules and beliefs (such as the pride parents feel when their child graduates from college).

Bodily reactions are the most obvious aspect of our emotional experience, because we can observe them easily. Such reactions span a wide range. They include, for example, the blush of embarrassment, the sweating palms that accompany nervousness, and the gestures such as playing with your hair or touching your face that go with discomfort. When you judge

VIEWPOINT Emotional isolation refers to the situation in which a person has no intimate with whom to share emotions. Even though the person may have a wide network of associates, there is no one person to relate to on an intimate level. In what ways might people seek to prevent or lessen emotional isolation?

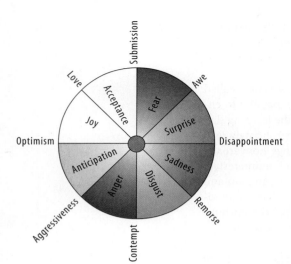

FIGURE 7.1

A Model of the Emotions

Do you agree with the basic assumptions of this model? For example, do you see love as a combination of joy and acceptance, and optimism as a combination of joy and anticipation?

From Robert Plutchik, *Emotion: A Psychoevolutionary Synthesis,* (figure 7.1) © 1980. Published by HarperCollins. Copyright © 2000 by Pearson Education. Reprinted by permission of Pearson Education, Inc.

people's emotions, you probably look to these nonverbal behaviors. You conclude that Ramon is happy to see you because of his smile and his open body posture. You conclude that Lisa is nervous from her damp hands, vocal hesitations, and awkward movements.

The mental or cognitive part of emotional experience involves the evaluations and interpretations you make on the basis of what you experience. For example, leading psychotherapist Albert Ellis (1988; Ellis & Harper, 1975), whose insights are used throughout this chapter, claims that your evaluations of what happens have a greater influence on your feelings than what actually happens. Let us say, for example, that your best friend, Sally, ignores you in the college cafeteria. The emotions you feel will depend on what you think this behavior means. You may feel pity if you figure that Sally is depressed because her father died. You may feel anger if you believe that Sally is simply rude and insensitive and snubbed you on purpose. Or you may feel sadness if you believe that Sally is no longer interested in being friends with you.

The cultural context—the culture you were raised in and/or the culture you live in—gives you a framework for both expressing feelings and interpreting the emotions of others. A colleague of mine gave a lecture in Beijing, China, to a group of Chinese college students. The students listened politely but made no comments and asked no questions after her lecture. At first my colleague concluded that the students were bored and uninterested. Later, however, she learned that Chinese students show respect by being quiet and seemingly passive. They think that asking questions would imply that she was not clear in her lecture. In other words, the culture—whether American or Chinese—influenced the interpretation of the students' feelings. Another example: In a recent study, Japanese students, when asked to judge the emotion shown in a computer icon, looked to the eyes to determine the emotion. Students from the United States, however, focused on the mouth (Yuki, Maddux, & Masuda, 2007; Masuda, Ellsworth, Mesquita, Leu, Tanida, & van de Veerdonk, 2008).

Emotions May Be Adaptive and Maladaptive

Emotions are often adaptive; that is, they can help you adjust appropriately to situations. For example, if you feel anxious about not doing well on an exam, it may lead you to study harder. If you fear losing your partner, you may behave more supportively and lovingly. If you're worried that someone might not like you, your worry may motivate you to be especially nice to the person. If you feel suspicious of someone following you down a dark street, you may take safety precautions. All of these situations are examples of emotions aiding you in accomplishing useful goals.

At other times, however, emotions may be maladaptive and may get in the way of your accomplishing your goals. For example, you may be so anxious about a test that you stop thinking and do more poorly than you would have if you walked in totally cold. Or you may fear losing your partner and as a result may become suspicious and accusatory, making your relationship even less likely to survive.

Another way in which emotions may create problems is in a tendency that some theorists have cleverly called catastrophizing (or awfulizing): taking a problem—even a minor one—and making it into a catastrophe. For example, you may feel that "If I don't do well on this test, I'll never get into law school" or "If this relationship doesn't work, I'm doomed." As you convince yourself of these impending catastrophes, your emotional responses can easily get out of hand (Bach & Wyden, 1968; Willson & Branch, 2006).

The important point is that emotions can work for you or against you. And the same is true of emotional communication. Some of it is good and is likely to lead to positive outcomes (a more secure relationship or a more positive interaction, say). But some of it is bad and may aggravate a conflict, alienate friends, or lessen your relationship satisfaction. Or emotional communication may simply be thought inappropriate and thus give others a bad impression (see photo and caption on p. 167).

Emotions Are Communicated Verbally and Nonverbally

Although emotions are especially salient in conflict situations and in relationship development and dissolution, they are actually a part of all messages. Emotions are always present—sometimes very strongly, sometimes only mildly. Therefore, they must be recognized as a part of the communication experience. This is not to say that emotions should always be talked about or that all emotions you feel should be expressed. Emotional feeling and emotional communication are two different things. In some instances you may want to say exactly what you feel, to reveal your emotions without any censorship. At other times, however, you may want to avoid revealing your emotions. For example, you might not want to reveal your frustration over a customer's indecision, or you might not want to share with your children your worries about finding a job.

Theorists do not agree over whether you can choose the emotions you feel. Some argue that you can; others argue that you cannot. You are, however, in control of the ways in which you express your emotions. Whether or not you choose to express your emotions will depend on your own attitudes about emotional expression. You may wish to explore these by taking the self-test later.

TEST YOURSELF

HOW DO YOU FEEL ABOUT COMMUNICATING FEELINGS?

Respond to each of the following statements with T if you feel the statement is a generally true description of your attitudes about expressing emotions, or with F if you feel the statement is a generally false description of your attitudes.

_____ 1. Expressing feelings is healthy; it reduces stress and prevents wasting energy on concealment.

_____ 2. Expressing feelings can lead to interpersonal relationship problems.

_____ 3. Expressing feelings can help others understand you.

_____ 4. Emotional expression is often an effective means of persuading others to do as you wish.

_____ 5. Expressing emotions may lead others to perceive you negatively.

_____ 6. Emotional expression can lead to greater and not less stress; expressing anger, for example, may actually increase your feelings of anger.

HOW DID YOU DO? These statements are arguments that are often made for and against expressing emotions. Statements 1, 3, and 4 are arguments made in favor of expressing emotions; 2, 5, and 6 are arguments made against expressing emotions. You can look at your responses as revealing (in part) your attitude favoring or opposing the expression of feelings. "True" responses to statements 1, 3, and 4 and "False" responses to statements 2, 5, and 6 would indicate a favorable attitude to expressing feelings. "False" responses to statements 1, 3, and 4 and "True" responses to statements 2, 5, and 6 indicate a negative attitude.

WHAT WILL YOU DO? There is evidence suggesting that expressing emotions can lead to all six outcomes—the positives and the negatives—so general suggestions for increasing your willingness to express your emotions are not offered. These potential consequences underscore the importance of critically assessing your options for emotional expression. Be flexible, remembering that what will work in one situation will not work in another.

If you decide to communicate your feelings, you need to make several decisions. For example, you have to choose how to do so—face-to-face or by letter, phone, e-mail, or office memo. And you have to choose the specific emotions you will and will not reveal. Finally, you have to choose the language in which you'll express your emotions.

As with most meanings, emotions are encoded both verbally and nonverbally. Your words, the emphasis you give them, and the gestures and facial expressions that accompany them all help to communicate your feelings. Conversely, you decode the emotional messages of others on the basis of both verbal and nonverbal cues. And of course emotions, like all messages, are most effectively communicated when verbal and nonverbal messages reinforce and complement each other.

Emotional Expression Is Governed by Display Rules

As explained in Chapter 6, different cultures' **display rules** govern what is and what is not permissible emotional communication. Even within U.S. culture itself, there are differences. For example, in one study Americans classified themselves into four categories: Caucasian, African American, Asian, and Hispanic/Latino. Just to make the point that different cultures teach different rules for the display of emotions, here are a few of the study's findings (Matsumoto, 1994): (1) Caucasians found the expression of contempt more appropriate than did Asians; (2) African Americans and Hispanics felt that showing disgust was less appropriate than did Caucasians; (3) Hispanics rated public displays of emotion as less appropriate than did Caucasians; and (4) Caucasians rated the expression of fear as more appropriate than did Hispanics.

Researchers agree that men and women experience emotions similarly (Oatley & Duncan, 1994; Cherulnik, 1979; Wade & Tavris, 2007). The differences that are observed are differences in emotional *expression*. Men and women seem to have different **gender display rules** for what is and what isn't appropriate to express, much as different cultures have different cultural display rules.

Women talk more about feelings and emotions and use communication for emotional expression more than men (Barbato & Perse, 1992). Perhaps because of this, they also express themselves facially more than men. Even junior and senior high schoolers show this gender difference. Research findings suggest that this difference may be due to differences in the brains of men and women; women's brains have a significantly larger inferior parietal lobule, which seems to account for women's greater awareness of feelings (Barta, 1999).

Women are also more likely to express socially acceptable emotions than are men (Brody, 1985). For example, women smile significantly more than men. In fact, women smile even when smiling is not appropriate—for example, when reprimanding a subordinate. Men, on the other hand, are more likely than women to express anger and aggression (Fischer, 1993; DePaulo, 1992; Wade & Tavris, 2007). Similarly, women are more effective at communicating happiness and men are more effective at communicating anger (Coats & Feldman, 1996). Women also cry more than men (Metts & Planalp, 2002).

Emotions Are Contagious

Emotional messages are often contagious (Cappella & Schreiber, 2006). If you've ever watched an infant and mother interacting, you can readily see how quickly the infant mimics the emotional expressions of the mother. If the mother smiles, the infant smiles; if the mother frowns, the infant frowns. As children get older, they begin to pick up more subtle expressions of emotions. For example, children quickly identify and often mimic a parent's anxiety or fear. Even among college roommates, the depression of one roommate spread to the other over a period of just three weeks (Joiner, 1994). In short, in **emotional contagion** emotions pass from one person to another; women are especially prone to this process (Doherty, Orimoto, Singelis, Hatfield, & Hebb, 1995; Cappella & Schreiber, 2006). In conversation and in small groups, the strong emotions of one person can easily prove contagious to others present; this can be productive when the emotions are productive or unproductive when the emotions are unproductive.

One view of this process goes like this:

1. Someone expresses an emotion—laughs, cries, leaps for joy.
2. You perceive this emotional expression.
3. You mimic this emotional expression, perhaps unconsciously.
4. The feedback you get from expressing the emotion creates in you a replication of the other person's feelings.

Another view of emotional contagion would hold that the process is under more conscious control. That is, you look at others who are expressing emotions to see how you should be feeling—you take nonverbal cues from those you observe—and then feel the feeling you feel you should be feeling.

You see another variant of intentional emotional contagion in attempts at persuasion that utilize **emotional appeals**. One popular appeal, which organizations use frequently in fund-raising for needy children, is to the emotion of pity. By showing you images of hungry and destitute children, these fund-raisers hope to get you to experience so much pity that you'll help finance their efforts. Similarly, people who beg for money often emphasize their difficulties in an effort to evoke pity and donations.

Emotional contagion also seems the goal of certain organizational display rules (www.bellomy-business.com, 2006, accessed March 4, 2008). For example, a company may require (or at least expect) that the sales force cheer enthusiastically as each new product is unveiled. This cheering is extremely useful and is likely to make the sales representatives more enthusiastic about and more emotionally committed to the product than if they didn't engage in this cheering.

Another popular appeal is to guilt. If someone does something for you, he or she may try to make you feel guilty unless you do something in return. Or someone may present himself or herself as in desperate need of money and make you feel guilty for having what

VIEWPOINT Having lost the Iowa Democratic primary for the 2008 presidential campaign and going into the New Hampshire primary, Hillary Clinton became tearful during an interview. To some, it showed Clinton as softer and more human than the common impression of her had been. To others, it suggested she was weak and would not be the person to be strong when the situation required. What's your impression of a female politician crying? Is it any different from your impression of a male politician crying?

VIEWPOINT Here are three theories offered to explain sex differences in emotional expression, similar to those noted in the discussion of gender differences in language (p. 109). Each of these provides a useful perspective for viewing often quite pronounced sex differences (Guerrero, Jones, & Boburka, 2006). Biological theory claims that differences in brains and chemistry account for the differences in the ability to express and detect emotions and for the different emotions displayed. Evolutionary theory claims that emotional expression was basic to survival; those who were good at it lived and passed on their genes to others and those who weren't good at it often died early with the result that their genes were not passed on. And, because men and women served widely differing functions, they each came to rely on different emotions and different ways of expressing and inhibiting emotions. Socialization theory claims that men and women are taught differently about emotions (and this, of course, varies with the culture) and have been socialized into expressing emotions as they do. Women are taught to smile and to express positive affect (it's the "feminine" thing to do), while men are taught to inhibit expressing sadness or fear (it's not "masculine" to display "weak" emotions).

you have and not sharing it. Sometimes people encourage others to feel guilt to make them more easily manipulated. If you can make a person feel guilty for having a great deal of money while others have little, you are on the road to persuading the person to give some of that money away.

With these principles of emotions and emotional expression as a foundation, we can now look at some of the obstacles to effective emotional expression.

Obstacles to Communicating Emotions

The expression of feelings is a part of most meaningful relationships. Yet it's often very difficult. Three major obstacles stand in the way of effective emotional communication: (1) society's rules and customs, (2) fear, and (3) inadequate interpersonal skills. Let's look more closely at each of these barriers.

Societal and Cultural Customs

If you grew up in the United States, you probably learned that many people frown on emotional expression. This attitude is especially prevalent in men and has been aptly called the "cowboy syndrome," after a pattern of behavior seen in the old Westerns (Balswick & Peck, 1971). The cowboy syndrome characterizes the closed and unexpressive male. This man is strong but silent. He never feels any of the softer emotions (such as compassion, love, or contentment). He would never ever cry, experience fear, or feel sorry for himself.

Unfortunately, many men grow up trying to live up to this unrealistic image. It's a syndrome that prevents open and honest expression. Boys are taught early in life not to cry and to not be "babies" if hurt. All this is not to suggest that men should communicate their

Motivational Appeals

Appeals to motives are commonplace. For example, if you want a friend to take a vacation with you, you're likely to appeal to such motives as the friend's desire for fun and excitement, and perhaps to the friend's hopes of meeting his or her true love. If you look at the advertisements for cruises and vacation packages, you'll see appeals to very similar motives. Fear appeals also are common: Persons who want to censor the Internet may appeal to your fear of children's accessing pornographic materials; those who want to restrict media portrayals of violence may appeal to your fear of increased violence in your community. Advertisers appeal to your vanity and your desire for increased sexual attractiveness in trying to sell you cosmetics and expensive clothing.

There can be no doubt that such motivational appeals are effective. But are they ethical?

What would you do?

Suppose you wanted to dissuade your teenage children from engaging in sexual relationships. Would it be ethical to use emotional appeals to fear—to scare them so that they'd avoid such relationships? Would it be ethical to use the same appeals if your goal were to get them to stop smoking?

emotions more openly. Unfortunately, there are many who will negatively evaluate men who express emotions openly and often; such men may be judged ineffective, insecure, or unmanly. In fact, some research shows that the reason men are reluctant to provide sensitive emotional support—to the degree that women do, for example—is that men don't want their behavior to be seen as feminine (Burleson, Holmstrom, & Gilstrap, 2005).

Nor are women exempt from restraints on emotional expression. At one time our society permitted and encouraged women to express emotions openly. The tide now is turning, especially for women in executive and managerial positions. Today the executive woman is being forced into the same cowboy syndrome. She is not allowed to cry or to show any of the once acceptable "soft" emotions. She is especially denied these feelings while she is on the job.

And, of course, organizations have their own cultural norms for the expression of emotions. For example, in many organizations employees are expected to pretend to be cheerful even when not and generally to display some emotions and to hide others. Unfortunately, differences between the emotions you feel and the emotions you express can create emotional dissonance, which in turn can lead to stress (Remland, 2006).

For both men and women, the best advice (as with any of the characteristics of communication effectiveness discussed in this book) is to express your emotions selectively. Carefully weigh the arguments for and against expressing your emotions. Consider the situation, the people you're with, the emotions themselves, and all of the elements that make up the communication act. And, most important, consider your choices for communicating emotions—not only what you'll say but also how you'll say it.

Fear

A variety of types of fear stand in the way of emotional expression. Emotional expression exposes a part of you that makes you vulnerable to attack. For example, if you express your love for another person, you risk being rejected. When you expose a weakness, you can more easily be hurt by uncaring or insensitive others. Of course, you may also fear hurting someone else by, say, voicing your feelings about past loves. Or you may be angry and want to say something but fear that you might hurt the person and then feel guilty yourself.

In addition, you may avoid revealing your emotions for fear of causing a conflict. Expressing your dislike for Pat's friends, for example, may create difficulties for the two of you, and you may not be willing to risk the argument and its aftermath. Because of fears such as these, you may deny to others and perhaps even to yourself that you have certain feelings. In fact, this kind of denial is the way many people were taught to deal with emotions.

As you can appreciate, fear can be adaptive; it may lead you to not say things you may be sorry for later. It may lead you to consider more carefully whether or not you should express yourself and how you might do it. But when it debilitates us and contradicts what logic and reason might tell us, then the fear becomes maladaptive.

Inadequate Interpersonal Skills

Perhaps the most important obstacle to effective emotional communication is lack of interpersonal skills. Many people simply don't know how to express their feelings. Some people, for example, can express anger only through violence or avoidance. Others can deal with anger only by blaming and accusing others. And many people cannot express love. They literally cannot say, "I love you."

Expressing negative feelings is doubly difficult. Many of us suppress or fail to communicate negative feelings for fear of offending the other person or making matters worse. But failing to express negative feelings will probably not help the relationship, especially if these feelings are concealed frequently and over a long time.

Both communicating your emotions and responding appropriately to the emotional expressions of others are as important as they are difficult (Burleson, 2003). And to complicate matters further, as noted in the self-test earlier in this chapter, emotional expression can be good but also can be bad. On the one hand, expressing emotions can be cathartic to yourself and may benefit a relationship. Expressing emotions can also help you air dissatisfactions and perhaps reduce or even eliminate them. Through emotional expression you can come to understand each other better, which may lead to a closer and more meaningful relationship.

VIEWPOINT People are more likely to receive expressions of positive affect positively and with approval, whereas negative affect is more likely to meet negative reactions (Sommers, 1984; Monahan, 1998; Metts & Planalp, 2002). But it's not always easy to determine how others will perceive an emotion; for example, jealousy, although a negative emotion, may be perceived positively, as a sign that you really care (Metts & Planalp, 2002, p. 359). What rule(s) do you follow in deciding whether or not to express your positive and your negative emotions?

On the other hand, expressing emotions may cause relationship difficulties. For example, expressing your dislike of a colleague's customary way of answering the phone may generate hostility; expressing jealousy when your partner spends time with friends may cause your partner to fear being controlled and losing autonomy.

Skills for Expressing Emotions

Much as emotions are a part of your psychological life, emotional expression is a part of your interpersonal life; it is not something you could avoid even if you wanted to. In specific cases you may decide to hide your emotions and not express them, but in other cases you'll want to express your emotions. If you do decide to express your emotions, you need first to engage in some self-reflection in which you analyze your feelings and second to describe your feelings.

Understand your Feelings

Your first step is intrapersonal. Here you ask yourself a few pertinent questions.

- "What am I feeling, and what made me feel this way?" That is, understand your emotions. Think about your emotions as objectively as possible. Identify, in terms as specific as possible, the antecedent conditions that may be influencing your feelings. Try to answer the question "Why am I feeling this way?" or "What happened to lead me to feel as I do?"
- "What exactly do I want to communicate?" Consider also whether your emotional expression will be a truthful expression of your feelings. When emotional expressions are faked—when, for example, you smile though feeling angry or say "I forgive you" when you don't—you may actually be creating emotional and physical stress (Grandey, 2000). Remember, too, the irreversibility of communication; once you communicate something, you cannot take it back.

Flexibility is a quality of thinking and behaving in which you vary your messages based on the unique situation in which you find yourself. One measure of flexibility asks you to consider how true you believe certain statements are—statements such as "People should be frank and spontaneous in conversation" or "When angry, a person should say nothing rather than say something he or she will be sorry for later." The "preferred" answer to all such questions is "sometimes true," underscoring the importance of flexibility in all interpersonal situations (Hart, Carlson, & Eadie, 1980). A more extensive test, by Matthew Martin and Rebecca Rubin (1994; also see Martin & Anderson, 1998) appears on the MyCommunicationLab website at www.mycommunicationlab.com. As you can appreciate, flexibility is especially important when communicating your feelings, be they positive or negative.

Increasing Flexibility. Here are a few ways to cultivate interpersonal flexibility.

- Realize that no two situations or people are exactly alike; consider what is different about this situation or person and take these differences into consideration as you construct your messages.
- Realize that communication always takes place in a context (Chapter 1); discover what that unique context is and ask yourself how it might influence your messages. Communicating bad news during a joyous celebration, for example, needs to be handled quite differently from communicating good news.
- Realize that everything is in a state of flux. Even if the way you communicated last month was effective, that doesn't mean it will be effective today or tomorrow. Realize too that sudden changes (the death of a lover or a serious illness) will influence what are and what are not appropriate messages.
- Realize that every situation offers you different options for communicating. Consider these options and try to predict the effects each option might have.

Working with Interpersonal Skills

The best way to examine your own flexibility is to take the self-test on MCL. After you compute your score, ask yourself what you can do to become more flexible, especially when you communicate emotions.

- "What are my communication choices?" Evaluate your communication options in terms of both effectiveness (what will work best and help you achieve your goal) and ethics (what is right or morally justified).

Describe Your Feelings

Your second step is interpersonal and may be best viewed as developing accurate descriptions of your feelings. Here are a few suggestions for being descriptive.

- *Be as specific as possible.* Consider, for example, the frequently heard "I feel bad." Does it mean "I feel guilty" (because I lied to my best friend)? "I feel lonely" (because I haven't had a date in the last two months)? "I feel depressed" (because I failed that last exam)? Specificity helps. Describe also the intensity with which you feel the emotion: "I feel so angry I'm thinking of quitting the job." "I feel so hurt I want to cry." Also describe any mixed feelings you might have. Very often feelings are a mixture of several emotions, sometimes even of conflicting emotions. Learn the vocabulary to describe your emotions and feelings in specific and concrete terms.

    Here is a list of terms for describing your emotions verbally. It's based on the eight primary emotions identified by Plutchik (refer to Figure 7.1). Notice that the terms included for each basic emotion provide you with lots of choices for expressing the intensity level you're feeling. For example, if you're extremely happy, then *bliss, ecstasy,* or *enchantment* might be an appropriate term. If you're mildly happy, then perhaps *contentment, satisfaction,* or *well-being* would be more accurate. Look over the list and try grouping the terms into three levels of intensity: high, middle, and low. Before doing that, however, look up the meanings of any words that are unfamiliar to you.

    Happiness: bliss, cheer, contentment, delight, ecstasy, enchantment, enjoyment, felicity, joy, rapture, gratification, pleasure, satisfaction, well-being
    Surprise: amazement, astonishment, awe, eye-opener, incredulity, jolt, revelation, shock, unexpectedness, wonder, startle, catch off-guard, unforeseen

Fear: anxiety, apprehension, awe, concern, consternation, dread, fright, misgiving, phobia, terror, trepidation, worry, qualm, terror

Anger: acrimony, annoyance, bitterness, displeasure, exasperation, fury, ire, irritation, outrage, rage, resentment, tantrum, umbrage, wrath, hostility

Sadness: dejected, depressed, dismal, distressed, grief, loneliness, melancholy, misery, sorrowful, unhappiness

Disgust: abhorrence, aversion, loathing, repugnance, repulsion, revulsion, sickness, nausea, offensiveness

Contempt: abhorrence, aversion, derision, disdain, disgust, distaste, indignity, insolence, ridicule, scorn, snobbery, revulsion, disrespect

Interest: attention, appeal, concern, curiosity, fascination, notice, spice, zest, absorb, engage, engross

- *Describe the reasons you're feeling as you are.* "I'm feeling guilty because I lied to my best friend." "I feel lonely; I haven't had a date for the last two months." "I'm really depressed from failing that last exam." If your feelings were influenced by something the person you're talking to did or said, describe this also. For example, "I felt so angry when you said you wouldn't help me". "I felt hurt when you didn't invite me to the party."

- *Address mixed feelings.* If you have mixed feelings—and you really want the other person to understand you—then address these mixed or conflicting feelings. "I want so much to stay with Pat and yet I fear I'm losing my identity." Or, "I feel anger and hatred, but at the same time I feel guilty for what I did."

- *In expressing feelings—inwardly or outwardly—try to anchor your emotions in the present.* Coupled with specific description and the identification of the reasons for your feelings, such statements might look like this: "I feel like a failure right now; I've erased this computer file three times today." "I felt foolish when I couldn't think of that formula." "I feel stupid when you point out my grammatical errors."

- *Own your feelings; take personal responsibility for your feelings.* Consider the following statements: "You make me angry." "You make me feel like a loser." "You make me feel stupid." "You make me feel like I don't belong here." In each of these statements, the speaker blames the other person for the way he or she is feeling. Of course, you know, on more sober reflection, that no one can make you feel anything. Others may do things or say things to you, but it is you who interpret them. That is, you develop feelings as a result of the interaction between what these people say, for example, and your own interpretations. **Owning feelings** means taking responsibility for them—acknowledging that your feelings are your feelings. The best way to own your statements is to use **I-messages** rather than the kinds of you-messages given above. With this acknowledgment of responsibility, the above statements would look like these: "I get angry when you come home late without calling." "I begin to think of myself as a loser when you criticize me in front of my friends." "I feel so stupid when you use medical terms that I don't understand." "When you ignore me in public, I feel like I don't belong here." These rephrased statements identify and describe your feelings about those behaviors; they don't attack the other person or demand that he or she change certain behaviors and consequently don't encourage defensiveness. With I-message statements, it's easier for the other person to acknowledge behaviors and to offer to change them.

- *Ask for what you want.* Depending on the emotions you're feeling, you may want the listener to assume a certain role or just listen or offer advice. Let the listener know what you want. Use I-messages to describe what, if anything, you want the listener to do: "I'm feeling sorry for myself right now; just give me some space. I'll give you a call in a few days." Or, more directly: "I'd prefer to be alone right now." Or, "I need advice." Or, "I just need someone to listen to me."

Handling Anger: A Special Case Illustration

As a kind of summary of the guidelines for expressing your emotions, this section looks at anger. **Anger** is one of the eight basic emotions identified in Plutchik's model (Figure 7.1). It's also an emotion that can create considerable problems if not managed properly.

Anger varies from mild annoyance to intense rage; increases in pulse rate and blood pressure usually accompany these feelings.

Anger is not always necessarily bad. In fact, anger may help you protect yourself, energizing you to fight or flee. Often, however, anger does prove destructive—as when, for example, you allow it to obscure reality or to become an obsession.

Anger doesn't just happen; you make it happen by your interpretation of events. Yet life events can contribute mightily. There are the road repairs that force you to detour so you wind up late for an important appointment. There are the moths that attack your favorite sweater. There's the water leak that ruins your carpet. People, too, can contribute to your anger: the driver who tailgates, the clerk who overcharges you, the supervisor who ignores your contributions to the company. But it is you who interpret these events and people in ways that stimulate you to generate anger.

Writing more than a hundred years ago, Charles Darwin observed in his *The Expression of the Emotions in Man and Animals* (1872) that "The free expression by outside signs of an emotion intensifies it . . . the repression, as far as this is possible, of all outside signs softens our emotions. He who gives way to violent gestures will increase his rage." Popular psychology ignored Darwin's implied admonition in the 1960s and '70s, when the suggested prescription for dealing with anger was to "let it all hang out" and "tell it like it is." Express your anger, many people advised, or risk its being bottled up and eventually exploding. This idea is called the **ventilation hypothesis**—the notion that expressing emotions allows you to ventilate your negative feelings and that this will have a beneficial effect on your physical health, your mental well-being, and even your interpersonal relationships (Spett, 2004; Kennedy-Moore & Watson, 1999).

Later thinking has returned to Darwin, however, and suggests that venting anger may not be the best strategy (Tavris, 1989). Expressing anger doesn't get rid of it but makes it grow: Angry expression increases anger, which promotes more angry expression, which increases anger, and on and on. Some support for this idea that expressing emotions makes them stronger comes from a study that compared (a) participants who felt emotions such as happiness and anger with (b) participants who both felt and expressed these emotions. The results of the study indicated that people who felt and expressed the emotions became emotionally aroused faster than did those who only felt the emotion (Hess, Kappas, McHugo, & Lanzetta, 1992). And of course this spiral of anger can make conflicts all the more serious and all the more difficult to manage.

A better strategy seems to be to reduce the anger. With this principle in mind, here are some suggestions for managing and communicating anger.

Anger Management: SCREAM Before You Scream Perhaps the most popular recommendation for dealing with anger is to count to 10. The purpose is to give you a cooling-off period, and the advice is not bad. A somewhat more difficult but probably far more effective strategy, however, would be to use that cooling-off period not merely for counting but for mindfully analyzing and ultimately managing your anger. The **anger management** procedure offered here is similar to those available in popular books on anger management but is couched in a communication framework. It's called SCREAM, an acronym for the major issues (that is, the major components of the communication process) that you need to consider:

1. *Self.* How important is this matter to you? Is it worth the high blood pressure and the general aggravation? For example, are you interpreting the "insult" as the other person intended, or could you be misperceiving the situation or the intent? Is an "insult" to you the same as an "insult" to your mother-in-law? Are you confusing factual with inferential knowledge? Are you sure that what you think happened really happened? Or might you be filling in the gaps with what could have or might have happened or with what you expected to happen?

2. *Context.* Is this the appropriate time and place to express your anger? Do you have to express your anger right now? Do you have to express it right here? Might a better time and place be arranged?

3. *Receiver.* Is this person the one to whom you wish to express your anger? For example, do you want to express your anger to your life partner if you're really angry with your supervisor for not recommending your promotion?

4. *Effect (immediate).* What effect do you want to achieve? Do you want to express your anger to help you get the promotion? To hurt the other person? To release pent-up emotions? To stand up for your rights? Each purpose would obviously require a different communication strategy. Consider, too, what may be the likely immediate effect of your anger display. For example, will the other person also become angry? And if so, is it possible that the entire situation will snowball and get out of hand?

5. *Aftermath (long-range).* What are the likely long-term repercussions of this expression of anger? What will be the effects on your relationship? Your continued employment?

6. *Messages.* Suppose that after this rather thorough analysis, you do decide to express your anger. What messages would be appropriate? How can you best communicate your feelings to achieve your desired results? This question brings us to the subject of anger communication.

Anger Communication Anger communication is not angry communication. In fact, it might be argued that the communication of anger ought to be especially calm and dispassionate. Here, then, are a few suggestions for communicating your anger in a nonangry way.

- *Get ready to communicate calmly and logically.* First, relax. Try to breathe deeply; think pleasant thoughts; perhaps tell yourself to "take it easy," "think rationally," and "calm down." Try to get rid of any unrealistic ideas you may have that might contribute to your anger. For example, ask yourself if this person's revealing something about your past to a third party is really all that serious or was really intended to hurt you.

- *Examine your communication choices.* In most situations you'll have a range of choices. There are lots of different ways to express yourself, so don't jump to the first possibility that comes to mind. Assess your options for the form of the communication— should you communicate face-to-face? By e-mail? By telephone? Similarly, assess your options for the timing of your communication, for the specific words and gestures you might use, for the physical setting, and so on.

- *Consider the advantages of delaying the expression of anger.* For example, consider writing the e-mail but sending it to yourself, at least until the next morning. Then the options of revising it or not sending it at all will still be open to you.

- *Remember that different cultures have different display rules*—norms for what is and what is not appropriate to display. Assess the culture you're in as well as the cultures of the other people involved, especially these cultures' display rules for communicating anger.

- *Apply the relevant skills of interpersonal communication.* For example, be specific, use I-messages, avoid allness, avoid polarized terms, and in general communicate with all the competence you can muster.

- *Recall the irreversibility of communication.* Once you say something, you'll not be able to erase or delete it from the mind of the other person.

These suggestions are not going to solve the problems of road rage, gang warfare, or domestic violence. Yet they may help—a bit—in reducing some of the negative consequences of anger and perhaps even some of the anger itself.

Skills for Responding to the Emotions of Others

Expressing your feelings is only half of the process of emotional communication; the other half is listening and responding to the feelings of others. Here are a few guidelines for making an often difficult process a little easier.

- *Look at nonverbal cues to understand the individual's feelings.* For example, overly long pauses, frequent hesitations, eye contact avoidance, or excessive fidgeting may be a sign of discomfort that it might we wise to talk about. Similarly, look for inconsistent messages, as when someone says that "everything is okay" while expressing facial sadness; these are often clues to mixed feelings. But be sure to use any verbal or nonverbal cues as hypotheses, never as conclusions. Check your perceptions before acting on them. Treat inferences as inferences and not as facts.

- *Look for cues as to what the person wants you to do.* Sometimes, all the person wants is for someone to listen. Don't equate (as the stereotypical male supposedly does) "responding to another's feelings" with "solving the other person's problems." Instead, provide a supportive atmosphere that encourages the person to express his or her feelings.
- *Use active listening techniques.* These will encourage the person to talk should he or she wish to. Paraphrase the speaker. Express understanding of the speaker's feelings. Ask questions as appropriate.
- *Empathize.* See the situation from the point of view of the speaker. Don't evaluate the other person's feelings. For example, comments such as "Don't cry; it wasn't worth it" or "You'll get promoted next year" can easily be interpreted to mean "Your feelings are wrong or inappropriate."
- *Focus on the other person.* Interjecting your own similar past situations is often useful for showing your understanding, but it may create problems if it refocuses the conversation away from the other person. Show interest by encouraging the person to explore his or her feelings. Use simple encouragers like "I see" or "I understand." Or ask questions to let the speaker know that you're listening and that you're interested.
- *Remember the irreversibility of communication.* Whether expressing emotion or responding to the emotions of others, it's useful to recall the irreversibility of communication. You won't be able to take back an insensitive or disconfirming response. Responses to another's emotional expressions are likely to have considerable impact, so be especially mindful to avoid inappropriate responding.

VIEWPOINT Marie and Tom have been married for several years. Marie is extremely expressive, yelling one minute, crying the next. By comparison, Tom is nonexpressive. This difference is now causing problems. Tom feels Marie reacts impulsively without thinking her feelings through; Marie feels Tom is unwilling to share his life with her. What skills do Marie and Tom need to learn?

Communicating with the Grief-Stricken: A Special Case Illustration

Communicating with people who are experiencing grief, a common but difficult type of communication interaction, requires special care (Zunin & Zunin, 1991). Consideration of this topic also will offer a useful recap of some of the principles of responding to the emotions of others.

A person may experience grief because of illness or death, the loss of a job or highly valued relationship (such as a friendship or romantic breakup), the loss of certain physical or mental abilities, the loss of material possessions (a house fire or stock losses), or the loss of some ability (for example, the loss of the ability to have children or to play the piano). Each situation seems to call for a somewhat different set of dos and don'ts.

A Problem Before considering specific suggestions for responding to a person experiencing grief, read the following expression of sympathy, what we might call "the problem."

> I just heard that Harry died—I mean—passed away. Excuse me. I'm so sorry. We all are. I know exactly how you feel. But, you know, it's for the best. I mean the man was suffering. I remember seeing him last month; he could hardly stand up, he was so weak. And he looked so sad, so lonely, so depressed. He must have been in constant pain. It's better this way; believe me. He's at peace now. And you'll get over it. You'll see. Time heals all wounds. It was the same way with me and you know how close we were. I mean we were devoted to each other. Everyone said we were the closet pair they ever saw. And I got over it. So, how about we'll go to dinner tonight? We'll take about old times. Come on. Come on. Don't be a spoilsport. I really need to get out. I've been in the house all week and you know what a drag that can be. So, do it for me; come to dinner. I won't take no for an answer; I'll pick you up at seven.

Obviously, this is not the way to talk to the grief-stricken. In fact, this paragraph was written to illustrate several popular mistakes. After you read the suggestions below, you may wish to return to this "expression of sympathy," reanalyze it, and rework it into an effective expression of sympathy.

A Solution   Here are some suggestions for communicating more effectively with the grief-stricken, offering at least some solutions to the above problem.

■ *Confirm the other person and the person's emotions.* A simple "You must be worried about finding another position" or "You must be feeling very alone right now" confirms the person's feelings. This type of expressive support lessens feelings of grief (Reed, 1993).

■ *Give the person permission to grieve.* Let the person know that it's acceptable and okay with you if he or she grieves in the ways that feel most comfortable—for example, crying or talking about old times. Don't try to change the subject or interject too often. As long as the person is talking and seems to be feeling better for it, be supportive.

■ *Avoid trying to focus on the bright side.* Avoid expressions such as "You're lucky you have some vision left" or "It's better this way; Pat was suffering so much." These expressions may easily be seen as telling people that their feelings should be redirected, that they should be feeling something different.

■ *Encourage the person to express feelings and talk about the loss.* Most people will welcome this opportunity. On the other hand, don't try to force people to talk about experiences or feelings they may not be willing to share.

Be especially sensitive to leave-taking cues. Behaviors such as fidgeting or looking at a clock, and statements such as "It's getting late" or "We can discuss this later," are hints that the other person is ready to end the conversation. Don't overstay your welcome.

■ *Let the person know you care and are available.* Saying you're sorry is a simple but effective way to let the person know you care. Express your empathy; let the grief-stricken person know that you can feel (to some extent) what he or she is going through. But don't assume that your feelings, however empathic you are, are the same in depth or in kind. At the same time, let the person know that you are available—"If you ever want to talk, I'm here" or "If there's anything I can do, please let me know."

Even when you follow the principles and do everything according to the book, you may find that your comments are not appreciated or are not at all effective in helping the person feel any better. Use these cues to help you readjust your messages.

Summary

This chapter explored the nature and principles of emotions in interpersonal communication, the obstacles to meaningful emotional communication, and some guidelines that will help you communicate your feelings and respond to the feelings of others more effectively.

Princples of Emotions and Emotional Messages

1. Emotions consist of a physical part (our physiological reactions), a cognitive part (our interpretations of our feelings), and a cultural part (our cultural traditions' influence on our emotional evaluations and expressions).

2. Emotions may be primary or blends. The primary emotions, according to Robert Plutchik, are joy, acceptance, fear, surprise, sadness, disgust, anger, and anticipation. Other emotions, such as love, awe, contempt, and aggressiveness, are blends of primary emotions.

3. There are different views as to how emotions are aroused. One proposed sequence is this: An event occurs, you respond physiologically, you interpret this arousal, and you experience emotion based on your interpretation.

4. Emotions are communicated verbally and nonverbally, and the way in which you express emotions is largely a matter of choice.

5. Cultural and gender display rules identify what emotions may be expressed, where, how, and by whom.

6. Emotions are often contagious.

Obstacles to Communicating Emotions

7. Among the obstacles to emotional communication are societal rules and customs, a fear of appearing weak or powerless, and a lack of skill in expressing emotions.

Skills for Expressing Emotions

8. Understand what you are feeling and what made you feel this way.
9. Formulate a communication goal; what exactly do you want to accomplish when expressing emotions?
10. Identify your communication choices and evaluate them.
11. Describe your feelings as accurately as possible, identify the reasons for your feelings, anchor your feelings and their expression in the present time, own your own feelings, and handle your anger as appropriate.

Skills for Responding to the Emotions of Others

12. Look for cues to understand the person's feelings. Listen for what is said and not said; look at the nonverbals, especially those that don't match the verbals.
13. Look for cues as to what the person wants you to do. Don't assume it's to solve their problem.
14. Use active listening techniques. Paraphrase, express understanding, and ask questions as appropriate.
15. Empathize. See the situation from the other person's perspective. Ask yourself what the other person may be feeling.
16. Focus on the other person. Avoid interpreting the situation from your own experiences.
17. Remember the irreversibility of communication. Once said, messages can't be erased, mentally or emotionally.

Key Terms

anger, **172**
anger management, **173**
blended emotions, **163**
cognitive labeling theory, **162**

display rules, **166**
emotions, **162**
emotional appeals, **167**
emotional contagion, **167**

emotional communication, **163**
gender display rules, **166**
I-messages, **172**
James-Lange theory, **162**

owning feelings, **172**
primary emotions, **163**
ventilation hypothesis, **173**

Critical Thinking Questions

1 Some societies permit and even expect men to show strong emotions. They expect men to cry, to show fear, to express anger openly. Other societies—including many groups within general U.S. culture—criticize men for experiencing and expressing such emotions. What has your culture taught you about gender and the expression of emotions—in particular, about the expression of strongly felt emotions and emotions that show weakness (such as fear, discomfort, or uncertainty)?

2 One implication of the cognitive labeling theory of emotions is that you and only you can make yourself feel angry or sad or anxious. This view is often phrased popularly as "Other people can hurt you physically, but only you can hurt yourself emotionally." Do you agree with this? What evidence can you advance to support or refute this position?

3 What has your experience revealed about the ways men and women express emotions? In what ways are men and women similar? In what ways are they different?

4 For each of the following situations, identify (1) the nature of the problem and (2) the one solution you would recommend to the parties involved.

■ Joe is extremely honest and open; he regularly says everything he feels without self-censorship. Not surprisingly, he often offends people. Joe is entering a new work environment and worries that his frankness may not be the best way to win friends and influence people.

■ Alex and Deirdre have dated steadily for the last four years. Deirdre is extremely unexpressive but believes that Alex—because of their long and close relationship—should know how she feels without her having to spell it out. When Alex doesn't respond appropriately, Deirdre becomes angry, saying that Alex doesn't really love her; if he did, he would know what she's feeling. Alex says this is crazy: "I'm no mind reader; if Deirdre wants something, she has the obligation to say so."

■ Tobin has recently been put in charge of a group of workers at a small printer repair firm. Tobin is extremely reserved and rarely reveals any emotion. He gives instructions, praises, and criticizes all with the same tone of voice and facial expressions. This has led the workers to feel he's insincere and isn't really feeling what he says.

Choice Points

1 *Dealing with Sadness and Joy.* The parents of your neighbor, who has lived next door to you for the last 10 years, were recently killed in a car accident. And now your neighbor, who has had many financial difficulties, will inherit a large estate. You meet in the hallway of your apartment house. Ask yourself: What does your neighbor want to hear? What do you say?

2 *Spending Time.* Your grandmother is dying and calls to ask you to spend some time with her. She says that she knows she is dying, that she wants you to know how much she has always loved you, and that her only regret in dying is not being able to see you anymore. You want her to feel comforted, and yet it's so emotional for you. Ask yourself: What do you say?

3 *Responding to Betrayal.* A colleague at work has revealed to other workers personal information about you that you confided in him and him alone. You're steaming as you pass a group of colleagues commenting on your current relationship problems. Ask yourself: What are some choices you have for reacting to this? What would you do first?

4 *The Crying Child.* A young child about six or seven years old is crying because the other children won't play with her. Ask yourself: What can you say to make the child feel better but without trying to solve the child's problems by asking the other children to play with this child?

5 *The Break In.* Fellow students have just had their dorm room broken into, their computer stolen, and their furnishings trashed.

They come to you and tell you what happened. Your room was not touched. Ask yourself: What might you say? What should you be sure you don't say?

6 *Responding Emotionally (or Not).* Your supervisor seems to constantly belittle your experience, which you thought was your strong point. Often your supervisor will say that your experiences were "in school" or "with only a few people" or some such negative phrase. You think your experience has more than prepared you for this job, and you want to make sure your supervisor knows this. Ask yourself: What are your options for communicating this feeling? What should you say?

7 *Giving Emotional Advice.* Your best friend tells you that he suspects his girlfriend is seeing someone else. He's extremely upset; he tells you that he wants to confront her with his suspicions but is afraid of what he'll hear. Ask yourself: What options does your friend have? What would you advise him to say?

MyCommunicationLab
Explorations

PEARSON
mycommunicationlab   www.mycommunicationlab.com

Exercises to help you understand the nature of emotional communication include ❶ Communicating Emotions Nonverbally, ❷ Communicating Your Emotions, ❸ Expressing Negative Feelings, ❹ Communicating Emotions Effectively, ❺ and Emotional Advice.

8 Conversational Messages

The Conversation Process	Organizational Conversation
Conversational Management	Conversational Problems:
Conversational Disclosure: Revealing Yourself	Prevention and Repair

Michael Clayton

Michael Clayton reveals some interesting perspectives on conversation; for example, the fact that the way you talk depends not only on the goal you hope to achieve, but on who you are and who you think the other person is. As you'll see in this chapter, conversation is a complex process and is at the center of all interpersonal interactions and relationships.

Conversation is the essence of interpersonal communication. These two concepts are so closely related that some communication researchers think of the words *conversation* and *interpersonal communication* as synonymous, as meaning essentially the same thing. Most researchers and theorists would claim that communication exists on a continuum such as that discussed in Chapter 1 (see especially Figure 1.1) and that interpersonal communication occupies some significant portion of the right side of this continuum. Exactly where impersonal ends and interpersonal begins is a matter of disagreement.

Conversation can be defined as "relatively informal social interaction in which the roles of speaker and hearer are exchanged in a nonautomatic fashion under the collaborative management of all parties" (McLaughlin, 1984). Examining conversation provides an excellent opportunity to look at verbal and nonverbal messages as they're used in day-to-day communications and thus serves as a useful culmination for this second part of the text.

The Conversation Process

It's convenient to divide up conversation into chunks or stages and to view each stage as requiring a choice as to what you'll say and how you'll say it. Here we divide the sequence into five steps: opening, feedforward, business, feedback, and closing (see Figure 8.1). These stages and the way people follow them will vary depending on the personalities of the communicators, their culture, the context in which the conversation occurs, the purpose of the conversation, and the entire host of factors considered throughout this text.

When reading about the process of conversation, keep in mind that not everyone speaks with the fluency and ease that many textbooks often assume. Speech and language disorders, for example, can seriously disrupt the conversation process when some elementary guidelines aren't followed. Table 8.1 offers suggestions for making such conversations run more smoothly.

Opening

The first step is to open the conversation, usually with some kind of greeting: "Hi. How are you?" "Hello, this is Joe." The greeting is a good example of **phatic communication**: It's a message that establishes a connection between two people and opens up the channels for more meaningful interaction. Openings, of course, may be nonverbal as well as verbal. A smile, kiss, or handshake may be as clear an opening as "Hello." Greetings are so common that they often go unnoticed. But when they're omitted—as when the doctor begins the conversation by saying, "What's wrong?"—you may feel uncomfortable and thrown off guard.

In normal conversation, the greeting is reciprocated with a greeting similar in degree of formality and intensity. When it isn't—when the other person turns away or responds coldly to your friendly "Good morning"—you know that something is wrong.

Openings are also generally consistent in tone with the main part of the conversation; a cheery "How ya doing today, bud?" is not normally followed by news of a family death, and

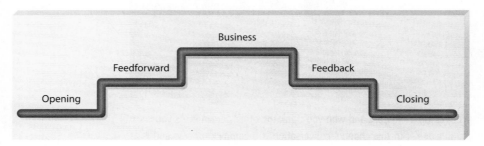

FIGURE 8.1

A Five-Stage Model of Conversation

This model of the stages of conversation is best seen as a way of talking about conversation and not as a hard-and-fast depiction of stages all conversations follow. As you review the model, consider how accurately it depicts conversation as you experience it. Can you develop a more accurate and more revealing model?

TABLE 8.1 Interpersonal Communication Tips
Between People with and without Speech and Language Disorders

| Demosthenes | Lewis Carroll | Winston Churchill | Mel Tillis |

Speech and language disorders vary widely—from fluency problems such as stuttering, to indistinct articulation, to difficulty in finding the right word, or aphasia. Following a few simple guidelines can facilitate communication between people with and without speech and language disorders.

If you're the person without a speech or language disorder:

1. Avoid finishing another's sentences. Although you may think you're helping the person who stutters or has word-finding difficulty, finishing the person's sentences may communicate the idea that you're impatient and don't want to spend the extra time necessary to interact effectively.

2. Avoid giving directions to the person with a speech disorder. Saying "slow down" or "relax" will often seem insulting and will make further communication more difficult.

3. Maintain eye contact. Show interest and at the same time avoid showing any signs of impatience or embarrassment.

4. Ask for clarification as needed. If you don't understand what the person said, ask him or her to repeat it. Don't pretend that you understand when you don't.

5. Don't treat people who have language problems like children. A person with aphasia, say, who has difficulty with names or nouns generally, is in no way childlike.

If you're the person with a speech or language disorder:

1. Let the other person know what your special needs are. For example, if you stutter, you might tell others that you have difficulty with certain sounds and so they need to be patient.

2. Demonstrate your own comfort. Show that you have a positive attitude toward the interpersonal situation. If you appear comfortable and positive, others will also.

Sources: These suggestions were drawn from a variety of sources: www.nsastutter.org/material/indep.php?matid=189, www.aphasia. org/, http://spot.pcc.edu/~rjacobs/career/communication_tips.htm, and www.dol.gov/odep/pubs/fact/comucate.htm (all accessed May 20, 2008).

a friendly conversation is not begun with insensitive openers: "Wow, you've gained a few pounds haven't you?"

Feedforward

At the second step, you usually provide some kind of feedforward (see Chapter 1), which gives the other person a general idea of the conversation's focus: "I've got to tell you about Jack," "Did you hear what happened in class yesterday?" or "We need to talk about our vacation plans." Feedforward also may identify the tone of the conversation ("I'm really depressed and need to talk with you") or the time required ("This will just take a minute") (Frentz, 1976; Reardon, 1987).

More formally we can identify at least four major functions of feedforward: to open the channels of communication, to preview the message, to disclaim, and to altercast.

- *To Open the Channels of Communication.* Phatic communication (also referred to as phatic communion) is information that tells you that the normal, expected, and accepted rules of interaction will be in effect. It tells you another person is willing to communicate. It's the "How are you" and "Nice weather" greetings that are designed to maintain rapport and friendly relationships (Placencia, 2004; Burnard, 2003). Similarly, listeners' short comments that are unrelated to the content of the conversation but that indicate interest and attention may also be considered phatic communication (McCarthy, 2003). Not surprisingly, phatic communication is important not only in face-to-face interaction but also in e-mail (Bloch, 2002).

- *To Preview the Message.* Feedforward messages may, for example, preview the content ("I'm afraid I have bad news for you"), the importance ("Listen to this before you make a move"), the form or style ("I'll tell you all the gory details"), and the positive or negative quality of subsequent messages ("You're not going to like this, but here's what I heard"). The subject heading on your e-mail well illustrates this function of feedforward, as do the phone numbers and names that come up on your caller ID.

- *To Disclaim.* The disclaimer is a statement that aims to ensure that your message will be understood as you want it to be and that it will not reflect negatively on you. For example, you might use a disclaimer when you think that what you're going to say may be met with opposition. Thus, you say "I'm not against immigration, but . . ." or "Don't think I'm homophobic, but . . ." (Disclaimers, as they function to prevent conversational problems, are discussed later in this chapter, pp. 201–202).

- *To Altercast.* Feedforward is often used to place the receiver in a specific role and to request responses in terms of this assumed role, a process called altercasting (Weinstein & Deutschberger, 1963; McLaughlin, 1984). For example, you might altercast by asking a friend, "As a future advertising executive, what would you think of corrective advertising?" This question casts your friend in the role of advertising executive (rather than parent, Democrat, or Baptist, for example) and asks that she or he answer from a particular perspective.

Conversational awkwardness often occurs when feedforwards are used inappropriately. For example, using overly long feedforwards may make the listener wonder whether you'll ever get to the business at hand and may make you seem disorganized and lacking in focus. Omitting feedforward before a truly shocking message (for example, the terminal illness of a friend or relative) can make you seem insensitive or uncaring.

Often the feedforward is combined with the opening, as when you see someone on campus, for example, and say, "Hey, listen to this" or when, in a work situation, someone says, "Well, folks, let's get the meeting going."

Here are a few suggestions for giving effective feedforward.

- Use feedforward to estimate the receptivity of the person to what you're going to say. For example, before asking for a date, you'd probably use feedforward to test the waters and to see if you're likely to get a "yes" response. You might ask if the other person enjoys going out to dinner or if he or she is dating anyone seriously. Before asking a friend for a loan, you'd probably feedforward your needy condition and say something like "I'm really strapped for cash and need to get my hands on $200 to pay my car loan" and wait for the other person to say (you hope), "Can I help?"

- Use feedforward that's consistent with your subsequent message. If your main message is one of bad news, then your feedforward needs to be serious and to help to prepare the other person for this bad news. You might, for example, say something like "I need to tell you something you're not going to want to hear. Let's sit down."

- The more important or complex the message, the more important and more extensive your feedforward needs to be. For example, in public speaking, in which the message is relatively long, the speaker is advised to give fairly extensive feedforward or what is called an orientation or preview. At the start of a business meeting, the leader may give feedforward in the form of an agenda or meeting schedule.

Business

The third step is the "business," the substance or focus of the conversation. The term *business* is used to emphasize that most conversations are goal directed. That is, you converse to fulfill one or several of the general purposes of interpersonal communication: to learn, relate, influence, play, or help (see Chapter 1). The term is also sufficiently general to incorporate all kinds of interactions. Not surprisingly, however, each culture has certain conversational **taboos**—topics or language that should be avoided, especially by "outsiders." For example, discussing bullfighting or illegal aliens can easily get you into difficulty in conversations with Mexicans, and politics and religion may pose problems in conversation with those from the Middle East (Axtell, 1994, 2007). In any case, the business is conducted through an exchange of speaker and listener roles. Brief, rather than long, speaking turns characterize most satisfying conversations.

In the business stage, you talk about Jack, what happened in class, or your vacation plans. This is obviously the longest part of the conversation and the reason for the opening and the feedforward.

Feedback

The fourth step is feedback (see Chapter 1), the reverse of the second step. Here you reflect back on the conversation to signal that, as far as you're concerned, the business is completed: "So you want to send Jack a get-well card," "Wasn't that the craziest class you ever heard of?" or "I'll call for reservations, and you'll shop for what we need."

Each feedback opportunity presents you with choices along at least the following five dimensions: positive–negative, person focused–message focused, immediate–delayed, low monitored–high monitored, and supportive–critical. To use feedback effectively, you need to make educated choices along these dimensions.

VIEWPOINT Greetings (whether face-to-face or computer-mediated) are a kind of feedforward and serve various functions (Knapp & Vangelisti, 2009; Krivonos & Knapp, 1975). For example, greetings may merely signal access, opening up the channels of communication for more meaningful interaction. Greetings also may reveal important information about the relationship; for example, a big smile and a warm "Hi, it's been a long time" signals that the relationship is still a friendly one. Greetings also may help maintain relationships. When workers in an office greet each other as they pass through the office, it assures them that even though they don't stop and talk for an extended period, they still have access to each other. What functions did your last three greetings serve?

- *Positive–Negative.* Feedback may be positive (you pay a compliment or pat someone on the back) or negative (you criticize someone or scowl). Positive feedback tells the speaker that he or she is on the right track and should continue communicating in essentially the same way. Negative feedback tells the speaker that something is wrong and that some adjustment should be made.
- *Person Focused–Message Focused.* Feedback may center on the person ("You're sweet" or "You have a great smile"). Or it may center on the message ("Can you repeat that number?" or "Your argument is a good one").
- *Immediate–Delayed.* In interpersonal situations, feedback is often sent immediately after the message is received; you smile or say something in response almost simultaneously with your receiving the message. In other communication situations, however, the feedback may be delayed. Instructor evaluation questionnaires completed at the end of a course provide feedback long after the class began. When you applaud or ask questions of a public speaker at the end of a lecture, the feedback is delayed. In interview situations, the feedback may come weeks afterward. In media situations, some feedback comes immediately through Nielsen ratings, and other feedback comes much later through viewing and buying patterns.
- *Low-Monitoring–High-Monitoring Feedback.* Varies from the spontaneous and totally honest reaction (low-monitored feedback) to the carefully constructed response designed to serve a specific purpose (high-monitored feedback). In most interpersonal situations, you probably give feedback spontaneously; you allow your responses to

show without any monitoring. At other times, however, you may be more guarded, as when your boss asks you how you like your job or when your grandfather asks what you think of his new earring.

- *Supportive–Critical.* Supportive feedback accepts the speaker and what the speaker says. It occurs, for example, when you console another, encourage him or her to talk, or otherwise confirm the person's definition of self. Critical feedback, on the other hand, is evaluative; it's judgmental. When you give critical feedback (whether positive or negative), you judge another's performance—as in, for example, coaching someone learning a new skill.

Realize that these categories are not exclusive. Feedback does not have to be either critical or supportive; it can be both. For example, in talking with someone who is trying to become a more effective interviewer, you might critically evaluate a practice interview but also express support for the effort. Similarly, you might respond to a friend's question immediately and then after a day or two elaborate on your response. Because each situation is unique, it's difficult to offer specific suggestions for making your conversational feedback more effective. But, with some adjustments for the specifics of the situation, the following guides might prove helpful:

- Focus on the behavior or the message rather than the motives behind the message or behavior. Say, for example, "You forgot my birthday" rather than "You don't love me."
- If your feedback is largely negative, try to begin with something positive. There are always positives if you look hard enough. The negatives will be much easier to take, after hearing some positives.
- Ask for feedback on your feedback, for example, say "Does this make sense?" "Do you understand what I want our relationship to be?"

The other half of the feedback equation is the person receiving the feedback (Robbins & Hunsaker, 2006). When you are the recipient of feedback, be sure to show your interest in feedback. This is vital information that will help you improve whatever you're doing. Encourage the feedback giver. Be open to hearing this feedback. Don't argue; don't be defensive.

Perhaps most important, check your perceptions. Do you understand the feedback? Ask questions. Not all feedback is easy to understand; after all, a wink, a backward head nod, or a smile can each signal a variety of different messages. When you don't understand the meaning of the feedback, ask for clarification (nondefensively, of course). Paraphrase the feedback you've just received to make sure you both understand it: "You'd be comfortable taking over the added responsibilities if I went back to school?"

Closing

The fifth and last step, the opposite of the first step, is the closing, the goodbye, which often reveals how satisfied the persons were with the conversation: "I hope you'll call soon" or "Don't call us, we'll call you." The closing also may be used to schedule future conversations: "Give me a call tomorrow night" or "Let's meet for lunch at twelve." When closings are indefinite or vague, conversation often becomes awkward; you're not quite sure if you should say goodbye or if you should wait for something else to be said.

In a way similar to the opening and the feedforward being combined, the closing and the feedback might be combined, as when you say: "Look, I've got to think more about this commitment, okay?"

Before reading about the process of conversation management, think of your own conversations, recalling both conversations that were satisfactory and some that were unsatisfactory. Think of a specific recent conversation as you respond to the self-test "How Satisfying Is Your Conversation?" Taking this test now will help highlight the characteristics of conversational behavior and the aspects that make some conversations satisfying and others unsatisfying.

✎ TEST YOURSELF

HOW SATISFYING IS YOUR CONVERSATION?

Respond to each of the following statements by recording the number best representing your feelings, using this scale: 1 = strongly agree, 2 = moderately agree, 3 = slightly agree, 4 = neutral, 5 = slightly disagree, 6 = moderately disagree, 7 = strongly disagree. Because this test was constructed before the advent of widespread use of computer-mediated communication, you might want to respond twice to each statement—once for face-to-face and once for computer-mediated communication (IM, chat, social networking, e-mail)—and compare your separate scores.

_____ 1. The other person let me know that I was communicating effectively.
_____ 2. Nothing was accomplished.
_____ 3. I would like to have another conversation like this one.
_____ 4. The other person genuinely wanted to get to know me.
_____ 5. I was very dissatisfied with the conversation.
_____ 6. I felt that during the conversation I was able to present myself as I wanted the other person to view me.
_____ 7. I was very satisfied with the conversation.
_____ 8. The other person expressed a lot of interest in what I had to say.
_____ 9. I did *not* enjoy the conversation.
_____ 10. The other person did *not* provide support for what he or she was saying.
_____ 11. I felt I could talk about anything with the other person.
_____ 12. We each got to say what we wanted.
_____ 13. I felt that we could laugh easily together.
_____ 14. The conversation flowed smoothly.
_____ 15. The other person frequently said things which added little to the conversation.
_____ 16. We talked about something I was *not* interested in.

HOW DID YOU DO? To compute your score, follow these steps:

1. Add the scores for items 1, 3, 4, 6, 7, 8, 11, 12, 13, and 14.
2. Reverse the scores for items 2, 5, 9, 10, 15, and 16 such that 7 becomes 1, 6 becomes 2, 5 becomes 3, 4 remains 4, 3 becomes 5, 2 becomes 6, and 1 becomes 7.
3. Add the reversed scores for items 2, 5, 9, 10, 15, and 16.
4. Add the totals from steps 1 and 3 to yield your communication satisfaction score.

You may interpret your score along the following scale:

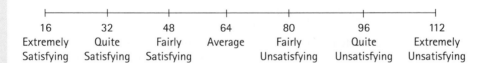

16	32	48	64	80	96	112
Extremely Satisfying	Quite Satisfying	Fairly Satisfying	Average	Fairly Unsatisfying	Quite Unsatisfying	Extremely Unsatisfying

WHAT WILL YOU DO? Before reading the remainder of this chapter, try to identify those qualities that make a conversation satisfying for you. What interpersonal qualities are most important to making a person a satisfying conversational partner? How might you cultivate these qualities? Table 8.2, p. 186, identifies some unsatisfying conversational partners that you'll likely want to avoid in your own conversations.

If you took the test twice, once for face-to-face conversation and once for CMC, which score was higher? That is, from which form of communication do you derive the greater satisfaction? How do you account for any differences? Interestingly enough, some research shows that, contrary to much popular thinking, CMC can yield greater satisfaction than face-to-face communication (Valkenburg & Peter, 2007).

Source: This test was developed by Michael Hecht and appeared in "The Conceptualization and Measurement of Interpersonal Communication Satisfaction," *Human Communication Research* 4 (1978): 253–264. It is reprinted by permission of the author.

TABLE 8.2 Unsatisfying Conversational Partners and How Not to Become One of Them

As you read this table, consider your own conversations. Have you met any of these people? Have you ever been one of these people?

Unsatisfying Conversational Partners	How Not to Become One of Them
The **Detour Taker** begins to talk about a topic and then goes off pursuing a totally different subject.	Follow a logical pattern in conversation, and avoid frequent and long detours.
The **Monologist** gives speeches rather than engaging in dialogue.	Give the other person a chance to speak and keep your own "lectures" short. Look for signs that indicate the listener's desire to speak.
The **Complainer** has many complaints and rarely tires of listing each of them.	Be positive; emphasize what's good before what's bad.
The **Moralist** evaluates and judges everyone and everything.	Avoid evaluation and judgment; see the world through the eyes of the other person.
The **Inactive Responder** gives no reaction regardless of what you say.	Respond overtly with verbal and nonverbal messages; let the other person see and hear that you're listening.
The **Story Teller** tells stories, too often substituting them for two-way conversation.	Talk about yourself in moderation; be other-oriented.
The **Interrogator** asks questions about everything, even about matters that are obvious or irrelevant.	Ask questions in moderation—to secure needed information and not to get every imaginable detail.
The **Egotist** talks only about topics that are self-related.	Be other-oriented; focus on the other person; listen as much as you speak.
The **Doomsayer** is the ultimate negative thinker; everything is a problem.	Be positive; talk about the good as well as the bad.
The **Arguer** listens only to find something to take issue with.	Be supportive, but argue and disagree when it's appropriate.
The **Thought Completer** "knows" exactly what you're going to say and so says it for you.	Don't interrupt; assume that the speaker wants to finish her or his own thoughts.
The **Self-Discloser** discloses more than you need or want to hear.	Disclose selectively, in ways appropriate to your relationship with the listener.
The **Advisor** regularly and consistently gives advice, whether you want it or not.	Don't assume that the expression of a problem is a request for a solution.
The **Psychiatrist** analyzes everything you say and mind-reads your motives.	Avoid playing the therapist as a regular role; be a friend, lover, or parent.

Conversational Management

Speakers and listeners have to work together to make conversation an effective and satisfying experience. **Conversational management** includes initiating, maintaining, and closing conversations.

Initiating Conversations

Several approaches to opening a conversation can be derived from the elements of the interpersonal communication process discussed in Chapter 1:

- *Self-references* say something about yourself. Such references may be of the "name, rank, and serial number" type—for example: "My name is Joe. I'm from Omaha." On the first day of class, students might say, "I'm worried about this class" or "I took this instructor last semester; she was excellent."
- *Other-references* say something about the other person or ask a question: "I like that sweater." "Didn't we meet at Charlie's?" Of course, there are pitfalls here. Generally, it's best not to comment on the person's race ("My uncle married a Korean"), the person's affectional orientation ("Nice to meet you; I have a gay brother"), or physical disability ("It must be awful to be confined to a wheelchair").

- *Relational references* say something about the two of you: for example, "May I buy you a drink?" "Would you like to dance?" or simply "May I join you?"
- *Context references* say something about the physical, social–psychological, cultural, or temporal context. The familiar "Do you have the time?" is a reference of this type. But you can be more creative and say, for example, "This restaurant seems very friendly" or "This Dali is fantastic."

As you know from experience, conversations are most satisfying when they're upbeat and positive. So it's generally best to lead off with something positive rather than something negative. Say, for example, "I like the music here" instead of "Don't you just hate this place?" Also, it's best not to be too revealing; disclosing too much too early in an interaction can make the other person feel uncomfortable.

Another way of looking at the process of initiating conversations is to examine the infamous "opening line," the opener designed to begin a romantic relationship.

Consider your own opening lines (or the opening lines that have been used on you). Let's say you're at a club and want to strike up a conversation—and perhaps spark a relationship. Which of the following are you most likely to use (Kleinke, 1986; Kleinke & Dean, 1990)?

- *Cute–flippant openers* are humorous, indirect, and ambiguous as to whether or not the person opening the conversation really wants an extended encounter. Examples: "Is that really your hair?" "Bet I can outdrink you."
- *Innocuous openers* are highly ambiguous as to whether these are simple comments that might be made to just anyone or whether they're in fact openers designed to initiate an extended encounter. Examples: "What do you think of the band?" "Could you show me how to work this machine?"
- *Direct openers* demonstrate clearly the speaker's interest in meeting the other person. Examples: "I feel a little embarrassed about this, but I'd like to meet you." "Would you like to have a drink after dinner?"

UNDERSTANDING INTERPERSONAL SKILLS

Expressiveness

Expressiveness is the skill of communicating genuine involvement; it entails, for example, taking responsibility for your thoughts and feelings, encouraging expressiveness or openness in others, and providing appropriate feedback. As you can easily appreciate, these are the qualities that make a conversation exciting and satisfying. Expressiveness includes both verbal and nonverbal messages and often involves revealing your emotions and your normally hidden self.

Communicating Expressiveness. Here are a few suggestions for communicating expressiveness.

- Vary your vocal rate, pitch, volume, and rhythm to convey involvement and interest. Vary your language; avoid clichés and trite expressions, which signal a lack of originality and personal involvement.
- Use appropriate gestures, especially gestures that focus on the other person rather than yourself. Maintain eye contact and lean toward the person; at the same time, avoid self-touching gestures or directing your eyes to others in the room.
- Give verbal and nonverbal feedback to show that you're listening. Such feedback promotes relationship satisfaction.
- Smile. Your smile is probably your most expressive feature and it will likely be much appreciated.
- Communicate expressiveness in ways that are culturally sensitive. Some cultures (Italian, for example) encourage expressiveness and teach children to be expressive. Other cultures (Japanese and Thai, for example) encourage a more reserved response style (Matsumoto, 1996). Some cultures (Arab and many Asian cultures, for example) consider expressiveness by women in business settings to be inappropriate (Lustig & Koester, 2006; Axtell, 1994; Hall & Hall, 1987).

Working with Interpersonal Skills

Think about the expressiveness of the people you know who are extremely popular and those who are significantly less popular. In what ways do these groups differ in expressiveness? How would you describe your own expressiveness?

One advantage of *cute-flippant* openers is that they're indirect enough to cushion any rejection. These are also, however, the lines least preferred by both men and women.

In contrast, both men and women generally like *innocuous* openers; they're indirect enough to allow for an easy out if the other person doesn't want to talk.

On *direct* openers, however, genders differ. Men like direct openers that are very clear in meaning, possibly because men are not used to having another person initiate a meeting. Women prefer openers that aren't too strong and that are relatively modest.

In e-mail conversations the situation is a bit different. Even before your message is opened, the receiver knows who the sender is, when the message was composed, and, from the title or subject line, something about the nature of your message. In addition to this general hint at the nature of the message, most e-mail users begin their e-mail with a kind of orientation or preface to what will follow, for example, "I'm writing to ask the name of your acupuncturist" or "I want to fill you in as to what happened at the party." Generally, such openers are direct and relate closely to what is to follow.

Maintaining Conversations

In maintaining conversations you follow a variety of principles and rules. Here we'll consider first the principles and maxims you follow in conversation, and second the ways in which the speaker and listener exchange turns in conversation.

The Principle of Cooperation During conversation you probably follow the principle of **cooperation,** implicitly agreeing with the other person to cooperate in trying to understand what each is saying (Grice, 1975; Lindblom, 2001). You cooperate largely by using four **conversational maxims**—principles that speakers and listeners in the United States and in many other cultures follow in conversation. Although the names for these maxims may be new, the principles themselves will be easily recognized from your own experiences.

The Maxim of Quantity Be as informative as necessary to communicate the intended meaning. Thus, in keeping with the **quantity maxim**, you include information that makes the meaning clear but omit what does not; you give neither too little nor too much information. You see people violate this maxim when they try to relate an incident and digress to give unnecessary information. You find yourself thinking or saying, "Get to the point; so what happened?" This maxim is also violated when necessary information is omitted. In this situation, you find yourself constantly interrupting to ask questions: "Where were they?" "When did this happen?" "Who else was there?"

This simple maxim is frequently violated in e-mail communication. Here, for example, are three ways in which e-mail often violates the maxim of quantity and some suggestions on how to avoid these violations.

- Chain e-mails often violate the maxim of quantity by sending people information they don't really need or want. Some people maintain lists of e-mail addresses and send all these people the same information. It's highly unlikely that everyone on these lists will need or want to read the long list of jokes you find so funny. *Suggestion:* Avoid chain e-mail (at least most of the time). When something comes along that you think someone you know would like to read, send it on to the specific one, two, or three people you know would like to receive it.
- When chain e-mails are used, they often contain the e-mail addresses of everyone on the chain. These extensive headers clog the system and also reveal e-mail addresses that some people may prefer to keep private or to share with others at their own discretion. *Suggestion:* When you do send chain e-mails (and in some situations, they serve useful purposes), conceal the e-mail addresses of your recipients by using some general description such as "undisclosed recipients."
- Large attachments take time to download and can create problems for people who do not have the latest technology. Not everyone wants to see the two hundred photos of your last vacation. *Suggestion:* Use attachments in moderation; find out first who would like to receive photos and who would not.

The Maxim of Quality Say what you know or assume to be true, and do not say what you know to be false. When you're in conversation, you assume that the other person's information is true—at least as far as he or she knows. When you speak with people who frequently violate the **quality maxim** by lying, exaggerating, or minimizing major problems, you come to distrust what such individuals are saying and wonder what is true and what is fabricated.

The Maxim of Relation Talk about what is relevant to the conversation. Thus, the **relation maxim** states, if you're talking about Pat and Chris and say, for example, "Money causes all sorts of relationship problems," it's assumed by others that your comment is somehow related to Pat and Chris. This principle is frequently violated by speakers who digress widely or frequently interject irrelevant comments, causing you to wonder how these comments are related to what you're discussing.

The Maxim of Manner Be clear, avoid ambiguities, be relatively brief, and organize your thoughts into a meaningful sequence. Thus, in accordance with the **manner maxim**, you use terms that the listener understands and clarify terms that you suspect the listener will not understand. When talking with a child, for example, you simplify your vocabulary. Similarly, you adjust your manner of speaking on the basis of the information you and the listener share. When talking to a close friend, for example, you can refer to mutual acquaintances and to experiences you've had together. When talking to a stranger, however, you'll either omit such references or explain them.

The four maxims just discussed aptly describe most conversations as they take place in much of the United States. Recognize, however, that maxims will vary from one culture to another. Here are two maxims appropriate in cultures other than that of the United States, but also appropriate to some degree throughout the United States:

- In Japanese conversations and group discussions, a maxim of *preserving peaceful relationships* with others may be observed (Midooka, 1990). Thus, for example, it would be considered inappropriate to argue and to directly demonstrate that another person is wrong. It would be inappropriate to contribute to another person's embarrassment or, worse, loss of face.
- The maxim of *self-denigration*, observed in the conversations of Chinese speakers, may require that you avoid taking credit for some accomplishment or make less of some ability or talent you have (Gu, 1990). To put yourself down in this way is a form of politeness that seeks to elevate the person to whom you're speaking.

The Principle of Dialogue Think about your own communication tendencies. Which of the following paired statements *generally* characterizes your interpersonal interactions?

- You frequently use negative criticism ("I didn't like that explanation") and negative personal judgments ("You're not a very good listener, are you?").

- You avoid negative criticism and negative personal judgments; you practice using positive criticism ("I like those first two explanations best; they were really well reasoned").

- You frequently use dysfunctional communication, such as expressing unwillingness to talk, or use messages that are unrelated to the topic of discussion ("There's no sense discussing this; I can see you're not rational").

- You keep the channels of communication open ("I really don't know what I did that offended you, but tell me. I don't want to hurt you again").

- You rarely demonstrate through paraphrase or summary that you understand the other person's meaning.

- You frequently paraphrase or summarize what the other person has said to ensure accurate understanding.

- You rarely request clarification of the other person's perspectives or ideas.

- You request clarification as necessary and ask for the other person's point of view because of a genuine interest in the other person's perspective.

- You frequently request personal positive statements or statements of self-approval ("How did you like the way I told that guy off? Clever, no?").

- You avoid requesting self-approval statements.

The statements in the left column are examples of monologue. The statements on the right are examples of dialogue. **Monologue** is communication in which one person speaks and the other listens; there's no real interaction among participants. The term *monologic communication* is an extension of this basic definition and refers to communication in which there is no genuine interaction, in which you speak without any real concern for the other person's feelings or attitudes. The monologic communicator is concerned only with his or her own goals and is interested in the other person only insofar as that person can be used to achieve those goals. In monologic interaction, you communicate what will advance your own goals, prove most persuasive, and benefit you.

Not surprisingly, effective communication is based not on monologue but on its opposite, *dialogue* (Buber, 1958; Brown & Keller, 1979; Thomlison, 1982; Yau-fair Ho, Chan, Peng, & Ng, 2001; McNamee & Gergen, 1999). In **dialogue**, there is two-way interaction. Each person is both speaker and listener, sender and receiver. In *dialogic communication* there is deep concern for the other person and for the relationship between the two people. The objective of dialogue is mutual understanding and empathy. There is respect for the other person, not because of what this person can do or give, but simply because this person is a human being and therefore deserves to be treated honestly and sincerely.

In a dialogic interaction, you respect the other person enough to allow that person the right to make his or her own choices without coercion, without the threat of punishment, without fear or social pressure. A dialogic communicator respects other people enough to believe that they can make their own decisions and implicitly or explicitly lets them know that whatever choices they make, they will still be respected as people.

The Principle of Turn Taking The defining feature of conversation is that the speaker and listener exchange roles throughout the interaction. You accomplish this through a wide variety of verbal and nonverbal cues that signal **conversational turns**—the changing (or maintaining) of the speaker or listener role during the conversation. In hearing people, turn taking is regulated by both audio and visual signals. Among blind speakers, the turn taking is governed in larger part by audio signals and often touch. Among deaf speakers, turn-taking signals are largely visual and also may involve touch (Coates & Sutton-Spence, 2001). Combining the insights of a variety of communication researchers (Duncan, 1972; Burgoon, Buller, & Woodall, 1996; Pearson & Spitzberg, 1990), let's look more closely at conversational turns in terms of cues that speakers use and cues that listeners use.

VIEWPOINT In dialogic interaction between, say, a fluent speaker and a person who has a severe physical or psychological communication problem, the more fluent speaker often tries to help the speaker with the problem communicate more effectively. In fact, some researchers have argued that the more competent communicator has an ethical responsibility to "equalize" the interaction by helping the other person to better convey his or her meaning (von Tetzchner & Jensen, 1999). Do you consider this an ethical responsibility?

Speaker Cues As a speaker, you regulate conversation through two major types of cues: turn-maintaining and turn-yielding. *Turn-maintaining cues* are designed to help you maintain the speaker's role. You can do this with a variety of cues; for example, by audibly inhaling to show that you have more to say, continuing a gesture or gestures to show that you have not completed the thought, avoiding eye contact with the listener so there's no indication that you're passing the speaking turn to him or her, sustaining your intonation pattern to indicate that you intend to say more, or vocalizing pauses ("er," "um") to prevent the listener from speaking and to show that you're still talking (Duncan, 1972; Burgoon, Buller, & Woodall, 1996). In most cases, speakers are expected to maintain relatively brief speaking turns and to turn over the speaking role willingly to the listener (when so signaled by the listener).

With *turn-yielding cues* you tell the listener that you're finished and wish to exchange the role of speaker for that of listener. These cues tell the listener (sometimes a specific listener) to take over the role of speaker. For example, at the end of a statement you might add some paralinguistic cue such as "eh?" that asks one of the listeners to assume the role of speaker. You can also indicate that you've finished speaking by dropping your intonation, by prolonged silence, by making direct eye contact with a listener, by asking some general question, or by nodding in the direction of a particular listener.

In much the same way that you expect a speaker to yield the role of speaker, you also expect the listener to willingly assume the speaking role. Those who don't may be regarded as reticent or unwilling to involve themselves and take equal responsibility for the conversation. For example, in an analysis of turn-taking violations in the conversations of marrieds, the most common violation found was that of no response. Forty-five percent of the 540 violations identified involved a lack of response to an invitation to assume the speaker role. Of these "no response" violations, 68 percent were committed by men and 32 percent by women. Other turn-taking violations include interruptions, delayed responses, and inappropriately brief responses. From this it's been argued that by means of these violations, all of which are committed more frequently by men, men often silence women in marital interactions (DeFrancisco, 1991).

Listener Cues As a listener, you can regulate the conversation by using a variety of cues. *Turn-requesting cues* let the speaker know that you'd like to take a turn as speaker. Sometimes you can do this by simply saying, "I'd like to say something," but often you do it more subtly through some vocalized "er" or "um" that tells the mindful speaker that you'd now like to speak. This request to speak is also often made with facial and mouth gestures. You can, for example, indicate a desire to speak by opening your eyes and mouth widely as if to say something, by beginning to gesture with your hand, or by leaning forward.

You can also indicate your reluctance to assume the role of speaker by using *turn-denying cues*. For example, intoning a slurred "I don't know" or a brief grunt signals you have nothing to say. Other ways to refuse a turn are to avoid eye contact with the speaker who wishes you to take on the role of speaker or to engage in some behavior that is incompatible with speaking—for example, coughing or blowing your nose.

Back-Channeling Cues and Interruptions Back-channeling cues are used to communicate various types of information back to the speaker *without* your assuming the role of speaker. Some researchers call these "acknowledgment tokens"—brief utterances such as "mm-hm," "uh-huh," and "yeah," the three most often used such tokens—that tell the speaker you're listening (Schegloff, 1982; Drummond & Hopper, 1993). Others call them "overlaps" to distinguish them from those interruptions that are aimed at taking over the speaker's turn (Tannen, 1994b). Back-channeling cues are generally supportive and confirming and show that you're listening and are involved in the interaction (Kennedy & Camden, 1988).

You can communicate a variety of messages with these back-channeling (overlaps, acknowledgment tokens) cues; here are four of the most important messages (Burgoon, Buller, & Woodall, 1996; Pearson & Spitzberg, 1990).

- *To indicate agreement or disagreement.* Smiles, nods of approval, brief comments such as "Right" and "Of course," or a vocalization like "uh-huh" signal agreement. Frowning, shaking your head, or making comments such as "No" or "Never" signal disagreement.
- *To indicate degree of involvement.* An attentive posture, forward leaning, and focused eye contact tell the speaker that you're involved in the conversation. An inattentive posture, backward leaning, and avoidance of eye contact communicate a lack of involvement.
- *To pace the speaker.* You ask the speaker to slow down by raising your hand near your ear and leaning forward, or to speed up by repeatedly nodding your head. Or you may cue the speaker verbally by asking the speaker to slow down or to speed up.
- *To ask for clarification.* Puzzled facial expressions, perhaps coupled with a forward lean, or direct interjection of "Who?," "When?," or "Where?" signal your need for clarification.

Interruptions, in contrast to back-channeling cues, are attempts to take over the role of the speaker. These are not supportive and are often disconfirming. Interruptions are often interpreted as attempts to change the topic to a subject that the interrupter knows more about or to emphasize the person's authority. Interruptions are seen as attempts to assert power and to maintain control. Not surprisingly, research finds that superiors (bosses and supervisors) and those in positions of authority (police officers and interviewers) interrupt those in inferior positions more than the other way around (Carroll, 1994; Ashcraft, 1998). In fact, it would probably strike you as strange to see a worker repeatedly interrupting a supervisor or a student repeatedly interrupting a professor.

Another and even more often studied aspect of interruption is that of gender difference. The popular belief is that men interrupt more than women. This belief, research finds, is

	To Speak	To Listen
Speaker	1 Turn-maintaining cues	2 Turn-yielding cues
Listener	3 Turn-requesting cues	4 Turn-denying cues

FIGURE 8.2

Turn Taking and Conversational Wants

Quadrant 1 represents the speaker who wishes to speak (continue to speak) and uses turn-maintaining cues; quadrant 2, the speaker who wishes to listen and uses turn-yielding cues; quadrant 3, the listener who wishes to speak and uses turn-requesting cues; and quadrant 4, the listener who wishes to listen (continue listening) and uses turn-denying cues. Back-channeling cues would appear in quadrant 4, as they are cues that listeners use while they continue to listen. Interruptions would appear in quadrant 3, though they're not so much cues that request a turn as takeovers of the speaker's position. Does this model allow for the representation of all conversational cues? Are there other types of cues that are not represented here?

basically accurate. Men interrupt both women and other men more than women do. For example, one analysis of 43 published studies on interruptions and gender differences showed that men interrupted significantly more than women (Anderson, 1998). In addition, the more malelike the person's gender identity—regardless of the person's biological sex—the more likely it is that the person will interrupt (Drass, 1986). Fathers, one research study shows, interrupt their children more than mothers do (Greif, 1980). These gender differences, however, are small. More important than gender in determining who interrupts is the specific type of situation; some contexts (for example, task-oriented situations) may call for more interruptions, whereas others (such as relationship discussions) may call for more back-channeling cues (Anderson, 1998).

The various turn-taking cues and how they correspond to the conversational wants of speaker and listener are summarized in Figure 8.2.

Closing Conversations

Closing a conversation is often a difficult task. It can be an awkward and uncomfortable part of interpersonal interaction. Here are a few suggestions you might consider:

- Reflect back on the conversation and briefly summarize it so as to bring it to a close. For example: "I'm glad I ran into you and found out what happened at that union meeting. I'll probably be seeing you at the meetings next week."
- Directly state the desire to end the conversation and to get on with other things. For example: "I'd like to continue talking, but I really have to run. I'll see you around."
- Refer to future interaction. For example: "Why don't we get together next week sometime and continue this discussion?"
- Ask for closure. For example: "Have I explained what you wanted to know?"
- State that you enjoyed the interaction. For example: "I really enjoyed talking with you."

Closing a conversation in e-mail follows the same principles as closing a face-to-face conversation. But exactly when you end the e-mail exchange is often not clear, partly because the absence of nonverbal cues creates ambiguity. For example, if you ask someone a question and the other person answers, do you then e-mail again and say "thanks"? If so, should the other person e-mail you back and say "It was my pleasure"? And, if so, should you then e-mail back and say "I appreciate your willingness to answer my questions"? And, if so, should the other person then respond with something like "It was no problem"?

On the one hand, you don't want to prolong the interaction more than necessary; on the other, you don't want to appear impolite. So how do you signal (politely) that the e-mail exchange should stop? Here are a few suggestions (Cohen, 2002).

- Include in your e-mail the notation NRN (No Reply Necessary).
- If you're replying with information the other person requested, end your message with something like "I hope this helps."

The Ethics of Gossip

Gossip is social talk that involves making evaluations about persons who are not present during the conversation; it generally occurs when two people talk about a third party (Eder & Enke, 1991; Wert & Salovey, 2004). As you obviously know, a large part of your conversation at work and in social situations is spent gossiping (Lachnit, 2001; Waddington, 2004; Carey, 2005). In fact, one study estimates that approximately two-thirds of people's conversation time is devoted to social topics, and that most of these topics can be considered gossip (Dunbar, 2004). Gossiping seems universal among all cultures (Laing, 1993), and among some it's a commonly accepted ritual (Hall, 1993). And, not surprisingly, gossip occupies a large part of Internet communication, as demonstrated by the growing popularity of such websites as Juicy Campus (www.JuicyCampus.com), which currently link 59 college campuses (Morgan, 2008).

As you might expect, gossiping often has ethical implications, and in many instances gossip is considered unethical. Some such instances generally identified as unethical are (Bok, 1983):

- when gossip is used to unfairly hurt another person; for example, spreading gossip about an office romance or an instructor's past indiscretions
- when you know that what you're saying is not true; for example, lying to make another person look bad
- when no one has the right to such personal information; for example, revealing the income of neighbors to others or revealing a fellow student's poor grades to other students
- when you've promised secrecy; for example, revealing something that you promised not to repeat to others.

What would you do?

Your best friend's romantic partner has come on to you on several occasions. What is your ethical obligation to your friend? If you decide to tell your friend, will it be ethical to tell other mutual friends? At what point does revealing this become unethical gossip?

- Title or head your message FYI (For Your Information), indicating that your message is just to keep someone in the loop.
- When you make a request for information, end your message with "thank you in advance."

With any of these closings, it should be clear to the other person that you're attempting to end the conversation. Obviously, you will have to use more direct methods with those who don't take these subtle hints or don't realize that both persons are responsible for the interpersonal interaction and for bringing it to a satisfactory close.

Conversational Disclosure: Revealing Yourself

One of the most important forms of interpersonal communication that you can engage in is talking about yourself, or self-disclosure. **Self-disclosure** means communicating information about yourself (usually information that you normally keep hidden) to another person. It may involve information about (1) your values, beliefs, and desires ("I believe in reincarnation"); (2) your behavior ("I shoplifted but was never caught"); or (3) your self-qualities or characteristics ("I'm dyslexic"). Overt and carefully planned statements about yourself as well as slips of the tongue would be classified as self-disclosing communications. Similarly, you could self-disclose nonverbally by, for example, wearing gang colors, a wedding ring, or a shirt with slogans that reveal your political or social concerns, such as "Pro-Life" or "Go Green." Self-disclosure also may involve your reactions to the feelings of others; for example, when you tell your friend that you're sorry she was fired.

VIEWPOINT At times self-disclosure occurs more in temporary than in permanent relationships—for example, between strangers on a train or plane, a kind of "in-flight intimacy" (McGill, 1985). In this situation, two people set up an intimate self-disclosing relationship during a brief travel period, but they don't pursue it beyond that point. In a similar way, you might set up a relationship with one or several people on the Internet and engage in significant disclosure. Perhaps knowing that you'll never see these other people and that they will never know where you live or work or what you look like makes it easier. Do you engage in such disclosure? If so, why?

Self-disclosure occurs in all forms of communication, not just interpersonal. It frequently occurs in small group settings, in public speeches, on television talk shows such as *Maury* and *Jerry Springer*, and even on *Leno* and *Letterman*. And self-disclosure can occur not only in face-to-face settings but also through the Internet. On social network sites, for example, a great deal of self-disclosure goes on, as it does when people reveal themselves in personal e-mails, newsgroups, and blog posts. In fact, research finds that reciprocal self-disclosure occurs more quickly and at higher levels online than it does in face-to-face interactions (Levine, 2000; Joinson, 2001).

You probably self-disclose for a variety of reasons. Perhaps you feel the need for catharsis—a need to get rid of guilt feelings or to confess some wrongdoing. You may also disclose to help the listener; to show the listener, for example, how you dealt with an addiction or succeeded in getting a promotion. Of course, you may self-disclose to encourage relationship growth, or to maintain or repair a relationship, or even as a strategy for ending a relationship.

Although self-disclosure may occur as a single message—for example, you tell a stranger on a train that you're thinking about getting a divorce—it's best viewed as a developing process in which information is exchanged between people in a relationship over the period of their relationship (Spencer, 1993, 1994). If we view it as a developing process, we can then appreciate how self-disclosure changes as the relationship changes; for example, as a relationship progresses from initial contact through involvement to intimacy, the self-disclosures increase. If the relationship deteriorates and perhaps dissolves, the disclosures will decrease. We can also appreciate how self-disclosure will differ depending on the type of relationship, on whether the other person is your friend, lover, parent, child, or counselor.

Self-disclosure involves at least one other individual; it cannot be an intrapersonal communication act. To qualify as self-disclosure, the information must be received and understood by another person. As you can appreciate, self-disclosure can vary from the relatively insignificant ("I'm a Sagittarius") to the highly revealing and deeply personal ("I'm currently in an abusive relationship" or "I'm almost always depressed").

The remaining discussion of this important concept will be more meaningful if you first consider your own willingness to self-disclose. How likely would you be to disclose the following items of information to, say, members of this class? Respond using a simple five-part scale (very likely, likely, not sure, unlikely, very unlikely):

1. Some of the happiest moments in your life.
2. Aspects of your personality that you don't like.
3. Your most embarrassing moment.
4. Your sexual fantasies.
5. Your greatest fears.

Thinking about your willingness to disclose these types of information—and you can easily add other things about yourself that you would and would not disclose—should get you started examining your own self-disclosing behavior.

Influences on Self-Disclosure

Many factors influence whether or not you disclose, what you disclose, and to whom you disclose. Among the most important factors are who you are, your culture, your gender, who your listeners are, and what your topic is.

- *Who you are:* Highly sociable and extroverted people self-disclose more than those who are less sociable and more introverted. People who are apprehensive about talking in general also self-disclose less than do those who are more comfortable in communicating. Competent people and those with high self-esteem engage in self-disclosure more than less competent people and those with low self-esteem (McCroskey & Wheeless, 1976; Dolgin, Meyer, & Schwartz, 1991).

■ *Your culture:* Different cultures view self-disclosure differently. People in the United States, for example, disclose more than do those in Great Britain, Germany, Japan, or Puerto Rico (Gudykunst, 1983). Americans also reported greater self-disclosure when communicating with other Americans than when communicating interculturally (Allen, Long, O'Mara, & Judd, 2003). In Japan it's considered undesirable for colleagues to reveal personal information, whereas in much of the United States it's expected (Barnlund, 1989; Hall & Hall, 1987).

■ *Your gender:* Research supports the popular belief that women disclose more than men (Stewart, Cooper, & Stewart, 2003). Women disclose more than men about their previous romantic relationships, their feelings about their closest same-sex friends, their greatest fears, and what they don't like about their partners (Sprecher, 1987). A notable exception occurs in initial encounters. Here men will disclose more intimately than women, perhaps "in order to control the relationship's development" (Derlega, Winstead, Wong, & Hunter, 1985).

■ *Your listeners:* Because you disclose on the basis of the support you receive, you disclose to people you like (Collins & Miller, 1994; Derlega, Winstead, Greene, Serovich, & Elwood, 2004) and to people you trust and love (Wheeless & Grotz, 1977; Sprecher & Hendrick, 2004). You also come to like those to whom you disclose (Berg & Archer, 1983). Not surprisingly, you're more likely to disclose to people who are close to you in age (Parker & Parrott, 1995).

■ *Your topic:* You're more likely to self-disclose about some topics than others; for example, you're more likely to disclose information about your job or hobbies than about your sex life or financial situation (Jourard, 1968, 1971a). You're also more likely to disclose favorable than unfavorable information. Generally, the more personal and negative the topic, the less likely you'll be to self-disclose.

VIEWPOINT In American culture we're more likely to disclose when the person we're with discloses. This dyadic effect (what one person does, the other person does likewise) probably leads us to feel more secure and reinforces our own self-disclosing behavior. Disclosures are also more intimate when they're made in response to the disclosures of others (Berg & Archer, 1983). This dyadic effect is not universal across all cultures, however. For example, although Americans are likely to follow the dyadic effect and reciprocate with explicit, verbal self-disclosure, Koreans aren't (Won-Doornick, 1985). As you can appreciate, this can easily cause intercultural differences; for example, an American might be insulted if his or her Korean counterpart didn't reciprocate with self-disclosures that were similar in depth.

Rewards and Dangers of Self-Disclosure

Research shows that self-disclosure has both significant rewards and dangers. In making choices about whether or not to disclose, consider both.

Rewards of Self-Disclosure Self-disclosure may help increase self-knowledge, communication and relationship effectiveness, and physiological well-being.

Self-disclosure helps you gain *greater self-knowledge*: a new perspective on yourself, a deeper understanding of your own behavior. Through self-disclosure you may bring to consciousness a great deal that you might otherwise keep from conscious analysis. Even self-acceptance is difficult without self-disclosure. You accept yourself largely through the eyes of others. Through self-disclosure and subsequent support, you'll see the positive responses to you; you'll see, for example, that others appreciate your sense of humor or ability to tell a good story or the values you espouse. And through these positive responses, you'll likely strengthen your positive self-concept.

Because you understand the messages of another person largely to the extent that you understand the person, self-disclosure is an essential condition for *communication and relationship effectiveness*. Self-disclosure helps you achieve a closer relationship with the person to whom you self-disclose and increases relationship satisfaction (Schmidt &

VIEWPOINT One of the stereotypes about gender differences in communication and widely reported in the popular writings on gender is that women talk more than men (http://itre.cis.upenn.edu/ ~myl/languagelog/archives/003420.html). But, a recent study of 396 college students finds that women and men talk about the same number of words per day, about 16,000; more precisely women spoke an average of 16,215 words while men spoke an average of 15,669 words, a difference that was statistically insignificant (Mehl, Vazire, Ramirez-Esparza, Slatcher, & Pennebaker, 2007). Do you own experiences support the stereotype, or these recent findings?

Cornelius, 1987; Sprecher, 1987; Meeks, Hendrick, & Hendrick, 1998). Within a sexual relationship, self-disclosure increases sexual rewards and general relationship satisfaction; after all, it's largely through self-disclosure that you learn what another person likes and dislikes. These two benefits increase sexual satisfaction (Byers & Demmons, 1999). Self-disclosure has also been studied as it relates to psychological abuse; research indicates that persons who engage in in-depth self-disclosure seem to experience less psychological abuse (Shirley, Powers, & Sawyer, 2007). The reason for this finding may be that people in abusive relationships tend to disclose less for fear that such disclosures will provide "reasons" for the abuse. Or it may be that freedom to disclose comes from a nonabusive, supportive, confirming relationship.

Self-disclosure seems to have a positive effect on *physiological health*. People who self-disclose are less vulnerable to illnesses (Pennebacker, 1991). Not surprisingly, health benefits also result from disclosing in e-mails (Sheese, Brown, & Graziano, 2004). For example, bereavement over the death of someone very close is linked to physical illness for those who bear this alone and in silence. But it's unrelated to any physical problems for those who share their grief with others.

Dangers of Self-Disclosure: Risks Ahead There are considerable potential personal, relational, and professional risks to self-disclosure.

If you self-disclose aspects of your life that vary greatly from the values of those to whom you disclose, you incur *personal risks*; you may experience rejection from even your closest friends and family members. Men and women who disclose that they have cheated on their relationship partner, have stolen, or are suffering from protracted depression, for example, may find their friends and family no longer wanting to be quite as close as before.

Even in close and long-lasting relationships, self-disclosure can pose *relational risks* (Bochner, 1984). Total self-disclosure may prove threatening to a relationship by causing a decrease in mutual attraction, trust, or any of the bonds holding the individuals together. Self-disclosures concerning infidelity, romantic fantasies, past indiscretions or crimes, lies, or hidden weaknesses and fears could easily have such negative effects.

Revealing political views or attitudes toward different religious or racial groups may open you to *professional risks* and create problems on the job, as may disclosing any health problems, such as being HIV positive (Fesko, 2001). Teachers who disclose former or current drug use or cohabitation with students may find themselves denied tenure, teaching at undesirable hours, and eventually falling victim to "budget cuts." Openly gay and lesbian personnel in the military, as well as in education, fire protection, law enforcement, or health-care agencies, to cite just a few examples, may find themselves confined to desk jobs, prevented from further advancement, or even charged with criminal behavior and fired.

In making your choice between disclosing and not disclosing, keep in mind—in addition to the advantages and dangers already noted—the irreversible nature of communication (discussed in Chapter 1). Regardless of how many times you may try to qualify something or take it back, once you have disclosed, you cannot undisclose. Nor can you erase the conclusions and inferences listeners have made on the basis of your disclosures.

Guidelines for Self-Disclosure

Because self-disclosure is so important and so delicate a matter, guidelines are offered here for (1) deciding whether and how to self-disclose, (2) responding to the disclosures of others, and (3) resisting pressures to self-disclose.

I just joined the social networking site Facebook and I'm confused about what is appropriate conversational information to include in my profile. All my friends have party pictures posted, but I've heard that employers use these sites to screen job applications. What do you suggest?

My best advice is to only put up pictures on Facebook or any social networking site that your grandmother could see. Remember that the Internet is a public space. Once something is posted, it is difficult to erase it. And, of course, people can make copies and send the information to others without your knowledge. Facebook and MySpace are socially oriented. LinkedIn and Plaxo focus on business usage; use these in your job searches. But it's a good idea to keep all your profiles respectable. What is it that you want people to know about you? More important, what information do you want to keep private? The private information should not be part of a conversation on Facebook or any social networking site.

For more information see Susan B. Barnes, *A Privacy Paradox: Social Networking in the United States* (2006), First Monday, 9:11 (www.uic.edu/htbin/cgiwrap/bin/ojs/index.php/fm/issue/view/203), or Susan B. Barnes, *Computer-Mediated Communication: Human-to-Human Communication across the Internet* (Boston: Allyn & Bacon, 2003); or visit http://emoticons.muller-godschalk.com.

Susan B. Barnes (Ph.D., New York University) is a professor in the Department of Communication at Rochester Institute of Technology and teaches courses in electronic communication and computer-mediated communication, while researching social media and electronic forms of communication. Dr. Barnes (Susan.Barnes@rit.edu) is the associate direction of the Social Computing Lab at RIT (social.it.rit.edu) and was recently awarded a grant from the national Science Foundation.

Guidelines for Making Self-Disclosures The following guidelines will help you ask yourself the right questions before you make a choice that must ultimately be your own.

- *Disclose out of appropriate motivation.* Self-disclosure should be motivated by a concern for the relationship, for the others involved, and for yourself. Avoid disclosing to hurt the listener; for example, people who tell their parents that they hindered their emotional development may be disclosing out of a desire to hurt and punish rather than a desire to improve the relationship.
- *Disclose in the appropriate context.* Before making any significant self-disclosure, ask whether this is the right time and place. Could a better time and place be arranged? Ask, too, whether this self-disclosure is appropriate to the relationship. Generally, the more intimate the disclosures, the closer the relationship should be. It's probably best to resist intimate disclosures (especially negative ones) with nonintimates or casual acquaintances, or in the early stages of a relationship.
- *Disclose gradually.* During your disclosures, give the other person a chance to reciprocate with his or her own disclosures. If reciprocal disclosures are not made, reassess your own self-disclosures. It may be a signal that for this person at this time and in this context, your disclosures are not welcome or appropriate.
- *Disclose without imposing burdens on yourself or others.* Carefully weigh the potential problems that you may incur as a result of your disclosure. Can you afford to lose your job if you disclose your arrest record? Is it wise to burden your mother-in-law with promises of secrecy to your disclosures of infidelity?

Guidelines for Facilitating and Responding to Self-Disclosures When someone discloses to you, it's usually a sign of trust and affection. In serving this most important receiver function, keep the following guidelines in mind. These guidelines will also help you facilitate the disclosures of another person.

- *Practice the skills of effective and active listening.* The skills of effective listening (Chapter 4) are especially important when you are listening to self-disclosures: Listen actively, listen for different levels of meaning, listen with empathy, and listen with an open mind. Express an understanding of the speaker's feelings to allow the speaker the opportunity to see them more objectively and through the eyes of another. Ask questions to ensure your own understanding and to signal your interest and attention.

- *Support and reinforce the discloser.* Express support for the person during and after the disclosures. Concentrate on understanding and empathizing with (rather than evaluating) the discloser. Make your supportiveness clear to the discloser through your verbal and nonverbal responses: Maintain eye contact, lean toward the speaker, ask relevant questions, and echo the speaker's thoughts and feelings.

- *Be willing to reciprocate.* When you make relevant and appropriate disclosures of your own in response to the other person's disclosures, you're demonstrating your understanding of the other's meanings and at the same time showing a willingness to communicate on this meaningful level.

- *Keep the disclosures confidential.* When a person discloses to you, it's because she or he wants you to know the feelings and thoughts that are communicated. If you reveal these disclosures to others, negative outcomes are inevitable and your relationship is almost sure to suffer. And be sure not to use the disclosures against the person. Many self-disclosures expose some kind of vulnerability or weakness. If you later

UNDERSTANDING INTERPERSONAL THEORY & RESEARCH

Online Relationship Theories

Here are two theories of online relationships that raise issues that are unique to online communication and that other theories do not address.

Social presence theory argues that the bandwidth of communication (the number of message cues exchanged) influences the degree to which the communication is personal or impersonal (Short, Williams, & Christie, 1976; Walther & Parks, 2002; Wood & Smith, 2005). When lots of cues are exchanged (especially nonverbal cues), as in face-to-face communication, you feel great social presence—the whole person is there for you to communicate with and exchange messages. When the bandwidth is smaller (as in e-mail or chat communication), then the communication is largely impersonal. So, for example, personal communication is easier to achieve in face-to-face situations (where tone of voice, facial expressions, eye contact, and similar nonverbal cues come into play) than in computer-mediated communication, which essentially contains only written cues.

It's more difficult, the theory goes, to communicate supportiveness, warmth, and friendliness in text-based chat or e-mail exchanges because of the smaller bandwidth. Of course, as video and audio components become more widely used, this distinction will fade.

Social information processing theory (SIP) argues, contrary to social presence theory, that whether you're communicating face-to-face or online, you can communicate the same degree of personal involvement and develop similar close relationships (Walther, 1992; Walther & Parks, 2002; Walther, 2008). The idea behind this theory is that communicators are clever people: Given whatever channel they have available to send and receive messages, they will make adjustments to communicate what they want and to develop the relationships they want. It is true that when the time span studied is limited—as it is in much of the research—that it is probably easier to communicate and develop relationships in face-to-face interaction than in online situations. But when the interaction occurs over an extended time period, as it often does in ongoing chat groups and in repeated e-mail exchanges, then the communication and the relationships can be as personal as those you develop in face-to-face situations.

Working with Theories and Research

How would you compare the level of closeness that you can communicate in face-to-face and in online situations? Do you feel it's more difficult (even impossible) to communicate, say, support, warmth, and friendship in online communication than in face-to-face communication?

turn around and use disclosures against the person who made them, you betray the confidence and trust invested in you. Regardless of how angry you may get, resist the temptation to use disclosures as weapons.

Guidelines for Resisting Pressure to Self-Disclose You may, on occasion, find yourself in a position where a friend, colleague, or romantic partner pressures you to self-disclose. In such situations, you may wish to weigh the pros and cons of self-disclosure and then make your decision as to whether and what you'll disclose. If your decision is not to disclose and you're still being pressured, then you need to say something. Here are a few suggestions.

- *Don't be pushed.* Although there may be certain legal or ethical reasons for disclosing, generally, if you don't want to disclose, you don't have to. Don't be pushed into disclosing because others are doing it or because you're asked to.
- *Be assertive in your refusal to disclose.* Say, very directly, "I'd rather not talk about that now" or "Now is not the time for this type of discussion." More specific guidelines for communicating assertiveness are offered in Chapter 5.
- *Delay a decision.* If you don't want to say no directly, but still don't want to disclose, delay the decision. Say something like "That's pretty personal; let me think about that before I make a fool of myself" or "This isn't really a good time (or place) to talk about this; I'll get back to you and we'll talk."
- *Be indirect and move to another topic.* Avoid the question and change the subject. This is a polite way of saying, "I'm not talking about it," and may be the preferred choice in certain situations. Most often people will get the hint and understand your refusal to disclose.

Organizational Conversation

Special forms of conversation seem to dominate in the workplace and deserve to be singled out for more extended discussion. Here we consider some of the formal and informal communications that occur in business or organizational settings.

Formal Communication

Formal workplace communication may be looked at in terms of its direction, whether upward, downward, or lateral. Let's survey each in turn and consider some suggestions for improving these organizational messages.

Upward Communication **Upward communication** consists of messages sent from the lower levels of a hierarchy to the upper levels—for example, from line worker to manager or from faculty member to dean. This type of communication usually is concerned with job-related activities and problems; ideas for change and suggestions for improvement; and feelings about the organization, work, other workers, or similar issues.

Upward communication is vital to the growth of any organization. It provides management with feedback on worker morale and possible sources of dissatisfaction and offers leaders the opportunity to acquire new ideas from workers. At the same time, it gives subordinates a sense of belonging to and being a part of the organization. Among the guidelines for improving upward communication are:

- Set up a nonthreatening system for upward communication that is acceptable to the cultural norms of the workforce, such as a suggestion box or periodic meetings. Realize that from a worker's point of view, upward communication involves risk.
- Be open to hearing worker comments, and eliminate unnecessary gatekeepers that prevent important messages from traveling up the organizational hierarchy (Callan, 1993).
- Be willing to listen to these messages even when they're critical.

Downward Communication **Downward communication** consists of messages sent from the higher levels to the lower levels of the hierarchy; for example, messages sent by managers to workers or by deans to faculty members. Common forms of downward communication include orders; explanations of procedures, goals, and changes; and appraisals of workers. Among the guidelines for effective downward communication are:

- Use a vocabulary known to the workers. Keep technical jargon to a minimum, especially with workers who are not native speakers of the managers' language.
- Provide workers with sufficient information for them to function effectively but avoid information overload.
- When criticizing, be especially careful not to damage the image of those singled out. Allow the person to save face.

Lateral Communication **Lateral communication** refers to messages between equals—manager to manager, worker to worker. Such messages may move within the same subdivision or department of the organization or across divisions. Lateral communication, for example, is the kind of communication that takes place between two history professors at Illinois State University, between a psychologist at Ohio State and a communicologist at Kent State University, and between a bond trader and an equities trader at a brokerage house.

Lateral communication facilitates the sharing of insights, methods, and problems. It helps the organization avoid some problems and to solve others. Lateral communication also builds morale and worker satisfaction. Good relationships and meaningful communication between workers are among the main sources of worker satisfaction. More generally, lateral communication serves the purpose of coordinating the various activities of the organization and enabling the various divisions to pool insights and expertise.

Among the guidelines for improving lateral communication are these:

- Recognize that your own specialty has a technical jargon that others outside your specialty might not know. Clarify when and as needed.
- See the entire organizational picture and recognize the importance of all areas. Seeing your own area as important and all others as unimportant does little to foster meaningful communication.
- Balance the needs of an organization that relies on cooperation and a system that rewards competition. In most cases it seems that cooperation can be increased without doing any individual damage.

Informal Communication: The Grapevine

As noted earlier, informal organizational messages may concern just about any topic germane to workers and the organization. These messages are called grapevine messages because of their resemblance to the patternless grapevines.

Grapevine messages don't follow any of the formal lines of communication established in an organization; rather, they seem to have a life of their own. Grapevine messages, like formal organizational messages, concern job-related issues—but the grapevine addresses topics that you want to discuss in a more interpersonal setting, such as issues that are not yet made public; the *real* relationship among the regional managers; or possible changes that are being considered but not yet finalized, like new rules on personal Internet usage. Not surprisingly, the grapevine also grows as the size of the organization increases. In fact, large organizations often have several grapevines; the grapevine among interns is not the same as the grapevine used by upper management, and the student grapevine is not the same as the faculty grapevine. Sometimes, of course, these systems, overlap; interns and management or students and faculty may exchange grapevine messages with each other.

The grapevine is most likely to be used when (Crampton, Hodge, & Mishra, 1998):

- Issues are considered important to the workers (the more important the topic, the more likely the grapevine will focus on it).
- There is ambiguity or uncertainty about what an organization is going to do (a lack of clarity encourages grapevine communication).
- A situation is perceived as threatening or insecure and anxiety may be running high.

One research study notes that during a crisis workers spend between 65 and 70 percent of their time on the grapevine. And even in noncrisis times, people in organizations spend between 10 and 15 percent of their time on the grapevine (Smith, 1996). As you can imagine, listening to grapevine messages will therefore give you insight into what workers consider important, what needs added clarification, and the issues that make workers anxious.

The grapevine is surprisingly accurate, with estimates of accuracy ranging from 75 to 95 percent. Workers hear about organizational matters first through the grapevine about 75 percent of the time. And perhaps equally important is the fact that workers believe the grapevine to be accurate—at times, more accurate than management's formal messages (Davis, 1980; Hellweg, 1992; Smith, 1996). Here are a few useful suggestions for dealing with the inevitable office grapevine:

- Understand the variety of purposes the grapevine serves. Its speed and general accuracy make it an ideal medium to carry many of the social communications that effectively bind workers together. So listen carefully; it will give you an insider's view of the organization and will help you understand those with whom you work.
- Treat grapevine information as tentative, as possibly but not necessarily true. Although grapevine information is generally accurate, it's often incomplete and ambiguous; it may also contain crucial distortions.
- Repeat only what you know or believe to be true, and indicate your own level of belief in your grapevine messages (for example, "I heard we're all getting a nice bonus, but it may be just wishful thinking from the mailroom staff").
- Tap into the grapevine. Whether you're a worker or a member of management, it's important to hear grapevine information. It may clue you into events that will affect your future with the organization, and it will help you network with others in the organization.
- Always assume that what you say in grapevine communication will be repeated to others (Smith, 1996; Hilton, 2000). So be mindful of your organizational communications; the potentially offensive joke that you e-mail a colleague can easily be forwarded to the very people who may take offense.

Conversational Problems: Prevention and Repair

In conversation you may anticipate a problem and seek to prevent it. Or you may discover that you said or did something that will lead to disapproval, and you may seek to excuse yourself. Here we'll look at just one example of a device to prevent potential conversational problems (the disclaimer) and one example of a device to repair conversational problems (the excuse). The purpose of these examples is simply to illustrate the complexity of these processes, not to present an exhaustive list of the ways conversational problems may be prevented or repaired.

Preventing Conversational Problems: The Disclaimer

Let's say, for example, that you fear your listeners will at first think a comment you're about to make is inappropriate, that they may rush to judge you without hearing your full account, or that they will think you're not in full possession of your faculties. In these cases, you may use some form of disclaimer. A **disclaimer** is a statement that aims to ensure that your message will be understood and will not reflect negatively on you (Hewitt & Stokes, 1975; McLaughlin, 1984). There are several types of disclaimer.

Hedging helps you to separate yourself from the message so that if your listeners reject your message, they need not reject you (for example, "I may be wrong here, but . . ."). If a hedge is seen as indicating a lack of certainty or conviction because of some inadequacy, it will decrease the attractiveness of both women and men (Wright & Hosman, 1983). However, it will will be more positively received if it is seen as indicating a lack of belief in allness (as indicating that no one can know all about any subject) as well as a belief that tentative statements are all a person can reasonably make (Hosman, 1989; Pearson, Turner, & Todd-Mancillas, 1991).

Credentialing helps you establish your special qualifications for saying what you're about to say ("Don't get me wrong, I'm not homophobic" or "As someone who telecommutes, I . . ."). *Sin licenses* ask listeners for permission to deviate in some way from some normally accepted convention ("I know this may not be the place to discuss business, but . . ."). *Cognitive disclaimers* help you make the case that you're in full possession of your faculties ("I know you'll think I'm crazy, but let me explain the logic of the case"). *Appeals for the suspension of judgment* ask listeners to hear you out before making a judgment ("Don't hang up on me until you hear my side of the story").

Generally, disclaimers are effective when you think you might offend listeners in telling a joke ("I don't usually like these types of jokes, but . . ."). In one study, for example, 11-year-old children were read a story about someone whose actions created negative effects. Some children heard the story with a disclaimer, and others heard the same story without the disclaimer. When the children were asked to indicate how the person should be punished, those who heard the story with the disclaimer recommended significantly lower punishments (Bennett, 1990).

Disclaimers, however, can also get you into trouble. For example, to preface remarks with "I'm no liar" may well lead listeners to think that perhaps you are lying. Also, if you use too many disclaimers, you may be perceived as someone who doesn't have any strong convictions or as one who wants to avoid responsibility for just about everything. This seems especially true of hedges.

In responding to statements containing disclaimers, it's often necessary to respond to both the disclaimer and to the statement. By doing so, you let the speaker know that you heard the disclaimer and that you aren't going to view this communication negatively. Appropriate responses might be: "I know you're no sexist, but I don't agree that . . ." or "Well, perhaps we should discuss the money now even if it doesn't seem right."

Repairing Conversational Problems: Excuses and Apologies

At times you may say the wrong thing; then, because you can't erase the message (communication really is irreversible), you may try to offer some kind of an explanation; you try to account for what happened. Perhaps the most common methods for doing so are the excuse and the apology, two closely related conversational accounts.

Excuses, central to all forms of communication and interaction, are "explanations or actions that lessen the negative implications of an actor's performance, thereby maintaining a positive image for oneself and others" (Snyder, 1984; Snyder, Higgins, & Stucky, 1983). Apologies are expressions of regret or sorrow for having done what you did or for what happened. Often the two are blended—*I didn't realize how fast I was driving* (the excuse); *I'm really sorry* (the apology). Let's separate them and look first at the excuse.

The Excuse Excuses seem especially in order when you do or say, or are accused of doing or saying, something that runs counter to what is expected, sanctioned, or considered "right" by others. Ideally, the excuse lessens the negative impact of the behavior.

The major motive for excuse making seems to be to maintain your self-esteem, to project a positive image to yourself and to others. Excuses also represent an effort to reduce stress: You may feel that if you can offer an excuse—especially a good one that is accepted by those around you—it will reduce the negative reaction and the subsequent stress that accompany a poor performance.

VIEWPOINT What kinds of disclaimers do you hear in informal groups at school? What kinds of excuses do you hear? How do these informal disclaimers and excuses differ from those you find on the job? What are the major effects that these disclaimers and excuses have, in your experience?

Excuses also may enable you to maintain effective interpersonal relationships even after some negative behavior. For example, after criticizing a friend's behavior and observing the negative reaction to your criticism, you might offer an excuse such as "Please forgive me; I'm really exhausted. I'm just not thinking straight." Excuses enable you to place your messages—even your possible failures—in a more favorable light.

Types of Excuses Different researchers have classified excuses into varied categories (Scott & Lyman, 1968; Cody & Dunn, 2007). One of the best typologies classifies excuses into three main types (Snyder, 1984):

- *I didn't do it:* Here you deny that you have done what you're being accused of. You may then bring up an alibi to prove you couldn't have done it, or perhaps you may accuse another person of doing what you're being blamed for ("I never said that" or "I wasn't even near the place when it happened"). These "I didn't do it" types are generally the worst excuses (unless they're true), because they fail to acknowledge responsibility and offer no assurance that this failure will not happen again. On the other hand, if you can demonstrate that you had no control over what happened and therefore cannot be held responsible, your excuse is likely to be highly persuasive (Heath, Stone, Darley, & Grannemann, 2003).
- *It wasn't so bad:* Here you admit to doing it but claim that the offense was not really so bad or perhaps that there was justification for the behavior ("I only padded the expense account, and even then only modestly" or "Sure, I hit him, but he was asking for it").
- *Yes, but:* Here you claim that extenuating circumstances accounted for the behavior; for example, that you weren't in control of yourself at the time or that you didn't intend to do what you did ("It was the liquor talking" or "I never intended to hurt him; I was actually trying to help").

Good and Bad Excuses The most important question for most people is what makes a good excuse and what makes a bad excuse (Snyder, 1984; Slade, 1995). How can you make good excuses and thus get out of problems, and how can you avoid bad excuses that only make matters worse?

Good excuse makers use excuses in moderation; bad excuse makers rely on excuses too often. Good excuse makers avoid blaming others, especially those they work with; bad excuse makers blame even their work colleagues. In a similar way, good excuse makers don't attribute their failure to others or to the company; bad excuse makers do. Good excuse makers acknowledge their own responsibility for the failure by noting that they did something wrong (not that they lack competence); bad excuse makers refuse to accept any responsibility for their failures. Not surprisingly, excuse makers who accept responsibility will be perceived as more credible, competent, and likable than those who deny responsibility (Dunn & Cody, 2000).

What makes one excuse effective and another ineffective will vary from one culture to another and will depend on factors already discussed. The culture's individualism–collectivism, its power distance, the value it places on assertiveness, and various other cultural tendencies will play a role (Tata, 2000).

The Apology In its most basic form, an apology is an expression of regret for something you did; it's a statement that you're sorry. And so the most basic of all apologies is simply: *I'm sorry.* In popular usage, the apology includes some admission of wrongdoing on the part of the person making the apology. Sometimes the wrongdoing is acknowledged explicitly (*I'm sorry I lied*) and sometimes only by implication (*I'm sorry you're so upset*).

In many cases the apology also includes a request for forgiveness (*Please forgive my lateness*) and some assurance that this won't happen again (*Please forgive my lateness; it won't happen again*).

According to the Harvard Business School Working Knowledge website (http://hbswk.hbs.edu/archive/3481.html, accessed May 20, 2008), apologies are useful for two main reasons. Apologies (1) help repair relationships (as you can easily imagine) and (2) repair the reputation of the wrongdoer. So, for example, if you do something wrong in your relationship, an apology will help you repair the relationship with your partner and perhaps reduce the level of conflict. At the same time, given that other people know about your behavior (just think *Jerry Springer*), an apology will help improve the image of you that they have in their minds.

An effective apology, like an effective excuse, must be crafted for the specific situation. Effective apologies to a longtime lover, to a parent, and to a new supervisor are likely to be very different, because the individuals are different and the relationships are different. And so the first rule of an effective apology is to take into consideration the uniqueness of the situation—the people, the context, the cultural rules, the relationship, the specific wrongdoing—for which you might want to apologize. Each situation will call for a somewhat different message of apology. Nevertheless, here are some general recommendations.

Some Dos for Effective Apologies

1. Do admit wrongdoing if indeed wrongdoing occurred. Accept responsibility. Own your own actions; don't try to pass them off as the work of someone else. Instead of "Smith drives so slow, it's a wonder I'm only 30 minutes late," say, "I should have taken traffic into consideration."
2. Do be apologetic. Say (and mean) the words *I'm sorry* or *What I did was wrong*.
3. Do state in specific rather than general terms what you've done. Instead of "I'm sorry for what I did," say, "I'm sorry for getting drunk at the party and flirting with everyone."
4. Do express understanding of how the other person feels and acknowledge the legitimacy of these feelings; for example, "You have every right to be angry; I should have called."
5. Do express your regret that this has created a problem for the other person: "I'm sorry I made you miss your appointment."
6. Do offer to correct the problem (whenever this is possible): "I'm sorry I didn't clean up the mess I made; I'll do it now."
7. Do give assurance that this will not happen again. Say, quite simply, "It won't happen again" or, better and more specifically, "I won't be late again."

Some Don'ts for Effective Apologies At the same time that you follow the suggestions for crafting an effective apology, try to avoid these common "don'ts."

1. Don't apologize when it isn't necessary.
2. Don't justify your behavior by mentioning that everyone does it, as in "Everyone leaves work early on Friday."
3. Don't justify your behavior by saying that the other person has done something equally wrong: "So I play poker; you play the lottery."
4. Don't qualify your responsibility by saying, for example, *I'm sorry if I did anything wrong* or expressing a lack of sincerity (*Okay, I'm sorry; it's obviously my fault—again*).
5. Don't accuse the other person of contributing to the problem. "I should have known you're overly anxious about receiving the figures exactly at 9:00 a.m."
6. Don't minimize the hurt that this may have caused. Avoid such comments as "So the figures arrived a little late. What's the big deal?"
7. Don't include excuses with the apology. Avoid such combinations as "I'm sorry the figures are late but I had so much other work to do." An excuse often takes back the apology and says, in effect, *I'm really not sorry, because there was good reason for what I've done, but I'm saying "I'm sorry" to cover all my bases and to make this uncomfortable situation go away.*
8. Don't take the easy way out and apologize through e-mail (unless the wrongdoing was committed in e-mail or e-mail is your only or main form of communication). Generally, it's better to use a more personal mode of communication—face-to-face or phone, for example. It's harder but it's more effective.

Summary

This chapter reviewed the process of conversation and discussed conversational stages, rules and principles for effective conversational management, self-disclosure in conversation, organizational conversation, and conversational repair.

The Conversation Process

1. The opening initiates and begins the conversation.
2. The feedforward previews or prefaces the major part of the conversation that is to follow.
3. The business is the major part of the conversation; it's the reason for the conversation.
4. The feedback summarizes or reflects back on the conversation.
5. The closing brings the conversation to an end.

Conversational Management

6. The initiation of conversations is often accomplished by means of self-references, other-references, relational references, and context references.
7. The maintenance of conversations depends on the principle of cooperation; the maxims of quantity, quality, relation, and manner; the principle of dialogue; and the principle of turn taking.
8. Ways to close conversations include reflecting back on the conversation, directly stating the desire to end the conversation, referring to future interactions, asking for closure, and expressing pleasure with interaction.

Conversational Disclosure: Revealing Yourself

9. Self-disclosure is revealing information about yourself to others, usually information that is normally hidden.
10. Self-disclosure is influenced by a variety of factors: who you are, your culture, your gender, your listeners, and your topic and channel.
11. Among the rewards of self-disclosure are self-knowledge, ability to cope, communication effectiveness, meaningfulness of relationships, and physiological health. Among the dangers are personal risks, relational risks, professional risks, and the fact that communication is irreversible; once something is said, you can't take it back.
12. In self-disclosing consider your motivation, the appropriateness of the disclosure to the person and context, the emergence (or absence) of reciprocal disclosure from the other person (the dyadic effect), and the possible burdens that the self-disclosure might impose on others and on yourself.
13. In responding to the disclosures of others, listen effectively, support and reinforce the discloser, keep disclosures confidential, and don't use disclosures as weapons.
14. In some situations you'll want to resist self-disclosing by being determined not to be pushed into it, being assertive and direct, or being indirect.

Organizational Conversation

15. Formal communication in an organization is sanctioned by the organization itself and is organizationally focused. Formal communication may be looked at in terms of its direction, whether upward, downward, or lateral. Upward communication consists of messages sent from the lower levels of a hierarchy to the upper levels—for example, from line worker to manager or from faculty member to dean. Downward communication consists of messages sent from higher levels to lower levels of a hierarchy; for example, messages sent by managers to workers or by deans to faculty members. Lateral communication refers to messages between equals—manager to manager, worker to worker. Such messages may move within the same subdivision or department of the organization or across divisions.
16. Informal messages are socially sanctioned. They are oriented not to the conduct of the business but to the individual members and their relationship to the organization and may concern just about any topic germane to workers and the organization. These messages follow no established organizational pathway and are called grapevine messages because of their resemblance to the patternless grapevines.

Conversational Problems: Prevention and Repair

17. One way to prevent conversational problems is to use the disclaimer, a statement that helps to ensure that your message will be understood and will not reflect negatively on you. Disclaimer types include hedging, credentialing, sin licenses, cognitive disclaimers, and appeals for the suspension of judgment.
18. Conversational repair often involves the excuse, an explanation designed to lessen the negative impact of a speaker's messages. Excuses generally come in three types: "I didn't do it," "It wasn't so bad," and "Yes, but."

Key Terms

back-channeling cues, **191**	dialogue, **190**	grapevine messages, **200**	quality maxim, **189**
conversation, **180**	disclaimer, **201**	interruptions, **191**	quantity maxim, **188**
conversational management, **186**	downward communication, **199**	lateral communication, **200**	relation maxim, **189**
conversational turns, **190**	excuse, **202**	manner maxim, **189**	self-disclosure, **193**
cooperation, **188**	gossip, **193**	monologue, **190**	upward communication, **199**

Critical Thinking Questions

1 Try collecting examples of disclaimers from your interpersonal interactions as well as from the media. Consider, for example, what type of disclaimer is being used. Why is it being used? Is the disclaimer appropriate? What other kinds of disclaimers could have been used more effectively?

2 Another way of looking at conversational rule violations is as breaches of etiquette. When you fail to follow the rules of etiquette, you're often breaking a conversational rule. A variety of websites focus on etiquette in different communication situations. For the etiquette of online conversation see www.internetiquette.org/; for Web etiquette see www.w3.org/Provider/Style/Etiquette.html; and for cell phone etiquette see www.cell-phone-etiquette.com/index.htm. Visit one or more of these websites and record any rules you find particularly applicable to interpersonal communication and conversation.

3 As explained in the text, research shows that hedging reflects negatively on both male and female speakers when it indicates a lack of certainty or conviction resulting from some inadequacy on the speaker's part. The hedging will be more positively received, however, if listeners feel it reflects the speaker's belief that tentative statements are the only kinds a person can reasonably make (Wright & Hosman, 1983; Hosman, 1989; Pearson, West, & Turner, 1995).

Do you find this to be true from your experience in using and listening to hedges?

4 Some researchers have pointed to a "disinhibition effect" that occurs in online communication. We seem less inhibited in communicating in e-mail or in chat groups, for example, than we do face-to-face. Among the reasons for this seems to be the fact that in online communication there is a certain degree of anonymity and invisibility (Suler, 2004). Does your relative anonymity in online communication lead you to communicate differently than you do in face-to-face interactions?

5 Realize that the more you reveal about yourself to others, the more areas of your life you expose to possible attack. Especially in the competitive context of work (or even romance), the more that others know about you, the more they'll be able to use against you. This simple fact has prompted power watcher Michael Korda (1975, p. 302) to advise that you "never reveal all of yourself to other people; hold something back in reserve so that people are never quite sure if they really know you." This advice is not to suggest that you be secretive; rather, Korda is advocating "remaining slightly mysterious, as if [you] were always capable of doing something surprising and unexpected." Do you agree with Korda? Why?

Choice Points

1 *Prefacing to Extremes.* A friend whom you talk to on the phone fairly regularly seems to take phatic communication to a new level—the preface is so long that it makes you want to get off the phone, and frequently you make excuses to do just that. Ask yourself: What are some things you might do to help your friend change this communication pattern?

2 *Expressing Yourself.* People have told you that they never can tell what you're thinking. Although you think this may well be an asset, you also want to have the ability to allow what you're thinking and feeling to be clear to others. Ask yourself: What might you do to make yourself more expressive in, say, work relationships? When first meeting another person? When meeting someone you may easily develop feelings for?

3 *Interrupting.* You're supervising a group of six people who are working to revise your college's website. But one member of the group interrupts so much that other members have simply stopped contributing. It's become a one-person group, and you can't have this. Ask yourself: What are some of the things that you might say to correct this situation without coming across as the bossy supervisor?

4 *Apologizing.* You borrowed a friend's car and got into an accident—and, to make matters worse, it was totally your fault. Ask yourself: What might you say that would help you explain

the situation, alleviate any anxiety your friend will have over the accident, and pave the way for a request to borrow the car again next week for the most important date of your life?

5 *Discouraging Self-Disclosure.* Your colleague at work reveals too much private information for your liking. You're really not interested in this person's sex life, financial woes, and medical problems. Ask yourself: What can you do to prevent this too-personal self-disclosure, at least to you?

6 *Refusing to Self-Disclose.* You've dated this person three or four times, and each time you're pressured to self-disclose past experiences and personal information you're simply not ready to talk about—at least, not at this early stage of the relationship. Ask yourself: What are some of the things you can say or do to resist this pressure to self-disclose? What might you say to discourage further requests that you reveal yourself?

7 *To Disclose or Not.* You discover that your close friend's romantic partner of the last two years is being unfaithful. You feel you have an obligation to tell your friend and decide to do so (though you still have doubts that this is the right thing to do). Ask yourself: What are some of the choices you have for communicating this information to your friend? What choice seems the most logical for this specific situation? After you formulate your response, take a look at Zhang and Merolla (2006).

MyCommunicationLab
Explorations

PEARSON
mycommunicationlab www.mycommunicationlab.com

This group of experiences deals with the conversation process and with a special aim to provide experience in effective and satisfying conversation. ❶ How Do You Open a Conversation? and ❷ How Do You Close a Conversation? provide practice in beginning and ending conversations effectively. ❸ Conversational Analysis: A Chance Meeting provides a dialogue that you can analyze for the elements and principles of conversation covered in this chapter. ❹ Giving and Taking Directions is a gamelike experience that will illustrate the difficulties in giving and taking directions and suggest how these difficult communication situations can be made more effective. ❺ Gender and the Topics of Conversation looks at gender differences in conversation. ❻ Responding Effectively in Conversation and ❼ The Qualities of Effectiveness are summary-type exercises that provide the opportunity to apply the qualities of effectiveness that you've already encountered to conversation. ❽ What Do You Have a Right to Know? explores a different perspective on self-disclosure; namely, the obligation to reveal parts of yourself. ❾ Disclosing Your Hidden Self presents an exciting class experience on the types of behaviors people keep hidden and the potential reactions to their disclosures. ❿ Weighing the Rewards and Dangers of Self-Disclosure presents a variety of scenarios of impending self-disclosure and asks you to consider the advantages and disadvantages of disclosing. ⓫ Time for Self-Disclosure explores the appropriateness of time in revealing certain information. ⓬ Formulating Excuses provides practice in developing and expressing excuses.

CHAPTER

9

Interpersonal Relationships: Stages and Theories

Relationship Stages   Relationship Theories

What Happens in Vegas

What Happens in Vegas provides an interesting perspective on the ways relationships may develop, one of the topics of this chapter. Here we explain the stages relationships go through and the theories that explain how relationships develop and why.

Contact with other human beings is so important that when you're deprived of it for long periods, depression sets in, self-doubt surfaces, and you may find it difficult to manage even the basics of daily life. Research shows clearly that the most important contributor to happiness—outranking money, job, and sex—is a close relationship with one other person (Freedman, 1978; Laroche & deGrace, 1997; Lu & Shih, 1997). The desire for relationships is universal; interpersonal relationships are important to men and to women, to homosexuals and to heterosexuals, to young and to old (Huston & Schwartz, 1995).

A good way to begin the study of interpersonal relationships is to examine your own relationships (past, present, or those you look forward to) by taking the self-test "What Do Your Relationships Do for You?" It highlights the advantages and the disadvantages that relationships serve.

TEST YOURSELF

WHAT DO YOUR RELATIONSHIPS DO FOR YOU?

Focus on your own relationships in general (friendship, romantic, family, and work), or focus on one particular relationship (say, your life partner or your child or your best friend), or focus on one type of relationship (say, friendships) and respond to the following by indicating the extent to which your relationship(s) serve each of these functions. Use a 10-point scale with 1 indicating that your relationship(s) never serves this function, 10 indicating that your relationship(s) always serves this function, and the numbers in between indicating levels between these extremes.

_____ 1. My relationships help to lessen my loneliness.
_____ 2. My relationships put uncomfortable pressure on me to expose my vulnerabilities.
_____ 3. My relationships help me to secure stimulation (intellectual, physical, and emotional).
_____ 4. My relationships increase my obligations.
_____ 5. My relationships help me gain in self-knowledge and in self-esteem.
_____ 6. My relationships prevent me from developing other relationships.
_____ 7. My relationships help enhance my physical and emotional health.
_____ 8. My relationships scare me because they may be difficult to dissolve.
_____ 9. My relationships maximize my pleasures and minimize my pains.
_____ 10. My relationships hurt me.

HOW DID YOU DO? The numbers from 1 to 10 that you used to respond to each statement should give you some idea of the advantages and disadvantages you see in your relationship.

The Advantages: The odd-numbered statements (1, 3, 5, 7, and 9) express what most people would consider advantages of interpersonal relationships.

(1) One of the major benefits of relationships is that they help to lessen loneliness (Rokach, 1998, Rokach & Brock, 1995). They make you feel that someone cares, that someone likes you, that someone will protect you, that someone ultimately will love you.

(3) As plants are heliotropic and orient themselves to light, humans are stimulotropic and orient themselves to sources of stimulation (M. Davis, 1973). Human contact is one of the best ways to secure this stimulation—intellectual, physical, and emotional.

(5) Through contact with others you learn about yourself and see yourself from different perspectives and in different roles, as a child or parent, as a coworker, as a manager, as a best friend. Healthy interpersonal relationships also help enhance self-esteem and self-worth. Simply having a friend or romantic partner makes you feel (at least most of the time) desirable and worthy.

(7) Research consistently shows that interpersonal relationships contribute significantly to physical and emotional health (Rosen, 1998; Goleman, 1995a, b; Rosengren et al., 1993; Pennebacker, 1991) and to personal happiness (Berscheid & Reis, 1998). Without close interpersonal relationships you're more likely to experience depression, which, in turn, contributes significantly to physical illness. Isolation, in fact, contributes as much to mortality as high blood pressure, high cholesterol, obesity, smoking, or lack of physical exercise (Goleman, 1995a).

(9) The most general function served by interpersonal relationships, and one that encompasses all the others, is that of maximizing pleasure and minimizing pain. Your good friends, for example, will make you feel even better about your good fortune and less hurt when you're confronted with hardships.

The Disadvantages: The even-numbered statements (2, 4, 6, 8, and 10) express disadvantages of interpersonal relationships.

(2) Close relationships put pressure on you to reveal yourself and to expose your vulnerabilities. While this is generally worthwhile in the context of a supporting and caring relationship, it may backfire if the relationship deteriorates and these weaknesses are used against you.

(4) Close relationships increase your obligations to these other people, sometimes to great extents. Your time is no longer entirely your own. And although you enter relationships to spend more time with these special people, you also incur time (and perhaps financial) obligations with which you may not be happy.

(6) Close relationships can lead you to abandon other relationships. Sometimes the termination of the other relationship involves someone you like but your partner can't stand. More often, however, it's simply a matter of time and energy; relationships take a lot of both, and you have less to give to these other and less intimate relationships.

(8) The closer your relationship, the more emotionally difficult it is to dissolve, a reality that may be uncomfortable for some people. And if money is involved, dissolving a relationship can often mean financial difficulties.

(10) And, of course, your partner may break your heart. Your partner may leave you—against all your pleading and promises. Your hurt will be in proportion to how much you care for and need your partner. If you care a great deal, you're likely to experience great hurt; if you care less, the hurt will be less—it's one of life's little ironies.

WHAT WILL YOU DO? One way to use this self-test is to consider how you might lessen the disadvantages of your interpersonal relationships. Consider, for example, if your own behaviors are contributing to the disadvantages. Do you bury yourself in one or two relationships and discourage the development of others? At the same time, consider how you can maximize the advantages that your relationships currently serve.

Relationship Stages

It's useful to look at interpersonal relationships as created and constructed by the individuals. That is, in any interpersonal relationship—say, between Pat and Chris—there are actually several relationships: (1) the relationship that Pat sees, (2) the relationship as Chris sees it, (3) the relationship that Pat wants and is striving for, (4) the relationship that Chris wants. And of course there are the many relationships that friends and relatives see and that they reflect back in their communications; for example, the relationship that Pat's mother, who dislikes Chris, sees and reflects in her communication with Pat and Chris is very likely to influence Pat and Chris in some ways. And then there's the relationship that a dispassionate researcher/observer would see. Looked at in this way, there are many interpersonal relationships in any interpersonal relationship.

This is not to say that there is no *real* relationship; it's just to say that there are many real relationships. And because there are these differently constructed relationships, people often disagree about a wide variety of issues and evaluate the relationship very differently. Regularly, on *Jerry Springer* and *Maury*, you see couples who view their relationship very differently. The first guest thinks all is going well until the second guest comes on and explodes—often identifying long-held dissatisfactions and behaviors that shock the partner.

One of the most obvious characteristics of relationships is that they occur in stages, moving from initial contact to greater intimacy and sometimes to dissolution. You and another person don't become intimate friends immediately upon meeting. Rather, you build an intimate

VIEWPOINT Among the advantages of online relationships is that they reduce the importance of physical characteristics and instead emphasize such factors as rapport, similarity, and self-disclosure and in the process promote relationships that are based on emotional intimacy rather than physical attraction (Cooper & Sportolari, 1997). What do you see as the main advantages of online relationships?

Ask the Researcher

Homosexual and Heterosexual Relationships

I'm gay, and I'm wondering just how this interpersonal relationship material applies to me. It seems most of the research concerns heterosexual relationships. Is any of this stuff really relevant to me?

Definitely. Researchers have found important similarities in the ways homosexual and heterosexual partners communicate. For example, they're similar in their expressed desires for affection, companionship, and commitment; and in relationship maintenance behaviors such as sharing tasks and time together, talking about the relationship, assuring the other, and interacting with supportive social networks. Also, long-term gay, lesbian, and heterosexual couples who are satisfied with their relationships similarly report that they contain the negative aspects of conflicts and are open and close with one another while also maintaining their individual privacy and identities.

All people in close relationships (homosexual and heterosexual) construct and continuously reconstruct their relationships through their exchange of verbal and nonverbal messages. Communication is the glue that holds people in a relationship. Because both partners make choices about how they'll communicate, they explicitly and implicitly "negotiate" the nature of their relationship in their exchanges. This process enables partners to construct traditional relationships or unique and highly complex relationships.

For more information see R. A. Mackey, M. A. Diemer, and B. A. O'Brien, "Relational Factors in Understanding Satisfaction in the Lasting Relationships of Same-Sex and Heterosexual Couples," *Journal of Homosexuality* 47 (2004): 111–136; and L. A. Baxter and B. M. Montgomery, *Relating: Dialogues and Dialectics* (New York: Guilford Press, 1996).

Barbara Montgomery (Ph.D., Purdue University) is professor of speech communication at Colorado State University–Pueblo.

---

relationship gradually, through a series of steps or stages. The same is true of most relationships (Mongeau & Henningsen, 2008).

The six-stage model presented in Figure 9.1 describes the main stages in most relationships. As shown in the figure, the six stages of relationships are contact, involvement, intimacy, deterioration, repair, and dissolution with each having an early and a late phase.

Relationship Movement Three types of arrows in the diagram depict different kinds of relationship movement.

- The *exit arrows* show that each stage offers the opportunity to exit the relationship. After saying "Hello" you can say "Goodbye" and exit. And, of course, you can end even the most intimate of relationships.
- The *vertical arrows* between the stages represent the fact that you can move to another stage: either to a stage that is more intense (say, from involvement to intimacy) or to a stage that is less intense (say, from intimacy to deterioration).
- The *self-reflexive arrows*—the arrows that return to the beginning of the same level or stage—signify that any relationship may become stabilized at any point. You may, for example, continue to maintain a relationship at the intimate level without its deteriorating or going back to the less intense stage of involvement. Or you may remain at the "Hello, how are you?" stage—the contact stage—without getting any further involved.

As you can imagine, movement from one stage to another depends largely on your communication skills—for example, your abilities to initiate a relationship, to present yourself as likable, to express affection, to self-disclose appropriately, and, when necessary, to dissolve the relationship with the least possible amount of acrimony (cf. Dindia & Timmerman, 2003).

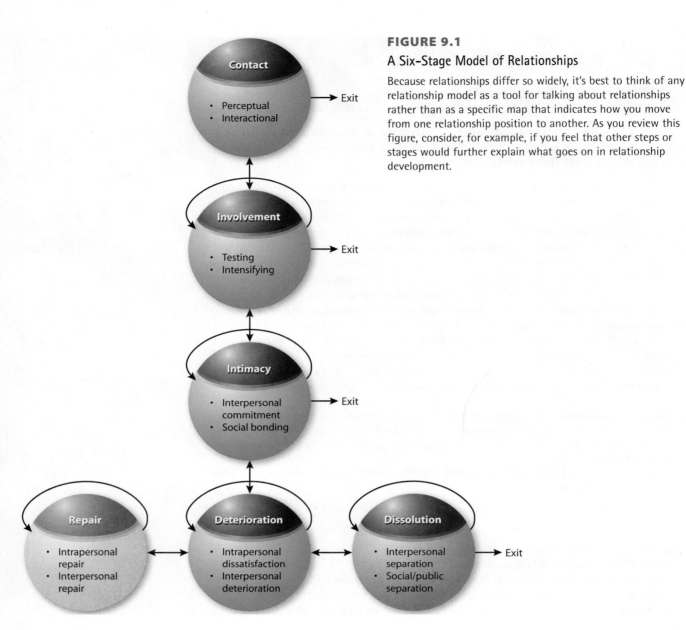

FIGURE 9.1

A Six-Stage Model of Relationships

Because relationships differ so widely, it's best to think of any relationship model as a tool for talking about relationships rather than as a specific map that indicates how you move from one relationship position to another. As you review this figure, consider, for example, if you feel that other steps or stages would further explain what goes on in relationship development.

Contact
- Perceptual
- Interactional
→ Exit

Involvement
- Testing
- Intensifying
→ Exit

Intimacy
- Interpersonal commitment
- Social bonding
→ Exit

Repair
- Intrapersonal repair
- Interpersonal repair

Deterioration
- Intrapersonal dissatisfaction
- Interpersonal deterioration

Dissolution
- Interpersonal separation
- Social/public separation
→ Exit

Relationship Turning Points Movement through the various stages usually is a gradual process; you don't jump from contact to involvement to intimacy. Rather, you progress gradually, a few degrees at a time. Yet there are often **turning points** (Baxter & Bullis, 1986). These are significant relationship events that have important consequences for the individuals and the relationship and may turn its direction or trajectory. For example, a relationship that is progressing slowly might experience a rapid rise after the first date, the first kiss, the first sexual encounter, or the first meeting with the partner's child.

Turning points can be positive, as the examples above would indicate, or negative. For example, the first realization that a partner has been unfaithful would likely be a significant turning point for many romantic relationships.

And, not surprisingly, turning points vary with culture. In some cultures the first sexual experience is a major turning point, whereas in others it may just be a minor progression in the normal dating process.

What constitutes a turning point will also vary with the relationship stage you are at. For example, an expensive and intimate gift may be a turning point at the involvement or even the deterioration stage; but it may be an ordinary event if you're at the intimate stage and such gifts are exchanged regularly.

Contact

At the initial phase of the **contact** stage, there is some kind of *perceptual contact*—you see, hear, read a message from or perhaps smell the person. From this you form a mental and physical picture—gender, approximate age, beliefs and values, height, and so on. After this perception, there is usually *interactional contact.* Here the contact is superficial and relatively impersonal. This is the stage at which you exchange basic information that is preliminary to any more intense involvement ("Hello, my name is Joe"). Here you initiate interaction ("May I join you?") and engage in invitational communication ("May I buy you a drink?"). The contact stage is the time of "first impressions." According to some researchers, it's at this stage—within the first four minutes of initial interaction—that you decide whether you want to pursue the relationship (Zunin & Zunin, 1972). Recall, in this connection, that communication is unrepeatable (Chapter 1, p. 25); consequently, you never have a second chance to make a first impression—a principle that's often overlooked when people don't think about it. Once you become mindful of the importance of first impressions, you're likely to reflect more carefully on your own verbal and nonverbal messages and on your choices of impression management strategies (Chapter 3, pp. 71–75).

At the contact stage in face-to-face interaction, physical appearance is especially important, because it's the characteristic most readily seen. Yet through verbal and nonverbal behaviors, qualities such as friendliness, warmth, openness, and dynamism also are revealed. In contrast, in computer-mediated contact, attitudinal sameness and wanting essentially the same things may be most influential in the beginning. This distinction, however, gets cloudy at times. For example, at least one online bulletin board contains a "missed connections" section where people post messages such as "I saw you on the bus and thought we connected, but you got off before I could say anything"—in the hope that the other person also felt a "missed connection" and also is hoping to make contact (J. Lee, 2005).

The contact stage is also the stage at which you'd begin flirting with a potential romantic partner. First, you'd engage in nonverbal flirting. The reason you'd likely use nonverbal messages first is that they are less direct and you're less accountable for any message that you send that may be rejected. For example, if your smile is not returned, there's no great loss of face. But if a verbal overture (say, "May I join you?") is responded to negatively, you'll likely feel a lot worse—your loss of face will be greater.

One watcher of nonverbal behaviors identifies six flirtatious nonverbals: maintaining an open body posture, raising your eyebrows, tilting your head to one side as if to get a better look at the other person, maintaining extra eye contact, leaning forward, and casting "sideways glances" that may be followed by a smile or some coy look (Luscombe, 2008). If these flirtatious behaviors yield some positive response, you're likely to flirt verbally—perhaps you'll ask if such an interesting person is here alone or if you may buy the person a drink.

Unfortunately, flirting also has a dark side. Overly aggressive flirting may easily be perceived as harassment or even stalking. One way to avoid being perceived as a harasser is to learn to distinguish the nonverbal cues that signal "I'm interested and just acting coy" (the six cues identified above are good starting points) from those that signal "I'm really not interested"—for example, the avoidance of eye contact, negative facial expressions, and one-word answers.

Involvement

At the **involvement** stage of a relationship, a sense of mutuality, of being connected develops. Here you experiment and try to learn more about the other person. At the initial phase

VIEWPOINT Throughout the life of a relationship, there exist "turning points," those jumps or leaps that project you from one relationship level to another. Do men and women, homosexuals and heterosexuals, and young and old see turning points in the same way? In what ways might different groups see turning points differently? Which turning points would be the most important to you?

of involvement, a kind of *testing* goes on. You want to see whether your initial judgment proves reasonable. So you may ask questions: "Where do you work?" "What are you majoring in?" If you want to get to know the person even better, you might continue your involvement by intensifying your interaction and by beginning to reveal yourself, though in a preliminary way. In a dating relationship, you might, for example, use a variety of strategies to help you move to the next stage and perhaps to intimacy. For example, you might increase contact with your partner; give your partner tokens of affection such as gifts, cards, or flowers; increase your own personal attractiveness; do things that suggest intensifying the relationship, such as flirting or making your partner jealous; and become more sexually intimate (Tolhuizen, 1989).

Throughout the relationship process, but especially during the involvement and early intimacy stages, you test your partner; you try to find out how your partner feels about the relationship. Among the strategies you might use are these (Baxter & Wilmot, 1984; Bell & Buerkel-Rothfuss, 1990):

- *Directness:* You ask your partner directly how he or she feels, or you disclose your own feelings on the assumption that your partner will also self-disclose.
- *Indirect suggestion:* You joke about a shared future together, touch more intimately, or hint that you're serious about the relationship, for example. Similar responses from your partner will mean that he or she wishes to increase the intimacy of the relationship.
- *Public presentation:* You may introduce your partner as your "boyfriend" or "girl-friend," for example, and see how your partner responds.
- *Separation:* You separate yourself physically to see how the other person responds. If your partner calls, then you know he or she is interested in the relationship.
- *Third party:* You ask mutual friends about your partner's feelings and intentions.

Intimacy

At the **intimacy** stage, you commit yourself still further to the other person and establish a relationship in which this individual becomes your best or closest friend, lover, or companion. Both the quantity and the quality of your interpersonal exchanges increase (Emmers-Sommer, 2004), and of course you also talk more and in greater detail about the relationship (Knobloch, Haunani, & Theiss, 2006). You also come to share each other's social networks, a practice followed by members of widely different cultures (Gao & Gudykunst, 1995).

Not surprisingly, your relationship satisfaction also increases with the move to this stage (Siavelis & Lamke, 1992). One research study defined intimacy as the feeling that you could be honest and open when talking about yourself, your thoughts, and your feelings that you don't reveal in other relationships (Mackey, Diemer, & O'Brien, 2000).

The intimacy stage usually divides itself into two phases. In the *interpersonal commitment* phase the two people commit themselves to each other in a private way. In the *social bonding* phase the commitment is made public—perhaps to family and friends, perhaps to the public at large. Here you and your partner become a unit, an identifiable pair.

When the intimacy stage involves a lifetime partnership, you face three main anxieties (Zimmer, 1986). A *security anxiety* leads you to worry that your partner may leave you for someone else or that he or she will be sexually unfaithful. A *fulfillment anxiety* involves concerns that you may not be able to achieve a close, warm, and special rapport or that you won't

VIEWPOINT Some cultures consider sexual relationships to be undesirable outside of marriage; others see sex as a normal part of intimacy and chastity as undesirable. Intercultural researchers (Hatfield & Rapson, 1996, p. 36) recall a meeting at which colleagues from Sweden and the United States were discussing ways of preventing AIDS. When members from the United States suggested teaching abstinence, Swedish members asked, "How will teenagers ever learn to become loving, considerate sexual partners if they don't practice?" "The silence that greeted the question," note the researchers, "was the sound of two cultures clashing." How have your cultural beliefs and values influenced what you consider appropriate relationship behavior?

Ethics in Interpersonal Communication

Your Obligation to Reveal Yourself

If you're in a close relationship, your influence on your partner is considerable, so you may have an obligation to reveal certain things about yourself. Conversely, you may feel that the other person—because he or she is so close to you—has an ethical obligation to reveal certain information to you.

Romantic Partner	Friend	At what point do you have an ethical obligation to reveal:
_____	_____	Age
_____	_____	History of family genetic disorders
_____	_____	HIV status
_____	_____	Past sexual experiences
_____	_____	Marital history
_____	_____	Annual salary and net financial worth
_____	_____	Affectional orientation
_____	_____	Attitudes toward other races and nationalities
_____	_____	Religious beliefs
_____	_____	Past criminal activity or incarceration

What would you do?

At what point in a relationship—if any—do you feel you would have an ethical obligation to reveal each of the 10 items of information listed here? Visualize a relationship as existing on a continuum from initial contact at 1 to extreme intimacy at 10, and use the numbers from 1 to 10 to indicate at what point you would feel your romantic partner or friend would have a right to know each type of information about you. If you feel you would never have the obligation to reveal this information, use 0. As you respond to these items, ask yourself: What gives one person the right to know personal information about another person?

be able to have an equal relationship. An *excitement anxiety* makes you worry that boredom and routine may set in or that you'll lose your freedom and become trapped.

Of course, not everyone strives for intimacy (Bartholomew, 1990; Thelen, Sherman, & Borst, 1998; Bumby & Hansen, 1997). Some people are so fearful of the consequences of intimacy that they actively avoid it. Others dismiss intimacy and defensively deny their need for more and deeper interpersonal contact. And still others, of course, are happy without an intimate relationship.

Deterioration

The **relationship deterioration** stage is characterized by a weakening of the bonds between the friends or lovers. The first phase of deterioration is usually *intrapersonal dissatisfaction*: You begin to experience personal dissatisfaction with everyday interactions and begin to view the future with your partner more negatively. If this dissatisfaction grows, you pass to the second phase, *interpersonal deterioration*. You withdraw and grow farther and farther apart. You share less of your free time. When you're together, there are more awkward silences, fewer disclosures, less physical contact, and a lack of psychological closeness. Conflicts become more common and their resolution more difficult.

Repair

The **relationship repair** stage is not always pursued. Some relational partners may pause during deterioration and try to repair their relationship. Others, however, may progress—without stopping, without thinking—to dissolution.

At the first repair phase, *intrapersonal repair*, you may analyze what went wrong and consider ways of solving your relational difficulties. You might at this stage consider changing your behaviors or perhaps changing your expectations of your partner. You might also evaluate the rewards of your relationship as it is now and the rewards to be gained if your relationship ended.

UNDERSTANDING INTERPERSONAL THEORY & RESEARCH

Relationship Commitment

An important factor influencing the course of relationship deterioration (as well as relationship maintenance) is the degree of *commitment* that you and your relationship partner have toward each other and toward the relationship. Not surprisingly, commitment is especially strong when individuals are satisfied with their relationship and grows weaker as individuals become less satisfied (Hirofumi, 2003). Three types of commitment are often distinguished and can be identified from your answers to the following questions (Johnson, 1973, 1982, 1991; Knapp & Taylor, 1994; Kurdek, 1995; Knapp & Vangelisti, 2009):

■ Do I have a *desire* to stay in this relationship? Do I have a desire to keep this relationship going?
■ Do I have a moral *obligation* to stay in this relationship?
■ Do I have to stay in this relationship? Is it a *necessity* for me to stay in this relationship?

All relationships are held together, in part, by commitment based on desire, obligation, or necessity, or on some combination of these factors. And the strength of the relationship, including its resistance to possible deterioration, is related to your degree of commitment. When a relationship shows signs of deterioration and yet there's a strong commitment to preserving it, you may well surmount the obstacles and reverse the process. For example, couples with high relationship commitment will avoid arguing about minor grievances and also will demonstrate greater supportiveness toward each other than will those with lower commitment (Roloff & Solomon, 2002). Similarly, those who have great commitment are likely to experience greater jealousy in a variety of situations (Rydell, McConnell, & Bringle, 2004). When commitment is weak and the individuals doubt that there are good reasons for staying together, the relationship deteriorates faster and more intensely.

Working with Theories and Research

Has commitment or the lack of it (on the part of either or both of you) ever influenced the progression of one of your relationships? What happened?

Should you decide that you wanted to repair your relationship, you might discuss this with your partner at the *interpersonal repair* phase—you might talk about the problems in the relationship, the changes you wanted to see, and perhaps what you'd be willing to do and what you'd want your partner to do. This is the stage of negotiating new agreements and new behaviors. You and your partner might try to repair your relationship by yourselves, or you might seek the advice of friends or family or perhaps go for professional counseling.

Dissolution

At the **relationship dissolution** stage, the bonds between the individuals are broken. In the beginning, dissolution usually takes the form of *interpersonal separation*, in which you may move into separate apartments and begin to lead lives apart from each other. If this separation proves acceptable and if the original relationship isn't repaired, you enter the phase of *social or public separation*. If the relationship is a marriage, this phase corresponds to divorce. In some cases the former partners change the definition of their relationship; for example, the "ex-lovers" become "friends" or "business partners." Avoidance of each other and a return to being "single" are among the primary characteristics of dissolution.

Dissolution also is the stage during which the ex-partners begin to look upon themselves as individuals rather than halves of a pair. They try to establish a new and different life, either alone or with another person. Some people, it's true, continue to live psychologically with a relationship that has already been dissolved; they frequent old meeting places, reread old love letters, daydream about all the good times, and fail to extricate themselves from a relationship that has died in every way except in their memory.

In cultures that emphasize continuity from one generation to the next and in which being "old-fashioned" is evaluated positively—as in, say, China—interpersonal relationships are likely to be long lasting and permanent. Those who maintain long-term relationships

TABLE 9.1 Knapp's Model of Interaction Stages

This model contains 10 stages: 5 stages that bring people together and 5 that separate them. This should further clarify the ways in which interpersonal communication changes as the relationship changes.

Coming Together The first five stages describe the processes of coming together and moving toward greater connection and intimacy.

Stage 1: Initiation	You perceive and interact with the other person; you try to present yourself in a positive light, "as a person who is pleasant, likable, understanding, and socially adept," and to open the channels of communication.
Stage 2: Experimenting	You try to learn about the other person; you try to find a topic or area of common experience or interest; you exchange basic information about yourselves. Small talk, according to this model, is the essence of this experimenting stage.
Stage 3: Intensifying	You interact on a more personal and intimate level; your speech becomes more informal and includes lots of terms that have meaning only for the two of you. This is also the stage at which you might exchange expressions of commitment to each other and to the relationship.
Stage 4: Integrating	You come together; you cultivate shared opinions and attitudes. "Intimacy trophies" (pins, rings) may be exchanged, and empathy seems to peak.
Stage 5: Bonding	You name the relationship for others; for example, you choose marriage or domestic partnership or designate yourselves as "exclusive partners." Here you commit yourselves to a "bonded future."

Coming Apart The next five stages describe the stages of coming apart and moving away from intimacy.

Stage 6: Differentiating	You begin to think of yourselves as different and distinct from each other. You start to emphasize differences between yourselves in thinking and in talking. This is the stage of "disengaging or uncoupling."
Stage 7: Circumscribing	You restrict communication, perhaps to topics that are safe and will not cause conflict. Your interpersonal exchanges decrease in both quantity and quality.
Stage 8: Stagnating	Your communication becomes relatively inactive; when you do communicate, it's with difficulty and awkwardness. Here the discussion rarely if ever focuses on the relationship; the communication comes to resemble that which you'd have with a stranger.
Stage 9: Avoiding	You physically separate; there is little or no face-to-face interaction. You may even disregard each other's messages, "showing cognitive and emotional detachment."
Stage 10: Terminating	You break the bonds that once held the relationship together and establish some kind of psychological or physical distance between you.

Sources: This model of relationship is adapted from Mark L. Knapp, *Social Intercourse: From Greeting to Goodbye* (Boston: Allyn & Bacon, 1978) and Mark L. Knapp and Anita L. Vangelisti, *Interpersonal Communication and Human Relationships*, 6th ed. (Boston: Allyn & Bacon, 2009), pp. 34–47. Copyright © by Pearson Education. Adapted by permission of the publisher.

tend to be rewarded, and those who break relationships tend to be punished. But in cultures in which change is seen as positive and being old-fashioned as negative—as in, say, the United States—interpersonal relationships are likely to be more temporary (Moghaddam, Taylor, & Wright, 1993). Here the rewards for long-term relationships and the punishments for broken relationships will be significantly less.

The stage model we've considered here is certainly not the only way you can look at relationships. Table 9.1 presents a somewhat different model to give you a different perspective on how to view relationships.

Relationship Theories

Several theories offer insight into why and how we develop and dissolve our relationships (Baxter & Braithwaite, 2008b). Here we'll examine six such theories: attraction, relationship rules, relationship dialectics, social penetration, social exchange, and equity.

Attraction Theory

Attraction theory holds that people form relationships on the basis of **attraction.** You are no doubt drawn, or attracted, to some people and not to others. In a similar way, some people are attracted to you and some are not. If you're like most people, then you're attracted to others on the basis of five major factors: similarity, proximity, reinforcement, physical attractivenes and personality, and socioeconomic and educational status.

Similarity If you could construct your mate, according to the **similarity** principle, it's likely that your mate would look, act, and think very much like you (Burleson, Samter, & Luccetti, 1992; Burleson, Kunkel, & Birch, 1994). Generally, people like those who are similar to them in nationality, race, abilities, physical characteristics, intelligence, and attitudes (Pornpitakpan, 2003).

Research also finds that you're more likely to help someone who is similar in race, attitude, general appearance, and even first name. Sometimes people are attracted to their opposites, in a pattern called **complementarity**; for example, a dominant person might be attracted to someone who is more submissive. Generally, however, people prefer those who are similar.

Proximity If you look around at people you find attractive, you will probably find that they are the people who live or work close to you. People who become friends are the people who have the greatest opportunity to interact with each other. *Proximity*, or physical closeness, is most important in the early stages of interaction—for example, during the first days of school (in class or in dormitories). The importance of proximity as a factor in attraction decreases, though always remaining significant, as the opportunity to interact with more distant others increases.

Reinforcement Not surprisingly, you're attracted to people who give rewards or reinforcements, which can range from a simple compliment to an expensive cruise. You're also attracted to people you reward (Jecker & Landy, 1969; Aronson, Wilson, & Akert, 2007). That is, you come to like people for whom you do favors; for example, you've probably increased your liking for persons after buying them an expensive present or going out of your way to do them a special favor. In these situations you justify your behavior by believing that the person was worth your efforts; otherwise, you'd have to admit to spending effort on people who don't deserve it.

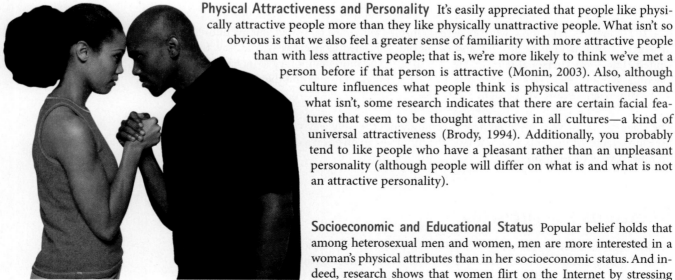

Physical Attractiveness and Personality It's easily appreciated that people like physically attractive people more than they like physically unattractive people. What isn't so obvious is that we also feel a greater sense of familiarity with more attractive people than with less attractive people; that is, we're more likely to think we've met a person before if that person is attractive (Monin, 2003). Also, although culture influences what people think is physical attractiveness and what isn't, some research indicates that there are certain facial features that seem to be thought attractive in all cultures—a kind of universal attractiveness (Brody, 1994). Additionally, you probably tend to like people who have a pleasant rather than an unpleasant personality (although people will differ on what is and what is not an attractive personality).

Socioeconomic and Educational Status Popular belief holds that among heterosexual men and women, men are more interested in a woman's physical attributes than in her socioeconomic status. And indeed, research shows that women flirt on the Internet by stressing their physical attributes, whereas men stress their socioeconomic status (Whitty, 2003b). Interestingly, there is evidence that men too consider a woman's socioeconomic status in making romantic relationship decisions—but whereas women find higher socioeconomic status more attractive, men find just the opposite. Men report greater likelihood of a romantic relationship with a woman lower in socioeconomic status than they are. Further, men find women with a higher educational level (which is often responsible for the higher socioeconomic status) less likable and less faithful and as a result see less likelihood of a romantic relationship with such women (Greitemeyer, 2007).

Relationship Rules Theory

You can gain an interesting perspective on interpersonal relationships by looking at them in terms of the rules that govern them (Shimanoff, 1980). The general assumption of **rules theory** is that relationships—friendship and love in particular—are held together by adherence to certain rules. When those rules are broken, the relationship may deteriorate and even dissolve.

Relationship rules theory helps us clarify several aspects of relationships. First, these rules help identify successful versus destructive relationship behavior. In addition, these rules help pinpoint more specifically why relationships break up and how they may be repaired. Further, if we know what the rules are, we will be better able to master the social skills involved in relationship development and maintenance. And because these rules vary from one culture to another, it is important to identify those unique to each culture so that intercultural relationships may be more effectively developed and maintained.

Friendship Rules One approach to friendship argues that friendships are maintained by rules (Argyle & Henderson, 1984; Argyle, 1986). When these rules are followed, the friendship is strong and mutually satisfying. When these rules are broken, the friendship suffers and may die. For example, the rules for keeping a friendship call for such behaviors as standing up for your friend in his or her absence, sharing information and feelings about successes, demonstrating emotional support for a friend, trusting and offering to help a friend in need, and trying to make a friend happy when you're together. On the other hand, a friendship is likely to be in trouble when one or both friends are intolerant of the other's friends, discuss confidences with third parties, fail to demonstrate positive support, nag, and/or fail to trust or confide in the other. The strategy for maintaining a friendship, then, depends on your knowing the rules and having the ability to apply the appropriate interpersonal skills (Trower, 1981; Blieszner & Adams, 1992).

Romantic Rules Other research has identified the rules that romantic relationships establish and follow. These rules, of course, will vary considerably from one culture to another. For example, the different attitudes toward permissiveness and sexual relations with which Chinese and American college students view dating influence the romantic rules each group will establish and live by (Tang & Zuo, 2000). Leslie Baxter (1986) has identified eight major romantic rules. Baxter argues that these rules keep the relationship together—or, when broken, lead to deterioration and eventually dissolution. The general form for each rule, as Baxter phrases it, is, "If parties are in a close relationship, they should …":

1. acknowledge each other's individual identities and lives beyond the relationship
2. express similar attitudes, beliefs, values, and interests
3. enhance each other's self-worth and self-esteem
4. be open, genuine, and authentic with each other
5. remain loyal and faithful to each other
6. have substantial shared time together
7. reap rewards commensurate with their investments relative to the other party
8. experience a mysterious and inexplicable "magic" in each other's presence

Family Rules Family communication research points to the importance of rules in defining and maintaining the family (Galvin, Bylund, & Brommel, 2008). Family rules concern three main interpersonal communication issues (Satir, 1983):

- What can you talk about? Can you talk about the family finances? Grandpa's drinking? Your sister's lifestyle?
- How can you talk about something? Can you joke about your brother's disability? Can you address directly questions of family history or family skeletons?
- To whom can you talk? Can you talk openly to extended family members such as cousins and aunts and uncles? Can you talk to close neighbors about family health issues?

All families teach rules for communication. Some of these are explicit, such as "Never contradict the family in front of outsiders" or "Never talk finances with outsiders." Other rules are unspoken; you deduce them as you learn the communication style of your family. For example, if financial issues are always discussed in secret and in hushed tones, then you rather logically infer that you shouldn't tell other more distant family members or neighbors about family finances.

Like the rules of friends and lovers, family rules tell you which behaviors will be rewarded (and therefore what you should do) and which will be punished (and therefore what you should not do). Rules also provide a kind of structure that defines the family as a cohesive unit and that distinguishes it from other similar families.

Not surprisingly, the rules a family develops are greatly influenced by the culture. Although there are many similarities among families throughout the world, there are also differences (Georgas et al., 2001). For example, members of collectivist cultures are more likely to restrict family information from outsiders as a way of protecting the family than are members of individualist cultures. But this tendency to protect the family can create serious problems in cases of wife abuse. Many women will not report spousal abuse because of this desire to protect the family image and not let others know that things aren't perfect at home (Dresser, 2005).

Family communication theorists argue that rules should be flexible so that special circumstances can be accommodated; for example, there are situations that necessitate changing the family dinner time, vacation plans, or savings goals (Noller & Fitzpatrick, 1993). Rules should also be negotiable so that all members can participate in their modification and feel a part of family government.

Relationship Dialectics Theory

Relationship dialectics theory argues that people in a relationship experience dynamic tensions between pairs of opposing motives or desires. Research generally finds three such pairs of opposites (Baxter, 2004; Baxter & Simon, 1993; Rawlins, 1989, 1992; Baxter & Braithwaite, 2007, 2008a):

The tension between *closedness and openness* has to do with the conflict between the desire to be in a closed, exclusive relationship and the wish to be in a relationship that is open to different people. Not surprisingly, this tension manifests itself most during the early stages of relationship development. You like the exclusiveness of your pairing, and yet you want also to relate to a larger group. Young heterosexual men, in interacting with women, use a pattern of messages that encourage closeness followed by messages that indicate a desire for distance followed by closeness messages followed by distancing messages—a clear example of the tension between the desire for closeness and the desire for autonomy (Korobov & Thorne, 2006)

Positiveness in interpersonal communication has to do with the use of positive rather than negative messages. For example, instead of the negative "I wish you wouldn't ignore my opinions," consider the positive alternative: "I feel good when you ask my opinions." Instead of the negative "You look horrible with long hair," consider the positive: "I think you look great with short hair." As you might expect, positive messages are important to creating and maintaining relationship satisfaction and are used more often by women, both in face-to-face and in computer-mediated communication, than by men (Gattis, Berns, Simpson, & Christensen, 2004; Adrianson, 2001). Interestingly enough, optimism—a generally positive outlook—has been found to positively correlate with relationship satisfaction and happiness; the more optimistic you are, the greater your relationship satisfaction and happiness are likely to be (Assad, Donnellan, & Conger, 2007).

Communicating Positiveness. Here are a few suggestions for communicating positiveness.

- Look for the positive in the person or in the person's work and compliment it. Compliment specifics; overly general compliments ("Your project was interesting") are rarely as effective as those that are specific and concrete ("Your proposal will boost efficiency and produce a great financial saving . . .").
- Express satisfaction nonverbally when communicating with others. For example, use friendly facial expressions, maintain a reasonably but appropriately close distance, and focus eye contact and avoid glancing away from the other person for long periods of time. At the same time, avoid negative teasing; this has been shown to lower satisfaction among couples (Horvath, 2004).
- Express positiveness with a recognition of cultural differences (Axtell, 2007; Dresser, 2005; Chen, 1992). For example, in the United States it's considered appropriate for a supervisor to compliment a worker for doing an exceptional job. But in many collectivist cultures this would be considered inappropriate, because it singles out one individual and separates that person from the group.

Working with Interpersonal Skills

Reflect on your own expressions of positiveness. Can you identify situations in which you could have expressed greater positiveness than you did? How might that have altered the situation? Can you identify situations in which your positiveness created interpersonal difficulties?

The tension between *autonomy and connection*, which seems to occur more often as the relationship progresses, involves the desire to remain an autonomous, independent individual but also to connect intimately to another person and to a relationship. You want to be close and connected with another person but you also want to be independent (Sahlstein, 2004). This tension, by the way, is a popular theme in women's magazines, which teach readers to want both autonomy and connection (Prusank, Duran, & DeLillo, 1993).

The tension between *novelty and predictability* centers on the competing desires for newness, different experiences, and adventure on the one hand and for sameness, stability, and predictability on the other. You're comfortable with being able to predict what will happen, and yet you also want newness, difference, novelty.

Each individual in a relationship may experience a somewhat different set of desires. For example, one person may want exclusivity above all, whereas that person's partner may want greater openness. There seem to be three main ways that you can use to deal with these tensions.

First, you can simply *accept the imbalance* as part of dating or as part of a committed relationship. You may even redefine it as a benefit and tell yourself something like: "I had been spending too much time at work. It's probably better that I come home earlier and don't work weekends"—accepting the closeness and giving up the autonomy.

Second, you can simply *exit the relationship*. For example, if the loss of autonomy is so great that you can't live with it, then you may choose to simply end the relationship and achieve your desired autonomy.

A third alternative is to *rebalance your life*. For example, if you find the primary relationship excessively predictable, you may seek to satisfy the need for novelty elsewhere, perhaps with a vacation to exotic places, perhaps with a different partner. If you find the relationship too connected (even suffocating), you may seek physical and psychological

space to meet your autonomy needs. You can also establish the balance you feel you need by negotiating with your partner; for example, agreeing that you will take separate vacations or that each of you will go out separately with old friends once or twice a week.

As you can appreciate, meeting your partner's needs while also meeting your own needs is one of the major relationship challenges you'll face. Knowing and empathizing with these tensions and discussing them seem useful (even necessary) tools for relationship maintenance and satisfaction.

Social Penetration Theory

Social penetration theory is a theory not of why relationships develop but of what happens when they do develop; it describes relationships in terms of the number of topics that people talk about and the degree of "personalness" of those topics (Altman & Taylor, 1973). The **breadth** of a relationship has to do with how many topics you and your partner talk about. The **depth** of a relationship involves the degree to which you penetrate the inner personality—the core—of the other individual.

We can represent an individual as a circle and divide that circle into various parts, as in Figure 9.2. This figure illustrates different models of social penetration. Each circle in the figure contains eight topic areas to depict breadth (identified as A through H) and five levels of intimacy to depict depth (represented by the concentric circles). Note that in circle 1, only three topic areas are penetrated. Of these, one is penetrated only to the first level and two to the second. In this type of interaction, three topic areas are discussed, and only at rather superficial levels. This is the type of relationship you might have with an acquaintance. Circle 2 represents a more intense relationship, one that has greater breadth and depth; more topics are discussed and to deeper levels of penetration. This is the type of relationship you might have with a friend. Circle 3 represents a still more intense relationship. Here there is considerable breadth (seven of the eight areas are penetrated) and depth (most of the areas are penetrated to the deepest levels). This is the type of relationship you might have with a lover or a parent.

When a relationship begins to deteriorate, the breadth and depth will, in many ways, reverse themselves, in a process called **depenetration**. For example, while ending a relationship, you might cut out certain topics from your interpersonal communications. At the same time, you might discuss the remaining topics in less depth. In some instances of relational deterioration, however, both the breadth and the depth of interaction increase. For example, when a couple breaks up and each is finally free from an oppressive relationship, they may—after some time—begin to discuss problems and feelings they would never have discussed when they were together. In fact, they may become extremely close friends and come to like each other more than when they were together. In these cases the breadth and depth of their relationship may increase rather than decrease (Baxter, 1983).

Social Exchange Theory

Social exchange theory claims that you develop relationships that will enable you to maximize your profits (Chadwick-Jones, 1976; Gergen, Greenberg, & Willis, 1980; Thibaut & Kelley, 1986; Stafford, 2008)—a theory based on an economic model of profits and losses. The theory begins with the following equation: Profits = Rewards − Costs.

FIGURE 9.2

Models of Social Penetration

How accurately do the concepts of breadth and depth express your communication in relationships of different intensities? Can you identify other aspects of messages that change as you go from talking with an acquaintance to talking with a friend or an intimate?

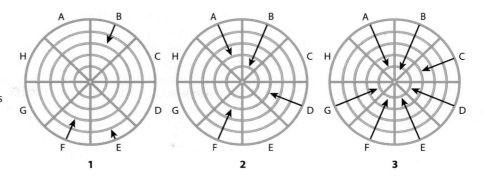

- **Rewards** are anything that you would incur costs to obtain. Research has identified six types of rewards in a love relationship: money, status, love, information, goods, and services (Baron & Byrne, 1984). For example, to get the reward of money, you might have to work rather than play. To earn the status of an A in an interpersonal communication course, you might have to write a term paper or study more than you want to.
- **Costs** are things that you normally try to avoid, that you consider unpleasant or difficult. Examples might include working overtime; washing dishes and ironing clothes; watching your partner's favorite television show, which you find boring; or doing favors for those you dislike.
- **Profit** is what results when the costs are subtracted from the rewards (Profit = Rewards − Costs).

Using this basic economic model, social exchange theory claims that you seek to develop the friendships and romantic relationships that will give you the greatest profits; that is, relationships in which the rewards are greater than the costs.

When you enter a relationship, you have in mind a **comparison level**—a general idea of the kinds of rewards and profits that you feel you ought to get out of such a relationship. This comparison level consists of your realistic expectations concerning what you feel you deserve from this relationship. For example, a study of married couples found that most people expect high levels of trust, mutual respect, love, and commitment. Couples' expectations are significantly lower for time spent together, privacy, sexual activity, and communication (Sabatelli & Pearce, 1986). When the rewards that you get equal or surpass your comparison level, you feel satisfied with your relationship.

However, you also have a comparison level for alternatives. That is, you compare the profits that you get from your current relationship with the profits you think you could get from alternative relationships. Thus, if you see that the profits from your present relationship are below the profits that you could get from an alternative relationship, you may decide to leave your current relationship and enter a new, more profitable relationship.

Equity Theory

Equity theory uses the ideas of social exchange, but goes a step farther and claims that you develop and maintain relationships in which the ratio of your rewards relative to your costs is approximately equal to your partner's (Walster, Walster, & Berscheid, 1978; Messick & Cook, 1983). For example, if you and a friend start a business in which you put up two-thirds of the money and your friend puts up one-third, equity would demand that you get two-thirds of the profits and your friend get one-third. In an *equitable relationship*, then, each party derives rewards that are proportional to the costs they each pay. If you contribute more toward the relationship than your partner, then equity requires that you should get greater rewards. If you both work equally hard, then equity demands that you should both get approximately equal rewards. Conversely, inequity will exist in a relationship if you pay more of the costs (for example, if you do more of the unpleasant tasks) but your partner enjoys more of the rewards. Inequity also will exist if you and your partner work equally hard but your partner gets more of the rewards. In this case you'd be underbenefited and your partner would be overbenefited.

Much research supports this theory that people want equity in their interpersonal relationships (Hatfield & Rapson, 2007; Ueleke et al., 1983). The general idea behind the theory is that if you are underbenefited (you get too little in proportion to what you put in), you'll be angry and dissatisfied. If, on the other hand, you are overbenefited (you get too much in proportion to what you put in), you'll feel guilty. Some research, however, has questioned this rather neat but intuitively unsatisfying assumption and finds that the overbenefited person is often quite happy and contented; guilt from getting more than you deserve seems easily forgotten (Noller & Fitzpatrick, 1993).

Equity theory puts into clear focus the sources of relational dissatisfaction seen every day. For example, in a relationship both partners may have full-time jobs, but one partner may also be expected to do the major share of the household chores. Thus, although both may be deriving equal rewards—they have equally good cars, they live in the same three-bedroom house, and so on—one partner is paying more of the costs. According to equity theory, this partner will be dissatisfied because of this lack of equity.

Equity theory claims that you will develop, maintain, and be satisfied with relationships that are equitable. You will not develop, will terminate, or will be dissatisfied with relationships that are inequitable. The greater the inequity, the greater the dissatisfaction and the greater the likelihood that the relationship will end.

Though each relationship is unique, relationships for many people possess similar characteristics. It is these general patterns that these theories try to explain. Taken together, the theories actually illuminate a great deal about why you develop relationships, the way relationships work, the ways you seek to maintain relationships, and the reasons why some relationships are satisfying and others are not. With an understanding of these aspects of relationships, you'll be in a better position to regulate and manage your own friendship, romantic, and family relationships—the topic of the next chapter.

Summary

This chapter introduced interpersonal relationships and focused on two areas: the stages you go through in developing and perhaps dissolving relationships, and the various theories of how and why interpersonal relationships develop and dissolve.

Relationship Stages

1. At the contact stage of a relationship you make perceptual contact and later interact with the person.
2. At the involvement stage you test your potential partner and, if this proves satisfactory, move on to intensifying your relationship.
3. At the intimacy stage you may make an interpersonal commitment and later enter the stage of social bonding, in which you publicly reveal your relationship status.
4. At the deterioration stage the bonds holding you together begin to weaken. Intrapersonal dissatisfaction later becomes interpersonal, when you discuss it with your partner and perhaps others.
5. At the repair stage you first engage in intrapersonal repair, analyzing what went wrong and perhaps what you can do to set things right; later you may engage in interpersonal repair, in which you and your partner consider ways to mend your deteriorating relationships.
6. At the dissolution stage you separate yourself from your partner and later perhaps separate socially and publicly.

Relationship Theories

7. Attraction theory holds that you develop relationships with those who are similar to you, who are physically close to you, who offer you reinforcement, whom you consider attractive physically and in personality, and who are of a desired socioeconomic and educational level.
8. Relationship rules theory holds that people maintain relationships with those who follow the rules the individuals have defined as essential to their relationship and dissolve relationships with those who don't follow the rules.
9. Relationship dialectics theory holds that relationships involve tensions between opposing needs and desires; for example, the opposing needs of connection with another person on the one hand and autonomy and independence on the other.
10. Social penetration theory focuses on the changes in breadth and depth of conversational topics that take place as partners move from one relationship stage to another.
11. Social exchange theory claims that we enter and maintain relationships in which the rewards are greater than the costs. When the costs become greater than the rewards, the relationship deteriorates.
12. Equity theory holds that you develop and maintain relationships in which your ratio of rewards compared to costs is approximately equal to your partner's.

Key Terms

Critical Thinking Questions

1 In 1967—after nine years of trials and appeals—the U.S. Supreme Court forbade any state laws against interracial marriage (Crohn, 1995). How would you describe the state of interracial romantic relationships today? What obstacles do such relationships face? What advantages do they offer?

2 Research finds that relationship dissolution is a significant influence on men who commit suicide, but not on women (Kposowa, 2000). Can you suggest any reasons for this finding?

3 At least one research study shows that in face-to-face relationships romanticism seems to increase on the basis of the amount of choice you have in selecting a partner. In countries where there is much choice, as in the United States and Europe, romanticism is high; in countries where there is less choice (as in India and parts of Africa), romanticism is lower (Medora, Larson, Hortacsu, & Dave, 2002). Internet dating provides greater choice than do face-to-face interactions, so does it follow that romanticism will be higher in Internet interactions?

4 According to some theories of gender differences in relationships, particularly evolutionary psychology or social Darwinism, men focus on youth and attractiveness in selecting a partner with whom to have children; women, on the other hand, seek men who have wealth and power in an attempt to achieve security. Some research casts doubt on this theory and suggests that both men and women who see themselves as especially attractive will seek partners who are also attractive. Similarly, those who are wealthy will seek others who have similar wealth (Angier, 2003). Which theory do you believe is more valid?

5 Can you supply personal examples that illustrate the three types of movement among the relationship stages—one example of a relationship that moved from one stage to another, one that remained at one stage for a long period, and one that ended?

6 Is the six-stage model presented here an adequate way to describe most interpersonal relationships as you understand them? How would you describe the stages of interpersonal relationships?

7 Do you "comparison shop" (compare your own relationship against potential alternative relationships) regardless of the type of relationship you're in? Or do you stop "shopping" when the relationship reaches a certain level of commitment?

8 Do a cost–benefit analysis of any one of your current relationships. In one column identify all the costs, and in the other column identify all the benefits you get from the relationship. Next, altercast: Playing the role of the person you just did an analysis of, do a cost–benefit analysis of yourself (as you think you might be seen by this person). What can you learn from this type of analysis?

9 How would you feel if you were in a relationship in which you and your partner contributed an equal share of the costs (that is, you each worked equally hard) but your partner derived significantly greater rewards?

Choice Points

1 *Refusing a Gift Positively.* A coworker with whom you're becoming friendly gives you a very intimate gift. You really don't know what this means. Ask yourself: What might you say to refuse the gift but not close off the possibility of dating?

2 *Ending the Relationship.* You want to break up your eight-month romantic relationship and still remain friends. Ask yourself: What are the possible contexts in which you might do this? What types of things can you say that might help you accomplish your dual goal?

3 *Moving through Relationship Stages.* Your current romantic partner seems to be moving too fast for your liking. You want to take things a lot slower, yet you don't want to turn this person off; this may be The One. Ask yourself: What might you say (and when and how might you say it) to get your partner to proceed more slowly?

4 *Meeting the Parents.* You're dating someone from a very different culture and have been invited to meet the parents and have a traditional ethnic dinner. Ask yourself: What might you do to make this potentially difficult situation go smoothly?

5 *Coming Clean.* You're getting ready to meet someone you've only communicated with over the Internet, and you're going to have to admit that you lied about your age and a few other things. Ask yourself: What do you have to come clean with most immediately? What are your options for expressing this? What seems the best option?

6 *Reducing Uncertainty.* You've been dating this person on and off for the last six months but you'd now like to move this relationship to a more exclusive arrangement. You're just not sure how your partner would feel about this. Ask yourself: What might you do to reduce the uncertainty and ambiguity? Specifically, what might you say to get some indication of whether your partner would or would not like to move this relationship toward greater intimacy?

PEARSON
mycommunicationlab   www.mycommunicationlab.com

The following exercises focus on interpersonal relationships and the communication that takes place at each stage. ❶ Analyzing Stage Talk and ❷ Learning to Hear Stage Talk provide opportunities to look at the various cues to the different relationship stages.

❸ Giving Repair Advice looks at relationship difficulties and encourages you to offer relationship repair advice based on the discussions in this chapter. ❹ Til This Do Us Part is an exercise that looks at some of the relationship issues that can break up a relationship.

CHAPTER
10

Interpersonal Relationships:
Development and Deterioration

Relationship Development

Relationship Maintenance

Relationship Deterioration

Relationship Repair

Relationship Dissolution

Sex and the City

Sex and the City tells the story of four women seeking romantic relationships. As they seek these relationships, they learn about themselves and about each other and about the friendship that binds them together no matter what happens. Perhaps most clearly illustrated in this film are the stages that relationships go through, from development to intimacy and (perhaps) to dissolution—the subject of this chapter.

The previous chapter discussed the general progression of relationships and some of the theories explaining the movement among the stages. We'll now consider how relationships develop, how they are maintained, how they deteriorate, how they may be repaired, and how they are dissolved. Let's look first at relationship development.

Relationship Development

Not surprisingly, many of the theories of interpersonal relationships discussed in Chapter 9 and elsewhere focus primarily on how relationships develop. So, in a sense, we have already covered this aspect of relationships. Here we'll briefly review these theories, focusing them more squarely on relationship development; we'll then look at the concept of the "relationship license."

Theories of Relationship Development

Relationship uncertainty reduction, attraction, rules, social exchange, and equity theories seem to have the most to say about how and why relationships develop.

- *Uncertainty reduction theory* (Chapter 3, pp. 70–71) describes relationship development as a process of reducing uncertainty about each other (Berger & Calabrese, 1975). Research is not consistent on whether or not reducing uncertainty increases or decreases liking for the other person. Some research claims that high uncertainty decreases liking; other research claims that high uncertainty increases liking and that it's familiarity that breeds contempt (Knobloch & Carpenter-Theune, 2004; Norton, Frost, & Ariely, 2007).
- *Attraction theory* (pp. 217–219) says that you'll develop relationships with those whom you interact with in close proximity; who reward you; whom you consider physically and psychologically attractive; and whom you see as similar to you, especially in terms of socioeconomic and educational status.
- *Rules theory* (pp. 219–220) describes friendship, love, and family relationships as interactions governed by series of rules that the participants agree to follow. When the rules are followed, the relationship develops; when they are not followed, the relationship is likely not to develop.
- *Social exchange theory* (pp. 222–223) claims that you will develop relationships that are profitable (that is, that give you more rewards than costs). If a potential relationship is seen as being more costly than rewarding, you'll likely not pursue that relationship.
- *Equity theory* (pp. 223–224) claims that you will develop relationships that you see as equitable—relationships in which the ratio of rewards to costs is about the same for each partner.

The Relationship License

Another concept especially relevant to the development of interpersonal relationships is what we might call the interpersonal license, or **relationship license**—a license to violate some relationship expectation, custom, or rule. As the relationship develops, so does the relationship license; it becomes broader as the relationship develops and becomes more restrictive as the relationship deteriorates. For example, long-term friends or romantic couples (say at the intimacy stage) may taste each other's food in a restaurant or may fix each other's clothing or pat each other on the rear. These are violations of rules that normally hold for non-intimates, for casual acquaintances or people in the initial stages of a relationship. In relationships that are deteriorating, the licenses become more limited or may be entirely withdrawn.

In some relationships the license is reciprocal; each person's license is the same. In other relationships it's nonreciprocal; one person has greater license than the other. For example, perhaps one person has license to come home at any time but the other is expected to stay on schedule. Or one person has license to spend the couple's money without explanation but the other has no such right. Or one perhaps has the right to be unfaithful but the other doesn't. For example, in some cultures, men are expected to have intimate relationships with many women, whereas women are expected to have relationships only with a legally approved partner. In this case a nonreciprocal license is built into the culture's rules. The non-reciprocal license is a good example of a lack of equity.

Part of the art of relationship communication is to negotiate the licenses that you want without giving up the privacy you want to retain. This negotiation is almost never made explicit; most often it is accomplished nonverbally and in small increments. The license to touch intimately, for example, is likely to be arrived at through a series of touches that increase gradually, beginning with touching that is highly impersonal.

Relationship Maintenance

Relationship maintenance behaviors are behaviors that serve to continue (maintain, retain) your relationship. (Behaviors directed at mending badly damaged or even broken relationships are considered under the topic of *repair,* pp. 237–240.) Of course, maintenance behaviors can serve a variety of functions. Some examples:

VIEWPOINT It's been argued that you don't actually develop attraction to those who are similar to you but rather are repulsed by those who are dissimilar (Rosenbaum, 1986). For example, you may be repulsed by those who disagree with you and therefore exclude them from those with whom you might develop a relationship. You're therefore left with a pool of possible partners whose attitudes are similar to yours. What do you think of this "repulsion hypothesis"? Do you and your relationship history more closely follow the predictions of repulsion theory or of attraction theory? Or might both dynamics be operating?

- to keep the relationship intact: to retain the semblance of a relationship, to prevent dissolution of the relationship
- to keep the relationship at its present stage: to prevent it from moving too far toward either less or greater intimacy
- to keep the relationship satisfying: to maintain an appropriate balance between rewards and penalties

Some people, after entering a relationship, assume that it will continue unless something catastrophic happens. Consequently, although they may seek to prevent any major mishaps, they're unlikely to engage in much maintenance behavior. Others will be ever on the lookout for something wrong and will seek to patch it up as quickly and as effectively as possible. In between lie most people, who will engage in maintenance behaviors when things are going wrong and when there is the possibility that the relationship can be improved.

Not surprisingly, a great deal of relationship maintenance takes place through e-mail (Stafford, Kline, & Dimmick, 1999; Howard, Rainie, & Jones, 2001). Because many relationships develop online, and because online contact is so easy to maintain even when partners are widely separated geographically, the use of e-mail is likely to increase in frequency and importance. The use of e-mail to maintain relationships is more common among women than men; women also find such e-mail contact more gratifying than do men (Boneva, Kraut, & Frohlich, 2001).

Reasons for Maintaining Relationships

The reasons for maintaining relationships are as numerous and as varied as the reasons for beginning them. Before looking at the specific reasons, let's look at what some of the theories predict.

Attraction theory holds that relationships are maintained when there is significant attraction, generally of the kind that led to the development of the relationship. Although both individuals, as well as their definitions of what constitutes attractiveness, may have changed, the importance of attraction—however defined—is likely to continue throughout the life of the relationship.

VIEWPOINT How would you feel if you were in a relationship in which you and your partner contributed an equal share of the costs (that is, you each worked equally hard), but your partner derived significantly greater rewards? How would you feel if you and your partner contributed an equal share of the costs, but you derived significantly greater rewards?

Social exchange theory holds that relationships will be maintained as long as the relationship is profitable—as long as the rewards exceed the costs. Note, of course, that what constitutes a reward and how significant that reward is can be defined only by the individual. More specifically, you're likely to maintain a relationship when it's more rewarding than what you expected (your comparison level). You're also likely to maintain your present relationship even when it falls short of your comparison level, as long as it's still higher than what you feel you could get elsewhere (your comparison level for alternatives). So even though you may think you deserve more, if you can't get more, then you're likely to stay put.

Equity theory holds that you maintain a relationship when you perceive relative equity. If you feel that both you and your partner are getting roughly the same rewards from the relationship proportional to the costs you're paying, then you're likely to maintain the relationship. If either person—but especially the person who is being shortchanged—perceives a lack of equity, the relationship may experience difficulty.

In addition to these theoretical predictions, let's look at some of the more popular and frequently cited reasons for relationship maintenance.

- *Emotional attachment:* Often you maintain a relationship because you love each other, you want to preserve your relationship, and you don't find alternative couplings as inviting or as potentially enjoyable.
- *Convenience:* The difficulties involved in finding another person to live with, another business partner, or another social escort may make it more convenient to stay together than to break up.
- *Children:* A couple may stay together because they feel, rightly or wrongly, that it's in the best interests of the children; or the children may provide a socially acceptable excuse to mask the real reason—convenience, financial advantage, fear of being alone, and so on.
- *Fear:* People may fear venturing into the outside world, being alone, facing others as "single," or even making it on one paycheck and so may elect to preserve their current relationship as the better alternative.
- *Inertia:* Some relationships are maintained because of inertia (the tendency for a body at rest to remain at rest and a body in motion to remain in motion); change seems too much trouble.
- *Commitment:* People may have a strong commitment to each other or to the relationship (Yela, 2000). In fact, recent research finds that women's commitment is more closely related to relationship maintenance and stability than any other factor (Sprecher, 2001).

Communication for Maintaining Relationships

One reason relationships last is that partners employ effective **relationship communication** to make them work. Interestingly enough, among married couples, the wives' use of maintenance strategies has a more significant effect on the satisfaction, love, and commitment that couples experience than does the husbands' use of such strategies (Weigel & Ballard-Reisch, 1999). This is not to say that men's maintenance strategies are ineffective; it's merely to say that in the average heterosexual married relationship, the couple is more influenced by the wife's maintenance behaviors.

There is conflicting research evidence on the value of electronic communication in maintaining relationships. In one study, for example, the researchers found that 55 percent of Internet users claimed that e-mail strengthened their family ties and 66 percent claimed that it improved their connections with close friends. Related to this is the finding that Internet users seem to experience significantly less social isolation than those who don't use the Internet. Only 8 percent of Internet users noted that they felt socially isolated, while 18 percent of nonusers reported feelings of social isolation (Raney, 2000). Another study reported contrary

UNDERSTANDING INTERPERSONAL SKILLS

Empathy

Empathy is feeling what another person feels from that person's point of view without losing your own identity. Empathy enables you to understand emotionally what another person is experiencing. (To sympathize, in contrast, is to feel *for* the person—to feel sorry or happy for the person, for example.) Women, research shows, are perceived as more empathic and engage in more empathic communication than do men (Nicolai & Demmel, 2007). So following these suggestions may come more easily to women.

Communicating Empathy. Empathy is best expressed in two distinct parts: thinking empathy and feeling empathy (Bellafiore, 2005). In thinking empathy you express an understanding of what the other person means. For example, when you paraphrase someone's comment, showing that you understand the meaning the person is trying to communicate, you're communicating thinking empathy. The second part is feeling empathy; here you express your feeling of what the other person is feeling. You demonstrate a similarity between what you're feeling and what the other person is feeling. Often you'll respond with both thinking and feeling empathy in the same brief response; for example, when a friend tells you of problems at home, you may respond by saying, for example, "Your problems at home do seem to be getting worse. I can imagine how you feel so angry at times."

Here are a few more specific suggestions to help you communicate both your feeling and your thinking empathy more effectively (Authier & Gustafson, 1982).

- Make it clear that you're trying to understand, not to evaluate, judge, or criticize.
- Focus your concentration: Maintain eye contact, an attentive posture, and physical closeness. Express involvement through facial expressions and gestures.
- Reflect back to the speaker the feelings that you think are being expressed, in order to check the accuracy of your perceptions and to show your commitment to understanding the speaker. Offer tentative statements about what you think the person is feeling; for example, "You seem really angry with your father" or "I hear some doubt in your voice."
- When appropriate, use your own self-disclosures to communicate your understanding; but be careful that you don't refocus the discussion on yourself.
- Address mixed messages so as to foster more open and honest communication. For example, if your friend verbally expresses contentment but shows nonverbal signs of depression, it may be prudent to question the possible discrepancy.

Working with Interpersonal Skills

In what situations would you appreciate others' showing empathy? What specifically might they do to demonstrate this empathy?

---

findings, claiming that the more people use the Internet, the less they communicate with family members in their home, the smaller their social circle, and the more they experience loneliness and depression (Kraut et al., 1999). The only reasonable conclusion seems to be that for some users the Internet strengthens social connections with friends and family, but for others it substitutes for face-to-face social interactions and connections.

Many researchers have focused on the maintenance strategies people use in their various relationships (Ayres, 1983; Dindia & Baxter, 1987; Dainton & Stafford, 1993; Guerrero, Eloy, & Wabnik, 1993; Canary, Stafford, Hause, & Wallace, 1993; Canary & Stafford, 1994). Here are some examples of how people maintain their relationships, presented in the form of suggestions for maintaining relationships.

- *Be nice.* Researchers call this *prosocial behavior.* You're polite, cheerful, and friendly; you avoid criticism; and you compromise even when it involves self-sacrifice. Prosocial behavior also includes talking about a shared future; for example, talking about a future vacation or buying a house together. It also includes acting affectionately and romantically.
- *Communicate.* You call just to say, "How are you?" or send cards or letters. Sometimes communication is merely "small talk" that is insignificant in itself but is engaged in because it preserves contact. Also included would be talking about the honesty and openness in the relationship and talking about shared feelings. Responding constructively in a conflict (even when your partner may act in ways harmful to the relationship) is another type of communicative maintenance strategy (Rusbult & Buunk, 1993).

- *Be open.* You engage in direct discussion and listen to the other—for example, you self-disclose, talk about what you want from the relationship, give advice, and express empathy.
- *Give assurances.* You assure the other person of the significance of the relationship—for example, you comfort the other, put your partner first, and express love.
- *Share joint activities.* You spend time with the other—for example, playing ball, visiting mutual friends, doing specific things as a couple (even cleaning the house), and sometimes just being together and talking with no concern for what is done. Controlling (eliminating or reducing) extrarelational activities would be another type of togetherness behavior (Rusbult & Buunk, 1993). Also included here would be ceremonial behaviors; for example, celebrating birthdays and anniversaries, discussing past pleasurable times, and eating at a favorite restaurant.
- *Be positive.* You try to make interactions pleasant and upbeat—for example, holding hands, giving in to make your partner happy, and doing favors. At the same time, you would avoid certain issues that might cause arguments.
- *Focus on improving yourself.* For example, you work on making yourself look especially good and attractive to the other person.

Relationship Deterioration

In *relationship deterioration,* as discussed in Chapter 9, there is a weakening of the bonds that hold people together. The process of deterioration may be gradual or sudden. For example, gradual deterioration may occur in a situation in which one of the parties in a relationship develops close ties with a new intimate, and this new relationship gradually pushes out the old. Sudden deterioration may occur when a rule that was essential to the relationship (for example, the rule of complete fidelity) is broken and both parties realize that the relationship cannot be sustained.

In terms of the theories introduced earlier, relationship deterioration can occur when you no longer find your partner attractive physically and in personality, when you no longer experience closeness, or when the differences become more important than the similarities. When relationships break up, it's generally the more attractive person who leaves (Blumstein & Schwartz, 1983). There is no denying the power of attractiveness in the development of relationships or the influence of its loss in the deterioration of relationships. According to social exchange theory, deterioration can set in when the costs begin to exceed the rewards. Similarly, a relationship may deteriorate when you feel that you could do better with someone else. Even if your relationship is less than you expected it to be, you probably will not dissolve it unless you perceive that another relationship (or being alone) will provide a greater profit. In terms of equity, deterioration can occur when you feel that you're putting more into the relationship than you're getting out of it or that your partner is benefiting from the relationship disproportionately.

Causes of Relationship Deterioration

There are as many reasons for relationship deterioration as there are people in relationships. Still, some general causes—applicable to a wide variety of relationship breakups—may be identified.

As a preface, recall that each of the benefits of relationships discussed in the self-test in Chapter 9 may, when no longer present, contribute to deterioration. For example, when loneliness is no longer reduced by the relationship (when one or both individuals feel lonely frequently or for prolonged periods), the relationship

VIEWPOINT In face-to-face relationships, emotional closeness compromises privacy; the closer you become, the less privacy you have. Research on online relationships, however, indicates that because you're more in control of what you reveal, you can develop close emotional relationships, but also maintain your privacy (Ben-Ze'ev, 2003). Do you find this to be true? If not, how would you express the relationship between emotional closeness and privacy online?

UNDERSTANDING INTERPERSONAL THEORY & RESEARCH

Jealousy

Jealousy is a reaction to relationship threat: If you feel that someone is moving in on your relationship partner, you may experience jealousy—especially if you feel that this interloper is succeeding.

Much research has reported that heterosexual men and women experience jealousy for different reasons, which are rooted in our evolutionary development (Buss, 2000; Buunk & Dijkstra, 2004; Buller, 2005). Basically, research finds that men experience jealousy if they fear that their partner is being *physically* intimate with another man, whereas women experience jealousy if they fear their partner's *emotional* intimacy with another woman. The evolutionary reason given is that among early humans men provided food and shelter for the family, so a man would resent his partner's physical intimacy with another because he would then be providing food and shelter for another man's child. Women depended on men for food and shelter, so a woman would become especially jealous when her partner was emotionally intimate with another, because this might mean he might leave her and she'd thus lose the food and shelter protection.

Not all research supports this finding, however, and not all theory supports this evolutionary explanation (Harris, 2003). For example, in a survey of Chinese men, only 25 percent reported that physical infidelity was the more distressing; 75 percent reported emotional infidelity to be more distressing.

Another commonly assumed gender difference is that jealous men are more prone to respond with violence. This assumption, however, does not seem to be accurate; men and women apparently are equally likely to respond with violence (Harris, 2003).

So what do you do (short of violence) when you experience jealousy? Communication researchers find several popular but generally negative interactive responses (Guerrero, Andersen, Jorgensen, Spitzberg, & Eloy, 1995; Dindia & Timmerman, 2003). A jealous person may:

■ nonverbally express displeasure; for example, cry or facially express hurt
■ threaten to become violent or actually engage in violence
■ direct verbal aggressiveness toward the partner; for example, be sarcastic or accusatory
■ withdraw affection from the partner or be abnormally silent, sometimes denying that anything is wrong

On the more positive side are responses known as "integrative communication": messages that attempt to work things out with the partner, such as self-disclosing feelings and being honest.

Working with Theories and Research

Examine your own jealousy or the jealousy you witness in others and especially the ways in which you or they have expressed this jealousy. What types of responses seem to promote relationship satisfaction? What types seem to damage the relationship?

---

may well be on the road to decay, because it's not serving a function it was entered into to serve. Similarly, when relationships no longer provide stimulation, gains in self-knowledge and self-esteem, enhancement of physical and emotional health, or maximizing of pleasures and minimizing of pain, they are likely to be in trouble.

Here are some additional causes of relationship deterioration.

■ *Poor communication:* Clearly, inadequate communication is one of the major causes of relationship breakdown. Communication that is excessively critical or unsupportive or disconfirming will create dissatisfaction that can easily lead to a breakdown in friendship, love, or family relationships.

■ *Third-party relationships:* People establish and maintain relationships to maximize their pleasure and minimize their pain. When these goals cease to be met, the relationship stands little chance of survival. In particular, when a new relationship (a new best friend, a new romantic partner) serves these needs better, the old relationship may deteriorate.

■ *Relationship changes:* The development of incompatible attitudes, vastly different intellectual interests and abilities, or major goal changes may contribute to relationship deterioration. The person who develops an addiction (to drugs, alcohol, or even stamp collecting) may likewise present the relationship with a serious problem.

■ *Sex- and work-related problems:* In romantic relationships, sexual problems cause great difficulties; for example, they rank among the top three problems in almost all studies of relationships (Blumstein & Schwartz, 1983). It's the quality of the sexual relationship,

VIEWPOINT Even though women are now firmly in the workplace, they're still the primary caregivers and perform the bulk of the household duties. Some years ago, in fact, Switzerland initiated a "fair play at home" campaign to get men to take on more of the household chores (Olson, 2002). If you were in charge of such a campaign in the United States, what would you say to men? What would you say to women?

not the quantity of sexual encounters, that seems crucial. When the quality is poor, outside affairs may be sought, and these contribute significantly to breakups for all couples, whether married or not. Similarly, problems associated with either partner's job often lead to trouble. Spending too much time at the office, earning too little money, and being unhappy in the job are examples of work-related issues that take their toll on a relationship.

- *Financial difficulties:* In surveys of problems among couples, financial worries loom large. Money is a major taboo topic for couples beginning a relationship, yet it often proves to be a cause of major problems as people settle into their relationship. One-fourth to one-third of all couples rank money as their primary problem; almost all rank it as one of their major problems (Blumstein & Schwartz, 1983). Money is so important in relationships because of its close connection with power. In relationships as in business, the person bringing in the most money wields the most power. This person has the final say, for example, on the purchase of expensive items as well as on decisions having nothing to do with money. The power that money brings quickly spreads to nonfinancial issues as well.
- *Beliefs about relationships:* If you and your partner have similar beliefs about relationships—and if these beliefs are realistic—then your relationship is likely to be strengthened. If, on the other hand, you and your partner hold widely different beliefs about, say, gender or financial expectations—and/or if your beliefs are unrealistic—then your relationship is more likely to experience instability and interpersonal distancing (Pasley, Kerpelman, & Guilbert, 2001; Goodwin & Gaines, 2004). The role of unrealistic beliefs is well illustrated in the self-test "What Do You Believe about Relationships?"

Effects of Relationship Deterioration

When relationships deteriorate, a variety of things happen. Although we're conditioned to view relationship deterioration as something negative, it's certainly not always negative and, in fact, may bring some positive benefits as well. On the negative side, perhaps the most obvious is a loss of all the benefits or rewards you enjoyed as a result of the relationship. Regardless of how unsatisfying the relationship may ultimately have been, it probably also had many good aspects. These are now lost.

There is also, generally, a loss of self-esteem. You may feel unworthy or perhaps guilty. You may blame yourself for doing the wrong things, for not doing the right things, or for being responsible for the losses you now confront. Of course, there are likely to be friends and family members who will give you a hard time, often implying that you're to blame.

There also are practical issues. The deterioration of a relationship often has financial implications, and you may now encounter money problems. Paying the rent, tuition, or outstanding loans by yourself may prove difficult. If the relationship is a marriage, then there are legal and perhaps religious implications. If there are children, the situation becomes even more complicated.

Communication in Relationship Deterioration

Relationship deterioration involves special communication patterns. These patterns are in part a response to the deterioration; you communicate the way you do because you feel that your relationship is in trouble. However, these patterns are also causative: The communication patterns you use largely determine the fate of your relationship. Here are a few communication patterns that are seen during relationship deterioration.

- *Withdrawal:* Nonverbally, withdrawal is seen in the greater space you need and in the speed with which tempers and other signs of disturbance arise when that space

TEST YOURSELF

WHAT DO YOU BELIEVE ABOUT RELATIONSHIPS?

On the line next to each statement, indicate whether you think the statement is TRUE (you agree with the statement to some extent) or FALSE (you disagree with the statement to some extent).

_____ 1. If a person has any questions about the relationship, then it means there is something wrong with it.

_____ 2. If my partner truly loved me, we would not have any quarrels.

_____ 3. If my partner really cared, he or she would always feel affection for me.

_____ 4. If my partner gets angry at me or is critical in public, this indicates he or she doesn't really love me.

_____ 5. My partner should know what is important to me without my having to tell him or her.

_____ 6. If I have to ask for something that I really want, it spoils it.

_____ 7. If my partner really cared, he or she would do what I ask.

_____ 8. A good relationship should not have any problems.

_____ 9. If people really love each other, they should not have to work on their relationship.

_____ 10. If my partner does something that upsets me, I think it is because he or she deliberately wants to hurt me.

_____ 11. When my partner disagrees with me in public, I think it is a sign that he or she doesn't care for me very much.

_____ 12. If my partner contradicts me, I think that he or she doesn't have much respect for me.

_____ 13. If my partner hurts my feelings, I think that it is because he or she is mean.

_____ 14. My partner always tries to get his or her own way.

_____ 15. My partner doesn't listen to what I have to say.

HOW DID YOU DO? Aaron Beck, one of the leading theorists in cognitive therapy and the author of the popular _Love Is Never Enough_, claims that all of these beliefs are unrealistic and may create problems in your interpersonal relationships. The test was developed to help people identify potential sources of difficulty for relationship development and maintenance. The more statements that you indicated you agree with, the more unrealistic your expectations are.

WHAT WILL YOU DO? If you hold any of these beliefs and you agree that they are counterproductive, what can you do about them? You may want to begin this analysis by reviewing the list—individually or in small groups—and identifying with hypothetical or real examples why each belief is unrealistic (or realistic).

Source: This test was taken from Aaron Beck, _Love Is Never Enough_, pp. 67–68. Copyright © 1988 by Aaron T. Beck, M.D. Reprinted by permission of Harper Collins Publishers, Inc. and Arthur Pine Associates, Inc. Beck notes that this test was adapted in part from the Relationship Belief Inventory of N. Epstein, J. L. Pretzer, and B. Fleming, "The Role of Cognitive Appraisal in Self-Reports of Marital Communication," _Behavior Therapy_ 18 (1987): 51–69.

is invaded. Other nonverbal signs of withdrawal include a decrease in eye contact and touching; less similarity in clothing; and fewer displays of items associated with the other person, such as bracelets, photographs, and rings (Miller & Parks, 1982; Knapp & Vangelisti, 2009). Verbally, withdrawal is marked by a decreased desire to talk and especially to listen. At times, you may use small talk not as a preliminary to serious conversation but as an alternative, perhaps to avoid confronting the serious issues.

- _Decline in self-disclosure:_ Self-disclosing communications decline significantly. If the relationship is dying, you may think self-disclosure not worth the effort. Or you may limit your self-disclosures because you feel that the other person may not accept them or can no longer be trusted to be supportive and empathic.

- _Deception:_ Deception increases as relationships break down. Sometimes this takes the form of clear-cut lies, which you or your partner may use to avoid arguments over such things as staying out all night, not calling, or being seen in the wrong place with the wrong person. At other times, lies may be used because of a feeling of shame; you may not want the other person to think less of you. One of the problems with deception is that it has a way of escalating, eventually creating a climate of distrust and disbelief.

■ *Positive and negative messages:* During deterioration there's an increase in negative and a decrease in positive messages. Once you praised the other's behaviors, but now you criticize them. Often the behaviors have not changed significantly; what has changed is your way of looking at them. What once was a cute habit now becomes annoying; what once was "different" now becomes inconsiderate. When a relationship is deteriorating, requests for pleasurable behaviors decrease ("Will you fix me my favorite dessert?") and requests to stop unpleasant or negative behaviors increase ("Will you stop monopolizing the phone?") (Lederer, 1984). Even the social niceties that accompany requests get lost as they deteriorate from "Would you please make me a cup of coffee, honey?" to "Get me some coffee, will you?" to "Where's my coffee?"

Figure 10.1 summarizes the changes in communication (discussed in this chapter and in Chapter 9) that take place as you move toward or away from intimacy. The general and most important point this figure makes is that communication effectiveness and satisfaction increase as you move toward intimacy and decrease as you move away from intimacy.

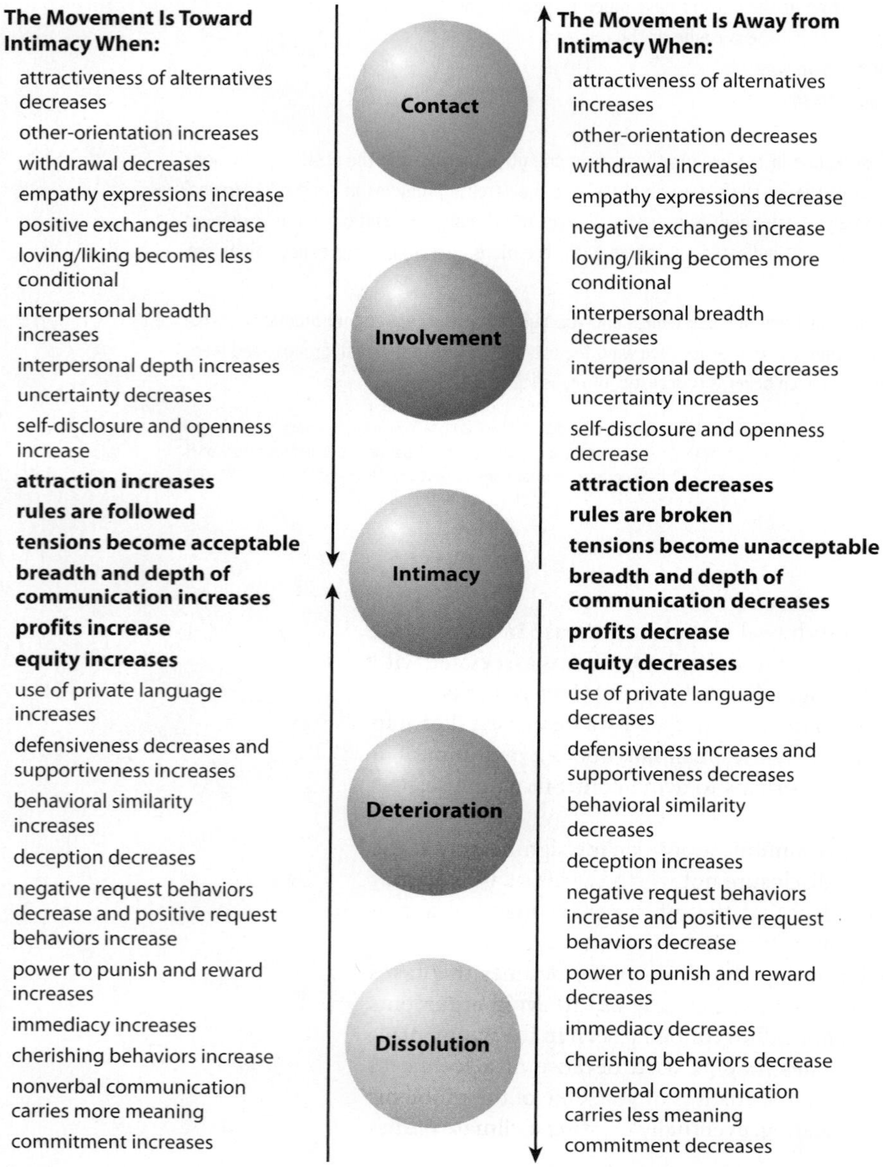

The Movement Is Toward Intimacy When:

attractiveness of alternatives decreases

other-orientation increases

withdrawal decreases

empathy expressions increase

positive exchanges increase

loving/liking becomes less conditional

interpersonal breadth increases

interpersonal depth increases

uncertainty decreases

self-disclosure and openness increase

attraction increases

rules are followed

tensions become acceptable

breadth and depth of communication increases

profits increase

equity increases

use of private language increases

defensiveness decreases and supportiveness increases

behavioral similarity increases

deception decreases

negative request behaviors decrease and positive request behaviors increase

power to punish and reward increases

immediacy increases

cherishing behaviors increase

nonverbal communication carries more meaning

commitment increases

Contact

Involvement

Intimacy

Deterioration

Dissolution

The Movement Is Away from Intimacy When:

attractiveness of alternatives increases

other-orientation decreases

withdrawal increases

empathy expressions decrease

negative exchanges increase

loving/liking becomes more conditional

interpersonal breadth decreases

interpersonal depth decreases

uncertainty increases

self-disclosure and openness decrease

attraction decreases

rules are broken

tensions become unacceptable

breadth and depth of communication decreases

profits decrease

equity decreases

use of private language decreases

defensiveness increases and supportiveness decreases

behavioral similarity decreases

deception increases

negative request behaviors increase and positive request behaviors decrease

power to punish and reward decreases

immediacy decreases

cherishing behaviors decrease

nonverbal communication carries less meaning

commitment decreases

FIGURE 10.1

Communication in Relationships

This summary of some of the changes that accompany increased intimacy and some that accompany decreased intimacy contains many of the findings discussed here and in Chapter 9. Changes related to the major theories discussed in Chapter 9 are noted here in boldface. Read down the list of changes with your own relationships in mind. What additional changes might you add to this list? Which changes do you fail to see in your own relationships or in relationships you've heard about?

The approach to ethics taken in this book from its inception has been information ethics. This position argues that people have the right to information relevant to the choices they make. From this basic premise several corollaries follow:

- Communications are ethical when they facilitate people's freedom of choice by presenting them with accurate information. Communications are unethical when they prevent people from securing such information or give them false or misleading information that will lead them to make choices they would not make if they had more accurate information.

- You have the right to information about yourself that others possess and that may influence the choices you make. Thus, for example, you have the right to face your accusers, to know the witnesses who will testify against you, to see your credit ratings, and to know what Social Security benefits you'll receive. On the other hand, you do not have the right to information that is none of your business, such as information about whether your neighbors are happy or argue a lot or receive food stamps.

- You have an obligation to reveal information that you possess that bears on the choices of other people and of your society. Thus, for example, you have an obligation to identify wrongdoing that you witness, to identify someone in a police lineup, to report criminal activity, and to testify at a trial when you possess pertinent information. This information is judged essential for society to accomplish its purposes and to make its legitimate choices.

What would you do?

Your best friend's husband is currently having an extramarital affair with a 15-year-old. Your friend suspects this is going on and asks if you know anything about it. Would it be ethical for you to lie and say you know nothing, or are you obligated to tell your friend what you know? Are you obligated to tell the police? What would you do in this situation?

Relationship Repair

If you wish to save a relationship, you may try to do so by changing your communication patterns and, in effect, putting into practice the insights and skills learned in this course. First, we'll look at some general ways to repair a relationship, and second, we'll examine ways to deal with repair when you are the only one who wants to change the relationship.

Interpersonal Repair

We can look at the strategies for repairing a relationship in terms of the following six suggestions, whose first letters conveniently spell out the word *REPAIR*, a useful reminder that repair is not a one-step but a multistep process (see Figure 10.2).

Recognize the Problem Your first step is to identify the problem and to recognize it both intellectually and emotionally. Specify what is wrong with your present relationship (in concrete terms) and what changes would be needed to make it better (again, in specific terms). Create a picture of your relationship as you would want it to be, and compare that picture to the way the relationship looks now. Specify the changes that would have to take place if the ideal picture were to replace the present picture.

Try also to see the problem from your partner's point of view and to have your partner see the problem from yours. Exchange these perspectives, empathically and with open minds. Try, too, to be descriptive when discussing grievances, taking special care to avoid such troublesome terms as "always" and "never." Own your feelings and thoughts; use I-messages and take responsibility for your feelings instead of blaming your partner.

Engage in Productive Communication and Conflict Resolution Interpersonal communication skills such as those discussed throughout the text (for example, other-orientation,

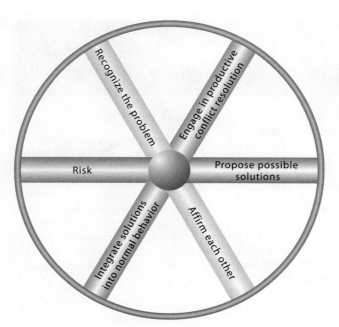

FIGURE 10.2

The Relationship Repair Wheel

The wheel seems an apt metaphor for the repair process; the specific repair strategies—the spokes—all work together in constant process. The wheel is difficult to get moving, but once in motion it becomes easier to turn. Also, it's easier to start when two people are pushing, but it is not impossible for one to move it in the right direction. What metaphor do you find helpful in thinking about relationship repair?

openness, confidence, immediacy, expressiveness, and empathy, considered in Understanding Interpersonal Skills boxes) are especially important during repair and are an essential part of any repair strategy. Here are several suggestions to refresh your memory.

- Look closely for relational messages that will help clarify motivations and needs. Respond to these messages as well as to the content messages.
- Exchange perspectives and see the situation as your partner does.
- Practice empathic and positive responses, even in conflict situations.
- Own your feelings and thoughts. Use I-messages and take responsibility for these feelings.
- Use active listening techniques to help your partner explore and express relevant thoughts and feelings.
- Remember the principle of irreversibility; think carefully before saying things you may later regret.
- Keep the channels of communication open. Be available to discuss problems, to negotiate solutions, and to practice new and more productive communication patterns.

Similarly, the skills of effective interpersonal conflict resolution are crucial in any attempt at relationship repair. If partners address relationship problems by deploying productive conflict resolution strategies, the difficulties may be resolved, and the relationship may actually emerge stronger and healthier. If, however, unproductive and destructive strategies are used, then the relationship may well deteriorate further. The nature and skills of conflict resolution are considered in depth in Chapter 12.

Pose Possible Solutions After the problem is identified, you discuss solutions—possible ways to lessen or eliminate the difficulty. Look for solutions that will enable both of you to win. Try to avoid "solutions" in which one person wins and the other loses. With such win–lose solutions, resentment and hostility are likely to fester.

Affirm Each Other Any strategy of relationship repair should incorporate supportiveness and positive evaluations. For example, happy couples engage in greater positive behavior exchange: They communicate more agreement, approval, and positive affect than do unhappy couples (Dindia & Fitzpatrick, 1985). Clearly, these behaviors result from the positive feelings the partners have for each other. However, it can also be argued that these expressions help to increase the positive regard each person has for the other.

One way to affirm another is to talk positively. Reverse negative communication patterns. For example, instead of withdrawing, talk about the causes of and the possible cures for your disagreements and problems. Reverse the tendency to hide your inner self. Disclose your feelings. Compliments, positive stroking, and all the nonverbals that say "I care" are especially important when you wish to reverse negative communication patterns.

Cherishing behaviors are an especially insightful way to affirm another person and to increase favor exchange (Lederer, 1984). **Cherishing behaviors** are those small gestures you enjoy receiving from your partner (a smile, a wink, a squeeze, a kiss). Cherishing behaviors should be (1) specific and positive, (2) focused on the present and future rather than related to issues about which the partners have argued in the past, (3) capable of being performed daily, and (4) easily executed. People can make a list of the cherishing behaviors they each wish to receive and then exchange lists. Each person then performs the cherishing behaviors desired by the partner. At first, these behaviors may seem self-conscious and awkward. In time, however, they will become a normal part of interaction.

VIEWPOINT One study found that of people who met on the Internet, those who meet in places of common interest, who communicate over a period of time before they meet in person, who manage barriers to greater closeness, and who manage conflict well are more likely to say together than couples who do not follow this general pattern (Baker, 2002). Based on your own experiences, how would you predict which couples would stay together and which would break apart?

Integrate Solutions into Normal Behavior Often solutions that are reached after an argument are followed for only a very short time; then the couple goes back to their previous, unproductive behavior patterns. Instead, integrate the solutions into your normal behavior; make them an integral part of your everyday relationship behavior. For example, make the exchange of favors, compliments, and cherishing behaviors a part of your normal relationship behavior.

Risk Take risks in trying to improve your relationship. Risk giving favors without any certainty of reciprocity. Risk rejection by making the first move to make up or by saying you're sorry. Be willing to change, to adapt, to take on new tasks and responsibilities.

Risk the possibility that a significant part of the problem is you—that you're being unreasonable or controlling or stingy and that this is causing problems and needs to be changed.

Intrapersonal Repair

One of the most important avenues to relationship repair originates with the principle of punctuation (see Chapter 1) and the idea that communication is circular rather than linear (see Chapter 1; Duncan & Rock, 1991). Let's consider an example involving Pat and Chris: Pat is highly critical of Chris; Chris is defensive and attacks Pat for being insensitive, overly negative, and unsupportive. If you view the communication process as beginning with Pat's being critical (that is, the stimulus) and with Chris's attacks being the response, you have a pattern such as occurs in Figure 10.3(A).

With this view, the only way to stop the unproductive communication pattern is for Pat to stop criticizing. But what if you are Chris and can't get Pat to stop being critical? What if Pat doesn't want to stop being critical?

You get a different view of the problem when you see communication as circular and apply the principle of punctuation. The result is a pattern such as appears in Figure 10.3(B).

Note that no assumptions are made about causes. Instead, the only assumption is that each response triggers another response; each response depends in part on the previous response. Therefore, the pattern can be broken at any point: Chris can stop Pat's criticism, for example, by not responding with attacks. Similarly, Pat can stop Chris's attacks by not responding with criticism.

In this view, either person can break an unproductive circle. Clearly, relationship communication can be most effectively improved when both parties change their unproductive

FIGURE 10.3(A)

A Stimulus–Response View of Relationship Problems

This view of the relationship process implies that one behavior is the stimulus and one behavior is the response. It implies that a pattern of behavior can be modified only if you change the stimulus, which will produce a different (more desirable) response.

patterns. Nevertheless, communication can be improved even if only one person changes and begins to use a more productive pattern. This is true to the extent that Pat's criticism depends on Chris's attacks and to the extent that Chris's attacks depend on Pat's criticism.

Relationship Dissolution

Some relationships, of course, do end. Sometimes there simply is not enough to hold the individuals together. Sometimes there are problems that cannot be resolved. Sometimes the costs are too high and the rewards too few, or the relationship is recognized as destructive and escape is the only alternative. As a relationship ends, you're confronted with two general issues: how to end the relationship, and how to deal with the inevitable problems that relationship endings cause.

Reasons for Relationship Dissolution

Let's begin by dispelling one great myth, and that is that relationship dissolution is always bad. It isn't, necessarily.

For a variety of reasons—some religious, some social, some economic, some interpersonal, and perhaps some based on an analysis of costs and benefits—people feel that relationships should last and that it's bad when they end. And so you often respond positively when a couple says they've been together for a long time; conversely, you'll probably respond with sadness and "I'm sorry" or "That's too bad" when you hear they're breaking up.

Upon more sober reflection, however, it should be clear that in some cases there are advantages to relationship dissolution. Often the relationship deserves to be dissolved. For example, friendships may become destructive or overly competitive—as can occur in a variety of work situations—and may be better put aside. If a "friend" makes your self-disclosures public or otherwise betrays your confidence, and if this becomes a pattern that's repeated over and over again, it may be time to move from the level of friendship to that of seldom-seen acquaintanceship.

Romantic relationships—whether dating, married, domestic partnership, or any other such relationship—may become unbalanced, with one person doing all the work and the other reaping all the benefits. If a romantic relationship becomes verbally or physically abusive, the relationship may be better dissolved.

Even in families, certain members or certain relationships within the family may become toxic. For example, sometimes partners, parents, or children become enablers, helping a family member to engage in destructive behavior—as when family members help to hide a person's alcoholism from friends and relatives and thus help the person continue drinking more comfortably and without social criticism. Gay and lesbian offspring who are rejected by their families after coming out may be better off away from homophobic (and guilt-instilling) parents, siblings, and other relatives. And the same can be said for a son or daughter who forms a permanent relationship with someone the family disapproves of and will not accept. In this case, the son or daughter may have to choose where his or her loyalty and primary affiliation must lie—with family or with the relationship partner. In at least some of these decisions, greater long-term satisfaction may come from severing family ties than from abandoning a productive and happy romantic relationship.

A related myth is to assume that when a relationship breaks up, one of the individuals must have done something wrong. But there are legitimate reasons for dissolution when

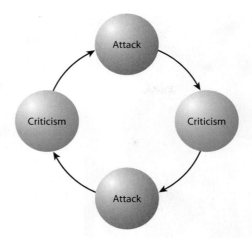

FIGURE 10.3(B)

A Circular View of Relationship Problems

Note that in this view of relationships, as distinguished from that depicted in Figure 10.3(A), relationship behaviors are seen in a circular pattern; no specific behavior is singled out as a stimulus and none as a response. The pattern can thus be broken by interference anywhere along the circle.

neither party has done anything wrong. People may develop different needs that cannot be met within the confines of the present relationship. Likewise, people sometimes experience changes in their interests and goals, recognize their true affectional orientation, or find a greater love—all legitimate reasons for relationship dissolution.

Conversely, it should not be assumed that because people stay together there is something noble about them or about their relationship. Long-lasting relationships are not necessarily better than relationships of short duration. The length of time people stay in a relationship actually says little about the nature of the relationship. Dramatic examples of this are seen daily on *Jerry Springer* and *Maury*, where guests describe long-term relationships that most people would find repulsive. Less dramatic examples are likely to be found everywhere else.

It's important to remember that we enter relationships for a variety of reasons and that in times of trouble it may be worth the effort to repair the relationship to get back what we had originally. The difficulty here is that we can never be sure if, after many failed efforts to repair the relationship, the next attempt might not succeed. The decision whether to stay in a relationship that does not fulfill your needs or is destructive or to end the relationship is not easy to make, as so many factors come into play. In the end, at some point, it may be best to say, "I tried and now I need to move on." Treating relationships as if they can be easily and appropriately discarded is unlikely to yield long-term benefits. Perhaps equally unlikely to yield long-term benefits is remaining in unproductive and destructive relationships.

Strategies of Disengagement

When you wish to exit a relationship, you need some way of explaining this—to yourself as well as to your partner. You need a strategy for getting out of a relationship that you no longer find satisfying or profitable. Five such strategies are presented below (Cody, 1982). As you read down the list, note that your choice of a strategy will depend on your goal. For example, you're more likely to remain friends if you use de-escalation than if you use justification or avoidance (Banks, Altendorf, Greene, & Cody, 1987).

- The use of a positive tone to preserve the relationship and to express positive feelings for the other person. For example, "I really care for you a great deal, but I'm not ready for such an intense relationship."
- Negative identity management to blame the other person for the breakup and to absolve yourself of the blame for the breakup. For example, "I can't stand your jealousy, your constant suspicions, your checking up on me. I need my freedom."
- Justification to give reasons for the breakup. For example, "I'm going away to college for four years; there's no point in not dating others."
- Behavioral de-escalation to reduce the intensity of the relationship. For example, you might avoid the other person, cut down on phone calls, or reduce the amount of time you spend together.
- De-escalation to reduce the exclusivity and hence the intensity of the relationship. For example, "I'm just not ready for an exclusive relationship. I think we should see other people."

Dealing with a Breakup

Regardless of the specific reason for the end of the relationship, relationship breakups are difficult to deal with; invariably they cause stress and emotional problems, and they may actually create as much pain in a person's brain as physical injuries (Eisenberger, Lieberman, & Williams, 2003). Women, it seems, experience greater depression and social dysfunction than men after relationship dissolution (Chung, Farmer, Grant, Newton, Payne, Perry, Saunders, Smith, & Stone, 2002). Consequently, it's important to give attention to self-repair. Here are a few suggestions to ease the difficulty that is sure to be experienced, whether the breakup is between friends or lovers or occurs because of death, separation, or the loss of affection and connection.

VIEWPOINT The media are currently teaching millions of people about interpersonal relationships by example and sometimes by explicit teaching, as with many talk shows. Take the viewpoint of the extraterrestrial who knows nothing about human interpersonal relationships (friendship, love, and family). What would this alien conclude from watching only Jerry Springer and Maury or only commercials or only soap operas or only news shows or only sitcoms or only television dramas? What would this alien conclude from all these shows put together?

Break the Loneliness–Depression Cycle The two most common feelings following the end of a relationship are loneliness and depression. These feelings are significant; treat them seriously. Realize that depression often leads to serious illness. In most cases, fortunately, loneliness and depression are temporary. Depression, for example, usually does not last longer than three or four days. Similarly, the loneliness that follows a breakup is generally linked to this specific situation and will fade when the situation changes. Grief—over the death of a loved one, say—may last a lot longer. When depression does last, is especially deep, or disturbs your normal functioning, it's time for professional help.

Take Time Out Resist the temptation to jump into a new relationship while the old one is still warm or before a new one can be assessed with some objectivity. At the same time, resist swearing off all relationships. Neither extreme works well.

Take time out for yourself. Renew your relationship with yourself. If you were in a long-term relationship, you probably saw yourself as part of a team, as part of a couple. Now get to know yourself as a unique individual, standing alone at present but fully capable of entering a meaningful relationship in the near future.

Bolster Self-Esteem When relationships fail, self-esteem often declines. This seems especially true for those who did not initiate the breakup (Collins & Clark, 1989). You may feel guilty for having caused the breakup or inadequate for not holding on to the relationship. You may feel unwanted and unloved. Your task is to regain a positive self-image.

Recognize, too, that having been in a relationship that failed—even if you view yourself as the main cause of the breakup—does not mean that you are a failure. Neither does it mean that you cannot succeed in a new and different relationship. It does mean that something went wrong with this one relationship. Ideally, it was a failure from which you have learned something important about yourself and about your relationship behavior.

Remove or Avoid Uncomfortable Symbols After any breakup, there are a variety of reminders—photographs, gifts, and letters, for example. Resist the temptation to throw these out. Instead, remove them. Give them to a friend to hold or put them in a closet where you'll not see them. If possible, avoid places you frequented together. These symbols will bring back uncomfortable memories. After you have achieved some emotional distance, you can go back and enjoy these as reminders of a once pleasant relationship. Support for this suggestion comes from research showing that the more vivid your memory of a broken love affair—a memory greatly aided by these relationship symbols—the greater your depression is likely to be (Harvey, Flanary, & Morgan, 1986).

Seek Support Many people feel they should bear their burdens alone. Men, in particular, have been taught that this is the only "manly" way to handle things. But seeking the support

Ask the Researcher

The Death of a Relationship

I recently lost my partner of 20 years in a car accident and am having lots of trouble dealing with this loss. Is there anything I can do to lessen the pain I feel?

The sudden loss of someone with whom you've had a long and intimate relationship can create lots of problems. The relationship has become part of your own identity, so losing your partner is like losing a part of your "self." You have lost not only your partner, but also your plans for the future, your emotional support, and perhaps even your financial support. Thus, you are now forced to be a different person than you were as a part of a relationship, and in this sense at least your loss is similar to the loss experienced by the dissolution of any intimate relationship. Your particular loss, however, is compounded because you didn't get to say good-bye. You may feel anger against the world, including the deceased, and you may even feel guilty that you were spared. Time may be the most important factor in healing such a loss; give yourself a chance to mourn and to learn to live alone.

For more information see C. A. Corr, C. M. Nabe, and D. M. Corr, *Death and Dying, Life and Living,* 2nd ed. (Pacific Grove, CA: Brooks/Cole, 1997); E. Kübler-Ross, *On Death and Dying* (New York: Macmillan, 1969, 1997); and H. S. Kushner, *When Bad Things Happen to Good People* (New York: Avon, 1981).

Shirlee A. Levin (M.A., University of Hawaii) is a professor of speech communication at the College of Southern Maryland, where she teaches courses in interpersonal communication, intercultural communication, groups and leadership, and the basic course. She has presented workshops for middle and high school students and faculty as well as for civic and religious groups. In 2003 she received the Community College Outstanding Educator Award from the National Communication Association, and she currently serves as president of the Maryland Communication Association.

of others is one of the best antidotes to the unhappiness caused when a relationship ends. Tell your friends and family of your situation—in only general terms, if you prefer—and make it clear that you want support. Seek out people who are positive and nurturing. Avoid negative individuals who will paint the world in even darker tones. Make the distinction between seeking support and seeking advice. If you feel you need advice, seek out a professional.

Avoid Repeating Negative Patterns Many people repeat their mistakes. They enter second and third relationships with the same blinders, faulty preconceptions, or unrealistic expectations with which they entered earlier involvements. Instead, use the knowledge gained from your failed relationship to prevent repeating the same patterns.

At the same time, don't become a prophet of doom. Don't see in every relationship vestiges of the old. Don't jump at the first conflict and say, "Here it goes all over again." Treat the new relationship as the unique relationship it is. Don't evaluate it through past experiences. Use past relationships and experiences as guides, not filters.

Summary

This chapter elaborated on the stages that interpersonal relationships may pass through—development, maintenance, deterioration, repair, and dissolution.

Relationship Development

1. Several general theories of interpersonal relationships focus on relationship development; for example, uncertainty reduction, attraction, rules, social exchange, and equity theories.

2. The relationship license increases as relationships develop toward intimacy and becomes more restrictive as relationships move toward dissolution.

Relationship Maintenance

3. Reasons for maintaining a relationship include emotional attachment, convenience, children, fear, inertia, and commitment.

4. Maintenance behaviors include being nice, communicating, being open, giving assurances, sharing joint activities, being positive, and improving yourself.

Relationship Deterioration

5. Relationship deterioration involves the weakening of the bonds holding people together. It occurs when one or both parties are unhappy with the current state of the relationship.
6. Among the causes of relationship deterioration are poor communication, third-party relationships, relationship changes, sex- and work-related problems, financial difficulties, and unrealistic beliefs about relationships.
7. Among the negative effects of relationship deterioration may be the loss of the good times and positive interactions, a loss of self-esteem, and financial problems.
8. Among the communication changes that occur during relationship deterioration are verbal and nonverbal withdrawal, a decline in self-disclosure, an increase in deception, and an increase in negative messages and decrease in positive messages.

Relationship Repair

9. In relationship repair people endeavor to correct the problems that beset a relationship and to bring the relationship to a more intimate, more positive state.

10. General repair strategies include repair: Recognizing the problem, Engaging in productive communication and conflict resolution, Posing possible solutions, Affirming each other, Integrating solutions into normal behavior, and Risking.
11. Repair isn't necessarily a two-person process; one person can break unproductive and destructive cycles.

Relationship Dissolution

12. Dissolution is the breaking or dissolving of the bonds that hold the relationship together.
13. Among the reasons for relationship dissolution are that the relationship no longer serves the needs it was created to meet, becomes less "profitable," or verbally or physically abusive.
14. Among disengagement strategies are positive tone, negative identity management, justification, behavioral de-escalation, and de-escalation of exclusivity.
15. Among the suggestions for dealing with relationship breakup are to break the loneliness-depression cycle, take time out, bolster self-esteem, remove uncomfortable symbols, seek support, and avoid repeating negative patterns.

Key Terms

disengagement, **241**
empathy, **231**
jealousy, **233**

relationship deterioration, **234**
relationship development, **228**

relationship dissolution, **240**
relationship license, **228**

relationship maintenance, **229**
relationship repair, **237**

Critical Thinking Questions

1 One way to improve communication during difficult times is to ask your partner to engage in positive behaviors rather than to stop negative behaviors. Consider how you might use this suggestion to replace such statements as the following: (1) "I hate it when you ignore me at business functions." (2) "I can't stand going to these cheap restaurants; when are you going to start spending a few bucks?" (3) "Stop being so negative; you criticize everything and everyone."

2 What practical suggestions for dealing with relationship deterioration, repair, or dissolution do the theories of attraction, social exchange, and equity offer?

3 Consider one of your own relationships that dissolved. What causes can you identify? Can you identify advantages of this dissolution?

4 How would you explain the finding that when relationships break up, it's the more attractive person who leaves first? What other factors might account for who leaves first?

5 How would you describe the relationship licenses that exist in your own relationships? In what cases might relationship problems be created because of the relationship licenses that exist within the relationship?

Choice Points

1 *Projecting an Image.* You're entering a new job and want to be perceived as likable and friendly but also as serious and conscientious. Ask yourself: What types of messages might help you achieve your dual goal? Which might you try first?

2 *Complaining.* Your partner complains constantly; no matter what the situation, your partner has a complaint about it. It's

becoming painful to listen to this and you want to stop it. Ask yourself: What are some of the things you might do to help lessen the complaining? Alternatively, what might you be doing to encourage the complaints, and therefore what might you stop doing?

3 *Jealousy.* Your partner is excessively jealous—at least from your point of view. You can't meet other people or even communicate with them online without your partner questioning your fidelity. You're fed up. Ask yourself: What might you do to reduce (or ideally stop) this jealousy without destroying the relationship?

4 *Virtual Infidelity.* You discover that your partner of the last 15 years is being unfaithful with someone online (and in another country). You understand that generally such infidelity is seen as a consequence of a failure in communication (Young, Griffin-Shelley, Cooper, O'Mara, & Buchanan, 2000). You want to discover the extent of this online relationship and your partner's intentions in regard to this affair. Ask yourself: What choices do you have for opening up this topic for honest conversation without making your partner defensive and hence uncommunicative?

MyCommunicationLab Explorations

This group of experiences deals with interpersonal relationships and their development, maintenance, deterioration, repair, and dissolution. ❶ Interpersonal Relationships in Songs and Greeting Cards explores the way cards and songs talk about relationships. ❷ Applying Theories to Problems provides an opportunity to apply the theories discussed in the previous chapter to common relationship problems discussed here. ❸ Male and Female looks at gender differences in relationships. ❹ Changing the Distance between You illustrates how relationship changes can be made. ❺ Relational Repair from Advice Columnists encourages you to critically examine the advice given by relationship columnists. ❻ How Can You Get Someone to Like You? looks at affinity-seeking strategies and how they're used to change people's perceptions. ❼ How Might You Repair Relationships? presents a variety of relationship problems and asks you to apply the insights gained here and from your own experience in suggesting repair strategies.

11 Interpersonal Relationship Types: Friendship, Love, Family, and Workplace

Friendship	Workplace Relationships
Love	Relationship Violence
Family	

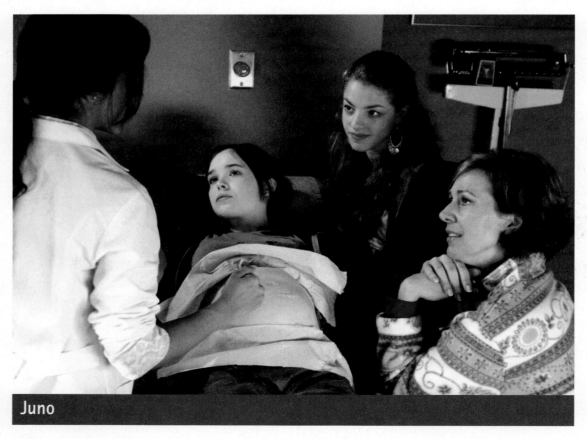

Juno

In *Juno* you see an excellent example of the interrelatedness among connected people—what happens to one person has an impact on friends, lovers, family, and extended others in various, often very different, ways. This interrelatedness is one of the themes of this chapter.

Now that the basic principles and stages of interpersonal relationships have been discussed, we can focus on specific relationship types. In this chapter we consider (1) friendship, (2) love, (3) family, and (4) workplace relationships, establishing what these are and exploring how interpersonal communication within each of these relationships can be made more effective. We'll also examine the dark side of some relationships in a section on relationship violence.

Friendship

Friendship has engaged the attention and imagination of poets, novelists, and artists of all kinds. On television, friendships have become almost as important as romantic pairings. And friendship also interests a range of interpersonal communication researchers (Samter, 2004). Throughout your life you'll meet many people, but out of this wide array you'll develop few relationships you would call friendships. Yet despite the low number of friendships you may form, their importance is great.

Definition and Characteristics

Friendship is an *interpersonal relationship* between two interdependent persons that is *mutually productive* and *characterized by mutual positive regard*. First, friendship is an interpersonal relationship; communication interactions must have taken place between the people. Further, the relationship involves a "personalistic focus" (Wright, 1978, 1984); friends react to each other as complete persons, as unique, genuine, and irreplaceable individuals.

Second, friendships must be mutually productive—they cannot be destructive to either person. Once destructiveness enters into a relationship, it can no longer be characterized as friendship. Lover relationships, marriage relationships, parent–child relationships, and just about any other possible relationship can be either destructive or productive, but friendship must enhance the potential of each person and can only be productive.

Third, friendships are characterized by mutual positive regard. Liking people is essential if we are to call them friends. Three major characteristics of friendship—trust, emotional support, and sharing of interests (Blieszner & Adams, 1992)—facilitate mutual positive regard.

When friends are especially close, the actions of one will impact more significantly on the other than they would if the friends were merely casual acquaintances. The closer friends are, the more interdependent they become. At the same time, however, the closer friends are, the more independent they are of, for example, the attitudes and behaviors of others. Also, the less they are influenced by the societal rules that govern more casual relationships. Close friends are likely to make up their own rules for interacting with each other; they decide what they will talk about and when, what they can say to each other without offending and what they can't, when and for what reasons they can call each other, and so on.

In North America friendships clearly are a matter of choice; you choose—within limits—who your friends will be. And most researchers define friendship as a voluntary relationship, a relationship of choice (Samter, 2004). The density of U.S. cities and the ease of communication and relocation does make many friendships voluntary. But throughout human history in many parts of the world—for example, in small villages miles away from urban centers, where people are born, live, and die without venturing much beyond their community—relationships traditionally have not been voluntary. In these settings you simply form relationships with those in your village. You don't have the luxury of selecting certain people to interact with and others to ignore. You must interact with and form friendships and romantic relationships with members of the community simply because these are the only people you come into contact with on a regular basis (Moghaddam, Taylor, & Wright, 1993). This situation is changing rapidly, however, as Internet use becomes near universal. With access to people from all over the world via the Internet, more and more relationships will become voluntary.

Friendship Types

Not all friendships are the same. But how do they differ? One way of answering this question is by distinguishing among three major types: friendships of reciprocity, receptivity, and association (Reisman, 1979, 1981).

The **friendship of reciprocity** is the ideal type, characterized by loyalty, self-sacrifice, mutual affection, and generosity. A friendship of reciprocity is based on equality: Each individual shares equally in giving and receiving the benefits and rewards of the relationship.

In the **friendship of receptivity**, in contrast, there is an imbalance in giving and receiving; one person is the primary giver and one the primary receiver. This is a positive imbalance, however, because each person gains something from the relationship. The different needs of both the person who receives and the person who gives affection are satisfied. This is the friendship that may develop between a teacher and a student or between a doctor and a patient. In fact, a difference in status is essential for the friendship of receptivity to develop.

The **friendship of association** is a transitory one. It might be described as a friendly relationship rather than a true friendship. Associative friendships are the kind we often have with classmates, neighbors, or coworkers. There is no great loyalty, no great trust, no great giving or receiving. The association is cordial but not intense.

Another way to look at friendship types is to compare face-to-face and online friendships. Not surprisingly, there is not yet enough research to draw clear distinctions between face-to-face and online friendships. Nevertheless, some differences are coming to light. For example, one study found that people viewed opposite-sex face-to-face friendships as more intimate than online friendships. Female–female online and face-to-face friendships, however, were rated equally—and male–male online friendships were rated as more intimate than face-to-face friendships (Haidar-Yassine, 2002). Another study found that face-to-face friendships involved more interdependence, greater breadth and depth, greater understanding, and greater commitment. Over time, however, as both types of friendships improved, the differences between face-to-face and online friendships decreased (Chan & Cheng, 2004).

Friendship Needs

For still another answer to the question of how friendships differ, consider the needs that friends serve. On the basis of your experiences or your predictions, you select as friends those who will help to satisfy your basic growth needs. Selecting friends on the basis of need satisfaction is similar to choosing a marriage partner, an employee, or any person who may be in a position to satisfy your needs. Thus, for example, if you need to be the center of attention or to be popular, you might select friends who allow you, and even encourage you, to be the center of attention or who tell you, verbally and nonverbally, that you're popular.

As your needs change, the qualities you look for in friendships also change. In many instances, old friends are dropped from your close circle to be replaced by new friends who better serve these new needs. One way to analyze the needs that friendships serve is to consider the values or rewards that you seek to gain through your friendships (Wright 1978, 1984). For example, depending on your needs, you may look for friends such as these:

- *Utility:* Someone who may have special talents, skills, or resources that will prove useful to you in achieving your specific goals and needs. For example, might you become friends with someone who is particularly bright, because such a person might assist you in getting better grades, in solving problems, or in getting a better job?
- *Affirmation:* Someone who will affirm your personal value and help you to recognize your attributes. For example, might you develop a friendship with someone because of that person's appreciation of your leadership abilities, your athletic prowess, or your sense of humor?
- *Ego support:* Someone who behaves in a supportive, encouraging, and helpful manner. For example, would you seek friendships that would help you view yourself as worthy and competent?
- *Stimulation:* Someone who introduces you to new ideas and new ways of seeing the world and helps you to expand your worldview. For example, would you form friendships with those who might bring you into contact with previously unfamiliar people, issues, religions, cultures, and experiences?
- *Security:* Someone who does nothing to hurt you or to emphasize or call attention to your inadequacies or weaknesses. For example, would you select friends because you wouldn't have to worry about their betraying you or making negative comments about you?

These benefits of face-to-face friends are very similar to those found for online friends: According to researchers, among the benefits of online friendships are recreation, support, safety, diversity, and networking possibilities (Reiner & Blanton, 1997).

Friendship and Communication

Friendships develop over time in stages. At one end of the friendship continuum are strangers, or two persons who have just met, and at the other end are intimate friends. What happens between these two extremes?

As you progress from the initial contact stage to intimate friendship, the depth and breadth of communications increase (see Chapter 9). You talk about issues that are closer and closer to your inner core. Similarly, the number of communication topics increases as your friendship becomes closer. As depth and breadth increase, so does the satisfaction you derive from the friendship. This increase in depth and breadth can and does occur in all forms of communication—face-to-face as well as online. It's interesting to note that establishing and maintaining friendships are the major reasons for Internet communication (instant messaging and texting, social network sites, and e-mail) among college students and among teens (Knox, Daniels, Sturdivant, & Zusman, 2001; Lenhart, Madden, Macgill, & Smith, 2007). And, not surprisingly, these forms of communication promote closeness and intimacy and often encourage online partners to meet face-to-face (Hu, Wood, Smith, & Westbrook, 2004).

Earlier (Chapter 9) we looked at the concept of dynamic tension in relationships, noting that there is a tension between, for example, autonomy and connection—the desire to be an individual but also to be connected to another person. Friendships also are defined by dynamic tensions (Rawlins, 1983). One tension is between the impulse to be open and to reveal personal thoughts and feelings on the one hand, and the impulse to protect yourself by not revealing personal information on the other. Also, there is the tension between being open and candid with your friend and being discreet. Because of these contradictory impulses, friendships don't always follow a straight path of increasing openness and candor. This is not to say that openness and candor don't increase as you progress from initial to casual to close friendships; they do. But the pattern does not follow a straight line; throughout the friendship development process, there are tensions that periodically restrict openness and candor.

There also are regressions that may temporarily pull the friendship back to a less intimate stage. Friendships stabilize at a level that is comfortable to both persons; some friendships will remain casual and others will remain close. Again, although friendship is presented in stages, there is not always a smooth progression to ever-increasing intimacy.

With these qualifications in mind, we can discuss three stages of friendship development and integrate some of the characteristics of effective interpersonal communication identified in Understanding Interpersonal Skills boxes (cf. Johnson, Wittenberg, Villagran, Mazur, & Villagran, 2003). The assumption made here is that as the friendship progresses from initial contact and acquaintanceship through casual friendship to close and intimate friendship, effective interpersonal communication increases. However, there is no assumption made that close relationships are necessarily the preferred type or that they're better than casual or temporary relationships. We need all types.

Contact The first stage of friendship development is an initial contact of some kind. This does not mean that what happened prior to the encounter is unimportant—quite the contrary. In fact, your prior history of friendships, your personal needs, and your readiness for friendship development are extremely important in determining whether the relationship will develop.

At the contact stage, the characteristics of effective interpersonal communication are usually present to only a small degree. You're guarded rather than open or expressive, lest you reveal aspects of yourself that might be viewed negatively. Because you don't yet know the other person, your ability to empathize with or to orient yourself significantly to the other is limited, and the relationship—at this stage, at least—is probably viewed as too temporary to be worth the effort. Because the other person is not well known to you, supportiveness, positiveness, and equality would all be difficult to manifest in any meaningful sense. The characteristics demonstrated are probably more the result of politeness than any genuine expression of positive regard.

At this stage, there is little genuine immediacy; you see yourselves as separate and distinct rather than as a unit. Any confidence that is demonstrated is probably more a function of the individual personalities than of the relationship. Because the relationship is so new and because the people don't know each other very well, the interaction often is characterized by awkwardness—for example, by overlong pauses, uncertainty about topics to be discussed, and ineffective exchanges of speaker and listener roles.

Involvement   In this second stage there is a dyadic consciousness, a clear sense of "we-ness," of togetherness; communication demonstrates a sense of immediacy. At this stage you participate in activities as a unit rather than as separate individuals. In the involvement period the other person is a casual friend—someone we would go with to the movies, sit with in the cafeteria or in class, or ride home with from school.

At this casual friendship stage, the qualities of effective interpersonal interaction begin to be seen more clearly. You start to express yourself openly and become interested in the other person's disclosures. You begin to own your feelings and thoughts and respond openly to his or her communications. Because you're beginning to understand this person, you empathize and demonstrate significant other-orientation. You also demonstrate supportiveness and develop a genuinely positive attitude both toward the other person and toward mutual communication situations. As you learn this person's needs and wants, you can stroke more effectively.

There is an ease at this stage, a coordination in the interaction between the two persons. You communicate with confidence, maintain appropriate eye contact and flexibility in body posture and gesturing, and use few of the adaptors that signal discomfort.

Close and Intimate Friendship   At the stage of close and intimate friendship, there is an intensification of the casual friendship; you and your friend see yourselves more as an exclusive unit, and each of you derives greater benefits (for example, emotional support) from intimate friendship than from casual friendship (Hays, 1989).

Because you know each other well (for example, you know each other's values, opinions, and attitudes), your uncertainty about each other has been significantly reduced—you're able to predict each other's behaviors with considerable accuracy. This knowledge makes significant interaction management possible, as well as greater positivity, supportiveness, and openness (Oswald, Clark, & Kelly, 2004). Similarly, it would seem logical to predict that you would be able to read the other's nonverbal signals more accurately and could use these signals as guides to your interactions—avoiding certain topics at certain times or offering consolation on the basis of facial expressions. However, there is some evidence to suggest that less close friends are better at judging when someone is concealing sadness and anger than are close and intimate friends (Sternglanz & DePaulo, 2004). In any case, at this stage you exchange significant messages of affection: messages that express fondness, liking, loving, and caring for the other person. Openness, self-disclosure, and emotional support become more important than shared activities (Fehr, 2004).

You become more other-oriented and more willing to make significant sacrifices for the other person. You'll go far out of your way for the benefit of this friend, and the friend does the same for you. You empathize and exchange perspectives a great deal more, and you expect in return that your friend will also empathize with you. With a genuinely positive feeling for this individual, your supportiveness and positive stroking become spontaneous. Because you see yourselves as an exclusive unit, equality and immediacy are in clear evidence. You view this friend as one who is important in your life; as a result, conflicts—inevitable in all close relationships—are important to resolve through compromise and understanding rather than through, for example, refusal to negotiate or a show of force.

You're willing to respond openly, confidently, and expressively to this person and to own your feelings and thoughts. Your supportiveness and positiveness are genuine expressions of the closeness you feel for this person. Each person in an intimate friendship is truly equal; each can initiate and each can respond; each can be active and each can be passive; each speaks and each listens.

Friendship, Culture, Gender, and Technology

Your friendships and the way you look at friendships will be influenced by your culture and gender and by technology. Let's look first at culture.

Culture and Friendships In the United States you can be friends with someone yet never really be expected to go much out of your way for this person. Many Middle Easterners, Asians, and Latin Americans would consider going significantly out of their way an absolutely essential ingredient in friendship; if you're not willing to sacrifice for your friend, then this person is not really your friend (Dresser, 2005).

Generally friendships are closer in collectivist cultures than in individualist cultures (see Chapter 2). In their emphasis on the group and on cooperating, collectivist cultures foster the development of close friendship bonds. Members of a collectivist culture are expected to help others in the group. When you help or do things for someone else, you increase your own attractiveness to this person, and this is certainly a good start for a friendship. Of course, the culture continues to reward these close associations.

Members of individualist cultures, on the other hand, are expected to look out for Number One, themselves. Consequently, they're more likely to compete and to try to do better than each other—conditions that don't support, generally at least, the development of friendships.

As noted in Chapter 2, these characteristics are extremes; most people have both collectivist and individualist values but have them in different degrees, and that is what we are talking about here—differences in degree of collectivist and individualist orientation.

Gender and Friendships Gender also influences your friendships—who becomes your friend and the way you look at friendships. Perhaps the best-documented finding—already noted in our discussion of self-disclosure—is that women self-disclose more than men (e.g., Dolgin, Meyer, & Schwartz, 1991). This difference holds throughout male and female friendships. Male friends self-disclose less often and with less intimate details than female friends do. Men generally don't view intimacy as a necessary quality of their friendships (Hart, 1990).

Women engage in significantly more affectional behaviors with their friends than do males; this difference may account for the greater difficulty men experience in beginning and maintaining close friendships (Hays, 1989). Women engage in more casual communication; they also share greater intimacy and more confidences with their friends than do men. Communication, in all its forms and functions, seems a much more important dimension of women's friendships.

When women and men were asked to evaluate their friendships, women rated their same-sex friendships higher in general quality, intimacy, enjoyment, and nurturance than did men (Sapadin, 1988). Men, in contrast, rated their opposite-sex friendships higher in quality, enjoyment, and nurturance than did women. Both men and women rated their opposite-sex friendships similarly in intimacy. These differences may be due, in part, to our society's suspicion of male friendships; as a result, a man may be reluctant to admit to having close relationship bonds with another man.

Men's friendships are often built around shared activities—attending a ball game, playing cards, working on a project at the office. Women's friendships, on the other hand, are built more around a sharing of feelings, support, and "personalism." An important element is similarity in status, in willingness to protect a friend in uncomfortable situations, and in academic major.

As we move further into the twenty-first century, the ways in which men and women develop and maintain their friendships will undoubtedly change considerably—as will all gender-related variables. In the meantime, given the present state of research in gender differences, be careful not to exaggerate and to treat small differences as if they were highly significant. Avoid stereotypes and avoid stressing opposites to the neglect of the huge number of similarities between men and women (Wright, 1988; Deaux & LaFrance, 1998).

Further, friendship researchers warn that even when we find differences, the reasons for them aren't always clear (Blieszner & Adams, 1992). Interesting examples are the findings that middle-aged men have more

Ethics in Interpersonal Communication

Relationship Ethics

The ethical issues and guidelines that operate within a friendship, romantic, family, or workplace relationship can be reviewed with the acronym ETHICS—empathy (Cheney & Tompkins, 1987), talk rather than force, honesty (Krebs, 1989), interaction management, confidentiality, and supportiveness (Johannesen, 2001).

- *Empathy:* People in relationships have an ethical obligation to try to understand what other individuals are feeling as well as thinking from those individuals' points of view.
- *Talk:* Decisions in a relationship should be arrived at by talk rather than by force—by persuasion, not by coercion.
- *Honesty:* Relationship communication should be honest and truthful.
- *Interaction management:* Relationship communication should be satisfying and comfortable and is the responsibility of all individuals.
- *Confidentiality:* People have a right to expect that what they say in confidence will not be revealed to others.
- *Supportiveness:* A supportive and cooperative climate should characterize the interpersonal interactions of people in relationships.

What would you do?

You're managing a team to select an architect for your company's new office complex. The problem is that Jack doesn't do any work and misses most of the meetings. You spoke with him about it, and he confided that he's going through a divorce and can't concentrate on the project. You feel sorry for Jack and have been carrying him for the last few months but realize now that you'll never be able to bring the project in on time if you don't replace Jack. Also, you don't want to get a negative appraisal because of Jack. What would you do in this situation?

---

friends than middle-aged women and that women have more intimate friendships (Fischer & Oliker, 1983). How can we explain these findings? Do men have more friends because they're friendlier than women, or because they have more opportunities to develop such friendships? Do women have more intimate friends because they have more opportunities to pursue such friendships, or because they have a greater psychological capacity for intimacy?

Technology and Friendships Perhaps even more obvious than the impact of culture of gender is the influence of technology on interpersonal relationships. Clearly, online interpersonal relationships are on the increase. The number of Internet users is rapidly increasing, and social networking sites such as Facebook and MySpace make it increasingly easy and interesting both to meet new friends and to keep in touch with old friends.

As relationships develop on the Internet, **network convergence** occurs; that is, as a relationship between two people develops, they begin to share their network of other communicators with each other (Parks, 1995; Parks & Floyd, 1996). This, of course, is similar to relationships formed through face-to-face contact. Online work groups, too, are on the increase and have been found to be more task oriented and more efficient than face-to-face groups (Lantz, 2001). Online groups also provide a sense of belonging that may once have been thought possible only through face-to-face interactions (Silverman, 2001).

Love

Of all the qualities of interpersonal relationships, none seems as important as love. "We are all born for love," noted famed British prime minister Benjamin Disraeli. "It is the principle of existence and its only end." **Love** is a feeling characterized by closeness and caring and by intimacy, passion, and commitment. It's also an interpersonal relationship developed, maintained, and sometimes destroyed through communication—and at the same time a relationship that can be greatly enhanced with communication skills (Dindia & Timmerman, 2003).

Although there are many theories about love, the conceptualization that captured the attention of interpersonal researchers and continues to receive research support is a model proposing that there is not one but six types of love (Lee, 1976; Kanemasa, Taniguchi, Daibo & Ishimori, 2004). View the descriptions of each type as broad characterizations that are generally but not always true. As a preface to this discussion of the types of love, you may wish to respond to the self-test "What Kind of Lover Are You?"

✐ TEST YOURSELF

WHAT KIND OF LOVER ARE YOU?

Respond to each of the following statements with T for true (if you believe the statement to be a generally accurate representation of your attitudes about love) or F for false (if you believe the statement does not adequately represent your attitudes about love).

_____ 1. My lover and I have the right physical "chemistry" between us.
_____ 2. I feel that my lover and I were meant for each other.
_____ 3. My lover and I really understand each other.
_____ 4. I believe that what my lover doesn't know about me won't hurt him or her.
_____ 5. My lover would get upset if he or she knew of some of the things I've done with other people.
_____ 6. When my lover gets too dependent on me, I want to back off a little.
_____ 7. I expect to always be friends with my lover.
_____ 8. Our love is really a deep friendship, not a mysterious, mystical emotion.
_____ 9. Our love relationship is the most satisfying because it developed from a good friendship.
_____ 10. In choosing my lover, I believed it was best to love someone with a similar background.
_____ 11. An important factor in choosing a partner is whether or not he or she would be a good parent.
_____ 12. One consideration in choosing my lover was how he or she would reflect on my career.
_____ 13. Sometimes I get so excited about being in love with my lover that I can't sleep.
_____ 14. When my lover doesn't pay attention to me, I feel sick all over.
_____ 15. I cannot relax if I suspect that my lover is with someone else.
_____ 16. I would rather suffer myself than let my lover suffer.
_____ 17. When my lover gets angry with me, I still love him or her fully and unconditionally.
_____ 18. I would endure all things for the sake of my lover.

HOW DID YOU DO? This scale, from Hendrick and Hendrick (1990), is based on the work of John Alan Lee (1976), as is the discussion of the six types of love that follows. The statements refer to the six types of love that we discuss in this section: eros, ludus, storge, pragma, mania, and agape. "True" answers represent your agreement and "false" answers your disagreement with the type of love to which the statements refer. Statements 1–3 are characteristic of the eros lover. If you answered true to these statements, you have a strong eros component to your love style. If you answered false, you have a weak eros component. Statements 4–6 refer to ludus love, 7–9 refer to storge love, 10–12 to pragma love, 13–15 to manic love, and 16–18 to agapic love.

WHAT WILL YOU DO? What things might you do to become more aware of the different love styles and to become a more well-rounded lover? How might you go about incorporating the qualities of effective interpersonal communication—for example, being more flexible, more polite, and more other-oriented—to become a more responsive, more exciting, more playful love partner?

Source: From "A Relationship Specific Version of the Love Attitude Scale" by C. Hendrick and S. Hendrick, *Journal of Social Behavior and Personality 5*, 1990. Reprinted by permission of Select Press.

Love Types

Let's look at each of Lee's (1976, 1988) six types of love:

- *Eros: Beauty and sexuality* (Statements 1–3 in the self-test). Like Narcissus, who fell in love with the beauty of his own image, the erotic lover focuses on beauty and physical

attractiveness, sometimes to the exclusion of qualities you might consider more important and more lasting. Also like Narcissus, the erotic lover has an idealized image of beauty that is unattainable in reality. Consequently, the erotic lover often feels unfulfilled. Not surprisingly, erotic lovers are particularly sensitive to physical imperfections in the ones they love.

- *Ludus: Entertainment and excitement* (Statements 4–6). Ludus love is experienced as a game, as fun. The better you can play the game, the greater the enjoyment. Love is not to be taken too seriously; emotions are to be held in check lest they get out of hand and make trouble; passions never rise to the point where they get out of control. A ludic lover is self-controlled, always aware of the need to manage love rather than allow it to be in control. Perhaps because of this need to control love, some researchers have proposed that ludic love tendencies may reveal tendencies to sexual aggression (Sarwer, Kalichman, Johnson, Early, et al., 1993). Not surprisingly, the ludic lover retains a partner only as long as the partner is interesting and amusing. When interest fades, it's time to change partners. Perhaps because love is a game, sexual fidelity is of little importance. In fact, recent research shows that people who score high on ludic love are more likely to engage in "extradyadic" dating and sex than those who score low on ludus (Wiederman & Hurd, 1999). And, not surprisingly, ludic lovers score high on narcissism (Campbell, Foster, & Finkel, 2002).

- *Storge: Peaceful and slow* (Statements 7–9). Storge love (a word that come from the Greek for "familial love") lacks passion and intensity. Storgic lovers set out not to find lovers but to establish a companionable relationship with someone they know and with whom they can share interests and activities. Storgic love is a gradual process of unfolding thoughts and feelings; the changes seem to come so slowly and so gradually that it's often difficult to define exactly where the relationship is at any point in time. Sex in storgic relationships comes late, and when it comes, it assumes no great importance.

- *Pragma: Practical and traditional* (Statements 10–12). The pragma lover is practical and seeks a relationship that will work. Pragma lovers want compatibility and a relationship in which their important needs and desires will be satisfied. They're concerned with the social qualifications of a potential mate even more than with personal qualities; family and background are extremely important to the pragma lover, who relies not so much on feelings as on logic. The pragma lover views love as a useful relationship that makes the rest of life easier. So the pragma lover asks such questions about a potential mate as "Will this person earn a good living?" "Can this person cook?" "Will this person help me advance in my career?" Pragma lovers' relationships rarely deteriorate. This is partly because pragma lovers choose their mates carefully and emphasize similarities. Another reason is that they have realistic romantic expectations.

- *Mania: Elation and depression* (Statements 13–15). Mania is characterized by extreme highs and extreme lows. The manic lover loves intensely and at the same time intensely worries about the loss of the love. This fear often prevents the manic lover from deriving as much pleasure as possible from the relationship. With little provocation, the manic lover may experience extreme jealousy. Manic love is obsessive; the manic lover must possess the beloved completely. In return, the manic lover wishes to be possessed, to be loved intensely. The manic lover's poor self-image seems capable of being improved only by love; self-worth comes from being loved rather than from any sense of inner satisfaction. Because love is so important, danger signs in a relationship are often ignored; the manic lover believes that if there is love, then nothing else matters.

- *Agape: Compassionate and selfless* (Statements 16–18). Agape is a compassionate, egoless, self-giving love. The agapic lover loves even people with whom he or she has no close ties. This lover loves the stranger on the road even though the two of them probably will never meet again. Agape is a spiritual love, offered without concern for personal reward or gain. This lover loves without expecting that the love will be reciprocated. Jesus, Buddha, and Gandhi preached this unqualified love, agape (Lee, 1976). In one sense, agape is more a philosophical kind of love than a love that most people have the strength to achieve. Not surprisingly people who believe in *yuan*, a Chinese concept that comes from the Buddhist belief in predestiny, are more likely to favor agapic (and pragmatic) love and less likely to favor erotic love (Goodwin & Findlay, 1997).

Each of these varieties of love can combine with others to form new and different patterns (for example, manic and ludic or storge and pragma). These six, however, identify the major types of love and illustrate the complexity of any love relationship. The six styles should also make it clear that different people want different things, that each person seeks satisfaction in a unique way. The love that may seem lifeless or crazy or boring to you may be ideal for someone else. At the same time, another person may see these very same negative qualities in the love you're seeking.

Remember, too, that love changes. A relationship that began as pragma may develop into ludus or eros. A relationship that began as erotic may develop into mania or storge. One approach sees this developmental process as having three major stages (Duck, 1986):

VIEWPOINT Researcher Robert Sternberg defines love as a combination of intimacy, passion, and commitment (Sternberg, 1986, 1988; Lemieux & Hale, 1999, 2001). *Intimacy*, the emotional aspect of love, includes sharing, communicating, and mutual support. *Passion*, the motivational aspect, consists of physical attraction and romantic passion. *Commitment*, the cognitive aspect, consists of the decisions you make concerning your lover. When you have all three aspects to about equal degrees, you have complete or consummate love. How does this definition match the meaning that you have for "love"?

- First stage: Eros, mania, and ludus (initial attraction)
- Second stage: Storge (as the relationship develops)
- Third stage: Pragma (as relationship bonds develop)

Love and Communication

How do you communicate when you're in love? What do you say? What do you do nonverbally? According to research, you exaggerate your beloved's virtues and minimize his or her faults. You share emotions and experiences and speak tenderly, with an extra degree of courtesy, to each other; "please," "thank you," and similar polite expressions abound. You frequently use "personalized communication." This type of communication includes secrets you keep from other people and messages that have meaning only within your specific relationship (Knapp, Ellis, & Williams, 1980). You also create and use personal idioms (and pet names): words, phrases, and gestures that carry meaning only for the particular relationship and that say you have a special language that signifies your special bond (Hopper, Knapp, & Scott, 1981). When outsiders try to use personal idioms—as they sometimes do—the expressions seem inappropriate, at times even an invasion of privacy.

You engage in significant self-disclosure. There is more confirmation and less disconfirmation among lovers than among either nonlovers or those who are going through romantic breakups. Not surprisingly, you also use more constructive conflict resolution strategies (see Chapter 12) if you feel your relationship is threatened (Gonzaga, Keltner, Londahl, & Smith, 2001). You're highly aware of what is and is not appropriate to say to the person you love. You know how to reward, but also how to punish, each other. In short, you know what to do to obtain the reaction you want.

Among your most often used means for communicating love are telling the person face-to-face or by telephone (in one survey 79 percent indicated they did it this way), expressing supportiveness, and talking things out and cooperating (Marston, Hecht, & Robers, 1987).

Nonverbally, you also communicate your love. Prolonged and focused eye contact is perhaps the clearest nonverbal indicator of love. So important is eye contact that its avoidance almost always triggers a "what's wrong?" response. You also have longer periods of silence than you do with friends (Guerrero, 1997). In addition, you display affiliative cues (signs that show you love the other person), including head nods, gestures, and forward leaning. And you give Duchenne smiles—smiles that are beyond voluntary control and that signal

In reading about the love styles, you may have felt that certain personality types are likely to favor one type of love over another. Here are personality traits that research finds people assign to each love style (Taraban & Hendrick 1995).

Which set of adjectives describing personality characteristics would you match with each love style (eros, ludus, storge, pragma, mania, and agape)?

1. inconsiderate, secretive, dishonest, selfish, and dangerous
2. honest, loyal, mature, caring, loving, and understanding
3. jealous, possessive, obsessed, emotional, and dependent
4. sexual, exciting, loving, happy, optimistic
5. committed, giving, caring, self-sacrificing, and loving
6. family-oriented, planning, careful, hard-working, and concerned

Very likely you perceived these personality factors in the same way as did the participants in research from which these traits were drawn: 1 = ludus, 2 = storge, 3 = mania, 4 = eros, 5 = agape, and 6 = pragma. Do note, of course, that these results do not imply that ludus lovers *are* inconsiderate, secretive, and dishonest. They merely mean that people in general (and perhaps you in particular) *think* of ludus lovers as inconsiderate, secretive, and dishonest.

Working with Theories and Research

How would you go about furthering this research on love styles and personality? What type of research might you undertake to increase our understanding of the relationship of personality and love style?

genuine joy (Gonzaga, Keltner, Londahl, & Smith, 2001). These smiles give you crow's-feet around the eyes, raise up your cheeks, and puff up the lower eyelids (Lemonick, 2005a).

You grow more aware not only of your loved one but also of your own physical self. Your muscle tone is heightened, for example. When you're in love you engage in preening gestures, especially immediately prior to meeting your lover, and you position your body attractively—stomach pulled in, shoulders square, legs arranged in appropriate masculine or feminine positions. Your speech may even have a somewhat different vocal quality. There is some evidence to show that sexual excitement enlarges the nasal membranes, which introduces a certain nasal quality into the voice (Davis, 1973).

You eliminate socially taboo adaptors, at least in the presence of the loved one. For example, you curtail scratching your head, picking your teeth, cleaning your ears, and passing wind. Interestingly enough, these adaptors often return after lovers have achieved a permanent relationship.

You touch more frequently and more intimately (Guerrero, 1997; Anderson, 2004). You also use more "tie signs," nonverbal gestures that show that you're together, such as holding hands, walking with arms entwined, kissing, and the like. You may even dress alike. The styles of clothes and even the colors selected by lovers are more similar than those worn by nonlovers.

Love, Culture, Gender, and Technology

Like friendship, love is heavily influenced by culture, gender, and technology (Dion & Dion, 1996; Wood & Smith, 2005). Let's consider first some of the cultural influences on the way you look at love and perhaps on the type of love you're seeking or maintaining.

Culture and Love Although most of the research on the six love styles has been done in the United States, some research has been conducted in other cultures (Bierhoff & Klein, 1991).

Asians have been found to be more friendship oriented in their love style than are Europeans (Dion & Dion, 1993b). Members of individualist cultures (for example, Europeans) are likely to place greater emphasis on romantic love and on individual fulfillment. Members of collectivist cultures are likely to spread their love over a large network of relatives

(Dion & Dion, 1993a). When compared to their Chinese counterparts, American men scored higher on ludic and agapic love and lower on erotic and pragma love. American men also are less likely to view emotional satisfaction as crucial to relationship maintenance (Sprecher & Toro-Morn, 2002).

One study finds a love style among Mexicans characterized as calm, compassionate, and deliberate (Leon, Philbrick, Parra, Escobedo, et al., 1994). In comparisons between love styles in the United States and France, it was found that people in the United States scored higher on storge and mania than the French; in contrast, the French scored higher on agape (Murstein, Merighi, & Vyse, 1991). In the United States Caucasian women scored higher on mania than African American women, whereas African American women scored higher on agape. Caucasian and African American men, however, scored very similarly; no statistically significant differences were found (Morrow, Clark, & Brock, 1995).

Gender and Love Gender also influences love. In the United States the differences between men and women in love are considered great. In poetry, novels, and the mass media, women and men are depicted as acting very differently when falling in love, being in love, and ending a love relationship. As Lord Byron put it in *Don Juan*, "Man's love is of man's life a thing apart, / 'Tis woman's whole existence." Women are portrayed as emotional, men as logical. Women are supposed to love intensely; men are supposed to love with detachment.

Women and men seem to experience love to a similar degree, and research continues to find great similarities between men's and women's conceptions of love (Rubin, 1973; Fehr & Broughton, 2001). However, women indicate greater love than men do for their same-sex friends. This may reflect a real difference between the sexes, or it may be a function of the greater social restrictions on men. A man is not supposed to admit his love for another man. Women are permitted greater freedom to communicate their love for other women.

Men and women also differ in the types of love they prefer (Hendrick, Hendrick, Foote, & Slapion-Foote, 1984). For example, on one version of the love self-test presented earlier, men scored higher on erotic and ludic love, whereas women scored higher on manic, pragmatic, and storgic love. No difference was found for agapic love.

Research finds that boys and girls differ somewhat in the age at which they first have sex. For example, a study in 2002 found that approximately 13 percent of girls and 15 percent of boys had sex before the age of 15. Interestingly enough, these percentages were lower than the figures from 1995, which were 19 percent for girls and 21 percent for boys (www.guttmacher.org, September 2006, accessed March 8, 2008). Boys and young men also report higher rates of sexual activity than do girls and young women (Regan et al., 2004). In the United States females marry for the first time at a younger age than men; in 2003 the median age for first marriage was 25.3 for females and 27.1 for males (www.census.gov, accessed August 19, 2005).

Much research finds that men place more emphasis on romance than women. For example, when college students were asked the question "If a man (woman) had all the other qualities you desired, would you marry this person if you were not in love with him (her)?" Approximately two-thirds of the men responded no, which seems to indicate that a high percentage were concerned with love and romance. However, less than one-third of the women responded no (LeVine, Sato, Hashimoto, & Verma, 1994). Further, when men and women were surveyed concerning their view on love—whether basically realistic or basically romantic—it was found that married women had a more realistic (less romantic) conception of love than did married men (Knapp & Vangelisti, 2009).

VIEWPOINT Men and women from different cultures were asked the following question: "If a man (woman) had all the other qualities you desired, would you marry this person if you were not in love with him (her)?" Results varied from one culture to another (Levine, Sato, Hashimoto, & Verma, 1994). For example, 50 percent of the respondents from Pakistan said yes, 49 percent of those from India said yes, and 19 percent from Thailand said yes. At the other extreme were those from Japan (only 2 percent said yes), the United States (only 3.5 percent said yes), and Brazil (only 4 percent said yes). How would you answer this question? How is your answer influenced by your culture?

Additional research also supports the view that men are more romantic. For example, "Men are more likely than women to believe in love at first sight, in love as the basis for marriage and for overcoming obstacles, and to believe that their partner and relationship will be perfect" (Sprecher & Metts, 1989). This difference seems to increase as the romantic relationship develops: Men become more romantic and women less romantic (Fengler, 1974).

One further gender difference may be noted, and that is the difference between men and women in breaking up a relationship (Blumstein & Schwartz, 1983; cf., Janus & Janus, 1993). Popular myth would have us believe that most love affairs break up as a result of the man's outside affair. But the research does not support this. When surveyed as to the reason for breaking up, only 15 percent of the men indicated that it was their interest in another partner, whereas 32 percent of the women noted this as a cause of the breakup. These findings are consistent with their partners' perceptions as well: 30 percent of the men (but only 15 percent of the women) noted that their partner's interest in another person was the reason for the breakup.

In their reactions to broken romantic affairs, women and men exhibit similarities and differences. For example, the tendency for women and men to recall only pleasant memories and to revisit places with past associations was about equal. However, men engaged in more dreaming about the lost partner and in more daydreaming generally as a reaction to the breakup than did women.

Technology and Love Perhaps even more important than culture and gender is the influence of technology on romantic relationships. In face-to-face relationships, you perceive the other person through nonverbal cues—you see the person's eyes, face, body—and you form impressions immediately. In online relationships of just a few years ago, physical attractiveness was signaled exclusively through words and self-descriptions (Levine, 2000). Under those circumstances, as you can appreciate, the face-to-face encounter strongly favored those who were physically attractive, whereas the online encounter favored those who were verbally adept at self-presentation and did not disadvantage less attractive individuals. Now, with photos, videos, and voice a part of many online dating and social networking sites, this distinction is fading—though it is probably not entirely erased. Certainly the face-to-face encounter still provides more nonverbal cues about the physical person.

Women, it seems, are more likely to form relationships on the Internet than men. About 72 percent of women and 55 percent of men had formed personal relationships online (Parks & Floyd, 1996). Not surprisingly, those who communicated more frequently formed more relationships.

There are many advantages to establishing relationships online. For example, online relationships are safe in terms of avoiding the potential for physical violence or sexually transmitted diseases. Unlike relationships established in face-to-face encounters, in which physical appearance tends to outweigh personality, Internet communication reveals people's inner qualities first. Rapport and mutual self-disclosure become more important than physical attractiveness in promoting intimacy (Cooper & Sportolari, 1997). And, contrary to some popular opinion, online relationships rely just as heavily on the ideals of trust, honesty, and commitment as do face-to-face relationships (Whitty & Gavin, 2001). Friendship and romantic interaction on the Internet are a natural boon to shut-ins and extremely shy people, for whom traditional ways of meeting others are often difficult. Computer talk is empowering for those with "physical disabilities or disfigurements," for whom face-to-face interactions are often superficial and often end with withdrawal (Lea & Spears, 1995; Bull & Rumsey, 1988). By eliminating the physical cues, computer talk equalizes the interaction and doesn't put the disfigured person, for example, at an immediate disadvantage in a society where physical attractiveness is so highly valued. On the Internet you're free to reveal as much or as little about your physical self as you wish, when you wish.

Another obvious advantage is that the number of people you can reach is so vast that it's relatively easy to find someone who matches what you're looking for. The situation is like finding a book that covers just what you need from a library of millions of volumes rather than from a collection holding only several thousand.

Of course, there are also disadvantages. For one thing, and depending on the technology you're using, you may not be able to see the other person in an online encounter. And even if you exchange photos, how certain can you be that the photos are of the person or that they were taken recently? In addition, you may not be able to hear the person's voice, and this too hinders you as you seek to develop a total picture of the other person.

Online, people can present a false self with little chance of detection; minors may present themselves as adults, and adults may present themselves as children in order to conduct illicit sexual communications and perhaps meetings. Similarly, people can present themselves as poor when they're rich, as mature when they're immature, as serious and committed when they're just enjoying the online experience. Although people can also misrepresent themselves in face-to-face relationships, the fact that it's easier to do online probably accounts for the greater frequency of misrepresentation in computer relationships (Cornwell & Lundgren, 2001).

Another potential disadvantage—though some might argue it is actually an advantage—is that computer interactions may become all consuming and may take the place of face-to-face interpersonal relationships.

Family

If you had to define the term **family**, you might reply that a family consists of a husband, a wife, and one or more children. When pressed, you might add that some families also include other relatives—in-laws, brothers and sisters, grandparents, aunts and uncles, and so on. But other types of relationships are, to their own members, "families." Table 11.1 provides a few statistics on the family as constituted in 1970 and in 2002.

TABLE 11.1 The Changing Face of the American Family

Here are a few statistics on the nature of the American family for 1970 and 2002, as reported by the *New York Times Almanac 2008* and *The World Almanac and Book of Facts 2008*, along with some trends these figures may indicate. What other trends do you see occurring in the family?

Family Characteristic	1970	2002	Trends
Number of members in average family	3.58	3.21	Reflects the tendency toward smaller families
Families without children	44.1%	52%	Reflects the growing number of families that are opting not to have children
Families headed by married couples	86.8%	76.3%	Reflects the growing trend for heterosexual couples to live as a family without marriage, for singles to have children, and for gay men and lesbians to form families
Females as heads of households	10.7%	17.7%	Reflects the growing number of women who have children without marriage and the increase in divorce and separation
Married-couple families	86.8%	76.3%	Reflects the growing trend for couples to form families without being married
Single-parent families	13%	27.8%	Reflects the growing trend for women (especially) to maintain families without a partner
Households headed by never-married women with children	248,000	4.3 million	Reflects the growing trend for women to have children and maintain a family without marriage
Children living with only one parent	12%	23%	Reflects the growing divorce rate and the increased number of children born to unwed mothers
Children between 25 and 34 living at home with parents	8% (11.9 million)	9.3% (19.2 million)	Reflects the increased economic difficulty of establishing a household and perhaps the increased divorce rate and later dates for marriage (especially true for men)

Ask the Researcher

Dysfunctional Family Patterns

I come from a classic dysfunctional family, and I'm determined to leave that behind me. But I have heard that family patterns repeat themselves. Is there anything I can do to stop this cycle from repeating and from preventing me from having a happy and productive family life myself?

Changing long-standing patterns of behavior is difficult. You've already taken a step toward changing by becoming aware of the pattern. Now you need to take time to understand the pattern—to figure out why family members engage in certain behaviors and avoid others. Understanding the pattern will help you recognize it when it crops up again. Another important step toward changing is being willing to differentiate yourself from your family. When you stop engaging in the pattern, you will be unlike other family members. You may feel marginalized and you may even be rejected. Before you can change, you need to be willing to be different. Finally, it is important to identify and practice an alternative pattern of behavior. It is easy to look at family members and see a pattern that is dysfunctional; it's much harder to come up with an alternative. Engaging in an alternative pattern will help prevent you from falling back into the old one.

For more information see L. Rubin, *The Transcendent Child: Tales of Triumph over the Past* (New York: Basic Books, 1996).

Anita L. Vangelisti (Ph.D., University of Texas at Austin) is professor of Communication Studies at the University of Texas at Austin. Her research focuses on the associations between communication and emotion in the context of close personal relationships. She is coeditor of the Cambridge University Press series on Advances in Personal Relationships and has served on the editorial boards of more than a dozen journals. Dr. Vangelisti has published numerous articles and chapters as well as several books.

One obvious example is the family without children, which in 2002 totaled 52 percent of the families in the United States. About 28 percent of American families are headed by a single parent.

Another obvious example is people living together in an exclusive relationship who are not married. For the most part these cohabitants live as if they were married: There is an exclusive sexual commitment; there may be children; there are shared financial responsibilities, shared time, and shared space. These relationships mirror traditional marriages, except that in marriage the union is recognized by a religious body, the state, or both; also, only marrieds can profit from federal benefits and protections.

Another example is the gay or lesbian couple who live together as "domestic partners" or in a "civil union"—relatively new terms for people living in a committed relationship—in households that have all the characteristics of a family. Many of these couples have children from previous heterosexual unions, through artificial insemination, or by adoption. Although accurate statistics are difficult to secure, primary relationships among gays and lesbians seem more common than the popular media lead us to believe. According to *Time Almanac with Information Please* (2005), the number of homosexual partners sharing a household is approximately 1 percent of all U.S. households (or 594,391 same-sex partner households). And, most relational experts agree, being in a committed relationship is the goal of most people, regardless of affectional orientation (Patterson, 2000; Kurdek, 2000, 2004; Fitzpatrick & Caughlin, 2002).

The communication principles that apply to the traditional nuclear family (the mother–father–child family) also apply to these other kinds of families. In the following discussion, the term **primary relationship** denotes the relationship between the two principal parties—the husband and wife, the lovers, the domestic partners, for example; and the term *family* denotes the broader constellation that includes children, relatives, and assorted significant others.

Characteristics of Families

All primary relationships and families have several qualities that further characterize this relationship type: defined roles, recognition of responsibilities, shared history and future, and shared living space.

Defined Roles Primary relationship partners have a relatively clear perception of the roles each person is expected to play in relation to the other and to the relationship as a whole. Each acquired the rules of his or her culture and social group; each knows approximately what his or her obligations, duties, privileges, and responsibilities are. The partners' roles might include those of wage earner, cook, house cleaner, child caregiver, social secretary, home decorator, plumber, carpenter, food shopper, money manager, and so on. At times the roles may be shared, but even then it's generally assumed that one person has primary responsibility for certain tasks and the other person for others.

Most heterosexual couples divide the roles rather traditionally, with the man as primary wage earner and maintenance person and the woman as primary cook, child rearer, and housekeeper. This is less true among more highly educated couples and those in the higher socioeconomic classes, where changes in traditional role assignments are first seen. However, among gay and lesbian couples, clear-cut, stereotypical male and female roles are not found. One research review, for example, noted that scientific studies "have consistently debunked this myth. Most contemporary gay relationships do not conform to traditional 'masculine' and 'feminine' roles; instead, role flexibility and turn taking are more common patterns. . . . In this sense, traditional heterosexual marriage is not the predominant model or script for current homosexual couples" (Peplau, 1988; Cloud, 2008).

Recognition of Responsibilities Family members see themselves as having certain obligations and responsibilities to one another. A single person does not have the same kinds of obligations to another as someone in a primary relationship. For example, individuals have an obligation to help each other financially. There are also emotional responsibilities: to offer comfort when our family members are distressed, to take pleasure in their pleasures, to feel their pain, to raise their spirits. Each person in a couple also has a temporal obligation to reserve some large block of time for the other. Time sharing seems important to all relationships, although each couple will define it differently.

Shared History and Future Primary relationships have a shared history and the prospect of a shared future. For a relationship to become primary, there must be some history, some significant past interaction. This interaction enables the members to get to know each other, to understand each other a little better, and ideally to like and even love each other. Similarly, the individuals view the relationship as having a potential future. Despite researchers' prediction that 50 percent of couples now entering first marriages will divorce (the rate is higher for second marriages) and that 41 percent of all persons of marriageable age will experience divorce, most couples entering a relationship such as marriage view it—ideally, at least—as permanent.

Shared Living Space In general American culture, persons in primary interpersonal relationships usually share the same living space. When living space is not shared, the situation is generally seen as "abnormal" or temporary, both by the culture as a whole and by the individuals involved in the relationship. Even those who live apart for significant periods probably perceive a shared space as the ideal and, in fact, usually do share some special space at least part of the time. In some other cultures, however, men and women don't share the same living space; the women may live with the children while the men live together in a communal arrangement (Harris, 1993).

Even in the United States, the number of long-distance relationships is not insignificant. For example, the Center for the Study of Long Distance Relationships (www.longdistancerelationships.net, accessed March 8, 2008) puts the number of married persons who do not share a living space at over 3,500,000, which is 2.9 percent of all U.S. marrieds. And the number of such relationships is increasing. Approximately 7 million couples (or 14 million people) consider themselves to be in long-distance relationships. It's been estimated that some 75 percent of college students have been at some point in their lives a part of a long-distance relationship, and at any one time some 25 to 50 percent of college students are in long-distance relationships (Stafford, 2004). Further, long-distance relationships do not seem to have less satisfaction, less commitment, less intimacy, or less durability than shared-space relationships, as long as the individuals are able to get together about once a month (Rohlfing, 1995; Stafford & Merolla, 2007).

One of the reasons for the increase in long-distance relationships is the economy, which often forces people to take jobs away from each other. Another reason is that long-distance relationships are one way of dealing with the inevitable tension between being connected and being independent noted in our earlier discussion of relationship dialectics (Chapter 9, pp. 220–222). A long-distance relationship allows you to have close connection with one person but also to have a great deal of autonomy and independence. The ease of long-distance communication through e-mail, cell and video phones, and chat rooms goes a long way to lessen the perception of psychological distance (www.richardbanks.com/trends, accessed March 8, 2008). Such frequent and easy communication can also make a long-distance relationship seem less lonely and more real than it might seem if communication were severely limited.

As you may know, colleges are mindful of the importance and impact of long-distance relationships, and many offer assistance for dealing with such relationships. For example, Penn State Erie (The Behrend College) at www.erie.psu.edu/student/counseling/longdistancerelationships/htm offers such "tips for success" as the following: Establish phone and webcam dates (and treat them seriously); e-mail; share plans; watch the same movie or read the same book and talk about it; visit (when you can); and, perhaps most important, maintain open communication.

Family Types

Based on responses from more than 1,000 couples to questions concerning their degree of sharing, their space needs, their conflicts, and the time they spend together, researchers have identified three basic types of primary relationships: traditionals, independents, and separates (Fitzpatrick, 1983, 1988, 1991; Noller & Fitzpatrick, 1993).

Traditional Couples If you are part of a "traditional" couple, you'll tend to agree with such statements as these (taken from Fitzpatrick's [1991; Noller & Fitzpatrick, 1993] Relational Dimensions Instrument):

- We tell each other how much we love or care about each other.
- We eat our meals at the same time every day.
- A woman should take her husband's last name when she marries.

Traditional couples share a basic belief system and philosophy of life. They see themselves as a blending of two persons into a single couple rather than as two separate individuals. They're interdependent and believe that each individual's independence must be sacrificed for the good of the relationship. Traditionals believe in mutual sharing and do little separately. This couple holds to the traditional gender roles, and there are seldom any role conflicts. There are few power struggles and few conflicts in general, because each person knows and adheres to a specified role within the relationship. In their communications, traditionals are highly responsive to each other. Traditionals lean toward each other, smile, talk a lot, interrupt each other, and finish each other's sentences.

Independent Couples If you are an "independent" you'll tend to agree with such statements as these:

- In marriage or close relationships, there should be no constraints or restrictions on individual freedom.
- I have my own private work space (study, workshop, utility room, etc.).
- I feel free to interrupt my mate when he or she is concentrating on something if he or she is in my presence.

Independent couples stress their individuality. The relationship is important, but never more important than each person's individual identity. Although independents spend a great deal of time together, they don't ritualize it, for example, with schedules. Each individual spends time with outside friends. Independents see themselves as relatively androgynous—as individuals who combine the traditionally feminine and the traditionally masculine roles and qualities. The communication between independents is responsive. They engage in conflict openly and without fear. Their disclosures are quite extensive and include high-risk and negative disclosures that are typically absent among traditionals.

Separate Couples If you are a "separate" you'll tend to agree with such statements as these:

- If I can avoid arguing about some problems, they will disappear.
- It is better to hide your true feelings in order to avoid hurting your mate.
- In our house, we keep a fairly regular daily time schedule.

Separate couples live together but view their relationship more as a matter of convenience than a result of their mutual love or closeness. They seem to have little desire to be together and, in fact, usually are together only at ritual functions, such as mealtime or holiday get-togethers. It's important to separates that each have his or her own physical as well as psychological space. Separates share little; each seems to prefer to go his or her own way. Separates hold relatively traditional values and beliefs about gender roles, and each person tries to follow the behaviors normally assigned to each role. What best characterizes this type, however, is that each person sees himself or herself as a separate individual and not as a part of a "we."

In addition to these three pure types, there also are combinations. For example, in the separate–traditional couple one individual is a separate and one a traditional. Another common pattern is the traditional–independent, in which one individual believes in the traditional view of relationships and one in autonomy and independence.

Family and Communication

One helpful way to understand families and primary relationships is in terms of the communication patterns that dominate the relationship. Four general communication patterns are identified here; each interpersonal relationship may then be viewed as a variation on one of these basic patterns.

The Equality Pattern The equality pattern probably exists more in theory than in practice, but it's a good starting point for looking at communication in primary relationships. It exists more among same-sex couples than in opposite-sex couples (Huston & Schwartz, 1995). In the equality pattern each person shares equally in the communication transactions; the roles played by each are equal. Thus, each person is accorded a similar degree of credibility; each is equally open to the ideas, opinions, and beliefs of the other; each engages in self-disclosure on a more or less equal basis. The communication is open, honest, direct, and free of the power plays that characterize so many other interpersonal relationships.

VIEWPOINT If you looked at the family from an evolutionary–Darwinian point of view, one research watcher notes, you'd have to conclude that families are "inherently unstable" and that it's necessity, not choice, that keeps them together. If they had better opportunities elsewhere, many family members would leave immediately (Goleman, 1995b). What do you see as the greatest advantages of family? What do you see as the greatest disadvantages?

There is no leader or follower, no opinion giver or opinion seeker; rather, both parties play these roles equally. Because of this basic equality, the communication exchanges themselves, over a substantial period, are equal. For example, the number of questions asked, the depth and frequency of self-disclosures, and the nonverbal behaviors of touching and eye gaze would all be about the same for both people.

Both parties share equally in decision-making processes—in insignificant decisions, such as which movie to attend, as well as in significant choices, such as where to send a child to school, whether to attend religious services, or what house to buy. Conflicts may occur with some frequency in equality relationships, but they're not seen as threatening to the individuals or to the relationship. They're viewed, rather, as exchanges of ideas, opinions, and values. These conflicts tend to be about content rather than relational issues (Chapter 12), and the couple has few power struggles within the relationship domain.

Equal relationships also are equitable. According to equity theory, family or relationship satisfaction will be highest when there is equity—when each partner gets a proportional share of the costs and the rewards of the relationship (Chapter 9). Dissatisfaction over inequities can lead to a "balancing of the scales" reaction. For example, an underbenefited partner may seek an outside affair as a way to get more relationship benefits—more love, more consideration, more support (Walster, Walster, & Traupmann, 1978; Noller & Fitzpatrick, 1993).

The Balanced Split Pattern

In the balanced split pattern, an equality relationship is maintained, but each person has authority over different domains. Each person is seen as an expert or a decision maker in different areas. For example, in the traditional nuclear family, the husband maintains high credibility in business matters and perhaps in politics. The wife maintains high credibility in such matters as child care and cooking. These gender roles are breaking down in many cultures, but they still define many families throughout the world (Hatfield & Rapson, 1996).

Conflict is generally viewed as nonthreatening by individuals in balanced split families, because each has specified areas of expertise. Consequently, the outcome of any conflict is almost predetermined.

The Unbalanced Split Pattern

In the unbalanced split relationship, one person dominates: One person is seen as an expert in more than half the areas of mutual communication. In many unions this "expertise" equates with control. Thus, in the unbalanced split, one person is more or less regularly in control of the relationship. In some cases this person is the more intelligent or more knowledgeable, but in many cases he or she is the more physically attractive or the higher wage earner. The less attractive or lower-income partner compensates by giving in to the other person, allowing the other to win arguments or to have his or her way in decision making.

The person in control makes more assertions, tells the other person what should or will be done, gives opinions freely, plays power games to maintain control, and seldom asks for opinions in return. The noncontrolling person, conversely, asks questions, seeks opinions, and looks to the other for decision-making leadership.

The Monopoly Pattern

In a monopoly relationship, one person is seen as the authority. This person lectures rather than communicating. Rarely does this person seek others' advice, and he or she always reserves the right to have the final say. In this type of couple, arguments are few—because both individuals already know who is boss and who will win any argument that may arise. When the authority is challenged, however, there are arguments and bitter conflicts. One reason the conflicts are so bitter is that these individuals have had no rehearsal for adequate conflict resolution. They don't know how to argue or how to disagree agreeably, so their conflict strategies frequently take the form of hurting the other person.

The controlling person tells the partner what is and what is not to be. The controlling person talks more frequently and goes off the topic of conversation more than does the noncontrolling partner (Palmer, 1989). The noncontrolling person looks to the other to give permission, to voice opinion leadership, and to make decisions, almost as a child looks to an all-knowing, all-powerful parent.

Families, Culture, Gender, and Technology

As with friendship and love, families too vary from one culture to another, are viewed differently by men and women, and are influenced by technology.

Culture and Gender and Families   In U.S. society, it is assumed in discussions of relationship development—such as the model presented in this text—that you voluntarily choose your relationship partners. You consciously choose to pursue certain relationships and not others. In some cases, your husband or wife is chosen to unite two families or to bring some financial advantage to your family or village. An arrangement such as this may have been entered into by your parents when you were an infant or even before you were born. In most cultures, of course, there's pressure to marry "the right" person and to be friends with certain people and not others.

Similarly, U.S. researchers study—and textbook authors write about—how relationships dissolve and how to survive relationship breakups. It's assumed that you have the right to exit an undesirable relationship. But in some cultures you cannot simply dissolve a relationship once it's formed or once there are children. In the practice of Roman Catholicism, once people are validly married, they're always married and cannot dissolve that relationship. More important in such cultures may be such issues as "How do you maintain a relationship that has problems?" "What can you do to survive in this unpleasant relationship?" or "How can you repair a troubled relationship?" (Moghaddam, Taylor, & Wright, 1993).

Further, your culture will influence the difficulty that you go through when relationships do break up. For example, married persons whose religion forbids divorce and remarriage will experience religious disapproval and condemnation as well as the same economic and social difficulties everyone else goes through. In the United States child custody almost invariably goes to the woman, and this presents an added emotional burden for the man. In Iran child custody goes to the man, which presents added emotional burdens for the woman. In India women experience greater difficulty than men in divorce because of their economic dependence on men, cultural beliefs about women, and the patriarchal order of the family (Amato, 1994). And it was only as recently as 2002 that the first wife in Jordan was granted a divorce. Prior to this, only men had been granted divorces (*New York Times*, May 15, 2002, p. A6).

In the United States both men and women can initiate relationships, and both can dissolve them. Both men and women are expected to derive satisfaction from their interpersonal relationships; and when that satisfaction isn't present, either person may seek to exit the relationship. In Iran, on the other hand, only the man has the right to dissolve a marriage without giving reasons.

Gay and lesbian families are accepted in some cultures and condemned in others. In some areas of the United States, "domestic partnerships" may be registered, and these grant gay men, lesbians, and (in some cases) unmarried heterosexuals rights that were formerly reserved only for married couples, such as health insurance benefits and the right to make decisions when one member is incapacitated. In Belgium, the Netherlands, Spain, South Africa, and Canada, same-sex couples can marry; in Norway, Sweden, and Denmark, same-sex relationship partners have the same rights as married partners. As of this writing, only one U.S. state—Massachusetts—has issued marriage licenses to same-sex couples. And, as mentioned in our discussion of heterosexism in Chapter 5, in many countries same-sex couples would be considered criminals and could face severe punishment—in some cultures, even death.

Technology and Families   You know from your own family interactions that technology has greatly changed communication among family members. Cell phones enable parents and children to keep in close touch in case of emergencies or just to chat. College students today stay in closer touch with their parents, in part because of the cell phone but also through e-mail and instant messaging.

On the other hand, some people—in some cases parents, in most cases children—become so absorbed with their online community that they have little time for their biological family members. In some cases, as in South Korea, Internet use seems to be contributing further to the already significant generational conflict between children and parents (Rhee & Kim, 2004). Similarly, a study on young people (ages 10 to 17) in the United States found that for both girls and boys, those who formed close online relationships were more likely to have low levels of communication with their parents and to be more "highly troubled" than those who don't form such close online relationships (Wolak, Mitchell, & Finkelhor, 2003).

In the case of adopted offspring, discovering birth parents is now a lot easier because of ready access to all sorts of data. Similarly, siblings that have been separated can more easily find one another—a process that may seem relatively unnecessary to most families in the United States but may be extremely important in war-torn countries where families have been separated through occupation or forced relocation.

Workplace Relationships

The workplace is a context in which all forms of communication take place and, not surprisingly, all kinds of relationships may be seen. This context is especially influenced by culture—both by the wider culture and by the particular culture of a given workplace. Like all cultures, workplace cultures have their own rituals, norms, and rules for communicating. These rules, whether in an interview situation or in a friendly conversation, delineate appropriate and inappropriate verbal and nonverbal behavior, specify rewards (or punishments for breaking the rules), and tell you what will help you get and keep a job and what won't. For example, the general advice given throughout this text is to emphasize your positive qualities, to highlight your abilities, and to minimize any negative characteristics or failings. But in some organizations—especially within collectivist wider cultures such as those of China, Korea, and Japan—workers are expected to show modesty (Copeland & Griggs, 1985). If you stress your own competencies too much, you may be seen as arrogant, brash, and unfit to work in an organization where teamwork and cooperation are emphasized.

When you join an organization, you learn the rules and norms of a culture different from, say, the college culture from which you came or from a former organization for which you worked. Put differently, and in terms of the concepts discussed in Chapter 2, you

UNDERSTANDING INTERPERSONAL SKILLS

Supportiveness

Supportiveness in communication is behavior that is descriptive rather than evaluative and provisional rather than certain (cf. Gibb, 1961). Descriptive messages state in relatively objective terms what you see or what you feel—as opposed to evaluative messages, which express your opinions and judgments. Descriptive messages may make others feel supported; judgmental or evaluative messages, on the other hand, may elicit defensiveness. (This doesn't mean that all evaluative communications meet a defensive response, of course. For example, the would-be actor who wants to improve technique often welcomes both positive and negative evaluations.) Similarly, provisional messages express an open-minded attitude and a willingness to hear opposing viewpoints. Certainty messages, on the other hand, tolerate no differences of opinion and are likely to engender defensiveness.

Communicating Supportiveness. Here are a few suggestions for communicating supportiveness by being descriptive and provisional, which will increase relationship satisfaction (Cramer, 2004).

- Avoid accusations or blame ("I should have stayed with my old job and not listened to your brother's advice").
- Avoid negative evaluative terms ("Didn't your sister look horrible in that red dress?").
- Avoid "preaching" ("You need to learn word processing and spreadsheet skills").
- Express your willingness to listen with an open mind and your readiness to consider changing your way of thinking and doing things.
- Ask for the opinions of others, and show that these are important to you. Resist the temptation to focus too much on your own way of seeing things.

Working with Interpersonal Skills

In what situations have you recently used supportiveness? In what situations have others responded to you with supportiveness? How was this supportiveness expressed? Try identifying situations in which supportiveness was not used but might have helped.

become acculturated, much as you would if you moved to a foreign country. As you can appreciate, it's essential to learn the organization's culture to know what the rules of the game are, especially the rules of communication. One issue that illustrates the influence of the specific workplace culture concerns the office romance, to which we now turn.

Romantic Relationships

Unlike television depictions, in which workers are always best friends who would do anything for one another and in which the characters move in and out of office romances with little difficulty—at least with no difficulty that can't be resolved in 24 minutes—real-life office romance can be complicated.

Opinions vary widely concerning workplace romances. Some organizations, on the assumption that romantic relationships are basically detrimental to the success of the workplace, have explicit rules prohibiting romantic involvements. In some organizations (including the military), members can be fired for such relationships. In other organizations, the prohibitions are unwritten and informal but nevertheless clearly in opposition to office romances. In one high-profile example, the president and CEO of Boeing Aircraft, Harry Stonecipher, was asked to step down after he admitted he had had an affair with a female executive, despite the fact that under his leadership Boeing's stock price had risen more than 30 percent. Boeing's reasons were that the affair "reflected poorly on his judgment" and that it was "inconsistent" with Boeing's code of conduct (http://cbs.marketwatch.com, accessed March 11, 2005). Yet in some other organizations the taboos against office romance are lessening, with a variety of business professionals supporting such relationships—or at least recognizing that such relationships are inevitable (Armour, 2003; Ward, 2003; Franklin, 2002).

On the positive side, the work environment seems a perfect place to meet a potential romantic partner. After all, by virtue of the fact that you're working in the same office, probably you both are interested in the same field, have similar training and ambitions, and will spend considerable time together—all factors that foster the development of a successful interpersonal relationship. Also, given that Americans are marrying later in life, they are less likely to meet prospective partners in school; so work seems the logical alternative. Published figures differ as to the frequency of office romances. According to a 2006 survey by CareerBuilder.com, 43 percent of U.S. workers said they had dated a fellow worker, and about one-third of these people got married (Voo, 2007). Another survey reported that 58 percent of workers had dated a coworker. Of these, 20 percent admitted to a romantic relationship with a boss and 15 percent to a relationship with someone they supervised (www.businessweek.com/debateroom/archives/2007/05/file_office_rom.html, accessed March 9, 2008). And of course even Bill and Melinda Gates met at work.

Office romances can lead to greater work satisfaction. For example, if you're romantically attracted to another worker, it can make going to work, working together, and even working added hours more enjoyable and more satisfying. If the relationship is good and mutually satisfying, the individuals are likely to develop empathy for each other and to act in ways that are supportive, cooperative, and friendly; in short, the workers are more likely to show all the characteristics of effective communication noted throughout this book.

However, even when the relationship is good for the two individuals, it may not be good for other workers. Seeing the loving couple together every day may generate office gossip that may prove destructive. Others may think the lovers are a team that has to be confronted as a pair, and that you can't criticize one without incurring the wrath of the other.

Workplace romantic relationships may cause problems for management when, for example, a promotion is to be made or relocation decisions are necessary. Can you legitimately ask one lover to move to Boston and the other to move to San Francisco? Will it prove difficult for management to promote one lover who then becomes the supervisor of the other?

The workplace also puts pressure on the individuals. Most organizations, at least in the United States, are highly competitive; one person's success often means another's failure. In this competitive context, the normal self-disclosures that regularly accompany increased intimacy (which often reveal weaknesses, doubts, and misgivings) may actually prove a liability.

When the romance goes bad or when it's one-sided, there are even more disadvantages. One obvious problem is that it can be stressful for the former lovers to see each other regularly and perhaps to work together. Other workers may feel they have to take sides, being supportive of one partner and critical of the other. This can easily cause friction throughout the organization. In addition, when an office romance breaks up, it's usually the more competent and employable person who leaves for another job, leaving the firm with the less valuable employee and the need to retrain someone to take over the departed lover's functions (Jones, 2004). Still another and perhaps more serious issue is the potential for charges of sexual harassment, especially if the romance was between a supervisor and a worker. Whether the charges are legitimate or are the result of an unhappy love affair and unrelated to the organization, management will find itself in the middle, facing lawsuits and time and money lost from investigating and ultimately acting on the charges.

The generally negative attitude of management toward office love affairs and the problems in dealing with the normal stress of both work and romance seem to present significant obstacles to such relationships and to the workplace, so workers are generally advised by management not to romance their colleagues. Friendships, on the other hand, seem the much safer course. Companies often encourage friendships by setting up sports teams, dinners, and lounge and exercise areas. In fact, research finds that office friendships increase employees' job satisfaction and commitment to the organization and decrease turnover (Morrison, 2004). And friendships often serve as the basis for mentoring and networking, topics to be discussed below.

It should also be noted that social networking sites, designed originally as places where people could make new friends and stay in touch with old ones, are increasingly being used for both mentoring and networking. Some sites are "by invitation only" and have been compared to gated communities or exclusive country clubs. These sites seem designed not for friendships but solely for mentoring and networking (MacMillan & Lehman, 2007). For example, Reuters Space (www.space.reuters.com) is a private online community specifically for hedge fund managers to network, and INmobile (www.INmobile.org) is designed for executives in the wireless industry.

Mentoring Relationships

In **mentoring** an experienced individual helps to train someone who is less experienced. (Mullen, 2005). Having a mentor, some organizational experts argue, is crucial for rising in a hierarchy and for developing your skills (Dahle, 2004). An accomplished teacher, for example, might mentor a younger teacher who has newly arrived or who has never taught before (Nelson, Pearson, & Kurylo, 2008). The mentor guides the new person through the organizational maze, teaches the strategies and techniques for success, and otherwise communicates his or her accumulated knowledge and experience to this "mentee."

The mentoring relationship provides an ideal learning environment. It's usually a one-on-one relationship between expert and novice, a relationship that is supportive and trusting. There's a mutual and open sharing of information and thoughts about the job. The relationship enables the novice to try out new skills under the guidance of an expert, to ask questions, and to obtain the feedback so necessary in learning complex skills. Mentoring is perhaps best characterized as a relationship in which the experienced and powerful mentor empowers the novice, giving the novice the tools and techniques for gaining the same power the mentor holds.

Not surprisingly, mentoring is frequently conducted online. One great advantage of e-mentoring is the flexibility it allows for communication. E-mail messages, for example, can be sent and received at times that are convenient for the individuals involved (Stewart, 2006). Further, because the individuals may be separated geographically, it's possible to have mentor-protégé relationships with people in foreign countries and in widely differing cultures—relationships that would be impossible without online communication. Still another advantage is that persons with disabilities (whether mentor or protégé) who cannot easily travel can still enjoy and profit from e-mentoring relationships (Burgstahler, 2007).

The mentoring relationship has been found to be one of the three primary paths for career achievement among African American men and women (Bridges, 1996). And in a study of middle-level managers, those who had mentors and participated in mentoring relationships were found to get more promotions and higher salaries than those who didn't have mentors (Scandura, 1992). More recent research also finds that college students benefit in a variety of ways from having a mentor. At the end of the first year, mentored students had a higher GPA, showed a higher retention rate, and had completed more credits than unmentored students (Campbell & Campbell, 2007).

At the same time, the mentor benefits from clarifying his or her thoughts, seeing the job from the perspective of a newcomer, and considering and formulating answers to a variety of questions. Much as a teacher learns from teaching, a mentor learns from mentoring.

Networking Relationships

In the popular mind, **networking** is often viewed simply as a technique for securing a job. But it actually has much broader applications and can be viewed as a process of using other people to help you solve your problems, or at least to offer insights that bear on your problem—for example, how to publish your manuscript, where to look for low-cost auto insurance, how to find an affordable apartment, or how to empty your cache.

Networking comes in at least two forms: informal and formal. Informal networking is what we do every day when we find ourselves in a new situation or are unable to answer questions. Thus, for example, if you're new at a school, you might ask someone in your class where to eat or where to shop for new clothes or who's the best teacher for interpersonal communication. In the same way, when you enter a new work environment, you might ask more experienced workers how to perform certain tasks or whom you should approach—or avoid—when you have questions.

Formal networking is the same thing, except that it's much more systematic and strategic. It's the establishment of connections with people who can help you—answer your questions, get you a job, help you get promoted, help you relocate or accomplish any task you want to accomplish.

At the most obvious level, you can network with people you already know. If you review the list of people in your acquaintance, you'll probably discover that you know a great number of people with very specialized knowledge who can be of assistance to you in a wide variety of ways. In some cultures (Brazil is one example) friendships are established in part because of potential networking connections (Rector & Neiva, 1996). You also can network with people who know people you know. Thus, you may contact a friend's friend to find out if the firm he or she works for is hiring. Or you may contact people you have no connection with. Perhaps you've read something that someone wrote or you've heard the person's name raised in connection with an area in which you're interested and you want to get more information. With e-mail addresses so readily available, it's now quite common to e-mail individuals who have particular expertise and ask them questions you might have.

The great value of networking, of course, is that it provides you with access to a wealth of specialized information. At the same time, it often makes accessing that information a lot easier than if you had to find it all by yourself.

In networking it's often recommended that you try to establish relationships that are mutually beneficial. After all, much as others are useful sources of information for you, you're likely to be a useful source of information for others. If you can provide others with helpful information, it's more likely that they will provide helpful information for you. In this way, a mutually satisfying and productive network is established.

Some networking experts advise you to develop files and directories of potentially useful sources that you can contact for needed information. For example, if you're a freelance artist, you might develop a list of people who might be in positions to offer you work or who might lead you to others who might offer such work. Authors, editors, art directors, administrative assistants, people in advertising, and a host of others might eventually provide useful leads for such work. Creating a directory of such people and keeping in contact with them on a fairly regular basis can often simplify your obtaining freelance work.

Formal networking requires that you take an active part in locating and establishing these connections. Be proactive; initiate contacts rather than waiting for them to come to you. Of course, this can be overdone; you don't want to rely on people to do work you can easily do yourself. Yet if you're also willing to help others, there is nothing wrong in asking these same people to help you. If you're respectful of their time and expertise, it's likely that your networking attempts will be responded to favorably. Following up your requests with thank-you notes will help you establish networks that can be ongoing, productive relationships rather than one-shot affairs.

Relationship Violence

In all interpersonal relationships—friendship, love, and family—there exists the possibility for what has come to be called "the dark side" of relationships. In any interpersonal interaction, there exists not only the potential for productive and meaningful communication but also the potential for unproductive and destructive communication. This dark side is perhaps most obvious in the various forms of relationship violence. Before reading about this important but often neglected topic, take the following self-test.

TEST YOURSELF

IS VIOLENCE A PART OF YOUR RELATIONSHIP?

Based on your present relationship or one you know, respond to the following questions with Yes if you do see yourself in the question or No if you do not see yourself here.

_____	1. Do you fear your partner's anger?
_____	2. Does your partner ever threaten you?
_____	3. Has your partner ever verbally abused you?
_____	4. Has your partner ever forced you to do something you didn't want to do?
_____	5. Has your partner ever hit (slapped, kicked, pushed) you?
_____	6. Has your partner isolated you from your friends or relatives?

HOW DID YOU DO? These six items are all signs of a violent partner and a violent relationship. You might also want to change the questions around a bit and ask yourself if your partner would answer "Yes" to any of these questions about you.

WHAT WILL YOU DO? If any of these questions describes your relationship, you may wish to seek professional help. Discussing these questions with your partner, which might seem the logical first step, could well create additional problems and perhaps incite violence. So you're better off discussing this with a school counselor or some other professional. At the same time, if any of these apply to you—if you yourself are prone to relationship violence—do likewise: Seek professional help. Additional suggestions are offered in the text of this section.

Source: These questions were drawn from a variety of sources; for example, SUNY at Buffalo Counseling Services (http://ub-counseling.buffalo.edu/warnings.shtml, accessed February 1, 2006); The American College of Obstetricians and Gynecologists, Women's Heath Care Physicians (www.acog.org/departments/dept_notice.cfm?recno=17&bulletin=198, accessed February 1, 2006); and the University of Texas at Austin, Counseling and Mental Health Center (http://www.utexas.edu/student/cmhc/booklets/relavio/relaviol.html, accessed February 1, 2006).

What Is Relationship Violence?

Three types of **relationship violence** may be distinguished: verbal or emotional abuse, physical abuse, and sexual abuse (Rice, 2007). In **verbal or emotional abuse,** the abuser may humiliate you; engage in economic abuse such as controlling the finances or preventing you from working; and/or isolate, criticize, or stalk you. Some research shows that people who use verbal or emotional abuse are more likely than others to escalate to physical abuse (Rancer & Avtgis, 2005). **Physical abuse** includes threats of violence as well as pushing, hitting, slapping, kicking, choking, throwing things at you, and breaking things. **Sexual abuse** involves touching that is unwanted, accusations of sexual infidelity without reason, forced sex, and references to you in abusive sexual terms.

A great deal of research has centered on trying to identify the warning signs of relationship violence. Here, for example, are a few signs compiled by the State University of New York at Buffalo; you might want to use this list to start thinking about your own relationship or those that you know of (http://ub-counseling.buffalo,edu/warnings/shtml, accessed February 1, 2006). It may be a warning sign if your partner:

- belittles, insults, or ignores you
- controls pieces of your life; for example, the way you dress or who you can be friends with
- gets jealous without reason
- can't handle sexual frustration without anger
- is so angry or threatening that you've changed your life so as not to provoke additional anger

The Effects of Relationship Violence

As you might expect, there are a variety of consequences to relationship violence: physical injuries, psychological injuries, and economic "injuries" (www.cdc.gov/ncic/factsheets/ipvfacts. htm, accessed May 7, 2007).

Perhaps the image that comes most quickly to mind when the issue of relationship violence is that of physical violence, and that element is certainly a big part of overall relationship violence. Physical injuries may range from scratches and bruises to broken bones, knife wounds, and central nervous system damage. Such injuries can range from minor to death.

Even when physical injuries are relatively minor, however, psychological injuries may be major; they may include, for example, depression, anxiety, fear of intimacy, and of course low self-esteem. In fact, relationship violence often attacks self-esteem to the point where the victims come to believe that the violence against them is justified.

In addition to the obvious physical and psychological injuries, consider the economic impact. It's been estimated that in the United States relationship violence costs approximately $6.2 billion for physical assaults and almost $500 million for rape. Interpersonal violence also results in lost days of work. The Center for Disease Control estimates that in this country interpersonal violence costs the equivalent of 32,000 full-time jobs in lost work each year. Additional economic costs are incurred when interpersonal violence prevents women from maintaining jobs or continuing their education.

The Alternatives to Relationship Violence

Here are some ways in which a nonviolent relationship looks when compared with a violent relationship (www.utexas.edu/student/cmhc/booklets/relavio/relaviol.html, accessed February 1, 2006).

- Instead of emotional abuse, there is fairness; you look for resolutions to conflict that will be fair to both of you.
- Instead of control and isolation, there is communication that makes the partner feel safe and comfortable expressing himself or herself.
- Instead of intimidation, there is mutual respect, mutual affirmation, and valuing of each other's opinions.
- Instead of economic abuse, the partners make financial decisions together.
- Instead of threats, there is accountability—each person accepts responsibility for his or her own behavior.
- Instead of one person's exercising power over the other, in a system in which one person is the boss and the other the servant, there is a fair distribution of responsibilities.
- Instead of sexual abuse, there is trust and respect for what each person wants and doesn't want.

Dealing with Relationship Violence

Whether you're a victim or a perpetrator of relationship violence, it is important to seek professional help (and, of course, the help of friends and family where appropriate). In addition, here are several further suggestions (www.utexas.edu/student/cmhc/booklets/relavio/relaviol.html, accessed February 1, 2006).

If your partner has been violent:

- Realize that you're not alone. There are other people who suffer similarly, and there is a mechanism in place to help you.
- Realize you're not at fault. You did not deserve to be the victim of violence.
- Plan for your safety. Violence, if it occurred once, is likely to occur again, and part of your thinking needs to be devoted to your own safety.
- Know your resources—the phone numbers you need to contact help, the locations of money and a spare set of keys.

If you are the violent partner:

- Realize that you too are not alone and that help and support are available.
- Know that you can change. It won't necessarily be easy or quick, but you can change.
- Own your own behaviors; take responsibility. This is an essential step if any change is to occur.

Relationship violence is not an inevitable part of interpersonal relationships; in fact, it occurs in a minority of relationships. Yet it's important to know that there is the potential for violence in all relationships, as there is the potential for friendship, love, support, and all the positive things we look for in relationships. Knowing the difference between productive and destructive relationships seems the best way to make sure that your own relationships are as you want them to be.

Summary

This chapter explored some major kinds of interpersonal relationships; specifically, friendship, love, family, and workplace relationships. It also examined relationship violence.

Friendship

1. Friendship is an interpersonal relationship between two persons that is mutually productive and is characterized by mutual positive regard.
2. One classification of the types of friendships identified friendships of (1) reciprocity, characterized by loyalty, self-sacrifice, mutual affection, and generosity; (2) receptivity, characterized by a comfortable and positive imbalance in the giving and receiving of rewards, in which each person's needs are satisfied by the exchange; and (3) association, a transitory relationship more like a friendly relationship than a true friendship.
3. Friendships serve a variety of needs and give us a variety of values, among which are the values of utility, affirmation, ego support, stimulation, and security.
4. Friendships develop in stages over time, from strangers at one end of the continuum to close and intimate ("best") friends at the other.
5. Friendships are influenced by culture, gender, and technology. For example, friendship demands vary between collectivist and individualist cultures. Women share more and are more intimate with same-sex friends than are men. Men's friendships are

often built around shared activities rather than shared intimacies. Online friends resemble face-to-face friends in these needs they serve but are often more diverse.

Love

6. Love is a feeling that may be characterized by closeness and caring and by intimacy, passion, and commitment.
7. Among the types of love: (1) Eros love focuses on beauty and sexuality, sometimes to the exclusion of other qualities; (2) ludus love is seen as a game and focuses on entertainment and excitement; (3) storge love is a kind of companionship, peaceful and slow; (4) pragma love is practical and traditional; (5) mania love is obsessive and possessive, characterized by elation and depression; and (6) agape love is compassionate and selfless, characterized as self-giving and altruistic.
8. Verbal and nonverbal messages echo the intimacy of a love relationship. With increased intimacy, you share more, speak in a more personalized style, engage in prolonged eye contact, and touch each other more often.
9. As an example of the impact of cultural differences on love, members of individualist cultures tend to place greater emphasis on romantic love than do members of collectivist cultures. In terms of gender differences, men generally score higher on erotic and ludic love, whereas women score higher on manic, pragmatic, and storgic love. Men also generally score

higher on romanticism than women. Many forms of technology, especially social networking sites, help people meet new romantic interests and maintain romantic relationships.

Family

10. Among the characteristics of families are: defined roles (members understand the roles each of them serves), recognition of responsibilities (members realize that each person has certain responsibilities to the relationship), shared history and future (members have an interactional past and an anticipated future together), and shared living space (generally, members live together).

11. Family types have been classified into (1) traditionals, who see themselves as a blending of two people into a single couple; (2) independents, who see themselves as primarily separate individuals and see their individuality as more important than the relationship or the connection between the individuals; and (3) separates, who see their relationship as a matter of convenience rather than of mutual love or connection.

12. Among the prominent communication patterns in families are: (1) equality, in which each person shares equally in the communication transactions and decision making; (2) balanced split, in which each person has authority over different but relatively equal domains; (3) unbalanced split, in which one person maintains authority and decision-making power over a wider range of issues than the other; and (4) monopoly, in which one person dominates and controls the relationship and the decisions made.

13. Families vary from one culture to another and are influenced in varied ways by new technologies.

Workplace Relationships

14. Romantic relationships in the workplace, although having a variety of benefits, are often frowned upon and often entail a variety of problems that would not arise in other contexts.

15. Mentoring relationships help you learn the ropes of an organization through the experience and knowledge of someone who has gone through the processes you'll be going through.

16. Networking helps you expand your areas of expertise and enables you to secure information bearing on a wide variety of problems you want to solve and questions you want to answer.

Relationship Violence

17. Relationship violence may consist of verbal or emotional, physical, or sexual abuse and has wide-ranging effects.

18. Alternatives to relationship violence include a variety of strategies that are largely the application of sound interpersonal communication principles.

Key Terms

agape, **254**	love, **252**	networking, **269**	relationship violence, **270**
eros, **253**	ludus, **254**	office romance, **267**	separate couples, **263**
family, **259**	mania, **254**	pragma, **254**	storge, **254**
friendship, **247**	mentoring, **268**	primary relationship, **261**	traditional couples, **262**
independent couples, **263**			

Critical Thinking Questions

1 When college students were asked to identify the features that characterize romantic love, the five elements most frequently noted were trust, sexual attraction, acceptance and tolerance, spending time together, and sharing thoughts and secrets (Regan, Kocan, & Whitlock, 1998). How would you characterize love? Would men and women characterize love similarly?

2 Psychotherapist Albert Ellis (1988) has argued that love and infatuation are actually the same emotion; he claims that we use the term "infatuation" to describe relationships that didn't work out and "love" to describe our current romantic relationships. How would you compare infatuation and love?

3 In a *Time* magazine article on romance, the author says: "The eventual goal of any couple is to pass beyond serial dating—beyond even the thrill of early love—and into what is known as companionate love [a love that is peaceful and based on friendship]" (Kluger, 2008). Do you believe this? Or is this one of the great myths of love?

4 How would you describe your own family in terms of (1) the characteristics of primary relationships and families discussed in this chapter (defined roles, recognition of responsibilities, shared history and future, and shared living space); (2) the most often used communication pattern (equality, balanced split, unbalanced split, or monopoly); and (3) the rules that are most important to your family? How would you describe the ideal family?

5 Although studies show there is no disadvantage in a child's growing up in a gay home (Goleman, 1992), the major argument made against granting adoption rights to gay men and lesbians is that the child will suffer. How do you account for this?

6 What are your feelings about romantic relationships in the workplace? Altercast—put yourself into both the position of the worker who sees great opportunities for relationships and the position of the manager who focuses on making sure the company makes money.

7 You want to establish a small mail-order business selling framed prints; you plan to buy the frames and prints separately and inexpensively at yard sales, restore them, and sell them. What types of network connections might be appropriate in this situation? How would you go about the actual networking?

Choice Points

1 *Asking a Favor.* You need to borrow $200 from your roommate, and you have no idea when you'll be able to pay it back. Ask yourself: What are some of the ways you might ask for this loan and at the same time not put your roommate in an awkward and uncomfortable position?

2 *From Friendship to Love.* You have a great friendship with a colleague at work, but recently these feelings of friendship are turning to feelings of love. Ask yourself: How can you move this friendship to love, or at least discover if the other person would be receptive to this change (cf. Marano, 2004)?

3 *Discovering Personal Information.* You're becoming romantically involved with someone from school, but before this relationship goes any farther, you want to know about this person's HIV status and adherence to safe sex practices. Ask yourself: What are some of the things that you might say that will elicit truthful information but at the same time will not create a rift in the relationship?

4 *Mentoring.* You've been asked to help mentor at-risk college freshmen—to help them adjust to the college experience and develop productive study habits. Ask yourself: What behaviors would contribute to effective mentoring in this situation? What behaviors should a mentor avoid in this situation?

5 *Apologizing.* You've been very successful in the stock market, so when you got the best tip ever, you shared it with three of your friends at work. Unfortunately, the stock tanked, your colleagues lost several thousand dollars each, and the situation at work is uncomfortable at best. Ask yourself: What might you say to these colleagues to reduce the tension and get things back to the way they were?

6 *Networking.* Pat, a colleague at work, has taken networking to its ultimate degree, constantly asking others for information without ever trying to find it without outside help. Oddly enough, Pat never shares when others try to network and learn something. Today Pat comes to you for a phone number that could easily be found through the company website. Ask yourself: What can you say to refuse this request and yet not create a major war within the company?

MyCommunicationLab
Explorations

PEARSON
mycommunicationlab www.mycommunicationlab.com

These experiences look at a variety of interpersonal relationships and the communication that takes place within these interactions. ❶ Friendship Behaviors stimulates you to look at friendship in terms of the responses friends are expected to have to a variety of situations. ❷ How Can You Talk Cherishing? examines a simple but powerful technique for increasing relationship satisfaction. ❸ Mate Preferences: I Prefer Someone Who . . . stimulates you to look at the kinds of qualities you look for in a mate. ❹ The Television Relationship provides a structured opportunity to look at relationships as presented in television sitcoms and dramas. ❺ The self-test How Romantic Are You? will enable you to measure your own degree of romanticism. ❻ To investigate your own couple preference, take the well-researched self-test What Type of Relationship Do You Prefer? The statements given in the section on Family Types come from this test.

CHAPTER
12

Interpersonal Conflict and Conflict Management

Preliminaries to Interpersonal Conflict

Principles of Interpersonal Conflict

Conflict Management Stages

Conflict Management Strategies

The Dark Knight

In *The Dark Knight* you see conflict taken to farcical proportions as Batman defends Gotham City against the chaos unleashed by the Joker, the most powerful of all Batman's enemies. This chapter focuses on conflict of a more realistic type, the kind of conflict you have with friends, lovers, and family.

This chapter addresses one of the most important topics in the study of interpersonal communication. As you'll see in this chapter, an understanding of interpersonal conflict and the skills for effective conflict management are essential to all forms of interpersonal interaction. After a few foundation concepts, this chapter focuses on the nature and principles of conflict, the stages of conflict management, and the strategies for managing conflict effectively.

Preliminaries to Interpersonal Conflict

Before considering the stages and strategies of conflict management, we need to define exactly what we mean by interpersonal conflict, some of the myths surrounding this concept, and some of the issues around which conflict often centers.

Definition of Conflict

You want to go to the movies with your partner. Your partner wants to stay home. Your insisting on going to the movies interferes with your partner's staying home, and your partner's determination to stay home interferes with your going to the movies. Your goals are incompatible; if your goal is achieved, your partner's goal is not. Conversely, if your partner's goal is achieved, your goal is not.

As this example illustrates, **interpersonal conflict** is disagreement between or among connected individuals who perceive their goals as incompatible: close friends, lovers, colleagues, family members (Hocker & Wilmot, 2007; Folger, Poole, & Stutman, 2005; Cahn & Abigail, 2007). More specifically, conflict occurs when people:

■ are interdependent (they're connected in some significant way); what one person does has an impact or an effect on the other person.
■ are mutually aware that their goals are incompatible; if one person's goal is achieved, then the other person's goal cannot be achieved. For example, if one person wants to buy a new car and the other person wants to pay down the mortgage, there is conflict. Note that this situation would not pose a conflict if the couple had unlimited resources, in which case they could both buy the car and pay down the mortgage.
■ perceive each other as interfering with the attainment of their own goals. For example, you may want to study, but your roommate may want to party; the attainment of either goal would interfere with the attainment of the other goal.

One of the implications of this concept of interdependency is that the greater the interdependency, (1) the greater the number of issues on which conflict can center, and (2) the greater the impact of the conflict and the conflict management interaction on the individuals and on the relationship. Put in terms of the concepts of breadth and depth discussed in relation to the social penetration model of relationships (Chapter 9, p. 222): As interdependency increases, so do breadth (the number of topics) and depth (the level to which topics are penetrated). When you think about it this way, it's easy to appreciate how important understanding interpersonal conflict and mastering the strategies of effective conflict management are to your relationship life. The diagram in Figure 12.1 is designed to illustrate this relationship.

Myths about Conflict

One of the problems many people have in dealing with **conflict** is that they may be operating on the basis of false assumptions about what conflict is and what it means. Think about your own assumptions about interpersonal and small group conflict, which were probably derived from the communications you witnessed in your family and in your social interactions. For example, do you think the following are true or false?

■ Conflict is best avoided. Time will generally solve any problem; most difficulties blow over given time.
■ If two people experience relationship conflict, it means their relationship is in trouble; conflict is a sign of a troubled relationship.
■ Conflict damages an interpersonal relationship.

FIGURE 12.1

Conflict and Interdependency

This figure illustrates that as interdependency increases, so do the potential and the importance of conflict. In this figure, a relationship of "classmates" is in the middle. Fill in the figure with relationships that are less interdependent and relationships that are more interdependent. How effectively does the relationship predicted in this figure depict your own interpersonal conflicts?

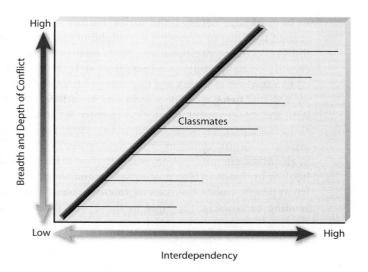

- Conflict is destructive because it reveals our negative selves—our pettiness, our need to be in control, our unreasonable expectations.
- In any conflict, there has to be a winner and a loser. Because goals are incompatible, someone has to win and someone has to lose.

Each of these statements is false—and, as we'll see in this chapter, these myths can easily interfere with your effectively dealing with conflict. It's not so much the conflict that creates problems as the way in which you approach and deal with the conflict. Some ways of approaching conflict can resolve difficulties and differences and can actually improve a relationship. Other ways can hurt the relationship; they can destroy self-esteem, create bitterness, and foster suspicion. And, perhaps most important, conflict does not mean that someone has to lose and someone has to win. Both can win. Your task, therefore, is not to try to create relationships that will be free of conflict but rather to learn appropriate and productive ways of managing conflict so that neither person emerges a loser.

Conflict Issues

Interpersonal conflicts cover a wide range of issues (Canary, 2003). Such conflicts may focus on goals to be pursued (for example, parents and child disagree on what college the child should attend or what romantic partner he or she should get involved with); on the allocation of resources such as money or time (for example, partners differ on how to spend their money); on decisions to be made (for example, spouses argue about whether to save or splurge a bonus); or on behaviors that are considered appropriate or desirable by one person but inappropriate or undesirable by the other (for example, two people disagree over whether one of them was flirting or drinking or not working as hard on the relationship).

In a study on the issues argued about by gay, lesbian, and heterosexual couples, researchers found that respondents identified six major issues that were virtually identical for all couples (Kurdek, 1994). These issues are arranged here in order, with the first being the most often mentioned. As you read this list, ask yourself how many of these issues you argue about.

- intimacy issues such as affection and sex
- power issues such as excessive demands or possessiveness, lack of equality in the relationship, friends, and leisure time
- personal flaws issues such as drinking or smoking, personal grooming, and driving style
- personal distance issues such as frequent absence and heavy school or job commitments
- social issues such as politics and social policies, parents, and personal values
- distrust issues such as previous lovers and lying

Another study found that any (or all) of four conditions generally led up to a couple's "first big fight": uncertainty over commitment, jealousy, violation of expectations, and/or personality differences (Siegert & Stamp, 1994).

In workplace settings, the major sources of conflict among top managers revolved around the issue of executive responsibility and coordination. Other conflicts focused on differences in organizational objectives, on how resources were to be allocated, and on what constituted an appropriate management style (Morrill, 1992).

In a study of same-sex and opposite-sex friends, the four issues most often argued about were shared living space or possessions, violations of friendship rules, the sharing of activities, and disagreement about ideas (Samter & Cupach, 1998).

In large part, the same conflicts you experience in face-to-face relationships can also arise in electronic communication. Yet there are a few conflict issues that seem to be unique to electronic communication, whether via e-mail, on social networking sites such as Facebook or MySpace, in blog postings, or on the phone. For the most part, such conflict results when people violate the rules of Internet courtesy discussed in Chapter 5. For example, sending commercial messages to those who didn't request them often creates conflict; sending a message to an entire listserv when it's relevant to only one member may annoy other members, who expect to receive messages relevant to the entire group and not personal exchanges between two people. Sending someone unsolicited mail (spamming or spimming), repeatedly sending the same mail, or posting the same message in lots of newsgroups even when the message is irrelevant to the focus of one or more groups, also will create conflict. Putting out purposely incorrect information or outrageous viewpoints to watch other people correct you or get emotionally upset by your message (trolling) can obviously lead to conflict, though some see it as fun. Other potential causes of such conflict include ill-timed cell phone calls, calling someone at work just to chat, or criticizing someone unfairly or posting an unflattering photo on social network sites.

Principles of Interpersonal Conflict

The importance and influence of conflict in all interpersonal relationships can be best appreciated if we understand some fundamental principles of this particular form of interaction. Here we look at (1) the inevitability of conflict, (2) conflict's positive and negative aspects, (3) conflict's focus on content and/or on relationships, (4) differing styles of conflict and their consequences, and (5) the influence of culture on conflict.

Conflict Is Inevitable

Conflict is a part of every interpersonal relationship, whether between parents and children, brothers and sisters, friends, lovers, or coworkers. One study found that on average couples, for example, have 182 conflicts each year (approximately 3.5 conflicts per week), each lasting on average 25 minutes, with another 30 minutes for sulking (www.24dash.com, accessed May 28, 2008).

The very fact that people are different, have had different histories, and have different goals will invariably produce differences. If the individuals are interdependent, as discussed earlier (see Figure 12.1), these differences may well lead to conflicts—and if so, the conflicts can focus on a wide variety of issues and be extremely personal.

Conflict Can Have Negative and Positive Effects

Even though interpersonal conflict is inevitable, the way you deal with conflict is crucial, for conflict can have both negative and positive effects depending on how it is handled.

Negative Effects Among the disadvantages of conflict is that it often leads to increased negative feelings. Many conflicts involve unfair fighting methods and focus largely on hurting the other person. If this happens, negative feelings are sure to increase. Conflict also may deplete energy better spent on other areas, especially when unproductive conflict strategies are used.

At times, conflict may lead you to close yourself off from the other individual. When you hide your feelings from your partner, you prevent meaningful communication and interaction; this, in turn, creates barriers to intimacy. Because the need for intimacy is so strong, one possible outcome is that one or both parties may seek intimacy elsewhere. This often leads to further conflict, mutual hurt, and resentment—all of which add heavily to the costs carried by the relationship. As the costs increase, the rewards may become more difficult to exchange. Here, then, is a situation in which costs increase and rewards decrease, a scenario that often results in relationship deterioration and eventual dissolution.

Positive Effects Among the advantages of conflict is that it forces you to examine a problem and work toward a potential solution. If you use productive conflict strategies, your relationship is likely to become stronger, healthier, and more satisfying than it was before.

Conflict often prevents hostilities and resentments from festering. Say you're annoyed at your partner, who comes home from work and then talks on the phone with colleagues for two hours instead of giving that time to you. If you say nothing, your annoyance is likely to grow. Further, by saying nothing you implicitly approve of such behavior, so it's likely that the phone calls will continue. Through your conflict and its resolution, you each let your needs be known: Your partner needs to review the day's work to gain assurance that it's been properly completed, and you have a need for your partner's attention. If you both can appreciate the legitimacy of these needs, then you stand a good chance of finding workable solutions. Perhaps your partner can make the phone calls after your attention needs are met. Perhaps you can delay your need for attention until your partner gets closure about work. Perhaps you can learn to provide for your partner's closure needs and in doing so get your own attention needs met. Again, you have win–win solutions; each of your needs are met.

Consider, too, that when you try to resolve conflict within an interpersonal relationship, you're saying that the relationship is worth the effort; otherwise, you'd walk away. Although there may be exceptions—as when you confront conflict to save face or to gratify some ego need—confronting a conflict often indicates concern, commitment, and a desire to protect and preserve the relationship.

Conflict Can Focus on Content and/or Relationship Issues

Using concepts developed earlier (Chapter 1), you can distinguish between content and relationship conflicts. *Content conflict* centers on objects, events, and persons in the world that are usually external to the people involved in the conflict. These include the millions of issues that you argue and fight about every day—the merits of a particular movie, what to watch on television, the fairness of the last examination, who should get promoted, the way to spend your savings.

Relationship conflicts are equally numerous and are concerned with the relationships between the individuals—with such issues as who's in charge, the equality or lack of it in the relationship, and who has the right to establish rules of behavior. Examples of relationship conflicts include those involving a younger brother who does not obey his older brother, two partners who each want an equal say in making vacation plans, or a mother and daughter who each want to have the final word concerning the daughter's lifestyle.

Relationship conflicts often are hidden and disguised as content conflicts. Thus, a conflict over where you should vacation may, on the content level, center on the advantages and disadvantages of Mexico versus Hawaii. On a relationship level, however, it may center on who has the greater right to select the place to vacation, who should win the argument, or who is the decision maker in the relationship.

Conflict Styles Have Consequences

As mentioned earlier, the way in which you engage in conflict has consequences for the resolution of the conflict and for the relationship between the conflicting parties. Figure 12.2 illustrates an approach to conflict that identifies five basic styles or ways of engaging in conflict and is especially relevant to an understanding of interpersonal conflicts (Blake & Mouton, 1984). The five styles, plotted along the dimensions of "concern for self" and "concern for the other person," provide insight into the ways people engage in conflict and into some of the advantages and disadvantages of each style. As you read through the following descriptions of these styles, try to identify your own often-used conflict style as well as the styles of those with whom you have close relationships.

Competing—I Win, You Lose The *competing* style represents great concern for your own needs and desires and little for those of others. As long as your needs are met, the conflict

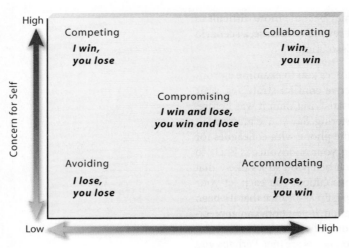

FIGURE 12.2

Five Conflict Styles

This figure is adapted from Blake and Mouton's (1984) approach to managerial leadership and conflict and illustrates five styles of conflict. As you read about these styles, consider your own conflict style and the styles of those with whom you interact most frequently. Most important, consider how you can make your own conflict style more effective.

has been dealt with successfully (for you). In conflict motivated by competitiveness, you'd be likely to be verbally aggressive while blaming the other person.

This style represents an *I win, you lose* philosophy. With this philosophy, you attempt to manage the conflict so that you win and the other person loses. As you can tell, this style might be appropriate in a courtroom or in buying a car, two situations in which one person benefits from the other person's losses. But in interpersonal situations this philosophy can easily lead to resentment in the person who lost, which in turn can easily morph into additional conflicts. Further, the fact that you win and the other person loses probably means that the conflict really hasn't been resolved, just concluded (for now).

Avoiding—I Lose, You Lose Using the *avoiding* style suggests that you are relatively unconcerned with your own or with the other's needs or desires. The avoider shrinks from any real communication about the problem, changes the topic when the problem is brought up, and generally withdraws from the scene both psychologically and physically.

As you can appreciate, this style does little to resolve any conflicts and may be viewed as an *I lose, you lose* philosophy. Interpersonal problems rarely go away of their own accord; rather, if they exist, they need to be faced and dealt with effectively. The avoidance philosophy just allows the conflict to fester and probably to grow, only to resurface in another guise.

Accommodating—I Lose, You Win In *accommodating* you sacrifice your own needs for the sake of the needs of the other person. Your major purpose is to maintain harmony and peace in the relationship or group. The accommodating style may help you attain the immediate goal of maintaining peace and perhaps satisfying the other person, but it does little to meet your own needs—which are unlikely to go away.

Accommodating represents an *I lose, you win* philosophy. And although this style may make your partner happy (at least on this occasion), it's not likely to prove a lasting resolution to an interpersonal conflict. You'll eventually sense the unfairness and inequity inherent in this approach to conflict, and you may easily come to resent your partner and perhaps even yourself.

Collaborating—I Win, You Win In *collaborating* your concern is with both your own and the other person's needs. Often considered the ideal, collaborating takes time and a willingness to communicate, and especially to listen to the perspectives and needs of the other person.

Ideally, collaborating will allow each person's needs to be being satisfied, an *I win, you win* situation. This is obviously the style that, ideally, you would use in most of your interpersonal conflict. Collaborating promotes resolutions in which both people get something.

Compromising—I Win and Lose, You Win and Lose The *compromising* style is in the middle; there's some concern for your own needs and some concern for the other's needs. Compromising is the kind of strategy you might refer to as "meeting each other halfway," "horse trading," or "give and take." This strategy is likely to result in maintaining peace, but there also will be dissatisfaction over the inevitable losses that have to be endured.

Compromising could be called an *I win and lose and you win and lose* strategy. There are lots of times when you can't both get exactly what you want. For example, you can't both get a new car if the available funds allow for only one. Still, you might each get a better car than what you now have—so you would win something, but not everything. You wouldn't get a new car, and the same would be true of your partner.

Conflict Is Influenced by Culture

As is true with all communication processes, conflict is influenced by the culture of the participants—and especially by their beliefs and values about conflict. Culture influences the topics people fight about as well as what are considered appropriate and inappropriate ways of dealing with conflict. For example, cohabiting 18-year-olds are more likely to have conflict with their parents over their living style if they live in the United States than if they live in Sweden, where cohabitation is much more accepted. Similarly, male infidelity is more likely to cause conflict among American couples than among southern European couples. Students from the United States are more likely to pursue a conflict with another United States student than with someone from another culture. Chinese students, on the other hand, are more likely to pursue a conflict with a non-Chinese than with another Chinese student (Leung, 1988).

The topics of conflicts also will depend on whether the culture is high or low context (see Chapter 2). In high-context cultures, conflicts are more likely to center on violations of collective or group norms and values. Conversely, in low-context cultures, conflicts are more likely to come up when individual norms are violated (Ting-Toomey, 1985).

Cultures also differ in how they define what constitutes conflict. For example, in some cultures it's quite common for women to be referred to negatively and to be seen as less than equal. To most people in the United States, this would constitute a clear basis for conflict. To some Japanese women, however, this isn't uncommon and isn't perceived as abusive (*New York Times*, February 11, 1996, pp. 1, 12). Further, Americans and Japanese differ in their views of the aim or purpose of conflict. The Japanese see conflicts and their resolution in terms of compromise; Americans, on the other hand, see conflict in terms of winning (Gelfand, Nishii, Holcombe, Dyer, Ohbuchi, & Fukuno, 2001). African Americans and European Americans engage in conflict in very different ways (Kochman, 1981; Hecht, Jackson, & Ribeau, 2003). The issues that cause and aggravate conflict, the conflict strategies that are expected and accepted, and the attitudes toward conflict vary from one group to the other.

Cultures vary widely in their responses to physical and verbal abuse. In some Asian and Hispanic cultures, for example, the fear of losing face or embarrassing the family is so great that people prefer not to report or reveal abuses. When looking over statistics, it may at first appear that little violence occurs in the families of certain cultures. Yet we know from research that wife beating is quite common in India, Taiwan, and Iran, for example (Counts, Brown, & Campbell, 1992; Hatfield & Rapson, 1996). In much of the United States, and in many other cultures as well, such abuse would not be tolerated no matter who was embarrassed or insulted.

Each culture seems to teach its members different views of conflict strategies (Tardiff, 2001). In one study, African American females were found to use more direct controlling strategies (for example, assuming control over the conflict and arguing persistently for their point of view) than did white females. White females, on the other hand, used more solution-oriented conflict styles than did African American females. African American and white men were similar in their conflict strategies; both avoided or withdrew from relationship conflict, preferring to keep quiet about their differences or make them seem insignificant

VIEWPOINT One of the most puzzling findings on violence is that many victims interpret it as a sign of love. For some reason, they see being beaten or verbally abused as a sign that their partner is fully in love with them. Also, many victims blame themselves for the violence instead of blaming their partners (Gelles & Cornell, 1985). Why do you think this is so? What part does force or violence play in conflicts in your own interpersonal relationships?

Not surprisingly, research finds significant gender differences in interpersonal conflict. For example, men are more apt to withdraw from a conflict situation than are women. It's been argued that this may be due to the fact that men become more psychologically and physiologically aroused during conflict (and retain this heightened level of arousal much longer) than do women and so may try to distance themselves and withdraw from the conflict to prevent further arousal (Gottman & Carrere, 1994; Goleman, 1995b). Another position would argue that men withdraw because the culture has taught men to avoid conflict; still another would claim that withdrawal is an expression of power.

Women, on the other hand, want to get closer to the conflict; they want to talk about it and re-solve it. Even adolescents reveal these differences. In research on boys and girls aged 11 to 17, boys withdrew more than girls (Lindeman, Harakka, & Keltikangas-Jarvinen, 1997; Heasley, Babbitt, & Bur-bach, 1995). Other research has found that women are more emotional and men are more logical when they argue. Women have been defined as conflict "feelers" and men as conflict "thinkers" (Sorenson, Hawkins, & Sorenson, 1995). Another difference is that women are more apt to reveal their negative feelings than are men (Schaap, Buunk, & Kerkstra, 1988; Canary, Cupach, & Messman, 1995).

It should be mentioned, however, that some research fails to support these stereotypical gender differences in conflict style—the differences that cartoons, situation comedies, and films portray so readily and so clearly. For example, several studies dealing with both college students and men and women in business found no significant differences in the ways men and women engage in conflict (Wilkins & Andersen, 1991; Canary & Hause, 1993; Gottman & Levenson, 1999).

Working with Theories and Research

New findings on gender differences continue to emerge, so update this discussion by logging on to your favourite search engine and searching for current research on "gender" and "conflict." What can you add to the discussion presented here?

(Ting-Toomey, 1986). Another example of this cultural influence on conflict is seen in the tendency of members of collectivist cultures to avoid conflict more, and to give greater importance to saving face, than members of individualist cultures (Dsilva & Whyte, 1998; Haar & Krabe, 1999; Cai & Fink, 2002; Oetzel & Ting-Toomey, 2003).

As in the wider culture, the cultural norms of organizations will influence the types of conflicts that occur and the ways in which they may be dealt with. In some work environments, for example, the expression of conflict with high-level management would not be tolerated; in others it might be welcomed. In individualist cultures there is greater tolerance for conflict within organizations, even when it may involve different levels of the hierarchy. In collectivist cultures there is less tolerance. And, not surprisingly, culture influences how conflicts will be resolved. For example, American managers (members of an individualistic culture) deal with workplace conflict by seeking to integrate the demands of the different sides; Chinese managers (members of a collectivist culture) are more likely to call on higher management to make decisions or to leave the conflict unresolved (Tinsley & Brett, 2001).

Another factor that influences conflict is your own position on the organizational hierarchy. For example, if you're a temporary worker in a large organization, you're not likely to have conflict with the CEO, because you'll probably never meet. But workplace conflicts with coworkers at your own level, or with those a level above or a level below, are much more likely to occur. When you experience conflict with, say, a supervisor, it's more likely to be job related—to focus on issues such as job satisfaction or organizational commitment. When you experience conflict with coworkers, it's more likely to be related to personal issues such as self-esteem or depression (Frone, 2000).

Conflict Management Stages

Before trying to manage or resolve a conflict, you need to prepare. Conflict resolution is an extremely important communication experience, and you don't want to enter it without adequate thought. Here are a few suggestions for preparing for resolving conflict.

Before the Conflict First, try to fight in private. When you air your conflicts in front of others, you create a variety of other problems. You may not be willing to be totally honest when third parties are present; you may feel you have to save face and therefore must win the fight at all costs. This may lead you to use strategies to win the argument rather than to resolve the conflict. You may become so absorbed by the image that others will have of you that you forget you have a relationship problem that needs to be resolved. Also, you run the risk of embarrassing your partner in front of others, and this embarrassment may create resentment and hostility.

Be sure you're each ready to fight. Although conflicts arise at the most inopportune times, you can choose the time to resolve them. Confronting your partner when she or he comes home after a hard day of work may not be the right time for resolving a conflict. Make sure you're both relatively free of other problems and ready to deal with the conflict at hand.

Know what you're fighting about. Sometimes people in a relationship become so hurt and angry that they lash out at the other person just to vent their own frustration. The problem at the center of the conflict (for example, the uncapped toothpaste tube) is merely an excuse to express anger. Any attempt to resolve this "problem" will be doomed to failure, because the problem addressed is not what is causing the conflict. Instead, the underlying hostility, anger, and frustration need to be addressed.

Fight about problems that can be solved. Fighting about past behaviors or about family members or situations over which you have no control solves nothing; instead, it creates additional difficulties. Any attempt at resolution will fail, because the problems are incapable of being solved. Often such conflicts are concealed attempts at expressing frustration or dissatisfaction.

Now that you're prepared for the conflict resolution interaction, refer to the model in Figure 12.3. It identifies the steps that will help you navigate through this process.

FIGURE 12.3

Stages in Conflict Resolution

This model of conflict resolution is essentially John Dewey's (1910) problem-solving sequence. The assumption made here is that a conflict to be resolved is essentially a problem to be solved and follows the same general sequence. As you read about this problem/conflict-solving sequence, try visualizing a specific conflict and how these several steps might help you resolve it.

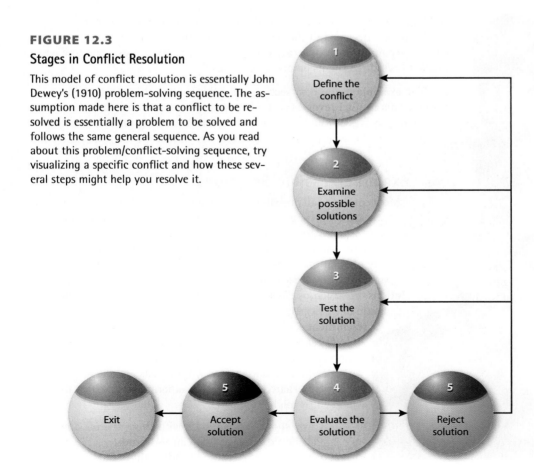

Define the Conflict

Your first and most essential step is to define the conflict. Here are several techniques to keep in mind.

- *Define both content and relationship issues.* Define the obvious content issues (who should do the dishes, who should take the kids to school) as well as the underlying relationship issues (who has been avoiding household responsibilities, whose time is more valuable).

- *Define the problem in specific terms.* Conflict defined in the abstract is difficult to deal with and resolve. It's one thing for a husband to say that his wife is "cold and unfeeling" and quite another to say that she does not call him at the office, kiss him when he comes home, or hold his hand when they're at a party. These behaviors can be agreed on and dealt with, but the abstract "cold and unfeeling" remains elusive.

- *Focus on the present.* Avoid **gunnysacking** (a term derived from the large burlap bag called a gunnysack)—the practice of storing up grievances so they may be unloaded at another time. Often, when one person gunnysacks, the other person gunnysacks; for example, the birthdays you forgot and the times you arrived late for dinner are all thrown at you. The result is two people dumping their stored-up grievances on each other with no real attention to the present problem.

- *Empathize.* Try to understand the nature of the conflict from the other person's point of view. Why is your partner disturbed that you're not doing the dishes? Why is your neighbor complaining about taking the kids to school? Once you have empathically understood the other person's feelings, validate those feelings when appropriate. If your partner is hurt or angry and you believe such feelings are legitimate and justified, say so: "You have a right to be angry; I shouldn't have said what I did about your mother. I'm sorry. But I still don't want to go on vacation with her." In expressing validation, you're not necessarily expressing agreement; you're merely stating that your partner has feelings that you recognize as legitimate.

  - *Avoid mind reading.* Don't try to read the other person's mind. Ask questions to make sure you understand the problem as the other person is experiencing it. Ask directly and simply: "Why are you insisting that I take the dog out now, when I have to call three clients before nine o'clock?"

The example in the next section will help us work through the remaining steps. This conflict revolves around Pat's not wanting to socialize with Chris's friends. Chris is devoted to these friends, but Pat actively dislikes them. Chris thinks they're wonderful and exciting; Pat thinks they're unpleasant and boring.

Examine Possible Solutions

Most conflicts can probably be resolved through a variety of solutions. Here are a few suggestions. Brainstorm by yourself or with your partner. Try not to inhibit or censor yourself or your partner as you generate these potential solutions. Once you have proposed a variety of solutions, look especially for solutions that will enable each party to win—to get something he or she wants. Avoid win–lose solutions, in which one person wins and one loses. Such outcomes will cause difficulty for the relationship by engendering frustration and resentment.

Carefully weigh the costs and the rewards that each solution entails. Most solutions will involve costs to one or both parties. Seek solutions in which the costs and the rewards will be evenly shared. For example, among the solutions that Pat and Chris might identify are these:

1. Chris should not interact with these friends anymore.
2. Pat should interact with Chris's friends.
3. Chris should see these friends without Pat.

Clearly solutions 1 and 2 are win–lose solutions. In solution 1, Pat wins and Chris loses; in 2, Chris wins and Pat loses. Solution 3 has some possibilities. Both might win and neither must necessarily lose. This potential solution, then, needs to be looked at more closely.

Test the Solution

First, test the solution mentally. How does it feel now? How will it feel tomorrow? Are you comfortable with it? In our example, will Pat be comfortable with Chris's socializing with these friends alone? Some of Chris's friends are attractive; will this cause difficulty for Pat and Chris's relationship? Will Chris give people too much to gossip about? Will Chris feel guilty? Will Chris enjoy seeing these friends without Pat?

Second, test the solution in practice. Put the solution into operation. How does it work? If it doesn't work, then discard it and try another solution. Give each solution a fair chance, but don't hang on to a solution when it's clear that it won't resolve the conflict.

Perhaps Chris might go out without Pat once to test this solution. Afterward, the couple can evaluate the experiment. Did the friends think there was something wrong with Chris's relationship with Pat? Did Chris feel guilty? Did Chris enjoy this new experience? How did Pat feel? Did Pat feel jealous? Lonely? Abandoned?

Evaluate the Solution

Did the solution help resolve the conflict? Is the situation better now than it was before the solution was tried? Share your feelings and evaluations of the solution.

Pat and Chris now need to share their perceptions of this possible solution. Would they be comfortable with this solution on a monthly basis? Is the solution worth the costs each will pay? Are the costs and rewards evenly distributed? Might other solutions be more effective?

Critical-thinking pioneer Edward deBono (1987) suggests that in analyzing problems, you use six "thinking hats" as a way of seeking different perspectives. With each hat you look at the problem from a different angle.

- *The fact hat* focuses attention on the facts and figures that bear on the problem. For example, how can Pat learn more about the rewards that Chris gets from the friends? How can Chris learn why Pat doesn't like these great friends?
- *The feeling hat* focuses attention on the emotional responses to the problem. How does Pat feel when Chris goes out with these friends? How does Chris feel when Pat refuses to meet them?
- *The negative argument hat* asks you to become the devil's advocate. How may this relationship deteriorate if Chris continues seeing these friends without Pat or if Pat resists interacting with Chris's friends?
- *The positive benefits hat* asks you to look at the upside. What are the opportunities that Chris's seeing friends without Pat might yield? What benefits might Pat and Chris get from this new arrangement?
- *The creative new idea hat* focuses on new ways of looking at the problem. In what other ways can Pat and Chris look at this problem? What other possible solutions might they consider?
- *The control of thinking hat* helps you analyze what you're doing; it asks you to reflect on your own thinking. Have Pat and Chris adequately defined the problem? Are they focusing too much on insignificant issues? Have they given enough attention to possible negative effects?

Accept or Reject the Solution

If you accept the solution, you're ready to put it into more permanent operation. Let's say that Pat is actually quite happy with the solution. Pat was able to use the evening to visit college friends.

Take a good look at your own conflict behaviors. What changes would you make? What conflict skills and strategies would you seek to integrate into your own interpersonal and small group conflict resolution behavior?

The next time Chris goes out with the friends Pat doesn't like, Pat intends to go out with some friends from college. Chris feels pretty good about seeing friends without Pat. Chris explains that they have both decided to see their friends separately and both are comfortable with this decision. If, however, either Pat or Chris feels unhappy with this solution, they will have to try out another solution or perhaps go back and redefine the problem and seek other ways to resolve it.

After the Conflict Even after the conflict is resolved, there is still work to be done. Often, after one conflict is supposedly settled, another conflict will emerge—because, for example, one person feels that he or she has been harmed and needs to retaliate and take revenge in order to restore a sense of self-worth (Kim & Smith, 1993). So it's especially important that the conflict be resolved and not be allowed to generate other, perhaps more significant conflicts.

Learn from the conflict and from the process you went through in trying to resolve it. For example, can you identify the fight strategies that merely aggravated the situation? Do you or your partner need a cooling-off period? Can you tell when minor issues are going to escalate into major arguments? Does avoidance make matters worse? What issues are particularly disturbing and likely to cause difficulties? Can they be avoided?

Keep the conflict in perspective. Be careful not to blow it out of proportion to the extent that you begin to define your relationship in terms of conflict. Avoid the tendency to see disagreement as inevitably leading to major blowups. Conflicts in most relationships actually occupy a very small percentage of the couple's time, and yet in recollection they often loom extremely large. Also, don't allow the conflict to undermine your own or your partner's self-esteem. Don't view yourself, your partner, or your relationship as a failure just because you had an argument or even lots of arguments.

Attack your negative feelings. Negative feelings frequently arise after an interpersonal conflict. Most often they arise because one or both parties used unfair fight strategies to undermine the other person—for example, personal rejection, manipulation, or force. Resolve to avoid such unfair tactics in the future, but at the same time let go of guilt and blame toward yourself and your partner. If you think it would help, discuss these feelings with your partner or even a therapist. Apologize for anything you did wrong. Your partner should do likewise; after all, both parties are usually responsible for the conflict (Coleman, 2002).

Increase the exchange of rewards and cherishing behaviors to demonstrate your positive feelings and to show you're over the conflict and want the relationship to survive and flourish.

Conflict Management Strategies

In managing conflict you can choose from a variety of strategies, which we will explore below. First, however, realize that the strategies you choose will be influenced by a variety of factors such as (1) the goals to be achieved, (2) your emotional state, (3) your cognitive assessment of the situation, (4) your personality and communication competence, and (5) your family history (Koerner & Fitzpatrick, 2002). Understanding these factors may help you select strategies that are more appropriate and more effective. Research finds that using productive conflict strategies can have lots of beneficial effects, whereas using inappropriate strategies may be linked to poorer psychological health (Weitzman & Weitzman, 2000; Weitzman, 2001; Neff & Harter, 2002).

1. The *goals* (short-term and long-term) you wish to achieve will influence what strategies seem appropriate to you. If you merely want to salvage this evening's date, you

may want to simply "give in" and basically ignore the difficulty. On the other hand, if you want to build a long-term relationship, you may want to fully analyze the cause of the problem and to seek strategies that will enable both parties to win.

2. Your *emotional state* will influence your strategies. You're unlikely to select the same strategies when you're sad as when you're angry. You will choose different strategies when you're seeking to apologize than when you're looking for revenge.

3. Your *cognitive assessment* of the situation will exert powerful influence. For example, your attitudes and beliefs about what is fair and equitable will influence your readiness to acknowledge the fairness in the other person's position. Your own assessment of who (if anyone) is the cause of the problem also will influence your conflict style. You may also assess the likely effects of your various options. For example, what do you risk if you fight with your boss by using blame or personal rejection? Do you risk alienating your teenager if you use force?

4. Your *personality and communication competence* will influence the way you engage in conflict. For example, if you're shy and unassertive, you may be more likely to try to avoid conflict than to fight actively. If you're extroverted and have a strong desire to state your position, then you may be more likely to fight actively and argue forcefully. And, of course, some people have greater tolerance for disagreement and consequently are more apt to let things slide and not become emotionally upset or hostile than are those with little tolerance for disagreement (Wrench, McCroskey, & Richmond, 2008; Teven, Richmond, & McCroskey, 1998).

5. Your *family history* will influence the strategies you use, the topics you choose to fight about, and perhaps your tendencies to obsess or to forget about interpersonal conflicts.

A wide variety of conflict resolution skills already have been covered in earlier chapters. For example, active listening (Chapter 4) is a skill that has wide application in conflict situations. Similarly, using I-messages rather than accusatory you-messages (Chapter 7) will contribute to effective interpersonal conflict resolution (Noller & Fitzpatrick, 1993). Of course, the characteristics of interpersonal competence covered in the Understanding Interpersonal Skills boxes throughout the text are clear and effective conflict resolution techniques.

The following discussion identifies additional strategies, detailing both the unproductive and destructive strategies that you'll want to avoid and the productive and constructive strategies that you'll want to use. It's important to see at the outset that the strategic choices you make (and do realize that you do have choices, something people frequently try to deny) will greatly affect both the specific interpersonal conflict and your relationship as a whole. For example, refusal messages, insults, accusations, and commands are likely to lead to conflict as well as to add to existing conflicts, delaying and perhaps preventing effective conflict management (Canary, Cody, & Manusov, 2003).

Win–Lose and Win–Win Strategies

As indicated in the discussion of conflict styles, when you look at interpersonal conflict in terms of winning and losing, you get four basic types: (1) A wins, B loses; (2) A loses, B wins; (3) A loses, B loses; and (4) A wins, B wins.

Obviously, win–win solutions are the most desirable. Perhaps the most important reason is that win–win solutions lead to mutual satisfaction and prevent the resentment that win–lose solutions often engender. Looking for and developing win–win solutions makes the next conflict less unpleasant; it becomes easier to see the conflict as "solving a problem" rather than as a "fight." Still another benefit of win–win solutions is that they promote mutual face-saving; both parties can feel good about themselves. Finally, people are more likely to abide by the decisions reached in a win–win outcome than they are in win–lose or lose–lose resolutions.

VIEWPOINT One study found that, generally at least, people are more positive in dealing with conflict in face-to-face situations than in computer-mediated communication (Zornoza, Ripoll, & Peiro, 2002). Do you notice this in your own interactions? If so, why do you think it's true? In what ways might you make your own online conflicts more positive?

UNDERSTANDING INTERPERSONAL SKILLS

Equality

In interpersonal communication the term **equality** refers to an attitude or approach that treats each person as an important and vital contributor to the interaction. In any situation, of course, there will be some inequality; one person will be higher in the organizational hierarchy, more knowledgeable, or more interpersonally effective. But despite this fact, an attitude of superiority is to be avoided. Interpersonal communication is generally more effective when it takes place in an atmosphere of equality.

Communicating Equality. Here are a few suggestions for communicating equality in all interactions, and especially in those involving conflict.

- Avoid "should" and "ought" statements (for example, "You really should call your mother more often" or "You should learn to speak up"). These statements put the listener in a one-down position.
- Make requests (especially courteous ones) and avoid demands (especially discourteous ones).
- Avoid interrupting; this signals an unequal relationship and implies that what you have to say is more important than what the other person is saying.
- Acknowledge the other person's contributions before expressing your own. Saying "I see," "I understand," or "That's right" lets the other person know you're listening and understanding.
- Recognize that different cultures treat equality very differently. In low-power-distance cultures there is greater equality than in high-power-distance cultures, in which status differences greatly influence interpersonal interactions.

Working with Interpersonal Skills

Think about your interpersonal interactions over the last few days. In what ways did you express equality? Can you identify situations in which you could have expressed greater equality? Would this have made a difference in the interaction?

In sum, you can look for solutions in which you or your side wins and the other person or side loses (win–lose solutions). Or you can look for solutions in which you and the other person both win (win–win solutions). Win–win solutions are always better. Too often, however, we fail even to consider the possibility of win–win solutions and what they might be.

Take an interpersonal example: Let's say that I want to spend our money on a new car (my old one is unreliable), but you want to spend it on a vacation (you're exhausted and feel the need for a rest). Through our conflict and its resolution, ideally, we learn what each really wants and may then be able to figure out a way for each of us to get what we want. I might accept a good used car, and you might accept a less expensive vacation. Or we might buy a used car and take an inexpensive road trip. Each of these win–win solutions will satisfy both of us; each of us wins, each of us gets what we wanted.

Avoidance and Active Fighting Strategies

Avoidance of conflict may involve actual physical flight; for example, leaving the scene of the conflict (walking out of the apartment or going to another part of the office), falling asleep, or blasting the stereo to drown out all conversation. It may also take the form of emotional or intellectual avoidance, whereby you leave the conflict psychologically by not dealing with the issues raised. Not surprisingly, as avoidance increases, relationship satisfaction decreases (Meeks, Hendrick, & Hendrick, 1998). Sometimes avoidance is a response to demands—a conflict pattern known as *demand–withdrawal*. Here one person makes demands and the other person, unwilling to accede to the demands, withdraws from the interaction (Canary, Cupach, & Messman, 1995; Sagrestano, Heavey, & Christensen, 2006; Guerrero, Andersen, & Afifi, 2007). This pattern is obviously unproductive, but either individual can easily break it—either by not making demands or by not withdrawing and instead participating actively in conflict management.

Although avoidance is an unproductive approach, this does not mean that taking time out to cool off is not a useful first strategy. Sometimes it is. When conflict is waged through e-mail or some social network site, for example, this is an easy-to-use and often effective strategy. By delaying your response until you've had time to think things out more logically and calmly, you'll be better able to respond constructively and to address possible resolutions to the conflict and get the relationship back to a less hostile stage.

Nonnegotiation is a special type of avoidance. Here you refuse to direct any attention to managing the conflict or to listen to the other person's argument. At times, nonnegotiation takes the form of hammering away at your own point of view until the other person gives in.

Another unproductive conflict strategy is the use of silencers. **Silencers** are conflict techniques that literally silence the other individual. Among the wide variety of silencers that exist, one frequently used technique is crying. When a person is unable to deal with a conflict or when winning seems unlikely, he or she may cry and thus silence the other person. Another silencer consists of feigning extreme emotionalism—yelling and screaming and pretending to be losing control. Still another is developing some physical reaction—headaches and shortness of breath are probably the most popular. One of the major problems with silencers is that you can never be certain whether they're strategies to win the argument or real physical reactions to which you should pay attention. Either way, however, the conflict remains unexamined and unresolved.

Instead of avoiding the issues or resorting to nonnegotiation or silencers, consider taking an active role in your interpersonal conflicts. If you wish to resolve conflicts, you need to confront them actively. Involve yourself on both sides of the communication exchange. Be an active participant as a speaker and as a listener; voice your own feelings and listen carefully to your partner's feelings.

An important part of active fighting involves taking responsibility for your thoughts and feelings. For example, when you disagree with your partner or find fault with her or his behavior, take responsibility for these feelings. Say, for example, "I disagree with . . ." or "I don't like it when you. . . ." Avoid statements that deny your responsibility, such as "Everybody thinks you're wrong about . . ." or "Chris thinks you shouldn't. . . ."

Force and Talk Strategies

When confronted with conflict, many people prefer not to deal with the issues but rather to force their position on the other person. The **force** may be emotional or physical. In either case, however, the issues are avoided, and the person who "wins" is the one who exerts the most force. This is the technique of warring nations, children, and even some normally sensible adults. It seems also to be the technique of those who are dissatisfied with the power they perceive themselves to have in a relationship (Ronfeldt, Kimerling, & Arias, 1998).

Ethics in Interpersonal Communication

Ethical Fighting

This chapter focused on the dimension of effectiveness versus ineffectiveness in conflict strategies. But all communication strategies also have an ethical dimension, and it is important to look at the ethical implications of conflict resolution strategies. For example:

■ Does conflict avoidance have an ethical dimension? For example, is it unethical for one relationship partner to refuse to discuss disagreements?

■ Can the use of physical force to influence another person ever be ethical? Can you identify a situation in which it would be appropriate for someone with greater physical strength to overpower another to compel the other to accept his or her point of view?

■ Are face-detracting strategies inherently unethical, or might it be appropriate to use them in certain situations? Can you identify such situations?

■ What are the ethical implications of verbal aggressiveness?

What would you do?

At your high-powered and highly stressful job, you sometimes smoke pot. This happens several times a month, but you don't use drugs at any other times. Your relationship partner—who you know hates drugs and despises people who use any recreational drug—asks you if you take drugs. Because it's such a limited use, and because you know that admitting this will cause a huge conflict in a relationship that's already having difficulties, you wonder if you can ethically lie about this.

VIEWPOINT Persons with disabilities are often singled out for verbal abuse and physical violence and are often ignored when they complain (Roeher Institute, 1995). What factors do you think contribute to abuse against persons with disabilities? Are these the same factors that contribute to abuse against women, against newly arrived immigrants, and/or against gay men and lesbians?

In one study more than 50 percent of single and married couples reported that they had experienced physical violence in their relationship. If we add symbolic violence (for example, threatening to hit the other person or throwing something), the percentages are above 60 percent for singles and above 70 percent for marrieds (Marshall & Rose, 1987). In other research 47 percent of a sample of 410 college students reported some experience with violence in a dating relationship (Deal & Wampler, 1986). In most cases the violence was reciprocal—each person in the relationship used violence.

The only real alternative to force is talk. For example, the qualities of openness, positiveness, and empathy (discussed in the Understanding Interpersonal Skills boxes in Chapters 4, 9, and 10) are suitable starting points. In addition, be sure to listen actively and openly (Chapter 4). This may be especially difficult in conflict situations; tempers may run high, and you may find yourself being attacked or at least disagreed with. Here are some suggestions for talking and listening more effectively in the conflict situation.

- *Act the role of the listener.* Also, think as a listener. Turn off the television, stereo, or computer; face the other person. Devote your total attention to what the other person is saying. Make sure you understand what the person is saying and feeling. One way to make sure is obviously to ask questions. Another way is to paraphrase what the other person is saying and ask for confirmation: "You feel that if we pooled our money and didn't have separate savings accounts, the relationship would be more equitable. Is that the way you feel?"
- *Express your support or empathy* for what the other person is saying and feeling: "I can understand how you feel. I know I control the finances and that can create a feeling of inequality." If appropriate, indicate your agreement: "You're right to be disturbed."
- *State your thoughts and feelings* on the issue as objectively as you can; if you disagree with what the other person said, then say so: "My problem is that when we did have equal access to the finances, you ran up so many bills that we still haven't recovered. To be honest with you, I'm worried the same thing will happen again."

Face-Detracting and Face-Enhancing Strategies

The discussion of politeness in Chapter 5 introduced the concepts of face and face-threatening messages (p. 105). As you might guess, these concepts have special relevance to interpersonal conflict. Face-detracting conflict strategies are those that attack either a person's positive face (for example, criticism of the person's contribution to a relationship or the person's abilities) or a person's negative face (for example, demands on a person's time or resources that attack the person's autonomy). Face-enhancing strategies are those that support and confirm a person's positive face (for example, praise, a pat on the back, or a sincere smile) or negative face (behaviors such as giving the person space and asking rather than demanding).

One popular but destructive face-detracting strategy is **beltlining** (Bach & Wyden, 1968). Much like fighters in a ring, each of us has an emotional "beltline." When you hit below it, you can inflict serious injury. When you hit above the belt, however, the person is able to absorb the blow. With most interpersonal relationships, especially those of long standing, you know where the other person's beltline is. You know, for example, that to hit Pat with the inability to have children is to hit below the belt. You know that to hit Chris with the failure to get a permanent job is to hit below the belt. This type of face-detracting strategy causes all persons involved added problems. Keep blows to areas your opponent can absorb and handle.

Another such face-detracting strategy is **blame**. Instead of focusing on a solution to a problem, some members try to affix blame on the other person. Whether true or not, blaming is generally unproductive for at least two reasons. First, it diverts attention away from the problem and from its potential solution. Second, it creates resentment that is likely to be responded to with resentment. The conflict then spirals into personal attacks, leaving the individuals and the relationship worse off than before the conflict was ever addressed.

Strategies that enhance positive face involve helping the other person to maintain a positive image, an image as competent and trustworthy, able and good. Even when you get what you want—say, in a bargaining situation—it's wise to help the other person retain positive face, because it makes it less likely that future conflicts will arise (Donahue, 1992). To enhance negative face, make few demands, respect another's time, give the other person space especially in times of stress, avoid inappropriate touching, and express respect for the other's point of view.

Confirming the other person's self-image (Chapter 5), listening supportively and actively (Chapter 4), using I-messages that avoid blaming the other person (Chapter 7), and using excuses and apologies as appropriate (Chapter 8) are additional and useful face-enhancing strategies.

Verbal Aggressiveness and Argumentativeness Strategies

An especially interesting perspective on conflict has emerged from work on verbal aggressiveness and argumentativeness (Infante & Rancer, 1982; Infante & Wigley, 1986; Infante, 1988; Rancer, 1998). Understanding these concepts will help you understand some of the reasons things go wrong and some of the ways in which you can use conflict to actually improve your relationships.

Ask the Researcher

Arguing Assertively

I'm very aggressive when I argue with friends, romantic partners, work colleagues, and so on. After all, I want to win the argument. So what's so wrong with my being aggressive when I argue?

Scholars agree that all arguing is assertive and that assertiveness is a positive and constructive trait. Highly assertive individuals, then, would approach arguing controversial issues with enjoyment. In fact, the challenge is in achieving individual goals. Yet two stumbling blocks to goal achievement hinge on relationship and situational factors. A competent communicator demonstrates flexibility and skill in adapting communicative behaviors in a wide variety of relationships and settings. For example, small group members high in argumentativeness are often perceived as stirring up conflict. Thus, it may be all right to always win arguments with friends and coworkers but not all right to always win arguments with a romantic partner or members of small groups. Trait researchers find that the situation and the relationship are key environmental factors warranting consideration. When training individuals to enhance assertiveness and argumentativeness abilities, trainers note the possible negative consequences of seeking to always win arguments, no matter what.

For more information see C. M. Anderson & A. S. Rancer (2007), "The Relationship between Argumentativeness, Verbal Aggressiveness, and Communication Satisfaction in Incarcerated Male Youth," *The Prison Journal* 87: 328–343.

Carolyn M. Anderson (Ph.D., Kent State University) is a professor in the School of Communication at the University of Akron (canders@uakron.edu) and teaches graduate and undergraduate courses in group decision making, leadership, and health communication. Dr. Anderson researches trait communication in interpersonal, group, organizational, family, and health settings. She serves the community as a consultant, public speaker, and trainer.

Verbal Aggressiveness   **Verbal aggressiveness** is an unproductive conflict strategy in which one person tries to win an argument by inflicting psychological pain, by attacking the other person's self-concept. It's a type of disconfirmation (and the opposite of confirmation) in that it seeks to discredit the individual's view of self (see Chapter 5). To explore this tendency further, take the accompanying self-test on verbal aggressiveness.

✎ TEST YOURSELF

HOW VERBALLY AGGRESSIVE ARE YOU?

This scale measures how people try to obtain compliance from others. For each statement, indicate the extent to which you feel it's true for you in your attempts to influence others. Use the following scale: 5 = strongly agree, 4 = agree, 3 = undecided, 2 = disagree, and 1 = strongly disagree.

_____   1. If individuals I am trying to influence really deserve it, I attack their character.

_____   2. When individuals are very stubborn, I use insults to soften their stubborness.

_____   3. When people behave in ways that are in very poor taste, I insult them in order to shock them into proper behavior.

_____   4. When people simply will not budge on a matter of importance, I lose my temper and say rather strong things to them.

_____   5. When individuals insult me, I get a lot of pleasure out of really telling them off.

_____   6. I like poking fun at people who do things that are stupid in order to stimulate their intelligence.

_____   7. When people do things that are mean or cruel, I attack their character in order to help correct their behavior.

_____   8. When nothing seems to work in trying to influence others, I yell and scream in order to get some movement from them.

_____   9. When I am unable to refute others' positions, I try to make them feel defensive in order to weaken their positions.

_____ 10. When people refuse to do a task I know is important without good reason, I tell them they are unreasonable.

HOW DID YOU DO?   To compute your verbal aggressiveness score, simply add up your responses. A total score of 30 would indicate the neutral point: not especially aggressive but not especially confirming of the other either. If you scored about 35, you would be considered moderately aggressive; and if you scored 40 or more, you'd be considered very aggressive. If you scored below the neutral point, you'd be considered less verbally aggressive and more confirming when interacting with others. In looking over your responses, make special note of the characteristics identified in the 10 statements that refer to the tendency to act verbally aggressive. Note those inappropriate behaviors that you're especially prone to commit.

WHAT WILL YOU DO?   Because verbal aggressiveness is likely to seriously reduce communication effectiveness, you probably want to reduce your tendencies to respond aggressively. Review the times when you acted verbally aggressive. What effect did such actions have on your subsequent interaction? What effect did they have on your relationship with the other person? What alternative ways of getting your point across might you have used? Might these have proved more effective? Perhaps the most general suggestion for reducing verbal aggressiveness is to increase your argumentativeness.

Source: From a 20-item scale developed by Infante and Wigley (1986) and factor analyzed by Beatty, Rudd, and Valencic (1999). Also see "Verbal Aggressiveness" by Dominic Infante and C. J. Wigley, _Communication Monographs_ 53 (1986); Michael J. Beatty, Jill E. Rudd, & Kristin Marie Valencic, "A Re-evaluation of the Verbal Aggressiveness Scale: One Factor or Two?," _Communication Research Reports_ 16 (1999): 10–17; and Levine, T. R., Beatty, M. J., Limon, S., Hamilton, M. A., Buck, R., & Chory-Assad, R. M. (2004, September). "The Dimensionality of the Verbal Aggressiveness Scale." _Communication Monographs_ 71: 245–268. Copyright © 1986 by the National Communication Association. Reprinted by permission of the publisher and authors.

Character attack, perhaps because it's extremely effective in inflicting psychological pain, is the most popular tactic of verbal aggressiveness. Other tactics include attacking the person's abilities, background, and physical appearance; cursing; teasing; ridiculing; threatening; swearing; and using various nonverbal emblems (Infante, Sabourin, Rudd, & Shannon, 1990).

Some researchers have argued that "unless aroused by verbal aggression, a hostile disposition remains latent in the form of unexpressed anger" (Infante, Chandler, & Rudd, 1989).

There is some evidence to show that people in violent relationships are more often verbally aggressive than people in nonviolent relationships (Sutter & Martin, 1998).

Because verbal aggressiveness does not help to resolve conflicts, results in loss of credibility for the person using it, and actually increases the credibility of the target of the aggressiveness, you may wonder why people act aggressively (Infante, Hartley, Martin, Higgins, et al., 1992; Infante, Riddle, Horvath, & Tumlin, 1992; Schrodt, 2003).

Communicating with an affirming style (for example, with smiles, a pleasant facial expression, touching, physical closeness, eye contact, nodding, warm and sincere voice, vocal variety) leads others to perceive less verbal aggression in an interaction than communicating with a nonaffirming style. The assumption people seem to make is that if your actions are affirming, then your messages are also, and if your actions are nonaffirming, then your messages are also (Infante, Rancer, & Jordan, 1996).

Argumentativeness Contrary to popular usage, the term **argumentativeness** refers to a quality to be cultivated rather than avoided. Argumentativeness is your willingness to argue for a point of view, your tendency to speak your mind on significant issues. It's the preferred alternative to verbal aggressiveness (Infante & Rancer, 1996; Hample, 2004). Before reading about ways to increase your argumentativeness, take the self-test "How Argumentative Are You?"

TEST YOURSELF

HOW ARGUMENTATIVE ARE YOU?

This questionnaire contains statements about your approach to debating controversial issues. Indicate how often each statement is true for you personally according to the following scale: 1 = almost never true, 2 = rarely true, 3 = occasionally true, 4 = often true, and 5 = almost always true.

_____ 1. While in an argument, I worry that the person I am arguing with will form a negative impression of me.

_____ 2. Arguing over controversial issues improves my intelligence.

_____ 3. I enjoy avoiding arguments.

_____ 4. I am energetic and enthusiastic when I argue.

_____ 5. Once I finish an argument, I promise myself that I will not get into another.

_____ 6. Arguing with a person creates more problems for me than it solves.

_____ 7. I have a pleasant, good feeling when I win a point in an argument.

_____ 8. When I finish arguing with someone, I feel nervous and upset.

_____ 9. I enjoy a good argument over a controversial issue.

_____ 10. I get an unpleasant feeling when I realize I am about to get into an argument.

_____ 11. I enjoy defending my point of view on an issue.

_____ 12. I am happy when I keep an argument from happening.

_____ 13. I do not like to miss the opportunity to argue a controversial issue.

_____ 14. I prefer being with people who rarely disagree with me.

_____ 15. I consider an argument an exciting intellectual challenge.

_____ 16. I find myself unable to think of effective points during an argument.

_____ 17. I feel refreshed and satisfied after an argument on a controversial issue.

_____ 18. I have the ability to do well in an argument.

_____ 19. I try to avoid getting into arguments.

_____ 20. I feel excitement when I expect that a conversation I am in is leading to an argument.

HOW DID YOU DO? To compute your argumentativeness score, follow these steps:

1. Add your scores on items 2, 4, 7, 9, 11, 13, 15, 17, 18, and 20.

2. Add 60 to the sum obtained in step 1.

3. Add your scores on items 1, 3, 5, 6, 8, 10, 12, 14, 16, and 19.

4. To compute your argumentativeness score, subtract the total obtained in step 3 from the total obtained in step 2.

The following guidelines will help you interpret your score: Scores between 73 and 100 indicate high argumentativeness; scores between 56 and 72 indicate moderate argumentativeness; and scores between 20 and 55 indicate low argumentativeness.

Generally, those who score high in argumentativeness have a strong tendency to state their position on controversial issues and to argue against the positions of others. A high scorer sees arguing as exciting and intellectually challenging, and as an opportunity to win a kind of contest.

The person who scores low in argumentativeness tries to prevent arguments. This person experiences satisfaction not from arguing but from avoiding arguments. The low argumentative person sees arguing as unpleasant and unsatisfying. Not surprisingly, this person has little confidence in his or her ability to argue effectively.

Finally, the moderately argumentative person possesses some of the qualities of the high argumentative person and some of the qualities of the low argumentative person.

WHAT WILL YOU DO? The researchers who developed this test note that both high and low argumentatives may experience communication difficulties. The high argumentative, for example, may argue needlessly, too often, and too forcefully. The low argumentative, on the other hand, may avoid taking a stand even when it seems necessary. Persons scoring somewhere in the middle are probably the more interpersonally skilled and adaptable, arguing when it is necessary but avoiding arguments that are needless and repetitive. Does your experience support this observation? What specific actions might you take to improve your argumentativeness?

Source: From Dominic Infante and Andrew Rancer, "A Conceptualization and Measure of Argumentativeness" *Journal of Personality Assessment* 46 (1982): 72–80. Copyright © 1982 by Taylor & Francis Informa UK Ltd.—Journals. Reproduced with permission of Taylor & Francis Informa UK Ltd.—Journals in the format Textbook via Copyright Clearance Center.

Differences between Argumentativeness and Verbal Aggressiveness As you can appreciate, there are numerous differences between argumentativeness and verbal aggressiveness. Here are just a few (Infante & Rancer, 1996; Rancer & Atvgis, 2006).

Argumentativeness	Verbal Aggressiveness
Is *constructive*; the outcomes are positive in a variety of communication situations (interpersonal, group, organizational, family, and intercultural)	Is destructive; the outcomes are negative in a variety of communication situations (interpersonal, group, organizational, family, and intercultural)
Leads to relationship *satisfaction*	Leads to relationship dissatisfaction, not surprising for a strategy that aims to attack another's self-concept
May prevent *relationship violence* especially in domestic relationships	May lead to relationship violence
Enhances *organizational life*; for example, subordinates prefer supervisors who encourage argumentativeness	Damages organizational life and demoralizes workers on varied levels
Enhances *parent–child communication* and enables parents to gain greater compliance	Prevents meaningful parent–child communication and makes corporal punishment more likely
Increases the user's *credibility*; argumentatives are seen as trustworthy, committed, and dynamic	Decreases the user's credibility, in part because it's seen as a tactic to discredit the opponent rather than address the argument
Increases the user's *power of persuasion* in varied communication contexts; argumentatives are more likely to be seen as leaders	Decreases the user's power of persuasion

Strategies for Cultivating Argumentativeness The following are some suggestions for cultivating argumentativeness. Ideally, most of these guidelines are already part of your interpersonal behavior (Infante, 1988). If any are not a part of your conflict behavior, consider how you can integrate them.

- Treat disagreements as objectively as possible. Avoid assuming that because someone takes issue with your position or your interpretation, they're attacking you as a person.
- Avoid attacking the other person (rather than the person's arguments), even if this would give you a tactical advantage. Center your arguments on issues rather than personalities.
- Reaffirm the other person's sense of competence. Compliment the other person as appropriate.
- Avoid interrupting. Allow the other person to state her or his position fully before you respond.
- Stress equality, and stress the similarities that you have with the other person (see the Understanding Interpersonal Skills box on p. 288). Stress your areas of agreement before attacking the disagreements.
- Express interest in the other person's position, attitude, and point of view.
- Avoid presenting your arguments too emotionally. Avoid using a loud voice or interjecting vulgar expressions, which will prove offensive and eventually ineffective.
- Allow the other person to save face. Never humiliate the other person.

Summary

This chapter examined principles of interpersonal conflict, conflict management stages, and some of the popular productive and unproductive conflict strategies.

Preliminaries to Interpersonal Conflict

1. Interpersonal conflict is a disagreement between connected individuals who each want something that is incompatible with what the other wants.
2. Interpersonal conflict is neither good nor bad, but, depending on how the disagreements are resolved, the conflict can strengthen or weaken a relationship.
3. Interpersonal conflicts arise from a variety of issues, including intimacy issues such as sex and affection, power issues such as possessiveness or lack of equity, and personal flaws issues such as drinking or smoking.

Principles of Interpersonal Conflict

4. Interpersonal conflict is inevitable; it's a fact of all relationships.
5. Conflict may have both negative and positive effects.
6. Conflict may focus on content (matters external to the relationship) or on relationship issues (matters integral to the nature of the relationship).
7. Conflict may be pursued with different styles, each of which has different consequences.
8. Conflict and the strategies used to resolve it are heavily influenced by culture.

Conflict Management Stages

9. Before the conflict: Try to fight in private, fight when you're ready, know what you're fighting about, and fight about problems that can be solved.

10. Define the conflict: Define the content and relationship issues in specific terms, avoiding gunnysacking and mind reading, and try to empathize with the other person.
11. Examine the possible solutions: Try to identify as many solutions as possible, look for win–win solutions, and carefully weigh the costs and rewards of each solution.
12. Test the solution mentally and in practice to see if it works.
13. Evaluate the tested solution from a variety of perspectives.
14. Accept the solution and integrate it into your behavior. Or reject the solution and begin again; for example, define the problem differently or look in other directions for possible solutions.
15. After the conflict: Learn something from the conflict, keep the conflict in perspective, attack your negative feelings, and increase the exchange of rewards.

Conflict Management Strategies

16. Seek out win–win solutions.
17. Become an active participant in the conflict; don't avoid the issues or the arguments of the other person.
18. Use talk to discuss the issues rather than trying to force the other person to accept your position.
19. Try to enhance the face, the self-esteem, of the person you're arguing with; avoid strategies that may cause the other person to lose face.
20. Argue the issues, focusing as objectively as possible on the points of disagreement; avoid being verbally aggressive or attacking the other person.

Key Terms

Critical Thinking Questions

1 What characters on television frequently demonstrate verbal aggressiveness? What characters frequently demonstrate argumentativeness? What distinguishes these types of characters?

2 Men generally score higher both in argumentativeness and in verbal aggressiveness than women. Men are also more apt to be perceived (by both men and women) as more argumentative and verbally aggressive than women (Nicotera & Rancer, 1994). Why do you think this is so?

3 What changes would you like to see your relational partners (friends, family members, romantic partners) make in their own verbal aggressiveness and argumentativeness? What might you do to more effectively regulate your own verbal aggressiveness and argumentativeness?

4 What does your own culture teach about conflict and its management? What strategies does it prohibit? Are some conflict strategies prohibited with certain people (say, your parents) but not with others (say, your friends)? Does your culture prescribe certain ways of dealing with conflict? Does it have different expectations for men and for women? To what degree have you internalized these teachings? What effect do these teachings have on your actual conflict behaviors?

5 What issues have you experienced conflict over in the last week or so? Try explaining the conflict(s) in terms of (1) content and relationship issues; (2) the strategies you used to manage the conflict; and (3) the outcome or aftermath of the conflict. If you had it to do over again, would you do anything differently?

6 For each of the following conflict scenarios, try generating as many win–win solutions as you feel the individuals could reasonably accept. Give yourself two minutes for each case. If possible, share your win–win solutions with other individuals or groups. Also, consider ways in which you might incorporate win–win strategies into your own conflict management behavior.

a. Pat and Chris won $4,500 in a state lottery. Pat wants to redecorate the living room, but Chris wants to save the money.

b. Sara and Margaret want to go to Canada and get married, but both sets of parents are adamantly opposed to same-sex marriage and want Sara and Margaret to stop seeing each other and enter therapy.

c. Pat is a fifth-grade teacher and is required to use a textbook on sex that contains a great many false and misleading statements. The principal demands that the textbook be followed without contradiction; Pat disagrees but needs the job.

7 Think about the major productive and unproductive conflict strategies discussed in this chapter as they might apply to the series of statements listed below. Assume that the statements are made by someone close to you. Try developing an unproductive response and an alternative productive response to any one or two of the statements.

a. "You just spend too much money; we need to save something for emergencies. You're leading us into bankruptcy."

b. "We need to move away from your parents; they're too possessive and intrude into every aspect of our lives. I can't stand it any more."

c. "Again, this report is simply inadequate. The spelling, grammar, and logical development are horrendous. You're going to have to learn how to do this or you can find another job."

Choice Points

1 *Escalating to Relationship Conflict.* Your own interpersonal conflicts often start out as content conflicts but quickly degenerate into relationship conflicts, and that's when things get ugly. Ask yourself: What types of things might you do to keep conflicts and their resolution focused on content and not on the relationship?

2 *Confronting a Problem.* Your next-door neighbor never puts out the garbage in time for pickup, so the garbage—often broken into by animals—remains until the next pickup. You're fed up with the rodents the garbage attracts, the smell, and the horrible appearance. Ask yourself: What might you say that could stop this problem and yet not make your neighbor hate you?

3 *Avoiding Conflict.* Your work team members all seem to have the same conflict style: avoidance. When alternatives are discussed or there is some kind of disagreement, they refuse to argue for one alternative or the other or even to participate in the discussion. You need spirited discussion and honest debate if your team is going to come up with appropriate solutions. Ask yourself: What are some of the things you can do to change this pattern of communication? Which would you try first?

4 *Talking Aggressively.* Your relationship partner is becoming more and more verbally aggressive, and you're having trouble with this new communication pattern. You want your partner to realize that this way of communicating is not productive and may ultimately destroy the relationship. Ask yourself: What options do you have for trying to lessen or even eliminate this verbal aggressiveness?

5 *Conflict Management.* Your dorm mate is very popular and has an open-door policy. So, throughout the day and evening, friends drop by to chat, borrow a book, check their e-mail, and do a range of things—all of which prevents you from studying. You need to resolve this problem. Ask yourself: What can you say to your roommate to begin to resolve this conflict?

MyCommunicationLab
Explorations

PEARSON mycommunicationlab www.mycommunicationlab.com

These experiences focus on interpersonal conflict, especially on understanding the nature of conflict and how you can more effectively resolve and manage conflict. ❶ Analyzing a Conflict Episode provides an opportunity to think critically about the messages used in a conflict interaction. ❷ Dealing with Conflict Starters looks at some of the messages that often begin conflicts. ❸ Generating Win–Win Solutions provides opportunities to experiment with strategies that can make conflict and its resolution more effective.

CHAPTER

13 Interpersonal Power and Influence

Principles of Power and Influence	Misuses of Power and Influence
Uses of Power and Influence	

Get Smart

In the movie *Get Smart,* and in the long-running TV series, you see a comedic power struggle between Control and KAOS. Power, however, is not something confined to spy agencies or nations; it's a part of all interpersonal relationships, as you'll see in this chapter. Understanding how power works and how it's exercised are crucial for interpersonal success, both personally and professionally.

This final chapter discusses one of the most important dimensions of interpersonal communication: power. Power influences what you do, when you do it, and with whom you do it. It influences your choice of friends, your romantic and family relationships, and your workplace relationships. Power also influences how successful you feel your relationships are; it also makes men appear "sexy" to women as well as to other men (Martin, 2005). Here we'll examine the key principles of power; the bases of power as applied to the relationship, the person, and the message; and two misuses of power: sexual harassment and power plays.

Principles of Power and Influence

Power is the ability of one person to influence what another person thinks or does. You have power over another person to the extent that you can influence what this person thinks or what this person does. And, conversely, another person has power over you to the extent that he or she can influence what you think or do. Perhaps the most important aspect of power to recognize is that *power is not reciprocal*: If one person has greater power, the other person must have less. If you are stronger than another person, then this person is weaker than you. If you are richer, then the other person must be poorer. In any one area—for example, strength or financial wealth—one person has more and, inevitably and by definition, the other person has less (is weaker or poorer).

We'll now consider some of the most important principles of power in interpersonal communication and relationships. These principles explain how power operates interpersonally and offer insight on how you can more effectively manage power.

Some People Are More Powerful Than Others

In the United States, all people are considered equal under the law and therefore equal in their entitlement to education, legal protection, and freedom of speech. But all people are not equal when it comes to just about everything else. Some are born into wealth, others into poverty. Some are born physically strong, good-looking, and healthy; others are born weak, less attractive, and with a variety of inherited illnesses.

Some people are born into power, and some of those who are not born powerful learn to become powerful. In short, some people control and others are controlled. Of course, the world is not quite that simple; some people exert power in certain areas of life, some in others. Some exert power in many areas, some in just a few.

Power bears a close relationship to interpersonal violence. For example, husbands who have less power in their relationship are more likely to be physically abusive toward their wives than husbands who have greater power (Babcock, Waltz, Jacobson, & Gottman, 1993). Further, in violent marriages the interpersonal power struggle is often characterized by unproductive and dysfunctional efforts at influence. For example, violent couples engage in greater blame and greater criticism of each other than do nonviolent couples (Rushe, 1996).

Power Can Be Shared

Some people would argue that power should be guarded—that by sharing it with others, you dilute your own power. Thus, the research scientist should not reveal successful research strategies to his or her assistants, because that would make them more powerful and the scientist less powerful, at least by comparison.

Another position would argue that by sharing your power, by empowering others, you actually grow in power. For adherents of this view, empowerment is not just an altruistic gesture on the part of, say, one relationship partner or a company's management; rather, it is a basic philosophy. According to this philosophy, empowered people are more likely to take a more personal interest in the relationship or in the job. Empowered people are proactive; they act and do not merely react. They're more likely to take on decision-making responsibilities, are willing to take risks, and are willing to take responsibility for their actions—all attributes that make relationships and business exciting and productive. In an interpersonal relationship (though the same would apply to a multinational organization), two empowered partners are more likely to effectively meet the challenges and difficulties most relationships will encounter.

Should you wish to empower others (your relational partner, an employee, another student, a sibling) to gain increased control over themselves and their environment, there are a variety of useful strategies.

- Raise the person's self-esteem. Resist faultfinding: It doesn't really benefit the faultfinder and certainly doesn't benefit the other person. Faultfinding disempowers others. Any criticism that is offered should be constructive. Be willing to offer your perspective—to lend an ear to a first-try singing effort or to read a new poem. Also, avoid verbal aggressiveness and abusiveness. Resist the temptation to win an argument with unfair tactics, tactics that are going to hurt the other person.
- Be open, positive, empathic, and supportive and treat the other person with an equality of respect. Be attentive and listen actively; this will tell the other person that he or she is important. After all, what greater praise could you pay than to give another person your time and energy?
- Share skills and share decision making. Be willing to relinquish control and allow the other person the freedom to make decisions. Encourage growth in all forms, academic and relational.

Power Can Be Increased or Decreased

Although people differ greatly in the amount of power they wield at any time and in any specific area, everyone can increase their power in some ways. You can lift weights and increase your physical power. You can learn the techniques of negotiation and increase your power in group situations. You can learn the principles of communication and increase your persuasive power.

Power can also be decreased. Probably the most common way to lose power is by unsuccessfully trying to control another's behavior. For example, the person who threatens you with punishment and then fails to carry out the threat loses power. Another way to lose power is to allow others to control you; for example, to allow others to take unfair advantage of you. When you don't confront these power tactics of others, you lose power yourself.

Power Follows the Principle of Less Interest

In any interpersonal relationship, the person who holds the power is the one less interested in and less dependent on the rewards and punishments controlled by the other person. If, for example, Pat can walk away from the rewards Chris controls or can suffer the punishments Chris can mete out, Pat controls the relationship. If, on the other hand, Pat needs the rewards Chris controls or is unable or unwilling to suffer the punishments Chris can administer, Chris maintains the power and controls the relationship. Put differently, Chris holds the relationship power to the degree that Chris is not dependent on the rewards and punishments under Pat's control.

The more a person needs a relationship, the less power that person has in it. The less a person needs a relationship, the greater that person's power. In a love relationship, for example, the person who maintains greater power is the one who would find it easier to break up the relationship. The person who is unwilling (or unable) to break up has little power, precisely because he or she is dependent on the relationship and the rewards provided by the other person.

Not surprisingly, if you perceive your partner as having greater power than you, you will probably be more likely to avoid confrontation and to refrain from criticism (Solomon & Samp, 1998).

Power Generates Privilege

When one person has power over another person, the person with power is generally assumed to have certain privileges, many of which are communication privileges. Put in terms of the relationship license discussed earlier (Chapter 10, pp. 228–229), power enlarges a person's license. And the greater the power difference, the greater is the license of the more powerful individual. Sometimes we're mindful of the privilege or license that comes with power. Most often, however, we seem to operate mindlessly, with no one questioning the power structure.

For example, consider the process of territorial encroachment (discussed in Chapter 6). A supervisor or boss can enter a subordinate's office, but the subordinate cannot enter a supervisor's office—at least, not without being asked. Very likely this power relationship is played out mindlessly by both the supervisor and the subordinate. Similarly, a teacher may invade a student's personal space and lean over the student's desk to inspect his or her work, but a student can't do that to a teacher.

Touch is another privilege. Generally, in any hierarchically organized group, higher-ups can touch those lower than they are. So a supervisor may touch the arm or rearrange the collar of a subordinate, but the other way around would seem unnatural in any hierarchical organization or culture. The general may touch the corporal, but not the other way around. The coach may touch the players, but the players may not touch the coach. The doctor may put his or her arm on a patient, but the patient would not do that to a doctor.

Those with power also have the privilege of having the final word, whether in an argument or a discussion. And, not surprisingly, the person with power is the one who normally wins an argument or whose thoughts and statements are given the most weight in a discussion.

Still another privilege is that those with power can break the rules; those with little power must follow the rules. The teacher may be late for class, but the students must be on time. The supervisor may be late for a meeting or conference call, but the subordinates must be on time, lest they be seen as violating the rules of the organization.

Power Has a Cultural Dimension

Recall the concept of power distance discussed in Chapter 2. There it was pointed out that cultures differ in the amount of power distance or discrepancy that exists between people and in the attitudes that people have about power, its legitimacy, and its desirability (Hofstede, 1983). In many Asian, African, and Arab cultures (as well as in many European cultures such as Italian and Greek), for example, there is a great power distance between men and women. Men have the greater power, and women are expected to recognize this and abide by its implications. Men, for example, make the important decisions and have the final word in any difference of opinion (Hatfield & Rapson, 1996).

In the United States the power distance between men and women is undergoing considerable changes. In many families men still have the greater power. Partly because they earn more money, they also make the more important decisions. As economic equality becomes more a reality than an ideal, however, this power difference may change. In contrast, in Arab cultures the man makes the more important decisions not because he earns more money but because he is the man—and men are simply given greater power.

Some cultures perpetuate the power difference by granting men greater educational opportunities. For example, although college education for women is taken for granted in most of the United States, it's the exception in many other cultures throughout the world.

In some Asian cultures persons in positions of authority—for example, teachers—have unquestioned power. Students do not contradict, criticize, or challenge teachers. This can easily create problems in the typical multicultural classroom. Students from cultures

VIEWPOINT Some theorists believe that computer-mediated communication will eventually eliminate the hierarchical structure of organizations, largely because it "encourages wider participation, greater candor, and an emphasis on merit over status" (Kollock & Smith, 1996, p. 109). If valid, this theory also would suggest that high-power-distance cultures will gradually move in the direction of low power distance and become more democratic. What evidence can you find bearing on this issue?

that teach that the teacher has unquestioned authority may have difficulty meeting the American teacher's expectation that students will interact critically with the material and develop interpretations of their own.

Bases of Power and Influence

One of the purposes of interpersonal communication is to influence; often you want to influence the attitudes or behaviors of a friend, lover, or family member. And, just as often, someone will want to influence what you think and what you do. At the same time, your friend, for example, may want to resist your influencing attempts; you, in turn, may want to resist the influencing attempts of others. These are the areas of interpersonal communication now called compliance-gaining and compliance-resisting. Let's look first at compliance-gaining.

Consider a specific situation. You're working in a car dealership and want to sell a car to the couple looking it over in your showroom. What strategies might you use to sell the car? What motives might you appeal to? What reasons could you give the couple for buying the car?

If you think for a moment about this, you're likely to come up with a variety of possible strategies. One research study, for example, identifies 64 such strategies (Kellerman & Cole, 1994). For convenience we can consider these strategies under three headings that are particularly appropriate to an interpersonal communication analysis of power: (1) power in the relationship, (2) power in the person, and (3) power in the message. An alternative typology is presented in the Understanding Interpersonal Theory and Research Box on compliance-gaining (p. 303).

Ask the Researcher

Achieving Power

How can I become powerful at work without appearing power hungry? Are there more subtle ways to express and gain power in the workplace? Any suggestions?

Powerful people often never show it. Instead, they simply act powerful. How do they do that? First, sound confident. Not pushy, but confident. Talk using reasonably intense language, striking metaphors, and vivid details, with a voice that is neither meek nor boisterous. Second, "own" the room. Stroll into meetings and reach out to others; make suggestions without hesitation. Sit where everyone can see you. Enter meetings with something for people to react to. Even if they change your suggestions, you still have framed the meeting. Third, look powerful—dress a bit better than others. Fourth, be better prepared than others. Know what you want to say and marshal good support for what you communicate. Create the agenda. Fifth, influence informally. Persuade face-to-face and one-on-one. Be the master of the "presell." Get buy-in before any formal meeting. Sixth, seek out crises; they are where you get discovered. Seventh, build alliances—make ideas "our" ideas rather than "my" idea.

For more information see Dale Carnegie, *How to Win Friends and Influence People*, ed. Arthur R. Pell (New York: Simon & Schuster, 1936/1982); Robert Cialdini, *Influence: The Psychology of Persuasion* (New York: William Morrow, 1993); and Robert Cialdini, *Influence: Science and Practice*, 4th ed. (Boston: Allyn & Bacon, 2000).

John Daly (Ph.D., Purdue University) is the Liddell Professor of Communication & Management at the University of Texas. He teaches and studies interpersonal communication and advocacy and has worked with numerous corporations on topics related to influence.

UNDERSTANDING INTERPERSONAL THEORY & RESEARCH

Compliance-Gaining (Another Typology)

A great deal of research has been done on compliance-gaining and compliance-resisting. One of the most interesting studies—in terms of its methodology and in terms of its conclusions—was that done by Robert Cialdini, who actually took jobs with various organizations that were in the business of gaining compliance (for example, he worked in sales, advertising, and public relations) and analyzed the techniques used. His research offers a six-part system of compliance-gaining strategies (Kenrick, Neuberg, and Cialdini, 2007).

- **Reciprocation.** If you can show that you did someone a similar favor, it will be easier to get that person to comply with your request now.
- **Commitment.** If you can get people to make an initial commitment, they're more likely to make subsequent commitments.
- **Authority.** If you can get others to see you as authoritative, you're that much closer to gaining compliance.
- **Social validation.** If you can make people believe that many others have done what you're requesting, they'll be more likely to follow.
- **Scarcity.** If you can make people believe that what you are selling, say, is scarce or rare, they'll be more apt to buy it.
- **Liking.** If you can make yourself likable, you'll find it easier to gain compliance; after all, everyone is more apt to do what a friend requests than what an enemy requests.

Working with Theories and Research

Examine your own experiences with compliance-gaining and try to recall situations in which these strategies were used, either by you or on you. Which of these strategies are you most likely to use with friends? With work colleagues?

Power in the Relationship

The bases of relationship power, research shows, can be conveniently classified into six types: referent, legitimate, expert, information or persuasion, reward, and coercive power (French & Raven, 1968; Raven, Centers, & Rodrigues, 1975; Raven, Schwarzwald, & Koslowsky, 1998). Each of these types of power offers a way of gaining compliance.

Before reading about these types of power, consider your own powers by responding to the following self-test, each item of which refers to a type of power discussed below.

Referent Power   If you can establish **referent power** over others (item 1 in the self-test) and make others wish to be like you or to be identified with you, you'll more easily gain their compliance. Referent power is the kind of power an older brother may have over a younger brother, because the younger brother wants to be like him. The assumption made by the younger brother is that he will be more like his older brother if he believes and behaves as his brother does. Once he decides to do so, it takes little effort for the older brother to exert influence over or gain compliance from the younger.

Referent power depends greatly on attractiveness and prestige; as they increase, so does identification and, consequently, your power to gain compliance. When you are well liked and well respected, are of the same gender as the other person, and have the same attitudes and experiences as the other person, your referent power is especially great.

Legitimate Power   If you are seen as having **legitimate power** over others (item 2)—if others believe you have the right, by virtue of your position, to influence or control their behavior—they'll logically be ready to comply with your requests. Legitimate power stems from our belief that certain people should have power over us, that they have a right to influence us because of who they are. Legitimate power usually derives from the roles people occupy. Teachers are often perceived to have legitimate power, and this is doubly true for religious teachers. Parents are seen as having legitimate power over their children.

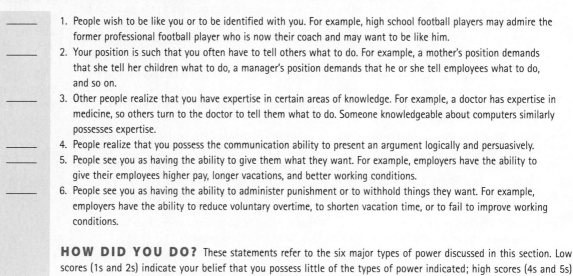

TEST YOURSELF

HOW POWERFUL ARE YOU?

For each statement, respond using a scale of 1 to 5 on which 1 = true of about 20 percent or less of the people you know; 2 = true of about 21 to 40 percent of the people you know; 3 = true of about 41 to 60 percent of the people you know; 4 = true of about 61 to 80 percent of the people you know; and 5 = true of about 81 percent or more of the people you know.

_____ 1. People wish to be like you or to be identified with you. For example, high school football players may admire the former professional football player who is now their coach and may want to be like him.

_____ 2. Your position is such that you often have to tell others what to do. For example, a mother's position demands that she tell her children what to do, a manager's position demands that he or she tell employees what to do, and so on.

_____ 3. Other people realize that you have expertise in certain areas of knowledge. For example, a doctor has expertise in medicine, so others turn to the doctor to tell them what to do. Someone knowledgeable about computers similarly possesses expertise.

_____ 4. People realize that you possess the communication ability to present an argument logically and persuasively.

_____ 5. People see you as having the ability to give them what they want. For example, employers have the ability to give their employees higher pay, longer vacations, and better working conditions.

_____ 6. People see you as having the ability to administer punishment or to withhold things they want. For example, employers have the ability to reduce voluntary overtime, to shorten vacation time, or to fail to improve working conditions.

HOW DID YOU DO? These statements refer to the six major types of power discussed in this section. Low scores (1s and 2s) indicate your belief that you possess little of the types of power indicated; high scores (4s and 5s) indicate your belief that you possess a great deal of those types of power.

WHAT WILL YOU DO? How satisfied are you with your level of power? If you're not satisfied, what might you do about it? A good starting place, of course, is to learn the skills of interpersonal communication discussed in this text. Consider the kinds of communication patterns that would help you communicate power in friendship, romantic, family, and workplace relationships.

Employers, judges, managers, doctors, and police officers are others who hold legitimate power in different areas.

Expert Power

You have **expert power** over others (item 3) when you are seen as having expertise or knowledge. Your knowledge—as perceived by others—gives you expert power. Usually expert power is subject specific. For example, when you're ill, you're influenced by the recommendation of someone with expert power related to your illness—say, a doctor. But you would not be influenced by the recommendation of someone to whom you don't attribute illness-related expert power—say, the mail carrier or a plumber. You give the lawyer expert power in matters of law and psychiatrists expert power in matters of the mind, but ideally you don't interchange them.

Your expert power increases when you're seen as unbiased and as having nothing to gain personally from influencing others. It decreases when you're seen as biased or as having something to gain from influencing others.

Information or Persuasion Power

You have **information or persuasion power** over others (item 4) when others see you as having the ability to communicate logically and persuasively. If others believe that you have persuasive ability, then you have persuasion power—the power to influence others' attitudes and behavior. If you're seen as possessing significant information and the ability to use that information in presenting a well-reasoned argument, then you have information power.

Reward and Coercive Powers You have **reward power** over others (item 5) if you have the ability to reward people. Rewards may be material (money, corner office, jewelry) or social (love, friendship, respect). If you're able to grant others some kind of reward, you have control over them to the extent that they want what you can give them. The degree of power you have is directly related to the perceived desirability of the reward. Teachers have reward power over students because they control grades, letters of recommendation, social approval, and so on. Students, in turn, have reward power over teachers because they control social approval, student evaluations of faculty, and various other rewards. Parents control rewards for children—food, television privileges, rights to the car, curfew times, and the like—and thus possess reward power.

You have **coercive power** over others (item 6) when you have the ability to administer punishments or remove rewards if others fail to yield to your influence. Usually, if you have reward power, you also have coercive power. Teachers not only may reward with high grades, favorable letters of recommendation, and social approval but also may punish with low grades, unfavorable letters, and social disapproval. Parents may deny as well as grant privileges to their children, and hence they possess coercive as well as reward power.

The strength of coercive power depends on two factors: (1) the magnitude of the punishment that can be administered and (2) the likelihood that the punishment will be administered as a result of noncompliance. When threatened by mild punishment or by punishment you think will not be administered, you're not as likely to do as directed as you would be if the threatened punishment were severe and highly likely to be administered.

Reward and coercive power are opposite sides of a coin, and the consequences of using them are quite different. First, if you have reward power, you're likely to be seen as more attractive. People like those who have the power to reward them and who do in fact reward them. Coercive power, on the other hand, decreases attractiveness; people dislike those who have the power to punish them or who threaten them with punishment, whether they actually follow through or not.

Second, when you use rewards to exert power, you don't incur the same costs as when you use punishment. When you exert reward power, you're dealing with a contented and happy individual. When you use coercive punishments, however, you must be prepared to incur anger and hostility, which may well be turned against you in the future.

Third, when you give a reward, it signals that you effectively exercised power and that you gained the compliance of the other person. You give the reward because the person did as you wanted. In the exercise of coercive power, however, the reverse is true. When you administer punishment, it shows that you have been ineffective in using the threat of coercive power and that there has been no compliance.

Fourth, when you exert coercive power, other bases of power frequently are diminished. There seems to be a boomerang effect in operation. People who exercise coercive power are seen as possessing less expert, legitimate, and referent power. Alternatively, when reward power is exerted, other bases of power increase.

People rarely use one base of power to influence others; usually, they use multiple power bases. For example, if you possess expert power, it's likely that you also possess information power and perhaps legitimate power as well. If you want to control the behavior of another person, you will probably use all three bases of power rather than relying on only one. As you can appreciate, certain individuals have numerous power bases at their disposal, whereas others seem to have few to none, which brings us back to our first principle: Some people are more powerful than others.

VIEWPOINT Research finds that men are generally perceived to have higher levels of expert and legitimate power than women and that women are generally perceived to have higher levels of referent power than men. When it comes to exerting influence, these findings suggest, women will have greater difficulty influencing others by communicating competence and authority than will men; men, on the other hand, will have greater difficulty influencing others using their referent power (Carli, 1999). What would you suggest that men do to increase referent power and that women do to increase expert and legitimate power?

Sometimes, attempts to gain the compliance of others through these power bases may backfire. At times, *negative power* operates. Each of the six power bases may, at times, have negative influence. For example, negative referent power is evident when a son rejects his father and wants to be his exact opposite. Negative coercive power may be seen when a child is warned against doing something under threat of punishment and then does exactly what he or she was told not to do; the threat of punishment may have made the forbidden behavior seem exciting or challenging.

Power in the Person

A great deal of your personal power, the power that resides in you as a person, depends on the **credibility** that you are seen to possess—the degree to which other people regard you as believable and therefore worth following. If others see you as competent and knowledgeable, of good character, and charismatic or dynamic, they will find you credible. As a result, you'll be more effective in influencing their attitudes, beliefs, values, and behavior. Credibility is not something you have or don't have in any objective sense; rather, it's a function of what other people think of you. Before reading any further take the self-test to examine your own credibility (p. 307).

Competence Your perceived competence is the knowledge and expertise that others see you as possessing; this is similar to expert and information power. The more knowledge and expertise others see you as having, the more likely they will believe you. Similarly, you're likely to believe a teacher or doctor if you think he or she is knowledgeable on the subject at hand.

Character People will see you as credible if they perceive you as being someone of high moral character, someone who is honest, and someone they can trust. If others feel that your intentions are good for them (rather than for your own personal gain), they'll think you credible and they'll believe you.

Charisma Charisma is a combination of your personality and dynamism as seen by other people. If you are seen as friendly and pleasant rather than aloof and reserved, dynamic rather than a hesitant and nonassertive speaker, you're likely to be seen as more credible.

Here are a few ways you can enhance your credibility:

- Express your expertise when appropriate. But don't overdo it.
- Stress your fairness. Everyone likes people who play fair and think about others fairly.
- Express concern for others; this will show your noble side and will reveal a part of you that says you've got character.
- Stress your concern for enduring values; this will show consistency and good moral character.
- Demonstrate a positive outlook; positive people are more likely to be believed and to be thought of highly than negative people.
- Be enthusiastic; it will help demonstrate your charisma.

Power in the Message

You can communicate power much as you communicate any other message. Here we consider power in the message; specifically, how you can communicate power through speaking, nonverbal communication, and listening.

TEST YOURSELF

HOW CREDIBLE ARE YOU INTERPERSONALLY?

Respond to each of the following phrases to indicate how you think a particularly important group of people (for example, your close friends, family, neighbors, or coworkers) see you when you interact interpersonally. Use the following scale: 5 = definitely true; 4 = probably true; 3 = neither true nor untrue; 2 = probably untrue; and 1 = definitely untrue.

_____ 1. People generally see me as knowledgeable

_____ 2. People see me as experienced

_____ 3. People see me as informed about what I'm talking about.

_____ 4. I'm seen as fair when I talk about controversial things.

_____ 5. People see me as concerned with who they are and what they want.

_____ 6. People see me as consistent over time.

_____ 7. People view me as an assertive individual.

_____ 8. I'm seen as enthusiastic.

_____ 9. People would consider me active rather than passive.

HOW DID YOU DO? This test focuses on the three qualities that confer credibility—your perceived competence, character, and charisma—and is based on a large body of research (for example, McCroskey [2007]; Riggio [1987]). Items 1 to 3 refer to your perceived competence: How competent or capable do you seem to be to other people? Items 4 to 6 refer to your perceived character: Do people see you as a good and moral person? Items 7 to 9 refer to your perceived charisma: Do others see you as dynamic and active rather than as static and passive? Total scores will range from a high of 45 to a low of 9. If you scored relatively high (say around 32 or higher), then you feel your others see you as credible. If you scored relatively low (say below 27), then you feel these people see you as lacking in credibility.

WHAT WILL YOU DO? Think about how you might go about increasing your credibility. What specific steps can you take to change any perception with which you may be unhappy? Are there specific things you can do to strengthen your competence, character, and/or charisma?

Speaking Power We can look at speaking power in at least two ways: the general verbal strategies that people use to influence others and the specific language they use.

General Verbal Strategies One team of researchers, on whom I draw here, groups verbal influence strategies into broad categories (Guerrero, Andersen, & Afifi, 2007). One such category is **direct requests** ("Can you get me a cup of coffee?" or "Please call for reservations"). This is the strategy that those in power would use and is actually the most common strategy used by both men and women. Another strategy is **bargaining** or **promising**, in which you agree to do something if the other person does something ("I'll clean up if you cook" or "We'll go out tomorrow; I want to watch the game tonight").

In **ingratiation** you act especially kindly; you suck up to the person so that eventually you'll get what you want ("You're such a great cook" _I don't want to cook tonight_ or "You write so well" _I hope you'll edit my term paper_). Another strategy is that of **manipulation**, in which you make the other person feel guilty or jealous enough to give you what you want ("Everyone else has an iPhone" _and you won't have to feel guilty for depriving me_ or "Pat called and asked if I'd go out this weekend" _unless you finally want to spend time together_).

In **threatening** you warn the other person that unpleasant things will happen if you don't get what you want ("I'll leave if you continue smoking" _so stop smoking if you don't want me to leave_ or "If you don't eat your veggies, you won't get any ice cream" _so finish your broccoli_).

Specific Language The ways in which powerfulness and powerlessness are communicated through specific language have received lots of research attention (Molloy, 1981;

UNDERSTANDING INTERPERSONAL SKILLS

Interaction Management

The term **interaction management** refers to the techniques and strategies by which you regulate and carry on interpersonal interactions. Effective interaction management results in an interaction that's satisfying to both parties. Neither person feels ignored or on stage; each contributes to, benefits from, and enjoys the interpersonal exchange.

Managing Communication Interactions. Of course, this entire text is devoted to the effective management of interpersonal interactions. Here, however, are a few specific suggestions.

- Maintain your role as speaker or listener and pass the opportunity to speak back and forth—through appropriate eye movements, vocal expressions, and body and facial gestures.
- Keep the conversation fluent, avoiding long and awkward pauses. For example, it's been found that patients are less satisfied with their interaction with their doctor when the silences between their comments and the doctor's responses are overly long (Rowland-Morin & Carroll, 1990).
- Communicate with verbal and nonverbal messages that are consistent and reinforce each other. Avoid sending mixed messages or contradictory signals—for example, a nonverbal message that contradicts the verbal message.

Kleinke, 1986; Johnson, 1987; Dillard & Marshall, 2003; Guerrero, Andersen, & Afifi, 2007). As you consider the major characteristics of powerful and powerless speech presented below, think of your own speech and whether or not you use these forms (or perhaps use them in certain communication situations but not in others).

- Hesitations; for example, "I er want to say that ah this one is er the best, you know?" (Hesitations make you sound unprepared and uncertain.)
- Too many intensifiers; for example, "Really, this was the greatest; it was truly phenomenal." (Too many intensifiers make everything sound the same and don't allow you to intensify what should be emphasized.)
- Disqualifiers; for example, "I didn't read the entire article, but . . ." or "I didn't actually see the accident, but. . . ." (Disqualifiers signal a lack of competence and a feeling of uncertainty.)
- Tag questions; for example, "That was a great movie, wasn't it?" "She's brilliant, don't you think?" (Tag questions ask for another's agreement and therefore may signal your need for agreement and your own uncertainty.)
- Self-critical statements; for example, "I'm not very good at this" or "This is my first interview." (Self-critical statements signal a lack of confidence and may make public your own inadequacies.)
- Slang and vulgar expressions; for example, "No problem!" "##!!!///*****!" (Slang and vulgarity signal low social class and hence little power.)

Compliance-Gaining Strategies Another way in which power is expressed in the message is in the use of compliance-gaining strategies. **Compliance-gaining strategies** are tactics aimed at influencing others to do what the user of the strategies wants them to do. Table 13.1 presents 16 compliance-gaining strategies. In reviewing these strategies, be mindful that compliance-gaining, like all interpersonal processes, involves two or more people in a transaction. Reading down the list may give the false impression that these strategies are one-way affairs, with one person using the strategy and the other person or persons complying. Actually, compliance-gaining is best viewed as a transactional, back-and-forth process. Conflict, compromise, renegotation of the goal, rejection of the strategy, and a host of other responses—in addition to simple compliance—are possible.

Realize too that all compliance requests involve an attack on negative face (see Chapter 5, pp. 104–105). Any request for compliance infringes on your autonomy. After all, if you

TABLE 13.1 Compliance-Gaining Strategies

These compliance-gaining strategies come from the research of Marwell and Schmitt (1967, 1990; also see Miller & Parks, 1982; Dillard, 1990; Dillard, Anderson, & Knobloch, 2002).

Compliance Strategy	Example
Pregiving. Pat rewards Chris and then requests compliance.	**Pat:** I'm glad you enjoyed dinner. How about going back to my place for a nightcap and whatever?
Liking. Pat is friendly in order to get Chris in a good mood so that Chris will comply with Pat's request.	**Pat:** (After giving Chris a back rub) I'd really like to relax and bowl a few games with Terry. Okay?
Promise. Pat promises to reward Chris if Chris complies with Pat's request.	**Pat:** I'll give you anything you want if you will just give me a divorce; just give me my freedom.
Threat. Pat threatens to punish Chris for noncompliance.	**Pat:** If you don't give me a divorce, you'll never see the kids again.
Aversive stimulation. Pat punishes Chris, making cessation contingent on compliance.	**Pat:** (Screams and cries and stops only when Chris complies.)
Positive expertise. Pat promises rewards for compliance because of "the nature of things."	**Pat:** If you follow the doctor's advice, you'll be fine.
Negative expertise. Pat promises punishment for noncompliance because of "the nature of things."	**Pat:** If you don't listen to the doctor, you're going to wind up back in the hospital.
Positive self-feelings. Pat promises that Chris will feel better if Chris complies with Pat's request.	**Pat:** You'll see. You'll be a lot better off without me; you'll feel better after the divorce.
Negative self-feelings. Pat promises that Chris will feel worse if Chris does not comply with Pat's request.	**Pat:** You'll hate yourself if you don't give me this divorce.
Positive altercasting. Pat argues that Chris should comply because a good person would comply.	**Pat:** Any intelligent person would grant their partner a divorce when the relationship has died.
Negative altercasting. Pat argues that Chris should comply because only a bad person would not comply.	**Pat:** Only a cruel and selfish neurotic could stand in the way of another's happiness.
Positive esteem. Pat tells Chris that people will think more highly of Chris if Chris complies with Pat's request.	**Pat:** Everyone will respect your decision to place your parents in an assisted living community.
Negative esteem. Pat tells Chris that people will think poorly of Chris if Chris does not comply with Pat's request.	**Pat:** Everyone will think that you're paranoid if you don't join the club.
Moral appeals. Pat argues that Chris should comply because it's moral to comply and immoral not to comply.	**Pat:** Any ethical person would return the mistaken overpayment.
Altruism. Pat asks Chris to comply because Pat needs this compliance (relying on Chris's desire to help).	**Pat:** I would feel so disappointed if you quit college now. Don't hurt me by quitting.
Debt. Pat asks Chris to comply because of the past favors given to Chris.	**Pat:** Look at how we sacrificed to send you to college.

wanted to do something, you would have done it already; you wouldn't have needed to wait for someone to ask you to do it. You're asked to do something, to comply with a request, because you would not have done it without the request.

And, not surprisingly, all compliance-resisting messages attack positive face. When you resist complying, you're in effect saying that you don't agree with what the person has asked. In fact, in most cases, you're telling the person that the request is unfair or unethical or somehow inappropriate. By directing attention to the inappropriateness of what the person asks—as you do when you refuse a request—you're saying in effect that the person has been impolite.

Nonverbal Power Much research has focused on the nonverbal factors related to your ability to persuade and influence others (Burgoon, Buller, & Woodall, 1996). For example, clothing and other artifactual symbols of authority help people to influence others. Research shows that others will be more easily influenced by someone in, for example, a respected uniform (such as that of police officer or doctor) than by someone in civilian clothes.

Ethics in Interpersonal Communication

The Ethics of Compliance-Gaining Strategies

The list of compliance-gaining strategies in Table 13.1 (p. 309) describes various techniques that people often use in their efforts to influence others. But is it ethical to use these approaches? For example, is it ethical to threaten another person? Is it ethical to make a person feel guilty by recalling the past favors you did for him or her and implying that there is a debt owed you? Is it ethical to imply that someone's image or self-esteem will be adversely affected if he or she doesn't comply with your request? Review the selected strategies in Table 13.1 and indicate the ethical implications of each strategy.

What would you do?

Because you've fallen behind schedule, you need your colleague's help to complete your current project on time. You wonder if it would be ethical to give your colleague an expensive watch she's been wanting, then ask for her help a few days later. You figure that if she accepted the watch, she'd find it difficult to refuse your request for help with your project. What would you do in this situation?

Affirmative nodding, facial expressions, and gestures help you express your concern for the other person and for the interaction and thus help you establish your charisma, an essential component of credibility. Self-manipulations (playing with your hair or touching your face, for example) and backward leaning will damage your persuasiveness.

Here are some popular suggestions for communicating power nonverbally in a business situation, most of which come from Lewis (1989). As you read this list, try to provide specific examples of these suggestions and how they might work in business, at home, or at school.

- Be sure to respond in kind to another's eyebrow flash (raising the eyebrow as a way of acknowledging another person).
- Avoid adaptors—self, other, and object—especially when you wish to communicate confidence and control.
- Use consistent packaging; be especially careful that your verbal and nonverbal messages don't contradict each other.
- When sitting, select chairs you can get in and out of easily; avoid deep plush chairs that you will sink into and will have trouble getting out of.
- To communicate confidence with your handshake, exert more pressure than usual and hold the grip a bit longer than normal.
- Other things being equal, dress relatively conservatively if you want to influence others; conservative clothing is usually associated with power and status. Trendy and fad clothing usually communicates a lack of power and status.
- Use facial expressions and gestures as appropriate; these help you express your concern for the other person as well as your comfort and control of the communication situation.
- Walk slowly and deliberately. To appear hurried is to appear as without power, as if you were rushing to meet the expectations of another person who had power over you.
- Maintain eye contact. People who maintain eye contact are judged to be more at ease and less afraid to engage in meaningful interaction than those who avoid eye contact. (Be aware, however, that in some contexts, if you use excessive or protracted direct eye contact, you may be seen as exercising coercive power; Aquinis & Henle, 2001.) When you break eye contact, direct your gaze downward; otherwise you'll communicate a lack of interest in the other person.
- Avoid vocalized pauses—the "ers" and "ahs" that frequently punctuate conversations when you're not quite sure of what to say next.
- Maintain reasonably close distances between yourself and those with whom you interact. If the distance is too far, you may be seen as fearful or uninvolved. If the distance is too close, you may be seen as pushy or overly aggressive.

Listening Power Much as you can communicate power and authority through words and through nonverbal expression, you also communicate power through listening. Throughout your listening, you're communicating messages to others, and these messages comment in some way on your power.

Powerful listeners listen actively. They focus and concentrate (with no real effort) on what is being said, especially on what people say they want or need (Fisher, 1995). Listen to phrases such as "I want," "It would help if I had," or "I'm looking for." Too, respond to what others have said. For example, preface comments with "In light of what you said about" or "If you feel strongly about."

Powerless listeners, on the other hand, listen passively; they may appear to be thinking about something else and only pretending to listen, and they rarely refer to what the other person has said when they do respond.

Powerful listeners respond visibly but in moderation; an occasional nod of agreement or a facial expression that says, "That's interesting" is usually sufficient. Responding with too little or too much reaction is likely to be perceived as evidence of powerlessness. Too little response says you aren't listening, and too much response says you aren't listening critically. Powerful listeners also use back-channeling cues—head nods and brief oral responses that say "I'm listening, I'm following you"—when appropriate. When no back-channeling cues are given, the speaker comes to wonder if the other person is really listening.

Powerful listeners maintain more focused eye contact than do those seen to have less power. In conversation, normal eye contact is intermittent—you glance at the speaker's face, then away, then back again, and so on. In a small group or public speaking situation, eye contact with the speaker is normally greater.

Adaptors—playing with your hair or a pencil—give the appearance of discomfort. Because of this, adaptors communicate a lack of power. These body movements show the listener to be more concerned with himself or herself than with the speaker. The absence of adaptors, on the other hand, makes the listener appear in control of the situation and comfortable in the role of listener.

Powerful listeners are more likely to maintain an open posture. When around a table or in an audience, they resist covering their abdomen or face with their hands. Persons who maintain a defensive posture with, for example, arms crossed may communicate a feeling of vulnerability and hence powerlessness.

Powerful listeners avoid interrupting the speaker in conversations or in small group situations. The reason is simple: Not interrupting is one of the rules of business communication that powerful people follow and powerless people don't. Completing the speaker's thoughts (or what the listener thinks is the speaker's thought) conveys a similar impression of powerlessness.

You also can signal power through visual dominance behavior (Exline, Ellyson, & Long, 1975), as mentioned in the discussion of eye communication in Chapter 6. For example, the average speaker maintains a high level of eye contact while listening and a lower level while speaking. When powerful individuals want to signal dominance, they may reverse this pattern. They may, for example, maintain a high level of eye contact while talking but a much lower level while listening.

Resisting Power and Influence

Let's say that someone you know asks you to do something you don't want to do, such as lend this person your term paper so he or she can copy it and turn it in to another teacher. Research with college students shows that there are four principal ways of responding (McLaughlin, Cody, & Robey, 1980; O'Hair, Cody, & O'Hair, 1991).

In **negotiation**, you attempt to accommodate to each other or to compromise in some way. In using this strategy to resist complying you might, for example, offer to meet the request halfway in a kind of compromise ("I'll let you read my paper but not copy it") or you might offer to help the person in some other way ("If you write a first draft, I'll go over it and try to make some comments"). If the request is a romantic one—for example, a request to go away for a ski weekend—you might resist by discussing your feelings and proposing an alternative; for example, "Let's double-date first."

In **nonnegotation**, you resist compliance without any attempt to compromise; you simply state your refusal to do as asked without any qualification. You might simply say, "No, I don't lend my papers out."

In **justification**, you resist compliance by giving reasons as to why you should not comply. You offer some kind of justification for not doing as requested. For example, you might justify your refusal by citing a negative consequence if you complied ("I'm afraid that I'd get caught, and then I'd fail the course") or a positive consequence of not complying ("You'll really enjoy writing this paper; it's a lot of fun").

In **identity management**, you resist by trying to manipulate the image of the person making the request. You might do this negatively or positively. In *negative identity management*, you might portray the person as unreasonable or unfair and say, for example, "That's really unfair of you to ask me to compromise my ethics." Or you might tell the person that it hurts that he or she would even think you would do such a thing.

You might also use *positive identity management*. Here you resist complying by making the other person feel good about himself or herself. For example, you might say, "You know this material much better than I do; you can easily do a much better paper yourself."

Both the use of and resistance to the imposition of power—like all forms of interpersonal communication—are transactional processes in which *all* elements are *inter*dependent; each element influences each other. Your attempts to gain influence, for example, will depend on the responses of the person you wish to influence. These responses in turn will influence your responses, and so on. Also, just as your relationship (its type, length, and degree of intimacy, for example) will influence the strategies you use, so the strategies you use will influence your relationship. Inappropriate strategies will have negative effects, just as positive strategies will have positive effects.

Misuses of Power and Influence

Although it would be nice to believe that power was usually wielded for the good of all, power often is used selfishly and unfairly. Here are two examples: sexual harassment and the use of power plays. In connection with sexual harassment, also take a look at Table 13.2.

Sexual Harassment

One type of unfair use of power is workplace **sexual harassment**, a form of behavior that violates Title VII of the Civil Rights Act of 1964 and as amended by the Civil Rights Act of 1991 (www.eeoc.gov/policy/vii.html, last modified January 15, 1997, accessed May 28, 2008). Of course sexual harassment is not confined to the workplace; it takes place in social settings and in educational settings, for example. Much of what is presented here is applicable to sexual harassment in general and not just to that which occurs in an organizational context.

Defining Sexual Harassment   The U.S. Equal Employment Opportunity Commission (EEOC) defines sexual harassment as follows (www.eeoc.gov/types/sexual_harassment.html, last modified March 4, 2008, accessed May 28, 2008):

> Unwelcome sexual advances, requests for sexual favors, and other verbal or physical conduct of a sexual nature constitute sexual harassment when this conduct explicitly or implicitly affects an individual's employment, unreasonably interferes with an individual's work performance, or creates an intimidating, hostile, and offensive work environment.

As you can see from this definition, sexual harassment falls into two general categories: *quid pro quo* (a term borrowed from the Latin, which literally means "something for something") and the creation of a hostile environment.

TABLE 13.2 Additional Types of Harassment

Although when we think of harassment, we most easily think of sexual harassment, there are a variety of other forms that harassment can take. All of these are power-driven and are communicated through a variety of verbal and nonverbal messages.

Nothing in this table should imply that harassment isn't at times perpetuated by the group that is usually harassed. For example, religious people may harass the nonreligious by trying to force their religious beliefs on nonbelievers, "praying for the nonbeliever," or warning of the terrible fates that await nonbelievers. Similarly, gay men and lesbians may harass heterosexuals, just as women may harass men, and those with disabilities may harass those without. And, of course, all groups have derogatory terms for "others."

The harassments highlighted here seem to be the most important in terms of type and the direction of the harassment (www.equalityhumanrights.com, print.employment.findlaw.com, www.eeoc.gov/types/religion, all accessed May 28, 2008).

Additional Types of Harassment	Examples
Race and color harassment. Harassment of another person because of that person's race or color, most often applied to minority and immigrant groups.	Using derogatory names or racial slurs; talking in stereotypes; acting superior and treating others as inferiors (for example, as less intelligent, less ethical, or less "civilized").
Affectional orientation harassment. Harassment based on a person's affectional orientation and generally directed at gay men and lesbians, transvestites, and transsexuals.	Using derogatory names, imitating stereotypical mannerisms, threatening outing, excluding same-sex partners from important functions.
Religious harassment. Harassment (sometimes referred to as creed harassment) that is based on a person's religious affiliation or religious beliefs.	Making offensive and stereotypical religious jokes; making fun of religious customs, symbols, or clothing; not accommodating to one religion while accommodating to others.
Academic harassment. Harassment in the form of statements or actions by senior faculty that interfere with a junior colleague's development, or statements or actions by a faculty member that interfere with students' ability to perform effectively.	Discriminating in counseling, being less attentive or supportive to junior faculty, grading students unfairly.
Status harassment. Harassment (usually) in the organizational setting, generally directed by those with power against those with less power; often takes the form of insulting comments to or treatment of workers by managers.	Criticizing publicly; giving unfair salary increases or witholding them; forcing workers to do unethical things (for example, pad an expense account); making insulting or sarcastic comments.
Disability harassment. Harassment against persons with disabilities, most often directed at persons with visual or hearing impairment or with physical, speech, or language disabilities.	Failing to adjust communications to the person with the disability; using language that demeans the person; intruding on physical aids (for example, sitting on a person's wheelchair).
Attractiveness harassment. Harassment directed at people low in attractiveness, often used against persons because of their weight or their lack of interpersonal popularity or physical attractiveness.	Using derogatory names, especially adjectives that highlight, for example, overweight; excluding people from gatherings because they're not very attractive or popular.
Citizenship harassment. Harassment based on a person's citizenship, generally directed against a person who is not a citizen.	Denying financial loans or medical benefits; using derogatory names.
Veteran harassment. Harassment based on a person's veteran status, used both against those who are veterans and those who aren't.	Using derogatory names for veterans that refer to wartime actions; using offensive names for those who have avoided military service.

In quid pro quo harassment, employment opportunities (as in hiring and promotion) are dependent on the granting of sexual favors. Conversely, quid pro quo harassment also involves situations in which reprisals and various negative consequences can result from the failure to grant such sexual favors. Put more generally, quid pro quo harassment occurs when employment consequences (positive or negative) hinge on a person's response to sexual advances.

Hostile environment harassment is much broader and includes all sexual behaviors (verbal and nonverbal) that make a worker uncomfortable. For example, putting sexually explicit pictures on the bulletin board, using sexually explicit screen savers, telling sexual jokes and stories, and using sexual and demeaning language or gestures all constitute sexual harassment. "Sexual harassment," notes one team of researchers, "refers to conduct, typically experienced as offensive in nature, in which unwanted sexual advances are made in the context of a relationship of unequal power or authority. The victims are subjected to verbal comments of a sexual nature, unconsented touching and requests for sexual favors" (Friedman, Boumil, & Taylor, 1992). Attorneys note that under the law "sexual harassment is any unwelcome sexual advance or conduct on the job that creates an intimidating, hostile or offensive working environment" (Petrocelli & Repa, 1992).

Recognizing Sexual Harassment

To determine whether behavior constitutes sexual harassment and to assess your own situation objectively rather than emotionally, ask yourself the following questions (VanHyning, 1993):

1. Is it real? Does this behavior have the meaning it seems to have?
2. Is it job related? Does this behavior have something to do with or will it influence the way you do your job?
3. Did you reject this behavior? Did you make your rejection of unwanted messages clear to the other person?
4. Have these types of messages persisted? Is there a pattern, a consistency to these messages?

If you answered yes to all four questions, then the behavior is likely to constitute sexual harassment (VanHyning, 1993).

Keep in mind three additional facts that are often misunderstood. First, members of either gender may sexually harass. Although most cases brought to public attention are committed by men against women, women may also harass men. Further, harassment may be committed by men against men and by women against women. Second, anyone in an organization can be guilty of sexual harassment. Although most cases of harassment involve harassment of subordinates by persons in authority, this is not a necessary condition. Coworkers, vendors, and even customers may be charged with sexual harassment. Third, sexual harassment is not limited to business organizations but can and does occur in schools; in hospitals; and in social, religious, and political organizations.

VIEWPOINT In one study, 10 to 15 percent of the students surveyed reported being harassed via e-mail or instant messaging (Finn, 2004). What is the state of online harassment on your campus? How would you describe the types of harassment some students experience?

Avoiding Sexual Harassment Behaviors

Three suggestions will help you avoid committing workplace harassment (Bravo & Cassedy, 1992). First, begin with the assumption that coworkers are not interested in your sexual advances, sexual stories and jokes, or sexual gestures. Second, listen and watch for negative reactions to any sex-related discussion. Use the suggestions and techniques discussed throughout this book (for example, perception checking and critical listening) to become aware of such reactions. When in doubt, find out; ask questions, for example. Third, avoid saying or doing anything that you think your parent, partner, or child would find offensive in the behavior of someone with whom she or he worked.

Responding to Sexual Harassment

Should you encounter sexual harassment and feel the need to do something about it, consider these suggestions recommended by workers in the field (Petrocelli & Repa, 1992; Bravo & Cassedy, 1992; Rubenstein, 1993):

1. *Talk to the harasser.* Tell this person, assertively, that you do not welcome the behavior and that you find it offensive. Simply informing Fred that his sexual jokes aren't appreciated and are seen as offensive may be sufficient to make him stop this joke telling. In some instances, unfortunately, such criticism goes unheeded, and the offensive behavior continues.

2. *Collect evidence.* Perhaps seek corroboration from others who have experienced similar harassment at the hands of the same individual, or create a log of the offensive behaviors.
3. *Begin with appropriate channels within the organization.* Most organizations have established channels to deal with such grievances. This step will in most cases eliminate any further harassment. In the event that it doesn't, you may consider going farther.
4. *File a complaint with an organization or governmental agency or perhaps take legal action.*
5. *Don't blame yourself.* Like many who are abused, you may tend to blame yourself, feeling that you're responsible for being harassed. You aren't; however, you may need to secure emotional support from friends or perhaps from a trained professional.

Power Plays

Power plays are patterns (not isolated instances) of behavior that are used repeatedly by one person to take unfair advantage of another person (Steiner, 1981). Power plays aim to deny you the right to make your own choices and come in a variety of forms.

Identifying Power Plays Power plays are not always easy to identify; often they seem to be only slight intrusions. But it's important to understand that their repeated use can prevent you from exercising your own rights. Let's look at a few of the major types to see how power plays are used and how they can be identified more easily.

One type is the "nobody upstairs" power play. In "nobody upstairs" the individual refuses to acknowledge your request, regardless of how or how many times you make it. One common form is the refusal to take no for an answer. Sometimes "nobody upstairs" takes the form of pleading ignorance of common socially accepted (but unspoken) rules, such as rules about knocking when you enter someone's room or refraining from opening another person's mail or wallet: "I didn't know you didn't want me to look in your wallet," or "Do you want me to knock the next time I come into your room?"

Another power play is "you owe me." Here others unilaterally do something for you and then demand something in return. They remind you of what they did for you and use this to get you to do what they want.

In "yougottobekidding," one person attacks the other by saying "You've got to be kidding" or some similar phrase, not out of surprise (which is fine) but out of a desire to put your ideas down: "You can't be serious." "You can't mean that." "You didn't say what I thought you said, did you?" The intention here is to express utter disbelief in the other's statement so as to make the statement and the person seem inadequate or stupid.

Responding to Power Plays The power plays discussed above are examples; but there are, of course, many others that you have no doubt met on occasion. What do you do when you recognize a power play? One commonly employed response is to ignore the power play and allow the other person to take control. Another response is to treat the power play as an isolated instance (rather than as a pattern of behavior) and object to it. For example, you might say quite simply, "Please don't come into my room without knocking first," or "Please don't look in my wallet without permission."

A third approach is a cooperative response (Steiner, 1981). In this response you do the following:

- *Express your feelings.* Tell the person that you're angry, annoyed, or disturbed by his or her behavior.
- *Describe the behavior to which you object.* Tell the person—in language that describes rather than evaluates—the specific behavior you object to; for example, reading your mail, saying you owe the person for something, or responding to everything you say with disbelief.
- *State a cooperative response you both can live with comfortably.* Tell the person—in a cooperative tone—what you want: For example: "I want you to knock before coming into my room," "I want you to stop telling me I owe you things," or "I want you to stop ridiculing my ideas."

A cooperative response to "nobody upstairs" might go something like this: "I'm angry (*expressing feelings*) that you persist in opening my mail. You have opened my mail four times this past week (*description of the behavior to which you object*). I want you to allow me to open my own mail. If there is anything in it that concerns you, I will let you know immediately" (*statement of cooperative response*).

Summary

This chapter discussed the importance of power and influence in interpersonal relationships, emphasizing the nature of power and its principles, different forms of power and influence, and examples of the misuse of power and influence.

Principles of Power and Influence

1. Some people are more powerful than others; some are born to power, others learn it.
2. Power can be shared. Empowering others enables them to gain power and control over themselves and over the environment. Empowering others has numerous advantages; for example, empowered people are more proactive and more responsible. Empowering others involves such strategies as being positive, avoiding verbal aggressiveness and abusiveness, and encouraging growth.
3. Power can be increased or decreased; power is never static.
4. Power follows the principle of less interest; generally, the less interest, the greater the power.
5. Power generates privilege.
6. Power has a cultural dimension; power is distributed differently in different cultures.

Bases of Power and Influence

7. Power in the relationship may be viewed in terms of six types of power: referent (B wants to be like A), legitimate (B believes that A has a right to influence or control B's behavior), expert (B regards A as having knowledge), information or persuasion (B attributes to A the ability to communicate effectively), reward (A has the ability to reward B), and coercive (A has the ability to punish B).
8. Power in the person may derives especially from personal credibility (a combination of perceived competence, character, and charisma).
9. Power in the message involves powerful speech, powerful nonverbal message, and powerful listening styles.
10. Among the strategies of resisting power and influence are negotiation, nonnegotiation, justification, and identity management.

Misuses of Power and Influence

11. Sexual harassment occurs when employment opportunities are made dependent on sexual favors and/or a hostile environment is created.
12. Power plays are patterns of behavior designed to take advantage of another person (including "nobody upstairs," "you owe me," and "yougottobekidding").
13. Possible responses to a power play include ignoring it, treating the power play as an isolated instance (and thus giving it little importance), and—the recommended response—cooperating.

Key Terms

coercive power, **305**

credibility, **306**

expert power, **304**

information or persuasion power, **304**

legitimate power, **303**

power, **299**

power plays, **315**

referent power, **303**

reward power, **305**

sexual harassment, **312**

Critical Thinking Questions

1 How satisfied are you with your command of each of the six bases of power? What might you do to increase those bases with which you're not satisfied?

2 How would you evaluate your own speaking, nonverbal, and listening power? What might you do to increase your power in these areas?

3 How would you use compliance-gaining strategies to influence someone to go on a date with you? How would you use compliance-resisting strategies to resist someone's persistent attempts to have you go on a date?

4 How is interpersonal power illustrated on prime-time television? For example: (1) Do male and female characters wield the same types of power? (2) Do the story lines in sitcoms and dramas reward the exercise of some types of power and punish the exercise of other types? (3) How do these programs deal with the process of empowering others? Is empowering rewarded? Are men and women portrayed as empowering in the same way?

5 A cooperative response to the power plays of others is clearly the recommended strategy, at least usually. But are there situations in which it might be more useful to ignore a power play?

In what types of interactions do you think ignoring might be used effectively? What reasons might you give for using such a strategy?

6 In each of the following three dyads, there is a power difference. One person is significantly richer, of higher status, more educated, or more attractive than the other. How might the power differences create communication difficulties when the individuals are engaged (1) in informal conversation and (2) in romantic encounters?

- a young nurse and the chief of surgery at a prestigious hospital
- an uneducated parent and the high school principal
- two coworkers, one extremely attractive and one extremely unattractive

Choice Points

1 *Harassing Behavior.* You notice that your colleague at work is being sexually harassed by a supervisor but says nothing. You bristle inside each time you see this happen. Ask yourself: What are some of the things you can do (if you think you should do anything, that is) that might help end this harassment?

2 *Confronting Power Plays.* One member of your study group uses the power play of "yougottobekidding," regardless of what you say. In one form or another, this member makes whatever you say appear inappropriate, unusable, or ill conceived. Ask yourself: How might you phrase a cooperative response to help put an end to this pattern of unfair communication?

3 *Gaining Recognition.* In your weekly meetings at work, the supervisor who serves as group leader consistently ignores your cues that you want to say something; also, when you do manage to say something, no one seems to react or take special note of your comments. You're determined to change this situation. Ask yourself: What can you do to turn things around?

4 *Explaining an Awkward Situation.* At your boss's house you're served shrimp for dinner, but shrimp makes you violently ill. Ask yourself: What can you say to explain the situation without making your boss feel badly?

5 *Asking for a Date.* You decide to ask the most popular person on campus for a date; the worst that could happen, you figure, is that you'll be rejected. Ask yourself: What options do you have for asking for this date? Consider, for example, the types of dates you might propose, the channels for communicating your desire for a date, and the actual messages you'd use in asking for a date. What option would you be most likely to select?

MyCommunicationLab Explorations

mycommunicationlab www.mycommunicationlab.com

These experiences focus on interpersonal power, its nature, and how it can be dealt with. ❶ Dyadic Power looks at selected dyads and asks you to identify the types of power that exist between them. ❷ Empowering Others offers scenarios in which you may effectively elect to empower other people. ❸ Power Plays presents situations in which power plays are used and provides the opportunity to develop and discuss strategies for dealing with them. ❹ Your beliefs about how easily other people can be manipulated are explored in the discussion and self-test of Machiavellianism. ❺ A discussion of the Knowledge Gap explores the relationship between knowledge and power.

Glossaries

Glossary of Interpersonal Communication Concepts

acculturation. The process by which your culture is modified or changed through contact with or exposure to another culture.

active listening. The process by which a listener expresses his or her understanding of the speaker's total message, including the verbal and nonverbal communication, the thoughts, and the feelings.

adaptors. Nonverbal behaviors that, when engaged in either in private or in public, serve some kind of need and occur in their entirety—for example, scratching your head until the itch is relieved.

adjustment. In verbal and nonverbal communications, the extent to which communicators share the same system of signals; this sharing makes effective communication possible.

affect displays. Movements of the facial area that convey emotional meaning such as anger, fear, or surprise.

affinity-seeking strategies. Behaviors designed to increase interpersonal attractiveness.

affirmation. The communication of support and approval.

ageism. Discrimination or prejudice based on age.

aggression. *See* **verbal aggression.**

allness. The illogical assumption that all can be known or said about a given person, issue, object, or event.

alter-adaptors. Body movements you make in response to your current interactions; for example, crossing your arms over your chest when someone unpleasant approaches or moving closer to someone you like.

altercasting. Placing the speaker in a specific role for a specific purpose and asking that he or she assume the perspective of this specific role; for example, "As a professor of communication, what would you say is . . .?"

ambiguity. The condition in which a message may be interpreted as having more than one meaning.

ambiguity tolerance. A characteristic of culture referring to the degree to which members of a culture feel comfortable with ambiguity and uncertainty.

anger. A generally unproductive emotion of strong feelings of displeasure, annoyance, or hostility.

anger management. The methods and techniques by which anger is controlled and managed.

apology. An expression of regret or sorrow for having done what you did or for what happened.

apprehension. *See* **communication apprehension.**

argumentativeness. Willingness to argue for your point of view, to speak your mind. Distinguished from **verbal aggressiveness.**

artifactual communication. A form of nonverbal communication involving the selection and arrangement of objects, for example, clothing, jewelry, hair styles, tattoos, and furniture.

assertiveness. A willingness to stand up for your rights but with respect for the rights of others.

assimilation. A process of message distortion in which messages are reworked to conform to your own attitudes, prejudices, needs, and values. *See also* **cultural assimilation.**

attention. The process of responding to a stimulus or stimuli; usually some consciousness of responding is implied.

attitude. A predisposition to respond for or against an object, person, or position.

attraction. The process by which one individual is emotionally drawn to another and finds that person satisfying to be with.

attraction theory. The theory that people develop relationships on the basis of attractiveness, proximity, and similarity.

attractiveness. Degree of physical appeal and/or pleasantness in personality.

attribution. The process of assigning causation or motivation to a person's behavior.

attribution theory. A theory concerned with the process of assigning causation or motivation to a person's behavior.

avoidance. An unproductive **interpersonal conflict** strategy in which a person takes mental or physical flight from the actual conflict.

back-channeling cues. Responses that a listener makes to a speaker while the speaker is speaking but which do not ask for the speaking role; for example, interjections such as "I understand" or "You said what?"

barriers to intercultural communication. Physical or psychological factors that prevent or hinder effective communication.

behavioral synchrony. Similarity in the behavior, usually nonverbal (such as postural stance or facial expressions), of two persons; generally taken as an indicator of liking.

belief. Confidence in the existence or truth of something; conviction.

beltlining. An unproductive **interpersonal conflict** strategy in which one person hits at a psychological or emotional level at which the other person cannot withstand the blow.

blame. An unproductive **interpersonal conflict** strategy in which we attribute the cause of the conflict to the other person or devote our energies to discovering who is the cause and avoid talking about the issues causing the conflict.

blended emotions. Emotions that are combinations of the primary emotions; for example, disappointment is a blend of surprise and sadness.

boundary marker. A **marker** that divides one person's territory from another's—for example, a fence.

breadth. In **social penetration theory,** the number of topics about which individuals in a relationship communicate.

bypassing. A type of miscommunication that occurs when the speaker and listener attribute different meanings to a message. Bypassing can occur when speaker and listener (1) use different words but give them the same meaning or (2) use the same words but give them different meanings.

captology. The study of the persuasive power of computer communication.

central marker. A **marker** or item that is placed in a territory to reserve it for a specific person—for example, a sweater thrown over a library chair to signal that the chair is taken.

certainty. An attitude of closed-mindedness that creates defensiveness among communicators. *Opposed to* **provisionalism.**

channel. The vehicle or medium through which signals are sent; for example, the vocal–auditory channel.

cherishing behaviors. Small behaviors we enjoy receiving from others, especially from our relational partner—for example, a kiss before the partner leaves for work.

chronemics. The study of the communicative nature of time, how a person's or culture's treatment of time reveals something about the person or culture; often divided into psychological and cultural time.

civil inattention. Polite ignoring of others (after a brief sign of awareness) so as not to invade their privacy.

cliché. An expression whose overuse calls attention to itself.

closed-mindedness. An unwillingness to receive certain communication messages.

code. A set of symbols used to translate a message from one form to another.

cognitive labeling theory. A theory of emotions which holds that you experience emotions according to the following steps: (1) An event occurs. (2) You respond physiologically. (3) You interpret this arousal—that is, you decide what emotion you're experiencing, and (4) you experience the emotion.

collectivist orientation. A cultural orientation in which the group's goals rather than the individual's are given greater importance and in which, for example, benevolence, tradition, and conformity are given special emphasis. *Opposed to* **individualist orientation.**

color communication. The use of color to communicate different meanings; each culture seems to define the meanings colors communicate somewhat differently.

communication. (1) The process or act of communicating; (2) the actual message or messages sent and received; (3) the study of the processes involved in the sending and receiving of messages.

communication apprehension. Fear or anxiety about communicating; usually identified as either trait apprehension (apprehensiveness in all communication situations) or state apprehension (apprehensiveness in specific communication situations).

communicology. The study of communication, particularly the subsection concerned with human communication.

competence. In **interpersonal communication,** knowledge about communication and the ability to engage in communication effectively. "Language competence" is a speaker's ability to use the language; it is a knowledge of the elements and rules of the language.

complementarity. A principle of **attraction** holding that you are attracted to people whose qualities you do not possess or you wish to possess, and to people who are opposite or different from yourself. *Opposed to* **similarity.**

complementary relationship. A relationship in which the behavior of one person serves as the stimulus for the complementary behavior of the other; in complementary relationships, behavioral differences are maximized.

compliance-gaining strategies. Behaviors designed to gain the agreement of others, to influence or persuade others to do as you wish.

compliance-resisting strategies. Behaviors directed at resisting the persuasive attempts of others.

computer-mediated communication. Communication between two or more people that takes place through a computer; for example, e-mail or instant messaging.

confidence. A quality of interpersonal effectiveness; a comfortable, at-ease feeling in interpersonal communication situations.

confirmation. A communication pattern that acknowledges another person's presence and indicates an acceptance of this person, this person's definition of self, and the relationship as defined or viewed by this person. *Opposed to* **rejection** and **disconfirmation.**

conflict. A disagreement or difference of opinion; a form of competition in which one person tries to bring a rival to surrender; a situation in which one person's behaviors are directed at preventing something or at interfering with or harming another individual. *See also* **interpersonal conflict.**

connotation. The feeling or emotional aspect of meaning, generally viewed as consisting of the evaluative (for example, good–bad), potency (strong–weak), and activity (fast–slow) dimensions. *Opposed to* **denotation.**

consistency. A process that influences you to maintain balance in your perceptions of messages or people; a process that causes you to see what you expect to see and to be uncomfortable when your perceptions run contrary to expectations.

contact. The first stage in **relationship development;** consists of "perceptual contact" (you see or hear the person) and "interactional contact" (you talk with the person).

content and relationship dimensions. Two aspects to which messages may refer: the world external to both speaker and listener (content) and the connections existing between the individuals who are interacting (relationship).

context. The physical, psychological, social, and temporal environment in which communication takes place.

conversation. Two-person communication that usually follows five stages: opening, feedforward, business, feedback, and closing.

conversational management. The management of the way in which messages are exchanged in **conversation.**

conversational maxims. Principles that are followed in **conversation** to ensure that the goal of the conversation is achieved.

conversational turns. The process of passing the speaker and listener roles during conversation.

cooperation. An interpersonal process by which individuals work together for a common end; the pooling of efforts to produce a mutually desired outcome. In conversation, an implicit agreement between speaker and listener to work together for mutual comprehension.

credibility. The perception of believability generally considered to consist of perceptions of competence, character, and charisma.

credibility strategies. Techniques by which you seek to establish your competence, character, and charisma.

critical thinking. The process of logically evaluating reasons and evidence and reaching a judgment on the basis of this analysis.

cultural assimilation. The process by which a person's culture is given up and he or she takes on the values and beliefs of another culture; as when, for example, an immigrant gives up his or her native culture to become a member of the new adopted culture.

cultural display. Signs that communicate a person's cultural identification, such as clothing or religious jewelry.

cultural display rules. Rules that identify what are and what are not appropriate forms of expression for members of the culture.

cultural rules. Standards and customs that are specific to a given culture.

cultural sensitivity. An attitude and way of behaving in which you're aware of, have a respect for, and acknowledge cultural differences.

cultural time. The meanings given to the ways time is treated in a particular culture.

culture. The relatively specialized elements of the lifestyle of a group of people that are passed on from one generation to the next through communication, not through genes.

culture shock. The reactions we experience at being in a culture very different from our own or from what we are used to.

date. An **extensional device** used to emphasize the notion of constant change and symbolized by a subscript: for example, John Smith$_{2000}$ is not John Smith$_{2010}$.

decoding. Taking a message in one form (for example, sound waves) and translating it into another form (for example, nerve impulses) from which meaning can be formulated. In human communication the decoder is the auditory mechanism; in electronic communication the decoder is, for example, the telephone earpiece. *See also* **encoding.**

defensiveness. An attitude of an individual or an atmosphere in a group characterized by threats, fear, and domination; messages evidencing evaluation, control, strategy, neutrality, superiority, and certainty are thought to lead to defensiveness. *Opposed to* **supportiveness.**

denial. Process by which you ignore or refuse to acknowledge your emotions to yourself or to others; one of the obstacles to the expression of emotion.

denotation. The objective or descriptive meaning of a word; the meaning you'd find in a dictionary. *Opposed to* **connotation.**

depenetration. A condition in which the **breadth** and **depth** of a relationship decrease.

depth. In **social penetration theory,** the degree to which the inner personality—the inner core of an individual—is penetrated in interpersonal interaction.

dialogue. A form of **communication** in which each person is both speaker and listener; communication characterized by involvement, concern, and respect for the other person. *Opposed to* **monologue.**

direct speech. Speech in which the speaker's intentions are stated clearly and directly.

disclaimer. Statement that asks the listener to receive what you say without its reflecting negatively on you.

disconfirmation. Process by which a person ignores or denies the right of another individual even to define himself or herself. *Opposed to* **rejection** and **confirmation.**

display rules. Rules or customs (of a culture or an organization) that govern what is and what is not permissible emotional communication.

downward communication. Communication from the higher levels of a hierarchy to the lower levels—for example, messages sent by managers to workers or from deans to faculty members.

dyadic communication. Two-person communication.

dyadic consciousness. An awareness on the part of the participants that an interpersonal relationship or pairing exists between them; distinguished from situations in which two individuals are together but do not see themselves as a unit or twosome.

dyadic effect. The tendency for the behaviors of one person to stimulate similar behaviors in the other interactant; often used to refer to the tendency for one person's self-disclosures to prompt the other also to self-disclose.

dyssemia. A condition in which an individual is unable to appropriately read the nonverbal messages of others or to communicate his or her own meanings nonverbally.

ear marker. A **marker** that identifies an item as belonging to a specific person—for example, a nameplate on a desk or initials on an attaché case.

effect. The outcome or consequence of an action or behavior; communication is assumed always to have some effect.

emblems. Nonverbal behaviors that directly translate words or phrases—for example, the signs for "OK" and "peace."

emotions. The feelings we have—for example, our feelings of guilt, anger, or love.

emotional appeals. Persuasive tactics directed at arousing emotional responses.

emotional communication. The expression of feelings—for example, feelings of guilt, happiness, or sorrow.

emotional contagion. The idea that the emotions of one person are often transferred to another person, much as a contagious disease is transmitted from one person to another.

empathy. The ability to feel another person's feeling; feeling or perceiving something as does another person.

encoding. Taking a message in one form (for example, nerve impulses) and translating it into another form (for example, sound waves). In human communication the encoder is the speaking mechanism; in electronic communication the encoder is, for example, the telephone mouthpiece. *See also* **decoding.**

enculturation. The process by which culture is transmitted from one generation to another.

E-prime. A form of the language that omits the verb *to be* except when it is used as an auxiliary or in statements of existence.

equality. An attitude that recognizes that each individual in a communication interaction is equal, that no one is superior to any other; encourages supportiveness. *Opposed to* **superiority.**

equilibrium theory. A theory of **proxemics** holding that intimacy and physical closeness are positively related; as a relationship becomes more intimate, the individuals will maintain shorter distances between themselves.

equity theory. A theory claming that you experience relational satisfaction when there is an equal distribution of rewards and costs between the two persons in the relationship.

etc. An **extensional device** used to emphasize the notion of infinite complexity; because you can never know all about anything, any statement about the world or an event must end with an explicit or implicit "et cetera."

ethics. The branch of philosophy that deals with the rightness or wrongness of actions; the study of moral values; in communication, the morality of message behavior.

ethnic identity. A commitment to the beliefs and philosophy of your culture; the degree to which you identify with your cultural group.

ethnocentrism. The tendency to see others and their behaviors through our own cultural filters, often as distortions of our own behaviors; the tendency to evaluate the values and beliefs of our own culture more positively than those of other cultures.

euphemism. A polite word or phrase used to substitute for some taboo or less polite term or phrase.

evaluating. Judging or placing a value on some person, object, or event; a stage in listening that involves thinking critically about and judging the message.

excuse. An explanation designed to lessen the negative consequences of something done or said.

expectancy violations theory. A theory of **proxemics** holding that people have certain expectations about space relationships. When an expectation is violated (say, a person stands too close to you or a romantic partner maintains abnormally large distances from you), the relationship comes into clearer focus and you wonder why this "normal distance" is being violated.

expressiveness. A quality of interpersonal effectiveness; genuine involvement in speaking and listening, conveyed verbally and nonverbally.

extensional devices. Linguistic devices proposed by Alfred Korzybski to make language a more accurate means for talking about the world. The extensional devices include **etc.**, **date**, and **index.**

extensional orientation. A tendency to give primary consideration to the world of experience and only secondary consideration to labels. *Opposed to* **intensional orientation.**

face-detracting conflict strategies. Strategies that attack a person's positive face (for example, comments that criticize the person's contribution to a relationship or the person's ability) or a person's negative face (for example, making demands on a person's time or resources that attack the person's autonomy).

face-enhancing strategies. Strategies that support and confirm a person's positive face (praise, a pat on the back, a sincere smile) or negative face (giving the person space and asking rather than demanding), for example.

facial feedback hypothesis. The hypothesis or theory that your facial expressions can produce physiological and emotional effects.

facial management techniques. Techniques used to mask certain emotions and to emphasize others; for example, intensifying your expression of happiness to make a friend feel good about a promotion.

fact–inference confusion. A misevaluation in which a person makes an inference, regards it as a fact, and acts on it as if it were a fact.

factual statement. A statement made by the observer after observation and limited to what is observed. *Opposed to* **inferential statement.**

family. A group of people who consider themselves related and connected to one another and among whom the actions of one member have consequences for others.

feedback. Information that is given back to the source. Feedback may come from the source's own messages (as when you hear what you're saying) or from the receiver(s) in forms such as applause, yawning, puzzled looks, questions, letters to the editor of a newspaper, increased or decreased subscriptions to a magazine. *See also* **negative feedback, positive feedback.**

feedforward. Information that is sent before a regular message, telling the listener something about what is to follow; a message that is prefatory to a more central message.

feminine culture. A culture in which both men and women are encouraged to be modest, oriented to maintaining the quality of life, and tender. Feminine cultures emphasize the quality of life and so socialize their people to be modest and to emphasize close interpersonal relationships. *Opposed to* **masculine culture.**

flexibility. A quality of thinking and behaving in which you vary your messages based on the unique situation in which you find yourself; the ability to adjust communication strategies and skills on the basis of the unique situation.

force. An unproductive **conflict** strategy in which you try to win an argument by physically or emotionally overpowering the other person, either by threat or by actual behavior.

friendship. An interpersonal relationship between two persons that is mutually productive, established and maintained through perceived mutual free choice, and characterized by mutual positive regard.

fundamental attribution error. In **attributions** of causality, the tendency to overvalue and give too much weight to the contribution of internal factors (the person's personality) and to undervalue and give too little weight to the contribution of external factors (the situation the person is in or the surrounding events).

gender display rules. Cultural rules that identify what are and what are not appropriate forms of expression for males and for females.

General Semantics. The study of the relationships among language, thought, and behavior.

gossip. Oral or written communication about someone not present, some third party, usually about matters that are private to this third party.

grapevine messages. Messages that do not follow any formal organizational structures; gossip related to a workplace or other community.

gunnysacking. An unproductive **conflict** strategy of storing up grievances—as if in a gunnysack—and holding them in readiness to dump on the opponent.

halo effect. The tendency to generalize a person's virtue or expertise from one area to other areas.

haptics. Technical term for the study of touch or **tactile communication.**

heterosexist language. Language that denigrates lesbians and gay men.

high ambiguity tolerance. Characteristic of cultures that are accepting of ambiguity and do not feel threatened by unknown situations; uncertainty is seen as a normal part of life, and people accept it as it comes.

high-context culture. A culture in which much of the information in communication messages is left implied; it's "understood." Meaning is considered to be in the context or in the person rather than explicitly coded in the verbal messages. **Collectivist cultures** are generally high context. *Opposed to* **low-context culture.**

home field advantage. The increased power that comes from being in your own territory.

home territories. Territories for which individuals have a sense of intimacy and over which they exercise control—for example, a teacher's office.

identity management. A strategy of resisting compliance by manipulating the image of the person making a request. Also used to refer to the strategies by which you present a favorable image of yourself and here is a synonym for **impression management.**

illustrators. Nonverbal behaviors that accompany and literally illustrate verbal messages—for example, upward movements of the head and hand that accompany the verbal "It's up there."

I-messages. Messages in which you accept responsibility for your personal thoughts and behaviors; messages in which you state your point of view explicitly. *Opposed to* **you-messages.**

image-confirming strategies. Techniques you use to communicate or to confirm your self-image, the image you want others to see.

immediacy. A quality of interpersonal effectiveness; a sense of contact and togetherness; a feeling that the speaker has an interest in and a liking for the other person.

implicit personality theory. A theory of personality, complete with rules about what characteristics go with what other characteristics, that you maintain and through which you perceive others.

impression formation. The process by which you perceive another person and ultimately come to some kind of evaluation or interpretation of this person.

impression management. The processes you go through to communicate the impression you want the other person to have of you; some writers use the term *self-presentation* or *identity management.*

inclusion. Principle of verbal interaction holding that all members should be a part of (included in) the interaction.

index. An **extensional device** used to emphasize the assumption that no two things are the same and symbolized by a subscript—for example, even though two people may both be politicians, politician$_{1[Smith]}$ is not politician$_{2[Jones]}$.

indirect speech. Speech that hides the speaker's true intentions; speech in which requests and observations are made indirectly.

indiscrimination. A misevaluation caused by categorizing people, events, or objects into a particular class and responding to them only as members of the class; a failure to recognize that each individual is unique.

individualist orientation. A cultural orientation that gives greater importance to the individual's than to the group's goals and preferences. *Opposed to* **collectivist orientation.**

inevitability. A principle of communication holding that communication cannot be avoided; all behavior in an interactional setting is communication.

inferential statement. A statement that can be made by anyone, is not limited to what is observed, and can be made at any time. *See also* **factual statement.**

informal time terms. Terms that express approximate rather than exact amounts of time; for example, "soon," "early," and "in a while."

information overload. A condition in which the amount or complexity of information is too great to be dealt with effectively by an individual, group, or organization.

in-group talk. Talk about a subject or in a vocabulary that some people present understand and others do not; has the effect of excluding those who don't understand.

insulation. A reaction to **territorial encroachment** in which you erect some sort of barrier between yourself and the would-be invaders; for example, a stone wall around your property, an unlisted phone number, or caller ID.

intensional orientation. A tendency to give primary consideration to the way things are labeled and only secondary consideration (if any) to the world of experience. *Opposed to* **extensional orientation.**

interaction management. A quality of interpersonal effectiveness in which the interaction is controlled and managed to the satisfaction of both parties; aspects of interaction management include effective management of conversational turns, fluency, and message consistency.

intercultural communication. Communication that takes place between persons of different cultures or between persons who have different cultural beliefs, values, or ways of behaving.

interpersonal communication. Communication between two persons or among a small group of persons, as distinguished from public or mass communication; communication of a personal nature, as distinguished from impersonal communication; communication between or among connected persons or those involved in a close relationship.

interpersonal conflict. A disagreement between two connected persons.

interpersonal effectiveness. The ability to accomplish interpersonal goals; interpersonal communication that is satisfying to both individuals.

interpersonal perception. The processes through which you become aware of, interpret, and evaluate people and their behavior.

interruptions. Verbal and nonverbal attempts to take over the role of the speaker.

intimacy. The closest interpersonal relationship; usually, the term denotes a close primary relationship.

intimacy claims. Obligations persons incur by virtue of being in a close and intimate relationship.

intimate distance. The closest distance in **proxemics**, ranging from touching to 18 inches.

intrapersonal communication. Communication with yourself.

involvement. The second stage in **relationship development,** in which you further advance the relationship, first testing each other and then intensifying your interaction.

irreversibility. A principle of communication holding that communication cannot be reversed; once something has been communicated, it cannot be uncommunicated.

James Lange theory. A theory of emotions which holds that you experience emotions in the following way: (1) An event occurs. (2) You respond physiologically. (3) You experience an emotion; for example, you feel joy or sadness.

jargon. The technical language of any specialized group, often a professional class, which is unintelligible to individuals not belonging to the group; shop talk. This glossary is an example of the jargon of a part of the communication field.

jealousy. A reaction (consisting of feelings, thoughts, and behaviors) to a physical or emotional threat to one or more of your significant relationships.

Johari window. A diagram of the four selves (open, blind, hidden, and unknown). The term *Johari* comes from the first names of Joseph Luft and Harry Ingham, who developed the model.

kinesics. The study of the communicative dimensions of facial and bodily movements.

language. The rules of syntax, semantics, and phonology by which sentences are created and understood; the name of any given language refers to the sentences that can be created in that language, such as English, Bantu, or Italian.

language relativity. See **linguistic relativity hypothesis.**

lateral communication. Communication between equals—manager to manager, worker to worker.

leave-taking cues. Verbal and nonverbal signals that indicate a person's desire to terminate a conversation.

leveling. A process of message distortion in which the number of details in a message is reduced as the message gets repeated from one person to another.

linguistic collusion. A response to **territorial encroachment** in which you speak in a language or jargon that the "invaders" don't understand and thus exclude them from the interaction. *See also* **withdrawal, turf defense,** and **insulation.**

linguistic relativity. The theory or hypothesis that the language you speak influences your perceptions of the world and your behaviors and that therefore people speaking widely differing languages will perceive and behave differently as a result of the language differences.

listening. An active process of receiving aural stimuli consisting of five stages: receiving, understanding, remembering, evaluating, and responding.

long-term memory. Memory that is (theoretically) unlimited in storage capacity and that holds information for long periods of time. *Opposed to* **short-term memory.**

love. An interpersonal relationship in which you feel closeness, caring, warmth, and excitement in relation to another person.

low ambiguity tolerance. Characteristic of cultures that are uncomfortable with ambiguity, do much to avoid uncertainty, and have a great deal of anxiety about not knowing what will happen next.

low-context culture. A culture in which most of the information in communication is explicitly stated in the verbal message rather than being left implied or assumed to be "understood." Low-context cultures are usually **individualist cultures.** *Opposed to* **high-context culture.**

manner maxim. A principle of **conversation** that holds that speakers cooperate by being clear and by organizing their thoughts into some meaningful and coherent pattern.

markers. Devices that signify that a certain territory belongs to a particular person. *See also* **boundary marker, central marker,** and **ear marker.**

masculine culture. A culture in which men are viewed as assertive, oriented to material success, and strong; women on the other hand are viewed as modest, focused on the quality of life, and tender. Masculine cultures emphasize success and so socialize their people to be assertive, ambitious, and competitive. *Opposed to* **feminine culture.**

matching hypothesis. The proposition that you date and mate people who are similar to yourself—who match you—in degree of physical attractiveness.

meaningfulness. A principle of **perception** that assumes that the behavior of people is sensible, stems from some logical antecedent, and is therefore meaningful rather than meaningless.

mentoring relationship. A relationship in which an experienced individual helps to train a less experienced person; for example, an accomplished teacher might mentor a younger teacher who has newly arrived or has never taught before.

mere exposure hypothesis. The theory that repeated or prolonged exposure to a stimulus may result in a change in attitude toward the stimulus object, generally in the direction of increased positiveness.

message. Any signal or combination of signals that serves as a **stimulus** for a receiver.

metacommunication. Communication about communication.

metalanguage. Language that refers to language.

metamessage. A message that makes reference to another message. For example, remarks such as "Did I make myself clear?" or "That's a lie" are metamessages, because they refer to other messages.

mindfulness and mindlessness. States of relative awareness. In a mindful state, you are aware of the logic and rationality of your behaviors and the logical connections existing among elements. In a mindless state, you're unaware of this logic and rationality.

mixed message. A message that communicates two different and often contradictory meanings; for example, a message that asks for two different (often incompatible) responses, such as "Leave me alone" combined with "Show me more attention." Often one meaning (usually the socially acceptable meaning) is communicated verbally and the other (usually the less socially acceptable meaning) nonverbally.

model. A representation of an object or process.

monochronic time orientation. A view of time in which things are done sequentially; one thing is scheduled at a time. *Opposed to* **polychronic time orientation.**

monologue. A form of **communication** in which one person speaks and the other listens; there's no real interaction among participants. *Opposed to* **dialogue.**

negative face. The desire to be autonomous, to have the right to do as you wish.

negative feedback. Feedback that serves a corrective function by informing the source that his or her message is not being received in the way intended. Looks of boredom, shouts of disagreement, letters critical of newspaper policy, and teachers' instructions on how better to approach a problem are examples of negative feedback that should (ideally) serve to redirect the speaker's behavior. *See also* **positive feedback.**

networking. Connecting with people who can help you accomplish a goal or help you find information related to your goal; for example, talking with many friends and other contacts when looking for a job.

neutrality. A response pattern lacking in personal involvement; encourages defensiveness. *Opposed to* **empathy.**

noise. Anything that interferes with your receiving a message as the source intended the message to be received. Noise is present in communication to the extent that the message received is not the message sent.

nonallness. The understanding that you can never know all about anything and that what you know, say, or hear is only a part of what there is to know, say, or hear.

nonnegotiation. An unproductive **conflict** strategy in which one individual refuses to discuss the conflict or to listen to the other person.

nonverbal communication. Communication without words; communication by means of space, gestures, facial expressions, touching, vocal variation, and silence, for example.

nonverbal dominance. Nonverbal behavior that allows one person to achieve psychological dominance over another.

object-adaptors. Movements that involve your manipulation of some object; for example, punching holes in a styrofoam coffee cup, clicking a ballpoint pen, or chewing on a pencil.

object language. Language used to communicate about objects, events, and relations in the world (rather than about words as in **metalanguage**).

occulesis. The study of the messages communicated by the eyes.

olfactory communication. Communication by smell.

openness. A quality of interpersonal effectiveness encompassing (1) your willingness to interact openly with others, to self-disclose as appropriate; (2) your willingness to react honestly to incoming stimuli; and (3) your willingness to own your own feelings and thoughts.

opinion. A tentative conclusion concerning some object, person, or event.

other-orientation. A quality of interpersonal effectiveness involving attentiveness, interest, and concern for the other person.

outing. The process whereby a person's affectional orientation is made public by another person without the consent of the gay man or lesbian.

overattribution. The tendency to attribute a great deal or even everything a person does to one or two characteristics.

owning feelings. The process by which you take responsibility for your own feelings instead of attributing them to others.

paralanguage. The vocal but nonverbal aspect of speech. Paralanguage consists of voice qualities (for example, pitch range, resonance, tempo); vocal characterizers (laughing or crying, yelling or whispering); vocal qualifiers (intensity, pitch height); and vocal segregates ("uh-uh," meaning "no," or "sh" meaning "silence").

passive listening. **Listening** that may be attentive and supportive but that occurs without the listener's talking or directing the speaker in any nonverbal way; also (used negatively), inattentive and uninvolved listening.

pauses. Silent periods in the normally fluent stream of speech. Pauses are of two types: filled or vocalized pauses (interruptions in speech that are filled with such vocalizations as "er" or "um") and unfilled pauses (silences of unusually long duration).

perception. The process by which you become aware of objects, events, and people through your senses.

perception checking. The process of verifying your understanding of some message, situation, or feeling.

perceptual accentuation. A process that leads you to see what you expect or want to see—for example, the tendency to see people you like as better looking and smarter than people you don't like.

personal distance. The second closest distance in **proxemics,** ranging from 18 inches to 4 feet.

personal rejection. An unproductive **conflict** strategy in which one person withholds love and affection and seeks to win the argument by getting the other person to break down under this withdrawal.

persuasion. The process of influencing attitudes and behavior.

phatic communication. Communication that is primarily social; communication designed to open the channels of communication rather than to communicate something about the external world. "Hello" and "How are you?" in everyday interaction are examples.

physical abuse. Behavior that involves threats of violence as well as pushing, hitting, slapping, kicking, choking, throwing things, and breaking things.

pitch. The highness or lowness of the vocal tone.

polarization. A form of fallacious reasoning by which only two extremes are considered; also referred to as "black-or-white" and "either/or" thinking or as a two-valued orientation.

politeness. Behavior that most people in a given culture would consider to represent "good manners"; may include consideration, respect, modesty, etc.

polychronic time orientation. A view of time in which several things may be scheduled or engaged in at the same time. *Opposed to* **monochronic time orientation.**

positive face. The desire to be viewed positively by others, to be thought of favorably.

positive feedback. Feedback that supports or reinforces the continuation of behavior along the same lines in which it is already proceeding, as when applause during a speech encourages the speaker to continue speaking this way. *See also* **negative feedback.**

positiveness. A characteristic of effective communication involving positive attitudes toward oneself, toward the interpersonal interaction, and toward expressing these attitudes to others (as in complimenting) along with acceptance and approval.

power. The ability to influence or control the behavior of another person; an inevitable part of interpersonal relationships.

power distances. A characteristic of culture referring to the degree to which there are power differences among the members. In high power-distance cultures there is great distance between those in authority and the regular citizenry; power is concentrated in the hands of a few. In low power-distance cultures power is more evenly distributed throughout the population.

power play. A consistent pattern of behavior in which one person tries to control the behavior of another.

primacy–recency. Phenomenon in interpersonal perception whereby we give more importance to that which occurs first (primacy) or to that which occurs last or most recently (recency).

primary affect displays. The communication of the six primary emotions: happiness, surprise, fear, anger, sadness, and disgust/contempt.

primary emotions. Basic emotions, usually identified as joy, acceptance, fear, surprise, sadness, disgust, anger, and anticipation.

primary relationship. The relationship between two people that they consider their most (or one of their most) important; for example, the relationship between husband and wife or domestic partners.

primary territory. Areas that you consider your exclusive preserve—for example, your room or office.

process. Ongoing activity; communication is referred to as a process to emphasize that it's always changing, always in motion.

projection. A psychological process whereby you attribute characteristics or feelings of your own to others; often, the process whereby you attribute your faults to others.

protection theory. A theory of **proxemics** holding that people establish a body buffer zone to protect themselves from unwanted closeness, touching, or attack.

provisionalism. An attitude of open-mindedness that leads to the development of a supportive relationship and atmosphere. *Opposed to* **certainty.**

proxemics. The study of the communicative function of space; the study of how people unconsciously structure spaces such as the distances between people in their interactions, the layouts of homes and offices, and even the design of cities.

proximity. Physical closeness—one of the qualities influencing interpersonal **attraction.** Also, as a principle of **perception,** the tendency to perceive people or events that are physically close as belonging together or representing some unit.

psychological time. Your emphasis on or orientation toward past, present, or future time.

public distance. The farthest distance in **proxemics,** ranging from 12 feet to more than 25 feet.

public territory. Areas that are open to all people—for example, restaurants or parks.

punctuation. The breaking up of continuous communication sequences into short sequences with identifiable beginnings and endings or stimuli and responses.

pupil dilation. The extent to which the pupil of the eye is expanded; generally, large pupils indicate positive emotional arousal.

pupillometrics. The study of communication through changes in the size of the pupils of the eyes.

Pygmalion effect. The condition in which you make a prediction of success, act as if the prediction were true, and thereby make it come true (for example, acting toward students as if they'll be successful influences them to become successful); a type of **self-fulfilling prophecy.**

quality maxim. A principle of **conversation** that holds that speakers cooperate by saying what they think is true and by not saying what they think is false.

quantity maxim. A principle of **conversation** that holds that speakers cooperate by being only as informative as necessary to communicate their intended meanings.

racist language. Language that denigrates, demeans, or is derogatory toward members of a particular race or ethnic group.

rate. The speed with which you speak, generally measured in words per minute.

receiver. Any person or thing that takes in messages. Receivers may be individuals listening to or reading a message, a group of persons hearing a speech, a scattered television audience, or machines that store information. *See also* **source.**

receiving. A stage in listening involving the hearing of and attending to the message.

reconciliation strategies. Behaviors designed to repair a broken relationship.

regulators. Nonverbal behaviors that regulate, monitor, or control the communications of another person.

rejection. A response to an individual that acknowledges the other person but expresses disagreement. *Opposed to* **confirmation** and **disconfirmation.**

relation maxim. A principle of **cooperation** in **conversation** that holds that speakers communicate by talking about what is relevant and by not talking about what isn't.

relationship communication. Communication between or among intimates or those in close relationships; the term is used by some theorists as synonymous with interpersonal communication.

relationship deterioration. The stage of a relationship during which the connecting bonds between the partners weaken and the partners begin drifting apart.

relationship development. The progress of an interpersonal relationship, which takes place over a series of six stages.

relationship dialectics theory. A theory that describes relationships in terms of the tensions between pairs of opposite, competing desires or motivations, such as the desire for autonomy and the desire to belong to someone, desires for novelty and for predictability, and desires for closedness and for openness.

relationship dimension. The dimension of messages that comments on the relationship between the speakers rather than on matters external to them.

relationship dissolution. The termination or end of an interpersonal relationship.

relationship license. Permission to violate some relationship expectation, custom, or rule.

relationship maintenance. Behaviors that help to continue and preserve a relationship; also, a stage of relationship stability in which the relationship does not progress or deteriorate significantly; a continuation as opposed to a dissolution (or an intensification) of a relationship.

relationship repair. A relationship stage in which one or both parties seek to improve a deteriorating relationship.

relationship violence. Generally considered to consist of **verbal or emotional abuse, physical abuse,** and/or **sexual abuse.**

remembering. A stage in listening referring to the retention of what you hear.

resemblance. As a principle of **perception**, the tendency to perceive people or events that are similar in appearance as belonging together.

responding. A stage in listening in which the listener answers or gives feedback to the speaker.

response. Any bit of overt or covert behavior.

role. The part an individual plays in a group; an individual's function or expected behavior.

rules theory. A theory that describes relationships as interactions governed by series of rules that couples agree to follow. When the rules are followed, a relationship is maintained; when they are broken, the relationship experiences difficulty.

schemata (singular: schema). Ways of organizing perceptions; mental templates or structures that help you organize the millions of items of information you come into contact with every day as well as those you already have in memory. Examples are general ideas about people (e.g., about Pat and Chris, Japanese, Baptists, or New Yorkers); about yourself (your qualities, abilities, and even liabilities); or about social roles (the characteristics of a police officer, professor, or multimillionaire CEO).

script. A type of **schema**; an organized body of information about some action, event, or procedure. A script is a general idea of how some event should play out or unfold, of the rules governing the events and their sequence.

secondary territory. Areas that do not belong to you but that you've occupied and which are therefore associated with you—for example, the seat you normally take in class.

selective exposure. Tendency of listeners to actively seek out information that supports their opinions and to actively avoid information that contradicts their existing opinions, beliefs, attitudes, and values.

self-acceptance. Being satisfied with yourself, your virtues and vices, your abilities and limitations.

self-adaptors. Movements that usually satisfy a physical need, generally serving to make you more comfortable; for example, scratching your head to relieve an itch, moistening your lips because they feel dry, or pushing your hair out of your eyes.

self-attribution. A process through which you seek to account for and understand the reasons and motivations for your own behaviors.

self-awareness. The degree to which you know yourself.

self-concept. Your self-image, the view you have of who you are.

self-deprecating strategies. Techniques you use to signal your incompetence or your inability to do some task so as to encourage another to help you out.

self-destructive beliefs. Beliefs that create problems, often beliefs that are unrealistic and set goals that are impossible to achieve.

self-disclosure. The process of revealing something about yourself to another—usually, revealing information that you'd normally keep hidden.

self-esteem. The value you place on yourself; your self-evaluation. Usually refers to the positive value people place on themselves.

self-fulfilling prophecy. Situation in which you make a prediction or prophecy and by making it cause it to come true. For example, expecting a person to be hostile, you act in a hostile manner toward this person and in so doing elicit hostile behavior in the person, thus confirming your prophecy.

self-handicapping strategies. Techniques you use to excuse possible failure; for example, setting up barriers or obstacles to make the task impossible so that when you fail, you won't be blamed or thought ineffective.

self-monitoring. Manipulating the image you present to others in interpersonal interactions so as to give the most favorable impression of yourself.

self-monitoring strategies. Techniques you use to carefully monitor (self-censor) what you say or do.

self-presentation. *See impression management.*

self-serving bias. A bias that operates in the self-attribution process, leading people to take credit for the positive consequences and to deny responsibility for the negative consequences of their behaviors.

semantics. The area of language study concerned with meaning.

sexist language. Language derogatory to members of one gender, generally women.

sexual abuse. Behavior that is unwanted and directed at a person's sexuality; for example, touching, accusations of sexual infidelity without reason, forced sex, and references to a person by abusive sexual terms.

sexual harassment. Unsolicited and unwanted verbal or nonverbal sexual messages.

short-term memory. Memory that is very limited in capacity; contains information that is quickly lost if it is not passed on to **long-term memory.**

shyness. Discomfort and uneasiness in interpersonal situations.

signal-to-noise ratio. A measure of what is meaningful (signal) versus what is interference (noise) relative to the participants and the context of an interaction.

silence. The absence of vocal communication; often misunderstood to refer to the absence of communication.

silencers. Unproductive **conflict** strategies (such as crying) that literally silence your opponent.

similarity. A principle of **attraction** holding that you're attracted to qualities similar to those you yourself possess and to people who are similar to yourself. *Opposed to* **complementarity.**

slang. Language used by special groups that the general society does not consider proper or standard.

social comparison processes. The processes by which you compare yourself (for example, your abilities, opinions, and values) with others and then assess and evaluate yourself on the basis of the comparison; one of the sources of **self-concept**.

social distance. The third farthest distance in **proxemics**, ranging from 4 feet to 12 feet; the distance at which business is usually conducted.

social exchange theory. A theory hypothesizing that you develop profitable relationships (those in which your rewards are greater than your costs) and that you avoid or terminate unprofitable relationships (those in which your costs exceed your rewards).

social information processing theory. A theory that claims, contrary to **social presence theory**, that whether you're communicating face-to-face or online, you can communicate the same degree of personal involvement and develop similar close relationships.

social penetration theory. A theory concerned with relationship development from the superficial to the intimate levels (**depth**) and from few to many areas of interpersonal interaction (**breadth**). See also **depenetration**.

social presence theory. A theory that argues that the bandwidth (the number of message cues exchanged) of communication influences the degree to which the communication is personal or impersonal. When lots of cues are exchanged (especially nonverbal cues), as in face-to-face communication, there is great social presence; when fewer cues are exchanged, as in e-mail, there is less social presence.

source. Any person or thing that creates messages; for example, an individual speaking, writing, or gesturing or a computer solving a problem. See also **receiver**.

speech. Messages conveyed via a vocal–auditory channel.

spiral of silence. A theory that argues that you're more likely to voice agreement than disagreement.

stability. Principle of **perception** holding that your perceptions of things and of people tend to be relatively consistent with your previous conceptions.

static evaluation. An orientation that fails to recognize that the world is constantly changing; an attitude that sees people and events as fixed rather than as ever changing.

status. The relative level each person occupies in a hierarchy; status always involves a comparison, and thus one person's status is only relative to the status of another. In the United States occupation, financial position, age, and educational level are significant determinants of social status.

stereotype. In communication, a fixed impression of a group of people through which we then perceive specific individuals; stereotypes are most often negative ("Martians are stupid, uneducated, and dirty") but also may be positive ("Venusians are scientific, industrious, and helpful").

stimulus. Any external or internal change that impinges on or arouses an organism.

stimulus–response models of communication. Models of communication that assume that the process of communication is linear, beginning with a stimulus that then leads to a response.

subjectivity. Principle of **perception** holding that your perceptions are not objective but are influenced by your wants and needs, your expectations and predictions.

superiority. A point of view or attitude that assumes that others are not equal to yourself; encourages **defensiveness**. Opposed to **equality**.

supportiveness. In communication, behavior that is descriptive rather than evaluative and provisional rather than certain; also, an attitude of an individual or an atmosphere in a group that is characterized by openness, absence of fear, and a genuine feeling of equality. Opposed to **defensiveness**.

symmetrical relationship. A relation between two or more persons in which one person's behavior serves as a stimulus for the same type of behavior in the other person(s); for example, a relationship in which anger in one person encourages anger in another person or in which a critical comment by one person leads the other person to respond in kind.

taboo. Forbidden; culturally censored. Taboo language is language that is frowned upon by polite society. Topics and specific words may be considered taboo—for example, death, sex, certain forms of illness, and various words denoting sexual activities and excretory functions.

tactile communication. Communication by touch; communication received by the skin.

temporal communication. The messages communicated by your time orientation and treatment of time.

territorial encroachment. The trespassing on, use of, or appropriation of one person's territory by another.

territoriality. A possessive or ownership reaction to an area of space or to particular objects.

theory. A general statement or principle applicable to various related phenomena.

touch. See **tactile communication**.

touch avoidance. The tendency to avoid touching and being touched by others.

transactional perspective. A point of view that sees communication as an ongoing process in which all elements are interdependent and influence one another.

turf defense. A response to **territorial encroachment** in which you defend your territory against invasion. You may simply say, "This is my seat," or you may start a fight as nations do. See also **withdrawal**, **insulation**, and **linguistic collusion**.

turning points. Significant relationship events that have important consequences for the individuals and the relationship and may alter the relationship's direction or trajectory.

uncertainty reduction theory. Applied to interpersonal relationships, theory holding that as relationships develop, uncertainty is reduced; relationship development is seen as a process through which individuals reduce their uncertainty about each other.

understanding. A stage in listening involving deciphering meaning from the message you hear.

universal of interpersonal communication. A feature of communication common to all interpersonal communication acts.

unproductive conflict strategies. Ways of engaging in conflict that generally prove counterproductive, including **avoidance, force, blame, silencers, gunnysacking,** and **beltlining.**

upward communication. Communication sent from the lower levels of a hierarchy to the upper levels—for example, from line worker to manager or from faculty member to dean.

unrepeatability. A characteristic of communication referring to the fact that all communication acts are unique and can never be repeated exactly.

value. Relative worth of something; a quality that makes something desirable or undesirable; ideals or customs about which we have emotional responses, whether positive or negative.

ventilation hypothesis. The assumption that expressing emotions (that is, giving vent to emotions) lessens their intensity.

verbal aggressiveness. An unproductive **conflict** strategy in which one person tries to win an argument by attacking the other person's **self-concept.**

verbal or emotional abuse. Behavior that is humiliating, isolating, or overly critical.

visual dominance. The use of your eyes to maintain a superior or dominant position; for example, when making an especially important point, you might look intently at the other person.

volume. The relative loudness of the voice.

win–lose strategies. Conflict management strategies that seek a resolution in which one person wins and the other loses.

win–win strategies. Conflict management strategies that seek a collaborative solution in which each person wins something.

withdrawal. A response to **territorial encroachment** in which you leave the scene, whether the country, home, office, or classroom. *See also* **turf defense, insulation,** and **linguistic collusion.**

you-messages. Messages in which you deny responsibility for your own thoughts and behaviors; messages that attribute your **perception** to another person; messages of blame. *Opposed to* **I-messages.**

Glossary of Interpersonal Communication Skills

abstractions. Use both abstract and specific terms when describing or explaining.

accommodation. Accommodate to the speaking style of your listeners in moderation. Too much mirroring of the other's style may appear manipulative.

active and inactive listening. Be an active listener: Paraphrase the speaker's meaning, express understanding of the speaker's feelings, and ask questions when necessary.

active interpersonal conflict. Engage in interpersonal conflict actively; be appropriately revealing, and listen to your partner.

advantages and disadvantages of relationships. In evaluating, entering, or dissolving relationships, consider both the advantages and the disadvantages.

allness. Avoid allness statements; they invariably misstate the reality and will often offend the other person.

analyzing your perceptions. Increase accuracy in interpersonal perception by identifying the influence of your physical and emotional states and making sure that you're not drawing conclusions from too little information.

anger management. Calm down as best you can; then consider your communication options and the relevant communication skills for expressing your feelings.

apologizing. Admit wrongdoing if indeed wrongdoing occurred and express your sorrow in specific rather than general terms; offer to correct the problem (whenever this is possible) and give assurance that this will not happen again.

appreciating cultural differences. Look at cultural differences not as deviations or deficiencies but as the differences they are. Recognizing different ways of doing things, however, does not necessarily mean accepting them.

appropriateness of self-disclosure. When thinking of disclosing, consider the legitimacy of your motives, the appropriateness of the disclosure, the listener's responses (is the dyadic effect operating?), and the potential burdens such disclosures might impose.

argumentativeness. Avoid aggressiveness (attacking the other person's self-concept); instead, focus logically on the issues, emphasize finding solutions, and work to ensure that what is said will result in positive self-feelings for both individuals.

artifactual communication. Use artifacts (for example, color, clothing, body adornment, space decoration) to communicate desired messages.

body movements. Use body and hand gestures to reinforce your communication purposes.

channel. Assess your channel options (for example, face-to-face, e-mail, leaving a voice-mail message) before communicating important messages.

checking perceptions. Increase accuracy in perception by (1) describing what you see or hear and the meaning you assign to it and (2) asking the other person if your perceptions are accurate.

communicating assertively. Describe the problem, say how the problem affects you, propose solutions, confirm your understanding, and reflect on your own assertiveness.

communicating power. Avoid powerless message forms such as hesitations, excessive intensifiers, disqualifiers, tag questions, one-word answers, self-critical statements, overly polite statements, and vulgar and slang expressions.

communication options. In light of the inevitability, irreversibility, and unrepeatability of messages, assess your communication options before communicating.

confirmation. When you wish to be confirming, acknowledge (verbally and/or nonverbally) others in your group and their contributions.

conflict styles. Choose your conflict style carefully; each style has consequences. In relationship conflict, look for win–win solutions rather than solutions in which one person wins and the other loses.

conflict, culture, and gender. Approach conflict with an understanding of the cultural and gender differences in attitudes toward what constitutes conflict and toward how it should be pursued.

connotative meanings. Clarify your connotative meanings if you have any doubts that your listeners might misunderstand you; as a listener, ask questions if you have doubts about the speaker's connotations.

content and relationship. Listen to both the content and the relationship aspects of messages, distinguish between them, and respond to both.

content and relationship conflicts. Analyze conflict messages in terms of content and relationship dimensions, and respond to each accordingly.

context adjustment. Adjust your messages to the physical, cultural, social–psychological, and temporal context.

conversational maxims. Follow (generally) the basic maxims of conversation, such as the maxims of quantity, quality, relations, manner, and politeness.

conversational rules. Observe the general rules for conversation (for example, keeping speaking turns relatively short and avoiding interrupting), but break them when there seems logical reason to do so.

conversational turns. Maintain relatively short conversational turns; after taking your turn, pass the speaker's turn to another person nonverbally or verbally.

cultural differences in listening. Be especially flexible when listening in a multicultural setting, realizing that people from other cultures give different listening cues and may operate with different rules for listening.

cultural identifiers. Use cultural identifiers that are sensitive to the desires of others; when appropriate, make clear the cultural identifiers you prefer.

cultural influences. Communicate with an understanding that culture influences communication in all its forms.

cultural influences on interpersonal relationships. Be aware that culture exerts influences on all types of relationships, encouraging some and discouraging others.

cultural sensitivity. Increase your cultural sensitivity by learning about different cultures, recognizing and facing your fears, recognizing relevant differences, and becoming conscious of the cultural rules of other cultures.

culture and perception. Increase accuracy in perception by learning as much as you can about the cultures of those with whom you interact.

dating statements. Date your statements to avoid thinking of the world as static and unchanging. Reflect the inevitability of change in your messages.

deciding to self-disclose. Consider the potential benefits (for example, self-knowledge, increased communication effectiveness, and physiological health) as well as the potential personal, relationship, and professional risks.

disclaimers. Use disclaimers if you feel you might be misunderstood. But avoid them when they're not necessary; too many disclaimers can make you appear unprepared or unwilling to state an opinion.

disconfirming language. Avoid sexist, heterosexist, racist, and ageist language, which is disconfirming and insulting and invariably creates communication barriers.

emotional communication. Communicate emotions effectively: (1) Describe feelings, (2) identify the reasons for the feelings, (3) anchor feelings to the present, and (4) own your feelings and messages.

emotional display. Express emotions and interpret the emotions of others in light of the cultural rules dictating what is and what isn't "appropriate."

emotionality in interpersonal communication. Recognize the inevitable emotionality in your thoughts and feelings, and include emotion as appropriate in your verbal and nonverbal messages.

emotional understanding. Identify and describe emotions (both positive and negative) clearly and specifically. Learn the vocabulary of emotional expression.

empathic and objective listening. Punctuate the interaction from the speaker's point of view, engage in dialogue, and seek to understand the speaker's thoughts and feelings.

empathic conflict. Engage in conflict with empathy rather than blame. Also, express this empathy ("I can understand how you must have felt").

empathy. Communicate empathy when appropriate: Resist evaluating the person, focus on the person, express active involvement through facial expressions and gestures, reflect back the feelings you think are being expressed, self-disclose, and address mixed messages.

ethnocentric thinking. Recognize your own ethnocentric thinking and be aware of how it influences your verbal and nonverbal messages.

evaluating. Try first to understand fully what the speaker means and then look to identify any biases or self-interests that might lead the speaker to give an unfair presentation.

excuse making. Use excuses in moderation; avoid blaming others; acknowledge and accept responsibility for the failure.

expressiveness. Communicate active involvement by using active listening, addressing mixed messages, using I-messages, and using appropriate variations in paralanguage and gestures.

eye movements. Use eye movements to seek feedback, exchange conversational turns, signal the nature of your relationship, or compensate for increased physical distance.

face-saving strategies. Use strategies that allow your opponents to save face; avoid beltlining, or hitting opponents with attacks that they will have difficulty absorbing and will resent.

facial messages. Use facial expressions to communicate involvement. In listening, look to the facial expressions of others as cues to their emotions and meaning.

facts and inferences. Distinguish facts (verifiably true past events) from inferences (guesses or hypotheses), and act on inferences with tentativeness.

feedback. Listen to both verbal and nonverbal feedback—from yourself and from others—and use these cues to help you adjust your messages.

feedforward. Use feedforward when you feel your listener needs background or when you want to ease into a particular topic, such as bad news.

flexibility. Because no two communication situations are identical, because everything is in a state of flux, and because everyone is different, cultivate flexibility and adjust your communication to the unique situation.

friendships. Establish friendships to help serve such needs as utility, ego support, stimulation, and security. At the same time, seek to serve your friends' similar needs.

fundamental attribution error. Avoid the fundamental attribution error, whereby you attribute someone's behavior solely to internal factors while minimizing or ignoring situational forces.

gender differences in listening. Understand that in general, women give more cues that they're listening and appear more supportive in their listening than men.

giving space. Give others the space they need. Look to the other person for any signs of spatial discomfort.

high- and low-context cultures. Adjust your messages and your listening in light of the differences between high- and low-context cultures.

I-messages. Use I-messages when communicating your feelings; take responsibility for your own feelings rather than attributing them to others.

immediacy. Maintain immediacy through close physical distances and eye contact and by smiling, using the other person's name, and focusing on the other's remarks.

implicit personality theory. Bring your implicit personality theory to your mindful state to subject your perceptions and conclusions to logical analysis.

increasing assertiveness. Increase assertiveness by analyzing the assertive messages of others, rehearsing assertive messages, and communicating assertively.

indirect messages. Use indirect messages when a more direct style might prove insulting or offensive, but be aware that they may create misunderstanding.

indiscrimination. Treat each situation and each person as unique (when possible) even when they're covered by the same label. Index key concepts.

individualist and collectivist cultures. Adjust your messages and your listening with an awareness of differences between individualist and collectivist cultures.

initial impressions. Guard against drawing impressions too quickly or from too little information and using initial impressions as filters; such filters can prevent you from forming more accurate perceptions on the basis of more information.

intensional orientation. Avoid intensional orientation. Look to people and things first and to labels second.

interaction management. Speak in relatively short conversational turns, avoid long and/or frequent pauses, and use verbal and nonverbal messages that are consistent.

intercultural communication. Become mindful of (1) differences between yourself and people who are culturally different, (2) differences within other cultural groups, and (3) cultural differences in meanings.

listening to the feelings of others. Empathize, focus on the other person, and encourage the person to explore his or her feelings.

managing relationship dissolution. Break the loneliness–depression cycle, take time out, bolster self-esteem, seek support from nourishing others, and avoid repeating negative patterns.

masculine and feminine cultures. Adjust your messages and your listening to allow for differences in cultural masculinity and femininity.

meanings depend on context. Look at the context for cues as to how you should interpret the meanings of messages.

meanings in people. When deciphering meaning, the best source is the person; meanings are in people. When in doubt, find out—from the source.

metacommunication. Metacommunicate when you want to clarify the way you're talking or what you're talking about by, for example, giving clear feedforward and paraphrasing your complex messages.

mindfulness. Increase your mindfulness by creating and recreating categories and being open to new information and points of view; also, beware of relying too heavily on first impressions.

negatives and positives of conflict. Approach conflict to minimize its negative aspects and to maximize the positive benefits of conflict and its resolution.

networking. Establish a network of relationships to provide insights into issues relevant to your personal and professional life, and be willing to lend your expertise to others.

noise management. Reduce physical, physiological, psychological, and semantic noise as best you can; use repetition and restatement and, when in doubt, ask if you're clear.

nonjudgmental and critical listening. Keep an open mind, avoid filtering out difficult messages, and recognize your own biases. When listening to make judgments, listen extra carefully, ask questions when in doubt, and check your perceptions before criticizing.

nonverbal communication and culture. Interpret the nonverbal cues of others with an awareness of the other person's cultural meanings (insofar as you can).

open expression in conflict. Try to express your feelings openly rather than resorting to silence or avoidance.

openness. Increase openness when appropriate by self-disclosing, responding spontaneously and honestly to those with whom you're interacting, and owning your own feelings and thoughts.

other orientation. Acknowledge the importance of the other person: use focused eye contact and appropriate facial expressions; smile, nod, and lean toward the other person.

overattribution. Avoid overattribution; rarely is any one factor an accurate explanation of complex human behavior.

packaging. Make your verbal and nonverbal messages consistent; inconsistencies often create uncertainty and misunderstanding.

paralanguage. Vary paralinguistic features to communicate nuances of meaning and to add interest and color to your messages.

perceptual shortcuts. Be mindful of your perceptual shortcuts so that they don't mislead you and result in inaccurate perceptions.

polarization. Avoid thinking and talking in extremes by using middle terms and qualifiers. But remember that too many qualifiers may make you appear unsure of yourself.

positiveness. Communicate positiveness by expressing your own satisfaction with the interaction and by complimenting others.

power distance. Adjust your messages and listening on the basis of the power-distance orientation of the culture in which you find yourself.

power plays. Respond to power plays with cooperative strategies: Express your feelings, describe the behavior to which you object, and state a cooperative response.

present-focus conflict. Focus your conflict resolution messages on the present; avoid gunnysacking, or dredging up and unloading old grievances.

problem-solving conflicts. Deal with interpersonal conflicts systematically as problems to be solved: Define the problem, examine possible solutions, test a solution, evaluate the solution, and accept or reject the solution.

receiving. Focus attention on both the verbal and the nonverbal messages; both communicate essential parts of the total meaning.

reducing uncertainty. Use passive, active, and interactive strategies to reduce uncertainty.

relationship messages. Formulate messages that are appropriate to the stage of the relationship. Also, listen to messages from relationship partners that may reveal differences in perceptions about your relationship stage.

relationship repair. Recognize the problem, engage in productive conflict resolution, pose possible solutions, affirm each other, integrate solutions into normal behavior, and take risks as appropriate.

remembering. Identify the central ideas, summarize the message in an easier-to-retain form, and repeat ideas (aloud or to yourself) to help you remember.

responding. Express support for the speaker using I-messages instead of you-messages.

responding to others' disclosures. Listen actively, support the discloser, and keep the disclosures confidential.

romantic workplace relationships. Before embarking on romantic relationships at work, be sure you have a clear understanding of the potential problems.

self-awareness. Increase self-awareness by listening to others, increasing your open self, and seeking out information to reduce blind spots.

self-concept. See yourself, as objectively as you can, through the eyes of others; compare yourself to similar (and admired) others; examine the influences of culture; and observe and evaluate your own message behaviors.

self-esteem. Raise your self-esteem: Challenge self-destructive beliefs, seek out nourishing people, work on projects that will result in success, and secure affirmation.

self-fulfilling prophecy. Take a second look at your perceptions when they correspond very closely to your initial expectations; the self-fulfilling prophecy may be at work.

self-serving bias. Become mindful of giving too much weight to internal factors (when explaining your positives) and too little weight to external factors (when explaining your negatives).

sexual harassment management. Talk to the harasser; if this doesn't stop the behavior, then consider collecting evidence, using appropriate channels within the organization, and filing a complaint.

sexual harassment messages. Avoid behaviors that are sexual in nature, that might be considered unreasonable, that are severe or pervasive, and that are unwelcome and offensive.

silence. Examine silence for meanings just as you would eye movements or body gestures.

spatial and proxemic conversational distances. Maintain distances that are comfortable and that are appropriate to the situation and to your relationship with the other person.

stereotypes. Focus on the individual rather than on the individual's membership in one group or another.

supportive conflict. Engage in conflict using a supportive approach, so as not to create defensiveness; avoid messages that evaluate or control, that are strategic or inappropriately neutral, or that express superiority or certainty.

surface and depth listening. Focus on both verbal and nonverbal messages, on both content and relationship messages, and on statements that refer back to the speaker. At the same time, do not avoid the surface or literal meaning.

talk, not force. Talk about problems rather than using physical or emotional force.

time cues. Be alert for time cues on the part of the person with whom you're interacting. Be especially sensitive to the person's leave-taking cues—remarks such as "It's getting late" or glances at his or her watch.

touch and touch avoidance. Respect the touch-avoidance tendencies of others; pay special attention to cultural and gender differences in touch preferences.

turn-taking cues. Respond to both the verbal and the nonverbal conversational turn-taking cues given you by others, and make your own cues clear to others.

understanding. Relate new information to what you already know, ask questions, and paraphrase what you think the speaker said to make sure you understand.

Bibliography

Bibliography

Abel, G. G., & Harlow, N. (2001). *The stop child molestation book.* Xlibris. (www.stopchildmolestation.org/pdfs/study.pdf).

Acor, A. A. (2001). Employers' perceptions of persons with body art and an experimental test regarding eyebrow piercing. Ph.D. dissertation, Marquette University. *Dissertation Abstracts International: Second B: The Sciences and Engineering* 61, 3885.

Adams-Price, C. E., Dalton, W. T., & Sumrall, R. (2004). Victim blaming in young, middle-aged, and older adults: Variations on the severity effect. *Journal of Adult Development* 11 (October), 289–295.

Adrianson, L. (2001). Gender and computer-mediated communication: Group processes in problem solving. *Computers in Human Behavior* 17, 71–94.

Afifi, W. A. (2007). Nonverbal communication. In *Explaining communication: Contemporary theories and exemplars* (pp. 39–60), B. B. Whaley & W. Samter (eds.). Mahwah, NJ: Erlbaum.

Afifi, W. A., & Johnson, M. L. (2005). The nature and function of tie-signs. In *The sourcebook of nonverbal measures: Going beyond words* (pp. 189–198), V. Manusov (ed.). Mahwah, NJ: Erlbaum.

Alessandra, T. (1986). How to listen effectively. *Speaking of success* (Video Tape Series). San Diego, CA: Levitz Sommer Productions.

Allen, J. L., Long, K. M., O'Mara, J., & Judd, B. B. (2003). Verbal and nonverbal orientations toward communication and the development of intracultural and intercultural relationships. *Journal of Intercultural Communication Research* 32 (September–December), 129–160.

Almeida, E. P. (2004). A discourse analysis of student perceptions of their communication competence. *Communication Education* 53 (October), 357–364.

Al-Simadi, F. A. (2000). Detection of deception behavior: A cross-cultural test. *Social Behavior & Personality* 28, 455–461.

Alsop, R. (2004). How to get hired: We asked recruiters what M.B.A. graduates are doing wrong. Ignore their advice at your peril. *Wall Street Journal* (September 22), R8.

Altman, I. (1975). *The environment and social behavior.* Monterey, CA: Brooks/Cole.

Altman, I., & Taylor, D. (1973). *Social penetration: The development of interpersonal relationships.* New York: Holt, Rinehart & Winston.

Amato, P. R. (1994). The impact of divorce on men and women in India and the United States. *Journal of Comparative Family Studies* 25, 207–221.

Andersen, P. A. (1991). Explaining intercultural differences in nonverbal communication. In *Intercultural communication: A reader,* 6th ed., L. A. Samovar & R. E. Porter (eds.). Belmont, CA: Wadsworth, pp. 286–296.

Andersen, P. A. (2004). *The complete idiot's guide to body language.* New York: Penguin Group.

Andersen, P. A., Guerrero, L. K., & Jones, S. M. (2006). Nonverbal behavior in intimate interactions and intimate relationships. In *The Sage handbook of nonverbal communication* (pp. 259–277), V. Manusov & M. L. Patterson (eds.). Thousand Oaks, CA: Sage.

Andersen, P. A., & Leibowitz, K. (1978). The development and nature of the construct touch avoidance. *Environmental Psychology and Nonverbal Behavior* 3, 89–106. Reprinted in DeVito & Hecht (1990).

Anderson, I. (2004). Explaining negative rape victim perception: Homophobia and the male rape victim. *Current Research in Social Psychology* 10 (November), np.

Anderson, K. J. (1998). Meta-analysis of gender effects on conversational interruption: Who, what, when, where, and how. *Sex Roles* 39 (August), 225–252.

Angier, N. (1995a). Powerhouse of senses: Smell, at last, gets its due. *New York Times* (February 14), C1, C6.

Angier, N. (1995b). Scientists mull role of empathy in man and beast. *New York Times* (May 9), C1, C6.

Angier, N. (2003). Opposites attract? Not in real life. *New York Times* 152 (July 8), F1, 6.

Aquinis, H., & Henle, C. A. (2001). Effects of nonverbal behavior on perceptions of a female employee's power bases. *Journal of Social Psychology* 141 (August), 537–549.

Argyle, M. (1986). Rules for social relationships in four cultures. *Australian Journal of Psychology* 38, 309–318.

Argyle, M. (1988). *Bodily communication,* 2d ed. New York: Methuen.

Argyle, M., & Dean, J. (1965). Eye contact, distance and affiliation. *Sociometry* 28, 289–304.

Argyle, M., & Henderson, M. (1984). The rules of friendship. *Journal of Social and Personal Relationships* 1, 211–237.

Argyle, M., & Ingham, R. (1972). Gaze, mutual gaze, and distance. *Semiotica* 1, 32–49.

Armour, S. (2003). Cupid finds work as office romance no longer taboo. *USA Today* (February 11), Money Section, 1.

Aronson, E., Wilson, T. D., & Akert, R. M. (2007). *Social psychology,* 6th ed. Boston: Allyn & Bacon.

Aronson, J., Cohen, J., & Nail, P. (1998). Self-affirmation theory: An update and appraisal. In *Cognitive dissonance* theory: *Revival with revisions and controversies,* E. Harmon-Jones & J. S. Mills (eds.). Washington, DC: American Psychological Association.

Arrindell, W. A., Steptoe, A., & Wardle, J. (2003). Higher levels of state depression in masculine than in feminine nations. *Behaviour Research and Therapy* 41 (July), 809–817.

Asch, S. (1946). Forming impressions of personality. *Journal of Abnormal and Social Psychology* 41, 258–290.

Ashcraft, M. H. (1998). *Fundamentals of cognition.* New York: Longman.

Aspinwall, L. G., & Taylor, S. E. (1993). Effects of social comparison direction, threat, and self-esteem on affect, evaluation, and expected success. *Journal of Personality and Social Psychology* 64, 708–722.

Assad, K. K., Donnellan, M. B., & Conger, R. D. (2007). Optimism: An enduring resource for romantic relationships. *Journal of Personality and Social Psychology* 93 (August), 285–297.

Aune, K. S. (2005). Assessing display rules in relationships. In *The sourcebook of nonverbal measures: Going beyond words* (pp. 151–162), V. Manusov (ed.). Mahwah, NJ: Erlbaum.

Aune, R. K., & Kikuchi, T. (1993). Effects of language intensity similarity on perceptions of credibility, relational attributions, and persuasion. *Journal of Language and Social Psychology* 12, 224–238.

Authier, J., & Gustafson, K. (1982). Microtraining: Focusing on specific skills. In *Interpersonal helping skills: A guide to training methods, programs, and resources,* E. K. Marshall, P. D. Kurtz, and Associates (eds.). San Francisco: Jossey-Bass, pp. 93–130.

Axtell, R. E. (1990). *Do's and taboos of hosting international visitors.* New York: Wiley.

Axtell, R. E. (2007). *Essential do's and taboos: The complete guide to international business and leisure travel.* Hoboken, NJ: Wiley.

Ayres, J. (1983). Strategies to maintain relationships: Their identification and perceived usage. *Communication Quarterly* 31, 62–67.

Babcock, J. C, Waltz, J., Jacobson, N. S., & Gottman, J. M. (1993). Power and violence: The relation between communication patterns, power discrepancies, and domestic violence. *Journal of Marriage and the Family* 60 (February), 70–78.

Bach, G. R., & Wyden, P. (1968). *The intimate enemy.* New York: Avon.

Bacon, B. (2004). *Meet me don't delete me: Internet dating: I've made all the mistakes so you don't have to.* Burbank, CA: Slapstick Publications.

Bailenson, J. N., Blascovich, J., Beall, A. C., & Loomis, J. M. (2001). Equilibrium theory revisited: Mutual gaze and personal space in virtual environments. *Presence: Teleoperators and Virtual Environments* 10 (December), 583–595.

Baker, A. (2002). What makes an online relationship successful? Clues from couples who met in cyberspace. *CyberPsychology and Behavior* 5 (August), 363–375.

Balswick, J. O., & Peck, C. (1971). The inexpressive male: A tragedy of American society? *The Family Coordinator* 20, 363–368.

Banks, S. P., Altendorf, D. M., Greene, J. O., & Cody, M. J. (1987). An examination of relationship disengagement: Perceptions, breakup strategies, and outcomes. *Western Journal of Speech Communication* 51, 19–41.

Barbato, C. A., & Perse, E. M. (1992). Interpersonal communication motives and the life position of elders. *Communication Research* 19, 516–531.

Barker, L. L. (1990). *Communication,* 5th ed. Englewood Cliffs, NJ: Prentice-Hall.

Barna, L. M. (1997). Stumbling blocks in intercultural communication. In *Intercultural communication: A reader,* 7th ed., L. A. Samovar & R. E. Porter (eds.). Belmont, CA: Wadsworth, pp. 337–346.

Barnlund, D. C. (1989). *Communicative styles of Japanese and Americans: Images and realities.* Belmont, CA: Wadsworth.

Baron, R. (1990). Countering the effects of destructive criticism: The relative efficacy of four interventions. *Journal of Applied Psychology* 75 (3), 235–245.

Baron, R. A., & Byrne, D. (1984). *Social psychology: Understanding human interaction* (4th ed.). Boston: Allyn & Bacon.

Barrett, L., & Godfrey, T. (1988). Listening. *Person Centered Review* 3 (November), 410–425.

Barta, P. (1999, December 16). Sex differences in the inferior parietal lobe. *Cerebral Cortex* (www.wired.com/news/technology/0,1282,33033,00.html).

Bartholomew, K. (1990). Avoidance of intimacy: An attachment perspective. *Journal of Social and Personal Relationships* 7, 147–178.

Basso, K. H. (1972). To give up on words: Silence in Apache culture. In *Language and social context,* Pier Paolo Giglioli (ed.). New York: Penguin.

Bateson, G. (1972). *Steps to an ecology of mind.* New York: Ballantine.

Baumeister, R. F., Bushman, B. J., & Campbell, W. K. (2000). Self-esteem, narcissism, and aggression: Does violence result from low self-esteem or from threatened egotism? *Current Directions in Psychological Science* 9 (February), 26–29.

Bavelas, J. B. (1990). Can one not communicate? Behaving and communicating: A reply to Motley. *Western Journal of Speech Communication* 54, 593–602.

Baxter, L. A. (1983). Relationship disengagement: An examination of the reversal hypothesis. *Western Journal of Speech Communication* 47, 85–98.

Baxter, L. A. (1986). Gender differences in the heterosexual relationship rules embedded in break-up accounts. *Journal of Social and Personal Relationships* 3, 289–306.

Baxter, L. A. (2004). Relationships as dialogues. *Personal Relationships* 11 (March), 1–22.

Baxter, L. A., & Braithwaite, D. O. (2007). Social dialectics: The contradiction of relating. In *Explaining communication: Contemporary theories and exemplars* (pp. 275–292), B. B. Whaley & W. Samter (eds.). Mahwah, NJ: Erlbaum.

Baxter, L. A., & Braithwaite, D. O. (2008a). Relational dialectics theory. In *Engaging theories in interpersonal communication: Multiple perspectives* (pp. 349–362), L. A. Baxter & D. O. Braithwaite (eds.). Los Angeles: Sage.

Baxter, L. A., & Braithwaite, D. O., eds. (2008b). *Engaging theories in interpersonal communication: Multiple perspectives.* Los Angeles: Sage.

Baxter, L. A., & Bullis, C. (1986). Turning points in developing romantic relationships. *Human Communication Research* 12, 469–493.

Baxter, L. A., & Simon, E. P. (1993). Relationship maintenance strategies and dialectical contradictions in personal relationships. *Journal of Social and Personal Relationships* 10, 225–242.

Baxter, L. A., & Wilmot, W. W. (1984). Secret tests: Social strategies for acquiring information about the state of the relationship. *Human Communication Research* 11, 171–201.

Beach, W. A. (1990). On (not) observing behavior interactionally. *Western Journal of Speech Communication* 54, 603–612.

Beatty, M. J., Rudd, J. E., & Valencic, K. M. (1999). A re-evaluation of the verbal aggressiveness scale: One factor or two? *Communication Research Reports* 16, 10–17.

Bell, R. A., & Buerkel-Rothfuss, N. L. (1990). S(he) loves me, s(he) loves me not: Predictors of relational information-seeking in courtship and beyond. *Communication Quarterly* 38, 64–82.

Bell, R. A., & Daly, J. A. (1984). The affinity-seeking function of communication. *Communication Monographs* 51, 91–115.

Bellafiore, D. (2005). *Interpersonal conflict and effective communication.* http://www.drbalternatives.com/articles/cc2.html. Accessed July 6, 2007.

Ben-Ze'ev, A. (2003). Primacy, emotional closeness, and openness in cyberspace. *Computers in Human Behavior* 19 (July), 451–467.

Bennett, M. (1990). Children's understanding of the mitigating function of disclaimers. *Journal of Social Psychology* 130, 29–37.

Berg, J. H., & Archer, R. L. (1983). The disclosure-liking relationship. *Human Communication Research* 10, 269–281.

Berger, C. R., & Bradac, J. J. (1982). *Language and social knowledge: Uncertainty in interpersonal relations.* London: Edward Arnold.

Berger, C. R., & Calabrese, R. J. (1975). Some explorations in initial interaction and beyond: Toward a theory of interpersonal communication. *Human Communication Research* 1, 99–112.

Berger, P. L., & Luckmann, T. (1980). *The social construction of reality.* New York: Irvington.

Bernstein, W. M., Stephan, W. G., & Davis, M. H. (1979). Explaining attributions for achievement: A path analytic approach. *Journal of Personality and Social Psychology* 37, 1810–1821.

Berry, J. N. III (2004). Can I quote you on that? *Library Journal* 129, 10.

Berry, J. W., Poortinga, Y. H., Segall, M. H., & Dasen, P. R. (1992). *Cross-cultural psychology: Research and applications.* Cambridge: Cambridge University Press.

Berscheid, E., & Reis, H. T. (1998). Attraction and close relationships. In *The handbook of social psychology,* 4th ed., Vol. 2, D. Gilbert, S. Fiske, & G. Lindzey (eds.). New York: W. H. Freeman, pp. 193–281.

Bierhoff, H. W., & Klein, R. (1991). Dimensionen der Liebe: Entwicklung einer Deutschsprachigen Skala zur Erfassung von Liebesstilen. *Zeitschrift for Differentielle und Diagnostische Psychologie* 12, 53–71.

Bishop, J. E. (1993). New research suggests that romance begins by falling nose over heels in love. *Wall Street Journal* (April 7), B1.

Black, H. K. (1999). A sense of the sacred: Altering or enhancing the self-portrait in older age? *Narrative Inquiry* 9, 327–345.

Blake, R. R., & Mouton, J. S. (1984). *The managerial grid III* (3d ed.). Houston, TX: Gulf Publishing.

Blieszner, R., & Adams, R. G. (1992). *Adult friendship.* Thousand Oaks, CA: Sage.

Blumstein, P., & Schwartz, P. (1983). *American couples: Money, work, sex.* New York: Morrow.

Bochner, A. (1984). The functions of human communication in interpersonal bonding. In *Handbook of rhetorical and communication theory,* C. C. Arnold & J. W. Bowers (eds.). Boston: Allyn & Bacon, pp. 544–621.

Bochner, S. (1994). Cross-cultural differences in the self-concept: A test of Hofstede's individualism/collectivism distinction. *Journal of Cross-Cultural Psychology* 25, 273–283.

Bochner, S., & Hesketh, B. (1994). Power distance, individualism/collectivism, and job-related attitudes in a culturally diverse work group. *Journal of Cross-Cultural Psychology* 25, 233–257.

Bodon, J., Powell, L., & Hickson III, M. (1999). Critiques of gate-keeping in scholarly journals: An analysis of perceptions and data. *Journal of the Association for Communication Administration* 28 (May), 60–70.

Bok, S. (1983). *Secrets.* New York: Vintage.

Bond, Jr., C. F., & Atoum, A. O. (2000). International deception. *Personality & Social Psychology Bulletin* 26 (March), 385–395.

Boneva, B., Kraut, R., & Frohlich, D. (2001). Using e-mail for personal relationships: The difference gender makes. *American Behavioral Scientist* 45, 530–549.

Borden, G. A. (1991). *Cultural orientation: An approach to understanding intercultural communication.* Englewood Cliffs, NJ: Prentice-Hall.

Bowen, F., & Blackmon, K. (2003). Spirals of silence: The dynamic of diversity on organizational voice. *Journal of Management Studies* 40 (September), 1393–1417.

Bower, B. (2001). Self-illusions come back to bite students. *Science News* 159, 148.

Bower, S. A., & Bower, G. H. (2005). *Asserting yourself: A practical guide for positive change.* Cambridge, MA: DaCapo Press.

Brashers, D. E. (2007). A theory of communication and uncertainty management. In *Explaining communication: Contemporary theories and exemplars* (pp. 201–218), B. B. Whaley & W. Samter (eds.). Mahwah, NJ: Erlbaum.

Bravo, E., & Cassedy, E. (1992). *The 9 to 5 guide to combating sexual harassment.* New York: Wiley.

Bridges, C. R. (1996). The characteristics of career achievement perceived by African American college administrators. *Journal of Black Studies* 26, 748–767.

Britnell, A. (2004). Culture shock-proofing. *Profit* 23 (November), 79–80.

Briton, N. J., & Hall, J. A. (1995). Beliefs about female and male nonverbal communication. *Sex Roles* 32, 79–90.

Brody, J. F. (1994). Notions of beauty transcend culture, new study suggests. *New York Times* (March 21), A14.

Brody, L. R. (1985). Gender differences in emotional development: A review of theories and research. *Journal of Personality* 53 (June), 102–149.

Brown, C. T., & Keller, P. W. (1979). *Monologue to dialogue: An exploration of interpersonal communication,* 2nd ed. Englewood Cliffs, NJ: Prentice-Hall.

Brown, P., & Levinson, S. C. (1987). *Politeness: Some universals of language usage.* Cambridge: Cambridge University Press.

Brownell, J. (2006). *Listening: Attitudes, principles, and skills,* 3d ed. Boston: Allyn & Bacon.

Buber, M. (1958). *I and thou,* 2nd ed. New York: Scribner's.

Bugental, J., & Zelen, S. (1950). Investigations into the "self-concept." I. The W-A-Y technique. *Journal of Personality* 18, 483–498.

Bull, R., & Rumsey, N. (1988). *The social psychology of facial appearance.* New York: Springer-Verlag.

Buller, D. B., LePoire, B. A., Aune, R. K., & Eloy, S. (1992). Social perceptions as mediators of the effect of speech rate similarity on compliance. *Human Communication Research* 19, 286–311.

Buller, D. J. (2005). *Adapting minds: Evolutionary psychology and the persistent quest for human nature.* Cambridge, MA: MIT Press.

Bumby, K. M., & Hansen, D. J. (1997). Intimacy deficits, fear of intimacy, and loneliness among sexual offenders. *Criminal Justice and Behavior* 24, 315–331.

Bunz, U., & Campbell, S. W. (2004). Politeness accommodation in electronic mail. *Communication Research Reports* 21 (winter), 11–25.

Burgoon, J. K. (1991). Relational message interpretations of touch, conversational distance, and posture. *Journal of Nonverbal Behavior* 15, 233–259.

Burgoon, J. K., & Bacue, A. E. (2003). Nonverbal communication skills. In *Handbook of communication and social interaction skills,* (pp. 179–220), J. O. Greene & B. R. Burleson (eds.). Mahwah, NJ: Lawrence Erlbaum.

Burgoon, J. K., Berger, C. R., & Waldron, V. R. (2000). Mindfulness and interpersonal communication. *Journal of Social Issues* 56, 105–127.

Burgoon, J. K., Buller, D. B., & Woodall, W. G. (1996). *Nonverbal communication: The unspoken dialogue,* 2d ed. New York: McGraw-Hill.

Burgoon, J. K., & Hoobler, G. D. (2002). Nonverbal signals. In *Handbook of Interpersonal Communication,* 3d ed. (pp. 240–299), M. L. Knapp & J. A. Daly (eds.). Thousand Oaks, CA: Sage.

Burgstahler, S. (2007). Managing an e-mentoring community to support students with disabilities: A case study. *Distance Education Report* 11 (July), 7–15.

Burleson, B. R. (2003). Emotional support skills. In *Handbook of communication and social interaction skills* (pp. 551–594), J. O. Greene & B. R. Burleson (eds.), Mahwah, NJ: Erlbaum.

Burleson, B. R., Holmstrom, A. J., & Gilstrap, C. M. (2005). 'Guys can't say *that* to guys': Four experiments assessing the normative motivation account for deficiencies in the emotional support provided by men. *Communication Monographs* 72 (December), 468–501.

Burleson, B. R., Kunkel, A. W., & Birch, J. D. (1994). Thoughts about talk in romantic relationships: Similarity makes for attraction (and happiness, too). *Communication Quarterly* 42 (summer), 259–273.

Burleson, B. R., Samter, W., & Luccetti, A. E. (1992). Similarity in communication values as a predictor of friendship choices: Studies of friends and best friends. *Southern Communication Journal* 57, 260–276.

Bushman, B. J., & Baumeister, R. F. (1998). Threatened egotism, narcissism, self-esteem, and direct and displaced aggression: Does self-love or self-hate lead to violence? *Journal of Personality and Social Psychology* 75, 219–229.

Buss, D. M. (2000). *The dangerous passion: Why jealousy is as necessary as love and sex.* New York: Free Press.

Buss, D. M., Shackelford, T. K., Kirkpatrick, L. A., Choe, J. C., Lim, H. K., Hasegawa, M., Hasegawa, T., & Bennett, K. (1999). Jealousy and the nature of beliefs about infidelity: Tests of competing hypotheses about sex differences in the United States, Korea, and Japan. *Personal Relationships* 6, 125–150.

Butler, P. E. (1981). *Talking to yourself: Learning the language of self-support.* New York: Harper & Row.

Buunk, B. P., & Dijkstra, P. (2004). Gender differences in rival characteristics that evoke jealousy in response to emotional versus sexual infidelity. *Personal Relationships* 11 (December), 395–408.

Byers, E. S., & Demmons, S. (1999). Sexual satisfaction and sexual self-disclosure within dating relationships. *Journal of Sex Research* 36, 180–189.

Cahn, D. D., & Abigail, R. A. (2007). *Managing conflict through communication,* 3rd ed. Boston: Allyn & Bacon.

Cai, D. A., & Fink, E. L. (2002). Conflict style differences between individualists and collectivists. *Communication Monographs* 69 (March), 67–87.

Callan, V. J. (1993). Subordinate–manager communication in different sex dyads: Consequences for job satisfaction. *Journal of Occupational & Organizational Psychology,* 66 (March), 1–15.

Camden, C., Motley, M. T., & Wilson, A. (1984). White lies in interpersonal communication: A taxonomy and preliminary investigation of social motivations. *Western Journal of Speech Communication* 48, 309–325.

Campbell, T. A., & Campbell, D. E. (2007). Outcomes of mentoring at-risk college students: Gender and ethnic matching effects. *Mentoring and Tutoring* 15 (May), 135–148.

Campbell, W. K., Foster, C. A., & Finkel, E. J. (2002). Does self-love lead to love for others? A story of narcissistic game playing. *Journal of Personality and Social Psychology* 83 (August), 340–354.

Canary, D. J. (2003). Managing interpersonal conflict: A model of events related to strategic choices. In *Handbook of communication and social interaction skills,* (pp. 515–550), J. O. Greene & B. R. Burleson (eds.). Mahwah, NJ: Lawrence Erlbaum.

Canary, D. J., Cody, M. J., & Manusov, V. L. (2003). *Interpersonal communication: A goals-based approach,* 3d ed. Boston: St. Bedford/St. Martins.

Canary, D. J., Cupach, W. R., & Messman, S. J. (1995). *Relationship conflict: Conflict in parent-child, friendship, and romantic relationships.* Thousand Oaks, CA: Sage.

Canary, D. J., & Hause, K. S. (1993). Is there any reason to research sex differences in communication? *Communication Quarterly* 41, 129–144.

Canary, D. J., & Stafford, L. (1994). Maintaining relationships through strategic and routine interaction. In *Communication and relational maintenance,* D. J. Canary & L. Stafford (eds.). New York: Academic Press.

Canary, D. J., Stafford, L., Hause, K. S., & Wallace, L. A. (1993). An inductive analysis of relational maintenance strategies: Comparisons among lovers, relatives, friends, and others. *Communication Research Reports* 10, 5–14.

Cappella, J. N., & Schreiber, D. M. (2006). The interaction management function of nonverbal cues. In *The Sage handbook of nonverbal communication* (pp. 361–379), V. Manusov & M. L. Patterson (eds.). Thousand Oaks, CA: Sage.

Carey, B. (2005). Have you heard? Gossip turns out to serve a purpose. *New York Times* (August 16), F1, F6.

Carli, L. L. (1999). Gender, interpersonal power, and social influence. *Journal of Social Issues* 55 (spring), 81–99.

Carlock, C. J., ed. (1999). *Enhancing self-esteem,* 3d ed. Philadelphia, PA: Accelerated Development, Inc.

Carroll, D. W. (1994). *Psychology of language,* 2d ed. Pacific Grove, CA: Brooks/Cole.

Carson, J. W., Carson, K. M., Gil, K. M., & Baucom, D. H. (2004). Mindfulness-based relationship enhancement. *Behavior Therapy* 35 (summer), 471–494.

Cashdan, E. (2001). Ethnocentrism and xenophobia: A cross-cultural study. *Current Anthropology* 42, 760–765.

Castleberry, S. B., & Shepherd, C. D. (1993). Effective interpersonal listening and personal selling. *Journal of Personal Selling and Sales Management* 13, 35–49.

Cawthon, S. W. (2001). Teaching strategies in inclusive classrooms with deaf students. *Journal of Deaf Studies and Deaf Education* 6, 212–225.

Chadwick-Jones, J. K. (1976). *Social exchange theory: Its structure and influence in social psychology.* New York: Academic Press.

Chan, D., K., & Cheng, G. H. (2004). A comparison of offline and online friendship qualities at different stages of relationship development. *Journal of Social and Personal Relationships* 21 (June), 305–320.

Chaney, R. H., Givens, C. A., Aoki, M. F., & Gombiner, M. L. (1989). Pupillary responses in recognizing awareness in persons with profound mental retardation. *Perceptual and Motor Skills* 69, 523–528.

Chang, H., & Holt, G. R. (1996). The changing Chinese interpersonal world: Popular themes in interpersonal communication books in modern Taiwan. *Communication Quarterly* 44, 85–106.

Chanowitz, B., & Langer, E. (1981). Premature cognitive commitment. *Journal of Personality and Social Psychology* 41, 1051–1063.

Chapdelaine, R. F., & Alexitch, L. R. (2004). Social skills difficulty: Model of culture shock for international graduate students. *Journal of College Student Development* 45 (March–April), 167–184.

Chen, G. (1992). Differences in self-disclosure patterns among Americans versus Chinese: A comparative study. Paper presented at the annual meeting of the Eastern Communication Association, Portland, ME.

Cheney, G., & Tompkins, P. K. (1987). Coming to terms with organizational identification and commitment. *Central States Speech Journal* 38, 1–15.

Cherulnik, P. D. (1979). Sex differences in the expression of emotion in a structured social encounter. *Sex Roles* 5 (August), 413–424.

Childress, H. (2004). Teenagers, territory and the appropriation of space. *Childhood: A Global Journal of Child Research* 11 (May), 195–205.

Cho, H. (2000). Asian in America: Cultural shyness can impede Asian Americans' success. *Northwest Asian Weekly* 19 (December 8), 6.

Christians, C. G., & Traber, M., eds. (1997). *Communication ethics and universal values.* Urbana, IL: University of Illinois Press.

Chung, L. C., & Ting-Toomey, S. (1999). Ethnic identity and relational expectations among Asian Americans. *Communication Research Reports* 16 (spring), 157–166.

Chung, M. C., Farmer, S., Grant, K., Newton, R., Payne, S., Perry, M., Saunders, J., Smith, C., & Stone, N. (2002). Gender differences in love styles and post traumatic reactions following relationship dissolution. *European Journal of Psychiatry* 16 (October–December), 210–220.

Clement, D. A., & Frandsen, K. D. (1976). On conceptual and empirical treatments of feedback in human communication. *Communication Monographs* 43, 11–28.

Cline, M. G. (1956). The influence of social context on the perception of faces. *Journal of Personality* 2, 142–185.

Cloud, J. (2008, January). Are gay relationships different? *Time,* 78–80.

Coates, J., & Sutton-Spence, R. (2001). Turn-taking patterns in deaf conversation. *Journal of Sociolinguistics* 5 (November), 507–529.

Coats, E. J., & Feldman, R. S. (1996, October). Gender differences in nonverbal correlates of social status. *Personality and Social Psychology Bulletin* 22, 1014–1022.

Cody, M. J. (1982). A typology of disengagement strategies and an examination of the role intimacy, reactions to inequity, and relational problems play in strategy selection. *Communication Monographs* 49, 148–170.

Cody, M. J., & Dunn, D. (2007). Accounts. In *Explaining communication: Contemporary theories and exemplars* (pp. 237–256), B. B. Whaley and W. Samter (eds.). Mahwah, NJ: Erlbaum.

Cohen, J. (2002, May 9). An e-mail affliction: The long good-bye. *New York Times*, G6.

Cohen, J. (2003). Parasocial breakups: Measuring individual differences in responses to the dissolution of parasocial relationships. *Mass Communication and Society* 6, 191–202.

Cohen, J. (2004). Parasocial break-up from favorite television characters: The role of attachment styles and relationship intensity. *Journal of Social and Personal Relationships* 21 (April), 187–202.

Coleman, P. (2002). *How to say it for couples: Communicating with tenderness, openness, and honesty.* Paramus, NJ: Prentice-Hall.

Colley, A., Todd, Z., Bland, M., Holmes, M., Khanom, N., & Pike, H. (2004). Style and content in e-mails and letters to male and female friends. *Journal of Language and Social Psychology* 23 (September), 369–378.

Collins, J. E., & Clark, L. F. (1989). Responsibility and rumination: The trouble with understanding the dissolution of a relationship. *Social Cognition* 7, 152–173.

Collins, N. L., & Miller, L. C. (1994). Self-disclosure and liking: A meta-analytic review. *Psychological Bulletin* 116 (November), 457–475.

Comer, L. B., & Drollinger, T. (1999). Active empathic listening and selling success: A conceptual framework. *Journal of Personal Selling and Sales Management,* 19, 15–29.

Conlin, M. (2002). Watch what you put in that office e-mail. *Business Week* (September 9), 114–115.

Constantine, M. G., Anderson, G. M., Berkel, L. A., Caldwell, L. D., & Utsey, S. O. (2005). Examining the cultural adjustment experiences of African international college students: A qualitative analysis. *Journal of Counseling Psychology* 52 (January), 57–66.

Cooley, C. H. (1922). *Human nature and the social order.* Rev. ed. New York: Scribner's.

Cooper, A., & Sportolari, L. (1997). Romance in cyberspace: Understanding online attraction. *Journal of Sex Education and Therapy* 22, 7–14.

Coover, G. E., & Murphy, S. T. (2000). The communicated self: Exploring the interaction between self and social context. *Human Communication Research* 26, 125–147.

Copeland, L., & Griggs, L. (1985). *Going international: How to make friends and deal effectively in the global marketplace.* New York: Random House.

Cornwell, B., & Lundgren, D. C. (2001). Love on the Internet: Involvement and misrepresentation in romantic relationships in cyberspace vs. realspace. *Computers in Human Behavior* 17, 197–211.

Counts, D. A., Brown, J. K., & Campbell, J. C. (1992). *Sanctions and sanctuary: Cultural perspectives on the beating of wives.* Boulder, CO: Westview Press.

Cramer, D. (2004). Emotional support, conflict, depression, and relationship satisfaction in a romantic partner. *Journal of Psychology: Interdisciplinary and Applied* 138 (November), 532–542.

Crampton, S. M., Hodge, J. W., & Mishra, J. M. (1998). The informal communication network: Factors influencing grapevine activity. *Public Personnel Management* 27 (winter), 569–584.

Crohn, J. (1995). *Mixed matches: How to create successful interracial, interethnic, and interfaith relationships.* New York: Fawcett.

Cross, E. E., & Madson, L. (1997). Models of the self: Self-construals and gender. *Psychological Bulletin* 122, 5–37.

Crusco, A. H., & Wetzel, C. G. (1984). The Midas touch: The effects of interpersonal touch on restaurant tipping. *Personality and Social Psychology Bulletin* 10, 512–517.

Dahle, C. (2004). Choosing a mentor? Cast a wide net. *New York Times* (July 25), BU 9.

Dainton, M., & Stafford, L. (1993). Routine maintenance behaviors: A comparison of relationship type, partner similarity, and sex differences. *Journal of Social and Personal Relationships* 10, 255–272.

Darwin, C. (1872). *The expression of the emotions in man and animals.* Chicago: University of Chicago Press (re-printed 1965).

Davis, K. (1980). Management communication and the grapevine. In *Intercom: Readings in organizational communication* (pp. 55–66), S. Ferguson & S. D. Ferguson (eds.). Rochelle Park, NJ: Hayden Books.

Davis, M. S. (1973). *Intimate relations.* New York: Free Press.

Davitz, J. R. (ed.). (1964). *The communication of emotional meaning.* New York: McGraw-Hill.

Deal, J. E., & Wampler, K. S. (1986). Dating violence: The primacy of previous experience. *Journal of Social and Personal Relationships* 3, 457–471.

Deaux, K., & LaFrance, M. (1998). Gender. In *The handbook of social psychology,* 4th ed., Vol. 1, D. Gilbert, S. Fiske, & G. Lindzey (eds.). New York: Freeman, pp. 788–828.

deBono, E. (1987). *The six thinking hats.* New York: Penguin.

DeFrancisco, V. (1991). The sound of silence: How men silence women in marital relations. *Discourse and Society* 2, 413–423.

Delia, J. G. (1977). Constructivism and the study of human communication. *Quarterly Journal of Speech* 63, 66–83.

Delia, J. G., O'Keefe, B. J., & O'Keefe, D. J. (1982). The constructivist approach to communication. In *Human communication theory: Comparative essays,* Frank E. X. Dance (ed.). New York: Harper & Row, pp. 147–191.

Dell, K. (2005). Just for dudes. *Time* (February, 14), B22.

DePaulo, B. M. (1992). Nonverbal behavior and self-presentation. *Psychological Bulletin* 111, 203–212.

Dereshiwsky, M. I., Moan, E. R., & Gahungu, A. (2002). Faculty perceptions regarding issues of civility in online instructional communication. *USDLA Journal* 16, No. 6 (June).

Derlega, V. J., Winstead, B. A., Greene, K., Serovich, J., & Elwood, W. N. (2004). Reasons for HIV disclosure/nondisclosure in close relationships: Testing a model of HIV-disclosure decision making. *Journal of Social and Clinical Psychology* 23 (December), 747–767.

Derlega, V. J., Winstead, B. A., Wong, P. T. P., & Hunter, S. (1985). Gender effects in an initial encounter: A case where men exceed women in disclosure. *Journal of Social and Personal Relationships* 2, 25–44.

DeVito, J. A. (1989). *The nonverbal communication workbook.* Prospect Heights, IL: Waveland Press.

DeVito, J. A. (2003a). MEDUSA messages. *Etc: A Review of General Semantics* 60 (fall), 241–245.

DeVito, J. A. (2003b). SCREAM before you scream. *Etc: A Review of General Semantics* 60 (spring), 42–45.

Dewey, J. (1910). *How we think.* Boston: Heath.

DiBaise, R., & Gunnoe, J. (2004). Gender and culture differences in touching behavior. *Journal of Social Psychology* 144 (February), 49–62.

Dillard, J. P., ed. (1990). *Seeking compliance: The production of interpersonal influence messages.* Scottsdale, AZ: Gorsuch Scarisbrick.

Dillard, J. P., Anderson, J. W., & Knobloch, L. K. (2002). Interpersonal influence. In *Handbook of interpersonal communication,* 3d ed. (pp. 425–474), M. L. Knapp & J. A. Daly (eds.). Thousand Oaks, CA: Sage.

Dillard, J. P., & Marshall, L. J. (2003). Persuasion as a social skill. In *Handbook of communication and social interaction skills* (pp. 479–514), J. O. Greene & B. R. Burleson (eds.). Mahwah, NJ: Lawrence Erlbaum.

Dindia, K., & Baxter, L. A. (1987). Strategies for maintaining and repairing marital relationships. *Journal of Social and Personal Relationships* 4, 143–158.

Dindia, K., & Fitzpatrick, M. A. (1985). Marital communication: Three approaches compared. In *Understanding personal relationships: An interdisciplinary approach,* S. Duck & D. Perlman (eds.). Thousand Oaks, CA: Sage, pp. 137–158.

Dindia, K., & Timmerman, L. (2003). Accomplishing romantic relationships. In *Handbook of communication and social interaction skills* (pp. 685–721), J. O. Greene & B. R. Burleson (eds.). Mahwah, NJ: Erlbaum.

Dion, K., Berscheid, E., & Walster, E. (1972). What is beautiful is good. *Journal of Personality and Social Psychology* 24, 285–290.

Dion, K. K., & Dion, K. L. (1993a). Individualistic and collectivist perspectives on gender and the cultural context of love and intimacy. *Journal of Social Issues* 49, 53–69.

Dion, K. K., & Dion, K. L. (1996). Cultural perspectives on romantic love. *Personal Relationships* 3, 5–17.

Dion, K. L., & Dion, K. K. (1993b). Gender and ethnocultural comparisons in styles of love. *Psychology of Women Quarterly* 17, 464–473.

Doherty, R. W., Orimoto, L., Singelis, T. M., Hatfield, E., & Hebb, J. (1995). Emotional contagion: Gender and occupational differences. *Psychology of Women Quarterly* 19, 355–371.

Dolgin, K. G., Meyer, L., & Schwartz, J. (1991). Effects of gender, target's gender, topic, and self-esteem on disclosure to best and middling friends. *Sex Roles* 25, 311–329.

Donahue, W. A. (with Kolt, R.). (1992). *Managing interpersonal conflict.* Thousand Oaks, CA: Sage.

Dorland, J. M., & Fisher, A. R. (2001). Gay, lesbian, and bisexual individuals' perception: An analogue study. *Counseling Psychologist* 29 (July), 532–547.

Dosey, M., & Meisels, M. (1976). Personal space and self-protection. *Journal of Personality and Social Psychology* 38, 959–965.

Douglas, W. (1994). The acquaintanceship process: An examination of uncertainty, information seeking, and social attraction during initial conversation. *Communication Research* 21, 154–176.

Dovidio, J. F., Gaertner, S. E., Kawakami, K., & Hodson, G. (2002). Why can't we just get along? Interpersonal biases and interracial distrust. *Cultural Diversity and Ethnic Minority Psychology* 8, 88–102.

Drass, K. A. (1986). The effect of gender identity on conversation. *Social Psychology Quarterly* 49, 294–301.

Dresser, N. (2005). *Multicultural manners: Essential rules of etiquette for the 21st Century, rev. ed.* New York: Wiley.

Drews, D. R., Allison, C. K., & Probst, J. R. (2000). Behavioral and self-concept differences in tattooed and nontattooed college students. *Psychological Reports* 86, 475–481.

Dreyfuss, H. (1971). *Symbol sourcebook.* New York: McGraw-Hill.

Drummond, K., & Hopper, R. (1993). Acknowledgment tokens in series. *Communication Reports* 6, 47–53.

Dsilva, M., & Whyte, L. O. (1998). Cultural differences in conflict styles: Vietnamese refugees and established residents. *The Howard Journal of Communication* 9, 57–68.

Duck, S. (1986). *Human relationships.* Thousand Oaks, CA: Sage.

Duke, M., & Nowicki, S., Jr. (2005). The Emory dyssemia index. In *The sourcebook of nonverbal measures: Going beyond words* (pp. 35–46), V. Manusov (ed.). Mahwah, NJ: Erlbaum.

Dunbar, N. E., & Burgoon, J. K. (2005). Measuring nonverbal dominance. In *The sourcebook of nonverbal measures: Going beyond words* (pp. 361–374), V. Manusov (ed.). Mahwah, NJ: Erlbaum.

Dunbar, R. I. M. (2004). Gossip in evolutionary perspective. *Review of General Psychology* 8 (June), 100–110.

Duncan, B. L., & Rock, J. W. (1991). *Overcoming relationship impasses: Ways to initiate change when your partner won't help.* New York: Plenum Press/Insight Books.

Duncan, S. D., Jr. (1972). Some signals and rules for taking speaking turns in conversation. *Journal of Personality and Social Psychology* 23, 283–292.

Dunn, D., & Cody, M. J. (2000). Account credibility and public image: Excuses, justifications, denials, and sexual harassment. *Communication Monographs* 67 (December), 372–391.

Durst, U. (2003). Evidence for linguistic relativity. *Pragmatics and Cognition* 11, 379–386.

Duval, T. S., & Silva, P. J. (2002). Self-awareness, probability of improvement, and the self-serving bias. *Journal of Personality and Social Psychology* 82, 49–61.

Dwyer, K. K. (2005). *Conquer your speech anxiety: Learning how to overcome your nervousness about public speaking,* 2nd ed. Belmont, CA: Wadsworth.

Eder, D., & Enke, J. L. (1991). The structure of gossip: Opportunities and constraints on collective expression among adolescents. *American Sociological Review* 56, 494–508.

Edstrom, A. (2004). Expression of disagreement by Venezuelans in conversation: Reconsidering the influence of culture. *Journal of Pragmatics* 36 (August), 1499–1508.

Edwards, R., & Bello, R. (2001). Interpretations of messages: The influence of equivocation, face-concerns, and ego-involvement. *Human Communication Research* 27, 597–631.

Ehrenhaus, P. (1988). Silence and symbolic expression. *Communication Monographs* 55, 41–57.

Einhorn, L. (2006). Using e-prime and English minus absolutisms to provide self-empathy. *Etc.: A Review of General Semantics* 63 (April), 180–186.

Eisenberger, N. I., Liberman, M. D., & Williams, K. D. (2003). Does rejection hurt? An fMRI study of social exclusion. *Science* 302 (October), 290–292.

Ekman, P. (1985). *Telling lies: Clues to deceit in the marketplace, politics, and marriage.* New York: Norton.

Ekman, P., & Friesen, W. V. (1969). The repertoire of nonverbal behavior: Categories, origins, usage, and coding. *Semiotica* 1, 49–98.

Ekman, P., Friesen, W. V., & Ellsworth, P. (1972). *Emotion in the human face: Guidelines for research and an integration of findings.* New York: Pergamon Press.

Elfenbein, H. A., & Ambady, N. (2002). Is there an in-group advantage in emotion recognition? *Psychological Bulletin* 128, 243–249.

Ellis, A. (1988). *How to stubbornly refuse to make yourself miserable about anything, yes anything.* Secaucus, NJ: Lyle Stuart.

Ellis, A., & Harper, R. A. (1975). *A new guide to rational living.* Hollywood, CA: Wilshire Books.

Ellis, K. (2004). The impact of perceived teacher confirmation on receiver apprehension, motivation, and learning. *Communication Education* 53 (January), 1–20.

Elmes, M. B., & Gemmill, G. (1990). The psychodynamics of mindlessness and dissent in small groups. *Small Group Research* 21, 28–44.

Emmers-Sommer, T. M. (2004). The effect of communication quality and quantity indicators on intimacy and relational satisfaction. *Journal of Social and Personal Relationships* 21 (June), 99–411.

Epstein, R. (2005). The loose screw awards: Psychology's top 10 misguided ideas. *Psychology Today* (February), 55–62.

Epstein, R. M., & Hundert, E. M. (2002). Defining and assessing professional competence. *JAMA: Journal of the American Medical Association* 287, 226–235.

Exline, R. V., Ellyson, S. L., & Long, B. (1975). Visual behavior as an aspect of power role relationships. In *Nonverbal communication of aggression,* P. Pliner, L. Krames, & T. Alloway (eds.). New York: Plenum Press.

Fagan, J., & Barnett, M. (2003). The relationship between maternal gatekeeping, paternal competence, mothers' attitudes about the father role, and father involvement. *Journal of Family Issues* 24 (November), 1020–1043.

Faigley, L. (2009). *The Penguin handbook,* 3d ed. New York: Longman.

Feeley, T. H., & deTurck, M. A. (1995). Global cue usage in behavioral lie detection. *Communication Quarterly* 43, 420–430.

Fehr, B. (2004). Intimacy expectations in same-sex friendships: A prototype interaction-pattern model. *Journal of Personality and Social Psychology* 86 (February), 265–284.

Fehr, B., & Broughton, R. (2001). Gender and personality differences in concepts of love: An interpersonal theory analysis. *Personal Relationships* 8, 115–136.

Fengler, A. P. (1974). Romantic love in courtship: Divergent paths of male and female students. *Journal of Comparative Family Studies* 5, 134–139.

Fernald, C. D. (1995). When in London . . .: Differences in disability language preferences among English-speaking countries. *Mental Retardation* 33, 99–103.

Ferraro, G. (2005). *Cultural dimension of international business,* 5th ed. Upper Saddle River, NJ: Prentice-Hall.

Fesko, S. L. (2001). Disclosure of HIV status in the workplace: Considerations and strategies. *Health and Social Work* 26 (November), 235–244.

Fife, E. M. (2007). Male friendship and competition: A dialectical analysis. *Ohio Communication Journal* 45, 41–64.

Finn, J. (2004). A survey of online harassment at a university campus. *English* 19 (April), 468–483.

Fischer, A. H. (1993). Sex differences in emotionality: Fact or stereotype? *Feminism & Psychology* 3, 303–318.

Fisher, D. (1995). *People power: 12 power principles to enrich your business, career, and personal networks.* Austin, TX: Bard & Stephen.

Fitzpatrick, M. A. (1983). Predicting couples' communication from couples' self-reports. In *Communication yearbook 7,* R. N. Bostrom (ed.). Thousand Oaks, CA: Sage, pp. 49–82.

Fitzpatrick, M. A. (1988). *Between husbands and wives: Communication in marriage.* Thousand Oaks, CA: Sage.

Fitzpatrick, M. A. (1991). Sex differences in marital conflict: Social psychophysiological versus cognitive explanations. *Text* 11, 341–364.

Fitzpatrick, M. A., & Caughlin, J. P. (2002). Interpersonal communication in family relationships. In *Handbook of interpersonal communication,* 3d ed., (pp. 726–777), M. L. Knapp & J. A. Daly. (eds.). Thousand Oaks, CA: Sage.

Fitzpatrick, M. A., Jandt, F. E., Myrick, F. L., & Edgar, T. (1994). Gay and lesbian couple relationships. In *Queer words, queer images: Communication and the construction of homosexuality* (pp. 265–285), Ringer, R. J. (ed.). New York: New York University Press.

Floyd, J. J. (1985). *Listening: A practical approach.* Glenview, IL: Scott, Foresman.

Floyd, K., & Mikkelson, A. C. (2005). In *The sourcebook of nonverbal measures: Going beyond words* (pp. 47–56), V. Manusov (ed.). Mahwah, NJ: Erlbaum.

Folger, J. P., Poole, M. S., & Stutman, R. K. (2009). *Working through conflict: A communication perspective,* 6th ed. Boston: Allyn & Bacon.

Forbes, G. B. (2001). College students with tattoos and piercings: Motives, family experiences, personality factors, and perception by others. *Psychological Reports* 89, 774–786.

Ford, S. (2003). "Dear Mr. Shawn": A lesson in e-mail pragmatics (netiquette). *TESOL Journal* 12 (spring), 39–40.

Foster, D. (2004). Standing on ceremony. *National Geographic Traveler* 21 (May–June), 97–99.

Fox, A. B., Bukatki, D., Hallahan, M., & Crawford, M. (2007). The medium makes a difference: Gender similarities and differences in instant messaging. *Journal of Language and Social Psychology* 26, 389–397.

Franklin, C. W., & Mizell, C. A. (1995). Some factors influencing success among African-American men: A preliminary study. *Journal of Men's Studies* 3, 191–204.

Franklin, R. (2002). Office romances: Conduct unbecoming? *Business Week Online* (February 14), np.

Fraser, B. (1990). Perspectives on politeness. *Journal of Pragmatics* 14, 219–236.

Freedman, J. (1978). *Happy people: What happiness is, who has it, and why.* New York: Ballantine.

French, J. R. P., Jr., & Raven, B. (1968). The bases of social power. In *Group dynamics: Research and theory,* 3d ed., D. Cartwright & A. Zander (eds.). New York: Harper & Row, pp. 259–269.

Frentz, T. (1976). A general approach to episodic structure. Paper presented at the Western Speech Association Convention, San Francisco. Cited in Reardon (1987).

Friedman, J., Boumil, M. M., & Taylor, B. E. (1992). *Sexual harassment.* Deerfield Beach, FL: Health Communications, Inc.

Frith, H. & Gleeson, K. (2004). Clothing and embodiment: Men managing body image and appearance. *Psychology of Men and Masculinity*, 5(1), 40–48.

Frone, M. R. (2000). Interpersonal conflict at work and psychological outcomes: Testing a model among young workers. *Journal of Occupational Health Psychology* 5, 246–255.

Fu, H., Watkins, D., & Hui, E. K. P. (2004). Personality correlates of the disposition towards interpersonal forgiveness: Chinese perspective. *International Journal of Psychology* 39 (August), 305–316.

Fuller, D. (2004). Electronic manners and netiquette. *Athletic Therapy Today* 9 (March), 40–41.

Furlow, F. B. (1996). The smell of love. *Psychology Today* 29, 38–45.

Galvin, K. M., Bylund, C. L., & Brommel, B. J. (2008). *Family communication: Cohesion and change,* 7th ed. Boston: Allyn & Bacon.

Gamble, T. K., & Gamble, M. W. (2003). *The gender communication connection.* Boston: Houghton Mifflin.

Gamson, J. (1998). Publicity traps: Television talk shows and lesbian, gay, bisexual, and transgender visibility. *Sexualities* 1 (February), 11–41.

Gao, G., & Gudykunst, W. B. (1995). Attributional confidence, perceived similarity, and network involvement in Chinese and American romantic relationships. *Communication Quarterly* 43, 431–445.

Gattis, K. S., Berns, S., Simpson, L. E., & Christensen, A. (2004). Birds of a feature or strange birds? Ties among personality dimensions, similarity, and marital quality. *Journal of Family Psychology* 18 (December), 564–574.

Gelfand, M. J., Nishii, L. H., Holcombe, K. M., Dyer, N., Ohbuchi, K., & Fukuno, M. (2001). Cultural influences on cognitive representations of conflict: Interpretations of conflict episodes in the United States and Japan. *Journal of Applied Psychology* 86, 1059–1074.

Gelles, R., & Cornell, C. (1985). *Intimate violence in families.* Thousand Oaks, CA: Sage.

Georgas, J., Mylonas, K., Bafiti, T., & Poortinga, Y. H. (2001). Functional relationships in the nuclear and extended family: A 16-culture study. *International Journal of Psychology* 36, 289–300.

Gergen, K. J., Greenberg, M. S., and Willis, R. H. (1980). *Social exchange: Advances in theory and research.* New York: Plenum Press.

Gibb, J. (1961). Defensive communication. *Journal of Communication* 11, 141–148.

Gibbs, N. (2005). Parents behaving badly. *Time* (February 21), 40–49.

Giles, D. C. (2001). Parasocial interaction: A review of the literature and a model for future research. *Media Psychology* 4, 279–305.

Giles, D. C., & Maltby, J. (2004). The role of media figures in adolescent development: Relations between autonomy, attachment, and interest in celebrities. *Personality and Individual Differences* 36 (March), 813–822.

Giles, H. (2008). Communication accommodation theory. In *Engaging theories in interpersonal communication: Multiple perspectives* (pp. 161–174), L. A. Baxter & D. O. Braithwaite (eds.). Los Angeles, CA: Sage.

Giles, H., & Ogay, T. (2007). In *Explaining communication: Contemporary theories and exemplars* (pp. 293–310), B. B. Whaley, & W. Samter (eds.). Mahwah, NJ: Erlbaum.

Gladstone, G. L., & Parker, G. B. (2002). When you're smiling, does the whole world smile with you? *Australasian Psychiatry* 10 (June), 144–146.

Goffman, E. (1967). *Interaction ritual: Essays on face-to-face behavior.* New York: Pantheon.

Goffman, E. (1971). *Relations in public: Microstudies of the public order.* New York: Harper Colophon.

Goldin-Meadow, S., Nusbaum, H., Kelly, S. D., & Wagner, S. (2001). Gesture—Psychological aspects. *Psychological Science* 12, 516–522.

Goldsmith, D. J. (2007). Brown and Levinson's politeness theory. In *Explaining communication: Contemporary theories and exemplars* (pp. 219–236), B. B. Whaley & W. Samter (eds.). Mahwah, NJ: Erlbaum.

Goldsmith, D. J. (2008). Politeness theory. In *Engaging theories in interpersonal communication: Multiple perspectives* (pp. 255–268), L. A. Baxter & D. O. Braithwaite (eds.). Los Angeles: Sage.

Goldsmith, D. J., & Fulfs, P. A. (1999). "You just don't have the evidence": An analysis of claims and evidence. In *Communication yearbook, 22* (pp. 1–49), M. E. Roloff (ed.). Thousand Oaks, CA: Sage.

Goleman, D. (1992). Studies find no disadvantage in growing up in a gay home. *New York Times* (December 2), C14.

Goleman, D. (1995a). *Emotional intelligence.* New York: Bantam.

Goleman, D. (1995b). For man and beast, language of love shares many traits. *New York Times* (February 14), C1, C9.

Gonzaga, G. C., Keltner, D., Londahl, E. A., & Smith, M. D. (2001). Love and the commitment problem in romantic relationships and friendships. *Journal of Personality and Social Psychology* 81 (August), 247–262.

Gonzalez, A., & Zimbardo, P. G. (1985). Time in perspective. *Psychology Today* 19, 20–26. Reprinted in DeVito & Hecht (1990).

Goodwin, R., & Findlay, C. (1997). "We were just fated together" . . . Chinese love and the concept of *yuan* in England and Hong Kong. *Personal Relationships* 4, 85–92.

Goodwin, R., & Gaines, S. O., Jr. (2004). Relationships beliefs and relationship quality across cultures: Country as a moderator of dysfunctional beliefs and relationship quality in three former Communist societies. *Personal Relationships* 11 (September), 267–279.

Gordon, T. (1975). *P.E.T.: Parent effectiveness training.* New York: New American Library.

Gosling, S. D., Ko, S. J., Mannarelli, T., & Morris, M. E. (2002). A room with a cue: Personality judgments based on offices and bedrooms. *Journal of Personality and Social Psychology* 82 (March), 379–398.

Gottman, J. M., & Carrere, S. (1994). Why can't men and women get along? Developmental roots and marital

inequities. In D. J. Canary and L. Stafford (eds.). *Communication and relational maintenance,* San Diego, CA: Academic Press, pp. 203–229.

Gottman, J. M., & Levenson, R. W. (1999). Dysfunctional marital conflict: Women are being unfairly blamed. *Journal of Divorce and Remarriage* 31, 1–17.

Gould, S. J. (1995). No more "wretched refuse." *New York Times* (June 7), A27.

Grace, S. L., & Cramer, K. L. (2003). The elusive nature of self-measurement: The self-construal scale versus the twenty statements test. *Journal of Social Psychology* 143 (October), 649–668.

Graham, E. E., Barbato, C. A., & Perse, E. M. (1993). The interpersonal communication motives model. *Communication Quarterly* 41, 172–186.

Graham, J. A., & Argyle, M. (1975). The effects of different patterns of gaze, combined with different facial expressions, on impression formation. *Journal of Movement Studies* 1, 178–182.

Graham, J. A., Bitti, P. R., & Argyle, M. (1975). A cross-cultural study of the communication of emotion by facial and gestural cues. *Journal of Human Movement Studies* 1, 68–77.

Grandey, A. A. (2000). Emotion regulation in the workplace: A new way to conceptualize emotional labor. *Journal of Occupational Health and Psychology* 5 (January), 95–110.

Greene, J. O. (2003). Models of adult communication skill acquisition: Practice and the course of performance improvement. In *Handbook of communication and social interaction skills,* J. O. Greene & B. R. Burleson (eds.). Mahwah, NJ: Erlbaum, pp. 51–92.

Greene, J. O., & Burleson, B. R. (eds.). (2003). *Handbook of communication and social interaction skills.* Mahwah, NJ: Erlbaum.

Greif, E. B. (1980). Sex differences in parent-child conversations. *Women's Studies International Quarterly* 3, 253–258.

Greitemeyer, T. (2007). What do men and women want in a partner? Are educated partners always more desirable? *Journal of Experimental Social Psychology* 43 (March), 180–194.

Grice, H. P. (1975). Logic and conversation. In *Syntax and semantics,* Vol. 3, *Speech acts,* P. Cole & J. L. Morgan (eds.). New York: Seminar Press, pp. 41–58.

Gross, T., Turner, E., & Cederholm, L. (1987). Building teams for global operation, *Management Review* (June), 32–36.

Gu, Y. (1990). Polite phenomena in modern Chinese. *Journal of Pragmatics* 14, 237–257.

Gudykunst, W. B., ed. (1983). *Intercultural communication theory: Current perspectives.* Thousand Oaks, CA: Sage.

Gudykunst, W. B. (1989). Culture and the development of interpersonal relationships. In *Communication yearbook 12,* J. A. Anderson (ed.). Thousand Oaks, CA: Sage, pp. 315–354.

Gudykunst, W. B. (1991). *Bridging differences: Effective intergroup communication.* Newbury Park, CA: Sage.

Gudykunst, W. B. (1993). Toward a theory of effective interpersonal and intergroup communication: An anxiety/uncertainty management (AUM) perspective. In *Intercultural communication competence,* R. L. Wiseman (ed.). Thousand Oaks, CA: Sage.

Gudykunst, W. B. (1994). *Bridging differences: Effective intergroup communication,* 2d ed. Thousand Oaks, CA: Sage.

Gudykunst, W. B., & Kim, Y. W. (1992). *Communicating with strangers: An approach to intercultural communication,* 2d ed. New York: Random House.

Gudykunst, W. B., & Ting-Toomey, S. (with Chua, E.) (1988). *Culture and interpersonal communication.* Thousand Oaks, CA: Sage.

Guéguen, N. (2003). Help on the Web: The effect of the same first name between the sender and the receptor in a request made by e-mail. *Psychological Record* 53 (summer), 459–466.

Guéguen, N., & Jacob, C. (2004). The effect of touch on tipping: An evaluation in a French bar. *International Journal of Hospitality Management* 24 (June), 295–299.

Guerin, B. (2003). Combating prejudice and racism: New interventions from a functional analysis of racist language. *Journal of Community and Applied Social Psychology* 13 (January), 29–45.

Guerrero, L. K. (1997). Nonverbal involvement across interactions with same-sex friends, opposite-sex friends, and romantic partners: Consistency or change? *Journal of Social and Personal Relationships* 14, 31–58.

Guerrero, L. K., & Andersen, P. A. (1991). The waxing and waning of relational intimacy: Touch as a function of relational stage, gender and touch avoidance. *Journal of Social and Personal Relationships* 8, 147–165.

Guerrero, L. K., Andersen, P. A., & Afifi, W. A. (2007). *Close encounters: Communication in relationships,* 2d ed. Thousand Oaks, CA: Sage.

Guerrero, L. K., Andersen, P. A., Jorgensen, P. F., Spitzberg, B. H., & Eloy, S. V. (1995). Coping with the green-eyed monster: Conceptualizing and measuring communicative response to romantic jealousy. *Western Journal of Communication* 59, 270–304.

Guerrero, L. K., DeVito, J. A., & Hecht, M. L., eds. (1999). *The nonverbal communication reader: Classic and contemporary readings.* Prospect Heights, IL: Waveland Press.

Guerrero, L. K., Eloy, S. V., & Wabnik, A. I. (1993). Linking maintenance strategies to relationship development and disengagement: A reconceptualization. *Journal of Social and Personal Relationships* 10, 273–282.

Guerrero, L. K., Jones, S. M., & Boburka, R. R. (2006). Sex differences in emotional communication. In *Sex differences and similarities in communication* (2d ed., pp. 241–262), K. Dindia & D. J. Canary (eds.). Mahwah, NJ: Erlbaum.

Haar, B. F., & Krabe, B. (1999). Strategies for resolving interpersonal conflicts in adolescence: A German-Indonesian comparison. *Journal of Cross-Cultural Psychology* 30, 667–683.

Haga, Y. (1988). Traits de langage et caractere japonais. *Cahiers de Sociologie Economique et Culturelle* 9, 105–109.

Haidar-Yassine, H. (2002). Internet friendships: Can virtual be real? *Dissertation Abstracts International: Section B: The Sciences & Engineering* 63 (5-B), 2651.

Hall, E. T. (1959). *The silent language.* Garden City, NY: Doubleday.

Hall, E. T. (1963). System for the notation of proxemic behavior. *American Anthropologist* 65, 1003–1026.

Hall, E. T. (1966). *The hidden dimension.* Garden City, NY: Doubleday.

Hall, E. T. (1976). *Beyond culture.* Garden City, NY: Anchor Press.

Hall, E. T., & Hall, M. R. (1987). *Hidden differences: Doing business with the Japanese.* New York: Anchor Books.

Hall, J. A. (1984). *Nonverbal sex differences.* Baltimore: Johns Hopkins University Press.

Hall, J. A. (2006). Women's and men's nonverbal communication: Similarities, differences, stereotypes, and origins. In *The Sage handbook of nonverbal communication* (pp. 201–218), V. Manusov & M. L. Patterson (eds.). Thousand Oaks, CA: Sage.

Hall, J. K. (1993). Tengo una bomba: The paralinguistic and linguistic conventions of the oral practice Chismeando. *Research on Language and Social Interaction* 26, 55–83.

Hamlin, J. K., Wynn, K., & Bloom, P. (2007). Babies prefer helpful to unhelpful social types. *Nature* 450 (November), 557–559.

Hample, D. (2004). Arguing skills. In *Handbook of communication and social interaction skills* (pp. 439–477), J. O. Greene & B. R. Burleson (eds.). Mahwah, NJ: Erlbaum.

Han, S., & Shavitt, S. (1994). Persuasion and culture: Advertising appeals in individualistic and collectivistic societies. *Journal of Experimental Social Psychology* 30, 326–350.

Haney, W. (1973). *Communication and organizational behavior: Text and cases,* 3d ed. Homewood, IL: Irwin.

Harris, C. R. (2003). A review of sex differences in sexual jealousy, including self-report data, psychophysiological responses, interpersonal violence, and morbid jealousy. *Personality and Social Psychology Review* 7, 102–128.

Harris, M. (1993). *Culture, people, nature: An introduction to general anthropology,* 6th ed. Boston: Allyn & Bacon.

Hart, F. (1990). The construction of masculinity in men's friendships: Misogyny, heterosexism and homophobia. *Resources for Feminist Research* 19, 60–67.

Hart, R. P., Carlson, R. E., & Eadie, W. F. (1980). Attitudes toward communication and the assessment of rhetorical sensitivity. *Communication Monographs* 47, 1–22.

Harvey, J. H., Flanary, R., & Morgan, M. (1986). Vivid memories of vivid loves gone by. *Journal of Social and Personal Relationships* 3, 359–373.

Hasart, J. K., & Hutchinson, K. L. (1993). The effects of eye-glasses on perceptions of interpersonal attraction. *Journal of Social Behavior and Personality* 8, 521–528.

Hasegawa, T., & Gudykunst, W. B. (1998). Silence in Japan and the United States. *Journal of Cross-Cultural Psychology* 29, 668–684.

Hatfield, E., & Rapson, R. L. (1996). *Love and sex: Cross-cultural perspectives.* Boston: Allyn & Bacon.

Hatfield, E., & Rapson, R. L. (2007). Equity theory. In *Encyclopedia of Social Psychology,* R. Baumeister & K. D. Vohs (eds.). Los Angeles: Sage.

Haugh, M. (2004). Revisiting the conceptualization of politeness in English and Japanese. *Multilingua* 23, 85–109.

Havlena, W. J., Holbrook, M. B., & Lehmann, D. R. (1989). Assessing the validity of emotional typologies. *Psychology and Marketing* 6 (Summer), 97–112.

Hayakawa, S. I., & Hayakawa, A. R. (1989). *Language in thought and action,* 5th ed. New York: Harcourt Brace Jovanovich.

Hays, R. B. (1989). The day-to-day functioning of close versus casual friendships. *Journal of Social and Personal Relationships* 6, 21–37.

Heasley, J. B. S., Babbitt, C. E., & Burbach, H. J. (1995). The role of social context in students' anticipatory reaction to a "fighting word." *Sociological Focus* 27, 281–283.

Heath, W. P., Stone, J., Darley, J. M., & Grannemann, B. D. (2003). Yes, I did it, but don't blame me: Perceptions of excuse defenses. *Journal of Psychiatry and Law* 31 (summer), 187–226.

Hecht, M. L., Jackson, R. L., & Ribeau, S. (2003). *African American communication: Exploring identity and culture,* 2d ed. Mahwah, NJ: Erlbaum.

Hellweg, S. A. (1992). Organizational grapevines. In *Readings in organizational communication* (pp. 159–172), K. L. Hutchinson (ed.). Dubuque, IA: William. C. Brown.

Hendrick, C., & Hendrick, S. (1990). A relationship-specific version of the love attitudes scale. In *Handbook of replication research in the behavioral and social sciences* (special issue), J. W. Heulip (ed.), *Journal of Social Behavior and Personality* 5, 239–254.

Hendrick, C., Hendrick, S., Foote, F. H., & Slapion-Foote, M. J. (1984). Do men and women love differently? *Journal of Social and Personal Relationships* 1, 177–195.

Henley, N. M. (1977). *Body politics: Power, sex, and nonverbal communication.* Englewood Cliffs, NJ: Prentice-Hall.

Hensley, W. E. (1996). A theory of the valenced other: The intersection of the looking-glass-self and social penetration. *Social Behavior and Personality* 24, 293–308.

Hess, E. H. (1975). *The tell-tale eye.* New York: Van Nostrand Reinhold.

Hess, E. H., Seltzer, A. L., & Schlien, J. M. (1965). Pupil response of hetero- and homosexual males to pictures of men and women: A pilot study. *Journal of Abnormal Psychology* 70, 165–168.

Hess, U., Kappas, A., McHugo, G. J., Lanzetta, J. T., et al. (1992). The facilitative effect of facial expression on the self-generation of emotion. *International Journal of Psychophysiology* 12, 251–265.

Hewitt, J. P. (1998). *The myth of self-esteem: Finding happiness and solving problems in America.* New York: St. Martin's Press.

Hewitt, J. P., & Stokes, R. (1975). Disclaimers. *American Sociological Review* 40, 1–11.

Hilton, L. (2000). They heard it through the grapevine. *South Florida Business Journal* 21 (August), 53.

Hirofumi, A. (2003). Closeness and interpersonal outcomes in same-sex friendships: An improvement of the investment model and explanation of closeness. *Japanese Journal of Experimental Social Psychology* 42 (March), 131–145.

Hocker, J. L., & Wilmot, W. W. (2007). *Interpersonal conflict,* 7th ed. New York: McGraw Hill.

Hoffmann, G. (2005). Rhetoric of Bush speeches: Purr words and snarl words. *Etc: A Review of General Semantics* 62 (April), 198–201.

Hofstede, G. (1983). National culture revisited. *Behavior Science Research* 18, 285–305.

Hofstede, G. (1997). *Cultures and organizations: Software of the mind.* New York: McGraw-Hill.

Hofstede, G. (2000). Masculine and feminine cultures. *Encyclopedia of psychology,* Vol. 5 (pp. 115–118), A. E. Kazdin (ed.). Washington, DC: American Psychological Association and Oxford University Press.

Hofstede, G., ed. (1998). *Masculinity and femininity: The taboo dimension of national cultures.* Thousand Oaks, CA: Sage.

Hoft, N. L. (1995). *International technical communication: How to export information about high technology.* New York: Wiley.

Holden, J. M. (1991). The most frequent personality priority pairings in marriage and marriage counseling. *Individual Psychology Journal of Adlerian Theory, Research, and Practice* 47, 392–398.

Holmes, J. (1995). *Women, men and politeness.* New York: Longman.

Hopper, R., Knapp, M. L., & Scott, L. (1981). Couples' personal idioms: Exploring intimate talk. *Journal of Communication* 31, 23–33.

Hornsey, J. J., Bath, M. T., & Gunthorpe, S. (2004). "You can criticize because you care": Identity attachment, constructiveness, and the intergroup sensitivity effect. *European Journal of Social Psychology* 34 (September–October), 499–518.

Hosman, L. A. (1989). The evaluative consequences of hedges, hesitations, and intensifiers: Powerful and powerless speech styles. *Human Communication Research* 15, 383–406.

How Americans Communicate (1999). http://www.natcom.org/Research/Roper/how_Americans_communicate.htm.

Howard, P. E. N., Rainie, L., & Jones, S. (2001). Days and nights on the Internet: The impact of a diffusing technology. *American Behavioral Scientist* 45, 383–404.

Hu, Y., Wood, J. F., Smith, V., & Westbrook, N. (2004). Friendships through IM: Examining the relationship between instant messaging and intimacy. *Journal of Computer-Mediated Communication* 10 (November), np.

Hunt, M. O. (2000). Status, religion, and the "belief in a just world": Comparing African Americans, Latinos, and whites. *Social Science Quarterly* 81 (March), 325–343.

Huston, M., & Schwartz, P. (1995). The relationships of lesbians and gay men. In *Under-studied relationships: Off the beaten track,* J. T. Wood, & S. Duck (eds.). Thousand Oaks, CA: Sage, pp. 89–121.

Imwalle, D. B., & Schillo, K. K. (2004). Masculinity and femininity: The taboo dimension of national cultures. *Archives of Sexual Behavior* 33 (April), 174–176.

Infante, D. A. (1988). *Arguing constructively.* Prospect Heights, IL: Waveland Press.

Infante, D. A., Chandler, T. A., & Rudd, J. E. (1989). Test of an argumentative skill deficiency model of interspousal violence. *Communication Monographs* 56, 163–177.

Infante, D. A., Hartley, K. C., Martin, M. M., Higgins, M. A., Bruning, S. D., & Hur, G. (1992). Initiating and reciprocating verbal aggression: Effects on credibility and credited valid arguments. *Communication Studies* 43, 182–190.

Infante, D. A., & Rancer, A. S. (1982). A conceptualization and measure of argumentativeness. *Journal of Personality Assessment* 46, 72–80.

Infante, D. A., & Rancer, A. S. (1996). Argumentativeness and verbal aggressiveness: A review of recent theory and research. In *Communication yearbook 19* (pp. 319–351), B. R. Burleson (ed.). Thousand Oaks, CA: Sage.

Infante, D. A., Rancer, A. S., & Jordan, F. F. (1996). Affirming and nonaffirming style, dyad sex, and the perception of argumentation and verbal aggression in an interpersonal dispute. *Human Communication Research* 22, 315–334.

Infante, D. A., Rancer, A. S., & Womack, D. F. (2003). *Building communication theory,* 4th ed. Prospect Heights, IL: Waveland Press.

Infante, D. A., Riddle, B. L., Horvath, C. L., & Tumlin, S. A. (1992). Verbal aggressiveness: Messages and reasons. *Communication Quarterly* 40, 116–126.

Infante, D. A., Sabourin, T. C., Rudd, J. E., & Shannon, E. A. (1990). Verbal aggression in violent and nonviolent marital disputes. *Communication Quarterly* 38, 361–371.

Infante, D. A., & Wigley, C. J. (1986). Verbal aggressiveness: An interpersonal model and measure. *Communication Monographs* 53, 61–69.

Iverson, J. M., & Goldin-Meadow, S., eds. (1999). *The nature and functions of gesture in children's communication.* San Francisco: Jossey-Bass.

Ivy, D. K., & Backlund, P. (2000). *Exploring gender-speak: Personal effectiveness in gender communication,* 2d ed. New York: McGraw-Hill.

Jackson, L. A., & Ervin, K. S. (1992). Height stereotypes of women and men: The liabilities of shortness for both sexes. *Journal of Social Psychology* 132, 433–445.

Jacobson, D. (1999). Impression formation in cyberspace: Online expectations and offline experiences in text-based virtual communities. *Journal of Computer Mediated Communication* 5, np.

Jaksa, J. A., & Pritchard, M. S. (1994). *Communication ethics: Methods of analysis,* 2d ed. Belmont, CA: Wadsworth.

Jambor, E., & Elliott, M. (2005). Self-esteem and coping strategies among deaf students. *Journal of Deaf Studies and Deaf Education* 10 (winter), 63–81.

Jandt, F. E. (2004). *An introduction to intercultural communication: Identities in a global community,* 4th ed. Thousand Oaks, CA: Sage.

Jandt, F. E. (2007). *An introduction to intercultural communication: Identities in a global community,* 5th ed. Thousand Oaks, CA: Sage.

Janus, S. S., & Janus, C. L. (1993). *The Janus report on sexual behavior.* New York: Wiley.

Jaworski, A. (1993). *The power of silence: Social and pragmatic perspectives.* Thousand Oaks, CA: Sage.

Jecker, J., & Landy, D. (1969). Liking a person as a function of doing him a favor. *Human Relations* 22, 371–378.

Johannesen, R. L. (2001). *Ethics in human communication,* 5th ed. Prospect Heights, IL: Waveland Press.

Johnson, A. J., Wittenberg, E., Villagran, M. M., Mazur, M., & Villagran, P. (2003). Relational progression as a dialectic: Examining turning points in communication among friends. *Communication Monographs* 70 (September), 230–249.

Johnson, C. E. (1987). An introduction to powerful and powerless talk in the classroom. *Communication Education* 36, 167–172.

Johnson, M. P. (1973). Commitment: A conceptual structure and empirical application. *Sociological Quarterly* 14, 395–406.

Johnson, M. P. (1982). Social and cognitive features of the dissolution of commitment to relationships. In *Personal Relationships 4: Dissolving Personal Relationships,* (pp. 51–73), S. Duck (ed.). New York: Academic Press.

Johnson, M. P. (1991). Commitment to personal relationships. In *Advances in personal relationships, Vol. 3* (pp. 117–143), W. H. Jones, & D. Perlman (eds.). London: Jessica Kingsley.

Johnson, S. D., & Bechler, C. (1998). Examining the relationship between listening effectiveness and leadership emergence: Perceptions, behaviors, and recall. *Small Group Research* 29, 452–471.

Johnson, S. M., & O'Connor, E. (2002). *The gay baby boom: The psychology of gay parenthood.* New York: New York University Press.

Joiner, T. E. (1994). Contagious depression: Existence, specificity to depressed symptoms, and the role of reassurance seeking. *Journal of Personality and Social Psychology* 67, 287–296.

Joinson, A. N. (2001). Self-disclosure in computer-mediated communication: The role of self-awareness and visual anonymity. *European Journal of Social Psychology* 31, 177–192.

Jones, B. C., DeBruine, L. M., Little, A. C., Burriss, R. P., & Feinberg, D. R. (2007). Social transmission of face preferences among humans. *Proceedings of the Royal Society* 274 (March 22), 899–903.

Jones, C., Berry, L., & Stevens, C. (2007). Synthesized speech intelligibility and persuasion: Speech rate and non-native listeners. *Computer Speech and Language* 21 (October), 641–651.

Jones, D. (2004). Cupid lurks in cubicles, so what's a worker to do? *USA Today* (April 2), Money Section, 5.

Jones, S. (2005). The touch log record: A behavioral communication measure. In *Applications of nonverbal communication* (pp. 67–82), R. E. Riggio & R. S. Feldman (eds.). Mahwah, NJ: Erlbaum.

Jones, S., & Yarbrough, A. E. (1985). A naturalistic study of the meanings of touch. *Communication Monographs* 52, 19–56. A version of this paper appears in DeVito & Hecht (1990).

Jörn, R. (2004). How to overcome ethnocentrism: Approaches to a culture of recognition by history in the twenty-first century. *History and Theory* 43 (December), 118–129.

Jourard, S. M. (1968). *Disclosing man to himself.* New York: Van Nostrand Reinhold.

Jourard, S. M. (1971). *Self-disclosure.* New York: Wiley.

Judge, T. A., & Cable, D. M. (2004). The effect of physical height on workplace success and income. *Journal of Applied Psychology* 89, 428–441.

Kallos, J. (2005). *Because netiquette matters! Your comprehensive reference guide to e-mail etiquette and proper technology use.* Philadelphia: Xlibris Corporation.

Kanemasa, Y., Taniguchi, J., Daibo, I., & Ishimori, M. (2004). Love styles and romantic love experiences in Japan. *Social Behavior and Personality: An International Journal* 32, 265–281.

Kanner, B. (1989). Color schemes. *New York Magazine* (April 3), 22–23.

Kapoor, S., Wolfe, A., & Blue, J. (1995). Universal values structure and individualism–collectivism: A U.S. test. *Communication Research Reports* 12, 112–123.

Katz, S. (2003). *Down to earth sociology: Introductory readings,* 12th ed. (pp. 313–320), J. W. Henslin (ed.). New York: Free Press.

Kearney, P., Plax, T. G., Richmond, V. P., & McCroskey, J. C. (1984). Power in the classroom IV: Alternatives to discipline. In *Communication Yearbook 8,* R. N. Bostrom (ed.). Thousand Oaks, CA: Sage, pp. 724–746.

Kearney, P., Plax, T. G., Richmond, V. P., & McCroskey, J. C. (1985). Power in the classroom III: Teacher communication techniques and messages. *Communication Education* 34, 19–28.

Keating, C. F. (2006). Why and how the silence self speaks volumes: Functional approaches to nonverbal impression management. In *The Sage handbook of nonverbal communication* (pp. 321–340), V. Manusov & M. L. Patterson (eds.). Thousand Oaks, CA: Sage.

Kellerman, K., & Cole, T. (1994). Classifying compliance gaining messages: Taxonomic disorder and strategic confusion. *Communication Theory* 1, 3–60.

Kennedy, C. W., & Camden, C. T. (1988). A new look at interruptions. *Western Journal of Speech Communication* 47, 45–58.

Kennedy-Moore, E., & Watson, J. C. (1999). *Expressing emotion: Myths, realities, and therapeutic strategies.* New York: Guilford Press.

Kenrick, D. T., Neuberg, S. L., and Cialdini, R. B. (2007). *Social psychology: Goals in interaction,* 4th ed. Boston: Allyn & Bacon.

Keyes, R. (1980). *The height of your life.* New York: Warner Books.

Kim, M., & Sharkey, W. F. (1995). Independent and interdependent construals of self: Explaining cultural patterns of interpersonal communication in multi-cultural organizational settings. *Communication Quarterly* 43, 20–38.

Kim, S. H., & Smith, R. H. (1993). Revenge and conflict escalation. *Negotiation Journal* 9, 37–43.

Kim, Y. Y. (1988). Communication and acculturation. In *Intercultural communication: A reader* (4th ed., pp. 344–354), L. A. Samovar & R. E. Porter (eds.). Belmont, CA: Wadsworth.

Kindred, J., & Roper, S. L. (2004). Making connections via instant messaging (IM): Student use of IM to maintain personal relationships. *Qualitative Research Reports in Communication* 5, 48–54.

Kirn, W. (2005). It's a glad, sad, mad world. *Time* (January 17), A65–A67.

Kleinke, C. L. (1986). *Meeting and understanding people.* New York: W. H. Freeman.

Kleinke, D. L., & Dean, G. O. (1990). Evaluation of men and women receiving positive and negative responses with various acquaintance strategies. *Journal of Social Behavior and Personality* 5, 369–377.

Kluger, J. (2005). The funny thing about laughter. *Time* (January 17), A25–A29.

Kluger, J. (2008, January 28). Why we love. *Time,* pp. 54–61.

Knapp, M. L. (1978). *Social intercourse: From greeting to goodbye.* Boston, MA: Allyn & Bacon.

Knapp, M. L. (2008). *Lying and deception in human interaction.* Boston: Pearson.

Knapp, M. L., Ellis, D., & Williams, B. A. (1980). Perceptions of communication behavior associated with relationship terms. *Communication Monographs* 47, 262–278.

Knapp, M. L., & Hall, J. (2002). *Nonverbal behavior in human interaction,* 3d ed. New York: Holt, Rinehart & Winston.

Knapp, M. L., & Taylor, E. H. (1994). Commitment and its communication in romantic relationships. In *Perspectives on close relationships,* A. L. Weber & J. H. Harvey (eds.). Boston: Allyn & Bacon, pp. 153–175.

Knapp, M. L., & Vangelisti, A. (2009). *Interpersonal communication and human relationships,* 6th ed. Boston: Allyn & Bacon.

Knobloch, L. K., & Carpenter-Theune, K. E. (2004). Topic avoidance in developing romantic relationships. *Communication Research* (April), 173–205.

Knobloch, L. K., Haunani, D., & Theiss, J. A. (2006). The role of intimacy in the production and perception of relationship talk within courtship. *Communication Research* 33 (August), 211–241.

Knobloch, L. K., & Solomon, D. H. (1999). Measuring the sources and content of relational uncertainty. *Communication Studies* 50 (winter), 261–278.

Knobloch, L. K., & Solomon, D. H. (2005). Measuring conversational equality at the relational level. In *The sourcebook of nonverbal measures: Going beyond words* (pp. 295–304), V. Manusov (ed.). Mahwah, NJ: Erlbaum.

Knox, D., Daniels, V., Sturdivant, L., & Zusman, M. E. (2001). College student use of the Internet for mate selection. *College Student Journal* 35, 158–160.

Kochman, T. (1981). *Black and white: Styles in conflict.* Chicago: University of Chicago Press.

Koerner, A. F., & Fitzpatrick, M. A. (2002). You never leave your family in a fight: The impact of family of origin on conflict behavior in romantic relationships. *Communication Studies* 53 (fall), 234–252.

Kollock, P., & Smith, M. (1996). Managing the virtual commons: Cooperation and conflict in computer communities. In *Computer-mediated communication: Linguistic, social, and cross-cultural perspectives* (pp. 109–128), S. Herring (ed.). Amsterdam: John Benjamins.

Koppelman, K. L., with Goodhart, R. L. (2005). *Understanding human differences: Multicultural education for a diverse America.* Boston: Allyn & Bacon.

Korda, M. (1975). *Power! How to get it, how to use it.* New York: Ballantine.

Korobov, N., & Thorne, A. (2006). Intimacy and distancing: Young men's conversations about romantic relationships. *Journal of Adolescent Research* 21, 27–55.

Korzybski, A. (1933). *Science and sanity.* Lakeville, CT: The International Non-Aristotelian Library.

Kposowa, A. J. (2000). Marital status and suicide in the National Longitudinal Mortality Study. *Journal of Epidemiology and Community Health,* 54 (April), 254–261.

Kramer, R. (1997). Leading by listening: An empirical test of Carl Rogers's theory of human relationship using interpersonal assessments of leaders by followers. *Dissertation Abstracts, International Section A. Humanities and Social Sciences* 58, 514.

Kraut, R., Patterson, M., Lundmarle, V., Kiesler, S., Mukopadhyay, & Scherlis, W. (1999). Internet paradox. *American Psychologist* 53, 1017–1031.

Krebs, G. L. (1989). *Organizational communication,* 2d ed. Boston: Allyn & Bacon.

Krivonos, P. D., & Knapp, M. L. (1975). Initiating communication: What do you say when you say hello? *Central States Speech Journal* 26, 115–125.

Kr|økke, C., & Sørensen, A. S. (2006). *Gender communication theories and analyses: From silence to performance.* Thousand Oaks, CA: Sage.

Kurdek, L. A. (1994). Areas of conflict for gay, lesbian, and heterosexual couples: What couples argue about influences relationship satisfaction. *Journal of Marriage and the Family* 56, 923–934.

Kurdek, L. A. (1995). Developmental changes in relationship quality in gay and lesbian cohabiting couples. *Developmental Psychology* 31, 86–93.

Kurdek, L. A. (2000). Attractions and constraints as determinants of relationship commitment: Longitudinal evidence from gay, lesbian, and heterosexual couples. *Personal Relationships* 7, 245–262.

Lachnit, C. (2001). Giving up gossip. *Workforce* 80 (July), 8.

Laing, M. (1993). Gossip: Does it play a role in the socialization of nurses? *Journal of Nursing Scholarship* 25, 37–43.

Lane, R. C., Koetting, M. G., & Bishop, J. (2002). Silence as communication in psychodynamic psychotherapy. *Clinical Psychology Review* 22 (September), 1091–1104.

Langer, E. J. (1989). *Mindfulness.* Reading, MA: Addison-Wesley.

Lantz, A. (2001). Meetings in a distributed group of experts: Comparing face-to-face, chat and collaborative virtual environments. *Behaviour and Information Technology* 20, 111–117.

Lanzetta, J. T., Cartwright-Smith, J., & Kleck, R. E. (1976). Effects of nonverbal dissimulations on emotional experience and autonomic arousal. *Journal of Personality and Social Psychology* 33, 354–370.

Laroche, C., & deGrace, G. R. (1997). Factors of satisfaction associated with happiness in adults. *Canadian Journal of Counseling* 31, 275–286.

Larsen, R. J., Kasimatis, M., & Frey, K. (1992). Facilitating the furrowed brow: An unobtrusive test of the facial feedback hypothesis applied to unpleasant affect. *Cognition and Emotion* 6, 321–338.

Lau, I., Chiu, C., & Hong, Y. (2001). I know what you know: Assumptions about others' knowledge and their effects on message construction. *Social Cognition* 19, 587–600.

Lauer, C. S. (2003). Listen to this. *Modern Healthcare* 33 (February 10), 34.

Lea, M., & Spears, R. (1995). Love at first byte? Building personal relationships over computer networks. In *Understudied relationships: Off the beaten track,* J. T. Wood & S. Duck (eds.). Thousand Oaks, CA: Sage, pp. 197–233.

Leathers, D., & Eaves, M. H. (2008). *Successful nonverbal communication: Principles and applications,* 4th ed. Boston: Allyn & Bacon.

Leavitt, H. J. (2005). *Top down: Why hierarchies are here to stay and how to manage them more effectively.* Cambridge, MA: Harvard Business School Publishing.

Lederer, W. J. (1984). *Creating a good relationship.* New York: Norton.

Lee, H. O., & Boster, F. J. (1992). Collectivism-individualism in perceptions of speech rate: A cross-cultural comparison. *Journal of Cross-Cultural Psychology* 23, 377–388.

Lee, J. (2005). Romance beckons (in case you missed it). *New York Times* (February 23), B4.

Lee, J. A. (1976). *The colors of love.* New York: Bantam.

Lee, J. A. (1988). Forbidden colors of love: Patterns of love and gay liberation. In *Gay relationships* (pp. 11–32), J. P. DeCecco (ed.). San Francisco: Haworth Press.

Lee, R. M. (2005). Resilience against discrimination: Ethnic identity and other-group orientation as protective factors for Korean Americans. *Journal of Counseling Psychology* 52 (January), 36–44.

Lemonick, M. D. (2005a). A smile doesn't always mean happy. *Time* (January 17), A29.

Lemonick, M. D. (2005b). Stealth attack on evaluation. *Time* (January 31), 53–54.

Lenhart, A., & Madden, M. (2007). Social Networking Websites and teens: An overview. *Pew Internet & American Life Project* (www.pewinternet.org).

Lenhart, A., Madden, M., Macgill, A. R., & Smith, A. (2007). Teens and social media: The use of social media gains a greater foothold in teen life as they embrace the conversational nature of inteaction online media. *Pew Internet & American Life Project.* http://www.pewinternet.org. Accessed May 20, 2008.

Leon, J. J., Philbrick, J. L., Parra, F., Escobedo, E., et al. (1994). Love styles among university students in Mexico. *Psychological Reports* 74, 307–310.

Leung, K. (1987). Some determinants of reactions to procedural models for conflict resolution: A cross-national study. *Journal of Personality and Social Psychology* 53, 898–908.

Leung, S. A. (2001). Editor's introduction. *Asian Journal of Counseling* 8, 107–109.

Levine, D. (2000). Virtual attraction: What rocks your boat. *CyberPsychology and Behavior* 3, 565–573.

Levine, M. (2004). Tell the doctor all your problems, but keep it to less than a minute. *New York Times* (June 1), F6.

Levine, T. R., Beatty, M. J., Limon, S., Hamilton, M. A., Buck, R., & Chory-Assad, R. M. (2004). The dimensionality of the verbal aggressiveness scale. *Communication Monographs* 71 (September), 245–268.

LeVine, R., Bartlett, K. (1984). Pace of life, punctuality, and coronary heart disease in six countries. *Journal of Cross-Cultural Psychology* 15, 233–255.

LeVine, R., Sato, S., Hashimoto, T., & Verma, J. (1994). Love and marriage in eleven cultures. Unpublished manuscript. California State University, Fresno, cited in Hatfield & Rapson (1996).

Levine, T. R., Kim, R. K., Park, H. S., & Hughes, M. (2006). Deception detection accuracy is a predictable linear function of message veracity base-rate: A formal test of Park and

Levine's probability model. *Communication Monographs* 73, 243–260.

Lewin, K. (1947). *Human relations.* New York: Harper & Row.

Lewis, D. (1989). *The secret language of success.* New York: Carroll & Graf.

Lewis, P. H. (1995). The new Internet gatekeepers. *New York Times* (November 13), D1, D6.

Li, H. Z. (1999). Communicating information in conversations: A cross-cultural comparison. *International Journal of Intercultural Relations* 23 (May), 387–409.

Lindblom, K. (2001). Cooperating with Grice: A cross-disciplinary metaperspective on uses of Grice's cooperative principle. *Journal of Pragmatics* 33, 1601–1623.

Lindeman, M., Harakka, T., & Keltikangas-Jarvinen, L. (1997). Age and gender differences in adolescents' reactions to conflict situations: Aggression, prosociality, and withdrawal. *Journal of Youth and Adolescence* 26, 339–351.

Lu, L., & Shih, J. B. (1997). Sources of happiness: A qualitative approach. *Journal of Social Psychology* 137, 181–188.

Lubin, J. S. (2004). How to stop the snubs that demoralize you and your colleagues. *Wall Street Journal* (December 7), B1.

Luft, J. (1984). *Group processes: An introduction to group dynamics,* 3d ed. Palo Alto, CA: Mayfield.

Lukens, J. (1978). Ethnocentric speech. *Ethnic Groups* 2, 35–53.

Lurie, A. (1983). *The language of clothes.* New York: Vintage.

Luscombe, B. (2008, January 28). Why we flirt. *Time,* pp. 62–65.

Lustig, M. W., & Koester, J. (2006). *Intercultural competence: Interpersonal communication across cultures,* 6th ed. Boston: Allyn & Bacon.

Lyman, S. M., & Scott, M. B. (1967). Territoriality: A neglected sociological dimension. *Social Problems* 15, 236–249.

Lyons, A., & Kashima, Y. (2003). How are stereotypes maintained through communication? The influence of stereotype sharedness. *Journal of Personality and Social Psychology* 85 (December), 989–1005.

Ma, K. (1996). *The modern Madame Butterfly: Fantasy and reality in Japanese cross-cultural relationships.* Rutland, VT: Charles E. Tuttle.

Mackey, R. A., Diemer, M. A., & O'Brien, B. A. (2000). Psychological intimacy in the lasting relationships of heterosexual and same-gender couples. *Sex Roles* 43, 201–227.

MacLachlan, J. (1979). What people really think of fast talkers. *Psychology Today* 13, 113–117.

MacMillan, D., & Lehman, P. (2007, November 15). Social networking with the elite. *Business Week* (www.businessweek.com.)

Madon, S., Guyll, M., & Spoth, R. L. (2004). The self-fulfilling prophecy as an intrafamily dynamic. *Journal of Family Psychology* 18, 459–469.

Mahaffey, A. L., Bryan, A., & Hutchison, K. E. (2005). Using startle eye blink to measure the affective component of antigay bias. *Basic and Applied Social Psychology* 27 (March), 37–45.

Main, F., & Oliver, R. (1988). Complementary, symmetrical, and parallel personality priorities as indicators of marital adjustment. *Individual Psychology Journal of Adlerian Theory, Research, and Practice* 44, 324–332.

Malandro, L. A., Barker, L. L., & Barker, D. A. (1989). *Nonverbal communication*, 2d ed. New York: Random House.

Mao, L. R. (1994). Beyond politeness theory: "Face" revisited and renewed. *Journal of Pragmatics* 21, 451–486.

Marano, H. E. (2004). Unconventional wisdom. *Psychology Today* 37 (May/June), 10–11.

Marano, H. E. (2008). The making of a perfectionist. *Psychology Today* 41 (March/April), 80–86.

Marsh, P. (1988). *Eye to eye: How people interact.* Topside, MA: Salem House.

Marshall, E. (1983). *Eye language: Understanding the eloquent eye.* New York: New Trend.

Marshall, L. L., & Rose, P. (1987). Gender, stress, and violence in the adult relationships of a sample of college students. *Journal of Social and Personal Relationships* 4, 229–316.

Marston, P. J., Hecht, M. L., & Robers, T. (1987). True love ways: The subjective experience and communication of romantic love. *Journal of Personal and Social Relationships* 4, 387–407.

Martin, G. N. (1998). Human electroencephalographic (EEG) response to olfactory stimulation: Two experiments using the aroma of food. *International Journal of Psychophysiology* 30, 287–302.

Martin, J. L. (2005). Is power sexy? *American Journal of Sociology* 111 (September), 408–446.

Martin, J. S., & Chaney, L. H. (2008). *Global business etiquette: A guide to international communication and customs.* Westport, CT: Praeger.

Martin, M. M., & Anderson, C. M. (1995). Roommate similarity: Are roommates who are similar in their communication traits more satisfied? *Communication Research Reports* 12, 46–52.

Martin, M. M., & Anderson, C. M. (1998). The cognitive flexibility scale: Three validity studies. *Communication Reports* 11 (winter), 1–9.

Martin, M. M., & Rubin, R. B. (1994). A new measure of cognitive flexibility. *Psychological Reports* 76, 623–626.

Martin, M. M., & Rubin, R. B. (1998). Affinity-seeking in initial interactions. *Southern Communication Journal* 63, 131–143.

Marwell, G., & Schmitt, D. R. (1967). Dimensions of compliance-gaining behavior: An empirical analysis. *Sociometry* 39, 350–364.

Marwell, G., & Schmitt, D. R. (1990). An introduction. In *Seeking compliance: The production of interpersonal influence messages,* J. P. Dillard (ed.). Scottsdale, AZ.: Gorsuch Scarisbrick, pp. 3–5.

Maslow, A., & Mintz, N. L. (1956). Effects of esthetic surroundings: I. Initial effects of three esthetic conditions upon perceiving energy and well-being in faces. *Journal of Psychology* 41, 247–254.

Masuda, T., Ellsworth, P. C., Mesquita, B., Leu, J., Tanida, S., & van de Veerdonk, E. (2008). Placing the face in context: Cultural differences in the perception of facial emotion. *Journal of Personality and Social Psychology* 94, 365–381.

Matsumoto, D. (1991). Cultural influences on facial expressions of emotion. *Southern Communication Journal* 56, 128–137.

Matsumoto, D. (1994). *People: Psychology from a cultural perspective.* Pacific Grove, CA: Brooks/Cole.

Matsumoto, D. (1996). *Culture and psychology.* Pacific Grove, CA: Brooks/Cole.

Matsumoto, D. (2006). Culture and nonverbal behavior. In *The Sage handbook of nonverbal communication* (pp. 219–236), V. Manusov & M. L. Patterson (eds.). Thousand Oaks, CA: Sage.

Matsumoto, D., & Kudoh, T. (1993). American-Japanese cultural differences in attributions of personality based on smiles. *Journal of Nonverbal Behavior* 17, 231–243.

Matsumoto, D., & Yoo, S. H. (2005). Culture and applied nonverbal communication. In *Applications of nonverbal communication* (pp. 259–277), R. E. Riggio & R. S. Feldman (eds.). Mahwah, NJ: Erlbaum.

Matsumoto, D., Yoo, S. H., Hirayama, S., & Petrova, G. (2005). Development and validation of a measure of display rule knowledge: The display rule assessment inventory. *Emotion* 5, 23–40.

Maynard, H. E. (1963). How to become a better premise detective. *Public Relations Journal* 19, 20–22.

McBroom, W. H., & Reed, F. W. (1992). Toward a reconceptualization of attitude-behavior consistency. Special Issue. Theoretical advances in social psychology. *Social Psychology Quarterly* 55, 205–216.

McCroskey, J. C. (1998). *Why we communicate the ways we do: A communibiological perspective.* Boston: Allyn & Bacon.

McCroskey, J. C. (2007). *An introduction to rhetorical communication,* 9th ed. Boston: Allyn & Bacon.

McCroskey, J. C., & Wheeless, L. (1976). *Introduction to human communication.* Boston: Allyn & Bacon.

McDevitt, M., Kiousis, S., & Wahl-Jorgensen, K. (2003). Spiral of moderation: Opinion expression in computer-mediated discussion. *International Journal of Public Opinion Research* 15 (winter), 454–470.

McDonald, E. J., McCabe, K., Yeh, M., Lau, A., Garland, A., & Hough, R. L. (2005). Cultural affiliation and self-esteem as predictors of internalizing symptoms among Mexican American adolescents. *Journal of Clinical Child and Adolescent Psychology* 34 (February), 163–171.

McGill, M. E. (1985). *The McGill report on male intimacy.* New York: Harper & Row.

McLaughlin, M. L. (1984). *Conversation: How talk is organized.* Thousand Oaks, CA: Sage.

McLaughlin, M. L., Cody, M. L., & Robey, C. S. (1980). Situational influences on the selection of strategies to resist compliance-gaining attempts. *Human Communication Research* 1, 14–36.

McNamee, S., & Gergen, K. J., eds. (1999). *Relational responsibility: Resources for sustainable dialogue.* Thousand Oaks, CA: Sage.

Medora, N. P., Larson, J. H., Hortascu, N., & Dave, P. (2002). Perceived attitudes towards romanticism: A cross-cultural study of American, Asian-Indian, and Turkish young adults. *Journal of Comparative Family Studies,* 33 (spring), 155–178.

Meeks, B. S., Hendrick, S. S., & Hendrick, C. (1998). Communication, love and relationship satisfaction. *Journal of Social and Personal Relationships* 15, 755–773.

Mehl, M. R., Vazire, S., Ramirez-Esparza, N., Slatcher, R. B., & Pennebaker, J. W. (2007, July). Are women really more talkative than men? *Science* 6, 82.

Merton, R. K. (1957). *Social theory and social structure.* New York: Free Press.

Messick, R. M., & Cook, K. S., eds. (1983). *Equity theory: Psychological and sociological perspectives.* New York: Praeger.

Messmer, M. (1999). Skills for a new millennium: Accounting and financial professionals. *Strategic Finance Magazine* (August), 10ff.

Metts, S., & Cupach, W. R. (2008). Face theory. In *Engaging theories in interpersonal communication: Multiple perspectives* (pp. 203–214), L. A. Baxter & D. O. Braithwaite (eds.). Los Angeles: Sage.

Metts, S., & Planalp, S. (2002). Emotional communication. In *Handbook of Interpersonal Communication,* 3d ed., (pp. 339–373), M. L. Knapp & J. A. Daly (eds.). Thousand Oaks, CA: Sage.

Midooka, K. (1990). Characteristics of Japanese style communication. *Media, Culture and Society* 12, 477–489.

Miller, G. R. (1978). The current state of theory and research in interpersonal communication. *Human Communication Research* 4, 164–178.

Miller, G. R. (1990). Interpersonal communication. In *Human communication: Theory and research* (pp. 91–122), G. L. Dahnke & G. W. Clatterbuck (eds.). Belmont, CA: Wadsworth.

Miller, G. R., & Parks, M. R. (1982). Communication in dissolving relationships. In *Personal relationships 4. Dissolving personal relationships,* S. Duck (ed.). New York: Academic Press, pp. 127–154.

Mintz, N. L. (1956). Effects of esthetic surroundings: II. Prolonged and repeated experience in a beautiful and ugly room. *Journal of Psychology* 41, 459–466.

Moghaddam, F. M., Taylor, D. M., & Wright, S. C. (1993). *Social psychology in cross-cultural perspective.* New York: W. H. Freeman.

Molloy, J. (1981). *Molloy's live for success.* New York: Bantam.

Monahan, J. L. (1998). I don't know it but I like you. *Human Communication Research* 24, 480–500.

Mongeau, P. A., & Henningsen, M. L. M. (2008). Stage theories of relationship development. In *Engaging theories in interpersonal communication: Multiple perspectives* (pp. 363–375), L. A. Baxter & D. O. Braithwaite (eds.). Los Angeles: Sage.

Monin, B. (2003). The warm glow heuristic: When liking leads to familiarity. *Journal of Personality and Social Psychology* 85 (December), 1035–1048.

Monk, A., Fellas, E., & Ley, E. (2004). Hearing only one side of normal and mobile phone conversations. *Behaviour & Information Technology* 23 (September–October), 301–306.

Moon, D. G. (1996). Concepts of "culture": Implications for intercultural communication research. *Communication Quarterly* 44, 70–84.

Morahan-Martin, J., & Schumacher, P. (2003). Loneliness and social uses of the Internet. *Computers in Human Behavior* 19 (November), 659–671.

Morgan, R. (2008, March 16). A crash course in online gossip. *New York Times,* Styles, p. 7.

Morreale, S. P., & Pearson, J. C. (2008). Why communication education is important: The centrality of the discipline in the 21st century. *Communication Education* 57 (April), 224–240.

Morreale, S. P., Osborn, M. M., & Pearson, J. C. (2000). Why communication is important: A rationale for the centrality of the study of communication. *Journal of the Association for Communication Administration* 29 (January), 1–25.

Morrill, C. (1992). Vengeance among executives. *Virginia Review of Sociology* 1, 51–76.

Morris, D. (1977). *Manwatching: A field guide to human behavior.* New York: Abrams.

Morris, D. (2002). *Peoplewatching.* New York: Vintage.

Morrison, E. W., Chen, Y., & Salgado, S. R. (2004). Cultural differences in newcomer feedback seeking: A comparison of the United States and Hong Kong. *Applied Psychology: An International Review* 53 (January), 1–22.

Morrison, R. (2004). Informal relationships in the workplace: Associations with job satisfaction, organizational commitment and turnover intentions. *New Zealand Journal of Psychology* 33, 114–128.

Morrow, G. D., Clark, E. M., & Brock, K. F. (1995). Individual and partner love styles: Implications for the quality of romantic involvements. *Journal of Social and Personal Relationships* 12, 363–387.

Mosteller, T. (2008). *Relativism: A guide for the perplexed.* London: Continuum.

Motley, M. T. (1990a). On whether one can(not) not communicate: An examination via traditional communication postulates. *Western Journal of Speech Communication* 54, 1–20.

Motley, M. T. (1990b). Communication as interaction: A reply to Beach and Bavelas. *Western Journal of Speech Communication* 54, 613–623.

Mottet, T., & Richmond, V. P. (1998). Verbal approach and avoidance items. *Communication Quarterly* 46, 25–40.

Mullen, C. A. (2005). *Mentorship primer.* New York: Peter Lang.

Murstein, B. I., Merighi, J. R., & Vyse, S. A. (1991). Love styles in the United States and France: A cross-cultural comparison. *Journal of Social and Clinical Psychology* 10, 37–46.

Myers, S. A., & Zhong, M. (2004). Perceived Chinese instructor use of affinity-seeking strategies and Chinese college student motivation. *Journal of Intercultural Communication Research* 33 (September–December), 119–130.

Neff, K. D., & Harter, S. (2002). The authenticity of conflict resolutions among adult couples: Does women's other-oriented behavior reflect their true selves? *Sex Roles* 47 (November), 403–417.

Nelson, P. E., Pearson, J. C., & Kurylo, A. (2008). Developing an intellectual communication. In *Getting the most from your graduate education in communication: A student's handbook*, Morreale, S., & Arneson, P. (eds.). Washington, DC: National Communication Association.

Neugarten, B. (1979). Time, age, and the life cycle. *American Journal of Psychiatry* 136, 887–894.

Neuliep, J. W., & Grohskopf, E. L. (2000). Uncertainty reduction and communication satisfaction during initial interaction: An initial test and replication of a new axiom. *Communication Reports* 13 (summer), 67–77.

Neuliep, J. W., & McCroskey, J. C. (1997). The development of a U.S. and generalized ethnocentrism scale. *Communication Research Reports* 14, 385–398.

Ng, S. H., He, A., & Loong, C. (2004). Tri-generational family conversations: Communication accommodation and brokering. *British Journal of Social Psychology* 43 (September), 449–464.

Nicholas, C. L. (2004). Gaydar: Eye-gaze as identity recognition among gay men and lesbians. *Sexuality and Culture: An Interdisciplinary Quarterly* 8 (winter), 60–86.

Nicolai, J., & Demmel, R. (2007). The impact of gender stereotypes on the evaluation of general practitioners' communication skills: An experimental study using transcripts of physician–patient encounters. *Patient Education and Counseling* 69 (December), 200–205.

Nicotera, A. M., & Rancer, A. S. (1994). The influence of sex on self-perceptions and social stereotyping of aggressive communication predispositions. *Western Journal of Communication* 58, 283–307.

Niemeier, S., & Dirven, R. (eds.). (2000). *Evidence for linguistic relativity.* Philadelphia: John Benjamins.

Noble, B. P. (1994, August 14). The gender wars: Talking peace. *New York Times,* p. 21.

Noelle-Neumann, E. (1973). Return to the concept of powerful mass media. In *Studies in broadcasting: An international annual of broadcasting science,* H. Eguchi & K. Sata (eds.). Tokyo: Nippon Hoso Kyokai, pp. 67–112.

Noelle-Neumann, E. (1980). Mass media and social change in developed societies. In *Mass communication review yearbook,* Vol. 1, G. C. Wilhoit & H. de Bock (eds.). Thousand Oaks, CA: Sage, pp. 657–678.

Noelle-Neumann, E. (1991). The theory of public opinion: The concept of the spiral of silence. *Communication yearbook/14,* J. A. Anderson (ed.). Thousand Oaks, CA: Sage, pp. 256–287.

Noller, P., & Fitzpatrick, M. A. (1993). *Communication in family relationships.* Englewood Cliffs, NJ: Prentice-Hall.

Norton, M. I., Frost, J. H., & Ariely, D. (2007). Less is more: The lure of ambiguity, or why familiarity breeds contempt. *Journal of Personality and Social Psychology* 92 (January), 97–105.

Oatley, K., & Duncan, E. (1994). The experience of emotions in everyday life. *Cognition and Emotion* 8, 369–381.

Ober, C., Weitkamp, L. R., Cox, N., Dytch, H., Kostyu, D., & Elias, S. (1997). *American Journal of Human Genetics* 61, 494–496.

Oberg, K. (1960). Cultural shock: Adjustment to new cultural environments. *Practical Anthropology* 7, 177–182.

Oetzel, J. G., & Ting-Toomey, S. (2003). Face concerns in interpersonal conflict: A cross-cultural empirical test of the face negotiation theory. *Communication Research* 30 (December), 599–624.

O'Hair, D., Cody, M. J., Goss, B., & Krayer, K. J. (1988). The effect of gender, deceit orientation and communicator style on macro-assessments of honesty. *Communication Quarterly* 36, 77–93.

O'Hair, D., Cody, M. J., & McLaughlin, M. L. (1981). Prepared lies, spontaneous lies, Machiavellianism, and nonverbal communication. *Human Communication Research* 7, 325–339.

O'Hair, M. J., Cody, M. J., & O'Hair, D. (1991). The impact of situational dimensions on compliance-resisting strategies: A comparison of methods. *Communication Quarterly* 39, 226–240.

Okrent, D. (2005). Numbed by the numbers, when they just don't add up. *New York Times* (January 23), Section 4, 2.

Olson, E. (2002). Switzerland tells its men: Wash that pot! Mop that floor! *New York Times,* A14.

Olson, E. (2006, April 6). Better not miss the buss. *New York Times,* pp. G1–G2.

Onishi, N. (2005). In Japan crash, time obsession may be culprit. *New York Times* (April 27), A1, A9.

Oswald, D. L., Clark, E. M., & Kelly, C. M. (2004). Friendship maintenance: An analysis of individual and dyad behaviors. *Journal of Social and Clinical Psychology* 23 (June), 413–441.

Owens, T. J., Stryker, S., & Goodman, N. (eds.) (2002). *Extending self-esteem research: Sociological and psychological currents.* Cambridge, MA: Cambridge University Press.

Palmer, M. T. (1989). Controlling conversations: Turns, topics, and interpersonal control. *Communication Monographs* 56, 1–18.

Parker, J. G. (2004). Planning and communication crucial to preventing workplace violence. *Safety and Health* 170 (September), 58–61.

Parker, R. G., & Parrott, R. (1995). Patterns of self-disclosure across social support networks: Elderly, middle-aged, and young adults. *International Journal of Aging and Human Development* 41, 281–297.

Parks, M. R. (1995). Webs of influence in interpersonal relationships. In *Communication and social influence processes,* C. R. Berger & M. E. Burgoon (eds.). East Lansing: Michigan State University Press, pp. 155–178.

Parks, M. R., & Floyd, K. (1996). Making friends in cyberspace. *Journal of Communication* 46, 80–97.

Pasley, K., Kerpelman, J., & Guilbert, D. E. (2001). Gendered conflict, identity disruption, and marital instability: Expanding Gottman's model. *Journal of Personal and Social Relationships* 18, 5–27.

Patterson, C. (2000). Family relationships of lesbians and gay men. *Journal of Marriage and the Family* 62, 1052–1067.

Paul, A. M. (2001). Self-help: Shattering the myths. *Psychology Today* 34, 60ff.

Pearson, J. C. (1993). *Communication in the family,* 2d ed. Boston: Allyn & Bacon.

Pearson, J. C., & Spitzberg, B. H. (1990). *Interpersonal communication: Concepts, components, and contexts,* 2d ed. Dubuque, IA: William C. Brown.

Pearson, J. C., Turner, L. H., & Todd-Mancillas, W. (1991). *Gender and communication,* 2d ed. Dubuque, IA: William C. Brown.

Pearson, J. C., West, R., & Turner, L. H. (1995). *Gender and communication,* 3d ed. Dubuque, IA: William C. Brown.

Penfield, J., ed. (1987). *Women and language in transition.* Albany: State University of New York Press.

Pennebacker, J. W. (1991). *Opening up: The healing power of confiding in others.* New York: Morrow.

Peplau, L. A. (1988). Research on homosexual couples: An overview. In *Gay relationships,* J. DeCecco (ed.). New York: Harrington Park Press, pp. 33–40.

Peterson, C. C. (1996). The ticking of the social clock: Adults' beliefs about the timing of transition events. *International Journal of Aging and Human Development* 42, 189–203.

Petrocelli, W., & Repa, B. K. (1992). *Sexual harassment on the job.* Berkeley, CA: Nolo Press.

Pinker, S. (1994). *The language instinct: How the mind creates language.* New York: Morrow.

Plaks, J. E., Grant, H., & Dweck, C. S. (2005). Violations of implicit theories and the sense of prediction and control: Implications for motivated person perception. *Journal of Personality and Social Psychology* 88 (February), 245–262.

Plutchik, R. (1980). *Emotion: A psycho-evolutionary synthesis.* New York: Harper & Row.

Pollack, A. (1996). Happy in the East (^—^) or smiling (:—) in the West. *New York Times* (August 12), D5.

Pornpitakpan, C. (2003). The effect of personality traits and perceived cultural similarity on attraction. *Journal of International Consumer Marketing* 15, 5–30.

Porter, R. H., & Moore, J. D. (1981). Human kin recognition by olfactory cues. *Physiology and Behavior* 27, 493–495.

Porter, S., Brit, A. R., Yuille, J. C., & Lehman, D. R. (2000). Negotiating false memories: Interviewer and rememberer

characteristics relate to memory distortion. *Psychological Science* 11 (November), 507–510.

Powell, M. (2005). *Behave yourself!: The essential guide to international etiquette.* Guilford, CT: Globe Pequot.

Prosky, P. S. (1992). Complementary and symmetrical couples. *Family Therapy* 19, 215–221.

Prusank, D. T., Duran, R. L., & DeLillo, D. A. (1993). Interpersonal relationships in women's magazines: Dating and relating in the 1970s and 1980s. *Journal of Social and Personal Relationships* 10, 307–320.

Rabinowitz, F. E. (1991). The male-to-male embrace: Breaking the touch taboo in a men's therapy group. *Journal of Counseling and Development* 69, 574–576.

Radford, M. H., Mann, L., Ohta, Y., & Nakane, Y. (1993). Differences between Australian and Japanese students in decisional self-esteem, decisional stress, and coping styles. *Journal of Cross-Cultural Psychology* 24, 284–297.

Rancer, A. S. (1998). Argumentativeness. In *Communication and Personality: Trait Perspectives,* J. C. McCroskey, J. A. Daly, M. M. Martin, & M. J. Beatty (eds.). Cresskill, NJ: Hampton Press, pp. 149–170.

Rancer, A. S., & Avtgis, T. A. (2006). *Argumentative and aggressive communication: Theory, research, and application.* Thousand Oaks, CA: Sage.

Raney, R. F. (2000). Study finds Internet of social benefit to users. *New York Times* (May 11), G7.

Rappaport, H., Enrich, K., & Wilson, A. (1985). Relation between ego identity and temporal perspective. *Journal of Personality and Social Psychology* 48, 1609–1620.

Rapsa, R., & Cusack, J. (1990). Psychiatric implications of tattoos. *American Family Physician* 41, 1481–1486.

Raven, B., Centers, C., & Rodrigues, A. (1975). The bases of conjugal power. In *Power in families,* R. E. Cromwell & D. H. Olson (eds.). New York: Halsted Press, pp. 217–234.

Raven, B. H., Schwarzwald, J., & Koslowsky, M. (1998). Conceptualizing and measuring a power/interaction model of interpersonal influence. *Journal of Applied Social Psychology* 28, 307–332.

Rawlins, W. K. (1983). Negotiating close friendship: The dialectic of conjunctive freedoms. *Human Communication Research* 9, 255–266.

Rawlins, W. K. (1989). A dialectical analysis of the tensions, functions, and strategic challenges of communication in young adult friendships. In *Communication yearbook 12,* (pp. 157–189), J. A. Andersen (ed.), Thousand Oaks, CA: Sage.

Rawlins, W. K. (1992). *Friendship matters: Communication, dialectics, and the life course.* Hawthorne, NY: Aldine DeGruyter.

Read, A. W. (2004). Language revision by deletion of absolutisms. *ETC: A Review of General Semantics* 61 (December), 456–462.

Reardon, K. K. (1987). *Where minds meet: Interpersonal communication.* Belmont, CA: Wadsworth.

Rector, M., & Neiva, E. (1996). Communication and personal relationships in Brazil. In *Communication in personal relationships across cultures,* W. B. Gudykunst, S. Ting-Toomey, & T. Nishida (eds.). Thousand Oaks, CA: Sage, pp. 156–173.

Reed, M. D. (1993, Fall). Sudden death and bereavement outcomes: The impact of resources on grief, symptomatology and detachment. *Suicide and Life-Threatening Behavior* 23, 204–220.

Regan, P. C., Durvasula, R., Howell, L., Ureno, O., & Rea, M. (2004). Gender, ethnicity, and the developmental timing of first sexual and romantic experiences. *Social Behavior and Personality: An International Journal* 32 (November), 667–676.

Regan, P. C., Kocan, E. R., & Whitlock, T. (1998). Ain't love grand! A prototype analysis of the concept of romantic love. *Journal of Social and Personal Relationships* 15, 411–420.

Reiner, D., & Blanton, K. (1997). *Person to person on the Internet.* Boston: AP Professional.

Reisenzein, R. (1983). The Schachter theory of emotion: Two decades later. *Psychological Bulletin* 94, 239–264.

Reisman, J. (1979). *Anatomy of friendship.* Lexington, MA: Lewis.

Reisman, J. M. (1981). Adult friendships. In *Personal relationships. 2: Developing personal relationships,* S. Duck & R. Gilmour (eds.). New York: Academic Press, pp. 205–230.

Remland, M. S. (2006). Uses and consequences of nonverbal communication in the context of organizational life. In *The Sage handbook of nonverbal communication* (pp. 501–519), V. Manusov & M. L. Patterson (eds.). Thousand Oaks, CA: Sage.

Rhee, K. Y., & Kim, W-B (2004). The adoption and use of the Internet in South Korea. *Journal of Computer Mediated Communication* 9 (4, July).

Rhee, S., Chang, J., & Rhee, J. (2003). Acculturation, communication patterns, and self-esteem among Asian and Caucasian American adolescents. *Adolescence* 38 (winter), 749–768.

Rice, M. (2007). Domestic violence. *National Center for PTSD Fact Sheet.* http://www.ncptsd.va.gov/ncmain/ncdocs/fact_shts/fs_domestic_violence.html. Accessed May 20, 2008.

Rich, A. L. (1974). *Interracial communication.* New York: Harper & Row.

Richards, I. A. (1951). Communication between men: The meaning of language. In *Cybernetics, Transactions of the Eighth Conference,* Heinz von Foerster (ed.).

Richmond, V. P., Davis, L. M., Saylor, K., & McCroskey, J. C. (1984). Power strategies in organizations: Communication techniques and messages. *Human Communication Research* 11, 85–108.

Richmond, V. P., & McCroskey, J. C. (1984). Power in the classroom II: Power and learning. *Communication Education* 33, 125–136.

Richmond, V. P., McCroskey, J. C., & Hickson, M. L. (2008). *Nonverbal behavior in interpersonal relations,* 6th ed. Boston: Allyn & Bacon.

Richmond, V. P., Smith, R., Heisel, A., & McCroskey, J. C. (2001). Nonverbal immediacy in the physician/patient relationship. *Communication Research Reports* 18, 211–216.

Riggio, R. E. (1987). *The charisma quotient.* New York: Dodd, Mead.

Riggio, R. E., & Feldman, R. S. (eds.). (2005). *Applications of nonverbal communication.* Mahwah, NJ: Erlbaum.

Rivlin, G. (2005). Hate Messages on Google Site Draw Concern. *New York Times* (February 7), C1, C7.

Roeher Institute (1995). *Harm's way: The many faces of violence and abuse against persons with disabilities.* North York (Ontario): Roeher Institute.

Rogers, C. (1970). *Carl Rogers on encounter groups.* New York: Harrow Books.

Rogers, C., & Farson, R. (1981). Active listening. In *Communication: Concepts and Processes,* 3d ed., J. DeVito (ed.). Englewood Cliffs, NJ: Prentice-Hall, pp. 137–147.

Rohlfing, M. E. (1995). "Doesn't anybody stay in one place anymore?" An exploration of the under-studied phenomenon of long-distance relationships. In *Under-studied relationships: Off the beaten track,* J. T. Wood & S. Duck (eds.). Thousand Oaks, CA: Sage, pp. 173–196.

Rokach, A. (1998). The relation of cultural background to the causes of loneliness. *Journal of Social and Clinical Psychology* 17, 75–88.

Rokach, A., & Brock, H. (1995). The effects of gender, marital status, and the chronicity and immediacy of loneliness. *Journal of Social Behavior and Personality* 19, 833–848.

Roloff, M. E., & Solomon, D. H. (2002). Conditions under which relational commitment leads to expressing or withholding relational complaints. *International Journal of Conflict Management* 13, 276–291.

Ronfeldt, H. M., Kimerling, R., & Arias, I. (1998). Satisfaction with relationship power and the perpetration of dating violence. *Journal of Marriage and the Family* 60 (February), 70–78.

Rosen, E. (1998). Think like a shrink. *Psychology Today* (October), 54–59.

Rosenbaum, M. E. (1986). The repulsion hypothesis. On the nondevelopment of relationships. *Journal of Personality and Social Psychology* 51, 1156–1166.

Rosengren, A., Orth-Gomér, K., Wedel, H., & Wilhelmsen, L. (1993). Stressful life events, social support, and mortality in men born in 1933. *British Medical Journal* (October 19). Cited in Goleman (1995a).

Rosenthal, R. (2002). The Pygmalion effect and its mediating mechanism. In *Improving academic achievement: Impact of psychological factors on education* (pp. 25–36), J. Aronson (ed.). San Diego, CA: Academic Press.

Rowland-Morin, P. A., & Carroll, J. G. (1990). Verbal communication skills and patient satisfaction: A study of doctor-patient interviews. *Evaluation and the Health Professions* 13, 168–185.

Ruben, B. D. (1985). Human communication and cross-cultural effectiveness. In *Intercultural Communication: A Reader,* 4th ed., L. A. Samovar & R. E. Porter (eds.). Belmont, CA: Wadsworth, pp. 338–346.

Rubenstein, C. (1993). Fighting sexual harassment in schools. *New York Times* (June 10), C8.

Rubin, D. C., Groth, E., & Goldsmith, D. J. (1984). Olfactory cues of autobiographical memory. *American Journal of Psychology* 97, 493–507.

Rubin, R. B., & Graham, E. E. (1988). Communication correlates of college success: An exploratory investigation. *Communication Education* 37, 14–27.

Rubin, R. B., & Martin, M. M. (1994). Development of a measure of interpersonal communication competence. *Communication Research Reports* 11, 33–44.

Rubin, R. B., & McHugh, M. (1987). Development of parasocial interaction relationships. *Journal of Broadcasting and Electronic Media* 31, 279–292.

Rubin, Z. (1973). *Liking and loving: An invitation to social psychology.* New York: Holt, Rinehart & Winston.

Rusbult, C. E., & Buunk, B. P. (1993). Commitment processes in close relationships: An interdependence analysis. *Journal of Social and Personal Relationships* 10, 175–204.

Rushe, R. H. (1996). Tactics of power and influence in violent marriages. *Dissertation abstracts international: Section B: The Sciences and Engineering* (University of Washington), 57, 1453.

Rydell, R. J., McConnell, A. R., & Bringle, R. G. (2004). Jealousy and commitment: Perceived threat and the effect of relationship alternatives. *Personal Relationships* 11 (December), 451–468.

Sabatelli, R. M., & Pearce, J. (1986). Exploring marital expectations. *Journal of Social and Personal Relationships* 3, 307–321.

Sagrestano, L. M., Heavey, C. L., & Christensen, A. (2006). Individual differences versus social structural approaches to explaining demand–withdrawal and social influence behaviors. In *Sex differences and similarities in communication*, 2d ed. (pp. 379–395), K. Dindia & D. J. Canary (eds.). Mahwah, NJ: Erlbaum.

Sagula, D., & Rice, K. G. (2004). The effectiveness of mindfulness training on the grieving process and emotional well-being of chronic pain patients. *Journal of Clinical Psychology in Medical Settings* 11 (December), 333–342.

Sahlstein, E. M. (2004). Relating at a distance: Negotiating being together and being apart in long-distance relationships. *Journal of Social and Personal Relationships* 21 (October), 689–710.

Samter, W. (2004). Friendship interaction skills across the life span. In *Handbook of communication and social interaction skills* (pp. 637–684), J. O. Greene & B. R. Burleson (eds.). Mahwah, NJ: Lawrence Erlbaum.

Samter, W., & Cupach, W. R. (1998). Friendly fire: Topics variations in conflict among same- and cross-sex friends. *Communication Studies* 49, 121–138.

Sanders, J. A., Wiseman, R. L., & Matz, S. I. (1991). Uncertainty reduction in acquaintance relationships in Ghana and the United States. In *Cross-cultural interpersonal communication*, S. Ting-Toomey & F. Korzenny (eds.). Thousand Oaks, CA: Sage, pp. 79–98.

Sapadin, L. A. (1988). Friendship and gender: Perspectives of professional men and women. *Journal of Social and Personal Relationships* 5, 387–403.

Sarwer, D. B., Kalichman, S. C., Johnson, J. R., Early, J., et al. (1993). Sexual aggression and love styles: An exploratory study. *Archives of Sexual Behavior* 22, 265–275.

Satir, V. (1983). *Conjoint Family Therapy,* 3d ed. Palo Alto, CA: Science and Behavior Books.

Savitsky, K., Epley, N., & Gilovich, T. (2001). Do others judge us as harshly as we think? Overestimating the impact of our failures, shortcomings, and mishaps. *Journal of Personality and Social Psychology* 81 (July), 44–56.

Scandura, T. (1992). Mentorship and career mobility: An empirical investigation. *Journal of Organizational Behavior* 13, 169–174.

Schaap, C., Buunk, B., & Kerkstra, A. (1988). Marital conflict resolution. In *Perspectives on marital interaction,* P. Noller & M. A. Fitzpatrick (eds.). Philadelphia: Multilingual Matters, pp. 203–244.

Schachter, S. (1971). *Emotion, obesity and crime.* New York: Academic Press.

Schegloff, E. (1982). Discourses as an interactional achievement: Some uses of "uh huh" and other things that come between sentences. In *Georgetown University roundtable on language and linguistics,* Deborah Tannen (ed.). Washington, DC: Georgetown University Press, pp. 71–93.

Scheufele, D. A., & Moy, P. (2000). Twenty-five years of the spiral of silence: A conceptual review and empirical outlook. *International Journal of Public Opinion Research* 12 (spring), 3–28.

Schmidt, T. O., & Cornelius, R. R. (1987). Self-disclosure in everyday life. *Journal of Social and Personal Relationships* 4, 365–373.

Schoeneman, T. J., & Rubanowitz, E. E. (1985). Attributions in the advice columns: Actors and observers, causes and reasons. *Personality and Social Psychology Bulletin* 11, 315–325.

Schott, G., & Selwyn, N. (2000). Examining the "male, antisocial" stereotype of high computer users. *Journal of Educational Computing Research* 23, 291–303.

Schrodt, P. (2003). Students' appraisals of instructors as a function of students' perceptions of instructors' aggressive communication. *Communication Education* 52 (April), 106–121.

Schutz, A. (1999). It was your fault! Self-serving biases in autobiographical accounts of conflicts in married couples. *Journal of Social and Personal Relationships* 16, 193–208.

Schwartz, E. (2005). Watch what you say. *InfoWorld* 27 (February 28), 8.

Schwartz, M., and the Task Force on Bias-Free Language of the Association of American University Presses (1995). *Guidelines for bias-free writing.* Bloomington: Indiana University Press.

Scott, M. L., & Lyman, S. M. (1968). Accounts. *American Sociological Review* 33, 46–62.

Seiter, J. S. (2007). Ingratiation and gratuity: The effect of complimenting customers on tipping behavior in restaurants. *Journal of Applied Social Psychology* 37 (March), 478–485.

Seiter, J. S., & Sandry, A. (2003). Pierced for success?: The effects of ear and nose piercing on perceptions of job candidates' credibility, attractiveness, and hirability. *Communication Research Reports* 20 (Fall), 287–298.

Serewicz, M. C. M., & Petronio, S. (2007). Communication privacy management theory. In *Explaining communication: Contemporary theories and exemplars* (pp. 257–274), B. B. Whaley, & W. Samter (eds.). Mahwah, NJ: Erlbaum.

Severin, W. J. & Tankard, J. W., Jr. (2001). *Communication theories: Origins, methods, and uses in the mass media.* Boston: Allyn & Bacon.

Shaw, L. H., & Grant, L. M. (2002). Users divided? Exploring the gender gap in Internet use. *CyberPsychology & Behavior* 5 (December), 517–527.

Sheese, B. E., Brown, E. L, & Graziano, W. G. (2004). Emotional expression in cyberspace: Searching for moderators of the Pennebaker disclosure effect via e-mail. *Health Psychology* 23 (September), 457–464.

Shelton, J. N., & Richeson, J. A. (2005). Intergroup contact and pluralistic ignorance. *Journal of Personality and Social Psychology* 88 (January), 91–107.

Sheppard, J. A., & Strathman, A. J. (1989). Attractiveness and height: The role of stature in dating preferences, frequency of dating, and perceptions of attractiveness. *Personality and Social Psychology* 15, 617–627.

Shibazaki, K., & Brennan, K. A. (1998). When birds of different features flock together: A preliminary comparison of intra-ethnic and inter-ethnic dating relationships. *Journal of Social and Personal Relationships* 15, 248–256.

Shimanoff, S. (1980). *Communication rules: Theory and research.* Thousand Oaks, CA: Sage.

Shirley, J. A., Powers, W. G., & Sawyer, C. R. (2007). Psychologically abusive relationships and self-disclosure orientations. *Human Communication* 10, 289–302.

Short, J., Williams, E., & Christie, B. (1976). *The social psychology of telecommunication.* London: Wiley.

Siavelis, R. L., & Lamke, L. K. (1992). Instrumentalness and expressiveness: Predictors of heterosexual relationship satisfaction. *Sex Roles* 26, 149–159.

Siegert, J. R., & Stamp, G. H. (1994). "Our first big fight" as a milestone in the development of close relationships. *Communication Monographs* 61, 345–360.

Silverman, T. (2001). Expanding community: The Internet and relational theory. *Community, Work and Family* 4, 231–237.

Singelis, T. M. (1994). The measurement of independent and interdependent self-construals. *Personality and Social Psychology Bulletin* 20, 580–591.

Singh, N., & Pereira, A. (2005). *The culturally customized web site.* Oxford, UK: Elsevier Butterworth-Heinemann.

Sizemore, D. S. (2004). Ethnic inclusion and exclusion. *Journal of Contemporary Ethnography* 33 (October), 534–570.

Skinner, M. (2002). In search of feedback. *Executive Excellence* (June), 18.

Slade, M. (1995). We forgot to write a headline. But it's not our fault. *New York Times* (February 19), 5.

Smith, A., & Williams, K. D. (2004). R U There? Ostracism by cell phone text messages. *Group Dynamics* 8 (December), 291–301.

Smith, B. (1996). Care and feeding of the office grapevine. *Management Review* 85 (February), 6.

Smith, C. S. (2002). Beware of green hats in China and other cross-cultural faux pas. *New York Times* (April 30), C11.

Smith, D. (2003, December 2). Doctors cultivate a skill: Listening. *New York Times*, p. 6.

Smith, M. H. (2003). Body adornment: Know the limits. *Nursing Management* 34 (February), 22–23.

Smith, R. (2004). The teaching of communication skills may be misguided. *British Medical Journal* 328 (April 10), 1–2.

Smith, S. M., & Shaffer, D. R. (1991). Celerity and cajolery: Rapid speech may promote or inhibit persuasion through its impact on message elaboration. *Personality and Social Psychology Bulletin* 17 (December), 663–669.

Smith, S. M., & Shaffer, D. R. (1995). Speed of speech and persuasion: Evidence for multiple effects. *Personality and Social Psychology Bulletin* 21 (October), 1051–1060.

Snyder, C. R. (1984). Excuses, excuses. *Psychology Today* 18, 50–55.

Snyder, C. R., Higgins, R. L., and Stucky, R. J. (1983). *Excuses: Masquerades in search of grace.* New York: Wiley.

Snyder, M. (1992). A gender-informed model of couple and family therapy: Relationship enhancement therapy. *Contemporary Family Therapy: An International Journal* 14 (February), 15–31.

Solomon, D. H., & Samp, J. A. (1998). Power and problem appraisal: Perceptual foundations of the chilling effect in dating relationships. *Journal of Social and Personal Relationships* 15, 191–209.

Sommer, K. L., Williams, K. D., Ciarocco, N. J., & Baumeister, R. F. (2001). When silence speaks louder than words: Explorations into the intrapsychic and interpersonal consequences of social ostracism. *Basic and Applied Social Psychology* 23, 225–243.

Sommers, S. (1984). Reported emotions and conventions of emotionality among college students. *Journal of Personality and Social Psychology* 46, 207–215.

Sorenson, P. S., Hawkins, K., & Sorenson, R. L. (1995). Gender, psychological type and conflict style preference. *Management Communication Quarterly* 9, 115–126.

Spencer, T. (1993). A new approach to assessing self-disclosure in conversation. Paper presented at the Annual Convention of the Western Speech Communication Association, Albuquerque, New Mexico.

Spencer, T. (1994). Transforming relationships through everyday talk. In *The Dynamics of Relationships: Vol. 4. Understanding Relationships,* S. Duck (ed.). Thousand Oaks, CA: Sage.

Spett, M. (2004). Expressing negative emotions: Healthy catharsis or sign of pathology? http://www.nj-act.org/article2.html. Accessed May 19, 2008.

Spitzberg, B. H. (1991). Intercultural communication competence. In *Intercultural communication: A reader*, L. A. Samovar & R. E. Porter (eds.). Belmont, CA: Wadsworth, pp. 353–365.

Spitzberg, B. H., & Cupach, W. R. (1989). *Handbook of interpersonal competence research.* New York: Springer-Verlag.

Spitzberg, B. H., & Hecht, M. L. (1984). A component model of relational competence. *Human Communication Research* 10, 575–599.

Sprecher, S. (1987). The effects of self-disclosure given and received on affection for an intimate partner and stability of the relationship. *Journal of Social and Personal Relationships* 4, 115–127.

Sprecher, S. (2001). Equity and social exchange in dating couples: Associations with satisfaction, commitment, and stability. *Journal of Marriage and the Family* 63 (August), 599–613.

Sprecher, S., & Hendrick, S. S. (2004). Self-disclosure in intimate relationships: Associations with individual and relationship characteristics over time. *Journal of Social and Clinical Psychology* 23 (December), 857–877.

Sprecher, S., & Metts, S. (1989). Development of the "Romantic Beliefs Scale" and examination of the effects of gender and gender-role orientation. *Journal of Social and Personal Relationships* 6, 387–411.

Sprecher, S., & Toro-Morn, M. (2002). A study of men and women from different sides of earth to determine if men are from Mars and women are from Venus in their beliefs about love and romantic relationships. *Sex Roles* 46 (March), 131–147.

Stafford, L. (2004). *Maintaining long-distance and cross-residential relationships.* Mahwah, NJ: Erlbaum.

Stafford, L. (2008). Social exchange theories. In *Engaging theories in interpersonal communication: Multiple perspectives* (pp. 377–390), L. A. Baxter & D. O. Braithwaite (eds.). Los Angeles: Sage.

Stafford, L., Kline, S. L., & Dimmick, J. (1999). Home e-mail: Relational maintenance and gratification opportunities. *Journal of Broadcasting and Electronic Media* 43, 659–669.

Stafford, L., & Merolla, A. J. (2007). Idealization, reunions, and stability in long-distance dating relationships. *Journal of Social and Personal Relations* 24, 37–54.

Stein, M. M., & Bowen, M. (2003). Building a customer satisfaction system: Effective listening when the customer speaks. *Journal of Organizational Excellence* 22 (summer), 23–34.

Steiner, C. (1981). *The other side of power.* New York: Grove.

Stephan, W. G., & Stephan, C. W. (1985). Intergroup anxiety. *Journal of Social Issues* 41, 157–175.

Stephen, R., & Zweigenhaft, R. L. (1986). The effect of tipping of a waitress touching male and female customers. *Journal of Social Psychology* 126 (February), 141–142.

Stephens, G. K., & Greer, C. R. (1995). Doing business in Mexico: Understanding cultural differences. *Organizational Dynamics* 24, 39–55.

Sternberg, R. J. (1986). A triangular theory of love. *Psychological Review* 93, 119–135.

Sternberg, R. J. (1988). *The triangle of love: Intimacy, passion, commitment.* New York: Basic Books.

Sternberg, R. J., & Weis, K. (2008). *The new psychology of love.* New Haven, CT: Yale University Press.

Sternglanz, R. W., & DePaulo, B. (2004). Reading nonverbal cues to emotions: The advantages and liabilities of relationship closeness. *Journal of Nonverbal Behavior* 28 (winter), 245–266.

Stewart, L. P., Cooper, P. J., & Stewart, A. D. (with Friedley, S. A.). (2003). *Communication and gender*, 4th ed. Boston: Allyn & Bacon.

Stewart, S. (2006). A pilot study of email in an e-mentoring relationship. *Journal of Telemedicine and Telecare* 12 (October), 83–85.

Strassberg, D. S., & Holty, S. (2003). An experimental study of women's Internet personal ads. *Archives of Sexual Behavior* 32 (June), 253–260.

Strecker, I. (1993). Cultural variations in the concept of "face." *Multilingua* 12, 119–141.

Suler, J. (2004). The online disinhibition effect. *CyberPsychology and Behavior* 7 (June), 321–326.

Sunnafrank, M., & Ramirez, A. (2004). At first sight: Persistent relational effects of get-acquainted conversations. *Journal of Social and Personal Relationships* 21 (June), 361–379.

Sutcliffe, K., Lewton, E., & Rosenthal, M. M. (2004). Communication failures: An insidious contributor to medical mishaps. *Academic Medicine* 79 (February), 186–194.

Sutter, D. L., & Martin, M. M. (1998). Verbal aggression during disengagement of dating relationships. *Communication Research Reports* 15, 318–326.

Tang, S., & Zuo, J. (2000). Dating attitudes and behaviors of American and Chinese college students. *The Social Science Journal* 37 (January), 67–78.

Tannen, D. (1990). *You just don't understand: Women and men in conversation.* New York: Morrow.

Tannen, D. (1994a). *Gender and discourse.* New York: Oxford University Press.

Tannen, D. (1994b). *Talking from 9 to 5.* New York: Morrow.

Taraban, C. B., & Hendrick, C. (1995). Personality perceptions associated with six styles of love. *Journal of Social and Personal Relationships* 12, 453–461.

Tardiff, T. (2001). Learning to say "no" in Chinese. *Early Education and Development* 12, 303–323.

Tata, J. (2000). Toward a theoretical framework of inter-cultural account-giving and account evaluation. *International Journal of Organizational Analysis* 8, 155–178.

Tavris, C. (1989). *Anger: The misunderstood emotion* (2nd ed.). New York: Simon & Schuster.

Teven, J. J., Richmond, V. P., & McCroskey, J. C. (1998). Measuring tolerance for disagreement. *Communication Research Reports* 15, 209–221.

Thelen, M. H., Sherman, M. D., & Borst, T. S. (1998). Fear of intimacy and attachment among rape survivors. *Behavior Modification* 22, 108–116.

Thibaut, J. W., & Kelley, H. H. (1959). *The social psychology of groups.* New York: Wiley. Reissued (1986). New Brunswick, NJ: Transaction Books.

Thomlison, D. (1982). *Toward interpersonal dialogue.* New York: Longman.

Thompson, C. A., & Klopf, D. W. (1991). An analysis of social style among disparate cultures. *Communication Research Reports* 8, 65–72.

Thompson, C. A., Klopf, D. W., & Ishii, S. (1991). A comparison of social style between Japanese and Americans. *Communication Research Reports* 8, 165–172.

Thorne, B., Kramarae, C., & Henley, N. (eds.). (1983). *Language, gender and society.* Rowley, MA: Newbury House.

Tierney, P., & Farmer, S. M. (2004). The Pygmalion process and employee creativity. *Journal of Management* 30 (June), 413–432.

Ting-Toomey, S. (1981). Ethnic identity and close friendship in Chinese-American college students. *International Journal of Intercultural Relations* 5, 383–406.

Ting-Toomey, S. (1985). Toward a theory of conflict and culture. *International and Intercultural Communication Annual* 9, 71–86.

Ting-Toomey, S. (1986). Conflict communication styles in black and white subjective cultures. In *Interethnic communication: Current research,* Y. Y. Kim (ed.). Thousand Oaks, CA: Sage, pp. 75–88.

Tinsley, C. H., & Brett, J. M. (2001). Managing workplace conflict in the United States and Hong Kong. *Organizational Behavior and Human Decision Processes* 85, 360–381.

Tolhuizen, J. H. (1986). Perceiving communication indicators of evolutionary changes in friendship. *Southern Speech Communication Journal* 52, 69–91.

Tolhuizen, J. H. (1989). Communication strategies for intensifying dating relationships: Identification, use, and structure. *Journal of Social and Personal Relationships* 6, 413–434.

Trager, G. L. (1958). Paralanguage: A first approximation. *Studies in Linguistics* 13, 1–12.

Trager, G. L. (1961). The typology of paralanguage. *Anthropological Linguistics* 3, 17–21.

Trower, P. (1981). Social skill disorder. In *Personal Relationships* 3, S. Duck & R. Gilmour (eds.). New York: Academic Press, pp. 97–110.

Tsiantar, D. (2005). The cost of incivility. *Time* (February 14), B5.

Tynes, B. M. (2007). Internet safety gone wild? Sacrificing the educational and psychosocial benefits of online social environments. *Journal of Adolescent Research* 22, 575–584.

Ueleke, W., et al. (1983). Inequity resolving behavior as a response to inequity in a hypothetical marital relationship. *A Quarterly Journal of Human Behavior* 20, 4–8.

Unger, F. L. (2001). Speech directed at able-bodied adults, disabled adults, and disabled adults with speech impairments. *Dissertation Abstracts International: Second B: The Sciences and Engineering,* 62, 1146.

Vainiomaki, T. (2004). Silence as a cultural sign. *Semiotica* 150, 347–361.

Valkenburg, P. M., & Peter, J. (2007). Online communication and adolescent well-being: Testing the stimulation versus the displacement hypothesis. *Journal of Computer-Mediated Communication* 12, article 2. http://jcmc.indiana.edu/vol12/issue4/Valkenburg.html. Accessed May 28, 2008.

VanHyning, M. (1993). *Crossed signals: How to say no to sexual harassment.* Los Angeles: Infotrends Press.

Varma, A., Toh, S. M, & Pichler, S. (2006). Ingratiation in job applications: Impact on selection decisions. *Journal of Managerial Psychology* 21, 200–210.

Veenendall, T. L., & Feinstein, M. C. (1995). *Let's talk about relationships: Cases in study.* Prospect Heights, IL: Waveland Press.

Velting, D. M. (1999). Personality and negative expectations: Trait structure of the Beck Hopelessness Scale. *Personality and Individual Differences* 26, 913–921.

Victor, D. (1992). *International business communication.* New York: HarperCollins.

von Tetzchner, S., & Jensen, K. (1999). Interacting with people who have severe communication problems: Ethical considerations. *International Journal of Disability, Development and Education* 46 (December), 453–462.

Vonk, R. (2002). Self-serving interpretations of flattery: Why ingratiation works. *Journal of Personality and Social Psychology* 82 (April), 515–526.

Voo, J. (2007). How to handle an office romance. http://www.cnn.com/2007/living/worklife/08/29/office.romance/index.html. Accessed May 20, 2008.

Vrij, A., & Mann, S. (2001). Telling and detecting lies in a high-stake situation: The case of a convicted murderer. *Applied Cognitive Psychology,* 15 (March–April), 187–203.

Waddington, K. (2004). Psst—spread the word—gossiping is good for you. *Practice Nurse* 27, 7–10.

Wade, C., & Tavris, C. (2007). *Psychology,* 9th ed. Upper Saddle River, NJ: Prentice-Hall.

Wade, N. (2002). Scent of a man is linked to a woman's selection. *New York Times* (January 22), F2.

Walster, E., Walster, G. W., & Berscheid, E. (1978). *Equity: Theory and research.* Boston: Allyn & Bacon.

Walster, E., Walster, G. W., & Traupmann, J. (1978). Equity and premarital sex. *Journal of Personality and Social Psychology* 36, 82–92.

Walther, J. B. (2008). Social information processing theory. In *Engaging theories in interpersonal communication: Multiple perspectives* (pp. 391–404), L. A. Baxter & D. O. Braithwaite (eds.). Los Angeles: Sage.

Walther, J. B., & Parks, M. R. (2002). Cues filtered out, cues filtered in: Computer-mediated communication and relationships. In *Handbook of interpersonal communication,* (pp. 529–563), M. L. Knapp and J. A. Daly (eds.). Thousand Oaks, CA: Sage.

Walther, J. D. (1992). Interpersonal effects in computer-mediated interaction: A relational perspective. *Communication Research* 19, 52–90.

Wan, C. (2004). The psychology of culture shock. *Asian Journal of Social Psychology* 7 (August), 233–234.

Ward, C., Bochner, S., & Furnham, A. (eds.). (2001). *The psychology of culture shock*. Hove, UK: Routledge.

Ward, S. F. (2003). Lawyers in love. *ABA Journal* 89 (September), 37.

Watzlawick, P. (1977). *How real is real? Confusion, disinformation, communication: An anecdotal introduction to communications theory*. New York: Vintage.

Watzlawick, P. (1978). *The language of change: Elements of therapeutic communication*. New York: Basic Books.

Watzlawick, P., Beavin, J. H., & Jackson, D. D. (1967). *Pragmatics of human communication: A study of interactional patterns, pathologies, and paradoxes*. New York: Norton.

Weathers, M. D., Frank, E. M., & Spell, L. A. (2002). Differences in the communication of affect: Members of the same race versus members of a different race. *Journal of Black Psychology* 28, 66–77.

Weigel, D. J., & Ballard-Reisch, D. S. (1999). Using paired data to test models of relational maintenance and marital quality. *Journal of Social and Personal Relationships* 16, 175–191.

Weinberg, H. L. (1959). *Levels of knowing and existence*. New York: Harper & Row.

Weitzman, P. F. (2001). Young adult women resolving interpersonal conflicts. *Journal of Adult Development* 8, 61–67.

Weitzman, P. F., & Weitzman, E. A. (2000). Interpersonal negotiation strategies in a sample of older women. *Journal of Clinical Geropsychology* 6, 41–51.

Wert, S. R., & Salovey, P. (2004). A social comparison account of gossip. *Review of General Psychology* 8 (June), 122–137.

Wertz, D. C., Sorenson, J. R., & Heeren, T. C. (1988). Can't get no (dis)satisfaction: Professional satisfaction with professional-client encounters. *Work and Occupations* 15, 36–54.

Westwood, R. I., Tang, F. F., & Kirkbride, P. S. (1992). Chinese conflict behavior: Cultural antecedents and behavioral consequences. *Organizational Development Journal* 10, 13–19.

Wheeless, L. R., & Grotz, J. (1977). The measurement of trust and its relationship to self-disclosure. *Human Communication Research* 3, 250–257.

Whitty, M. T. (2003a). Cyber-flirting: Playing at love on the Internet. *Theory and Psychology* 13 (June), 339–357.

Whitty, M. T. (2003b). Logging onto love: An examination of men's and women's flirting behaviour both offline and on the Internet. *Australian Journal of Psychology* 55, 68–72.

Whitty, M., & Gavin, J. (2001). Age/sex/location: Uncovering the social cues in the development of online relationships. *CyberPsychology and Behavior* 4, 623–630.

Wiederman, M. W., & Hurd, C. (1999). Extradyadic involvement during dating. *Journal of Social and Personal Relationships* 16, 265–274.

Wilkins, B. M., & Andersen, P. A. (1991). Gender differences and similarities in management communication: A meta-analysis. *Management Communication Quarterly* 5, 6–35.

Willis, J., & Todorov, A. (2006). First impressions: Making up your mind after a 100-Ms exposure to a face. *Psychological Science* 17 (July), 592–598.

Willson, R., & Branch, R. (2006). *Cognitive behavioural therapy for dummies*. West Sussex, England: Wiley.

Wilson, S. R., & Sabee, C. M. (2003). Explicating communicative competence as a theoretical term. In *Handbook of communication and social interaction skills* (pp. 3–50), J. O. Greene & B. R. Burleson (eds.). Mahwah, NJ: Erlbaum.

Windy, D., & Constantinou, D. (2005). *Assertiveness step by step*. London: Sheldon Press.

Winquist, L. A., Mohr, C. D., & Kenny, D. A. (1998). The female positivity effect in the perception of others. *Journal of Research in Personality* 32, 370–388.

Witcher, S. K. (1999, August 9–15). Chief executives in Asia find listening difficult. *Asian Wall Street Journal Weekly* 21, p. 11.

Wolak, J., Mitchell, K. J., & Finkelhor, D. (2003). Escaping or connecting? Characteristics of youth who form close online relationships. *Journal of Adolescence* 26 (February), 105–119.

Wolpe, J. (1958). *Psychotherapy by reciprocal inhibition*. Stanford, CA: Stanford University Press.

Won-Doornink, M. J. (1985). Self-disclosure and reciprocity in conversation: A cross-national study. *Social Psychology Quarterly* 48, 97–107.

Wood, A. F., & Smith, M. J. (2005). *Online communication: Linking technology, identity, and culture*. Mahwah, NJ: Lawrence Erlbaum.

Wood, J. T. (1994). *Gendered lives: Communication, gender, and culture*. Belmont, CA: Wadsworth.

Woodzicka, A. A., & LaFrance, M. (2005). Working on a smile: Responding to sexual provocation in the workplace. In *Applications of nonverbal communication* (pp. 141–160), R. E. Riggio & R. S. Feldman (eds.). Mahwah, NJ: Erlbaum.

Wrench, J. S., McCroskey, J. C., & Richmond, V. P. (2008). *Human communication in everyday life: Explanations and applications*. Boston: Allyn & Bacon.

Wright, J., & Chung, M. C. (2001). Mastery or mystery? Therapeutic writing: A review of the literature. *British Journal of Guidance and Counseling* 29 (August), 277–291.

Wright, J. W., & Hosman, L. A. (1983). Language style and sex bias in the courtroom: The effects of male and female use of hedges and intensifiers on impression formation. *Southern Speech Communication Journal* 48, 137–152.

Wright, P. H. (1978). Toward a theory of friendship based on a conception of self. *Human Communication Research* 4, 196–207.

Wright, P. H. (1984). Self-referent motivation and the intrinsic quality of friendship. *Journal of Social and Personal Relationships* 1, 115–130.

Wright, P. H. (1988). Interpreting research on gender differences in friendship: A case for moderation and a plea for caution. *Journal of Social and Personal Relationships* 5, 367–373.

Yau-fair Ho, D., Chan, S. F., Peng, S., & Ng, A. K. (2001). The dialogical self: Converging East–West constructions. *Culture and Psychology* 7, 393–408.

Yau-fair Ho, D., Chan, S. F., Peng, S., & Ng, A. K. (2001). The dialogical self: Converging East–West constructions. *Culture and Psychology* 7, 393–408.

Yela, C. (2000). Predictors of and factors related to loving and sexual satisfaction for men and women. *European Review of Applied Psychology* 50, 235–243.

Young, K. S., Griffin-Shelley, E., Cooper, A., O'Mara, J., & Buchanan, J. (2000). Online infidelity: A new dimension in couple relationships with implications for evaluation and treatment. *Sexual Addiction and Compulsivity* 7, 59–74.

Yuki, M., Maddux, W. W., Masuda, T. (2007). Are the windows to the soul the same in the East and West? Cultural differences in using the eyes and mouth as cues to recognize emotions in Japan and the United States. *Journal of Experimental Social Psychology* 43, 303–311.

Zhang, S., & Merolla, A. (2006). Communicating dislike of close friends' romantic partners. *Communication Research Reports* 23(3), 179–186

Zimmer, T. A. (1986). Premarital anxieties. *Journal of Social and Personal Relationships* 3, 149–159.

Zornoza, A., Ripoll, P., & Peiró, J. M. (2002). Conflict management in groups that work in two different communication contexts: Face-to-face and computer-mediated communication. *Small Group Research* 33 (October), 481–508.

Zuckerman, M., Klorman, R., Larrance, D. T., & Spiegel, N. H. (1981). Facial, autonomic, and subjective components of emotion: The facial feedback hypothesis versus the externalizer-internalizer distinction. *Journal of Personality and Social Psychology* 41, 929–944.

Zunin, L. M., & Zunin, H. S. (1991). *The art of condolence: What to write, what to say, what to do at a time of loss.* New York: Harper Perennial.

Zunin, L. M., & Zunin, N. B. (1972). *Contact: The first four minutes.* Los Angeles: Nash.

Index

Index

Note: Italicized letters *f, t,* and *b* following page numbers indicate figures, tables, and boxes, respectively.

Culture (*continued*)
emotions and, 166–170, 168*b*
equality and, 288*b*
ethics and, 35*b*
ethnocentrism in, 48, 50–51, 51*t*
excluding talk use and, 106
expressiveness and, 187*b*
eye contact and, 47, 133, 154
family and, 220, 265
fears of, recognizing and facing, 44
feedback and, 88
feminine, 38–39
friendship and, 251, 269
gatekeeping and, 11
gesture and, 153, 154*t*
gossip and, 193*b*
grief and, 45
high-ambiguity-tolerant, 39–40
high-context, 41–42, 281
homosexual relationships and, 265
identifiers of, 117–118
immediacy and, 134*b*
individualist (*See* Individualist culture)
invitations and, 45, 48
listening and, 87–88
love and, 256–257
low-ambiguity-tolerant, 39–40
low-context, 41–42, 281
masculine, 38–39
model of intercultural communication, 43, 43*f*
nature of, 30–31
networking and, 269
noncontact, 155
nonverbal communication and, 46, 88, 130, 153–158, 154*t*
perception and, 63, 71
perspectives of, 34–35
politeness and, 105–106
positiveness and, 221*b*
power and, 36, 38, 301–302
praise and, 108
rate of speech and, 155
regulators and, 130
relationships and, 216–217
relevance of, 32–34

research on, 43–44
self-awareness and, 58
self-concept and, 55*f,* 56
self-disclosure and, 195
self-test of cultural beliefs, 32
self-test on cultural orientation, 37–38
self-test on ethnocentrism, 50
sensitivity to, 33, 42*b,* 71, 117–118
sexuality and, 214*b*
silence and, 155
theories of, 30
time orientation and, 150, 156–158
touch and, 155
uncertainty reduction and, 44
views on rape and, 61*b*
workplace relationships and, 266–267, 269
Culture shock, 45*b*
Cute-flippant openers, 187, 188

D

Daly, John, 302*b*
Dark side of communication
allness, 124
blame, 290–291
criticism, hurtful, 109
deception, 124
disconfirmation, 112
emotional vulnerability, 210*b*
fact–inference confusion, 124
fallacious reasoning, 84
harassment, 213, 312–314, 313*t*
image confirming strategies, 75
intensional orientation, 124
interpersonal communication, ignoble use of, 19
jealousy, 233*b*
maladaptive emotions 164–165
media violence, 165*b*
polarization, 124
power plays, 315–316
racial profiling, 66
racism, 112–113
self-disclosure dangers, 196
sexual harassment, 213, 312–314, 313*t*
static evaluation, 124
stereotypes, 196

verbal aggressiveness, 292*b,* 292–294
Darwinism, social, 30
Date device in static evaluation, 123
Dating. *See* Relationships
Deaf people
communication between hearing people and, 82*t*
self-esteem of, 60
Deception. *See* Lying
Decoding, 9–10
Decoration of space, 145–146
Defensiveness, 266*b*
Deintensifying, 132
Delayed feedback, 183
Demographics, 32
Denotation, 102
Depenetration, 222
Depression, 242, 254
Depth listening, 91–93
Depth of topics, 222
Destructive criticism, 108
Deterioration of relationships, 212*f,* 215, 232–236, 236*f*
Detour takers, 186*t*
Development of relationships, 212*f,* 213–215, 217–224, 228–229, 249–250
Dialectics theory, relationship, 220–222
Dialogue
defined, 190
with impaired speaker, ethics in, 190*b*
principle of, 189–190
Direct openers, 187, 188
Direct requests, 307
Directness of messages, 105, 106*b,* 107*b,* 109*b,* 214
Disabilities. *See also* Blind people; Deaf people
ableist language and, 112
communication tips for people with and without, 49*t*
harassment and, 313*t*
violence against people with, 290*b*
Disclaimers, 182, 201–202, 202*b*
Disconfirmation, 112–116, 113*t*
Display rules
cultural, 147, 154, 166–167

Credits

Text Credits

Page 3: Reprinted by permission of Sherwyn P. Morreale.

Page 31: Reprinted from *International Journal of Intercultural Relations*, 5, Stella Ting-Toomey, "Ethnic Identity and Close Friendship in Chinese-American College Students," pp. 383–406. Copyright © 1981 with permission from Elsevier.

Page 33: Reprinted by permission of Molefi Asante.

Page 57: Reprinted by permission of Linda Costigan Lederman.

Page 89: Reprinted by permission of Deborah Borisoff.

Page 104: Reprinted by permission of Teresa L. Thompson, Ph.D. Copyright © 2005.

Page 135: Reprinted by permission of Kelly A. Rocca.

Page 165: Reprinted by permission of Elizabeth M. Perse.

Page 197: Reprinted by permission of Susan B. Barnes.

Page 211: Reprinted by permission of Barbara M. Montgomery.

Page 243: Reprinted by permission of Prof. Shirlee A. Levin, College of Southern Maryland.

Page 260: Reprinted by permission of Carolyn M. Anderson, Professor, School of Communication, University of Akron, Akron, OH 44325.

Page 262: From Mary Anne Fitzpatrick's Relational Dimensions Instrument. Copyright © Mary Anne Fitzpatrick.

Page 274: Reprinted by permission of Anita Vangelisti.

Page 302: Reprinted by permission of John Daly.

Photo Credits

Chapter 1
Page 1: ©MGM/Courtesy Everett Collection; 8: Chris Jackson/Getty Images; 10, top: Imagebroker/Alamy; 10, bottom: Ariel Skelley/Corbis; 11: Lauren Nicole/Digital Vision/ Getty Images Royalty Free; 12: (Table 1.2) left to right: Pearson Education; Everett Collection; STAN HONDA/AFP/Getty Images; Daniel Barry/Getty Images; 13: Helen Norman/Corbis; 15: Journal-Courier/Valerie Berta/The Image Works; 22: image100/Alamy Royalty Free.

Chapter 2
Page 29: ©Sony Pictures Classics/courtesy Everett Collection; 34: Don Smetzer/PhotoEdit, Inc.; 36: Xinhua News Agency/WPN; 39: Rubberball Productions/Getty Images Royalty Free; 40: AP Images; 44: Digital Vision/SuperStock Royalty Free; 46: ©HBO/Everett Collection; 47: JupiterImages/Creatas/Alamy Royalty Free; 49: (Table 2.1) left to right: ©New York Daily News, L. P. Reprinted with permission; PA Photos/Landov; AP Images/ Andy King; AP Images/Nevada Appeal, Chad Lundquist.

Chapter 3
Page 54: ©Universal Pictures/Courtesy Everett Collection; 58: Erik Dreyer/Stone/Getty Images; 60: Masterfile Royalty Free; 63: Michael Newman/PhotoEdit, Inc.; 64: Corbis Royalty Free; 66: Chip East/Reuters/Corbis.

Chapter 4

Page 78: ©Walt Disney Co./Everett Collection; 82: (Table 4.1) left to right: Ludwig van Beethoven (1770–1827) Composing his "Missa Solemnis," 1819 (oil on canvas), Stieler, Joseph Carl (1781–1858)/Beethoven Haus, Bonn, Germany/The Bridgeman Art Library; The Granger Collection, New York; AP Images/Robert E. Klein; Kelsey McNeal/© ABC/Everett Collection; 83: Everett Collection; 86: Toby Burrows/Digital Vision/Getty Images Royalty Free; 88: ©Design Pics Inc./Alamy Royalty Free; 91: Myrleen Ferguson Cate/PhotoEdit, Inc.

Chapter 5

Page 98: ©MGM/Courtesy Everett Collection; 99: Comstock Images/Jupiter Images Royalty Free; 105: Photodisc/Getty Images Royalty Free; 106: AP Images/Tim Larsen; 107: Craig Sjodin/© ABC/Everett Collection; 111: Garry A. Conner/Index Stock Imagery; 114: Robert A. Maass/Corbis; 120: Bob Daemmrich/The Image Works; 123: Brand X Pictures/Getty Images Royalty Free.

Chapter 6

Page 128: ©20thCentFox/Everett Collection; 131: joSon/Photodisc/Getty Images Royalty Free; 136: Bob Daemmrich/The Image Works; 145: PhotoDisc/Getty Images; 148: Stockdisc/Picture Quest Royalty Free; 152: JGI/Blend Images/Getty Images; 155: ©Radius Images/Alamy Royalty Free.

Chapter 7

Page 161: ©Paramount/Everett Collection; 163: David Young-Wolff/PhotoEdit, Inc.; 167: REUTERS/Brian Snyder/Landov; 168, left: Blend Images/Alamy Royalty Free; 168, right: Thomas Northcut/Riser/Getty Images Rights Ready; 170: SW Productions/Photodisc/Getty Images Royalty Free; 175, 176: JupiterImages/BananaStock/Alamy Royalty Free.

Chapter 8

Page 179: ©Warner Bros/Courtesy Everett Collection; 181: (Table 8.1) left to right: The Granger Collection, New York; Al Francekevich/Photographer's Choice/Getty Images; Bettmann/Corbis; AP Images/Jeff Adkins; 183: Mark Liebowitz/Masterfile; 190: The Kobal Collection/Picture Desk; 194: ColorBlind Images/Blend Images/Alamy Royalty Free; 195: Denis Felix/Taxi/Getty Images; 196: James Marshall/The Image Works; 202: Jeff Greenberg/PhotoEdit, Inc.

Chapter 9

Page 208: ©20thCentFox/Everett Collection; 210: PRNewsFoto/Engage/Newscom; 213: Marilyn Humphries/The Image Works; 214: Gary A. Conner/PhotoEdit, Inc.; 218: Stockdisc/PictureQuest Royalty Free; 220: Photodisc/Getty Images Royalty Free; 222: ©Warner Bros/Everett Collection.

Chapter 10

Page 227: ©New Line Cinema/Everett Collection; 228: Digital Vision/Getty Images Royalty Free; 229: Stockbyte/Getty Images Royalty Free; 230: Bruce Ayers/Getty Images; 232: Blend Images/Alamy Royalty Free; 234: Masterfile Royalty Free; 239: Chip Simons/Taxi/Getty Images; 242: ©Warner Bros/Everett Collection.

Chapter 11

Page 246: ©Fox Searchlight/Everett Collection; 251: Rubberball/Jupiter Images Royalty Free; 254: Stockdisc/Getty Images Royalty Free; 255: ©Columbia Pictures/Everett Collection; 257: Michael Newman/PhotoEdit Inc.; 263: Marmaduke St. John/Alamy Royalty Free.

Chapter 12

Page 275: Warner Bros/Everett Collection; 281: Index Stock Imagery; 284: Corbis Royalty-Free/Jupiter Images Royalty Free; 285: Rubberball/Jupiter Images Royalty Free; 286: Bob Daemmrich/The Image Works; 287: Alexander Walter/Taxi/Getty Images; 290: David R. Frazier Photolibrary.

Chapter 13

Page 298: ©Warner Bros/Everett Collection; 299: Corbis Royalty Free; 300: Image Source Black/Alamy Royalty Free; 301: Carsten Koall/Visum/The Image Works; 305: Ariel Skelley/Corbis; 306: Jack Hollingsworth/Photodisc/Getty Images Royalty Free; 314: PBWPIX/Alamy.